Rajasthan

a Lonely Planet travel survival kit

Michelle Coxall
Sarina Singh

D1368928

Rajasthan

1st edition

Published by
Lonely Planet Publications
Head Office: PO Box 617, Hawthorn, Vic 3122, Australia
Branches: 155 Filbert St, Suite 251, Oakland, CA 94607, USA
               10 Barley Mow Passage, Chiswick, London W4 4PH, UK
               71 bis rue du Cardinal Lemoine, 75005 Paris, France

Printed by
Colorcraft Ltd, Hong Kong
Printed in China

Photographs by
Sara-Jane Cleland   Adam McCrow
Michelle Coxall   Sanjay Singh Badnor
Richard I'Anson

Front cover: Sam Sand Dunes, near Jaisalmer (Michelle Coxall)

This Edition
January 1997

Although the authors and publisher have tried to make the information as accurate as possible, they accept no responsibility for any loss, injury or inconvenience sustained by any person using this book.

National Library of Australia Cataloguing in Publication Data

Coxall, Michelle
   Rajasthan

   1st ed.
   Includes index.
   ISBN 0 86442 470 1

   1. Rajasthan (India) – Guidebooks. I. Singh, Sarina, 1968-.
   II. Title. (Series : Lonely Planet travel survival kit).

914.440452

text & maps © Lonely Planet 1997
photos © photographers as indicated 1997
Jaisalmer climate chart compiled from information supplied by Patrick J Tyson, © Patrick J Tyson, 1997

Michelle Coxall

Michelle trained as an editor with Lonely Planet before leaving to work with the Tibetan community in Dharamsala in northern India. She stayed on in India to update the Gujarat chapter of LP's *India* guide, and returned the following year to co-author *Indian Himalaya*, Lonely Planet's new guide to the region. Her recent (fourth) visit to India to co-author this book has left her as fascinated, bewildered and intrigued with this extraordinary country as she was after her previous three visits.

Sarina Singh

After completing a business degree in Melbourne, destiny summoned Sarina to India. After recovering from malaria, she pursued a marketing traineeship with Sheraton Hotels. She later abandoned hotels for newspapers, working as a freelance journalist and foreign correspondent. Writing mainly about India, she also travelled to Africa, Nepal, the Middle East and Pakistan, where she interviewed a notorious Mujahideen warlord at his hideout. She is currently writing a television documentary series about contemporary Indian royalty.

From the Authors

Michelle Coxall I would like to thank the following people in Rajasthan, who willingly offered their help and advice: Laxmi Kant Jangid, at the Hotel Shiv Shekhawati, Jhunjhunu; Ramesh and Rajesh Jangid, at the Tourist Pension, Nawalgarh; Chander Prakash, at Anjali Exporter, Jaisalmer; and my trusty rickshaw-wallah (badge No 2297), Chhotu Singh in Jaipur, for whom nothing was too much trouble. Also thanks to Claudia Dreykluft, my travelling companion in Bikaner.

Thanks to Jo Horsburgh, editor at Lonely Planet, for assistance and encouragement well beyond the call of duty, and to Chris, for walking the dog and everything else.

Sarina Singh First and foremost, a very special thank you to Sanjay Singh Badnor for his prolific assistance, enthusiasm and greatly treasured friendship. Many thanks to Khem Singh for his generosity and for introducing speleology to my vocab! Thanks also to the travellers I met along the way for their tips and to the gracious people of Rajasthan who helped, especially in Udaipur.

In Melbourne, I'm deeply grateful to Camille Gautam (currently lost somewhere in Africa) for her help and to my parents for baby-sitting my canine companion Susha. At Lonely Planet, a huge thank you to Sharan Kaur for her guidance and encouragement, to Michelle Coxall for her constant support, to Jo Horsburgh and David Andrew for their adroit editing and to Sue Galley for having faith in me.

I'd like to dedicate this book to my dear friends in Mumbai: Amit, Swati and Parth Jhaveri – for their kindness.

From the Publisher

This book was edited by Jo Horsburgh, Anne Mulvaney, David Andrew and Jane Rawson. Adam McCrow was responsible for the design, layout and illustrations, with Margaret Jung and Tamsin Wilson contributing additional illustrations. Paul Piaia drew all the maps. Thanks to Simon Bracken and Adam McCrow for the cover design, Kerrie Williams for the index, and to Sharan Kaur and Valerie Tellini, who did the final checking. Special thanks to the authors, Michelle Coxall and Sarina Singh, for their high standards and patient replies to even the most trivial editorial queries.

Warning & Request

Things change – prices go up, schedules change, good places go bad and bad places go bankrupt – nothing stays the same. So, if you find things better or worse, recently opened or long since closed, please tell us and help make the next edition even more accurate and useful.

We value all of the feedback we receive from travellers. Julie Young co-ordinates a small team who reads and acknowledges every letter, postcard and email, and ensures that every morsel of information finds its way to the appropriate authors, editors and publishers.

Everyone who writes to us will find their name in the next edition of the appropriate guide and will also receive a free subscription to our quarterly newsletter, *Planet Talk*. The very best contributions will be rewarded with a free Lonely Planet guide.

Excerpts from your correspondence may appear in updates (which we add to the end pages of reprints); new editions of this guide; in our newsletter, *Planet Talk*; or in the Postcards section of our Web site – so please let us know if you don't want your letter published or your name acknowledged.

Contents

Map Legend

BOUNDARIES

.... International Boundary

.... Regional Boundary

ROUTES

.... Freeway

.... Highway

.... Major Road

.... Unsealed Road or Track

.... City Road

.... City Street

.... Railway

.... Underground Railway

.... Tram

.... Walking Track

.... Walking Tour

.... Ferry Route

.... Cable Car or Chairlift

AREA FEATURES

.... Parks

.... Built-Up Area

.... Pedestrian Mall

.... Market

.... Cemetery

.... Reef

.... Beach or Desert

.... Rocks

HYDROGRAPHIC FEATURES

.... Coastline

.... River, Creek

.... Intermittent River or Creek

.... Rapids, Waterfalls

.... Lake, Intermittent Lake

.... Canal

.... Swamp

SYMBOLS

✪ CAPITAL		.... National Capital
◉ Capital		.... Regional Capital
CITY		.... Major City
● City		.... City
● Town		.... Town
● Village		.... Village
■	▼	.... Place to Stay, Place to Eat
☎	🍴	.... Cafe, Pub or Bar
✉	☎	.... Post Office, Telephone
❶	❸	.... Tourist Information, Bank
◗	🅿	.... Transport, Parking
🏛	🏠	.... Museum, Youth Hostel
⚏	Å	Caravan Park, Camping Ground
🈯	➡	.... Church, Cathedral
🌙	🏯	.... Mosque, Temple
🛕	🕉	...... Sikh Temple, Hindu Temple
✚	★	.... Hospital, Police Station
◔	🅿	.... Embassy, Petrol Station
✈	✝	.... Airport, Airfield
▭	✿	.... Swimming Pool, Gardens
❖	🐘	.... Shopping Centre, Zoo
⚜	▣	...Winery or Vineyard, Picnic Site
←	A25	One Way Street, Route Number
🏛	⚒	.... Stately Home, Monument
🏯	▣	.... Castle, Tomb
⌒	⌂	.... Cave, Hut or Chalet
▲	※	.... Mountain or Hill, Lookout
🗼	⊿	.... Lighthouse, Shipwreck
)(	◎	.... Pass, Spring
🏴	⚡	.... Beach, Surf Beach
	∴	...... Archaeological Site or Ruins
		.... Ancient or City Wall
		.... Cliff or Escarpment, Tunnel
		.... Railway Station

Note: not all symbols displayed above appear in this book

Introduction

The colourful, exotic state of Rajasthan encapsulates the essence of India. This is the home of the Rajputs, a group of warrior clans who variously claim descent from the sun, the moon and the flames of a sacrificial fire, who controlled this part of India for over 1000 years. The Rajputs' highly evolved code of chivalry and honour is akin to that of the mediaeval European knights. They were fiercely independent and renowned for their valour and pride, preferring, when defeat was imminent in battle, to die an honourable death rather than to treat with the enemy. For the Rajput women, this translated into occasions of grim mass self-destruction known as *jauhar*, in which they threw themselves onto massive funeral pyres rather than face dishonour at the hands of the enemy.

Fiercely defending their territories to the death, the Rajputs entrenched themselves in

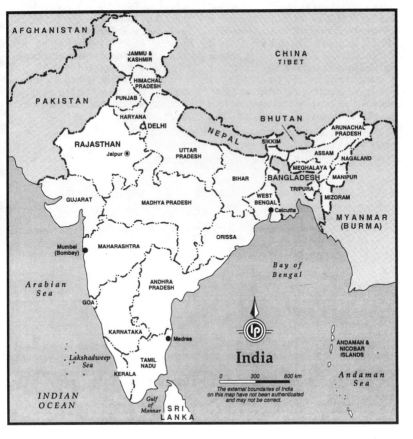

9

this harsh desert land, building huge forts such as those at Chittorgarh, Jodhpur and Jaisalmer, which still stand today.

Rajasthan is also replete with beautiful palaces, containing fountains, gardens, mirrored halls and airy galleries. Today, many of these have been converted into luxury hotels.

Perhaps the most lasting impression that visitors take away with them after travelling through this state is that of colour. In Rajasthan, colour – apparent in turbans, in the long skirts known as *ghagharas* worn by Rajasthani women, and in their *odhnis*, or headscarves – reaches new heights of luminosity and vividness. Iridescent yellows, shocking pinks, emerald greens, turquoise blues and splashes of brilliant reds and oranges seem to be reinventions of traditional colours. The effect is dazzling, and you'll experience it everywhere – a group of village women crowded around a stall in a busy bazaar; a sea of coloured turbans on a crowded bus; or even in the middle of the desert, as a lone, iridescent pink turbaned villager leads his camel home across the parched land. In a land characterised by desert wastelands and sandy monotone landscapes, the Rajasthanis have created beauty amid the starkness of the landscape, introducing colours which challenge the bleached, arid land.

Rajasthan is one of the most popular tourist destinations in India, but this vast state can easily accommodate its visitors – there's simply so much to see, from national parks such as Keoladeo Ghana, Bharatpur and Sariska, thriving cities such as Jaipur and Jodhpur, romantic forts and palaces, the beautiful towns of Udaipur and Pushkar, set beside picturesque lakes, the painted *havelis* (mansions) of Shekhawati, and the incomparably exotic fort of Jaisalmer. And then, of course, there are the ubiquitous camels, gaily caparisoned, threading their way through the streets and bazaars, waiting patiently at the traffic lights in Jaipur, or silhouetted against the sunset on the Sam sand dunes.

Finally, in contrast to the sometimes inhospitable land, there is a fine tradition of hospitality in Rajasthan, and the visitor is treated as a privileged guest.

Facts about Rajasthan

HISTORY
Early History
The north-western region of India, which incorporates Rajasthan, remained in early history for the most part independent from the great empires consolidating their hold on the subcontinent. Buddhism failed to make substantial inroads here; the Mauryan Empire (321-184 BC), whose most renowned emperor Ashoka converted to Buddhism in 262 BC, had minimal impact in Rajasthan. However, there are Buddhist caves and *stupas* (Buddhist shrines) at Jhalawar, in southern Rajasthan.

Ancient Hindu scriptural epics make reference to sites in present-day Rajasthan. The holy pilgrimage site of Pushkar is mentioned in both the *Mahabharata* and *Ramayana.*

Emergence of the Rajputs
The fall of the Gupta Empire, which held dominance in northern India for nearly 300 years, until the early 5th century, was followed by a period of instability as various local chieftains sought to gain supremacy. Various powers rose and fell in northern India. Stability was only restored with the emergence of the Gurjara Pratiharas, the earliest of the Rajput (from 'Rajputra', or Sons of Princes) dynasties which were later to hold the balance of power throughout Rajasthan.

The emergence of the Rajput warrior clans in the 6th and 7th centuries played the greatest role in the subsequent history of Rajasthan. From these clans emerged the name Rajputana, by which the collection of princely states came to be known during the Muslim invasion of India. The Rajputs, who fled aggressors in their homelands in Gujarat, Punjab and Uttar Pradesh, settled in the region, subjugating the indigenous tribes, the Bhils and Mers. There is also some evidence to suggest that some of the Rajput clans can trace their emergence to the arrival of foreign invaders such as the White Huns, who may have settled and been assimilated into the region, and other invaders and settlers from central Asia.

Whatever their actual historical origins, the Rajputs have evolved a complex mythological genealogy. This ancestry can be divided into two main branches: the Suryavansa, or Race of the Sun (Solar Race), which claims direct descent from Rama; and the Induvansa, or Race of the Moon (Lunar Race), which claims descent from Krishna. Later a third branch was added, the Agnikula, or 'Fire Born'. These people claim that they were manifested from the flames of a sacrificial fire on Mt Abu. From these three principal races emerged the 36 Rajput clans.

As they were predominantly of lower castes, the Rajputs should not in theory have aspired to warrior status, which was an occupation reserved for those in the upper echelons of the caste hierarchy. Their (albeit contrived) celestial origins, however, enabled them to claim descent from the Kshatriya, or martial caste, which in the caste hierarchy falls only just below that of the Brahmins.

The Rajput clans gave rise to dynasties such as the Chauhans, the Sisodias, the Kachhwahas and the Rathores. The Chauhans of the Agnikula Race emerged in the 12th century and were renowned for their valour. Their territories included the Sapadalaksha kingdom, which encompassed a vast area including present-day Jaipur, Ranthambhore, part of Mewar, the western portion of Bundi district, Ajmer, Kishangarh and even, at one time, Delhi. Branches of the Chauhans also ruled territories known as Ananta (in present-day Shekhawati), and Saptasatabhumi.

The Sisodias of the Suryavansa Race, originally from Gujarat, migrated to Rajasthan in the mid-7th century and reigned over Mewar, which encompassed Udaipur and Chittorgarh.

The Kachhwahas, originally from Gwalior in Madhya Pradesh, travelled west in the

12th century. They built the massive fortress at Amber, the capital later being shifted to Jaipur. Like the Sisodias, they belonged to the Suryavansa Race.

Also belonging to the Suryavansa Race, the Rathores (earlier known as Rastrakutas) travelled from Kanauj, in Uttar Pradesh. Initially they settled in Pali, south of present-day Jodhpur, but later moved to Mandore in 1381 and ruled over Marwar (Jodhpur). Later they commenced construction on the stunning Meherangarh Fort at Jodhpur.

The Bhattis, who belong to the Induvansa Race, driven from their homeland in the Punjab by the Turks, installed themselves at Jaisalmer in 1156. They remained more or less entrenched in their desert kingdom until they were integrated into the state of Rajasthan following Independence.

The Warrior Legacy

The first external threat to the dominance of the Rajputs was that posed by the Arabs who took over Sind in 713. The Gurjara Pratiharas' response to the Arab threat was largely defensive. The Arabs were repulsed by the Gurjara Pratiharas led by their king, Nagabhata I, founder of the Pratihara Empire. The Arabs also tested their strength against the Rastrakutas. Unfortunately, when not pitting their wits against the Arabs, the Pratiharas and Rastrakutas were busy fighting each other.

By the third decade of the 8th century, a new threat was emerging in the form of the Turks, who had occupied Ghazni in Afghanistan.

Around 1001 AD, Mahmud of Ghazni's army descended upon India, destroying infidel temples and carrying off everything of value that could be moved. The Rajputs were not immune from these incursions; a confederation of Rajput rulers assembled a vast army and marched northwards to meet the advancing Turks. Unfortunately, however, it was a case of too little, too late, and they were decisively and crushingly vanquished. The Pratiharas, then centred at Kanauj, fled the city before the Turks arrived, and in their absence the temples of

Kanauj, as with so many others in northern India, were sacked and desecrated.

Towards the end of the 12th century, Mohammed of Ghori invaded India to take up where Mahmud of Ghazni had left off. He met with a collection of princely states which failed to mount a united front. Although initially repulsed, Ghori later triumphed, and Delhi and Ajmer were lost to the Muslims. Ajmer remained a Muslim stronghold over the centuries, apart from a brief period when it was retaken by the Rathores. Today it is an important Muslim place of pilgrimage.

The Rajputs vs the Sultans of Delhi

Mohammed of Ghori was killed in 1206, and his successor, Qutb-ud-din, became the first of the Sultans of Delhi. Within 20 years, the Muslims had brought the whole of the Ganges basin under their control.

In 1297, Ala-ud-din Khilji pushed the Muslim borders south into Gujarat. Ala-ud-din mounted a protracted siege of the massive fort at Ranthambhore, which was at the time ruled by the Rajput chief Hammir Deva. Hammir was reported as dead (although it's unknown if he did actually die in the siege) and upon hearing of their chief's demise, the womenfolk of the fortress collectively threw themselves on a pyre, thus performing the first instance of *jauhar*, or collective sacrifice, in the history of the Rajputs. Alu-ud-din later went on to sack the fortress at Chittorgarh in 1303, held by the Sisodia clan. According to tradition, Alu-ud-din had heard repute of the great beauty of Padmini, the consort of the Sisodian chief, and resolved to carry her off with him. Like Ranthambhore before it, Chittorgarh also fell to the Muslim leader.

The Rajputs vs the Mughals

The Delhi sultanate weakened at the beginning of the 16th century, and the Rajputs took advantage of this to restore and expand their territories. At this time the kingdom of Mewar, ruled by the Sisodias under the leadership of Rana Sangram Singh, gained pre-eminence among the Rajput states. Under this leader, Mewar pushed its bound aries far beyond its original territory, posing a formidable threat to the new Mughal Empire which was emerging under the leadership of Babur (reigned 1527-30).

Babur, a descendent of both Timur and Genghis Khan, marched into Punjab from his capital at Kabul in Afghanistan in 1525 and defeated the Sultan of Delhi at Panipat. He then focused his attention on the Rajput princely states, many of whom, anticipating his designs, had banded together to form a united front under Rana Sangram Singh.

Unfortunately, when the inevitable confrontation took place, the Rajputs were defeated by Babur. They sustained great losses, with many Rajput chiefs falling in the fray, including Rana Sangram Singh himself, who reputedly had no less than 80 wounds on his body suffered during both this and previous campaigns.

The defeat shook the very foundations of the princely states. Mewar's confidence was shattered by the death of its illustrious leader, and its territories contracted following subsequent attacks by the Sultan of Gujarat.

At this time Marwar, under its ruler Maldeo, emerged as the strongest of the Rajput states, and it recorded a victory against the claimant to the Mughal throne, Sher Shah. However, none of the Rajputs was able to withstand the formidable threat posed by the most renowned of the Mughal emperors, Akbar (reigned 1556-1605).

Recognising that the Rajputs could not be conquered by mere force alone, Akbar contracted a marriage alliance with a princess of the important Kachhwaha clan who held Amber (and later founded Jaipur). The Kachhwahas, unlike their other Rajput brethren at the time, aligned themselves with the powerful Mughals, and even sent troops to aid them in times of battle.

Akbar also used more conventional methods to assert his dominance over the Rajputs, wresting Ajmer from the Rathores of Marwar which had been briefly restored to the Rajputs under Maldeo. All the important Rajput states eventually acknowledged Mughal sovereignty and became vassal states of the Mughal Empire, except Mewar,

The Mughal emperor Akbar ruled from 1556 to 1605, and was probably the greatest of the Mughal rulers, who dominated northern India for three centuries.

which fiercely clung to its independence, refusing to pay homage to the infidels.

An uneasy truce was thus maintained between the Rajputs and the Mughal emperors, until the reign of Aurangzeb, the last great Mughal emperor, when relations were characterised by mutual hostility.

Aurangzeb devoted his resources to extending the empire's boundaries. The punitive taxes which he levied on his subjects to pay for his military exploits and his religious zealotry eventually secured his downfall.

The Rajputs were united in their opposition to Aurangzeb, and the Rathores and Sisodias raised arms against him. It didn't take long for revolts by the enemies of Aurangzeb to break out on all sides and, with his death in 1707, the Mughal Empire's fortunes rapidly declined.

The Rajputs vs the Marathas

Following the death of Aurangzeb and the dissolution of the Mughal Empire came the Marathas. They first rose to prominence with

Shivaji who, between 1646 and 1680, performed feats of arms and heroism across central India. The Maratha Empire continued under the Peshwas, hereditary government ministers who became the real rulers. They gradually took over more and more of the weakening Mughal Empire's powers, first by supplying troops and then by actually taking control of Mughal land.

The Marathas conducted numerous raids on the Rajputs, and the latter, too busy fighting among themselves, laid themselves wide open to these aggressions, resulting in numerous defeats in battle, the loss of territories and the inevitable decline of the Rajput states.

The Emergence of the British
In the early 19th century, the East India Company, a London trading company which had a monopoly on trade in India, was taken over by the British Government, and India was effectively under British control.

Meanwhile, the Marathas continued to mount raids on the Rajputs. Initially the British adopted a policy of neutrality towards the feuding parties. However, the British eventually stepped into the fray, negotiating treaties with the leaders of the main Rajput states. British protection was offered in return for Rajput support.

Weakened by habitual fighting between themselves and in their skirmishes with the Marathas, one by one the princely states forfeited their independence in exchange for this protection. British residents were gradually installed in the princely states. The British ultimately eliminated the Maratha threat, but by this stage the Rajputs were effectively reduced to puppet leaders and lackeys of the British.

While the Rajput leaders enjoyed the status and prestige of their positions, discontent was manifesting itself among numbers of their subjects, which broke out in rebellion in 1857. This rebellion proved to be a precursor to widespread opposition to British rule throughout India. It was Mohandas Gandhi, later to be known as Mahatma Gandhi, who galvanised the peasants and villagers into the

non-violent resistance which was to spearhead the nationalist movement.

Road to Independence
By the time WWII was concluded, Indian independence was inevitable. The war dealt a deathblow to colonialism and the myth of European superiority, and Britain no longer had the power nor the desire to maintain a vast empire. Within India, however, a major problem had developed: the large Muslim minority had realised that an independent India would also be a Hindu-dominated India.

The country was divided along purely religious lines, with the Muslim League, led by Muhammad Ali Jinnah, speaking for the Muslims, and the Congress Party led by Jawaharlal Nehru, representing the Hindu population.

Gandhi was absolutely opposed to the severing of the Muslim dominated regions from the prospective new nation. However, Jinnah was intransigent: 'I will have India divided, or India destroyed,' was his uncompromising demand. The new viceroy, Louis Mountbatten, made a last-ditch attempt to convince the rival factions that a united India was a more sensible proposition, but the reluctant decision was made to divide the country. Independence was finally instituted on 15 August 1947, with the concomitant partitioning of the nascent country. The result was a Hindu-dominated India and a Muslim-dominated West and East Pakistan.

Emergence of the State of Rajasthan
It took some time for the boundaries of the proposed new state of Rajasthan to be defined. In 1948, Rajasthan comprised the south and south-eastern states of Rajputana. With the merger of Mewar, Udaipur became the capital of the United State of Rajasthan. The Maharana of Udaipur was invested with the title of *rajpramukh* (head of state). Manikya Lal Varma was appointed as prime minister of the new state, which was inaugurated on 18 April 1948.

Almost from the outset the prime minister came into opposition with the rajpramukh over the constitution of the state government ministry. Varma wanted to form a ministry of all Congress members. The rajpramukh was keen to have his own candidates installed from among the *jagirdars*, or feudal lords. Jagirdars traditionally acted as intermediaries between the tillers of the soil (the peasants) and the state, taking rent or produce from the tenants and paying tribute to the princely ruler. They were symbols of the old feudal order, for whom millions of inhabitants of Rajputana were held in serfdom. Varma was keen to abolish the age-old system of *jagirdari* and, with Nehru's support, was able to install his own Congress ministry and do away with this feudal relic.

Still retaining their independence from India were Jaipur and the desert kingdoms of Bikaner, Jodhpur and Jaisalmer. From a security point of view, it was vital to the new Indian Union to ensure that the desert kingdoms, which were contiguous with Pakistan, were integrated into the new nation. The princes finally agreed to sign the Instrument of Accession, and the kingdoms of Bikaner, Jodhpur, Jaisalmer and Jaipur were merged in 1949. The Maharaja of Jaipur, Man Singh II, was invested with the title of rajpramukh. Jaipur became the capital of the new state of Rajasthan. Heera Lal Shastri was installed as the first premier of Rajasthan.

Later in 1949, the United State of Matsya, comprising the former kingdoms of Bharatpur, Alwar, Karauli and Dholpur, was incorporated into Rajasthan. As a consequence, Rajasthan became the second largest state in India, exceeded in geographical area only by the central Indian state of Madhya Pradesh. Rajasthan attained its current dimensions in November 1956 with the additions of Ajmer-Merwara, Abu Rd and a part of Dilwara, originally part of the princely kingdom of Sirohi which had been divided between Gujarat and Rajasthan.

The princes of the former kingdoms were constitutionally granted handsome remuneration in the form of privy purses to assist them in the discharge of their financial obligations (and to keep them in the style to which they had become accustomed). In 1970, Indira Gandhi (daughter of India's first prime minister, Jawaharlal Nehru), who had come to power in 1966, commenced undertakings to discontinue the privy purses, which were abolished in 1971.

Rajasthan Today
Many of the former rulers of Rajasthan continue to use the title of maharaja for social purposes. The only power this title holds today is as a status symbol. Since the privy purse abolition, the princes have had to financially support themselves. Some hastily sold valuable heirlooms and properties for literally nothing, in a desperate attempt to pay bills.

While a handful of princes squandered their family fortunes, others refused to surrender their heritage, and turned their hands to business, politics or other vocations. Many decided to convert their palaces into hotels as a means of earning income. Some of these palace-hotels have become prime tourist destinations in India, such as the Lake Palace Hotel in Udaipur, the Rambagh Palace in Jaipur and the Umaid Bhawan Palace in Jodhpur. The revenue earned from such hotels has enabled the maharajas to maintain their properties, sustain time-honoured family traditions and continue to lead a comfortable lifestyle.

However, not all palaces are on the tourist circuit and cannot rely purely on tourism as a source of steady income. Many palaces and forts are tucked away in remote parts of Rajasthan, and have been reluctantly handed over to the government, because the owners were simply unable to maintain them. Unfortunately, many of these rich vestiges of India's royal past are poorly maintained.

GEOGRAPHY & GEOLOGY
The state of Rajasthan covers some 342,000 sq km in the north-western region of India. It is divided into six administrative zones: Mewat (Alwar region); Marwar (Jodhpur region); Mewar (Udaipur region); Dhundhar (Jaipur region); Hadoti (Kota region); and Shekhawati (Sikar region).

Hills of Rajasthan

The state is dissected by the Aravalli Range, which extends diagonally across Rajasthan from the north-east to the south-west, inhibiting the movement of the Thar Desert eastwards. In places, the Aravalli is over 750m high, although the average elevation of the state falls between 100 and 350m above sea level. The highest point of the range is known as Guru Shikhar, which rises 1721m above mean sea level, and is the highest peak of Mt Abu. The Aravalli may be the oldest existing mountain range in the world. There is a second hilly spur, the Vindhyas, in the southernmost regions of Rajasthan.

Rivers

The Aravalli Range effectively divides Rajasthan's two principal river systems. The Chambal, which is the only perennial river in the state, rises in Madhya Pradesh from the northern slopes of the Vindhyas, entering Rajasthan at Chaurasigarh. It forms part of the eastern border between Rajasthan and Madhya Pradesh. Supplemented by its tributaries, the Kali Sindh, Alnia, Kunu, Parbati, Eru, Mej, Chakan and Banas, it flows north-westwards, draining into the Yamuna River which courses across northern India, finally entering the sea at the Bay of Bengal.

The southern region of Rajasthan is drained by the Mahi and Sabarmati rivers, while the Luni, which rises about seven km north of Ajmer in the Aravalli at the confluence of the Saraswati and Sagarmati rivers, is the only river in western Rajasthan. It flows for 482 km before draining into the Arabian Sea at the Rann of Kutch in Gujarat. The Luni is seasonal, and comparatively shallow, although at places it is over two km wide. Its main tributaries are the Lilri, Raipur, Sukri, Bandi, Mitri, Jawai Khari, Sagi and Johari, which all rise in the Aravalli.

Marusthali – Region of Death

The arid desert region in the west of the state is known as Marusthali, or the Region of Death. This sandy wasteland extends between the Aravalli Range to the east and the Sulaiman Kirthar Range to the west. This is the Thar Desert, which is the eastern extension of the great Saharo-Tharian desert expanse. It encompasses 68% of the state's geographical area and represents 61% of the area covered by desert in India.

In Rajasthan, the arid zone includes the districts of Jaisalmer and Bikaner, the north-western regions of Barmer and Jodhpur districts, the western section of Nagaur and Churu districts, and the southern portion of Ganganagar district. The desert, the greatest part of which lies in Rajasthan, also extends into the neighbouring states of Gujarat Punjab and Haryana, and across the international border into Pakistan.

The sandy plains are periodically relieved by low rugged and barren slopes. The sand dunes of Marusthali, which comprise about 60% of the desert region, are formed partly by the erosion of these low eminences, and partly from sand carried from the Rann of Kutch in Gujarat by south-westerly winds.

It is hard to imagine that this now desolate region was once covered by massive forests and was host to various large animals. In 1996, two amateur palaeontologists discovered animal fossils in the Thar Desert which possibly date from some 300 million years ago. They include those of dinosaurs and their primitive ancestors. Fourteen km from Jaisalmer is the Akal Wood Fossil Park where fossils have been recovered which date from nearly 185 million years ago. Plant fossils as young as 45 million years old indicate that, geologically, the desertification of Rajasthan is relatively recent and an ongoing evolution.

Semi-Arid Transitional Plain

It is difficult to identify exactly where the desert region merges into the semi-arid region, which encompasses about 25% of the geographical area of the state. The semi-arid zone is characterised by a larger distribution of rock protrusions and numerous short water courses. It lies between the Aravalli Range and the Thar Desert, extending

Top Left: A young boy beats the dhol, Jaisalmer.
Top Right: Snake charmer playing the poongi, Pushkar.
Bottom Left: Traditional dancer at Shilpgram, near Udaipur.
Bottom Right: A musician playing the kamayacha, Jaisalmer.

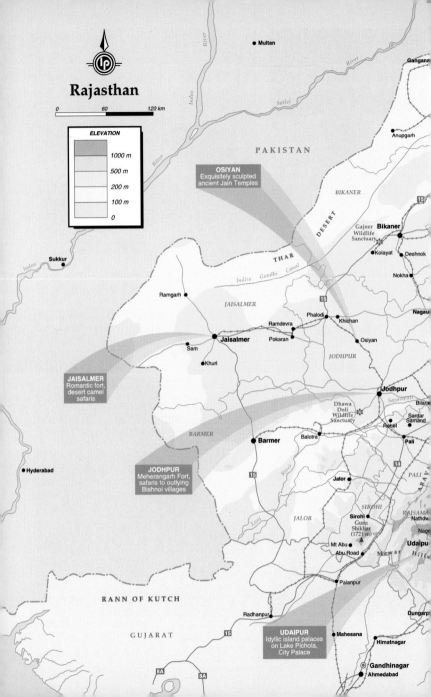

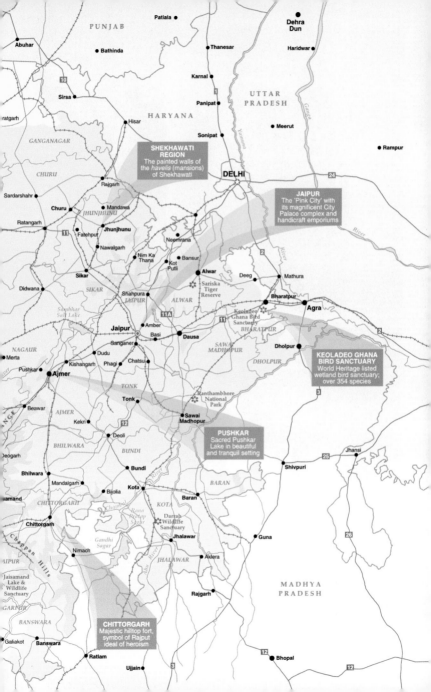

Top Left: Camel-wallah, Sam Sand Dunes, near Jaisalmer.
Top Right: Bhil people at a village near Bijaipur.
Bottom Left: A sadhu, or holy man, with his body covered in ash, lies beside a temple near Jaipur.
Bottom Right: Woman with nose ring, Jaipur.

westwards from the Aravalli, and encompassing the Ghaggar River Plain, parts of Shekhawati, and the Luni River Basin. The undulating terrain of the Shekhawati region acts to catch and contain rainwater, which is collected in depressions forming salt lakes. The Luni River forms a natural barrier between the desert and semi-arid region, inhibiting the movement of the desert eastwards.

Eastern Plains

The Eastern Plains is a large undulating region to the east of the Aravalli Range, which comprises two distinct areas, the Plain of Mewar, which contains the Banas River Basin, to the north of Udaipur, and the Chappan Plains, to Udaipur's south. The Plain of Mewar encompasses sections of Bhilwara and Bundi, all of Tonk district and most of Ajmer, Jaipur, Sawai Madhopur and Dholpur districts. It is drained by the Banas River and its tributaries which flow south-eastwards before joining the Chambal River on the Madhya Pradesh-Rajasthan border. The Chappan Plains comprises the two southernmost districts of Banswara and Dungarpur, and is drained by the Mahi River and its tributaries, which eventually flow into the Arabian Sea. The region is characterised by various low eminences.

Hadoti Plateau

This zone falls to the east and south-east of the Eastern Plains, and is characterised by hill folds and ridges, most notably around Chittorgarh, Bundi and Ranthambhore. It is the major catchment area for the Chambal River, which is flanked, particularly in the environs of Dholpur, by rugged and precipitous gorges. The region lying between the Banas and Chambal rivers is characterised by scarpland, composed of sandstone, while the area encompassing Jhalawar, Kota, parts of Chittorgarh, Bhilwara and Bundi forms a tableland traversed by the tributaries of the Chambal. The valleys formed by these rivers are rich in black soil.

CLIMATE

The climate of Rajasthan can be neatly divided into four different seasons: pre-monsoon, monsoon, post-monsoon and winter. Pre-monsoon, which extends from April to June, is the hottest season, with temperatures ranging from 32°C to 45°C. There is little relief from the scorching onslaught of the heat, particularly in the arid zone to the west and north-west of the Aravalli Range, where temperatures often climb above 45°C, particularly in May and June. Mt Abu registers the lowest temperatures at this time. In the desert regions, the temperature plummets as night falls. Prevailing winds are from the west and, in the desert sometimes carry dust storms (known locally as *andhis*). The only compensation is that the winds are usually accompanied by a slight reduction in temperatures, and sometimes, by light showers.

The monsoon is a welcome arrival in late June in the eastern and south-eastern regions of the state, falling in mid-July in the desert zones. It is preceded by dust and thunderstorms. Unless the rains are insubstantial, the monsoon is accompanied by a decrease in temperatures, with average maximum temperatures of between 29.5°C to 32.2°C in the south and south-east of Rajasthan, and an average of above 37.7°C in the north and north-western regions. Over 90% of Rajasthan's precipitation occurs during the monsoon period, and humidity is greatest at this time, particularly in August, although it's less evident in the desert zone.

The third season is the post-monsoon. The monsoon has generally passed over the entire state by mid-September. It is followed by a second hot season, with relatively uniform temperatures registered across the state at this time. In October, the average maximum temperature is 33°C to 38°C, and the minimum is between 18°C and 20°C.

The fourth season, and the one of most interest to visitors, is the winter, or cold season, which extends from December to March. There is a marked variation in maximum and minimum temperatures, and regional variations across the state. January

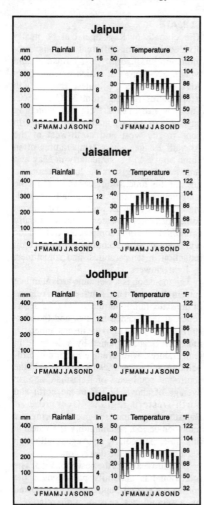

Jaipur

| mm | Rainfall | in | °C | Temperature | °F |

Jaisalmer

| mm | Rainfall | in | °C | Temperature | °F |

Jodhpur

| mm | Rainfall | in | °C | Temperature | °F |

Udaipur

| mm | Rainfall | in | °C | Temperature | °F |

predominantly from the north and north-east. At this time, relative humidity ranges from between 50% to 60% in the morning, and 25% to 35% in the afternoon.

There is a wide variation in the distribution of rainfall across the state, with a reduction in the volume of rain as you proceed further west. In the south-east, over 1500 mm can be expected, with most rain (about 90% of the annual rainfall) falling during the monsoon period (mid-June to mid-September), and an average of 55 days of rain. At the western extremity of Rajasthan, less than 100 mm may be registered in any one year, and rainfall is received on an average of only 15 days in the year.

ECOLOGY & ENVIRONMENT
Desertification
The greatest threat faced by the inhabitants of Rajasthan today is that of desertification. While this is in part a natural phenomenon which has occurred over the ages as geological factors have given rise to warmer and drier climates, the process is exacerbated by the problem of a burgeoning human and animal population endeavouring to utilise ever-diminishing resources. The Thar Desert is the most densely populated desert in the world, with an average of 61 people per sq km, as opposed to only three people per sq km in deserts elsewhere in the world. Further pressure is placed on this fragile region by the density of livestock: while the ratio of livestock to humans elsewhere in the country is 1:05, in the desert, it is 1:2.

An acute shortage of water, salinity, erosion, periodic droughts, overgrazing, overcultivation and overconsumption of scanty vegetation for fuel and timber requirements all either contribute to or are a consequence of the continuing desertification of Rajasthan. As inhabitants scour the landscape for wood fuel, some species of vegetation are severely threatened. The roots of *Calligonum polygonoides*, which is one of the few species found on sand dunes, are used for fuel, and the removal of this plant is severely affecting the stability of the sand dunes. Once common in Jodhpur district,

is the coolest month of the year. Average temperatures at the following centres are as follows (minimums are in parentheses): Bikaner, 22°C (9°C); Jaipur, 22.8°C (9°C); Ajmer, 22.8°C (7.7°C); Jodhpur, 24.4°C (9°C); and Kota, 25°C (10.5°C). There is slight precipitation in the north and north-eastern regions of the state, and light winds,

this plant is now completely absent here. Rohira has all but disappeared from the arid zone. The wood of this plant, known locally as Marwar teak, is highly prized for furniture construction, and traditionally was used in the carved architraves and window frames of *havelis* (mansions).

A Marwari proverb illustrates the destructive effects of overgrazing on the desert:

Oont chhode Akaro, Bakri chhode Kangro
The camel consumes everything other than ak (a thorny shrub), but the goat devours even that, leaving only the pebbles.

Periodic droughts are commonplace in Rajasthan, and are the main contributor to famine. Droughts are caused by the unreliability of the monsoon; in any five years, two may be considered as drought years. In the desert regions, it is not uncommon for one in every three years to be stricken by drought. The success of crops is also threatened by scorching heat; sandy soils which are at the best of times not particularly fertile, being notably nutrient deficient, particularly in nitrogen; intermittent dust storms which smother and destroy crops; and few underground water resources. Although Rajasthan constitutes some 10.4% of the total Indian geographical area, it has only about 1% of India's available water resources.

In western Rajasthan, even in good years, cultivation barely meets subsistence requirements. The number of rainy days in any one year is an average of only 15, and there is a very high rate of evaporation. The main river system, the Luni, which runs through this region, is not perennial. Ground water is often unfit for animal and human consumption, and irrigation is practically nonexistent.

It is not just the arid zones which are threatened due to over-utilisation of resources. The dense forests which covered the Aravalli Range prior to Independence are thinning rapidly. Prior to Independence, villagers were forbidden from encroaching on these forests, which were the preserves of the maharajas and barons who hunted large animals here. However, following Independence, huge stands of trees were felled to meet increasing timber, fuel and fodder requirements. This trend is continuing, with a 41.5% reduction in forest cover between 1972 and 1975, and 1980 and 1984.

The alarming disappearance of the forests of the Aravalli has provoked government intervention, and some areas are now closed periodically to enable the forest to regenerate. However, the closed regions are poorly policed by lowly paid guards who are eminently susceptible to bribes by pastoralists desperate to find fodder for their livestock. Local inhabitants are also entitled to take dry wood from the forests. However, there is simply not enough wood for everyone, which compels villagers to enter the forests and ringbark healthy trees, returning later to remove the dead timber.

Pollution

Pollution and deforestation are damaging many parts of southern Rajasthan. Marble mining has been particularly damaging to the environment, resulting in substantial deforestation and pollution. Industrial waste has largely been responsible for air, water and noise pollution. To address the issue of water pollution, the government has introduced policies which restrict building and development around lakes and rivers.

It's too late, unfortunately, for the village of Bichri, only 15 km from Udaipur, where most of the village's canals are contaminated with sulphurous sludge which was released indiscriminately by various chemical plants in the district. Over 350 hectares of prime wetland has been rendered a desolate wasteland and the water in dozens of wells in the vicinity of the factories is unfit for human consumption. The companies continued to manufacture highly toxic chemicals without official permission. Despite a Supreme Court order to safely store effluents, chemical waste was released into streams or mixed with soil and deposited in various places in a crude attempt to hide it, with the result that these toxic effluents have seeped into the ground water.

Conservation

According to scientists, the most efficient means to combat the process of desertification is afforestation. Not only will afforestation programmes provide food, fodder, fuel and timber, but trees stabilise the earth and act as windbreaks, therefore lessening the damage caused by sandstorms. The sparse vegetation in the arid zone is both in a very degraded condition and extremely slow growing, a further cause for alarm.

The first official recognition of the advancement of the Thar Desert and its alarming ramifications for the inhabitants of the arid zone occurred in 1951. As a direct result of this finding, the Desert Afforestation Research Station was established in Jodhpur in 1952, which in 1959 became the Central Arid Zone Research Institute, to conduct research into the problems of desertification. This is the most important institute of its type in south Asia.

The most important work being conducted by the institute is the stabilising of shifting sand dunes; the establishment of silvipastoral and fuelwood plantations; planting of windbreaks which reduce wind speed and subsequent erosion; rehabilitation of degraded forests; and afforestation of barren hill slopes, among other endeavours.

Some of the work carried out at the institute has been the subject of criticism by conservationists. They claim that, rather than protecting and preserving the desert ecosystem, massive endeavours to irrigate and afforest the arid zone fundamentally alter its fragile composition.

An afforestation project on the banks of the Indira Gandhi (Rajasthan) Canal has come under attack. The indigenous *Calligonum polygonoides*, which has already completely disappeared from some regions in the arid zone, is being uprooted and replaced with fast-growing species such as *Eucalyptus hybrid* and *Acacia tortilis*. *Calligonum polygonoides*, with its deep and widespreading root system, is an important stabiliser of sand dunes. Further, the inhabitants who have been allocated land in the environs of the canal from which their fields are irrigated have uprooted this shrub in order to raise crops. This has resulted in heavy siltation of a portion of the canal in Jaisalmer district and, where shrubs have been uprooted, shifting sand dunes have become prevalent, rendering much of this area a wasteland.

Animal husbandry is the traditional livelihood of the majority of the inhabitants of the 11 desert districts of Rajasthan, forming the major staple of the economy. Intensive planting of non-native species in the name of afforestation reduces traditional grazing grounds. In addition to upsetting the finely balanced desert ecosystem, such species are of little nutritional or practical use to villagers. Environmentalists argue that development should work not counter to, but in harmony with, the desert ecosystem. It should promote the generation and conservation of desert species which are finely attuned and adapted to the fragile environment and provide food, fodder and fuel.

Indira Gandhi Canal Project

It has been suggested that the massive Indira Gandhi Canal project, which is connected with the Bhakra Dam in Punjab, was concerned more with economics (opening up large arid belts for cash crops which are managed by wealthy landowners rather than the rural poor) than with ecological concerns and conservation. Indigenous plants have suffered, further adding to the degeneration of the arid zone. Also, critics suggest that the canal has incorporated traditional grazing grounds to which graziers are now denied access, and has been a key factor in the introduction of ecologically unsound cash crops, chemical fertilisers and pesticides. They argue that the command area has been exposed to over-irrigation which has destroyed fragile soil constituents. They suggest that traditional crops, which would provide nourishment and sustenance to local inhabitants and which require less irrigation, and traditional grazing grounds *(gochars)* could have been established. ∎

Conservation Organisations
There are several non-profit voluntary organisations in Rajasthan working at the grass-roots level to regenerate the ecosystem and promote environmentally sustainable development.

Bhinasar Gochar Andolan works to promote pasture systems and the use of traditional technology. It argues that every village should be considered a self-sufficient unit and that villagers should make collective decisions about development in their region. It has an underlying philosophy of multidimensional development which includes education, health, training, and social and cultural equality. The organisation has had some success in the growing of khejri seedlings in nurseries, one of the most important and useful plants of the desert, but considered for many years by scientists to be too difficult to propagate in nurseries. For more information, contact: Shubhu Patwa, Journalist, Bhinasar, Bikaner 334403; ☎ (0151) 52-3205 (home), 61-505 (work).

Tarun Bharat Sangh (Young India Organisation) is involved in water harvesting projects, comprising the construction of small dams which collect rain-fed water. Traditional technology, local labour and materials are utilised, and dams are shared by communities via small irrigation channels. For more information, write to: Rajendra Singh, Tarun Bharat Sangh, PO Bhikampura Kisori, District Alwar 301022.

Ubeshwar Vikas Mandal is concerned with the afforestation of hilly areas. For more information, write to: Kisor Sant, Ubeshwar Vikas Mandal, 10-C Fatehpura, Udaipur 313001.

The **Central Arid Zone Research Institute**, in Jodhpur, has a small pictorial museum. It is open Monday to Saturday from 10 am to 5 pm, and includes a photographic exhibition illustrating the work of the institute. For more information, write to: Central Arid Zone Research Institute (CAZRI), Jodhpur, 342003. ■

FLORA & FAUNA
Flora

Vegetation in the desert zone is sparse, with only a limited range of very slow-growing thorny trees and shrubs, and some grasses, which have adapted to the hostile conditions. The most common tree species are the ubiquitous khejri *(Prosopis cineraria)* and various strains of acacia. Rajasthan also has some dry teak forest, dry mixed deciduous forest, bamboo brakes and subtropical hill forests. Forest stocks are dwindling, however, as inhabitants scour the landscape for fuel and fodder. Forests, most of which are in very poor condition, cover only just over 9% of the state, mostly to the east of the Aravalli Range.

The hardy khejri, which is held sacred by the Bishnoi tribes of Jodhpur district, is the most prolific tree of the arid zone. It is extremely drought resistant, due to its deep root system. The thorny twigs are used for barriers between fields to keep sheep and goats away from crops. The leaves are dried and used for fodder. The tree also produces a bean-shaped fruit, which can be eaten ripe or unripe. When unripe, it is cooked and eaten as *sangri*. The wood is used to make furniture and the branches also burnt for fuel. The twigs are used in the sacred fire burnt at marriage ceremonies.

Another tree found distributed across the arid zone is rohira *(Tecoma undulata)*, the pods of which have medicinal value in the relief of abscesses; the wood is used in furniture construction. The Central Arid Zone Research Institute has had some success introducing faster-growing exotic species to the desert zone, including various species of acacia.

Grasses of the arid zone include sewan *(Lasiurus sindicus)*, which is found over large areas, dhaman *(Cenchrus ciliaris)*, boor *(Cenchrus jwarancusa)* and bharut *(Cenchrus catharticus)*. The last of these is abundant in times of drought, when it serves as a staple for the poor.

There are various species of shrubs in the arid zone, including *Calligonum polygonoides*, known locally as phog, which, with its extensive root system, acts to stabilise sand dunes. The wood is used in construction (when green), the branches serve as camel fodder, and the pods, which are known as lasson, are eaten as vegetables. Other shrub species include the leafless khair *(Capparis decidua)*, ak *(Calotropis procera)* and thor *(Euphorbia caduca)*. Khair not only has strong and durable wood which is resistant to white ants, but produces a fruit which can be eaten fresh or preserved. Ak prospers in sandy soil, and both ak and thor produce a juice which is taken as a cough elixir. The leaves of thor, known as papri, are eaten as a vegetable.

Keoladeo Ghana National Park, in Bharatpur district, has nearly 280 species of plants, including numerous herbs. Common trees found in the park include *Acacia nilotica*, *Acacia leucophloea*, *Prosopis juliflora* and *Prosopis cinerarea*.

Ranthambhore National Park, in Sawai Madhopur district, also has a variety of vegetation, with 306 species having been identified, including 73 tree species, 13 shrubs and various perennial and annual climbers. There are 30 species of grasses, eight of which are valuable as fodder, and two of which are perennial. Over 100 species of vegetation have medicinal value.

Fauna

Despite the inhospitable terrain, Rajasthan hosts a wide variety of mammals and birds. Mammals of the arid zone have, by necessity, adapted to the hostile environment in order to survive. Some mammals of the Thar Desert supplement their fluid intake with insects, which are composed of between 65% and 80% water, and water-bearing plants. Others retain water for longer periods. Means of adapting to the extremes in temperature include burrowing in the sand or venturing out only at night, when the temperature plummets.

Antelopes & Gazelles Despite the paucity of blackbuck antelope numbers in most parts of Rajasthan, there are still substantial populations in Jodhpur district, where these animals are afforded special protection by the Bishnoi tribes who live here. Blackbucks

The chinkara is remarkable for its swiftness and its ability to survive for long periods without water.

feature fine spiralling horns in mature males which can be up to 60 cm long.

It is also partly due to the efforts of the Bishnoi that populations of chinkara, or Indian gazelle, are still found in the arid zone. Chinkaras are slighter than blackbucks, standing some 100 cm tall, and live in smaller herds, sometimes with no more than three members. They are very well adapted to the desert, thriving on wild grasses and various types of shrubs.

Another member of the *Bovidae* family is the nilgai, or bluebull, a large, stocky animal whose front legs are longer than its rear legs, giving it an ungainly, sloping stance. Nilgai are found in most parts of India, and in Rajasthan are found on open plains (although not in the extreme west of the state) and in the foothills of the Aravalli Range.

The Cat Family There are various representatives of the cat family in Rajasthan. Probably the most well known is the Indian tiger. Tigers were once found right along the length of the Aravalli Range. However, due to being hunted almost to the point of extinction by Rajasthan's princely rulers, and later by animal poachers trading in illegal skins, and due to the reduction in their habitat as a consequence of encroachment by farmers, they are now found only at Ranthambhore and Sariska national parks, both of which are administered by Project Tiger.

The leopard, or panther, is rarely seen, but inhabits rocky declivities in the Aravalli, as well as parts of Jaipur and Jodhpur districts.

A much smaller specimen of the cat family is the jungle cat, which is about 60 cm long, excluding the tail, and weighs between five and six kg. The jungle cat is notable for its long limbs and short tail (about 25 cm long), and is able to kill animals larger than itself. It is generally nocturnal, but may hunt in the morning and evenings. It may be seen at the Keoladeo Ghana National Park.

Smaller than the jungle cat is the Indian desert cat, which is about the size of a domestic moggie, but is covered in spots, other than on the tail, flanks and cheeks, which are striped. The desert cat was once fairly well distributed in the Thar Desert, but is now rarely seen.

The Dog Family The jackal is renowned for its unearthly howling, which enables jackals to locate each other and form packs. Once quite common in Rajasthan, they were found close to villages where they preyed on livestock. Reduction of their habitat and hunting for their skins has drastically reduced jackal numbers. They are nocturnal, and feed on rodents, lizards, small mammals and carrion.

The wolf once roamed in large numbers in the desert zone, but was hunted almost to the point of extinction by farmers who lost numbers of their herds to this predator. Over recent decades, they have begun to make a reappearance due to concerted conservation endeavours. Wolves protect themselves from the scorching heat of the desert by digging burrows in sand dunes. In the desert zone, they live in pairs rather than packs. Their prey consists of domestic animals, rodents, small mammals and birds.

The desert fox is a subspecies of the red fox, and was once prolific in the Thar Desert, but due to hunting and loss of habitat, its numbers are now drastically reduced. A close cousin of the desert fox is the Indian fox, which used to be found in the arid zone, although not in the extreme west. Like the desert fox, its numbers have dramatically declined, and now it is found in Rajasthan only in national parks.

Rodents The largest of the rodents found in Rajasthan, or in all of India for that matter, is the crested porcupine. In the arid zone, the crested porcupine is found in the environs of hills and near fixed sand dunes. It is seldom seen, as it only ventures out at night, and is herbivorous.

There are several gerbils in the arid zone, including the nocturnal ratod, the blight of farmers, as it wreaks havoc on crops. The ratod is the largest gerbil in the Thar Desert, and is widely distributed, although it is not found on sand dunes. It is about the same size as a house rat.

A smaller version is the desert gerbil. Like the ratod, the desert gerbil is the bane of farmers, descending in vast numbers on crops and causing untold damage. The burrowing activity of these pests contributes towards desertification: in the arid zone, between 12,000 and 15,000 burrows have been identified per hectare. Each burrow opening requires the shifting of one kg of soil, which is carried by the high velocity winds, contributing towards soil erosion and dust storms. A distinctive characteristic of the desert gerbil is the manner in which it alerts its fellows to danger. When sensing danger, gerbils thump the earth with their hind feet and the entire colony flees to their burrows.

Found in India only in the Indian desert is the hairy footed gerbil, which thrives in extremely arid regions, and is commonly found in sand dunes. It feeds on all vegetable matter, and supplements its fluid intake with the consumption of insects.

There are various species of rats and mice in the desert region. The mole rat owes its name to its distinctive mole-like appearance, accentuated by diminutive ears. It has a short tail and a reddish-brown coat. This destructive little fellow gnaws away the bark around the main stems of trees from its underground burrow, eventually causing the death of the tree.

The lesser bandicoot is found all over India, although those found in Rajasthan are smaller than those of South India. This is a relatively new arrival to Rajasthan, having colonised those areas abutting the Indira Gandhi Canal where irrigation has been introduced. It is similar in appearance to the common house rat, although has a shorter tail, and is a major pest to farmers.

Monkeys Two types of monkey are found in Rajasthan, the rhesus monkey and the more gangly langur. The rhesus is found predominantly in the vicinity of the Aravalli Range. It has a distinctive red face and red rump, and lives in large groups headed by a dominant male. Rhesus monkeys are often found in or near human habitations, upon which they have become dependent for food.

The langur is covered by brownish-grey fur and has a black face with prominent eyebrows. It is herbivorous and, like the rhesus, can be found in or near human settlements.

Bats Bats found in Rajasthan include a sub-species of the pigmy pipistrelle, the *Pipistrellus mimus glaucillus*, a diminutive

The Hanuman langur may be encountered at some temples.

bat which can be found living between the walls of houses or beneath tree bark.

The disconcerting-looking Indian false vampire is a carnivore, living on small rodents, other rats, lizards and small birds. It has enormous ears in proportion to its head and powerful wings. It is found in eastern Rajasthan.

Insectivores Mammals found in Rajasthan belonging to this group include the nocturnal Indian shrew, which is found throughout

Royal Hunts

The Rajputs, particularly the princes, were once passionate hunters and were greatly admired for their shooting skills. Hunting, or *shikhar*, was considered an important part of an Indian prince's upbringing, right up until the first half of this century. A handful of princesses were even encouraged to excel at this elite sport. Children as young as 10 years old, lugging heavy rifles, would participate in hunts, eager to return to the palace with an animal of some sort.

Indeed in India, hunting was the 'sport of kings' and many princes toured the world in search of new and unusual animals to add to their collection. Stuffed tigers, lion-skin rugs (complete with head), zebra-fur lamps and mounted animal trophies filled many of Rajasthan's palaces.

Some maharajas believed that hunting was necessary to maintain a crucial balance of wildlife. Others claimed it was their duty to protect their subjects from the many dangerous animals that lurked around villages.

But hunting was not the sport of Indian princes alone. The British were also very keen hunters and organised elaborate shooting expeditions. During their heyday in India, the British Raj, English lords, viceroys and other dignitaries often joined the maharajas on killing sprees through the jungles. Trudging through the forest atop elephants, they were mainly in search of the big jungle cats – lions, tigers, panthers and leopards. But almost anything that came in their path would do, from wild boar to spotted deer.

Today hunting is illegal in India. A number of maharajas have become staunch conservationists and have played an active role in protecting the country's dwindling wildlife population. Nowadays, it is the lucrative international poaching trade that threatens some of India's wildlife with extinction. ∎

Rajasthan, although predominantly in the Aravalli Range and the semi-arid Shekhawati region. It is also known as a musk rat, but does not belong to the rodent family, and can be distinguished from a rat by its prominent, flexible nose.

Other insectivores include two species of hedgehog: the Indian hedgehog and the desert hedgehog. Both are nocturnal creatures. The desert hedgehog is larger, and is prolific in the desert region. It protects itself from predators by rolling into a ball, with its sharp quills a deterrent to attack.

The Indian hedgehog rarely ventures into the extreme arid zones, but is found in Jodhpur district and Shekhawati.

Other Mammals The wild boar belongs to the pig family and, once prolific in Rajasthan, its numbers are now confined to the south-eastern Aravalli Range, around Mt Abu, and in the vicinity of the new Indira Gandhi Canal. It has tiny eyes, small tusks, a stocky frame and a short, fine tail. The hunting of wild boar was a favourite occupation of the maharajas of Rajasthan.

The sloth bear inhabits forested regions, and in Rajasthan can be found on the western slopes of the Aravalli Range. The average length of the sloth bear is some 150 cm, and it stands 75 cm at the shoulder. It is covered in long black hair, other than on the muzzle. It feeds on vegetation and insects, although has been known to eat carrion.

The striped hyena defies categorisation, resembling a dog but having various feline-like anatomical features, such as the teeth. It is found in Rajasthan on rocky terrain, and is a nocturnal creature, feeding on carrion and occasionally killing ailing sheep or goats.

The desert hare is found in desert grasslands, and poses a nuisance to farmers, as it feeds on crops. It also ringbarks saplings by tearing the bark near the base of the stem, a bane to conservationists engaged in reafforestation.

Two types of mongoose can be found in Rajasthan: the small Indian mongoose and the Indian grey mongoose, or common mongoose. The small Indian mongoose is found in the arid zone and lives on insects, small rodents, lizards, birds and even snakes. The Indian grey mongoose is larger than its cousin, and enjoys, when it can get it, poultry. They also climb trees to divest nests of eggs.

A civet which is a subspecies of the small Indian civet inhabits the Thar Desert. It is a long, lean animal with an elongated head and short limbs, and is nocturnal. It feeds on poultry, insects, lizards, rodents and eggs.

The Indian pangolin is rare in Rajasthan, although not unknown. It is a curious creature with an armour of overlapping scales which are in fact flattened hairs or spines. When it is threatened, the pangolin rolls itself into an almost impenetrable ball. Its diet consists of ants and termites.

Birdlife There is an abundance of birdlife in Rajasthan and no less than 450 species have been identified in the state. The Keoladeo Ghana National Park, near Bharatpur in eastern Rajasthan, is an internationally renowned bird sanctuary.

Birds of the Forests The forests of the Aravalli Range provide habitat for numerous birds. These include orioles, hornbills, mynas, kingfishers, swallows, parakeets, warblers, robins, flycatchers, peacocks, quails, doves, barbets, bee-eaters, woodpeckers and drongos, among others.

The peacock, the elegant national bird, is represented frequently in Rajasthani art.

In the Sitamata-Pratapgarh area can be seen lorikeets, which are found nowhere else in the state. The forests of Darrah are home to the Alexandrine parakeet. Birds of prey include numerous species of owl (great horned, dusky, brown fishing and collared scops, and spotted owlet), eagles (spotted and tawny), white-eyed buzzards, black winged kites and shikras.

Birds of the Wetlands The wetlands in eastern Rajasthan encompass India's most important bird sanctuary: the Keoladeo Ghana National Park. Other wetlands include those encompassed by Sariska and Ranthambhore national parks, Jaisamand Lake in Udaipur district and Sadar Samand Lake in Jodhpur district. Keoladeo Ghana has the widest variety of species, and all species mentioned in this section are found at Keoladeo Ghana National Park.

Migratory species include spoonbills, herons, cormorants, storks, openbills, ibis and egrets, among others.

Wintering waterfowl include common, marbled, falcated and Baikal teal, pintail, gadwall, shoveler, coot, wigeon, bar-headed and greylag geese, brahminy and common pochard. Waders include snipe, sandpipers and plovers. Several terrestrial species include the Siberian crane, which only winters at Keoladeo, the monogamous sarus, which inhabits the park year round, and the beautiful demoiselle crane. In Keoladeo, species resident throughout the year include moorhens, egrets, herons, storks and cormorants.

Birds of prey at Keoladeo include various types of eagles (greater spotted, steppe, imperial, Spanish imperial, fishing), vultures (white-backed and scavenger) and owls (spotted, dusky horned and mottled wood). Other birds of prey include the pallid and marsh harrier, sparrowhawk, kestrel and goshawk.

Birds of the Grasslands Grasslands, which are rich in insects on which birds feed, can be found throughout Rajasthan. Some of the better grassland zones to spot birds are the Tal Chhapar Sanctuary in Churu district (northern Rajasthan); Sorsan, near Kota (southern Rajasthan); Sonkalia, near Ajmer (eastern Rajasthan); and in the environs of the Indira Gandhi Canal (western Rajasthan).

The vulture, a bird of prey, actually feeds on carrion.

Common birds of the grasslands include various species of lark, including the short-toed, crested, sky and crowned finch-lark. Quails, including grey, rain, common and bush, can also be seen in the grasslands, as can several types of shrike (grey, rufous-backed and bay-backed), mynas, drongos and partridges. Migratory birds include the lesser florican, which can be seen during the monsoon, and the houbara bustard, which winters at the grasslands. Birds of prey include falcons, eagles, hawks, kites, kestrels and harriers.

Birds of the Desert The Thar Desert also has a prolific variety of birdlife. At the small village of Khichan, about 135 km from Jodhpur, vast flocks of demoiselle cranes descend on fields in the morning and evening from the last week of August, or first week of September, to the end of March. Other winter visitors to the desert include houbara and common cranes.

Water is of course scarce in the desert, so at the water holes that do exist, flocks of birds can be seen in their hundreds. These water holes attract large flocks of imperial, spotted, pintail and Indian sandgrouse in the early mornings. Other desert dwellers include drongos, common and bush quail, blue tailed and little green bee-eaters and grey partridges.

Birds of prey in the desert include eagles (steppe and tawny), buzzards (honey and long-legged), goshawks, peregrine falcons, kestrels, and various types of buzzard. The most notable of the desert and dry grassland dwellers is the impressive great Indian bustard, which stands some 40 cm high and can weigh up to 14 kg.

The little green bee-eater is commonly seen perched on posts and wires from where it sallies forth after its favourite food – bees.

Endangered Species
Tigers While some of Rajasthan's wildlife is perishing as a consequence of encroachment on its habitat, other species are falling at the hands of poachers. It is estimated that since 1990 over 20 tigers have been slaughtered at Ranthambhore National Park. After its skin is removed, the bones inevitably find their way to China, where they form the basis of 'tiger wine', believed to have healing properties. The penis is coveted for its alleged aphrodisiac powers. The skin and claws can fetch up to US$6000 in Nepal.

National parks and sanctuaries are proving to be lucrative hunting grounds for poachers. Frequently, only main roads in parks are patrolled by often poorly paid guards, so poachers can trespass without fear of detection. In July 1992, Badia, one of Ranthambhore's more committed trackers, was brutally murdered – allegedly by poachers, who have still not been convicted.

The Cult of Conservation
The Bishnoi cult, which now has adherents in Haryana, Gujarat and Uttar Pradesh, was founded by Guru Jambhoji in the late 15th century in Bikaner district. It stresses the conservation and protection of all living things, conforming to the 29 *(bishnoi)* principles outlined by Guru Jambhoji. It is due to the vigilance of the Bishnoi tribes in the environs of Jodhpur that animals such as the blackbuck are flourishing in this area. ■

Strict measures have been implemented in order to stop the lucrative international trade in tiger skins and bones, including severe penalties imposed on offenders. According to the chief wildlife warden in Jaipur, it is now almost easier to kill a human being than a tiger at Ranthambhore National Park! Nevertheless, the smaller animals on which tigers prey are still hunted by local villagers, and the survival of this beautiful, endangered animal still hangs in the balance.

Other Fauna The habitat of the animals of the Thar Desert is being steadily destroyed by overgrazing and over-utilisation of desert resources. Some mammals which once thrived in the arid zone have now completely vanished from this region, such as the wolf, cheetah, caracal and wild ass. Several other species are on the endangered list, including the desert fox, jackal, panther, blackbuck (Indian antelope) and chinkara (Indian gazelle).

There has been some reversal in the fate of the great Indian bustard, whose numbers have dwindled alarmingly due to hunting and as a consequence of its eggs being trampled by livestock. The establishment of the Desert National Park has seen a healthy increase in bustard numbers, and its future is no longer in immediate peril. The population of great Indian bustards in the Desert National Park in western Rajasthan accounts for 50% of the total population (estimated at 1500) in all of India.

Hunting & Human Encroachment The tiger is not the only animal to fall at the hands of human beings. Although not necessarily in immediate danger of extinction, other large mammals, such as the spotted deer, blackbuck, sambar, chowsingha, bluebull, wild boar and chinkara are hunted for their meat, skins or antlers. Smaller mammals such as mongooses, squirrels, jungle cats, hares and jackals are killed for their fur. The skins of reptiles supply the lucrative handbag, shoe and belt market. Fish are indiscriminately killed by dynamiting rivers or by application of poison. Monkeys are trapped and exported to foreign private collectors. Birds and small mammals are captured in nets. Large carnivores such as tigers and leopards are poisoned with baits, or killed or wounded in spring traps which snare their limbs. Wild boars are killed by consuming baits which literally explode inside them.

NATIONAL PARKS & SANCTUARIES

Rajasthan has several world-renowned sanctuaries and national parks, and numerous other sanctuaries. Some of these, such as Ranthambhore and Sariska, were originally the hunting reserves of the maharajas. Other parks, such as the Desert National Park & Sanctuary in western Rajasthan have been established to protect and preserve the unique plants and animals found in the arid zone.

Wildlife Conservation Organisations & Resources
Library There is a library at the offices of the Chief Wildlife Warden in Jaipur where visitors are welcome with prior permission. Contact Mr MS Yadav, Technical Assistant to the Chief Wildlife Warden, Van Bhawan (near Secretariat), Jaipur (☎ (0141) 38-3367).

World Wide Fund for Nature (WWF) WWF in Delhi publishes both annual and quarterly journals on issues relating to wildlife conservation in India. Contact World Wide Fund for Nature, 172-B Max Mueller Marg, Lodhi Estate, New Delhi 110003 (☎ (011) 461-6352; fax 462-6837).

Bombay Natural History Society The society conducts studies on habits and habitats of birds and wildlife, as well as initiating programmes to promote their preservation. For further information contact the society at Hornbill House, Dr Salim Ali Chowk, Shaheed Bhagat Singh Rd, Mumbai (Bombay) 400023 (☎ (022) 284-3869; fax 283-7615). ■

Eastern Rajasthan

Ranthambhore National Park Ranthambhore was established as a sanctuary in 1955, came under the administration of Project Tiger in 1973 and was declared a national park in 1980. It encompasses an area of 1334 sq km in eastern Rajasthan, on the eastern edge of the Thar Desert, and within its precincts is an ancient fort. There is a wide range of fauna, including, apart from the elusive tiger (according to the last census, there are 27 tigers at Ranthambhore), cheetals, leopards, nilgai (bluebull), chinkara (Indian gazelle), sambar (India's largest deer), the threatened wild boar, hyenas, jackals and sloth bears. The artificial lakes at Ranthambhore also support a wide variety of birdlife, with no less than 270 species represented, including some migratory visitors. There is an excellent infrastructure in place for visits, including organised safaris, and accommodation to suit all pockets. The closest town, Sawai Madhopur, is easily accessible by rail, being on the Jaipur to Kota line. Best time to visit: October to April.

Sariska National Park Tigers are also the big attraction at this national park, encompassing 800 sq km of predominantly dry mixed deciduous forest astride the Aravalli Range in Alwar district, 107 km from Jaipur and 200 km from Delhi. Sariska was once the exclusive hunting ground of the maharajas of Alwar (the royal hunting lodge is now a beautiful luxury hotel). It was established as a sanctuary in 1958, and incorporated into Project Tiger in 1979. As at Ranthambhore, tigers are elusive, but other large mammals at the park include leopards, cheetals, chinkara, chowsingha (four-horned antelopes), the threatened ratel (honey badger), wild dogs and more. There is also an ancient fort and several ancient temples. Safaris can be organised at the Forest Reception Office at the park, and there are three places to stay: a forest rest house, tourist bungalow and the upmarket Hotel Sariska Palace. The closest large town is Alwar, which lies 36 km to the north-east, and is connected with both Delhi and Jaipur by regular train and bus services. Best time to visit: November to May.

Keoladeo Ghana National Park This is India's best known bird sanctuary (usually just called Bharatpur). It features large numbers of breeding waterbirds and thousands of migratory birds, including some from Siberia and China. The network of crossroads and tracks through the sanctuary increases opportunities to see the birds, deer and other wildlife. There is a good infrastructure in place for visitors, with rickshaw-wallahs trained in bird identification waiting outside the park gates to guide visitors through this beautiful park. There is accommodation to suit all budgets, both near the park entrance, and in Bharatpur. Bharatpur, only five km from the sanctuary, is easiest to access from Jaipur by bus. Best time to visit: October to March, July to August (wetlands).

Southern Rajasthan

Jaisamand Sanctuary This 62 sq km sanctuary was established in 1957 adjacent to the artificial Jaisamand Lake, which was built in the 17th century by Maharaja Jai Singh. Apart from the range of wildlife which can be seen here, the lake itself is well worth visiting, with beautiful *chhatris*, or cenotaphs, around its perimeters. The lake encourages a wide variety of birds, both resident and migratory, and is also inhabited by crocodiles, while the dry deciduous forest is home to cheetal, leopard, chinkara and wild boar. There are several places to stay, including a tourist bungalow, forest rest house and upmarket hotel. The sanctuary is 48 km south-east of Udaipur. Best time to visit: November to June.

Darrah Wildlife Sanctuary This sanctuary encompasses 250 sq km of dry deciduous forest, 50 km from Kota. Mammals which inhabit the sanctuary include leopards, chinkaras, spotted deer, sambars, the threatened wild boar, wolves and sloth bears. There is a forest rest house at Darrah, which also has rail connections. Contact the Wildlife Warden, Darrah Wildlife Sanctuary, Kamalpura, Kota. Best time to visit: February to May.

National Chambal Wildlife Sanctuary This 548 sq km sanctuary extends into neighbouring Madhya Pradesh, encompassing a sizeable stretch of the Chambal River, Rajasthan's only perennial river. The sanctuary was primarily established to protect the rare gharial, a type of thin-snouted fish-eating crocodile. Gharial can be seen basking on the river banks from the safety of boats, which can be hired in Kota. Other wildlife inhabiting the park (but less likely to be observed) are wolves, chinkara, blackbuck, wild boar and the rare (in Rajasthan, in any case) caracal. The sanctuary is easily accessible from Kota. Best time to visit: October to March.

Kumbhalgarh Sanctuary This sanctuary is adjacent to the historic Kumbhalgarh Fort, 84 km north of Udaipur, and encompasses 560 sq km in the Aravalli Range. It is best known for its wolves, which roam in packs of up to 40 animals. The sanctuary is also the habitat of the rare chowsingha, or four horned antelope, and also harbours populations of sloth bears, nilgai, wild boar, leopards, panthers, sambar and jackals. It's one of the few reserves that allows people to enter on horseback. There is mid-range accommodation available. Best time to visit: October to June.

Mt Abu Wildlife Sanctuary This 290 sq km sanctuary is the location of the highest peak in the Aravalli, Guru Shikhar (1721m). The sanctuary encompasses both dry mixed deciduous and subtropical forest, and has some large mammals, including wild boar, sambar, chinkara, (rarely seen) leopards and sloth bears. It is easily accessible from Mt Abu, eight km distant. Best time to visit: March to June.

Sitamata Wildlife Sanctuary This sanctuary covers 423 sq km of mainly deciduous forest. Wildlife includes deer, sambar, caracal and wild boar. It is 65 km south-east of Udaipur. Best time to visit: March to July.

Northern Rajasthan
Tal Chhapar Wildlife Sanctuary This sanctuary encompasses 70 sq km of grassland 95 km to the south-west of Churu. It has populations of blackbuck, chinkara, desert fox and desert cat, and both resident and migratory birds, such as various types of eagle (short-toed, tawny and imperial) and sparrowhawks. In September, large flocks of harriers visit Tal Chhapar, including Montagu's and marsh harriers, and smaller flocks of hen and pallid harriers. Demoiselle cranes are also winter visitors, Indian rollers can be seen in September and October, and bee-eaters, skylarks, ring and brown doves and crested larks are resident throughout the year. There is a forest rest house at Chhapar. Best time to visit: September to March.

Western Rajasthan
Desert National Park & Sanctuary This national park lies 42 km to the south-west of Jaisalmer, and was established in 1980 in order to preserve the fragile desert ecosystem and thus protect the range of drought-resistant species which inhabit it. It encompasses an area of 3162 sq km, an arid zone of sand dunes, thorn forest, scrub and sandy wastelands. There is a good representative selection of desert dwellers within the park, including blackbucks, chinkaras, nilgais, wolves, desert foxes, desert cats and crested porcupines. There are 43 species of reptiles and numerous bird species, most notable of which is the great Indian bustard, which is thriving in this region as a direct result of the establishment of the national park.

The national park should be avoided during the summer months, when temperatures soar to over 50°C. You will need to bring a good supply of drinking water at any time. Villagers may let rooms, or there are several rest houses in the park environs. Contact the Deputy Director, Desert National Park, Jaisalmer. Best time to visit: September to March.

Dhawa Doli Wildlife Sanctuary This sanctuary lies 40 km south-west of Jodhpur on the Barmer road, and has populations of blackbucks, partridges, desert foxes and nilgais. It is possible to visit the sanctuary on tours from Jodhpur. Best time to visit: October to February.

Gajner Wildlife Sanctuary This tiny (10 sq km) sanctuary is 32 km from Bikaner on the Jaisalmer road. It has a good representative variety of desert species, including desert cats and desert foxes, as well as chinkaras and blackbucks. There is upmarket accommodation in the village of Gajner. Best time to visit: October to March.

Khichan Khichan is a small village which lies only a few km from the large town of Phalodi, between Jodhpur and Jaisalmer, about 135 km from the former. It has not yet been listed as a wildlife sanctuary, but bird lovers shouldn't fail to visit. From late August/early September to the end of March, it's possible to witness the spectacular site of hundreds of demoiselle cranes descending on the fields around the village, which feed on grain distributed by villagers. To observe the cranes of Khichan, you need to advise in advance of your visit. See the Western Rajasthan chapter for details. Best time to visit: September to March.

GOVERNMENT & POLITICS
National
India has a parliamentary system of government. At the national level there is an upper house (Lok Sabha) and a lower house (Rajya Sabha). There are also state governments with legislative assemblies (Vidhan Sabha). The two national houses and the various state houses elect the Indian president, who is a figurehead – the prime minister wields the real power.

There is a strict division between the activities handled by the states and by the national government. The police force, education, agriculture and industry are reserved for the state governments. Certain other areas are jointly administered by the two levels of government.

The central government has the controversial right to assume power in any state if the situation in that state is deemed to be unmanageable. Known as President's Rule, it has been enforced either because the law and order situation is out of control or because there is a political stalemate.

In the May 1996 national elections, the Congress Party, which has ruled India for all but four years since Independence in 1948 lost its majority. The national government now comprises a coalition calling itself the United Front and is led by Deve Gowda. This alliance has effectively blocked the Hindu nationalist Bharatiya Janata Party (BJP), which won the greatest percentage of the vote without achieving a majority, from power.

State

Following the formation of the state of Rajasthan, executive and legislative powers were wielded by the rajpramukh, Man Singh II of Jaipur, who was assisted in the execution of his duties by the state ministry, whom he appointed. The chief minister, or premier, was Heera Lal Shashtri. The central government wielded jurisdiction over defence, external affairs and communications, and retained 'general control' over administration of the state, meaning that the rajpramukh had to comply with occasional central government interference. The title of rajpramukh was replaced by that of governor in 1956, a position which held little political weight.

The ministry headed by Shashtri was replaced by a council of ministers headed by CS Venkatachari in January 1951, which in turn was replaced three months later by that headed by Jainarain Vyas. The ministries were appointed by the rajpramukh, not democratically elected by their constituents. It was not until February 1952 that the first general election to the state assembly was held. Until this time, the inhabitants of Rajasthan had had little experience of democratic processes, with monarchical rule being virtually absolute.

Since Rajasthan has had an elected government, it has been ruled by various parties: Congress, the Janata People's Party, and by a coalition of the BJP and the Janata Dal. At various times it has also been subjected to President's Rule. In the 1996 state election, the BJP-Janata Dal coalition led by Bhairon Singh Shekhawat retained power.

ECONOMY

Prior to Independence, princely rulers derived revenue from rent, customs duty, transit duty imposed on traders and merchants passing through their respective kingdoms, and excise duty imposed on liquor and narcotic drugs. Some maharajas derived revenue from state-owned railways, or from forestry and mining. After the annual tribute payable to the British government was deducted, remaining revenue was spent on maintaining the state's army, on law enforcement, and on sustaining the princes' often extravagant lifestyles. Little of the funds derived from tax and non-tax sources were spent on public amenities or civic services such as health and education.

In the immediate post-Independence period, Rajasthan was one of India's poorest states, a situation exacerbated not only by its feudal legacy, but by the ravages wreaked on the region by periodic droughts and famines. Currently, the per capita income is below the national average with, in 1993-94, an average annual income of Rs 1760, as against the national average of Rs 2282.

Agriculture

Today agriculture and animal husbandry form the mainstay of the state's economy, representing, in the period 1994-95, 44.79% of the state's revenue, and in 1993-94, 40.51%, as against only 31.74% for the country as a whole. Droughts, which have become more frequent over recent years, are a major drain on state resources. For example, famine relief in 1987-88 exceeded the state's entire proposed budget for that year.

Despite massive expenditure on irrigation, agricultural output has fluctuated dramatically over the years. Actual grain production has increased since 1951, even though some years there have been much greater crop yields than others. The production of oilseeds has increased 24 fold, sugarcane production has more than doubled, and cotton has increased from just over 100,000 bales to over one million bales in 1994-95.

The number of livestock has also risen dramatically and is now almost double 1951 figures, being a total of some 40 million head. This represents an alarming trend, as overgrazing is substantially contributing to environmental degradation and desertification. The focus regarding livestock in the current five year economic plan is on increasing productivity and improving livestock health, with improvement in veterinary facilities, rather than increasing herds.

Substantial funds have also been directed towards afforestation, which will inhibit the advancement of desertification and soil erosion, and address the state's fuelwood deficits.

Industry

The production of textiles is the most important contributor to the industrial sector, and Rajasthan is one of India's major textile producers. In 1992-93, there were 30 textile mills in the state, employing around 50,000 people. The state produces almost half of the total national output of polyester viscose yarn, contributing some Rs 400 million to the national economy.

About 15,000 people are employed in the cement industry, which is the state's largest manufacturing industry, and this industry is continuing to grow. The production of sugar also contributes to the state economy, as does the mining of marble and sandstone, a trade in which the states of Rajputana have been engaged for centuries.

Handicrafts

In order to promote the growth of the handicraft sector and generate employment, the state government has run a large number of training programmes in which trainees receive a stipend as an incentive to attend. Over 11,000 people have been trained in carpet weaving under this programme. The Rajasthan Small Industries Corporation trains Scheduled Tribes in furniture making near Udaipur.

The state government has exempted most craft items from sales tax, so it is difficult to estimate the revenue earned from this sector, as it doesn't go into the state coffers. In 1994, there were over 166,000 small-scale industries, including cotton and wool spinning, carpet making, block-printing, gem cutting and polishing, ivory carving, pottery and brassware production, leather goods production, marble carving and enamelling, among others. It is estimated that more than 600,000 people are employed in this sector.

Infrastructure

A measure developed by the Centre for Monitoring Indian Economy (CMIF), which attaches a numerical value to the development of infrastructure such as roads, irrigation, education, health, transport and other facilities provided by states (which in turn can be used to gauge the relative prosperity of a given state), indicates that Rajasthan is well below the national average in terms of expenditure on infrastructure. It has consistently ranked third lowest out of the 15 major states for the last decade or so, with only trouble-torn Jammu & Kashmir, and Madhya Pradesh, India's largest state, falling below it on the index.

POPULATION & PEOPLE

According to the last national census (1991) the population of Rajasthan is 54.4 million, an alarming increase of some 38 million since the first census was conducted in 1951 shortly after Independence. In fact, Rajasthan registered the highest growth rate out of 17 of India's major states, and is well above the national growth rate of 23.5%.

There are various hypotheses for this phenomenal growth. Despite still being periodically ravaged by drought, Rajasthan no longer suffers from the famines which decimated populations in times past, as improved transport infrastructure and communications enables the stricken inhabitants to receive aid in the form of grain and fodder. Rajasthan is still a relatively poor state, and there is a direct correlation between poverty and the size of families. The perpetual desire for 'an heir and a spare' encourages parents to keep trying for two male offspring.

While the average number of people per sq km is 142, densities vary drastically according to region.

Hindus represent around 89% of the state's population. Scheduled Castes and Tribes form 17.29% and 12.44% of the state's population respectively.

About 8% of Rajasthan's population is Muslim, most of whom are Sunnite. There is a small affluent community of Shi'ite Muslims in south-eastern Rajasthan known as the Bohras.

Tribal People of Rajasthan

The main tribes of Rajasthan are the Bhils and the Minas, who were the original inhabitants of the area now called Rajasthan, but who were forced into the Aravalli Range by the Aryan invasion. Smaller tribes include the Sahariyas, Damariyas, Garasias and the Gaduliya Lohars.

Bhils The Bhils are an important tribal group and traditionally inhabited the south-eastern corner of the state – the area around Udaipur, Chittorgarh and Dungarpur – although the largest concentrations of them are found in neighbouring Madhya Pradesh.

Legend has it that the Bhils were fine archers, hence their name, which can be traced to the Tamil word *vil*, meaning bow. Bhil bowmen are mentioned in both the *Mahabharata* and the *Ramayana*. They were highly regarded as warriors, and the Rajput rulers relied heavily on them to thwart the invading Marathas and Mughals. In fact, some scholars suggest that the Rajputs owe their warrior propensities to their exposure to the Bhils, whom they emulated. The British formed a Mewar Bhil Corps in the 1820s in recognition of the Bhils' martial tradition.

Although originally food gatherers, the Bhils these days have taken up small-scale agriculture, or have abandoned the land altogether and taken up city residence and employment. The literacy rate of the Bhils, particularly the women, used to be one of the lowest of any group in the country which made them prime targets for exploitation and bonded labour. This trend is now being reversed, and the fortunes of the Bhils are improving accordingly. Several Bhils have even entered state parliament, becoming MLAs, including, in one instance, a Bhil woman.

Those Bhils who can afford it engage in polygamy. Marriages of love, as opposed to arranged marriages which are the norm in India, are condoned.

The Baneshwar Festival is a Bhil festival held near Dungarpur in February each year, and large numbers of Bhils gather for four days of singing, dancing and worship. Holi is another important time for the Bhils.

Witchcraft, magic and superstition are deeply rooted aspects of Bhil culture.

Minas The Minas are the second largest tribal group in the state after the Bhils, and are the most widely spread. They live in the regions of Shekhawati and eastern Rajasthan. Scholars are still disagreed as to whether the Minas are an indigenous tribe, or whether they migrated to the region from central Asia. The name Mina is derived from *meen*, or fish, and the Minas claim descent from the fish incarnation of Vishnu. Originally they were a ruling tribe, but their downfall was a long drawn-out affair. It began with the Rajputs and was completed when the British government declared them a criminal tribe in 1924, mainly to stop them trying to regain their territory from the Rajputs. In their skirmishes with the Rajputs, the Minas resorted to various unorthodox means such as demanding 'protection money' from villagers to curtail their dacoit activities.

Following Independence, their ignominious status as a 'criminal tribe' was lifted. However, their culture was by this time more or less totally destroyed, and they have been given protection as a Scheduled Tribe.

With the withdrawal of the Criminal Tribes Act, the Minas took to agriculture. As is the case with the Bhils, the literacy rate among the Minas was very low, but is improving.

Marriage is generally within the tribe. This is arranged by the parents and most marriages take place when the children are quite young.

Gaduliya Lohars The Gaduliya Lohars were originally a martial Rajput tribe, but these days are nomadic blacksmiths. Their traditional territory was Mewar (Udaipur) and they fought with the maharana against the Mughals. With typical Rajput chivalry, they made a vow to the maharana that they would only enter his fort at Chittorgarh after he had overcome the Mughals. As he died without achieving this, the clan was forced to become nomadic. When Nehru was in power he led a group of Gaduliya Lohars into Chittorgarh Fort, with the hope that they would then resettle in their former lands, but they preferred to remain nomadic.

Garasias The Garasias are a small Rajput tribe found in the Abu Road area of southern Rajasthan. It is thought that they intermingled with the Bhils to some extent, which is supported by the fact that bows and arrows are widely used.

The marriage ceremony is curious in that the couple elope, and a sum of money is paid to the father of the bride. If the marriage fails, the bride returns home, with a small sum of money to give to the father. Widows are not entitled to a share of their husband's property, and so generally remarry.

Sahariyas The Sahariyas are thought to be of Bhil origin, and live in the areas of Kota, Dungarpur and Sawai Madhopur in the south-east of the state. They are one of the least educated tribes in the country, with a literacy rate of only 5% and, as unskilled labourers, have been cruelly exploited.

As all members of the clan are considered to be related, marriages are arranged outside the tribe. Their food and worship traditions are closely related to Hindu customs. ∎

Female Infanticide

The mortality rate of female infants is greater than that of males. In 1991, there were 913 females per 1000 males in Rajasthan; the national figure was 929 per 1000. The dowry system, which requires the parents of the bride to ply the bridegroom's family with enormous gifts of cash and goods, ensures the continued undesirability of girl children, and the lower status of women in Rajasthani society.

The practice of killing newborn female infants was not unknown in Rajasthan prior to Independence, particularly among Rajput families, who were compelled according to tradition to pay vast sums in dowry to a girl's in-laws upon her marriage. Some analysts suggest that female infanticide may still take place in remote rural areas. Less vigilant post-natal care of female infants as opposed to male infants contributes to a higher mortality rate among girls. More affluent members of society had, until it was outlawed recently, recourse to tests such as amniocentesis and chorionic villus sampling (CVS) which revealed the sex of unborn children, enabling female foetuses to be aborted. It is not unlikely that, for the right fee, doctors in large cities such as Jaipur could be persuaded to still provide this service, in addition to abortion, where requested. ■

The Gujjars, who profess Hinduism, dwell in eastern Rajasthan, including Jaipur, Udaipur, Alwar, Kota and Bharatpur. They are divided into two groups, the Laur and the Khari.

The nomadic Rabari, or Raika, are also Hindu. They are divided into two groups, the Marus, who breed camels, and the Chalkias, who breed sheep and goats.

The affluent Oswals hail from Osiyan, near Jodhpur, and are successful in trade and commerce. They are predominantly Jain, although a few profess Vaishnavism. Oswal women are compelled to observe strict purdah, or seclusion.

See Tribal People of Rajasthan later in this section for information on Rajasthan's tribal people.

EDUCATION

Despite the vast improvement in educational facilities in Rajasthan in recent years, Rajasthan has the second lowest literacy rate in India – only 38.8%, as compared to the national average of 52.11%. Only the extremely poor state of Bihar in north-east India has a poorer literacy record. This depressing state of affairs is worsened when a breakdown of male and female literacy is considered: female literacy is only 20.48% (all-India: 39.3%), which is the lowest percentage of female literacy in *any* of the states and territories of India. In order to improve these statistics, the National Literacy Mission has introduced the Integrated Child Development Scheme (ICDS) in Rajasthan, which has established preschool programmes and provides supplementary food to improve child nutrition.

At the formation of the state of Rajasthan the state possessed only one university, in Jaipur. There are now six universities, and the state government is currently establishing a Sanskrit university. Since Independence, five medical colleges have been founded, as well as several technical and engineering colleges. There are 166 colleges, of which 97 are private, over 1200 higher secondary and senior higher secondary schools, 3200 secondary schools, 11,000 upper primary schools and 34,000 primary schools.

ARTS

The celebration of beauty in Rajasthan is abundantly evident in its traditional arts and crafts, as well as in everyday domestic items and tools of the Rajputs' trade such as swords and knives.

Traditionally, the maharajas commissioned fine artistic works to adorn their palaces and to convey a degree of opulence befitting their esteemed status; the flourishing of the arts in Rajasthan is due, in a good degree, to the patronage of Rajasthan's princely rulers.

Today the artisans are producing goods for the large number of foreign visitors to Rajasthan, most of whom are less discerning than your average king. Nevertheless, institutions such as the National Awards for

Master Craftsmen encourage artisans to strive for artistic excellence and perpetuate Rajasthan's fine artistic tradition.

Music and dance are integral to all celebrations and festivals, and Rajasthan has a rich tradition of regional folk dances. In some dances, whole communities participate, others are performed only by men or by women. There is also a tradition of itinerant performers who interpret popular or religious myths and legends through song, dance and drama, or who in the past received patronage at royal courts and performed for the pleasure of kings and their entourages.

Dance

Many tribal groups in southern Rajasthan have maintained old forms of folk dance. The *ghoomer* is a type of ceremonial dance performed only by women on special occasions, such as festivals or weddings. On the occasion of sacred festivals such as Navratri, women perform the ghoomer for the deities. This dance varies in different communities and regions. In Udaipur, the dancers join a circle and carry sticks which they rhythmically strike together.

The Bhil tribal people of southern Rajasthan perform a special dance during the festival of Holi in March known as the *gir*, which is performed only by men, who hold sticks which they beat together. The *gir-ghoomer* is performed by both men and women, dressed in traditional costume. At the commencement of the dance, participants form two circles. The women, who form a small inner circle, are encompassed by the men, who form a large circle around them, and who determine the rhythm of the dance by the beating together of sticks and striking of drums. As the dance proceeds, the participants change places, with the men forming the inner circle.

The *dandiya* is performed by both men and women as part of the exuberant Holi celebrations, and is particularly notable in Jodhpur district. Participants form a circle and beat together small sticks accompanied by musicians. Also performed during Holi, in eastern Rajasthan, is the *gindar*, which is

danced throughout the night. In an unusual show of tolerance, caste Hindus perform this dance with Dalits, or Untouchables.

The *neja* is danced by the Minas of Kherwara and Dungarpur just after Holi. In this dance, a coconut is placed on a large pole, and while men endeavour to dislodge it, women rhythmically beat sticks and strike the men with whips.

A form of the classical *kathak* dance, which is more commonly associated with Lucknow in Uttar Pradesh, is performed in Jaipur. This dance was traditionally performed by males only, but today it is danced by both boys and girls, the latter of whom dress as males. Kathak interprets through dance the stories of Krishna and his consort, Radha, and entails dramatic facial expressions, especially through the movement of the eyes and eyebrows, and dexterous movement of the neck and wrists.

The *terahtal*, which is derived from the Hindi word for '13', is performed with the aid of 13 cymbals, which are fastened to the bodies of the female dancers who are accompanied by male singers and drummers. It is performed in honour of the local deity, Ramdev, and can be seen at the Ramdevra Festival which is held in August or September at the small village of Ramdevra, near Pokaran in western Rajasthan.

The *gir* is a dance performed only by men of the Bhil tribal group.

Music

Folk music is a vital part of Rajasthani culture. Through songs the legendary battles of the Rajputs are told. The music engenders both a spirit of identity and provides entertainment as relief from the daily grind of wrenching a living from the inhospitable land.

Percussion Instruments The most common instrument found in the villages of Rajasthan is the *dhol*, or drum. Goat skin is stretched over both ends of the dhol, one end being beaten with the hand, and the other with a stick. There is also a smaller version of the dhol, the *dholak*, which is one of the most common instruments of northern India. Another type of drum is the *ektara*, which is played during devotional ceremonies by priests. The ektara consists of a gourd over which skin is stretched. This membrane is beaten with a finger or with a stick of bamboo.

Matas are played in pairs by two musicians. A mata is an earthenware pot over the opening of which a skin is stretched. It is a popular instrument of the Bhopas, a caste of professional storytellers. The *chara* is also an earthenware pot, but the mouth is left open, and into this the musician sometimes blows, creating a deep, resonant booming sound. The sides of the pot are struck with the right hand on which is worn a ring. Sometimes the musician accompanies the performance with dance steps. The chara is traditionally played by the Meghwal caste who are found along the Indo-Pakistan border.

The *naupat* is played during marriage ceremonies, and consists of two drums, a *nagada*, which is the male form of the drum, and the *jheel*, which is the female form. The *chang* is a large drum played generally by one, but sometimes two, musicians. It is frequently played during the festival of Holi. The drummer beats the centre of the drum with his left hand and the rim of the instrument with a stick held in his right hand. The *duff* is also played during Holi. This is a large tambourine consisting of a rim of iron or wood, and a membrane of goat's skin.

The *chang* and the *duff* are played during festivals.

The *nagada*, different from the male form of the naupat mentioned above, consists of two drums of different sizes which are played together. One drum is made of iron and the other of copper. Over the larger of the two is stretched buffalo skin, while the smaller nagada has camel skin. They were traditionally beaten during battles. The *khanzari* is a small drum encircled with brass or iron bells which is traditionally played by Kalbelias, or snake charmers. The *tabla* is a pair of drums and is played by classical musicians throughout India.

Wind Instruments Wind instruments include the *kariya*, which is a brass instrument once played in the courts of the maharajas, and also on the battlefield. The *mashak* is a wind instrument played by the Bhopas of Bhaironji. The *surnai* is played by the Jogis of the Bhil areas, the Dholis, and the Langas of Jaisalmer. The mouthpiece contains a *jhajoor*, or tar-leaf reed.

The *narh* is a four holed flute which is made from a form of desert grass known as kangore, and was traditionally played by shepherds to amuse themselves on their lonely vigils. Kangore was once obtained from Pakistan, but due to hostilities between India and Pakistan, and hence reduced opportunities to obtain kangore, there are few narh players left in Rajasthan.

Another type of wind instrument is the *satara*, consisting of two flutes which are played simultaneously. One of the flutes contains holes which, as with conventional flutes, enables different pitches to be achieved by covering or uncovering them with the fingers. Holes are absent in the second flute, which when played gives a steady drone. The satara is a popular instrument with the Bhils and Meghwals, and is played by shepherds.

One of the most well known instruments of the desert is the *poongi*, also known as a *murli*. This is the traditional snake charmers' flute, the bulge in its centre formed by a gourd. The different pitches attained are enabled by reeds of different lengths. It is played in the desert regions by folk musicians such as Langas and Manganiyars.

The *bankiya* is found in the Mewar (Udaipur) region, and is a form of trumpet, with sound produced by blowing in small holes at one end of the instrument.

The *morchang* is a small iron instrument which is held in the mouth by the teeth. Breathing in or out causes the central reed to vibrate, and various tones are achieved by moving the hand along the length of the instrument.

Stringed Instruments The two stringed *rawanahattha*, a bowed instrument, is played by Bhopas in honour of their deity, Pabuji. One of the two strings is made of horse hair, and the other is formed from several thin threads which are twisted together to form one string. The bowl is made from a coconut shell, and the main body of the instrument from bamboo.

The *kamayacha* is a stringed instrument played by the professional Muslim caste singers known as Manganiyars, who perform in small groups of three of four people. The kamayacha is played by means of a bow, drawn across the strings which are made of animal gut. The bowl of the instrument is of wood, with a membrane stretched across it.

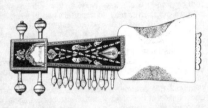

The *sarangi* is a stringed instrument that is played with a bow.

A well known stringed instrument of Rajasthan is the *sarangi*, of which there are various types. The *Sindhi sarangi* is used to accompany Sarangiya Langas, Muslim singers who perform for Muslim patrons. A smaller version of this instrument, the *Gujratan sarangi*, is also played by these singers. There is another group of Langas, the Surnayia Langas, who play an oboe-like instrument, but who do not sing. Yet another type of sarangi is the *jogiya sarangi*, which is traditionally played by snake charmers who hail from the Barmer and Jodhpur districts.

The stringed *srimandal* is very rarely seen today, and only a few musicians in Jaisalmer district still excel at this instrument. It consists of a rectangular shaped board over which are stretched 17 or 18 strings. One string, known as the *mandrasa*, is plucked throughout the performance to provide the drone, while the other strings are dexterously plucked to give the melody. Other stringed instruments include the *revaj*, *dusaka*, *apang* and *dilruba*, the last of which is played with a bow.

The five stringed *tandoora* is played by plucking the strings and beating the rhythm on the bowl of the instrument. It is often used to accompany the dance known as the *terahtal*, which is performed in honour of Ramdev.

The *sitar*, which is a classical instrument as opposed to a folk instrument, is played in Rajasthan. It dates from the 12th century and was introduced to India by the Muslims.

Folk Songs Folk songs are commonly ballads which relate heroic deeds or love stories, and religious or devotional songs, which are known as *bhajans* and *banis*, and are often accompanied by percussion instruments such as ektaras or dholaks. Various communities specialise in professional singing, such as the Dhadhis, the Dholis, the Mangamars, and the Nats, among others. Hindu prostitutes known as Patars, and Muslim prostitutes known as Kancharis, are renowned for their singing, as are the Muslim Mirasis, who specialise in folk songs called *mands* which almost approximate classical singing. ■

The drone of the snake charmer's *poongi* evokes the desert.

Patrons & Performers

Musicians and minstrels play an integral role in Rajasthani society, not only in providing entertainment, but in maintaining a tradition which is deeply rooted in community life. There are various castes and communities of professional musicians such as the Muslim Manganiyars, Langas and Dholis. They belong to subcastes of the lowest caste.

Professional musicians receive patronage not only from ruling families, but from ordinary people, both high and low caste, who pay for the performers' services with livestock, cash or a portion of the patron's crop. They play an important role in the cultural life and cohesiveness of society and are essential for the ceremonies which accompany birth, marriage and death. The musician's responsibility at a death ceremony includes holding a vigil at the cremation ground for 12 days and reciting lamentations dedicated to the deceased.

As patronage is hereditary, the virtuosity (or lack of it) of the performer does not influence the relationship. A *jajman* (patron) cannot 'fire' a musician who exhibits little talent. The relationship must be maintained, in the hope that the musician may produce a son or grandson who shows more promise. Musicians are attached not just to a single family, but to the entire family line. A breakdown in this relationship is detrimental to societal structure, so certain mechanisms have evolved to ensure the continuation of the bond. A patron can endure social stigma if his family's performer withdraws their services, so it is in his best interests to preserve the relationship. A musician can express their displeasure of a patron by refusing to recite *subhraj*, poems dedicated to the patron's family. If this fails to bring the patron around, the musician can take the more drastic step of removing the strings from his instrument and symbolically burying them. The worst insult which can be made towards a patron by a musician is to make an effigy of him which is tied to the tail of a donkey, paraded through the patron's village and repeatedly beaten with a shoe. The patron is then denied the services of all musicians belonging to their persecutor's caste, and as musicians are essential at important social functions, the patron is effectively socially ostracised and may, for example, be compelled to marry his children to members of a lower caste.

In addition to receiving patronage from ordinary people, musicians were also patronised, prior to Independence, by the jagirdars, or feudal lords. Most of the musicians who performed for the jagirdars belonged to the Damani caste, a subgroup of the Dholis. Unfortunately, when the jagirdari system was abolished after Independence, the Damanis lost their patrons. Many were compelled to seek employment in fields unrelated to music, spelling the death knell for various forms of traditional music which had formed part of the Damanis' repertoire. ∎

In the region of Marwar (Jodhpur), the *loor*, or *luvar*, is performed only by women. The participants stand opposite each other in two lines, and at a given beat of the drum, advance rapidly towards each other singing, and then retreat to their original position.

Performed mostly by the Bhil women of Udaipur, the *gauri* dance depicts legends associated with Shiva and Parvati. Participants form a semi-circle and perform a series of steps in time with drum beats.

Snake charmers, known as Kalbelias, and their wives, often complement their performances with dances such as the *shankaria*, which portrays a romantic tale. The Siddha Jats of Bikaner are renowned for their spectacular fire dance, which entails dancing on hot coals which reputedly leave no burns.

A traditional dance of Shekhawati is the *kacchi ghori*. The dancers, all of whom are men, ride mock wooden horses and brandish swords in mock battles. They are accompanied by a singer and musicians.

The *ramlila* and the *rasalila* are performed in honour of Rama and Krishna respectively, and are danced to the accompaniment of harmoniums and drums.

Puppetry

The traditional puppeteers, known as *kathputlis* or *putli-wallahs*, of Rajasthan originally hailed from Nagaur district. The itinerant kathputli emerged in the last century, when performers travelled from village to village to secure their livelihood. The skilled puppeteers relay stories through narration, music and dance. The kathputlis are among the most impoverished of Rajasthan's traditional entertainers, and are often compelled to work as farm labourers to supplement their meagre income.

Many of the kathputlis make their own

Karna the Dacoit

The most famous (or infamous) player of the narh (flute) was Karna Ram Bheel, who was equally well known for his enormous moustache, said to be 2.35m long. When not producing sweet melodies on his narh, Karna, allegedly to earn his place in the annals of folklore, was a ruthless dacoit who showed his victims no mercy. He was eventually apprehended for murder and thrown in prison.

He appeared for all intents and purposes to be a reformed man on his release, being content to play his narh and display his fine moustache, which earned him a place in the *Guinness Book of Records*. However, when his lands were appropriated by a man called Allabaksh, he became so enraged that he tied up the offender and refused to release him. Entreaties on behalf of the captive Allabaksh fell on deaf ears, and when one of Karna's former accomplices, Iliyas, acting in Karna's best interests, liberated Allabaksh, Karna, in abject fury, shot him dead.

Iliyas' sons vowed to avenge their father, and one night Karna was ambushed on his camel cart, and his head severed from his body. The head, with magnificent moustache intact, was carried off by the sons of Iliyas and placed on their father's grave. ■

puppets from wood or clay. Common themes employed in the stories of the kathputlis are those pertaining to romance, such as the story of Dhola Maru. The stories are re-enacted by the puppeteers.

The puppeteer is usually male, but he is generally assisted in his performance by his wife, who plays the dholak, and sings. Today there is less demand for the kathputlis, although the regions of Lunicha, Kuchaman and Khakholi, on the eastern fringes of the Thar Desert, still have a lively tradition of kathputli performers. In order to supplement their low incomes, kathputlis have been compelled to wander further afield in search of paying audiences, necessitating long journeys throughout northern India in the winter months. Up to a dozen families may set out on these journeys, pitching tents at night and carrying all their possessions on their backs.

Acrobats

Like Rajasthan's puppeteers, its community of acrobats, who belong to the Nat community, are very poor, and often have to supplement their low income by begging. The itinerant Nats travel around the countryside performing acrobatic feats such as tightrope walking and balancing on long bamboo poles for the entertainment of villagers. There is still a substantial community of Nats in Chittorgarh district.

Literature

Rajasthan has a tradition of written literature which dates back to the 9th century, at which time it is believed *Khuman Raso*, the tale of a Mewari hero, was written by Dalapat Vijaya. The epic *Prithviraj Raso*, which celebrates the life of Maharaja Prithviraj Chauhan, was written by Chand Bardai in the mediaeval period. While Rajasthan has produced several talented writers in the post-Independence period, few of their works have been translated into English.

Marwari is the dialect most commonly used by Rajasthani writers. A form of literary Rajasthani, known as Dingal, evolved in the 15th century for the communication of poetry and ballads telling of the exploits of heroes and warriors.

Popular literature is embodied in folk tales which were related orally by bards down through the centuries. Tales include love stories such as those of Dhola Maru (see The Legend of Dhola Maru in the introduction to the Northern Rajasthan chapter) and the tragic tale of the beautiful princess Mumal (described on the following page), tales of heroic exploits, religious legends, fables containing morals for children and stories recounting the dastardly deeds of notorious *dacoits* (bandits), among others.

In addition to folk tales are folk songs and ballads, the latter of which are frequently concerned with the virtue and heroism of deified folk heroes such as Pabuji, who died while fulfilling a promise which took him away from his marriage. *Pabuji-ka-phad* is a style of folk poetry performed by the nomadic

Bhopas, devotees of Pabuji, who complement the narrative with painted scrolls showing the various events in the life of Pabuji.

Khyals are a form of folk literature through which Rajasthan's folk literature is conveyed. Tales, legends and historical events are communicated through khyals which may include plays, songs, sayings and storytelling. When sung, they are often accompanied by a tambourine-drum known as a *duff*. The most renowned khyals were those performed by the Nautankis of Bharatpur, who incorporated athletic leaps and the beating of drums with their recitations.

The folk literature of Rajasthan, which glorifies heroism, chivalry, virtue and honourable death and sacrifice, has probably had a greater influence than any other in engendering the image in popular consciousness of the brave Rajput warrior.

Pottery

According to tradition, the first potter was created by Lord Shiva, who required a vessel for ceremonial purposes on the occasion of his wedding to Sati. This potter was named Rudrapal, and it is from him that the potters' caste, known as the Kumbhars, are descended. Many potters today still take the name Rudrapal, in honour of their legendary forebear.

Of all the arts of Rajasthan, pottery has the longest lineage, with fragments of pottery recovered from Kalibangan which date probably from the Harappan era (around 2500 BC). Prior to the beginning of the first millennium, potters in the environs of present-day Bikaner were decorating red pottery with black designs.

Today, different regions of Rajasthan produce different types of pottery, the most famous of which is the blue pottery of Jaipur. Blue glazed pottery originated in China, and later passed to Persia, from where it was introduced to India by the Muslims. The blue glazed work was first evident on tiles which adorned the palaces and cenotaphs of the Mughal rulers. Later the technique was applied to pottery.

In most centres the production of this highly glazed pottery declined during the era of the Mughal emperor Aurangzeb. However, the tradition was revived in Jaipur in the mid-19th century.

The pieces are decorated with images representing legends, ornamental devices and floral motifs, and depictions of animals. They are then painted with a coat of cobalt or copper oxide. After receiving a final coat of glaze, they are baked in a kiln for up to three days.

Every village in Rajasthan has a resident potter, who not only produces domestic

Mumal & Mahendra

Upon first laying eyes on her, Mahendra of Umarkot lost his heart to the beautiful princess Mumal. Every night he raced to her chamber, borne by a swift camel by the name of Chekal. As Mahendra had to travel at night to visit Mumal, who lived in the distant village of Ludarwa, he had little energy left to perform husbandly duties to the satisfaction of his eight wives. Suspecting his nocturnal visits to the princess of renowned beauty, the aggrieved wives beat Mahendra's trusty camel Chekal within almost an inch of his life, rendering him completely and permanently lame. Mumal was thus compelled to solicit the services of a camel not of the calibre of the bruised and battered Chekal, which subsequently lost its way.

In the meantime, Mumal's sister Sumal, of rather more homely appearance than Mumal, decided to pay a visit to her sister. Sumal was in the habit of wearing men's clothes, and fell asleep next to Mumal who was exhausted from her midnight vigil awaiting Mahendra. Mumal had failed to appear at the usual hour due to the disorientation of his surrogate camel. When Mahendra finally made his way to Mumal's apartment, he was confronted by the rather disconcerting sight of Mumal lying next to what appeared to be, for all intents and purposes, another man. Mahendra fled from the chamber, vowing never to lay eyes on Mumal again, and bitterly cursing the inconstancy of women. Mumal waited every night for her absent lover, finally pining away with grief. When Mahendra heard of her death, and of the misunderstanding which had kept him from visiting her, he went mad. ∎

vessels, but is required to produce clay images of the deities for ceremonial purposes. The most striking of these sacred images are produced in the village of Molela, north of Udaipur in southern Rajasthan. Here potters work with terracotta formed from clay and donkeys' dung, continuing a tradition which dates back to the Harappan era.

Sculpture & Stonework

Rajasthan is known for the fine quality of marble and sandstone extracted from the numerous quarries in the state. This has given rise to a tradition of stonemasons and sculptors. Some of the more famous quarries include those at Makrana, from which the marble used in the Taj Mahal was mined. Also built using marble from these mines were the exquisite Dilwara Jain temples at Mt Abu.

The quarries of Dungarpur yield a soft chironatic stone which is used for carving images of the deities. When this stone is oiled, it becomes a rich, lustrous black. Due to their divine subject matter, sculptors producing these images are required to work according to guidelines laid down in the *Shilpa-Shashtra*, an ancient Hindu treatise on sculpture and architecture. In most cases, producing an image of a deity can entail the work of two or more sculptors. An apprentice would be responsible for carving the crude image and liberating it from the stone block, but the fine work which imparts expression and dignity to the image is given to a master sculptor.

The finest sculptors of the day were commissioned to work on the beautiful temples of Rajasthan, and some of the best work can be seen in the temples of the Jains. The Dilwara temples at Mt Abu feature exquisite carvings. No less inspiring are the Jain temples within the fort walls at Jaisalmer, the superb Jain and Hindu temples at Osiyan in western Rajasthan, which date from the 8th to the 12th centuries, and the beautiful 15th century Jain temples at Ranakpur, in southern Rajasthan.

Jaipur is the centre of marble carving in Rajasthan. Here artisans create marble

Saraswati, 12th century Jain marble statue

images of the deities as well as domestic utensils such as bowls for grinding spices and kneading dough.

At centres such as Ajmer, Udaipur, Jodhpur, Bikaner and Jaipur can be seen very fine examples of *jali*, or stone tracery, worked on screens and panels in the palaces of these cities. Jali screens offer protection from the elements while also allowing the passage of ventilation through the intricate geometric patterns which comprise the screen. They are frequently found in the windows of the *zenanas*, or women's quarters, enabling the women in purdah to view the events of the courts without being seen themselves. Jali screens are sculptured from both sandstone and marble.

Painting

The history of painting in Rajasthan can be traced to the prehistoric period, as evidenced by the discovery of paintings in rock shelters in the Chambal Valley. Fragments of paintings found on pottery shards recovered from Kalibangan, Ahar and Gilund, among other places, indicate the antiquity of the pictorial art tradition in Rajasthan.

From the 11th century, pictorial art was recorded on palm leaf, and in subsequent centuries, on paper. These were predominantly religious paintings which illustrated ancient Jain manuscripts. The influence of these early paintings is evident in the paintings of the 15th century. Remnants of paintings dating from this period are evident at Kumbhalgarh and Chittorgarh forts. Common themes employed include religious mythology, especially that concerning Krishna and Radha, romance and interpretations of poems written about a musical mode or melody *(ragamala)*.

Miniature Painting The most characteristic paintings of Rajasthan are miniatures, small paintings crammed with detail and executed in vegetable and mineral colours, generally on hand-made paper, but also painted on ivory, marble, wood, cloth and leather.

Miniature painting flourished in Rajasthan during the 18th and 19th centuries.

Various schools of miniature painting began to emerge in the 17th century. Although employing common themes, there were distinct differences in paintings produced in different regions. The most important regional schools of painting were those of Mewar (Udaipur), Marwar (encompassing Bikaner, Jaisalmer and Jodhpur), Amber (Jaipur; also known as the Dhundhar school), Kishangarh (flourished in the 18th century) and Hadoti (Bundi; in 1624 divided into Bundi and Kota).

The Bundi school produced some magnificent work, which other schools endeavoured to emulate, employing rich colours and idealised subject matter, often against a lush jungle background. In the late 18th century, Bundi artists created unusual paintings with half the surface left white, and just a few figures painted against this in pale colours. The Kota school, which emerged in the 19th century, is renowned for its depictions of shikhars, or royal hunts.

Also producing distinctive paintings were the artists of Kishangarh. The Kishangarh school emerged in the second half of the 17th century under the patronage of Raja Man Singh. The school flourished under a later ruler, Sawant Singh, who ascended the *gaddi*, or throne, in 1706. The portrayal of Krishna's consort, Radha, was a common theme employed, and it is believed that a local beauty, Bani Thani, who had won the heart of Sawant Singh, was the model for these paintings. The greatest works of the Kishangarh school were produced by the master artist Nihal Chand. The Kishangarh school is also known for its romantic miniatures.

The artists of Amber, and of the later capital of Jaipur, received the patronage of successive Kachhwaha rulers, and this area was one of the most prolific centres for painting. Much of the work from Jaipur was influenced by Mughal artistic styles.

The patronage of the royal family of Mewar and the pursuit of all artistic endeavours here afforded a fertile environment for the flourishing of miniature painting. Mewar is famous for its paintings depicting court life. These were produced for the various maharanas of Mewar from the early 18th century. The paintings are large and detailed, portraying festivals, ceremonies, elephant fights and hunts. Human faces had distinctive features such as almond-shaped eyes and prominent noses.

The paintings of Jodhpur, belonging to the Marwar school, featured distinctive vivid colours and heroic, bewhiskered men accompanied by dainty maidens. The paintings of Bikaner were greatly influenced by the Mughals, as many master Mughal painters, known as Ustas, were encouraged to attend the Bikaner court.

The Rajasthani painters used colours derived from minerals, ochres and vegetables. The vibrant colours still evident today in miniatures and frescoes in some of the royal palaces were derived from crushed semi-precious stones, while the gold and silver colouring is in fact finely pounded pure gold and silver leaf.

Portrait & Courtly Painting Rajput exposure to the Mughal courts in the first half of the 17th century gave rise to a new mode of painting, the royal portrait. Bikaner, with its close association with the Mughals, was one of the first schools to adopt the new style. Throughout the subsequent evolution of Rajasthani painting, while the Rajputs borrowed from the Mughals, the new modes of representation were for the most part incorporated within traditional forms of depiction. Rajasthani paintings remained, despite adaptation of Mughal themes, much more idealised, abstract and stylised than their Mughal counterparts.

The 18th century saw less emphasis on religious themes and the illustration of manuscripts, and more on secular themes. Paintings commonly depicted maharajas engaged in various activities, such as hunting, visiting the zenana, attending the *durbar* (royal court) or fulfilling religious obligations, such as presiding at the Holi celebrations. Mewar became the main centre for the production of these courtly themes.

A distinct difference in the paintings of the Rajputs and those of the Mughals in the 18th century was in the use of colour. While the Mughals employed muted colours which afforded a sense of shadow and depth to paintings, the Rajputs used bold primary colours which rendered their paintings two dimensional and abstract. It is not unusual to see Rajasthani miniatures of this period in which the subjects appear to 'float', captured in limbo between the foreground and background, the earth and the sky.

The 19th century heralded a decline in the execution of portraits in Rajasthan, perhaps reflecting a decline in the relative power of the maharajas as the British began to erode their dominance and, as a consequence, divest them of their heroic status.

Cloth Painting The town of Nathdwara, 48 km from Udaipur, is an important centre for the production of *pichwai* paintings, which are religious paintings on home-spun cloth hung behind images of Krishna, who in Nathdwara is worshipped as Sri Nathji. The paintings were introduced by members of a Vaishnavite sect known as the Vallabh Sampradhya.

The large cloths are painted to evoke a particular mood, generally associated with the legends of Krishna, such as the rasalila. In the rasalila, Krishna, in order to please the *gopis* (milkmaids), manifested himself numerous times and was thus able to dance individually beside every maiden (the circular nature of this dance also makes the rasalila a popular theme on the interior of domes in temples and chhatris). Traditionally pichwai paintings were executed in colours derived from natural minerals and vegetables, with red and yellow predominating; today, however, they are mass-produced for the tourist market and are of little artistic value.

Another form of cloth painting is the *phad*, a painted scroll which is used by the nomadic Bhopas to illustrate legends associated with the deified hero Pabuji. The Bhopa, assisted by his wife, the Bhopi, travels from village to village, dancing, singing and pointing to relevant sections of the scroll at pertinent moments to assist the narrative. The paintings are executed by a subset of the Chhipa caste, the Joshis, who hail from the regions of Bhilwara and Chittorgarh.

Domestic Painting The region of Shekhawati, in northern Rajasthan, is reputed for its extraordinary painted havelis. This form of painting is covered in more detail in the colour section on architecture.

The folk art form of *mandana* is also evident in Rajasthan, in which houses are decorated with floral and geometric designs in red chalk, or with vegetation motifs which indicate the various seasons.

Textiles

Rajasthan is famous for its vibrantly coloured textiles. Cotton cloth is produced by the Julaha, or weaver, caste. The cloth produced by the weavers in the village of Kaithoon, in Kota district, is the most highly prized. It is known as *masuria*, and is woven from both cotton and silk. Saris made of this cloth fetch top prices around the country.

The basic cloth receives one or several of various treatments to achieve its rich blaze of colour, including dyeing, block-printing and numerous forms of embroidery and appliqué.

Tie-Die Cloth Of the dyeing processes, the method producing the most intricate and interesting result is that of *bandhani*, or tie and dye. Basically this entails knotting parts of the fabric; when the fabric is dyed, the knotted sections retain their original colour. Alternatively, after the fabric is knotted, it is bleached, resulting in the unknotted sections of the fabric being paler than the knotted sections.

The intricate work of tying the cloth is the preserve of women and girl children. Different patterns can be created by employing different methods. *Loharia* (which translates as 'ripples') is striped diagonally and is used in saris and turbans. Diagonal patterns of dots are formed by the *jaaldar* and *beldar* processes. *Ekdali* features small circles and

squares; *shikari* employs animal and human motifs, which are drawn before the cloth is dyed. In *tikunthi*, circles and squares appear in groups of three; in *chaubasi*, they appear in groups of four; and in *satbandi*, in groups of seven. The dominant colours used in bandhani tie and dye are yellow, red, green and pink.

One of the most intricate designs is attained using a technique where the cloth is first folded, and then pressed with wooden blocks embedded with nails, which causes raised impressions on the cloth. These raised points are then gathered up and tied, and the cloth then dyed. The brilliant results are then worn as headscarves *(odhnis)*. *Pomacha* and *sikari-bandhej* odhnis are also highly sought. The former features lotus motifs against a white or pink background. A yellow background indicates that the wearer has recently given birth. Sikari-bandhej odhnis are produced in Sikar, in the region of Shekhawati, and feature designs of birds and animals.

Printed Cloth There are two forms of printing – block-printing, and reverse or resist printing. In block-printing, wooden blocks known as *buntis* or *chhapas*, on which incisions form the basic design, are dipped in dye and applied directly to the cloth. In the second mode of printing, part of the cloth is covered with a dye-resistant substance such as wax, and the cloth is then dyed. The waxed sections of course retain their original colour, and the wax or other substance (such as clay) is washed off. These original colour sections are then block-printed.

The village of Sanganer, near Jaipur, is famous for its block-printed fabric – Sanganeri prints, generally featuring floral motifs, are exported around the world. Every day, thousands of metres of fabric can be seen drying in long swathes on the banks of the Saraswati River.

The village of Bagru is also renowned for its block-prints, which feature predominantly zigzag motifs. The city of Barmer, in western Rajasthan, produces resist-printed cloth featuring geometric designs in blue and red on both sides which is known as *ajrakh*, and is generally worn only by men as shawls and turbans. Jaisalmer specialises in resist printing, which is only executed at night and in the winter months.

In the town of Nathdwara, in southern Rajasthan, finely printed cloth depicting religious themes, particularly centred around the life of Sri Nathji, the presiding deity, was used, along with pichwai paintings (see Cloth Painting earlier), to adorn temples. The tradition continues today, with pilgrims purchasing these cloths as religious mementos.

Dyes Before the introduction of synthetic dyes, all colours were derived from natural sources such as vegetables, minerals and even insects. Yellow was derived from turmeric and buttermilk; green from banana leaves; orange from saffron and jasmine; black from iron rust; blue from indigo; red from sugarcane and sunflowers; and purple from the kirmiz insect. Colours were either fast *(pacca)* or fleeting *(kacha)*. Fast colours are generally more muted than fleeting colours, consisting of browns, blues and greens, while the vibrant yellows, oranges and pinks are generally kacha colours.

Appliqué & Embroidery The third method of adorning cloth is embroidery and appliqué, and this usually takes place after the cloth has been printed or tie-dyed. A visit to any of the museums in the palaces of Rajasthan's former princely rulers gives an indication of the superlative quality of the embroidery of this state, evident in the collections of richly brocaded royal vestments. During the period of the Mughals, embroidery workshops known as *kaarkhanas* were established to train artisans so that the royal families would have an abundant supply of richly embroidered cloth. Finely stitched tapestries were also executed for the royal courts which received their inspiration from miniature paintings.

In Bikaner, designs using double stitching result in the pattern appearing on both sides of the cloth. In Shekhawati, the Jats embroider motifs of animals and birds on their odhnis and *ghagharas* (long, gathered skirts). Chainstitch is employed in Alwar district against a bold background. Tiny mirrors are stitched into garments in Jaisalmer, an artistic device which is widely employed in Gujarat. Beautifully embroidered cloths are also produced for domestic livestock, and ornately bedecked camels are a wonderfully common sight at the Pushkar Camel Fair.

Carpets & Weaving

Before the emergence of the Muslims in India, the tradition of carpet making was unknown in the country. Floor coverings consisted of small mats, called *jajams*, on which only one person could sit. Carpet weaving took off in the 16th century under the patronage of the great Mughal emperor Akbar, who commissioned the establishment of various carpet-weaving factories, including one at Jaipur.

In Jaipur, pile carpets were produced under the tutorship of Persian weavers. Some of these carpets were enormous, requiring the construction of vast looms, in order to produce carpets for the royal durbar halls. There is an exquisite collection of carpets both at the museum in the City Palace, and at the Albert Hall museum, both in Jaipur.

In the 19th century, Maharaja Sawai Ram Singh II of Jaipur established a carpet factory at the Jaipur jail, and soon other jails introduced carpet-making units. Some of the most beautiful *durries*, or flat cotton carpets, were produced by prisoners in jails – Bikaner jail was well known for the excellence of its durries.

Following the demise of the princely states, both the quality and quantity of carpets produced in Rajasthan declined, without the patronage of the royal families. However, recent government training initiatives have seen the revival of this craft, and fine quality carpets are being produced in Bikaner, Jodhpur, Jaipur, Kota and other centres.

In the desert regions, where temperatures plummet when the sun goes down, blankets and shawls are vital. Shawls are woven of soft, fine wool, while blankets are woven of coarse, hand-spun wool, and are known as *pattus* or *kheis*. They often feature a coloured border in a contrasting colour.

Jewellery

In even the poorest villages of Rajasthan, women, and often men, can be seen bedecked in elaborate silver jewellery – bracelets, rings, nose rings, toe rings, ankle bracelets, pendants worn on the forehead and breast. The quality of the jewellery indicates the relative economic status of the wearer (or more accurately, of her husband) – one woman may wear ornaments weighing up to five kg! Very rarely are these objects of pure silver. Usually the silver is mixed with copper to make it more malleable, although it is still of a very high grade – generally above 90%. Villagers and tribal groups of different regions can be identified by their ornaments, and these ornaments also indicate the caste to which they belong.

Unfortunately, few antique pieces have survived in their original condition, inevitably being melted down and refashioned into another article according to the dictates of fashion.

The princely rulers invested much of their wealth in ornaments of silver and gold, usually encrusted with precious and semi-precious gems. It was the founder of Amber, Maharaja Man Singh I, who introduced the beautiful *meenakari*, or enamelwork, to Rajasthan, around the end of the 17th century. Man Singh enticed five master meenakari workers from Lahore to his royal court, and established a tradition of fine enamelwork that continues in Jaipur to this day.

The oldest extant example of meenakari work is the Jaipur staff. It is 132 cm long and comprises 33 segments of gold upon each of which is exquisite enamelwork featuring floral and animal designs. The handle of the staff is of solid jade. The maharaja bore this staff with him to Delhi when he was summoned to the royal court by Emperor Akbar.

Both silver and gold can be used as a base for meenakari. However, only a limited number of colours, including gold, blue, green and yellow, can be adhered to silver, whereas all available colours can be applied to gold, making it the preferred medium of enamellers.

Jaipur enamellers use the *champleve* method, in which engravings are made on the object to be enamelled, and these are then flooded with the enamel colour. Each colour has to be individually fired, so those colours which are most resistant to heat are applied first, as they will be re-fired with the addition of each new colour. As a rule, white is the first colour applied, and red the last.

The final object is the work of a succession of master artisans – the *sonar*, or goldsmith; the *chattera*, who engraves the piece; and the *minakar*, or enameller. *Kundan* jewellery features precious gems on one side, and meenakari work on the reverse, requiring the expertise of a *kundansaz*, who applies the gems.

Meenakari of Jaipur has particularly vibrant colour. The rich, ruby red the Jaipur minakars produce is highly prized. Jaipur is also an important gem-cutting and polishing region.

Woodwork

Given the paucity of wood in most parts of Rajasthan, it is not surprising that stone sculpture is more prevalent than woodcarving. Nevertheless, there is a tradition of woodcarving which dates back many centuries. Unfortunately, few of the mediaeval pieces have survived, having succumbed to Rajasthan's arid climate or to white ants.

Shekhawati was an important centre for woodcarving. Here the woodcarver's talent can be seen in finely wrought doors, and door and window frames. Also in Shekhawati were produced *pidas*, low, folding chairs which featured decorative carving. Bikaner was also an important centre for woodcarving, for its ornately carved doors and lintels, and particularly for latticed screen windows (jalis).

The heads of the puppets of the kathputli were usually carved from wood, and then painted with the requisite (ferocious, heroic, lovelorn) expression. Wooden boxes featuring several layers of lacquer were popular in the 19th century, a craft which was probably introduced from Sind (now in Punjab).

Lacquered ware is produced in Jaipur, Jodhpur, Sawai Madhopur and Udaipur. Jaipur and Jodhpur are known for their lac bangles and bracelets. The wooden item to receive the lacquer treatment is first rubbed with liquid clay, and then, when dry, the design is stencilled with the aid of charcoal. Liquid clay, applied with very fine brushes of squirrel hair, is then used to trace the design, which becomes raised with each successive layer. The surface is then coated with paint, and gold leaf applied.

The village of Bassi, near Chittorgarh, is known for the production of puppets and toys, particularly for images of Ishar and Gauri which feature in the Gangaur Festival. Carved wooden horses, honouring the trusty steed of the deified hero, Ramdevji, are offered at his temple during the annual Ramdevji Festival. The woodcarvers of Barmer use sheesham and rohira wood, the latter, known locally as 'Marwar teak' and possessing excellent qualities for carving, has now unfortunately almost vanished from the desert zone.

Ivory Carving

It is believed that the art of ivory carving in India dates back at least to the 2nd century BC. In Rajasthan, the main centres for this art form are Jaipur, Udaipur and Bharatpur, where master carvers were once patronised by the royal courts. Jaipur was famed in the mid-17th century for its carved ivory hand fans. Jodhpur specialises in ivory bangles, which are worn in great number to cover the entire arm. The bangles increase in size from the wrist to just below the shoulder. The ivory inlaid doors of the Bikaner Palace are famed for their beauty and artisanship. While carved ivory items can still be purchased in centres such as Jaipur, the export of ivory items from India is illegal. That is, it is illegal to take ivory in any shape or form out of the country.

Leatherwork

Leather craft has a long history in Rajasthan. As working with leather is considered an 'unclean' profession, it is performed by the lowest caste in the Hindu caste hierarchy, the Sudras. Tanning is carried out by the Chamar caste. Cobblers throughout Rajasthan belong to a caste known as Mochis. Leather shoes known as *jootis*, or *mojdis* are produced in Jodhpur and Jaipur, among other centres. Jootis often feature ornate embroidery known as *kashida*: in Jodhpur, the embroidery is applied direct to the leather, while in Jaipur, it is worked on velvet with which the shoes are covered. Embroidery is always executed by women. Other forms of ornamentation include fancy stitching on the uppers, and appliqué. Strangely, there is no 'right' or 'left' foot: both shoes are identical, but due to the softness of the leather, eventually they conform to the shape of the wearer's foot.

Alwar is reputed for its beautiful leather book bindings, a craft which flourished under Maharaja Banni Singh in the early 19th century. One of the finest works, a beautifully worked leather cover for the famous copy of *Gulistan (A Rose Garden)*, by Shekh Muslihud-din-Sadi, can now be seen on display in the Alwar museum at the City Palace complex. Bikaner is known for its production of *kopis*, or camel-hide water bottles.

SOCIETY & CONDUCT
Traditional Culture

Birth The birth of a boy child is greeted with great rejoicing and celebration. The birth is broadcast by an elderly female member of the husband's family who beats a copper *thali* (plate) to inform the neighbours of the good news. However, the birth of a girl child is considered a cause of commiseration, and there is no joyous celebration. A folk saying sums up the typical attitude towards girl children:

Beti bhali no ek
It is not worth having even one daughter.

In order to ward off evil spirits known as *dakins* or *chureils* who prey on young infants, a ceremony is performed shortly after birth. The death of a newborn child is attributed to the malevolent machinations of these spirits.

Around 20 days following birth, at an hour deemed auspicious by the priest, a ceremony known as *panghat poojan* is performed at the local village well in worship of the water god. The new mother is permitted, after this ceremony, to recommence her domestic duties.

The birth of a girl child is not considered a calamity in all communities. There are several communities, mostly belonging to the Scheduled Castes and Tribes, which demand a bride price, or *reet*, on the marriage of their daughters. Young men who are unable to pay reet are either condemned to bachelorhood, or are compelled to exchange their sisters or female cousins in a multiple marriage transaction.

Adoption Adoption is a common solution in Rajasthan to the problem of a lack of a male heir, and one resorted to in the past by numerous maharajas. The adoption ceremony is performed before a group of representatives from the community, and entails the smearing of vermilion on the forehead of the adoptee, and the placing of a turban on his head.

Marriage Marriages are, almost without exception, arranged by parents, the engagement being announced after a suitable match is found and the horoscopes of the prospective partners compared by a priest and found to be compatible. The father of the girl traditionally sends her future father-in-law a coconut. Once the coconut has been received, the marriage is inevitable. Cross-caste marriages, once socially taboo, are now performed occasionally, and are generally the result of a love match.

Although outlawed by government, child marriages are not uncommon in rural areas, and the Sahariya tribal people arrange marriages while the child is still in the womb. Often a group of children are married simultaneously, to reduce costs, although the new-lyweds return to the family home until they reach maturity. On attaining puberty, girls are given gifts by their parents and then dispatched with due ceremony to their in-laws' homes. Several days in the year are considered auspicious for marriage, and on such days, thousands of child marriages are performed throughout Rajasthan. The authorities generally turn a blind eye to these proceedings, after receiving requisite baksheesh. Some of those who have actively opposed this custom have been violently assaulted.

Spring, especially around the festival of Holi, is a popular time for weddings, although the actual date of marriage is determined by a Brahmin priest. Around Holi in Jaipur, Jodhpur and the other towns and cities of Rajasthan, it's not uncommon to see marriage processions along the busy streets. The (usually) terror-stricken groom, resplendent in traditional Rajput warrior costume, is borne aloft on a white horse, surrounded by his friends and family, and the marriage party, known as the *baraat*, is led by a brightly decorated float which is pulled through the streets, on which a singer and musicians blast out the latest Hindi movie love songs through megaphones. Hired helpers carry heavy and ornate fluorescent lights on their shoulders to illuminate the procession.

Traditionally, the bridegroom proceeded to the home of the bride, where, after piercing with a sword a shield-shaped device known as a *toran* over the doorway, and thus symbolically 'winning' his bride from her family, the groom entered the family home to claim her. This was not necessarily an easy process, as traditionally the prospective bride was allowed to fend off her suitor with a sword. If the husband-to-be survived the attack, he could claim her! Today brides strike their future husbands with bunches of sweets rather than sword strokes.

Following the marriage, according to Rajasthani tradition the groom is plied with numerous seemingly nonsensical riddles by his new female in-laws. The main object of the riddles is to unsettle and embarrass the groom, and often the riddles have a ribald sexual content.

Polygamy Prior to the dissolution of the princely states, it was not unusual for a maharaja to have at least several wives, who were known as *ranis*. Polygamy flourished during the mediaeval period when more wives ensured more male progeny, and hence more warriors to fight in the not infrequent battles and skirmishes of the Rajputs.

The ability to be able to support a large harem became a symbol of power and affluence, and even this century, one maharaja boasted more than 300 women, which constituted a vast drain on the state's financial reserves! Gayatri Devi, the jet-setting wife of the last maharaja of Jaipur, Man Singh II, who socialised with, among others, Queen Elizabeth II of England and Prince Philip, was Man Singh's third wife. Polygamy is still practised by those members of the Bhil and Mina tribes who can afford to maintain more than one wife.

Dowry System Unfortunately, the dowry system is entrenched in Rajasthan, and the parents of girl children can be plunged into terrible debt endeavouring to retain their honour by sending their daughter to her in-laws' home with appropriate gifts of cash, jewellery, electrical goods such as TVs and radios, and even motor scooters in some instances.

If the family of the bridegroom believes that the dowry is not adequate, further demands can be made on the bride's family. Bride-burning, or dowry death, is not unknown in Rajasthan and, as in other parts of India, the deaths of new brides in 'stove fires' are not uncommon. Some of these are attributed to the murderous impulses and greed of in-laws, who kill their daughter-in-law to enable their son to remarry and hence claim another dowry. A poet from Rajasthan has written 'How is the stove so wise that it distinguishes between a daughter-in-law and mother-in-law?' A new law was passed in 1996 prohibiting the demand for dowry by a prospective bride's in-laws. However, it is unlikely that in the short term this will serve to reverse the age-old tradition of dowry, particularly in rural India.

Divorce & Remarriage Traditionally, among the Jats, Gujjars and Scheduled Castes and Tribes, a woman is permitted to remarry following the death of her husband. However, the new husband is required to pay compensation both to the relatives of the former husband and to the bride's parents. Remarriage of widows was once forbidden by the Hindu upper castes, but is gradually becoming more prevalent and accepted. Divorce, also once forbidden, is now also becoming more prevalent among these castes. If a woman wishes to obtain a divorce to marry another man, compensation is payable to the former husband and his family.

Purdah Prior to Independence and the dissolution of the princely states, purdah, or isolation of married women, was prevalent among the upper echelons of society, particularly among the Rajputs. Maintaining a woman in purdah reflected favourably on her husband, a symbol of his wealth and position.

The women of the royal harems were ensconced in zenanas, rarely venturing beyond the palace precincts, and viewed by no man other than their husband (and the palace eunuchs). If they did leave their cloistered quarters, the women were transported in covered vehicles under heavy escort.

Lower caste women were veiled from the eyes of men by their head scarves. Only the nomads and tribal women were free from the constraints imposed by purdah. Today purdah is considered a relic of the feudal past and, other than in the Muslim communities and among the Oswal Jains, is generally not observed.

Death Twelve days following cremation, if the deceased was the male head of the family, a symbolic turban-tying ceremony is performed, in which his successor is recognised by his family and the community.

In rural areas, a death feast known variously as *mosar*, *barwa*, *kariyawar* or *terwa* is often held 12 or 13 days after death by the family of the deceased. The mourning relatives are reminded of their obligations to perform a death feast by community leaders who call on the family three days following the death, regardless of the family's financial ability to discharge this obligation. Frequently these unwelcome visitors are conveniently accompanied by the *bohara*, or village moneylender.

Death feasts can be expensive and elaborate affairs, often plunging those who hold them into debt, and it has been known for the bohara to call on the bereaved family shortly after the death feast and seize their possessions in lieu of payment. However, the custom of mosar is entrenched, and to fail in this duty to the deceased would reflect poorly on both the family of the deceased and the honour of the deceased person.

In 1922, some 50,000 people were fed at the death feast of Maharaja Madho Singh of Jaipur. It has been known for some people to celebrate the mosar feast in their lifetime, for fear that their relatives would fail to honour them in this way after their death. The state government has enacted laws to limit the numbers of guests at these feasts, with little success. In one instance, an altercation between the police and mourners at a death feast resulted in the deaths of scores of people.

Very affluent families may erect a chhatri to commemorate the deceased. This practice was common in Shekhawati, where some of the wealthy merchant families, such as the Poddars, have left a legacy of architecturally impressive and beautiful chhatris.

Sati The practice of sati, or voluntary self-immolation by a widow on her husband's funeral pyre, is believed to date from the Vedic era. It is named after Shiva's wife, Sati, who self-immolated when her father insulted Shiva by refusing to invite him to a feast. In Rajasthan, there are numerous instances of sati, especially among the ruling Rajputs, when the wives of maharajas threw themselves on their husbands' pyres, both to honour their dead husband, and to avoid the ignominy of widowhood.

Widows, rather than being treated with compassion and solicitude on the deaths of their husbands, were divested of their wealth and rich vestments, cursed and hounded and

The Death by Fire of Roop Kunwar

On 4 September 1987, India was plunged into controversy when an 18 year old recently widowed woman, Roop Kunwar, burned to death on her husband's funeral pyre at the village of Deorala in the district of Sikar. According to the dead girl's family and the entire village of Deorala, Roop Kunwar voluntarily ascended the funeral pyre and calmly recited prayers while she was consumed by flames. Sceptics have alleged that the young woman, who had only been married seven months, was drugged and forcibly thrown on the fire.

What is equally as shocking as the fact that a young woman should perish by fire, whether voluntarily or involuntarily, is that in the late 20th century the alleged act of sati was glorified and the victim deified. Roop Kunwar was deified not just by superstitious rural folk, but by hundreds of thousands of people around the country. Within one week of Roop Kunwar's death, Deorala had become a major pilgrimage site, attracting no less than *half a million* pilgrims, most of whom left substantial donations for a temple to be built in her honour. Among the thousands of pilgrims who visited the site of the calamity were several members of both the state and central governments.

On 27 September, the prime minister, Rajiv Gandhi, issued a statement declaring the circumstances of the death of Roop Kunwar 'utterly reprehensible and barbaric'. In December 1987, a law was passed by the central government banning sati, with family members of persons committing sati to be divested of their right to inherit her property. Persons charged with 'glorifying' sati would be prohibited from contesting elections. In addition, *sati melas*, or fairs, were banned.

Despite these measures, the incontestable power of the sati still holds sway over the population, both educated and uneducated. Women still reverently pay homage at shrines erected in honour of satis, believing that they have the power to make barren women fertile, or cure terminal illnesses. The reverence in which sati is evidently still held is exemplified in the extraordinarily lavish temple of Rani Sati in Jhunjhunu, in Shekhawati, which commemorates the self-immolation of a woman on her husband's funeral pyre in 1595. This temple receives the second highest amount of donations of any temple in India. ■

considered living symbols of misfortune. There are also examples in Rajput history of not only wives, but maids, slaves and other domestic hands perishing on the funeral pyre of a deceased ruler.

There are several examples in Rajput history of sati performed on a mass scale (jauhar), when defeat in battle was imminent and the women of the royal court preferred to face death, rather than dishonour at the hands of the enemy.

In 1846, the princely state of Jaipur was the first state in Rajasthan to outlaw sati after prompting by the British government, and it was soon followed by other states. Mewar resisted the ban, and in 1861 Queen Victoria was compelled to issue a proclamation forbidding the practice of sati. Intermittent cases of sati have taken place over subsequent years.

Traditional Beliefs & Practices

Evil spirits, or ghosts, known as *bhuuts* or *dakins*, which possess the minds of their hapless victims, can be dislodged with the assistance of a priest, known as a *jogi* or a *bhopa* (the Bhil name for a priest). Bhuuts and dakins are also blamed for natural disasters such as droughts, famines and crop failure, and are propitiated accordingly to avert calamity. They are known to frequent crossroads. The Balaji exorcism temple, 80 km to the east of Jaipur, is visited by those seeking relief from possession by a bhuut or dakin.

Barren women are feared by new mothers, as it is believed that a barren women will conceive if she secures the hair or a fragment of clothing from an infant, who will die as a consequence.

The crossing of a cobra or cat in front of a person is considered a bad omen, as is confronting a goldsmith, a cart laden with firewood, or a woman carrying an empty pitcher. A person setting out on a long journey who is confronted by any of these inauspicious signs would do well to delay their journey.

However, meeting a married woman with a pitcher full of water is an auspicious sign, auguring well for a good journey. Also considered good luck is the braying of a donkey or the cheeping of a sparrow. Friday is considered a lucky day, and work commenced on this day is guaranteed success. Monday, however, is not considered a good day for commencing new projects, and journeys to the east are never undertaken on a Monday.

It is considered unlucky to have hair cut on a Tuesday, and barber stalls remain closed on this day throughout the state.

Deceased ancestors are worshipped as *pitars* (men) and *pitaris* (women who die before their husbands). On the anniversary of the death of the pitar or pitari, food must be offered to a Brahmin, a cow, a crow and a dog. These ancestors are also collectively worshipped on a particular fortnight of the year known as Shraddha Paksha.

The Caste System

The caste system, integral to Hinduism, dominates the social organisation of Rajasthan, as it does most of India. Although its origins are hazy, it seems to have been developed by the Brahmins, or priest class, in order to maintain their superiority over the indigenous Dravidians. Eventually, the caste system became formalised into four distinct classes, each with rules of conduct and behaviour. These four castes, in order of hierarchy, are said to have come from Brahma's mouth (Brahmins; priest caste), arms (Kshatriyas; warrior caste), thighs (Vaisyas; caste of tradespeople and farmers) and feet (Sudras; caste of farmers and peasants). These basic castes are then subdivided into numerous lesser divisions. Beneath all the castes are the Dalits and Scheduled Castes (formerly known as Harijans and Untouchables), who have no caste. A Hindu cannot change his or her caste – you're born into it and are stuck with it for the rest of your lifetime.

In Rajasthan, there are some local variations on the caste system. The most important variation is the Rajput caste. The Rajputs are traditionally warriors and claim lineage to the Kshatriyas. In Rajasthan, there are also communities of Jats and Gujjars who are traditionally engaged in farming and animal husbandry. In Rajasthan, the tribal groups, known as Scheduled Tribes, belong to the Dalits, the lowest casteless class for whom all the most menial and degrading tasks are reserved.

Prior to Independence and merger into the Indian Union, the martial Rajputs wielded the most power. The Rajputs comprised various clans, or *khamps*, according to their dynastic families. Due to the integration of the princely kingdoms into the state of Rajasthan, and the abolition of the system of jagirdari, the Rajputs were nudged from their positions of power by the Brahmins. The Brahmins can be subdivided into two groups, Chhanayatis and non-Chhanayatis, between whom intermarriage is traditionally forbidden.

Below the Rajputs in Rajasthan's caste hierarchy, the Vaisyas can be divided into two groups: those who profess Jainism, and those professing Vaishnavism, or worship of the god Vishnu. The Oswals, who hail from Osiyan, fall loosely into this caste classification. Below the Vaisyas, the Jats today play an active role in the administration and politics of the state. They are generally vegetarian and profess Vaishnavism.

Women in Society

Rural women in Rajasthan are one of the most economically and socially disadvantaged groups, unable to hold property in their own right, and receiving little, if any, education. Some measures have been undertaken by the central and state governments to enhance the status of rural women in Indian society. Development of Women & Child in Rural Areas, or DWACRA, is a central government initiative aimed at encouraging and promoting the economic empowerment of women.

In Jaipur, the Women & Child Development Department (☎ (0141) 51-7561) is administering programmes to increase awareness among rural women about issues which directly impinge on them, including child marriage, purdah, dowry, and lack of education for girl children. Small meetings known as *jajams* are held at the village level to educate the women.

Legislation has recently been passed which requires that 30% of seats in local elections to *gram panchayats* (one village, or two to three villages), *panchayat sammitis* (village clusters) and *zila parishads* (district committees) must be reserved for women across India. The state government of Rajasthan has gone one step further by passing a law requiring that 30% of the headpersons of gram panchayats and panchayat sammitis must be village women.

There are dozens of voluntary organisations in Rajasthan working towards the economic and social empowerment of women. Care Rajasthan, the Urmal Trust and Sewa Mandir all run important programmes in this area.

Village Life

Traditional village huts are known as *jhonpas*. They are generally small, single storey dwellings, with the walls composed of mud and straw, and a thatched roof. The hearth is usually built in part of the *adgaliya*, or verandah, which fronts the dwelling. There are no windows in jhonpas, and the door is generally of split bamboo. The floor is of packed earth coated with mud and dung. More affluent village members may build a house of stone. Next to the dwelling is a separate building of the same materials, known as a *chhan* or *dogla*. This is where livestock and grain are kept.

Around the hut, and sometimes around the entire village, is erected a barrier of thorns, which keeps wild animals and livestock from wandering into the domestic area.

Water, or its absence, is a big problem in the arid zones. Some 24,000 villages in Rajasthan have no drinking water, and the burden of carrying water, sometimes more than two or three km, belongs to women. A paucity of fuelwood also necessitates villagers having to scour the countryside for a meagre load which is then carried many km back to the hearth. Villagers who own livestock prepare cakes of cow dung in the summer, which is burnt as fuel throughout the year.

Women prepare meals with the aid of a handmill *(chakki)*, a mortar *(okhli)* and pestle *(moosal)*. Meals are carried out to the men working in the fields and women also help in the fields during the harvest.

Desert villages are naturally found close to available water sources, and village size is dependent on water availability and land productivity, resulting in small communities which are relatively isolated from each other. In order to trade their goods and purchase livestock, members of these isolated communities attend regular markets and fairs *(melas)*, which are opportunities for inter-village socialising. These colourful fairs can range from small local gatherings to enormous fairs, such as the Pushkar Camel Fair.

Dos & Don'ts

Religious Etiquette Particular care should be taken when attending a religious place (temple, shrine) or event. Dress and behave appropriately – don't wear shorts or singlet tops (this applies to men and women) and do not smoke or hold hands. Remove your shoes before entering the holy place, and never touch a carving or statue of a deity. In some places, such as mosques, you will be required to cover your head. For religious reasons, do not touch local people on the head and similarly never direct the soles of your feet at a person, religious shrine, or image of a deity, as this may cause offence. Never touch another person with your feet.

Photographic Etiquette You should be sensitive about taking photos of people, especially women, who may find it offensive – always ask first. Taking photos at a death ceremony, or a religious ceremony or of people bathing (in baths or rivers) may cause offence.

Food Etiquette Never throw food into a fire whether at a camp site in the desert or in a home. It is also expedient not to touch food or cooking utensils that local people will use. You should use your right hand for all social interactions, whether passing money or food or any other item. Eat with your right hand only. If you are invited to dine with a family,

always take off your shoes and wash your hands before taking your meal. The hearth is the sacred centre of the home, so never approach it unless you have been invited to do so.

Washing Nudity is completely unacceptable and a swimsuit must be worn even when bathing in a remote location.

Guest Etiquette Never enter the kitchen unless you have been invited to do so, and always remove your shoes before entering. Similarly, never enter the area where drinking water is stored unless you have removed your shoes. Do not touch terracotta vessels in which water is kept – ask your host to serve you.

RELIGION
Hinduism

Hinduism is the dominant religion of Rajasthan, professed by 89.32% of the state's population. Hinduism is one of the oldest extant religions, with firm roots extending back to beyond 1000 BC.

Hinduism today has a number of holy books, the most important being the four *Vedas* (Divine Knowledge) which are the foundation of Hindu philosophy. The *Upanishads*, contained within the *Vedas*, delve into the metaphysical nature of the universe and the soul.

Also important is the *Mahabharata* (Great War of the Bharatas), an epic poem containing over 220,000 lines. It describes the battles between the Kauravas and Pandavas, who were descendants of the Induvansa (Lunar Race). In it is the story of Rama, and it is probable that the most famous Hindu epic, the *Ramayana*, was based on this. The *Bhagavad Gita* is a famous episode of the *Mahabharata* where Krishna relates his philosophies to Arjuna.

Hindu Philosophy & Practice Basically the religion postulates that we will all go through a series of rebirths or reincarnations that eventually lead to *moksha*, the spiritual salvation which frees one from the cycle of rebirths. With each rebirth you can move closer to or further from eventual moksha; the deciding factor is your *karma*, which is literally a law of cause and effect. Bad actions during your life result in bad karma, which ends in a lower reincarnation. Conversely, if your deeds and actions have been good you will reincarnate on a higher level and be a step closer to eventual freedom from rebirth.

Dharma, or the natural law, defines the total social, ethical and spiritual harmony of your life. There are three categories of dharma, the first being the eternal harmony which involves the whole universe. The second category is the dharma that controls castes and the relations between castes. The third dharma is the moral code which an individual should follow.

The Hindu religion has three basic practices. They are *puja*, or worship, the cremation of the dead, and the rules and regulations of the caste system. See the Society & Conduct section of this chapter for details about the caste system.

A *guru* is not so much a teacher as a spiritual guide, somebody who by example or simply by their presence indicates what path you should follow. In a spiritual search one always needs a guru. A *sadhu* is an individual on a spiritual search. They're an easily recognised group, usually wandering around half-naked, smeared in dust with their hair and beard matted.

Hindu Pantheon Westerners may have trouble understanding Hinduism principally because of its vast pantheon of gods. In fact you can look upon all the different gods simply as pictorial representations of the many attributes of a god. The one omnipresent god usually has three physical representations. Brahma is the creator, Vishnu is the preserver and Shiva is the destroyer and reproducer.

Each god has an associated animal known as the 'vehicle' on which they ride, as well as a consort with certain attributes and abilities.

Brahma, despite his supreme position, appears much less often than Vishnu or Shiva. Brahma has four arms and four heads, which symbolise his all-seeing presence.

Vishnu, the preserver, is usually shown in one of the physical forms in which he has visited earth. In all, Vishnu has paid nine visits and on his 10th he is expected as Kalki, riding a horse. On earlier visits he appeared in animal form, as in his boar or man-lion (Narsingh) incarnations, but on visit seven he appeared as Rama, regarded as the personification of the ideal man and the hero of the *Ramayana*. Rama's consort is Sita. Rama also managed to provide a number of secondary gods including his helpful ally Hanuman, the monkey god, who is one of the most popular deities of Rajasthan.

On visit eight Vishnu came as Krishna, who was brought up with peasants and thus became a great favourite of the working classes. Krishna is widely revered throughout Rajasthan. He is renowned for his exploits with the gopis and his consorts are Radha, the head of the gopis, Rukmani and Satyabhama. Krishna is often blue in colour and plays a flute. Vishnu's last incarnation was on visit nine, as the Buddha. This was probably a ploy to bring the Buddhist splinter group back into the Hindu fold.

Durga, the terrible, is the dark side of Parvati, Shiva's wife.

When Vishnu appears as Vishnu, rather than one of his incarnations, he sits on a couch made from the coils of a serpent and in his hands he holds two symbols, the conch shell and the discus. Vishnu's vehicle is the half-man half-eagle known as the Garuda. His consort is the beautiful Lakshmi (Laxmi) who came from the sea and is the goddess of wealth and prosperity.

Shiva's creative role is symbolised by the frequently worshipped *lingam* (phallus). Shiva rides on the bull Nandi and his matted hair is said to have Ganga, the goddess of the river Ganges, in it. Some of the most ancient temples in Rajasthan are dedicated to Shiva, as the Pratihara dynasty, which ruled from the 8th to the 10th centuries, was Shaivite.

Shiva's consort is Parvati, the beautiful. In Rajasthan she is worshipped during the Teej festival which celebrates her marriage to Shiva. Parvati has, however, a dark side when she appears as Durga, the terrible. In this role she holds weapons in her 10 hands and rides a tiger. As Kali, the fiercest of the gods, she demands sacrifices and wears a garland of skulls. The Bhil and Mina tribal people are devotees of Kali. In Rajasthan, she is worshipped by women as Gauri, and honoured during the Gangaur Festival which takes place across Rajasthan just after Holi. Kali usually handles the destructive side of Shiva's personality.

Shiva and Parvati have two children. Ganesh is the elephant-headed god of prosperity and wisdom, and is probably the most popular of all the gods. Ganesh obtained his elephant head due to his father's notorious temper. Coming back from a long trip, Shiva discovered Parvati in her chambers with a young man. Not pausing to think that their son might have grown up a little during his absence, Shiva lopped his head off. He was then forced by Parvati to bring his son back to life but could only do so by giving him the head of the first living thing he saw – which happened to be an elephant. Ganesh's vehicle is a rat. Shiva and Parvati's other son is Kartikkaya, the god of war.

In Rajasthan, the most important temple to Ganesh is at the Ranthambhore Fort.

Ganesh is the god of prosperity and wisdom.

Every year thousands of invitations are sent to the elephant god, care of the Ranthambhore Fort, to request Ganesh's presence at weddings!

A variety of lesser gods and goddesses also make up the Hindu pantheon. Most temples are dedicated to one or other of the gods, but curiously there are very few Brahma temples – Rajasthan has the honour of being the site of one of only two temples honouring Brahma in the entire country, at Pushkar, in eastern Rajasthan. Most Hindus profess to be either Vaishnavites (followers of Vishnu) or Shaivites (followers of Shiva). The cow is, of course, the holy animal of Hinduism.

Worship of the snake god, Sheshnag, is widespread across Rajasthan.

Folk Gods & Goddesses Rajasthan has numerous folk gods and goddesses, many of whom are deified local heroes. In addition to these folk deities, every family pays homage to a clan goddess, or *kuldevi*.

The deified folk hero Ramdev has an important temple near Pokaran in western Rajasthan. He is revered for spurning caste distinctions and for his aid to the poor and sick.

Pabuji often features in the stories of the Bhopas, Rajasthan's professional story tellers. According to tradition, Pabuji entered a transaction with a woman called Devalde, in which, in return for a mare, he vowed to protect her cows from all harm. The time to fulfil this obligation came, inconveniently, during the celebration of Pabuji's own marriage. Recalling his vow, Pabuji immediately went to the aid of the threatened livestock. During the ensuing battle, he, along with all the male members of his family, perished at the hands of a villain by the name of Jind Raj Khinchi.

In order to preserve the family line, Pabuji's sister-in-law cut open her own belly and produced Pabuji's nephew, Nandio, before committing sati on her husband's funeral pyre. An annual festival is held at Kodumand, in Jaisalmer district, the birthplace of Pabuji, at which Bhopas perform Pabuji-ka-phad, poetry recitations in praise of Pabuji.

Gogaji was a warrior who lived in the 11th century and could cure snakebite – victims of snakebite are brought before his shrine by devotees, who include both Hindus and Muslims. Also believed to cure snakebite if propitiated accordingly is Tejaji. According to tradition, while pursuing *dacoits* (villains) who had rustled his father-in-law's cows, Teja was confronted by a snake which was poised to strike him. Teja pleaded with the snake to let him pass so that he could recover the cows, and promised to return later. The snake relented, and Teja duly returned, bloody and bruised from his confrontation with the dacoits. The snake was reluctant to bite Teja on his wounds, so Teja offered the snake his tongue. So impressed was the snake, that it decreed that anyone honouring Teja by wearing a thread in his name would be cured of snakebite. Other deified heroe include a father and son, Mehaji and Harbhu

Goddesses, generally incarnations o Devi, or Shakti, the Mother Goddess include the fierce Chamunda Mata, an incar nation of Durga; Sheetala Mata, the goddes of smallpox, whom parents propitiate i order to spare their children from this afflic tion; Kela Devi; and Karni Mata, worshippe at Deshnok, near Bikaner.

Aaiji, a Rajput woman who lived in th 15th century and is believed to be an incar nation of Shakti, is worshipped at Bilara, i the district of Jodhpur.

Women who have committed sati on thei husbands' funeral pyres are also frequentl revered as goddesses, such as Rani Sati, wh has an elaborate temple in her honour i Jhunjhunu, in Shekhawati.

Barren women pay homage to the go Bhairon, an incarnation of Shiva, at hi shrines which are usually found under kheji trees. In order to be blessed with a child, th woman is required to leave a garmen hanging from the branches of the tree, an often these can be seen fluttering ove shrines to Bhairon. The ubiquitous kheji tree of Rajasthan is worshipped during th festival of Dussehra, and the banyan an peepul trees, both considered sacred, are als worshipped on special days.

Jainism

The Jain religion is contemporaneous wit Buddhism and bears many similarities t both it and Hinduism. It was founded aroun 500 BC by Mahavira, the 24th and last of th Jain prophets, known as *tirthankars*, or finder of the Path. The Jains tend to be commerciall successful and have an influence dispropor tionate to their actual numbers.

In Rajasthan, Jains number only 1.82% o the population. There are, nevertheless numerous beautiful Jain temples in this state as Jainism was for the most part tolerated b the Rajput rulers, some of whom funded th construction of these temples.

The religion originally evolved as reformist movement against the dominanc of priests and the complicated rituals o

Brahmanism, and it rejected the caste system. Jains believe that the universe is infinite and was not created by a deity. They also believe in reincarnation and eventual spiritual salvation, or moksha, through following the path of the tirthankars. One factor in the search for salvation is *ahimsa*, or reverence for all life and the avoidance of injury to all living things. Due to this belief, Jains are strict vegetarians and some monks actually cover their mouths with a piece of cloth in order to avoid the risk of accidentally swallowing an insect.

The Jains are divided into two sects, the white-robed Shvetambara and the Digambara. The Digambaras are the more austere sect; their name literally means Sky Clad since, as a sign of their contempt for material possessions, they do not even wear clothes.

The Jains constructed extraordinary temple complexes, notable for the large number of similar buildings clustered together in one place. While those in Rajasthan are not quite as spectacular as the hilltop 'temple city' at Palitana, in Gujarat, the Jain temple complexes of Mt Abu, Ranakpur and Jaisalmer, and the Jain temples at Osiyan and Bikaner, are known for their beautiful sculpture and architectural symmetry.

Other Religions

Muslims, followers of the Islamic religion, represent 7.28% of the state's population, therefore constituting the second largest religious group in the state. Most Muslims today are Sunnites, followers of the succession from the caliph, while the others are Shias or Shi'ites who follow the descendants of Ali. There is a small community of Shi'ite Muslims, known as Bohras, in south-eastern Rajasthan. The most important pilgrimage site for Muslims in Rajasthan is the Dargah, the tomb of a Sufi saint, Khwaja Muin-ud-in Chishti, at Ajmer.

In Rajasthan, 1.44% of the population processes Sikhism. Most of Rajasthan's Sikhs live in Ganganagar district.

There is a very small population of Christians in Rajasthan, amounting to only 0.12% of the population. They are found predominantly in Ajmer and Jaipur, where there are several Catholic and Protestant churches. The Buddhist population is negligible in Rajasthan, representing only 0.01% of the population.

LANGUAGE

Rajasthani is the collective name for the various dialects spoken in Rajasthan. There are five main regional dialects: Marwari, Mewari, Dhundhari, Mewati and Hadoti. Marwari, spoken by 16.27% of the population, is the most commonly spoken dialect. Other dialects include Bhili and Bagri. Hindi, spoken by 92.97% of the population, is the most widely spoken language in Rajasthan, and the most useful language with which to communicate across the state. Other languages spoken in Rajasthan include Punjabi (spoken by 1.84% of the population), Urdu (0.77%), Sindhi (0.34%) and Gujarati (0.08%).

English is widely spoken by people working in the hospitality industry, such as hotels and restaurants, and at important tourist attractions such as forts and palaces. English-speaking guides are available in towns and cities such as Jaipur, Udaipur, Jodhpur, Bikaner and Jaisalmer. In Jaipur, it's also possible to hire Spanish, German and French-speaking guides.

In the rural areas, little if any English is spoken, and attempts at a few Hindi phrases will greatly enhance your enjoyment of travelling through these more remote regions. One word which you will probably hear frequently during your travels in Rajasthan is *padharo*, meaning 'Please come/You're welcome'. The small hole-in-the-wall eateries which are known elsewhere in India as *dhabas* are often referred to as *bhojnalyas* in Rajasthan.

Beware of *acha*, that all-purpose word for 'OK'. It can also mean 'OK, I understand what you mean, but it isn't OK'.

Hindi

See Lonely Planet's *Hindi/Urdu phrasebook* for a comprehensive list of Hindi words and phrases.

Basics

Hello/Goodbye.	namaste
Excuse me.	maaf kijiyeh
Please.	meharbani seh
Thank you.	shukriya
Yes/No.	haan/nahin
Do you speak English?	kya aap angrezi samajhte hain?
I don't understand.	meri samajh mei nahin aaya
What is your name?	aap ka shubh naam kya hai?
How are you?	aap kaiseh hain?
Very well, thank you.	bahut acha, shukriya
What is the time?	kitneh bajeh hain?

Getting Around & Accommodation

Where is the ...?	... kahan hai?
bus stop	bas staap
hotel	hotal
station	steshan
How far is ...?	... kitni duur hai?
How do I get to ...?	... kojane ke liyeh kaiseh jaana parega?
What street is this?	ye kaun sii ... hai?
When will the next bus leave?	agli bas kab jaaegi?
Which bus goes to ...?	... kaun sii bas jaati hai?
Are there rooms available?	koi kamra khaali hai?
How much is it per night?	ek raat ke kitneh paise lagein-ge?
Is a bathroom attached?	saath meh baathroom hai?

Food & Shopping

I/we would like some food.	khaana chaahiyeh
Do you have drinking water?	piineh kaa paani hai?
Show me the menu.	mujheh minu dikhaiyeh
I only eat vegetarian food.	main shakahaari huun

The bill please.	bill de dijiyeh
How much?	kitneh
	paiseh/kitneh hai?
This is expensive.	yeh bahut mehnga hai
fruit	phal
vegetables	sabzi
sugar	chini
rice	chaaval
water	paani
tea	chai
coffee	kaafi
milk	dudh
chemist/pharmacy	davai kii dukaan
market	baazaar/markit
shop	dukaan

Health

Where is the ...?	... kahaan hai?
doctor	doktar
dentist	daanton kaa doktar
hospital	haspataal
My stomach is upset.	meraa peit kharaab hai
It hurts here.	yahaan dard hai
I'm allergic to penicillin.	mujhe penicilin se elargii hai
medicine	dava-ee
pregnant	garbhvatii
prescription	priskripshan

Numbers

Whereas we count in tens, hundreds, thousands, millions and billions, the Indian numbering system goes tens, hundreds, thousands, hundred thousands, ten millions. A hundred thousand is a *lakh,* and 10 millions is a *crore.*

These two words are almost always used in place of their English equivalent. Thus you will see 10 lakh rather than one million and one crore rather than 10 million. Furthermore, the numerals are generally written that way too – thus three hundred thousand appears as 3,00,000 not 300,000, and one million, five hundred thousand would appear numerically as 1,05,00,000 (one crore, five lakh) not 10,500,000. If you say something costs five crore or is worth 10 lakh, it always means 'of rupees'.

1	*ek*	15	*pandranh*
2	*do*	16	*solanh*
3	*tin*	17	*staranh*
4	*char*	18	*aatharanh*
5	*panch*	19	*unnis*
6	*chhe*	20	*bis*
7	*saat*	21	*ikkis*
8	*aath*	30	*tis*
9	*nau*	40	*chalis*
10	*das*	50	*panchas*
11	*gyaranh*	60	*saath*
12	*baranh*	70	*sattar*
13	*teranh*	80	*assi*
14	*chodanh*	90	*nabbe*
		100	*so*
		200	*do so*
		1000	*ek hazaar*
		100,000	*lakh*
		10,000,000	*crore*

Facts for the Visitor

PLANNING
When to Go
The best time to visit Rajasthan is in the cooler winter months (December to February), when the days are warm and sunny with average temperatures across the state in the mid-20s, and cool nights. However, hotel prices are at a premium in winter. The days begin to heat up in March, but are generally still pleasant. The post-monsoon season, from mid-September to the end of November, is also pleasant, with average maximum temperatures in October in the mid-30s and an average minimum of around 20°C.

The winter season corresponds with some of Rajasthan's most colourful festivals, such as the Desert Festival in Jaisalmer, the Camel Festival at Bikaner and the Nagaur Cattle Fair. March is also an excellent time to visit Rajasthan, as this corresponds with India's most exuberant festival – Holi. Rajasthan's own Gangaur festival is celebrated in March-April, as is Udaipur's Mewar Festival and Jaipur's Elephant Festival. The Pushkar Camel Fair takes place in November.

Winter is also a good time to visit Rajasthan's best known wildlife sanctuaries, Keoladeo Ghana Bird Sanctuary, Ranthambhore National Park and Sariska Wildlife Sanctuary. For more information, see National Parks & Wildlife Sanctuaries in the Facts about Rajasthan chapter.

Maps
The Discover India Series has a very good map of Rajasthan at a scale of 1:1,200,000, clearly showing rail routes, major highways and roads. Lonely Planet's *India & Bangladesh* travel atlas is a handy reference to the entire Indian subcontinent. Its coverage of Rajasthan is excellent, with symbols clearly showing sites of ancient forts, national parks and sanctuaries and other sites of interest to visitors. The maps have been checked on the ground by Lonely Planet authors and travel

information is provided in English, French Dutch, Spanish and Japanese.

There is a stall outside the tourist reception centre in Delhi (see under Tourist Office later in this chapter) which sells maps of Rajasthan.

What to Bring
The usual travellers' rule applies – bring a little as possible. It's much better to have to buy something you've left behind than find you have too much and need to get rid of it

Clothes Light, cool cotton clothes are the best bet for day wear, with a light sweater or pullover for nights, which can get surprisingly chilly, especially in the winter month In some centres, such as Jaipur, Pushkar an Udaipur, western-style clothes can be purchased off the peg at ridiculously low price or you can have clothes made to measure in the small tailor shops found in all but the tiniest villages.

Modesty rates highly in India, as in mo Asian countries. Although men wearing shorts is accepted as a western eccentricity they should at least be of a decent length Unless women want to draw (even greater than usual) attention to themselves, the shouldn't wear shorts or sleeveless tops. A reasonable clothes list would include:

- underwear and swimming gear
- one pair of cotton trousers
- one pair of shorts (men only)
- one long (ankle-length) cotton skirt (women)
- a few T-shirts or short-sleeved cotton shirts
- sweater for cold nights
- one pair of sneakers or shoes plus socks
- sandals
- thongs (handy to wear when showering in commo bathrooms)
- a set of 'dress up' clothes (for dining at the Lak Palace in Udaipur!)
- a straw or cotton hat

Bedding A sleeping bag can be a hassle t carry, but can serve as something to sleep i (also avoiding unsavoury-looking hotel bedding), a cushion on hard train seats, a pillow on long bus journeys or a bed top-cover (since cheaper hotels rarely give you one). If you're planning a camel safari, a sleeping bag can come in very handy. If you're sleeping out on the dunes, it can get surprisingly chilly, and the blankets which are provided on the safaris are never warm enough.

A sheet sleeping bag can be very useful, particularly on overnight train trips or if you don't trust the hotel's sheets. Mosquito nets are rare, so your own sheet or sheet sleeping bag will also help to keep mosquitoes at bay.

Some travellers find that a plastic sheet is useful for a number of reasons, including to bedbug-proof unhealthy-looking beds. Others have recommended an inflatable pillow as a useful accessory. These are widely available for Rs 30.

Toilet Paper Indian sewerage systems are generally overloaded enough without having to cope with toilet paper as well. However, if you can't adapt to the Indian method of a jug of water and your left hand, toilet paper is widely available in the larger cities and popular travellers' centres, such as Pushkar and Jaisalmer. A receptacle for used toilet paper is sometimes provided in toilets – use it!

Toiletries Soap, toothpaste and other toiletries are readily available, although hair conditioner often comes in the 'shampoo and conditioner in one' format, so if you don't use this stuff, bring your own conditioner. Astringent is useful for cleaning away the grime at the end of the day – bring cotton-balls for application. A universal sink plug is worth having since few cheaper hotels have plugs. A nailbrush can be extremely useful. Tampons are not readily available in Rajasthan – bring a supply. Sanitary pads are widely available in larger towns and cities.

Men can safely leave their shaving gear at home. One of the pleasures of Indian travel is a shave in a barber shop every few days. With AIDS becoming more widespread in India, however, choose a barber shop that looks clean, and make sure that a fresh blade is used. For just a few rupees you'll get the full treatment – lathering, followed by a shave, then the process is repeated, and finally there's the hot, damp towel and sometimes talcum powder. You may also get a scalp massage thrown in.

Miscellaneous Items It's amazing how many things you wish you had with you when you're in India. For budget travellers, a padlock is a virtual necessity. Most cheap hotels and quite a number of mid-range places have doors locked by a flimsy latch and padlock. You'll find having your own sturdy lock on the door does wonders for your peace of mind.

A knife (preferably Swiss Army) has a whole range of uses, and can be particularly good for peeling fruit. Some travellers rhapsodise about the usefulness of a miniature electric element to boil water in a cup. A sarong is a handy item – it can be used as a bed sheet, an item of clothing, an emergency towel, and a pillow on trains!

Insect repellent can also be extremely useful. Pick up an electric mosquito zapper in Delhi or Jaipur. Power cuts are not uncommon in Rajasthan ('load shedding' as it is euphemistically known) and there's little street lighting at night so a torch (flashlight) and candles are essential. A mosquito net can be very useful, especially in notorious mosquito zones such as Pushkar.

Bring along a spare set of specs and your spectacle prescription if you're short-sighted. Earplugs are useful for light sleepers, and even heavier sleepers can have difficulty shutting out the din in some hotels. Eye shades can also be handy.

In Rajasthan, a sun hat and sunglasses are essential. A water bottle should always be by your side; and also, if you're not drinking bottled water, have water purification tablets (which also reduces the amount of plastic bottles seen on dumps around

India). High-factor sunscreen cream is becoming more widely available, but it's *expensive*! Lip balm is especially useful in the desert regions, where the sun can really pack a punch.

Some travellers bring a reasonably heavy duty chain to secure their pack to the luggage racks of trains and buses. Some women carry a high-pitched whistle which may act as a deterrent to would-be assailants. See the Health section later in this chapter for details about medical supplies.

SUGGESTED ITINERARIES

Although Rajasthan's places of interest are scattered over a vast geographical area, an excellent rail network means that you can cover large distances very efficiently, and visit many of Rajasthan's sites in just several weeks.

Rajasthan's most important sites include Jaipur, the historic Chittorgarh Fort, romantic Udaipur, Ranthambhore National Park, the desert city of Jaisalmer, bustling Jodhpur, and Bharatpur, home of the Keoladeo Ghana National Park. In two weeks or longer you could take in all of these, as well as Agra (in Uttar Pradesh). A short camel trek in the environs of Jaisalmer, or a visit to the holy town of Pushkar, or the beautiful palace of Deeg, or Alwar, en route back to Delhi, might also be possible.

In three to four weeks, you could visit all of the above places and take in the Shekhawati region of northern Rajasthan, with its magnificent painted *havelis*, or mansions, as well as the desert city of Bikaner, which has a stunning fort. Bird lovers should stop at Khichan, between Jodhpur and Jaisalmer, to witness the spectacular sight of thousands of demoiselle cranes descending on the fields around this village to feed on grain distributed by villagers.

In four to five weeks you could enjoy an extended camel trek in the environs of Jaisalmer, Pushkar or Shekhawati, a horse safari in southern Rajasthan, and visit Rajasthan's only hill-station, Mt Abu, worth visiting especially for its beautiful Jain temples.

HIGHLIGHTS

While there are plenty of ancient fortresses and palaces, beautiful temple complexes and fine national parks and sanctuaries in Rajasthan, one of the highlights of a visit to Rajasthan is simply travelling through what is probably the most colourful region of India. Rajasthanis adorn themselves in garments of the most astonishingly vibrant colours. Villagers bedeck themselves in chunky and elaborate silver jewellery.

Jaipur

You could easily spend several days in Jaipur itself: arts and crafts from around Rajasthan are assembled in the emporiums of the capital city, and it's a great place to shop. When you've exhausted yourself shopping a refreshing drink at the luxurious Rambagh Palace hotel's Polo Bar, accompanied by the strains of traditional Rajasthani folk musicians, might serve to revive you. You could then stroll to the adjacent polo grounds and watch a game of horse polo (in March only, the polo season), or wander through the artisans' quarters of the old city and watch master craftspeople at work.

In Sanganer, a small village near Jaipur, you can see vast lengths of colourful fabric drying on the riverbanks, or watch yards of it unfurl as it is held at either end by women from the printing and dyeing communities.

Eastern Rajasthan

Also set around a lake is the holy town of Pushkar, in eastern Rajasthan. The setting is beautiful, with tiny whitewashed buildings and temples along the shore of this small, perfectly round lake. A diminutive hill, with a small temple perched on top of it, serves as a backdrop. The main bazaar is crammed with shops selling brightly coloured clothes in western styles, miniature paintings and other artefacts. There are numerous salubrious places to eat (but no alcohol – this is a holy town), some great second-hand bookshops, and in the evening you can sit on the verandah of your guest house, looking out over the lake and listen to the resounding rhythm of drums, beaten by priests to herald he close of the day. In November, Pushkar hosts its annual Camel Fair, and at this time thousands of inhabitants from the villages of Rajasthan throng to the small town to buy and trade camels.

Alwar and Deeg, both in eastern Rajasthan, have stunning palaces which are not often visited by tourists.

Southern Rajasthan

Udaipur may well be the most romantic city in Rajasthan, if not all of India. Beautiful palaces, temples and havelis flank the shores of Lake Pichola, in the centre of which is Jagmandir Island and the luxurious Lake Palace hotel, a vision in white. Even if you can't afford to stay at the Lake Palace, there are numerous budget and mid-range guest houses right on the lake shore which offer superlative views out across the lake.

Despite its massive size and historic importance, few travellers make their way to Chittorgarh. Many Rajasthanis consider that the Chittorgarh Fort epitomises the essence of Rajput bravery.

Northern Rajasthan

The Shekhawati region of northern Rajasthan is a feast of colour. Here, thousands of havelis feature paintings both on the internal and external walls. The havelis were built by rich merchants who spared no expense constructing elaborate homes as symbols of their elevated financial and social status. The paintings represent an extraordinary cultural tapestry, recording for prosperity the inventions of the day, such as steam locomotives and treadle sewing machines.

Western Rajasthan

Jaisalmer is another travellers' favourite. Its massive fort rises like an apparition after the long bus or train journey across the dead flat desert. Contained within its walls, reached by an enormous stone ramp, are dozens of cobblestone-lined alleyways concealing temples and bazaars. Up on the ramparts enormous stone balls are perched, once deadly missiles which were pushed down onto the heads of invading enemies. There are dozens of great budget places to stay, plenty of good restaurants and desert panoramas to take your breath away.

Forty-two km from Jaisalmer are the Sam sand dunes, where even the most jaded seen-it-all traveller will find it hard to resist playing Lawrence of Arabia. Visions of caparisoned camels and their drivers silhouetted against the sun might verge on the clichéd, but this is in fact what you'll see here. Despite the tourist hype, it is a strangely evocative experience, with musicians playing as the sun sets over the Thar Desert.

Jodhpur's fort is another grand edifice in stone testifying to the warrior spirit of the Rajputs. It's a massive, cannon-ball-pocked monolith which affords brilliant views over the city from its battlements, and its museum houses one of the most fabulous collections of artefacts dating from the days of the maharajas.

Bikaner is a bustling and chaotic desert city. The main attraction here is the city's massive fort, but you can also lose yourself for hours in the labyrinthine streets of the old city, or take day trips to a camel breeding farm (more interesting than you might suspect) and the Karni Mata Temple at Deshnok. Just when you thought you'd got a handle on Hinduism, this temple will leave you perplexed again, for here, thousands of rats are revered as the incarnate souls of dead storytellers!

Wildlife Sanctuaries

Eastern Rajasthan has the state's most important and notable wildlife sanctuaries. Tigers are the attraction at Ranthambhore and Sariska, but even if you miss out on seeing these elusive big cats, you are virtually guaranteed sightings of other large mammals such as chinkara, sambar, nilgai and wild boar. To enjoy a visit to Keoladeo Ghana National Park near Bharatpur, it's not necessary to be a budding ornithologist. Here you can view at close hand thousands of birds representing hundreds of different species in a beautiful wetland setting.

Safaris

If you want the ultimate desert experience you're a perfect candidate for a camel safari. They're possible in the environs of Pushkar and Jaisalmer, or in the Shekhawati region. It's also possible to take extended horse safaris in southern Rajasthan. For more information, see the Activities section of this chapter, or the relevant sections in individual chapters.

TOURIST OFFICES
Local Tourist Offices

There are Rajasthan Tourism Development Corporation (RTDC) tourist offices and tourist reception centres in most of the places of interest to visitors in Rajasthan, including offices at Jaipur, Ajmer, Alwar, Amber, Bharatpur, Bikaner, Bundi, Chittorgarh, Jaisalmer, Jhunjhunu, Jodhpur, Kota, Mt Abu, Sawai Madhopur and Udaipur. They range from the extraordinarily helpful to the fairly useless. However, you can usually pick up glossy brochures and maps at even the most inefficient of them, as well as a copy of *Atithi* (Guest), which is a tourist publication produced by the RTDC. Addresses are given in relevant sections throughout the book. In addition, there are several Rajasthan tourist offices in other Indian cities, including:

Ahmedabad
    Bharatiya Hotel Incorporated, 11 Neptune Towers, Opposite Nehru Bridge, Ashram Rd (☎ (079) 46-5048; fax 42-0925)
Calcutta
    1st Floor, 2 Ganesh Chandra Ave (☎ (033) 27-9740)
Delhi
    Bikaner House, Pandara Rd, New Delhi (☎ (011) 338-3837; fax 338-2823)
Madras
    28 Commander-in-Chief Rd (☎ (044) 827-2093)
Mumbai (Bombay)
    230 Dr DN Rd (☎ (022) 283-5603; fax 204-4162)

Government of India tourist offices in the four international gateways to India include:

Calcutta
    4 Shakespeare Sarani (☎ (033) 242-1402, 242-3521)
Delhi
    88 Janpath, New Delhi (☎ (011) 332-0005)
Madras
    154 Anna Salai (☎ (044) 852-4295)
Mumbai (Bombay)
    123 Maharishi Karve Rd, Churchgate (☎ (022) 203-2932)

Beware of touts, particularly in New Delhi, who hang around the national tourist office to hustle you into nearby privately operated tourist concerns claiming that these are the official Government of India tourist offices. Note the above address.

Tourist Offices Abroad

The Government of India Department of Tourism maintains a string of tourist offices in other countries where you can get brochures, leaflets and some information about India. The tourist office leaflets and brochures often have high quality information and are worth getting hold of. However, some of the foreign offices are not always as useful for obtaining information as those within India. There are also smaller 'promotion offices' in Osaka (Japan) and in Dallas, Miami, San Francisco and Washington DC (USA).

Australia
    Level 1, 17 Castlereagh St, Sydney, NSW 2000 (☎ (02) 9232-1600; fax 9223-3003)
Canada
    60 Bloor St West, Suite No 1003, Toronto, Ontario M4W 3B8 (☎ (416) 962-3787; fax 962-6279)
France
    8 Blvd de la Madeleine, 75009 Paris (☎ (01) 42 65 83 86; fax 42 65 01 16)
Germany
    Kaiserstrasse 77-III, D-6000 Frankfurt-am-Main-1 (☎ (069) 23-5423; fax 23-4724)
Italy
    Via Albricci 9, 20122 Milan (☎ (02) 80-4952; fax 7202-1681)
Japan
    Pearl Bldg, 9-18 Ginza, 7-Chome, Chuo ku, Tokyo 104 (☎ (03) 571-5062; fax 571-5235)
Malaysia
    Wisma HLA, Lot 203 Jalan Raja Chulan, 50200 Kuala Lumpur (☎ (03) 242-5285; fax 242-5301)

ADAM MCCROW

MICHELLE COXALL

Top: Safari camel, Sam Sand Dunes, near Jaisalmer.
Bottom: Belch.

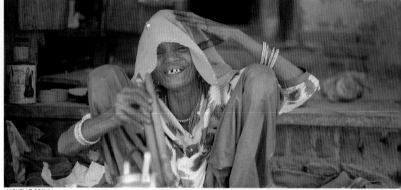

Top: Lac bangle maker, Fatehpur.
Middle: Chai-wallah, Lakshmangarh.
Bottom: Rickshaw-wallah, Alwar.

The Netherlands
      Rokin 9-15, 1012 KK Amsterdam
      (☎ (020) 620-8991; fax 38-3059)
Singapore
      United House, 20 Kramat Lane, Singapore 0922
      (☎ 235-3800; fax 235-8677)
Sweden
      Sveavagen 9-11, S-III 57, Stockholm 11157
      (☎ (08) 21-5081; fax 21-0186)
Switzerland
      1-3 Rue de Chantepoulet, 1201 Geneva
      (☎ (022) 732-1813; fax 731-5660)
Thailand
      Kentucky Fried Chicken Bldg, 3rd Floor, 62/5
      Thaniya Rd, Bangkok 10500 (☎ (02) 235-2585)
UK
      7 Cork St, London W1X 2AB
      (☎ (0171) 437-3677; fax 494-1048)
USA
      30 Rockefeller Plaza, 15 North Mezzanine, New
      York NY 10112
      (☎ (212) 586-4901; fax 582-3274)
      3550 Wilshire Blvd, Suite 204, Los Angeles CA
      90010 (☎ (213) 380-8855; fax 380-6111)

VISAS & DOCUMENTS

Passport

You must have a passport with you all the time; it's the most basic travel document. Ensure that your passport will be valid for the entire period you intend to remain overseas. If your passport is lost or stolen, immediately contact your country's embassy or consulate in Delhi.

Visas

Virtually everybody needs a visa to visit India. The application is (in theory) straightforward and the visas are usually issued with a minimum of fuss.

Tourist visas come in a variety of flavours and are shown in the visa table below. Note that with a three month visa, your entry to India must be within 30 days from the date

of issue of the visa. Also, the six month visa is valid from the date of issue of the visa, not the date you enter India. This means that if you enter India five months after the visa was issued, it will be valid only for one month, not the full six months. If you enter India the day after it was issued, you can stay for the full six months. We get many letters from travellers who get caught out, thinking a six month visa gives them a six month stay in India. Very few embassies issue one year tourist visas, although travellers have recently reported that it is possible to obtain a one year Indian visa in the Netherlands, valid from date of issue.

The cost of the visa varies depending on your nationality. Currently, for a 15 day/three month/six month visa, Brits pay UK£3/13/26, and Aussies pay A$17/40/70. Most other nationalities are charged much the same.

Pakistan The high commission in Islamabad is quite efficient, although if there is an Indian embassy in your home country they may have to fax there to check that you are not a thief, wanted by the police or in some other way undesirable. The process takes a few days, and of course you have to pay for the fax.

Thailand It now takes four working days for non-Thai nationals to obtain an Indian visa.

Sri Lanka In addition to the Indian embassy in Colombo, travellers have reported that it is possible to obtain an Indian visa in Kandy. Visas take approximately one week to be issued. The office is located on the uphill road 100m after the Royal Palace Park, on the left, near the Castle Hill Guest House.

Indian Visas			
Duration	*Valid from*	*Entries*	*Extendible*
15 days	entry to India	single	No
15 days	entry to India	double	No
3 months	entry to India	multiple	No
6 months	issue of visa	multiple	Yes

Nepal According to a recent report from travellers, it is no longer possible to get a new Indian visa in Kathmandu if you already have a six month visa in your passport. Some travellers have managed to get a short visa extension, however, by having their visas changed to six months from date of entry instead of from date of issue.

Visa Extensions Only six month tourist visas are extendible. If you want to stay in India beyond the 180 days from the date of issue of your visa, *regardless of your date of entry into India*, you're going to have to try to extend your visa. Extensions are not given as a matter of routine. If you have already been in the country for six months, it can be difficult to get an extension, and then you may only be given a month. If you've been in India less than six months the chances are much better. A one month extension costs anything from Rs 600 to Rs 800, and four photos are required.

Applications for visa extensions can be made at Foreigners' Registration Offices (see below), and in all state and district capitals at the office of the Superintendent of Police.

If you stay beyond four months you are also supposed to get an income tax clearance before you leave. See the upcoming Tax Clearance Certificates section for details.

Foreigners' Registration Offices Visa extensions are issued by Foreigners' Registration offices. The main offices include:

Calcutta
    237 Acharya JC Bose Rd (☎ (033) 247-3301)
Delhi
    1st Floor, Hans Bhavan, Tilak Bridge, New Delhi
    (☎ (011) 331-9489)
Madras
    Shashtri Bhavan Annexe, 26 Haddows Rd
    (☎ (044) 827-8210)
Mumbai (Bombay)
    Special Branch II, Annexe 2, Office of the Commissioner of Police (Greater Mumbai), Dadabhoy Naoroji Rd (☎ (022) 262-0446)

Tax Clearance Certificates
If you stay in India for more than 120 days you need a 'tax clearance certificate' to leave the country. This supposedly proves that your time in India was financed with your own money, not by working in India or by selling things or playing the black market.

Basically all you have to do is find the Foreign Section of the Income Tax Department in Delhi, Calcutta, Madras or Mumbai (Bombay) and turn up with your passport, visa extension form, any other similar paperwork and a handful of bank exchange receipts (to show you really have been changing foreign currency into rupees officially). You fill in a form and wait for anything from 10 minutes to a couple of hours. You're then given your tax clearance certificate and away you go. We've never yet heard from anyone who has actually been asked for this document on departure.

Photocopies
It's a good idea to carry photocopies of your important travel documents, which obviously should be kept separate from the originals in the event that these are lost or stolen.

Take a photocopy of the first page of your passport (with your personal details and photograph), as well as a copy of the page with your Indian visa. A photocopy of your travel insurance policy could be handy. Keep a record of the travellers' cheques you have exchanged, where they were encashed, the amount and serial number. Encashment receipts should also be kept separate from your travellers' cheques. Photocopy your airline ticket and your credit card. It's not a bad idea to leave photocopies of your important travel documents with a friend or relative at home.

Restricted Areas
There are some places in Rajasthan where foreigners cannot go unless they have special permission from the relevant authorities. Due to the hostilities between India and Pakistan, foreigners are prohibited from approaching within 50 km of the Indo-Pakistan border. Special permission is required from the

Collector's office in Jaisalmer to travel to most of Rajasthan west of National Highway No 15, due to its proximity to the Pakistan border, and is only issued in exceptional circumstances. The only places exempted are Amar Sagar, Bada Bagh, Lodhruva, Kuldhara, Akal, Sam, Ramkund, Khuri and Mool Sagar.

Permission is required from the District Magistrate or Superintendent of Police in Barmer to travel to the Kiradu temple complex, about 35 km from Barmer near the Pakistan border.

Onward Tickets

Many Indian embassies and consulates will not issue a visa to enter India unless you are holding an onward ticket, which is taken as sufficient evidence that you intend to leave the country.

Travel Insurance

A travel insurance policy to cover theft, loss and medical problems is a wise idea. There is a wide variety of policies and your travel agent will have recommendations. The international student travel policies handled by STA Travel, Council Travel and other student travel organisations are usually good value. Some policies offer a range of medical-expense options. The more expensive options are chiefly for countries like the USA which have extremely high medical costs. Check the small print:

Some policies specifically exclude 'dangerous activities' which can include motorcycling and even trekking. If such activities are on your agenda you don't want that sort of policy. A locally acquired motorcycle licence may not be valid under your policy.

You may prefer a policy which pays doctors or hospitals direct rather than you having to pay on the spot and claim later. If you have to claim later make sure you keep all documentation. Some policies ask you to call back (reverse charges) to a centre in your home country where an immediate assessment of your problem is made.

Check if the policy covers ambulances, an emergency helicopter airlift out of a remote region, or an emergency flight home. If you have to stretch out you will need two seats and somebody has to pay for them!

Driving Licence & Permits

If you are planning to drive in India, get an International Driving Permit from your local national motoring organisation. In some centres, such as Delhi, it's possible to hire motorcycles. An International Permit can also be used for other identification purposes, such as plain old bicycle hire.

Other Documents

A health certificate, while not necessary in India, may well be required for onward travel. Student cards are virtually useless these days – many student concessions have either been eliminated or replaced by 'youth fares' or similar age concessions. Similarly, a Youth Hostel (Hostelling International – HI) card is not generally required for India's many hostels, but you do pay slightly less at official youth hostels if you have one.

It's worth having a batch of passport photos for visa applications and for obtaining permits to remote regions. If you run out, Indian photo studios will do excellent portraits at pleasantly low prices.

Visas for Neighbouring Countries

Bhutan Although Bhutan is an independent country, India has firm control over foreign policy and most other things. Applications to visit Bhutan must be made through the Director of Tourism, Ministry of Finance, Tachichho Dzong, Thimpu, Bhutan; or through the Bhutan Foreign Mission (☎ (011) 60-9217; fax 687-6710), Chandragupta Marg, Chanakyapuri, New Delhi 110021, India; or through the Bhutanese mission in New York. And don't hold your breath – unless you have high-up Indian connections or a personal friend in the Bhutanese aristocracy, you needn't expect to get a permit. Very few permits are issued for overland travel. The only way around these restrictions is to book an organised tour, and these don't come cheap.

Myanmar (Burma) The embassy in Delhi is fast and efficient and issues four week visas.

There is *no* Burmese consulate in Calcutta, although there is one in Kathmandu in Nepal and Dhaka in Bangladesh.

Nepal The Nepalese Embassy in Delhi is on Barakhamba Rd, New Delhi, quite close to Connaught Place, not out at Chanakyapuri like most other embassies. It is open Monday to Friday from 10 am to 1 pm. Single entry, 30 day visas take 24 hours and cost US$25 (payable in rupees). A 30 day visa is available on arrival in Nepal for US$25, and can be extended, but doing so involves rather a lot of form filling and queuing – it's better to have a visa in advance, if possible.

There is also a consulate in Calcutta, and they issue visas on the spot. You'll need one passport photo and the rupee equivalent of US$25.

Sri Lanka Most western nationalities do not need a visa to visit Sri Lanka, but there are diplomatic offices in Delhi, Mumbai, and Madras.

Thailand There are Thai embassies in Delhi and Calcutta. One month visas cost about US$10 and are issued in 24 hours. They can be extended in Thailand. If you are flying into and out of Thailand and don't intend to stay more than 15 days, a visa is not required, but you cannot extend your period of stay.

EMBASSIES
Indian Embassies Abroad
India's embassies, consulates and high commissions include:

Australia
    3-5 Moonah Place, Yarralumla, ACT 2600
    (☎ (06) 273-3999; fax 273-3328)
    Level 27, 25 Bligh St, Sydney, NSW 2000
    (☎ (02) 9223-9500; fax 9223-9246)
    13 Munro St, Coburg, Melbourne, Vic 3058
    (☎ (03) 9386-7399; fax 9384-1609)
    The India Centre, 49 Bennett St, Perth, WA 6004
    (☎ (09) 221-1485; fax 221-1206)
Bangladesh
    120 Road 2, Dhamondi, Dhaka
    (☎ (02) 50-3606; fax 86-3662)
    1253/1256 OR Nizam Rd, Mehdi Bagh,
    Chittagong (☎ (031) 21-1007; fax 22-5178)

Belgium
    217 Chaussee de Vleurgat, 1050 Brussels
    (☎ (02) 640-9802; fax 648-9638)
Bhutan
    India House Estate, Thimpu, Bhutan
    (☎ (0975) 22-162; fax 23-195)
Canada
    10 Springfield Rd, Ottawa K1M 1C9
    (☎ (613) 744-3751; fax 744-0913)
China
    1 Ri Tan Dong Lu, Beijing
    (☎ (01) 532-1908; fax 532-4684)
Denmark
    Vangehusvej 15, 2100 Copenhagen
    (☎ (045) 3118-2888; fax 3927-0218)
France
    15 rue Alfred Dehodencq, 75016 Paris
    (☎ (01) 40 50 70 70; fax 40 50 09 96)
Germany
    Adenauerallee 262, 53113 Bonn 1
    (☎ (0228) 54-050; fax 54-05154)
Israel
    4 Kaufman St, Sharbat House, Tel Aviv 68012
    (☎ (03) 58-4585; fax 510-1434)
Italy
    Via XX Settembre 5, 00187 Rome
    (☎ (06) 488-4642; fax 481-9539)
Japan
    2-2-11 Kudan Minami, Chiyoda-ku, Tokyo 10.
    (☎ (03) 3262-2391; fax 3234-4866)
Myanmar (Burma)
    545-547 Merchant St, Yangon (Rangoon)
    (☎ (01) 82-550; fax 89-562)
Nepal
    Lainchaur, GPO Box 292, Kathmandu
    (☎ (071) 41-1940; fax 41-3132)
The Netherlands
    Buitenrustweg 2, 252 KD, The Hague
    (☎ (070) 346-9771; fax 361-7072)
New Zealand
    180 Molesworth St, Wellington
    (☎ (04) 473-6390; fax 499-0665)
Pakistan
    G5 Diplomatic Enclave, Islamabad
    (☎ (051) 81-4371; fax 82-0742)
    India House, 3 Fatima Jinnah Rd, Karachi
    (☎ (021) 52-2275; fax 568-0929)
South Africa
    Sanlam Centre, Johannesburg
    (☎ (011) 333-1525; fax 333-0690)
Sri Lanka
    36-38 Galle Rd, Colombo 3
    (☎ (01) 421-605; fax 44-6403)
Thailand
    46 Soi 23 (Prasarnmitr), Sukhumvit Rd, Bangk○
    (☎ (02) 258-0300; fax 258-4627)
    113 Bumruangrat Rd, Chiang Mai 50000
    (☎ (053) 24-3066; fax 24-7879)

UK

  India House, Aldwych, London WC2B 4NA
  (☎ (0171) 836-8484; fax 836-4331)
  8219 Augusta St, Birmingham B18 6DS
  (☎ (0121) 212-2782; fax 212-2786)

USA

  2107 Massachusetts Ave NW, Washington DC
  20008 (☎ (202) 939-7000; fax 939-7027)
  3 East 64th St, Manhattan, New York, NY 10021-
  7097 (☎ (212) 879-7800; fax 988-6423)
  540 Arguello Blvd, San Francisco, CA 94118
  (☎ (415) 668-0662; fax 668-2073)

Foreign Embassies & High Commissions in India

Most foreign diplomatic missions are in the nation's capital, Delhi, but there are also quite a few consulates in the other major cities of Mumbai, Calcutta and Madras. Embassies and consulates in New Delhi include the following (the telephone area code for New Delhi is 011):

Australia

  1/50-G Shantipath, Chanakyapuri
  (☎ 688-8223; fax 687-4126)

Austria

  EP-13 Chandragupta Marg, Chanakyapuri
  (☎ 60-1238; fax 688-6929)

Bangladesh

  56 Ring Rd, Lajpat Nagar-III
  (☎ 683-4668; fax 683-9237)

Belgium

  50-N Shantipath, Chanakyapuri
  (☎ 608-295; fax 688-5821)

Bhutan

  Chandragupta Marg, Chanakyapuri
  (☎ 60-9217; fax 687-6710)

Canada

  7/8 Shantipath, Chanakyapuri
  (☎ 687-6500; fax 687-0031)

China

  50-D Shantipath, Chanakyapuri
  (☎ 60-0328; fax 688-5486)

Denmark

  11 Aurangzeb Rd (☎ 301-0900; fax 301-0961)

Finland

  E-3 Nyaya Marg, Chanakyapuri
  (☎ 611-5258; fax 688-6713)

France

  2/50-E Shantipath, Chanakyapuri
  (☎ 611-8790; fax 687-2305)

Germany

  6/50-G Shantipath, Chanakyapuri
  (☎ 60-4861; fax 687-3117)

Ireland

  13 Jor Bagh Rd (☎ 461-7435; fax 469-7053)

Israel

  3 Aurangzeb Rd (☎ 301-3238; fax 301-4298)

Italy

  50-E Chandragupta Marg, Chanakyapuri
  (☎ 611-4355; fax 687-3889)

Japan

  4-5/50-G Shantipath, Chanakyapuri
  (☎ 687-6581)

Myanmar (Burma)

  3/50-F Nyaya Marg, Chanakyapuri
  (☎ 60-0251; fax 687-7942)

Nepal

  Barakhamba Rd (☎ 332-8191; fax 332-6857)

The Netherlands

  6/50-F Shantipath, Chanakyapuri
  (☎ 688-4951; fax 688-4856)

New Zealand

  50-N Nyaya Marg, Chanakyapuri
  (☎ 688-3170; fax 687-2317)

Norway

  50-C Shantipath, Chanakyapuri
  (☎ 687-3532; fax 687-3814)

Pakistan

  2/50-G Shantipath, Chanakyapuri
  (☎ 60-0603; fax 637-2339)

South Africa

  B-18 Vasant Marg, Vasant Vihar
  (☎ 611-9411, 611-3505)

Spain

  12 Prithviraj Rd (☎ 379-2085; fax 379-3375)

Sri Lanka

  27 Kautilya Marg, Chanakyapuri
  (☎ 301-0201; fax 301-5295)

Sweden

  Nyaya Marg, Chanakyapuri
  (☎ 687 5760; fax 688-5401)

Switzerland

  Nyaya Marg, Chanakyapuri
  (☎ 60-4225; fax 687-3093)

Thailand

  56-N Nyaya Marg, Chanakyapuri
  (☎ 60-5679; fax 687-2029)

UK

  50 Shantipath, Chanakyapuri
  (☎ 687-2161; fax 687-2882)

USA

  Shantipath, Chanakyapuri (☎ 60-0651)

CUSTOMS

The usual duty-free regulations apply for India; that is, one bottle of whisky and 200 cigarettes.

You're allowed to bring in all sorts of western technological wonders, but big items, such as video cameras, are likely to be entered on a 'Tourist Baggage Re-Export' form to ensure you take them out with you when you go. This also used to be the case with laptop computers, but some travellers have reported that it is no longer necessary. It's not necessary to declare still cameras, even if you have more than one.

Note that if you are entering India from Nepal you are not entitled to import anything free of duty.

MONEY
Costs
Whatever budget you decide to travel on, you can be assured that you'll be getting a whole lot more for your money than in most other countries – Rajasthan is fantastic value.

If you stay in luxurious converted forts and palaces, fly between the main cities of Rajasthan, and spend up big in the emporiums in Jaipur, you can spend a lot of money. The Royal suite at the Rambagh Palace hotel in Jaipur will set you back a mere US$675 per night!

At the other extreme, if you scrimp and save, stay in dormitories or the cheapest hotels, always travel in ordinary public buses, and learn to exist on *dhal* (curried lentil gravy) and rice, you can see Rajasthan on less than US$7 a day.

Most travellers will probably be looking for something between these extremes. If so, for US$15 to US$20 a day on average, you'll stay in reasonable hotels, eat in regular restaurants but occasionally splash out on a fancy meal, and take auto-rickshaws rather than a bus.

Carrying Money
A money belt worn around your waist beneath your clothes is probably one of the safest ways of carrying important documents such as your passport and travellers' cheques on your person. Some travellers prefer a pouch attached to a string which is worn around the neck, with the pouch against the chest concealed beneath a shirt or jumper. It is now possible to purchase innocuous looking leather belts from travel goods suppliers which a have a secret compartment in which you could hide your 'emergency stash'.

Travellers' Cheques
Although it's usually not a problem to change travellers' cheques, it's best to stick to the well known brands – American Express, Visa, Thomas Cook, Citibank and Barclays – as more obscure ones may cause problems. Occasionally a bank won't accept a certain type of cheque – Visa and Citibank in particular – and for this reason it's worth carrying more than one flavour.

A few simple measures should be taken to facilitate the replacement of travellers' cheques, should they be stolen. See Stolen Travellers' Cheques in the Dangers & Annoyances section later in this chapter.

Credit Cards
Credit cards are widely accepted at curio shops and larger hotels in major cities such as Jaipur and Jodhpur, as well as in popular travellers' centres such as Udaipur and Jaisalmer.

With MasterCard, Japanese Credit Bureau or Visa cards you can to obtain cash rupees in Jaipur on the spot. With American Express you can get dollar or sterling travellers' cheques in Delhi, but you must have a personal cheque to cover the amount, although counter cheques are available if you ask for them.

International Transfers
Don't run out of money in India unless you have a credit card against which you can draw travellers' cheques or cash. Having money transferred through the banking system can be time consuming. It's usually straightforward if you use a foreign bank, Thomas Cook or American Express in Delhi; elsewhere it may take a fortnight and will be a hassle.

If you do have money sent to you in India, specify the bank, the branch and the address of the bank you want it sent to.

Currency
The rupee (Rs) is divided into 100 paise (p). There are coins of five, 10, 20, 25 and 50 paise, Rs one, two and five (rare), and notes of Rs one, two, five, 10, 20, 50, 100 and 500.

In 1996, the Reserve Bank of India

decided to stop printing notes of Rs one, two and five.

You are not allowed to bring Indian currency into the country or take it out of the country. You are allowed to bring in unlimited amounts of foreign currency or travellers' cheques, but you are supposed to declare anything over US$10,000 on arrival.

One of the most annoying things about India is that no-one ever seems to have *any* change, and you'll find on numerous occasions you'll be left waiting for five minutes while a shopkeeper hawks your Rs 100 note around other shops to secure change.

Banknotes

Indian currency notes circulate far longer than in the west and the small notes in particular become very tatty – some should carry a government health warning! A note can have holes right through it (most do in fact, as they are bundled together with staples when new) and be quite acceptable but if it's slightly torn at the top or bottom on the crease line then it's no good and you'll have trouble spending it. Even a missing corner makes a bill unacceptable. The answer to this is to check your change carefully – often the tear can be cleverly concealed beneath a judiciously placed thumb – or simply accept it philosophically or think of clever uses for it. Use damaged notes for official purposes. I'd love to pay the Rs 300 departure tax with 300 totally disreputable Rs 1 notes – although someone who did just that wrote to say he had some trouble getting them to accept it! Some banks have special counters where torn notes will be exchanged for good ones, but who wants to visit banks more than necessary? ∎

At the time of going to press, the exchange rates were as follows:

A$1	=	Rs 28.50
C$1	=	Rs 26.10
DM1	=	Rs 23.80
FFr1	=	Rs 7.00
Jap¥100	=	Rs 33.00
Nep Rs100	=	Rs 63.00
NZ$1	=	Rs 24.80
Sin$1	=	Rs 25.40
US$1	=	Rs 35.70
UK£1	=	Rs 55.60

Outside the main cities, the State Bank of India is usually the place to change money, although occasionally you'll be directed to another bank, such as the State Bank of Bikaner & Jaipur or the Bank of Baroda. In the more remote regions, few banks offer exchange facilities, so utilise the banks in the main tourist centres before heading out into the desert – although you'll have no trouble changing money at Bikaner or Jaisalmer. Some banks charge an encashment fee, which may be levied for the entire transaction, or on each cheque. Find out how much the bank is going to charge to exchange your cheques before you sign them.

Black Market

The rupee is a fully convertible currency, that is, the rate is set by the market not the government. For this reason there's not much of a black market, although you can get a couple of rupees more for your dollars or pounds cash. In the major tourist centres you will have constant offers to change money. There's little risk involved although it is officially illegal.

Encashment Certificates

All money is supposed to be changed at official banks or moneychangers, and you are supposed to be given an encashment certificate for each transaction. In practice, some people surreptitiously bring rupees into the country with them – they can be bought at a discount price in places such as Singapore or Bangkok. Indian rupees can be

Currency Exchange

In Delhi and other gateway cities you can change most foreign currencies or travellers' cheques – Australian dollars, Deutschmarks, yen or whatever – but in Rajasthan it's best to stick to US dollars or pounds sterling. Thomas Cook and American Express are both popular travellers' cheques, and can be exchanged readily in most major tourist centres.

Beggars

All sorts of stories about beggars do the rounds of the travellers' hang-outs, many of them with little basis in fact. Stories such as rupee millionaire beggars, people (usually kids) being deliberately mutilated by their parents so they can beg, and a beggars' Mafia are all common.

It's a matter of personal choice how you approach the issue of beggars and baksheesh. Some people feel it is best to give nothing to any beggar, believing it 'only encourages them' and preferring to contribute in a voluntary capacity; others give away loose change when they have it; some benevolent souls have even been known to exchange large notes for handfuls of rupees so that they always have change on hand specifically for this purpose; unfortunately, others insulate themselves entirely and give nothing in any way. ■

brought in fairly openly from Nepal and again you can get a slightly better rate there.

Banks will usually give you an encashment certificate, but occasionally they don't bother. It is worth getting them, especially if you want to re-exchange excess rupees for hard currency when you depart India.

The other reason for saving encashment certificates is that if you stay in India longer than four months, you have to get an income tax clearance. See Tax Clearance Certificates earlier in this chapter for details.

Baksheesh

In most Asian countries tipping is virtually unknown, but India is an exception to that rule – although tipping has a rather different role in India than in the west. The term *baksheesh*, which encompasses tipping and a lot more besides, aptly describes the concept of tipping in India. You 'tip' not so much for good service, but to get things done.

Judicious baksheesh will open closed doors, find missing letters and perform other small miracles. Tipping is not necessary for taxis nor for cheaper restaurants, but if you're going to be using something repeatedly, an initial tip will ensure the standards are kept up.

In tourist restaurants or hotels, where service is usually tacked on in any case, the normal 10% figure usually applies. In smaller places, where tipping is optional, you need only tip a few rupees, not a percent-

The Art of Haggling

The friendly art of haggling is an absolute must in most parts of Rajasthan, unless you don't mind paying above the market value. Shopkeepers in cities like Udaipur, Jaipur and Jodhpur are accustomed to tourists who have lots of money and little time to spend it. This means that when you ask a shopkeeper 'How much?', the reply will probably be 'very good price', but more often than not that price is daylight robbery. How much you're being fleeced usually varies according to how gullible you look. It's not unusual to be charged at least double the 'real' price.

So how do you know if you're being over-charged and need to strike back with some serious haggling? Well, you are safe in government emporiums and some larger shops, where the prices are usually fixed (often quite high). But in most other shops that cater primarily to tourists, it's probably worth haggling. The kind of places that usually fall into this category are handicraft, carpet, painting, jewellery, souvenir and clothing shops.

If you have absolutely no idea of what something should really cost, start by slashing the price by at least half. Shopkeepers will probably look frightfully aghast and tell you that this is impossible, as it's the very price they had to pay for the item themselves. This is the usual story. But now the shopkeeper knows that you're not going to be taken for a ride. This is when the battle for a bargain begins and it's up to you and the salesperson to negotiate a price. You'll find that many shopkeepers lower their so called 'final price' if you proceed to head out of the shop and tell them that you'll 'think about it'.

Ultimately, once you start bargaining, usually it's just a matter of time before the prices come down. And remember, don't be afraid to haggle. It's all part and parcel of shopping in India, and although sometimes exhausting, it can also be a lot of fun. ■

age of the bill. Hotel porters usually get about Rs 1 per bag; other possible tipping levels are Rs 1 to Rs 2 for bike-watching, Rs 10 for train conductors or station porters performing miracles for you, and Rs 5 to Rs 15 for extra services from hotel staff.

POST & COMMUNICATIONS
Post
The Indian postal and poste restante services are generally excellent. Expected letters almost always are there and letters you send almost invariably reach their destination, although they take up to three weeks. American Express, in its major city locations, offers an alternative to the poste restante system.

Have letters addressed to you with your surname in capitals and underlined, followed by the poste restante, GPO, and the city or town in question. Many 'lost' letters are simply misfiled under given (Christian) names, so always check under both your names. Letters sent via poste restante are generally held for one month only, after which, if unclaimed, they are returned to the sender (although a clerk at the GPO in Jaipur advised that poste restante letters are held here for two weeks only).

You can often buy stamps at good hotels, saving a lot of queuing in crowded post offices.

Postal Rates It costs Rs 6 to send a postcard or aerogramme anywhere in the world from India, and Rs 11 for a standard letter (up to 20g).

Posting Parcels Most people discover how to do this the hard way, in which case it'll take half a day. Go about it as described below, which can still take up to an hour:

- Take the parcel to a tailor and tell him you'd like it stitched up in cheap linen. Negotiate the price first.
- Go to the post office with your parcel and ask for the necessary customs declaration forms. Fill them in and glue one to the parcel. The other will be stitched onto it. To avoid excise duty at the delivery end it's best to specify that the contents are a 'gift'. Be careful how much you declare the contents to be worth. If you specify over Rs 1000, your parcel will not be accepted without a bank clearance certificate. You can imagine the hassles involved in getting one of these so always state the value as less than Rs 1000.
- Have the parcel weighed and franked at the parcel counter.

Note that small parcels up to two kg (considered 'packets' rather than 'parcels') can be sent at letter mail rates, which are much cheaper than parcel rates. For example, a compact 500g parcel sent airmail to Australia is only Rs 150 instead of approximately Rs 750.

Parcel Post Rates					
Airmail					
Weight (kg)			*Destination & Cost (Rs)*		
	USA	*UK*	*Australia*	*Japan*	*Netherlands*
1	790	795	970	845	675
2	1276	1055	1490	1105	935
3	1750	1315	2010	1365	1195
4	2030	1575	2530	1625	1455
5	2716	1835	3050	1885	1715
Seamail					
Weight (kg)			*Destination & Cost (Rs)*		
	USA	*UK*	*Australia*	*Japan*	*Netherlands*
1	369	573	486	617	456
2	647	735	595	736	576
5	937	921	731	879	743
10	1581	1201	996	1118	973
15	2269	1601	1273	1431	1248

If you are just sending books or printed matter, these can go by bookpost, which is considerably cheaper than parcel post, but the package must be wrapped a certain way: make sure that the package can either be opened for inspection along the way, or that it is just wrapped in brown paper or cardboard and tied with string, with the two ends exposed so that the contents are visible. To protect the books, it might be worthwhile first wrapping them in clear plastic. No customs declaration form is necessary for such parcels.

The maximum weight for a bookpost parcel is two kg, which costs Rs 210 (seapost) to destinations around the world. Rates for airmail bookpost are: 200g, Rs 45; 250g, Rs 54; 500g, Rs 102; 760g, Rs 159; one kg, Rs 195; 1260g, Rs 252; 1500, Rs 288; two kg, Rs 363.

Be cautious with places which offer to mail things to your home address after you have bought them. Government emporiums are usually OK. In New Delhi, some places offer a comprehensive parcel packing service and will also offer to post the parcel for you. No matter how many travellers' testimonies you are shown guaranteeing that parcels arrived at their destinations, it pays to take the parcel to the post office yourself.

Sending parcels in the other direction (to you in India) is an extremely hit-and-miss affair. Don't count on anything bigger than a letter getting to you. And don't count on a letter getting to you if there's anything of market value inside it.

Telephone

The telephone system in India is generally very good. Most places are hooked up to the STD/ISD network, so making interstate and international calls is simplicity itself from even the smallest town.

Everywhere you'll come across private STD/ISD call booths with direct local, interstate and international dialling. These phones are usually found in shops or other businesses, but are well signposted with large 'STD/ISD' signs advertising the service. A digital meter lets you keep an eye on what the call is costing, and gives you a printout at the end. You then just pay the shop owner – quick, painless and a far cry from the not so distant past when a night spent at a telegraph office waiting for a line was not unusual. Direct international calls from these phones cost around Rs 70 per minute depending on the country you are calling. To make an international call, you will need to dial the following:

00 (international access code from India) + country code (of the country you are calling) + area code + local number

In some centres, STD/ISD booths may offer a 'call back' service – you ring your folks or friends, give them the number of the booth and wait for them to call you back. The booth operator will charge about Rs 2 to Rs 3 per minute for this service, in addition to the cost of the preliminary call. Advise your callers how long you intend to wait at the booth in the event that they have trouble getting back to you. The number your callers dial will be as follows:

(caller's country international access code) + 91 (international country code for India) + area code + local number (booth number)

The Central Telegraph Offices/Telecom offices in major towns are usually reasonably efficient. Some are open 24 hours.

Home Country Direct Phone Numbers

Country	Number
Australia	0006117
Canada	000167
Germany	0004917
Italy	0003917
Japan	0008117
The Netherlands	0003117
New Zealand	0006417
Singapore	0006517
Spain	0003417
Taiwan	00088617
Thailand	0006617
UK	0004417
USA	000117

Also available is the Home Country Direct service, which gives you access to the international operator in your home country. You can then make reverse charge (collect) or credit card calls, although this is not always easy. If you are calling from a hotel beware of exorbitant connection charges on these sorts of calls. You may also have trouble convincing the owner of the telephone you are using that they are not going to get charged for the call. The countries and numbers to dial are listed in the Home Country Direct Phone numbers table.

Fax

Fax rates at the telegraph office at the Jaipur central post office are Rs 60 per page for neighbouring countries, Rs 95 per page to other Asian destinations, Africa, Europe, Australia and New Zealand, and Rs 110 to the USA and Canada. This fax office is open 24 hours. Rates within India are Rs 30 per page for A4 size transmissions, and Rs 15 for A4/2 sheet transmissions.

It's possible to receive faxes at telegraph offices. Fax numbers at telegraph offices around Rajasthan, in Delhi and at Agra are as follows:

Town	Fax Number
Agra	(0562) 26-9626, 36-1146
Ajmer	(0145) 42-7004
Alwar	(0144) 23-805
Barmer	(02982) 20-328
Bikaner	(0151) 52-7673
Bharatpur	(05644) 21-170
Bundi	(0747) 22-850
Chittorgarh	(01472) 40-072
Jaipur	(0141) 36-2018, 38-1525
Jaisalmer	(02992) 52-634
Jodhpur	(0291) 33-194
Kota	(0744) 24-446
Mt Abu	(029742) 3576
New Delhi	(011) 331-3411, 331-3412
Pushkar	(0145) 81-2282
Udaipur	(0294) 52-5959

Many of the STD/ISD booths also have a fax machine for public use.

Telegrams

Telegrams sent from the telegraphic office at the central post office in Jaipur cost Rs 2.50 per word to the USA, and Rs 2 to all other destinations.

BOOKS
Lonely Planet

It's pleasing to be able to say that for more information on India and its neighbours, and for travel beyond India, most of the best guides come from Lonely Planet! Lonely Planet's award-winning *India* is now in its 6th edition. One of Lonely Planet's most successful and popular titles, this is the most comprehensive guide to the country you'll find.

Lonely Planet's handy pocket-sized city guide *Delhi* has all the information you need to find your way around this often chaotic city.

The Himalayan region is well covered, with both a trekking guide and a regular travel guide. *Trekking in the Indian Himalaya* is by Garry Weare, who has spent years discovering the best trekking routes in the Himalayan region, and his guide is full of practical descriptions and excellent maps. Lonely Planet's new guide, *Indian Himalaya* has loads of information on the hill stations, Tibetan centres and pilgrimage spots of the Indian Himalaya.

Lonely Planet guides to other countries in the South Asian region include: *Nepal, Trekking in the Nepal Himalaya, Tibet, Karakoram Highway, Pakistan, Bangladesh, Myanmar, Sri Lanka, Maldives,* and *South-East Asia.*

Guidebooks

While there are numerous glossy coffee-table type books on Rajasthan, there is a paucity of good, practical travel guides to Rajasthan. Insight Guides' *Rajasthan* guide is an attractive volume with fine photographs and excellent essays on the arts, culture and history of Rajasthan. It is, however, a little short on practical travel information, but is a good souvenir to take home with you. Insight also has a book on the 'golden triangle' – *Delhi, Jaipur & Agra.* While the coverage of these cities is good, it's obviously not very helpful if you're planning to get off the main tourist circuit into the heart of the state. In a similar vein is Odyssey Guides' *Delhi, Agra & Jaipur*, and *Delhi, Agra & Jaipur* by Sondeep Shankar & Sumi Krishna Chauhan. Nelles Guides' *Northern India* devotes a small section to Rajasthan.

Travel Writing

In Rajasthan (Lonely Planet, 1996) by Royina Grewal gives a fascinating insider's view of the people and places encountered in the state; this book is one of the many exciting titles in Lonely Planet's travel literature series, Journeys. Robyn Davidson's *Desert Places* (Viking, UK, 1996) is an account of the author's journey by camel with the Rabari (Rajasthani nomads) on their annual migration through the Thar Desert. It gives a compelling insight into both the plight of the nomads and the solo woman traveller in Rajasthan.

Princely Rule

A Princess Remembers by Gayatri Devi and Santha Rama Rau (paperback, Tarang Paperbacks, New Delhi, 1992) is the memoirs of the maharani of Jaipur, Gayatri Devi, wife of the last maharaja, Man Singh II. It's easy reading and provides a fascinating insight into the bygone days of Indian royalty.

A Desert Kingdom: The Rajputs of Bikaner by Naveen Patnaik (George Widenfeld & Nicholson Ltd, UK, 1990) is a fine hardback volume featuring magnificent old B&W photos from the private collection of Maharaja Ganga Singh of Bikaner, who ascended the throne in 1885 at the age of seven. It includes an interesting commentary and historical analysis of his rule.

Maharana by Brian Masters (hardback, Mapin Publishing, Ahmedabad, 1990) traces the history of the rulers of Udaipur, the world's oldest ruling dynasty, which spans 76 generations.

Maharaja: The spectacular heritage of princely India (Thames & Hudson, UK, 1988), with text by Andrew Robinson and superb photographs by the well known Japanese photographer Sumio Uchiyama portrays the past and present heritage of princely India and covers a range of royal families, predominantly from Rajasthan.

The House of Marwar by Dhananajaya Singh (hardback, Lustre Press, New Delhi, 1994) outlines the history of the royal house of Jodhpur from the first ruler in the early 13th century, right up to the present Maharaja of Jodhpur. The book contains a small collection of black & white photos of royalty.

Coffee-Table Books

Jaipur: The last destination, with text by Aman Nath and photographs by Samar Singh Jodha (India Book House Pvt Ltd, Bombay, 1993), is a magnificent prize winning hardback volume with historical notes, beautiful photographs, essays on Jaipur's maharajas and the textiles, arts and crafts of the pink city. It's not cheap, however, at Rs 2500.

Rajasthan: An enduring romance is an attractive hardback volume by Sunil Mehra (Lustre Press Pvt Ltd, Delhi, 1993). *Rajasthan*, text by Gerard Busquet and photos by Pierre Toutain (hardback, Harrap Columbus, London, 1988), is predominantly pictorial, with a variety of colour photographs reflecting the vibrant places and people of Rajasthan.

Rajasthan: India's enchanted land is a finely presented paperback volume. The photographs are by Raghubir Singh, who grew up in Jaipur, and there's a foreword by the famous director Satyajit Ray (Time Books International, New Delhi, 1989).

Arts & Crafts

Arts & Crafts of Rajasthan, edited by Aman Nath & Francis Wacziarg (Thames & Hudson, UK, 1987), is a beautiful hardback volume with fine photographs contributed by both editors. The accompanying essays are informative and interesting.

Arts & Artists of Rajasthan by RK Vashistha (Abhinav Publications, New Delhi, 1995) is a hardback volume covering the period from the 7th to the 19th centuries, particularly concentrating on the art centres of Mewar (Udaipur). There are numerous colour and B&W plates with extensive notes, as well as short biographies on notable artists.

The City Palace Museum Udaipur, with text by Andrew Topsfield and photos by Pankaj Shah (hardback, Mapin Publishing, Ahmedabad, 1990), provides an interesting visual and historical background of the Mewar paintings at the City Palace Museum in Udaipur.

Ateliers of the Rajput Courts (Lalit Khala Akademi, New Delhi, 1983) is a series of beautiful colour plates of Rajasthani miniatures which are part of the Lalit Khala series (portfolio No 39). The accompanying text is by Raj K Tandan. The prints are loose leaf, so could be easily framed.

The Painted Havelis of Shekhawati

The growing interest in the magnificent painted havelis of Shekhawati has spawned a number of books on the region. The definitive guide to the region is Ilay Cooper's *The Painted Towns of Shekhawati* (Mapin Publishing, Ahmedabad, 1994). It's not only a practical guide to the region, with notes for easy location and identification of paintings and maps of the most important towns, but has very good essays on the history of the region, painting techniques, layout of havelis, and more.

Other books on this subject are: *Shekhawati: Rajasthan's painted homes*, with text by Pankaj Rajesh and photographs by Karoki Lewis (Lustre Press, New Delhi); *Rajasthan: The painted walls of Shekhavati* by Francis Wacziarg & Aman Nath (Croom Helm, London, 1982); and *Shekhawati: Rajasthan's painted homes* (Lustre Press, New Delhi, 1995), with text by Pankaj Rakesh and photographs by Karoki Lewis.

Architecture

The Royal Palaces of India, with text by George Michell and photographs by Antonio Martinelli (Thames & Hudson, London, 1994), is the most comprehensive book to the forts and palaces of India. The text is complemented with excellent photographs, and there are also some archaeological maps. It's

incredibly detailed, giving information on the kitchen layout, bathrooms, women's quarters, and more.

The Forts of India, by Virginia Fass with a foreword by the son of the last maharaja of Jaipur (Collins, London, 1986), is a large hardback volume with both B&W and colour photographs and substantial historical notes.

Flora

A classic text on the flora of the arid zone is E Blatter & F Hallberg's *The Flora of the Indian Desert* (Scientific Publishers, Jodhpur, 1984; first published in *The Journal of the Bombay Natural History Society*, 1918-1921). This is very much a technical reference, with detailed field notes and descriptions, but the notes on traditional uses of the plants of the Thar Desert are interesting.

Wildlife

The Tiger's Destiny by Valmik Thapar (text) and Fateh Singh Rathore (photographs) (Time Books International, London, 1992) deals with the besieged tigers of Ranthambhore National Park.

Specifically dealing with the prolific bird-life of Keoladeo Ghana National Park is *Bharatpur: Bird paradise*, by Martin Ewans (text) and Thakur Dalip Singh et al (photographs) (Lustre Press Pty Ltd, New Delhi, 1992). This paperback edition has both colour and black & white photos with good notes on numerous species.

Mammals of the Thar Desert by Ishwar Prakash (Scientific Publishers, Jodhpur, 1994) is a small hardback volume which gives detailed descriptions and field notes of the various mammals of the arid zone, accompanied by good line drawings.

Novels

Virgin Princess: An historical novel of Mewar (Udaipur, India) – the world's oldest dynasty by Jane Richardson (India Book Distributors, Bombay, 1991) is an interesting if badly written romantic tale.

Raj by Gita Mehta (Penguin, New Delhi, 1990) is the more convincingly told story of a young Rajput princess who is contracted in marriage to an arrogant prince.

History & Culture

Annals & Antiquities of Rajasthan by Captain James Tod is probably the text most cited by historians writing about Rajasthan. A classic text, it was originally published in 1829-32. Published by Oriental Books Reprint Corporation, New Delhi, it comes in a two volume set at Rs 250 per volume, or a cheaper three volume set which costs Rs 400 for the set. It's also available in an attractive antique reproduction mock-leather three volume set for Rs 1500.

Cultural History of Rajasthan by Kalyan Kumar Ganguli (hardback, Sundeep Prakashan, Delhi, 1983) is a scholarly text which provides a comprehensive historical and cultural analysis of Rajputana.

Folklore of Rajasthan, by DR Ahuja (National Book Trust, New Delhi, 1980), is a handy paperback book which considers the cultural heritage of Rajasthan and its people, with chapters on folk music and dance, customs and traditions, myths and mythology, and more.

For an assessment of the position of women in Indian society, it is well worth getting hold of *May You Be the Mother of One Hundred Sons* (Penguin, 1991) by Elizabeth Bumiller. Her book offers some excellent insights into the plight of women in general and rural women in particular.

For those interested in the continuing and often shocking and sad story of India's tribal people, there is the scholarly *Tribes of India – the Struggle for Survival* (1982) by Christoph von Führer-Haimendorf.

The Idea of Rajasthan, edited by Karine Schomer et al (American Institute of Indian Studies, New Delhi, 1994), is a two volume set of contemporary essays by various scholars on the historical and cultural influences which have contributed towards Rajasthani identity.

Politics

Rajasthan: Polity, Economy & Society by BL Panagariya & NC Pahariya (Rawat Publica-

tions, Jaipur, 1996) is a well written text which concentrates on the formation and composition of the state of Rajasthan in the post-Independence period, the government of the state to the present day, as well as the state's economy, development and cultural heritage.

ONLINE SERVICES

There are numerous online services relevant to India, but services come and go with some frequency. Check the Lonely Planet home page on the Internet (http://www.lonely planet.com) for up-to-date information about online services.

FILMS

Latcho Drom (Safe Journey), France, 1992-93, directed by Tony Gatlif, traces the lives of gypsy dancers and musicians from India to the Middle East, Eastern Europe and Spain. The film opens in the Rajasthan desert with stunning desert vistas and evocative scenes of traditional music and dance by the Rajasthani nomads, as seen through the eyes of a young boy.

NEWSPAPERS & MAGAZINES

English-language dailies include the *Times of India*, the *Hindustan Times*, the *Indian Express* and the *Statesman*; many feel the *Express* is the best of the bunch.

Weekly news magazines include *Frontline*, *India Today*, *The Week*, *Sunday* and the *Illustrated Weekly of India*. They're widely available at bookshops and train and bus stations.

The only English-language paper which is published in Rajasthan is *Rajasthan Pattrik*, with its headquarters in Jaipur. It is widely distributed in its Hindi edition, but is extremely difficult to obtain in the English edition. It serves the small expat community living in Rajasthan.

RADIO & TV

The revolution in the TV network has been the introduction of cable TV. It's amazing to see satellite dishes, even in the remotest villages. The result is that viewers can tune in to the BBC and, broadcasting from Hong Kong, Murdoch's Star TV, Prime Sports and V (an MTV-type Hindi music channel). Z TV is a local Hindi cable channel. The national broadcaster is Doordarshan.

PHOTOGRAPHY
Film
Colour print film processing facilities are readily available in larger cities. Film is relatively cheap and the quality is usually (but not always) good. Kodak 100 colour print film costs around Rs 140 for a roll of 36. Always check the use-by date on local film stock. Heat and humidity can play havoc with film, even if the use-by date hasn't been exceeded. Developing costs are around Rs 25, plus Rs 5 per photo for printing.

If you're taking slides bring the film with you. Colour slide film is only available in the major cities. Colour slides can be developed only in Delhi, and quality is not guaranteed. A better bet is to carry your film home with you. Kodachrome and other 'includes developing' film will have to be sent overseas. It's up to you whether you send it straight back and face the risk of delay and damage, or carry it back with you at the end of your trip.

Equipment
A UV filter permanently fitted to your lens will not only cut down ultraviolet light, but will protect your lens. Spare batteries should be carried at all times. Serious photographers will consider bringing a tripod and fast film (400 ASA) for temple and fort interior shots.

Exposure
In the desert you should allow for the extreme light intensity, and take care not to overexpose your shots. In general, photography is best done in the early morning and late afternoon. The stark midday sun eliminates shadows rendering less depth to your photographs. The long shadows at the end of the day can enhance the wave-like ripples on sand dunes and emphasise the character lines on faces. Beware of taking photographs directly into the sunset at the Sam sand dunes if you're taking a portrait of a camel-wallah and his beast, unless you want your subjects to be rendered as silhouettes.

Restrictions & Photographing People
Be careful what you photograph. India is touchy about places of military importance – this can include railway stations, bridges, airports, military installations and sensitive border regions. Some temples prohibit photography in the *mandapa* (forechamber of a temple) and inner sanctum. If in doubt, ask. Many temples in Rajasthan, and numerous forts and palaces, levy a fee to bring a still camera or video camera onto the premises. You have to pay up front – generally around Rs 25 for a still camera and Rs 50 for a video camera – and there's no refund if you decide not to take any pictures after all.

Some people are more than happy to be photographed, but care should be taken in pointing cameras at women. Again, if in doubt, ask. A zoom is a less intrusive means of taking portraits – even when you've obtained permission to take a portrait, shoving a lens in your subject's face can be disconcerting. A reasonable distance between you and your subject will help to reduce your subject's discomfort, and will result in more natural shots.

Protecting Your Camera & Film
Film manufacturers warn that, once exposed, film should be developed as quickly as possible; in practice the film seems to last, even in India's summer heat, without deterioration for months. If you're going to be carrying exposed film for long, consult a specialist photography handbook about ways of enhancing preservation. Try to keep your film cool, and protect it in water and air-proof containers if you're travelling during the monsoon. Silicone sachets distributed around your gear will help to absorb moisture.

It's worthwhile investing in a lead-lined (X-ray proof) bag, as repeated exposure to X-ray (even so-called 'film proof' X-ray) can damage film. *Never* put your film in baggage which will be placed in the cargo holds of aeroplanes. It will probably be subjected to large doses of X-ray which will spoil or completely ruin it.

Professional photographers suggest that, in the desert, your camera should be kept in a white bag, as black surfaces absorb heat much faster than white ones. Try to keep your camera and film as much as possible in the shade.

TIME

India is 5½ hours ahead of GMT/UTC, 4½ hours behind Australian EST and 10½ hours ahead of American EST. It is officially known as IST – Indian Standard Time, although many Indians prefer to think it stands for Indian Stretchable Time!

ELECTRICITY
Voltage & Cycle

The electric current is 230-240V AC, 50 cycles. Electricity is widely available in the main towns and cities and tourist destinations. Many of the remote villages still remain without electricity. Those that have electricity usually use it for powering irrigation equipment – very few village homes are electrified.

Plugs & Sockets

Sockets are of a three round-pin variety, similar (but not identical) to European sockets. European round-pin plugs will go into the sockets, but as the pins on Indian plugs are somewhat thicker, the fit is loose and connection is not always guaranteed.

WEIGHTS & MEASURES

Although India is officially metricated, imperial weights and measures are still used in some areas of commerce. A conversion chart is included on the inside back cover of the book.

LAUNDRY

All of the top-end hotels, most of the mid-range hotels and some of the budget hotels and guest houses offer a laundry service, and costs are minimal.

Dhobi-Wallahs

After a gruelling day of trekking through sultry deserts on camel-back or climbing to hilltop fortresses, all you want to do when you get back to your hotel is get out of those grimy clothes. There are no laundrettes in Rajasthan and you probably can't afford the luxury of having everything (right down to your underwear) dry-cleaned. Don't despair! You won't have to sacrifice that special meal in a palace-hotel to pay unexpected dry-cleaning bills, for there's a *dhobi-wallah* just around the corner.

If you're staying at one of Rajasthan's smaller hotels or guest houses, there will probably be a knock on your door every morning and a laundry boy will collect all those dusty, sweaty clothes you wore yesterday. The very same clothes will reappear that evening, washed and ironed with loving care, and all for just a few rupees per item. But what happened to your clothes between their departure and return?

Well, they certainly did not get anywhere near a washing machine. First of all they're collected and taken to the *dhobi ghat*. A ghat is a place with water and a dhobi-wallah is a washerperson, so the dhobi ghat is where the dhobi-wallahs ply their trade and wash clothes.

Then the clothes are separated – all the white shirts are washed together, all the grey trousers, all the pink skirts, all the blue jeans. By now, if this was the west, your clothes would either be hopelessly lost or you'd need a computer to keep track of them all. But no multi-programmed miracle of technology can wash as clean as an enthusiastic dhobi-wallah, although admittedly after a few visits to the Indian laundry your clothes do begin to look distinctly thinner. Buttons also tend to get shattered, so bring some spare. Zips, lace, bras and underpants sometimes fare likewise.

Once clean, the clothes are strung out on miles of clothesline to quickly dry in the glorious Indian sun. They're then taken to the ironing sheds where primitive irons press your jeans like they've never been pressed before. Not just your jeans – your socks, your T-shirts, even your underwear will come back with knife-edge creases. Then the Indian miracle takes place. Out of the hundreds, even thousands of items washed that day, somehow your very own brown socks, blue jeans, favourite T-shirts, striped boxer shorts and purple underwear all find their way back together and head for your hotel room. A system of marking clothes, known only to the dhobis, is the real reason behind this feat. They say criminals have been tracked down simply by those telltale 'dhobi marks'. ∎

HEALTH

Travel health depends on your predeparture preparations, your day-to-day health care while travelling and how you handle any medical problem or emergency that does develop. While the list of potential dangers can seem quite frightening, with a little luck, some basic precautions and adequate information, few travellers experience more than upset stomachs. For information about health insurance, see under Travel Insurance earlier in this chapter.

Travel Health Guides

There are a number of books on travel health:

Staying Healthy in Asia, Africa & Latin America by Dirk Schroeder (Moon Publications, 1994). Probably the best all-round guide to carry, as it's compact but very detailed and well organised.

Travellers' Health by Dr Richard Dawood (Oxford University Press, 1992). Comprehensive, easy to read, authoritative and also highly recommended, although it's rather large to lug around.

Where There is No Doctor by David Werner (Macmillan, 1994). A very detailed guide intended for someone, such as a Peace Corps worker, going to work in a developing country, rather than for the average traveller.

Travel with Children by Maureen Wheeler (Lonely Planet Publications, 1995). Includes basic advice on travel health for young children.

There are also a number of excellent travel health sites on the Internet. From the Lonely Planet home page, *http://www.lonelyplanet. com*, there are links, at *http://www.lonely planet.com/health/health.htm/h-link.htm*, to the World Health Organisation, Centers for Diseases Control & Prevention in Atlanta, Georgia, and Stanford University Travel Medicine Service.

Predeparture Planning

Medical Kit It's wise to carry a small, straightforward medical kit. The kit should include:

- Aspirin or paracetamol (acetaminophen in the USA) – for pain or fever.
- Antihistamine (such as Benadryl) – useful as a decongestant for colds and allergies, to ease the itch from insect bites or stings, and to help prevent motion sickness. There are several antihistamines on the

market, all with different pros and cons (eg a tendency to cause drowsiness), so it's worth discussing your requirements with a pharmacist or doctor. Antihistamines may cause sedation and interact with alcohol so care should be taken when using them.

- Antibiotics – useful if you're travelling well off the beaten track, but they must be prescribed and you should carry the prescription with you.
- Loperamide (eg Imodium) or Lomotil for diarrhoea; prochlorperazine (eg Stemetil) or metaclopramide (eg Maxalon) for nausea and vomiting. Anti-diarrhoea medication should not be given to children under the age of 12.
- Rehydration mixture – for treatment of severe diarrhoea. This is particularly important if travelling with children, but is recommended for everyone.
- Antiseptic such as povidone-iodine (eg Betadine), which comes as a solution, ointment, powder and impregnated swabs – for cuts and grazes.
- Multi-vitamins are a worthwhile consideration, especially for long trips when dietary vitamin intake may be inadequate. Men, women and children each have different vitamin requirements so obtain multi-vitamin tablets which are specific to age and gender.
- Calamine lotion or Stingose spray – to ease irritation from bites or stings.
- Bandages and Band-Aids – for minor injuries.
- Scissors, tweezers and a thermometer (note that mercury thermometers are prohibited by airlines).
- Cold and flu tablets and throat lozenges
- Insect repellent, sunscreen, lip balm and water purification tablets.
- A couple of syringes, in case you need injections in a country with medical hygiene problems. Ask your doctor for a note explaining why they have been prescribed.

Ideally, antibiotics should be administered only under medical supervision and should never be taken indiscriminately. Take only the recommended dose at the prescribed intervals and continue using the antibiotic for the prescribed period, even if the illness seems to be cured earlier. Antibiotics are quite specific to the infections they can treat. Stop immediately if there are any serious adverse reactions and don't use the antibiotic at all if you are unsure that you have the correct one. Some individuals are allergic to commonly prescribed antibiotics such as penicillin and sulpha drugs. It would be sensible to always carry a list of your allergies when travelling.

In many countries, if a medicine is available at all it will generally be available over the counter and the price will be much cheaper than in the west. However, be careful if buying drugs in developing countries, particularly where the expiry date may have passed or correct storage conditions may not have been followed. Bogus drugs are common and it's possible that drugs which are no longer recommended, or have even been banned, in the west are still being dispensed in many Third World countries.

In many countries it may be a good idea to leave unwanted medicines, syringes etc with a local clinic, rather than carry them home.

Various so-called 'AIDS kits' are available in the UK and other western countries, and these have all the gear necessary for blood transfusions and injections. If you are going to be in India for a long time and intend to get off the beaten track, they can be a good idea. In fact even in many places where there are plenty of tourists – such as Jaisalmer – the medical facilities are extremely basic. Having your own sterile equipment could be worthwhile if you have an accident and are hospitalised. For such a kit to be useful for a blood transfusion, however, it needs to have the plastic tube which carries the blood from the bag or bottle, as well as the intravenous needle which actually goes into the arm – some kits have the latter but not the former.

Health Preparations Make sure you're healthy before you start travelling. If you are embarking on a long trip make sure your teeth are OK; there are lots of places where a visit to the dentist would be the last thing you'd want.

If you wear glasses, take a spare pair and your prescription. Replacing your glasses can be a real problem, although in many places you can get new spectacles made up quickly, cheaply and competently.

If you require a particular medication take an adequate supply, as it may not be available locally. Take the prescription or, better still, part of the packaging showing the generic rather than the brand name (which may not be locally available), as it will make getting

replacements easier. It's a wise idea to have a legible prescription with you to show you legally use the medication – it's surprising how often over-the-counter drugs in one country are illegal without a prescription or even banned in another.

Immunisations Vaccinations provide protection against diseases you might meet along the way.

It is important to understand the distinction between vaccines recommended for travel in certain areas and those required by law. Essentially the number of vaccines subject to international health regulations has been dramatically reduced over the last 10 years. Currently yellow fever is the only vaccine subject to international health regulations. Vaccination as an entry requirement is usually only enforced when coming from an infected area.

If you are coming from an infected area (many South American and African countries), you must have a yellow fever vaccination certificate or you will be destined for up to six days in isolation. The same applies if your aeroplane has come from an infected area and has not been disinfected, or by a ship that touched port up to 30 days before arriving in India, if it has not been disinfected.

Smallpox has now been wiped out worldwide, so immunisation is no longer necessary. Occasionally travellers face bureaucratic problems regarding cholera vaccine even though all countries have dropped it as a health requirement for travel.

All vaccinations should be recorded on an International Health Certificate, which is available from your physician or government health department.

Plan ahead for getting your vaccinations: some of them require an initial shot followed by a booster, while some vaccinations should not be given together. It is recommended you seek medical advice at least six weeks prior to travel.

Most travellers from western countries will have been immunised against various diseases during childhood but your doctor may still recommend booster shots against measles or polio, diseases still prevalent in India and many developing countries. The period of protection offered by vaccinations differs widely and some are contraindicated if you are pregnant.

In some countries immunisations are available from airport or government health centres. Travel agents or airline offices will tell you where. Vaccinations include:

Tetanus & Diphtheria
Boosters are necessary every 10 years and protection is highly recommended.

Polio
A booster of either the oral or injected vaccine is required every 10 years to maintain your immunity after childhood vaccination. Polio is a very serious, easily transmitted disease which is still prevalent in the Indian Himalaya and many developing countries.

Typhoid
Available either as an injection or oral capsules. Protection lasts from one to five years depending on the vaccine, and is useful if you are travelling for long in rural, tropical areas. You may get some side effects such as pain at the injection site, fever, headache and a general unwell feeling. A single dose injectable vaccine, Typhim Vi, has few side effects, but is more expensive. Side effects are unusual with the oral form but occasionally an individual will have stomach cramps.

Hepatitis A
The most common travel-acquired illness which can be prevented by vaccination. Protection can be provided in two ways – either with the antibody gamma globulin or with a new vaccine called Havrix 1440.
Havrix 1440 provides long-term immunity (possibly more than 10 years) after an initial course of two injections and a booster at 6-12 months. It may be more expensive than gamma globulin but certainly has many advantages, including length of protection and ease of administration. It is important to know that being a vaccine it will take about three weeks to provide satisfactory protection – hence the need for careful planning prior to travel.
Gamma globulin is not a vaccination but a ready-made antibody which has proven very successful in reducing the chances of hepatitis infection. It should also be given as close as possible to departure because it is at its most effective in the first few weeks after administration and the effectiveness tapers off gradually between three and six months.

Hepatitis B
Travellers at risk of contact (see Infectious Diseases section) are strongly advised to be vaccinated, especially if they are children or will have close contact with children. The vaccination course comprises three injections given over a six month period then boosters every three to five years. The initial course of injections can be given over as short a period as 28 days then boosted after 12 months if more rapid protection is required.

Meningococcal Meningitis
The risk area for this disease is northern India and Nepal. Travellers to Rajasthan should consider having this vaccination. The vaccination is usually recommended for those who will be in the risk area for seven days or longer. A single injection will give good protection against the A, C, W and Y groups of the bacteria for at least a year. The vaccine is not, however, recommended for children under two years, because they do not develop satisfactory immunity from it.

Tuberculosis (TB)
TB risk should be considered for people travelling for more than three months. As most healthy adults do not develop symptoms, a skin test before and after travel to determine whether exposure has occurred is recommended. Vaccination for children who will be travelling for more than three months is also recommended.

Rabies
Pretravel rabies vaccination involves having three injections over 21 to 28 days and should be considered by those who will spend a month or longer in a country where rabies is common, especially if they are cycling, handling animals, caving, travelling to remote areas, or are children (who may not report a bite). If someone who has been vaccinated is bitten or scratched by an animal they will require two booster injections of vaccine.

Japanese B Encephalitis
Vaccination is usually considered for those spending a month or longer in a risk area, for those making repeated trips to a risk area or those visiting during an epidemic. The vaccination course consists of three injections given over 30 days. The vaccine has been associated with serious allergic reactions so the decision to have it should be balanced against the risk of contracting the illness.

Basic Rules

Care in what you eat and drink is the most important health rule; stomach upsets are the most likely travel health problem (between 30% and 50% of travellers in a two week stay experience these) but the majority of these upsets will be relatively minor. Don't become paranoid; trying the local food is part of the experience of travel, after all.

Water The number one rule is *don't drink the water* and that includes ice. If you don't know for certain that the water is safe always assume the worst. Reputable brands of bottled water or soft drinks are generally fine, although in some places bottles refilled with tap water are not unknown. Only use water from containers with a serrated seal – not tops or corks. Take care with fruit juice, particularly if water may have been added. Milk should be treated with suspicion, as it is often unpasteurised. Boiled milk is fine if it is kept hygienically and yoghurt is always good. Tea or coffee should also be OK, since the water should have been boiled.

Water Purification The simplest way of purifying water is to boil it thoroughly. Vigorous boiling for five minutes should be satisfactory; however, at high altitude water boils at a lower temperature, so germs are less likely to be killed. If you cannot boil water, it should be treated chemically. Chlorine tablets (Puritabs, Steritabs or other brands) will kill many pathogens, but not those pathogens causing giardia and amoebic cysts. Iodine is very effective in purifying water and is available in tablet form (such as Potable Aqua), but follow the directions carefully and remember that too much iodine can be harmful.

If you can't find tablets, tincture of iodine (2%) or iodine crystals can be used. Four drops of tincture of iodine per litre or quart of clear water is the recommended dosage; the treated water should be left to stand for 20 to 30 minutes before drinking. Iodine crystals can also be used to purify water but this is a more complicated process, as you have to first prepare a saturated iodine solution. Iodine loses its effectiveness if exposed to air or damp so keep it in a tightly sealed container. Flavoured powder will disguise the taste of treated water and is a good idea if you are travelling with children.

Consider purchasing a water filter for a long trip. They filter out parasites, bacteria and viruses and, although expensive, they are more cost effective than buying bottled water.

Food There is an old colonial adage which says: 'If you can cook it, boil it or peel it you can eat it...otherwise forget it'. Salads and fruit should be washed with purified water or peeled where possible. Ice cream is usually OK if it is a reputable brand name, but beware of street vendors and of ice cream that has melted and been refrozen. Thoroughly cooked food is safest but not if it has been left to cool or if it has been reheated. Shellfish such as mussels, oysters and clams should be avoided as well as undercooked meat, particularly in the form of mince. Steaming does not make shellfish safe for eating.

If a place looks clean and well run and if the vendor also looks clean and healthy, then the food is probably safe. In general, places that are packed with travellers or locals will be fine, while empty restaurants are questionable. The food in busy restaurants is cooked and eaten quite quickly with little standing around and is probably not reheated.

Nutrition If your food is poor or if you're travelling hard and fast and therefore missing meals, or if you simply lose your appetite, you can soon start to lose weight and place your health at risk.

Make sure your diet is well balanced. Eggs, tofu, beans, *dhal* and nuts are all safe ways to get protein. Fruit you can peel (bananas, oranges or mandarins, for example) is always safe and a good source of vitamins. Try to eat plenty of grains (including rice) and bread. Remember that although food is generally safer if it is cooked well, overcooked food loses much of its nutritional value. If your diet isn't well balanced or if your food intake is insufficient, it's a good idea to take vitamin and iron pills.

In hot climates make sure you drink enough – don't rely on feeling thirsty to indicate when you should drink. Not needing to urinate or very dark yellow urine is a danger sign. Always carry a water bottle with you on long trips. Excessive sweating can lead to loss of salt and therefore muscle cramping. Salt tablets are not a good idea as a preventive, but in places where salt is not used much, adding salt to food can help.

Everyday Health Normal body temperature is 37°C (98.6°F); more than 2°C (4°F) higher indicates a 'high' fever. The normal adult pulse rate is 60 to 100 per minute (children 80 to 100, babies 100 to 140). You should know how to take a temperature and a pulse rate. As a general rule the pulse increases about 20 beats per minute for each °C (2°F) rise in fever.

Respiration (breathing) rate is also an indicator of illness. Count the number of breaths per minute: between 12 and 20 is normal for adults and older children (up to 30 for younger children, 40 for babies). People with a high fever or serious respiratory illness (such as pneumonia) breathe more quickly than normal. More than 40 shallow breaths a minute usually means pneumonia.

In western countries with safe water and excellent human waste disposal systems we often take good health for granted. In years gone by, when public health facilities were not as good as they are today, certain rules attached to eating and drinking were observed, such as washing your hands before a meal. It is important for people travelling in areas of poor sanitation to be aware of this and adjust their own personal hygiene habits.

Clean your teeth with purified water rather than straight from the tap. Avoid climatic extremes: keep out of the sun when it's hot, dress warmly when it's cold. Avoid potential diseases by dressing sensibly – you can get worm infections through walking barefoot. You can avoid insect bites by covering bare skin when insects are around, by screening windows or beds and by using insect repellents. Seek local advice: and in situations where there is no information, discretion is the better part of valour.

Medical Problems & Treatment

Potential medical problems can be broken down into several areas. Firstly there are the problems caused by extremes of temperature, altitude or motion. Then there are diseases and illnesses caused through poor environmental sanitation, insect bites or stings, and animal or human contact. Simple cuts, bites and scratches can also cause problems.

Self-diagnosis and treatment can be risky, so wherever possible seek qualified help. Although we do give drug dosages in this section, they are for emergency use only. Medical advice should be sought where possible before administering any drugs.

An embassy or consulate can usually recommend a good place to go for such advice. So can five star hotels, although they often recommend doctors with five star prices. (This is when that medical insurance really comes in useful!) In some places standards of medical attention are so low that for some ailments the best advice is to get on a plane and go somewhere else.

Environmental Hazards

Sunburn In the desert, the tropics or at high altitude you can get sunburnt surprisingly quickly, even through cloud. Use a sunscreen and take extra care to cover areas which don't normally see sun, such as your feet. A hat provides added protection, and you should also use zinc cream or some other barrier cream for your nose and lips. Calamine lotion is good for mild sunburn.

Prickly Heat Prickly heat is an itchy rash caused by excessive perspiration trapped under the skin. It usually strikes people who have just arrived in a hot climate and whose pores have not yet opened sufficiently to cope with greater sweating. Keeping cool by bathing often, using a mild talcum powder or even resorting to air-conditioning may help until you acclimatise.

Heat Exhaustion Dehydration or salt deficiency can cause heat exhaustion. Take time to acclimatise to high temperatures and make sure you get sufficient liquids. Wear loose clothing and a broad-brimmed hat. Do not do anything too physically demanding.

Salt deficiency is characterised by fatigue, lethargy, headaches, giddiness and muscle cramps and in this case salt tablets may help. Vomiting or diarrhoea can deplete your liquid and salt levels. Anhydrotic heat exhaustion, caused by an inability to sweat, is quite rare. Unlike the other forms of heat exhaustion, it is likely to strike people who have been in a hot climate for some time, rather than newcomers.

Heat Stroke This serious, sometimes fatal, condition can occur if the body's heat-regulating mechanism breaks down and the body temperature rises to dangerous levels. Long, continuous periods of exposure to high temperatures can leave you vulnerable to heat stroke. You should avoid excessive alcohol or strenuous activity when you first arrive in a hot climate.

The symptoms are feeling unwell, not sweating very much or at all and a high body temperature (39°C to 41°C or 102°F to 106°F). Where sweating has ceased the skin becomes flushed and red. Severe, throbbing headaches and lack of co-ordination will also occur, and the sufferer may be confused or aggressive. Eventually the victim will become delirious or convulse. Hospitalisation is essential, but in the interim get victims out of the sun, remove their clothing, cover them with a wet sheet or towel and then fan continuously.

Fungal Infections Fungal infections, which occur with greater frequency in hot weather, are most likely to occur on the scalp, between the toes or fingers (athlete's foot), in the groin (jock itch or crotch rot) and on the body (ringworm). You get ringworm (which is a fungal infection, not a worm) from infected animals or by walking on damp areas, like shower floors.

To prevent fungal infections wear loose, comfortable clothes, avoid artificial fibres, wash frequently and dry carefully. If you do get an infection, wash the infected area daily with a disinfectant or medicated soap and water, and rinse and dry well. Apply an antifungal powder like the widely available Tinaderm. Try to expose the infected area to air or sunlight as much as possible and wash all towels and underwear in hot water as well as changing them often. Wear flipflops (thongs) in common showers.

Hypothermia Too much cold is just as dangerous as too much heat, particularly if it leads to hypothermia. This is unlikely to be a problem in Rajasthan, even though in the desert temperatures can plunge at night.

Motion Sickness Eating lightly before and during a trip will reduce the chances of motion sickness. If you are prone to motion sickness, try to find a place that minimises disturbance – near the wing on aircraft, close to midships on boats, near the centre on buses. Fresh air usually helps; reading and cigarette smoke don't. Commercial motion-sickness preparations, which can cause drowsiness, have to be taken before the trip commences; when you're feeling sick it's too late. Ginger (available in capsules) and peppermint (including mint-flavoured sweets) are natural preventives.

Jet Lag Jet lag is experienced when a person travels by air across more than three time zones (each time zone usually represents a one hour time difference). It occurs because many of the functions of the human body (such as temperature, pulse rate and emptying of the bladder and bowels) are regulated by internal 24 hour cycles called circadian rhythms. When we travel long distances rapidly, our bodies take time to adjust to the 'new time' of our destination, and we may experience fatigue, disorientation, insomnia, anxiety, impaired concentration and loss of appetite. These effects will usually be gone within three days of arrival, but there are ways of minimising the impact of jet lag:

- Rest for a couple of days before departure; try to avoid late nights and last-minute dashes for travellers' cheques, passport etc.

- Try to select flight schedules that minimise sleep deprivation; arriving late in the day means you can go to sleep soon after you arrive. For very long flights, try to organise a stopover.
- Avoid excessive eating (which bloats the stomach) and alcohol (which causes dehydration) during the flight. Instead, drink plenty of non-carbonated, non-alcoholic drinks such as fruit juice or water.
- Avoid smoking, as this reduces the amount of oxygen in the aeroplane cabin even further and causes greater fatigue.
- Make yourself comfortable by wearing loose-fitting clothes and perhaps bringing an eye mask and ear plugs to help you sleep.

Infectious Diseases

Diarrhoea A change of water, food or climate can cause the runs; diarrhoea caused by contaminated food or water is more serious. Despite all your precautions you may still have a mild bout of travellers' diarrhoea but a few rushed toilet trips with no other symptoms is not indicative of a serious problem. Moderate diarrhoea, involving half-a-dozen loose movements in a day, is more of a nuisance.

Dehydration is the main danger with any diarrhoea, particularly for children in whom dehydration can occur quite quickly. Fluid replacement remains the mainstay of management. Weak black tea with a little sugar, soda water, or soft drinks allowed to go flat and diluted 50% with water are all good. With severe diarrhoea a rehydrating solution is necessary to replace minerals and salts. Commercially available ORS (oral rehydration salts) are very useful; add the contents of one sachet to a litre of boiled or bottled water. In an emergency you can make up a solution of eight teaspoons of sugar to a litre of boiled water and eat salted cracker biscuits. You should stick to a bland diet as you recover.

Lomotil or Imodium can be used to bring relief from the symptoms, although they do not actually cure the problem. Only use these drugs if absolutely necessary – eg if you *must* travel. For children under 12 years, Lomotil and Imodium are not recommended. Under all circumstances fluid replacement is the most important thing to remember. Do not use these drugs if the person has a high fever or is severely dehydrated.

In certain situations antibiotics may be indicated:

- Watery diarrhoea with blood and mucus. (Gut paralysing drugs like Imodium or Lomotil should be avoided in this situation.)
- Watery diarrhoea with fever and lethargy.
- Persistent diarrhoea not improving after 48 hours.
- Severe diarrhoea, if it is logistically difficult to stay in one place.

The recommended drugs (adults only) would be either norfloxacin 400 mg twice daily for three days or ciprofloxacin 500 mg twice daily for three days.

The drug bismuth subsalicylate has also been used successfully. It is not available in some countries, including Australia. The dosage for adults is two tablets or 30 ml and for children it is one tablet or 10 ml. This dose can be repeated every 30 minutes to one hour, with no more than eight doses in a 24 hour period.

The drug of choice for children would be co-trimoxazole (Bactrim, Septrin, Resprim) with dosage dependent on weight. A five day course is also given.

Giardiasis The parasite causing this intestinal disorder is present in contaminated water. The symptoms are stomach cramps, nausea, a bloated stomach, watery, foul-smelling diarrhoea and frequent gas. Giardiasis can appear several weeks after you have been exposed to the parasite. The symptoms may disappear for a few days and then return; this can go on for several weeks. Tinidazole, known as Fasigyn, or metronidazole (Flagyl) are the recommended drugs for treatment. Either can be used in a single treatment dose. Antibiotics are of no use.

Dysentery This serious illness is caused by contaminated food or water and is characterised by severe diarrhoea, often with blood or mucus in the stool. There are two kinds of dysentery. Bacillary dysentery is characterised by a high fever and rapid onset; headache, vomiting and stomach pains are also symptoms. It generally does not last longer than a week, but it is highly contagious.

Amoebic dysentery is often more gradual in the onset of symptoms, with cramping abdominal pain and vomiting less likely; fever may not be present. It is not a self-limiting disease: it will persist until treated and can recur and cause long-term health problems.

A stool test is necessary to diagnose which kind of dysentery you have, so you should seek medical help urgently. In case of an emergency, the drugs norfloxacin or cipro-floxacin can be used as presumptive treatment for bacillary dysentery, and metronidazole (Flagyl) for amoebic dysentery.

For bacillary dysentery, norfloxacin 400 mg twice daily for seven days or cipro-floxacin 500 mg twice daily for seven days are the recommended dosages.

If you're unable to find either of these drugs, then a useful alternative is co-trimoxazole 160/800 mg (Bactrim, Septrin, Resprim) twice daily for seven days. This is a sulpha drug and must not be used by people with a sulpha allergy.

In the case of children the drug co-trimoxazole is a reasonable first-line treatment. For amoebic dysentery, the recommended adult dosage of metronidazole (Flagyl) is one 750 mg to 800 mg capsule three times daily for five days. Children aged between eight and 12 years should have half the adult dose; the dosage for younger children is one-third the adult dose.

An alternative to Flagyl is Fasigyn, taken as a two gram daily dose for three days. Alcohol must be avoided during treatment and for 48 hours afterwards.

Cholera Cholera vaccination is not very effective. The bacteria responsible for this disease are waterborne, so attention to the rules of eating and drinking should protect the traveller.

Outbreaks of cholera are generally widely reported, so you can avoid such problem areas. The disease is characterised by a sudden onset of acute diarrhoea with 'rice water' stools, vomiting, muscular cramps, and extreme weakness. You need medical help – but treat for dehydration, which can be extreme, and if there is an appreciable delay in getting to hospital then begin taking tetracycline. The adult dose is 250 mg four times daily. It is not recommended for children aged eight years or under nor for pregnant women. An alternative drug is Ampicillin. People with allergies to penicillin should not take Ampicillin. Remember that while antibiotics might kill the bacteria, it is a toxin produced by the bacteria which causes the massive fluid loss. Fluid replacement is by far the most important aspect of treatment.

Typhoid Typhoid fever is another gut infection that travels the faecal-oral route – that is, contaminated water and food are responsible. Vaccination against typhoid is not totally effective and it is one of the most dangerous infections, so medical help must be sought.

In its early stages typhoid resembles many other illnesses: sufferers may feel like they have a bad cold or flu on the way, as early symptoms are a headache, a sore throat, and a fever which rises a little each day until it is around 40°C (104°F) or more. The victim's pulse is often slow relative to the degree of fever present and gets slower as the fever rises – unlike a normal fever where the pulse increases. There may also be vomiting, diarrhoea or constipation.

In the second week the high fever and slow pulse continue and a few pink spots may appear on the body; trembling, delirium, weakness, weight loss and dehydration are other symptoms. If there are no further complications, the fever and other symptoms will slowly diminish during the third week. However, you must get medical help before this because pneumonia (acute infection of the lungs) or peritonitis (perforated bowel) are common complications, and because typhoid is very infectious.

The fever should be treated by keeping the victim cool and dehydration should also be watched for.

The drug of choice is ciprofloxacin at a dose of one gram daily for 14 days. It is quite expensive and may not be available. The alternative, chloramphenicol, has been the mainstay of treatment for many years. In many countries it is still the recommended antibiotic but there are fewer side effects with Ampicillin. The adult dosage is two 250 mg capsules, four times a day. Children aged between eight and 12 years should have half the adult dose; younger children should have one-third the adult dose.

People who are allergic to penicillin should not be given Ampicillin.

Plague There was an outbreak of pneumonic plague in 1994 in Surat, Gujarat, although the risk to travellers is tiny.

Viral Gastroenteritis This is caused not by bacteria but, as the name suggests, by a virus. It is characterised by stomach cramps, diarrhoea, and sometimes by vomiting and/or a slight fever. All you can do is rest and drink lots of fluids.

Hepatitis Hepatitis is a general term for inflammation of the liver. There are many causes of this condition: drugs, alcohol and infections are but a few.

The discovery of new strains has led to a virtual alphabet soup, with hepatitis A, B, C, D, E and others. These letters identify specific agents that cause viral hepatitis. Viral hepatitis is an infection of the liver, which can lead to jaundice (yellow skin), fever, lethargy and digestive problems. It can have no symptoms at all, with the infected person not knowing that they have the disease. Travellers shouldn't be too paranoid about this apparent proliferation of hepatitis strains; hep C, D, E and G are fairly rare (so far) and following the same precautions as for A and B should be all that's necessary to avoid them.

Viral hepatitis can be divided into two groups on the basis of how it is spread. The first route of transmission is via contaminated food and water (leading to Hepatitis A and E), and the second route is via blood and bodily fluids (resulting in Hepatitis B, C and D).

Hepatitis A This is a very common disease in most countries, including India. Most people in developing countries are infected as children; they often don't develop symptoms, but do develop life-long immunity. The disease poses a real threat to the traveller, as people are unlikely to have been exposed to hepatitis A in developed countries.

The symptoms are fever, chills, headache, fatigue, feelings of weakness and aches and pains, followed by loss of appetite, nausea, vomiting, abdominal pain, dark urine, light-coloured faeces, jaundiced skin and the whites of the eyes may turn yellow. In some cases you may feel unwell, tired, have no appetite, experience aches and pains and be jaundiced. You should seek medical advice, but in general there is not much you can do apart from resting, drinking lots of fluids, eating lightly and avoiding fatty foods. People who have had hepatitis must forego alcohol for six months after the illness, as hepatitis attacks the liver and it needs that amount of time to recover.

The routes of transmission are via contaminated water, shellfish contaminated by sewerage, or foodstuffs sold by food handlers with poor standards of hygiene.

Taking care with what you eat and drink can go a long way towards preventing this disease. But this is a very infectious virus, so if there is any risk of exposure, additional cover is highly recommended. This cover comes in two forms: Gamma globulin and Havrix 1440. Gamma globulin is an injection where you are given the antibodies for hepatitis A, which provide immunity for a limited time. Havrix 1440 is a vaccine, where you develop your own antibodies, which gives lasting immunity.

Hepatitis B This is also a very common disease, with almost 300 million chronic carriers in the world. Hepatitis B, which used to be called serum hepatitis, is spread through contact with infected blood, blood products or bodily fluids, for example through sexual contact, unsterilised needles and blood transfusions. Other risk situations include having a shave or tattoo in a local shop, or having your body pierced. The symptoms of type B are much the same as type A except that they are more severe and may lead to irreparable liver damage or even liver cancer.

Although there is no treatment for hepatitis B, a cheap and effective vaccine is available; the only problem is that for long-lasting cover you need a six month course. People who should receive a hepatitis B vaccination include anyone who anticipates contact with blood or other bodily secretions, either as a health-care worker or through sexual contact with the local population, and particularly those who intend to stay in the country for a long period of time.

Hepatitis C This is another recently defined virus. It is a concern because it seems to lead to liver disease more rapidly than hepatitis B.

The virus is spread by contact with blood – usually via contaminated transfusions or shared needles. Avoiding these is the only means of prevention, as there is no available vaccine.

Hepatitis D Often referred to as the 'Delta' virus, this infection only occurs in chronic carriers of hepatitis B. It is transmitted by blood and bodily fluids. Again there is no vaccine for this virus, so avoidance is the best prevention. The risk to travellers is certainly limited.

Hepatitis E This is a very recently discovered virus, of which little is yet known. Epidemics occur, including in India, generally causing mild hepatitis, although it can be very serious in pregnant women.

Care with water supplies is the only current prevention, as there are no specific vaccines for this type of hepatitis. At present it doesn't appear to be too great a risk for travellers.

Intestinal Worms These parasites are most common in rural, tropical areas, and a stool test when you return home is not a bad idea. They can be present on unwashed vegetables or in undercooked meat and you can pick them up through your skin by walking in bare feet. Infestations may not show up for some time, and although they are generally not serious, if left untreated they can cause severe health problems. A stool test is necessary to pinpoint the problem and medication is often available over the counter.

Tetanus This potentially fatal disease is found worldwide, occurring more commonly in undeveloped tropical areas. It is difficult to treat but is preventable with immunisation. Tetanus occurs when a wound becomes infected by a germ which lives in the faeces of horses and other animals, so clean all cuts, punctures and animal bites. Tetanus is also known as lockjaw, and the first symptom may be discomfort in swallowing, or stiffening of the jaw and neck; this is followed by painful convulsions of the jaw and whole body.

Rabies Rabies is a fatal viral infection found in many countries and is caused by a bite or scratch by an infected animal. Dogs are noted carriers as are monkeys and cats. Any bite, scratch or even lick from a warm-blooded, furry animal should be cleaned immediately and thoroughly. Scrub with soap and running water, and then clean with an alcohol or iodine solution. If there is any possibility that the animal is infected, medical help should be sought immediately to prevent the onset of symptoms and death.

In a person who has not been immunised against rabies, treatment involves having five injections of vaccine and one of immunoglobulin over 28 days starting as soon as possible after the exposure. Even if the animal is not rabid, all bites should be treated seriously as they can become infected or can result in tetanus. A rabies vaccination is now available and should be considered if you are in a high-risk category – for example, if you intend to explore caves (bat bites can be dangerous), work with animals, or travel so far off the beaten track that medical help is more than two days away.

Meningococcal Meningitis This disease is a bacterial infection of the lining of the brain. It is found in Nepal and India.

Trekkers to rural areas should be particularly careful, as the disease is caught by close contact with people who carry it in their throats and noses, who spread it through coughs and sneezes and may not be aware that they are carriers.

This very serious disease attacks the brain and can be fatal. A scattered, blotchy rash, fever, severe headache, sensitivity to light and neck stiffness which prevents forward bending of the head are the first symptoms. Death can occur within a few hours, so immediate treatment is important.

Treatment is large doses of penicillin given intravenously, or, if that is not possible, intramuscularly (ie in the buttocks). Vaccination offers good protection for over a year, but you should also check for reports of current epidemics.

Tuberculosis (TB) There is a worldwide resurgence of tuberculosis. It is a bacterial infection which is usually transmitted from person to person by coughing but may be transmitted through consumption of unpasteurised milk. Milk that has been boiled is safe to drink, and the souring of milk to make yoghurt or cheese also kills the bacilli. Typically many months of contact with the infected person is required before the disease is passed on. The usual site of the disease is the lungs, although other organs may be involved. Most infected people never develop symptoms. In those who do, especially infants, symptoms may arise within weeks of the infection occurring and may be severe. In most, however, the disease lies dormant for many years until, for some reason, the infected person becomes physically run down. Symptoms include fever, weight loss, night sweats and coughing.

Sexually Transmitted Diseases Sexual contact with an infected sexual partner spreads these diseases. While abstinence is the only 100% preventive, using condoms is also effective. Gonorrhoea, herpes and syphilis are the most common of these diseases; sores, blisters or rashes around the genitals, discharges or pain when urinating are common symptoms. In some STDs, such as wart virus or chlamydia, symptoms may be less marked or not observed at all in women. Syphilis symptoms eventually disappear completely but the disease continues and can cause severe problems in later years. The treatment of gonorrhoea and syphilis is with antibiotics.

There are numerous other sexually transmitted diseases, for most of which effective treatment is available. However, there is no cure for herpes and there is also currently no cure for AIDS.

HIV/AIDS HIV, the Human Immunodeficiency Virus, may develop into AIDS, Acquired Immune Deficiency Syndrome. HIV is a major problem in many countries, including India. Any exposure to blood, blood products or bodily fluids may put the individual at risk. In many developing countries transmission is predominantly through heterosexual sexual activity. This is quite different from industrialised countries where transmission is mostly through contact between homosexual or bisexual males, or via contaminated needles shared by IV drug users. Apart from abstinence, the most effective preventive is always to practise safe sex using condoms. Without a blood test, it is impossible to detect the HIV-positive status of an otherwise healthy-looking person.

HIV/AIDS can also be spread through infected blood transfusions; most developing countries cannot afford to screen blood for transfusions. It can also be spread by dirty needles – vaccinations, acupuncture, tattooing and ear or nose piercing can potentially be as dangerous as intravenous drug use if the equipment is not clean. If you do need an injection, ask to see the syringe unwrapped in front of you, or better still, take a needle and syringe pack with you overseas – it is a cheap insurance package against infection with HIV.

Fear of HIV infection should never preclude treatment for serious medical conditions.

Although there may be a risk of infection, it is very small indeed.

The AIDS situation in India is quite serious; an article in *Navbharat Times* a few years ago estimated that 30% of the 100,000 prostitutes in Mumbai are HIV positive. Further, a random survey of truck drivers revealed that 25% were HIV positive and most did not know anything about AIDS.

Insect-Borne Diseases

Malaria This serious disease is spread by mosquito bites.

If you are travelling in areas in which the disease is endemic, which in India is everywhere, except the Himalayan region at certain times of the year, it is extremely important to take malarial prophylactics. Symptoms include headaches, fever, chills and sweating which may subside and recur. Without treatment malaria can develop more serious, potentially fatal effects.

Antimalarial drugs do not prevent you from being infected but kill the parasites during a stage in their development.

There are a number of different types of malaria. The one of most concern is falciparum malaria. This is responsible for the very serious cerebral malaria. Falciparum is the predominant form in many malaria-prone areas of the world, including Africa, South-East Asia and Papua New Guinea. It has also been reported in India. Contrary to popular belief cerebral malaria is not a new strain.

Chloroquine plus proguanil anti-malarials are recommended, but expert advice should be sought, as there are many factors to consider when deciding on the type of antimalarial medication, including the area to be visited, the risk of exposure to malaria-carrying mosquitoes, your current medical condition, and your age and pregnancy status.

It is also important to discuss the side-effect profile of the medication, so you can work out some level of risk versus benefit ratio. It is also very important to be sure of the correct dosage of the medication prescribed to you. Some people have inadvertently taken weekly medication (chloroquine) on a daily basis, with disastrous effects. While discuss-

ing dosages for prevention of malaria, it is often advisable to include the dosages required for treatment, especially if your trip is through a high-risk area that would isolate you from medical care.

The main messages are as follows.

Primary prevention must always be in the form of mosquito-avoidance measures. The mosquitoes that transmit malaria bite from dusk to dawn and during this period travellers are advised to:
• wear light coloured clothing
• wear long pants and long sleeved shirts
• use mosquito repellents containing the compound DEET on exposed areas (overuse of DEET may be harmful, especially to children, but its use is considered preferable to being bitten by disease-transmitting mosquitoes)
• avoid highly scented perfumes or aftershave
• use a mosquito net – it may be worth taking your own

While no antimalarial is 100% effective, taking the most appropriate drug significantly reduces the risk of contracting the disease.

No-one should ever die from malaria. It can be diagnosed by a simple blood test. Symptoms range from fever, chills and sweating, headache and abdominal pains to a vague feeling of ill-health, so seek examination immediately if there is any suggestion of malaria.

Contrary to popular belief, once a traveller contracts malaria he/she does not have it for life. One of the parasites may lie dormant in the liver but this can also be eradicated using a specific medication. Malaria is curable, as long as the traveller seeks medical help when symptoms occur.

Dengue Fever There is no prophylactic available for this mosquito-spread disease the main preventive measure is to avoid mosquito bites. A sudden onset of fever, head aches and severe joint and muscle pains are the first signs before a rash starts on the trunk of the body and spreads to the limbs and face After a further few days, the fever will subside and recovery will begin. Serious complications are not common but full recovery can take up to a month or more.

Typhus Typhus is spread by ticks, mites or lice. It begins with fever, chills, headache and muscle pains followed a few days later by a body rash. There is often a large painful sore at the site of the bite and nearby lymph nodes are swollen and painful. Typhus is uncommon in travellers, but can be treated under medical supervision.

Tick typhus is spread by ticks. Seek local advice on areas where ticks pose a danger and always check your skin carefully for ticks after walking in a danger area such as a tropical forest. A strong insect repellent can help, and serious walkers in tick areas should consider having their boots and trousers impregnated with benzyl benzoate and dibutylphthalate.

Filariasis This is a mosquito-transmitted parasitic infection common in India. There is a range of possible manifestations of the infection, depending on which filarial parasite species has caused the infection. Symptoms include fever, pain and swelling of the lymph glands; inflammation of lymph drainage areas; swelling of a limb or the scrotum; skin rashes and blindness. Treatment is available to eliminate the parasites from the body, but some of the damage they cause may not be reversible. Medical advice should be obtained promptly if the infection is suspected.

Leishmaniasis A group of parasitic diseases transmitted by sandfly bites is common in India. Cutaneous leishmaniasis affects the skin tissue causing ulceration and disfigurement and visceral leishmaniasis affects the cells of internal organs. The disease rarely causes serious illness, but it is often misdiagnosed and therefore treated incorrectly. Treatment of the disease is with drugs containing antimony.

Avoiding sandfly bites is the best precaution. The bites generally occur at night, are usually painless, only slightly itchy and are yet another reason to cover up and apply repellent, especially between late afternoon and dawn.

Japanese B Encephalitis This viral infection of the brain is transmitted by mosquitoes. It is usually a severe illness with a high mortality rate. Most cases occur in rural areas because part of the life cycle of the virus takes place in pigs or wading birds. Symptoms include fever, headache, vomiting, neck stiffness, pain in the eyes when looking at light, alteration in consciousness, seizures and paralysis or muscle weakness. Correct diagnosis and treatment require hospitalisation. Vaccination is recommended for those intending to spend more than a month in a rural risk area during the rainy season, for those making repeated trips into a risk area or who are planning to stay for a year or more in a risk area, and for those visiting an area where there is an epidemic. The disease is not common in travellers.

Cuts, Bites & Stings

Cuts & Scratches Skin punctures can easily become infected in hot climates and may be difficult to heal. Treat any cut with an antiseptic such as povidone-iodine. Where possible avoid bandages and Band-Aids, which can keep wounds wet.

Bites & Stings Bee and wasp stings are usually painful rather than dangerous. Calamine lotion will give relief and ice packs will reduce the pain and swelling. There are some spiders with dangerous bites but antivenenes are usually available. Again, local advice is the best suggestion.

Snakes To minimise your chances of being bitten always wear boots, socks and long trousers when walking through undergrowth where snakes may be present. Don't put your hands into holes and crevices, and be careful when collecting firewood.

Snake bites do not cause instantaneous death and antivenenes are usually available. Keep the victim calm and still, wrap the bitten limb tightly, as you would for a sprained ankle, and then attach a splint to immobilise it. Then seek medical help, if possible *with* the dead snake for identification. Don't attempt to catch the snake if there is even a remote possibility of being bitten again. Tourniquets and sucking out the poison are now comprehensively discredited.

Bedbugs & Lice Bedbugs live in various places, but particularly in dirty mattresses and bedding. Spots of blood on bedclothes or on the wall around the bed can be read as a suggestion to find another hotel. Bedbugs leave itchy bites in neat rows. Calamine lotion or Stingose spray may help.

All lice cause itching and discomfort. They make themselves at home in your hair (head lice), your clothing (body lice) or in your pubic hair (crabs). You catch lice through direct contact with infected people or by sharing combs, clothing and the like. Powder or shampoo treatment will kill the lice and infected clothing should then be washed in very hot water.

Leeches & Ticks Leeches may be present in damp rainforest conditions; they attach themselves to your skin to suck your blood. Trekkers often get them on their legs or in their boots. Salt or a lighted cigarette end will make them fall off. Do not pull them off, as the bite is then more likely to become infected. An insect repellent may keep them away. You should always check your body if you have been walking through a tick-infested area, as ticks can cause skin infections and other more serious diseases. If a tick is found attached, press down around the tick's head with tweezers, grab the head and gently pull upwards. Avoid pulling the rear of the body, as this may squeeze the tick's gut contents through the attached mouth parts into the skin, increasing the risk of infection and disease. Smearing chemicals on the tick will not make it let go and is not recommended.

Women's Health
Gynaecological Problems
Poor diet, lowered resistance due to the use of antibiotics for stomach upsets and even contraceptive pills can lead to vaginal infections when travelling in hot climates. Keeping the genital area clean, and wearing skirts or loose-fitting trousers and cotton underwear will help to prevent infections.

Yeast infections, characterised by a rash, itch and discharge, can be treated with a vinegar or lemon-juice douche, or with yoghurt. Nystatin miconazole or clotrimazole suppositories are the usual medical prescription. Trichomoniasis and gardnerella are more serious infections; symptoms are a smelly discharge and a burning sensation when urinating. Male sexual partners must also be treated, and if a vinegar-water douche is not effective, medical attention should be sought. Metronidazole (Flagyl) is the prescribed drug.

Pregnancy Most miscarriages occur during the first three months of pregnancy, so this is the most risky time to travel as far as your own health is concerned. Miscarriage is not uncommon, and can occasionally lead to severe bleeding. The last three months should also be spent within reasonable distance of good medical care. A baby born as early as 24 weeks stands a chance of survival, but only in a good modern hospital. Pregnant women should avoid all unnecessary medication, but vaccinations and malarial prophylactics should still be taken where possible. Additional care should be taken to prevent illness and particular attention should be paid to diet and nutrition. Alcohol and nicotine, for example, should be avoided.

Women travellers often find that their periods become irregular or even cease while they're on the road. Remember that a missed period in these circumstances doesn't necessarily indicate pregnancy. There are health posts or Family Planning clinics in many urban centres in developing countries, where you can seek advice and have a urine test to determine whether or not you are pregnant.

Hospitals
Although India does have a few excellent hospitals such as the Christian Medical College Hospital in Vellore, Tamil Nadu, the Breach Candy Hospital in Mumbai and the

All India Institute of Medical Sciences in Delhi, most Indian cities do not have the quality of medical care available in the West. Usually hospitals run by western missionaries have better facilities than government hospitals where long queues are common. Unless you have something very unusual, these Christian-run hospitals are the best places to head for in an emergency.

India also has many qualified doctors with their own private clinics which can be quite good and, in some cases, as good as anything available anywhere in the world. The usual fee for a clinic visit is about Rs 80; Rs 200 for a specialist. Home calls usually cost about Rs 100.

WOMEN TRAVELLERS

Foreign women travelling in India have always been viewed by Indian men as free and easy, based largely on what they believe to be true from watching cheap western soapies. Women have been hassled, stared at, spied on in hotel rooms, and often groped, although the situation was rarely threatening.

Recently, however, the situation has become more difficult for women travellers, mainly because the 'sexual revolution' which swept the west 25 years ago has now hit India. Movies and magazines are much more explicit, and the widespread billboard advertisements for condoms often quote passages from the Kama Sutra and depict naked or semi-naked women and men. The message getting through to the middle-class Indian male is that sex before and outside of marriage is less of a taboo than in the past, and so foreign women are seen as even more free and easy than ever before.

Rajasthan is, unfortunately, no exception, and women travelling alone will find themselves constantly the centre of unsolicited male attention.

Close attention to standards of dress will go a long way to minimising problems for female travellers. The light cotton drawstring skirts that many foreign women pick up in India are really sari petticoats and to wear them in the street is rather like going out half dressed. Ways of blending into the Indian background include avoiding sleeveless blouses, skirts that are too short and, of course, the bra-less look.

Getting stared at is something which you'll have to get used to. Don't return male stares, as this will be considered a come-on; just ignore them. Dark glasses can help. Other harassment likely to be encountered includes obscene comments, touching-up and jeering, particularly by groups of youths.

Getting involved in inane conversations with men is also considered a turn-on. Keep discussions down to a necessary minimum unless you're interested in getting hassled. If you get the uncomfortable feeling he's encroaching on your space, the chances are that he is. A firm request to keep away is usually enough. Firmly return any errant limbs, put some item of luggage in between you and if all else fails, find a new spot. You're also within your rights to tell him to shove off!

Being a woman also has some advantages. There is often a special ladies' queue for train tickets or even a ladies' quota and ladies' compartments. One woman wrote that these ladies' carriages were often nearly empty – another said that they were full of screaming children. Special ladies' facilities are also sometimes found in cinemas and other places.

GAY & LESBIAN TRAVELLERS

While overt displays of affection between members of the opposite sex, such as cuddling and hand-holding, are frowned upon in India, it is not unusual to see Indian men holding hands with each other or engaged in other close affectionate behaviour. This does not necessarily suggest that they are gay. The gay movement in India is confined almost exclusively to larger cities such as Delhi and Mumbai. As with relations between heterosexual western couples travelling in India – both married and unmarried – gay and lesbian travellers should exercise discretion and refrain from displaying overt affection towards each other in public.

Legal Status Homosexual relations for men are illegal in India. Section 377 of the national legislation forbids 'carnal intercourse against the order of nature' (that is, anal intercourse). The penalties for transgression can be up to life imprisonment. There is no legislation forbidding lesbian relations.

DISABLED TRAVELLERS

Travelling in India can entail some fairly rigorous challenges, even for the able-bodied traveller – long bus trips in crowded vehicles between remote villages and endless queues in the scorching heat at bus and train stations can test even the hardiest traveller. For the mobility impaired traveller, these challenges are increased many-fold. Few buildings have wheelchair access; toilets have certainly not been designed to accommodate wheelchairs; footpaths, where they exist (only in larger towns), are generally riddled with potholes and crevices, littered with obstacles and packed with throngs of people, severely restricting mobility.

Nevertheless, increasing numbers of disabled travellers are taking on the challenge of travel in India. Seeing the mobility impaired locals in the city of Jaipur whizz through the traffic at breakneck speed in modified hand-powered bicycles might even serve as inspiration! If your mobility is restricted you will require a strong, able-bodied companion to accompany you, and it would be well worth considering hiring a private vehicle and driver.

SENIOR TRAVELLERS

Unless your mobility is impaired (see above under Disabled Travellers), or you are vision impaired or in any other way incapacitated, and are in reasonable health, there is no reason why the senior traveller should not consider India as a potential holiday destination. It may be helpful to discuss your proposed trip with your local GP.

TRAVELLING WITH CHILDREN

The numbers of intrepid souls travelling around India accompanied by one, or even two, young children, seems to be on the increase. Children can often enhance your encounters with local people, as they often possess little of the self-consciousness and sense of the cultural differences which can inhibit interaction between adults. Nevertheless, travelling with children can be hard work, and ideally the burden needs to be shared between two adults. For more information, see the Health section earlier in this chapter, and get hold of a copy of Lonely Planet's *Travel with Children* (1995) by Maureen Wheeler.

DANGERS & ANNOYANCES
Theft

Never leave those most important valuables (passport, tickets, health certificates, money, travellers' cheques) in your room; they should be with you at all times. Either have a stout leather passport wallet on your belt, or a passport pouch under your shirt, or simply extra internal pockets in your clothing. On trains at night keep your gear near you; padlocking a bag to a luggage rack can be useful, and some of the newer trains have loops under the seats which you can chain things to. Never walk around with valuables casually slung over your shoulder. Take extra care in crowded public transport.

Thieves are particularly prevalent on train routes where there are lots of tourists. The Delhi to Agra *Shatabdi Express* service is notorious; Delhi to Jaipur, Jaipur to Ajmer and Jodhpur to Jaisalmer are other routes to take care on. Train departure time, when the confusion and crowds are at their worst, is the time to be most careful. Just as the train is about to leave, you are distracted by someone while his or her accomplice is stealing your bag from by your feet. Airports are another place to be careful, especially when international arrivals take place in the middle of the night, when you are unlikely to be at your most alert.

From time to time there are also drugging episodes. Travellers meet somebody on a train or bus or in a town, start talking and are then offered a cup of tea or something similar. Hours later they wake up with a headache and all their gear gone, the tea having been full of

Festivals & Ceremonies

Rajasthan hosts some of India's most spectacular *melas* (fairs) and festivals. The sight of thousands of colourfully garbed villagers assembled in one place is spectacle enough, but these melas and celebrations often feature colourful and intricate dances involving dozens of participants, further contributing to the spectacle.

Fairs and festivals may be purely commercial in nature, such as the Nagaur Cattle Fair, purely religious, such as Gangaur, which commemorates the love between Shiva and Parvati, a combination of both, such as the Pushkar Camel Fair, which is held at the sacred Pushkar Lake, or seasonal, celebrating the seasons. Whatever their impetus, fairs and festivals afford an integral social function, enabling villagers from remote regions to meet and mingle, marriage alliances to be contracted, livestock deals to be struck and rural issues (for example, market prices, drought control measures) to be discussed.

At all festivals, as much attention to detail in dress is accorded the animal participants as to the human ones. Camels are adorned with colourful tassels and bridles, magnificently embroidered or mirrored rugs and ornaments known as *gorbandhs*, which are made by new brides for their husbands' camels.

SANJAY SINGH BADNOR

SANJAY SINGH BADNOR

Top: Folk singers in the Sam Sand Dunes, near Jaisalmer.

Bottom: A dance performance at a local festival, Jhalawar.

Rajasthan's oldest, most well known and arguably most spectacular festival is the Pushkar Camel Fair, which is held annually in November at the small village of Pushkar, near Ajmer. This fair fulfils both a religious and commercial role, enabling thousands of devotees from around the country to bathe in the sacred Pushkar Lake on the auspicious date of Kartik Purnima , while also providing a temporary marketplace for traders in livestock to parade their elaborately bedecked and groomed beasts before potential buyers. It is a spectacle *par excellence*, with thousands of participants, Ferris wheels, a 'tent city' established to accommodate everyone, and of course, plenty of camels.

SARA-JANE CLELAND

SARA-JANE CLELAND

SARA-JANE CLELAND

Top, Middle & Bottom: Scenes from the Pushkar Camel Fair.

ADAM MCCROW

Top: Dressed for the occasion – Jaisalmer Desert Festival.

Bottom: Hirsute hopefuls in traditional garb line up in the Mr Desert competition, Jaisalmer Desert Festival.

ADAM MCCROW

Some festivals have been established purely to attract overseas visitors, such as Jaisalmer's Desert Festival, which is held each year in late January/early February, corresponding with the peak tourist season. Despite its blatant rupee-driven impetus, if you're in camel's spit of Jaisalmer, it's a spectacle which shouldn't be missed, with villagers and townspeople donning traditional garb, dozens of elaborately caparisoned camels, traditional dances and music, camel polo matches and more. This is a great time to visit the Sam Sand Dunes near Jaisalmer, when traditional musicians attempt to outdo each other in musical virtuosity, and camel races take place across the dunes. The Mr Desert competition attracts a swag of mustachioed hopefuls.

Festivals which are celebrated nationwide, such as Holi and Diwali appear, when celebrated in this state, to be injected with that curious Rajasthani element of verve and zest which sets them apart from the rest of the country. Holi, for example, the Festival of Colours, which takes place in March, truly lives up to its name in Rajasthan, where the flinging of coloured dye achieves new heights of spirited abandon. In the days of the princely states, subjects gleefully threw coloured water at their maharajas, and princes played Holi with the ladies of the *zenana* (women's quarters). Even today, in Jaisalmer and Udaipur, Holi revellers enter the former royal compounds and engage in uninhibited colour drenching of their former rulers. Westerners are, of course, not immune from the revelry, and your best bet, should you find yourself in Rajasthan at this time, is to don your oldest clothes and resign yourself to being completely drenched with wet and often indelible colour. Men and women, old and young, rich and poor – everyone enters into the spirit of Holi, with faces, hair and clothes smeared in pink, yellow and green dye. Even the cows lumbering through the streets are an unsettling and vibrant pink!

Weddings are also celebrated with typical Rajasthani enthusiasm. During the peak wedding season – around February and March – marriage parties, known as *baraats*, can be seen parading through the streets of towns and villages across the state, led by a motorised or hand-pulled 'stage' on which a singer waxes lyrical upon the virtues of love (despite the fact that most marriages are arranged!), his voice amplified 100-fold through a bank of loudspeakers. Astride a white horse, the groom is borne to a gaily decorated *mandap* (pavilion), usually at the bride's house, where the vows are made and the guests are entertained by hired entertainers such as musicians, *hijiras* (eunuchs who dress effeminately) and singers.

Traditional dances play a large role in the celebration of religious festivals such as Navratri and Dussehra, during both of which women dance the *ghoomer*. During Holi, the Bhil tribal people dance the *gir*. In either August or September, in the small village of Ramdevra in western Rajasthan, female dancers perform the *terahtal* in honour of the local deity Ramdevji.

Left: Children smeared with coloured dyes during the festivities of Holi, Jaisalmer.

Right: Hijiras make appearances at births and weddings.

MICHELLE COXALL

MICHELLE COXALL

sleeping pills. Don't accept drinks or food from strangers no matter how friendly they seem, particularly if you're on your own.

Beware also of your fellow travellers. Unhappily there are more than a few backpackers who make the money go further by helping themselves to other people's.

If you do have something stolen, you're going to have to report it to the police. You'll also need a statement proving you have done so if you want to claim on insurance.

Insurance companies, despite their rosy promises of full protection and speedy settlement of claims, are just as disbelieving as the Indian police and will often attempt every devious trick in the book to avoid paying out on a baggage claim.

Stolen Travellers' Cheques If you're unlucky enough to have things stolen, some precautions can ease the pain. All travellers' cheques are replaceable, although this does you little immediate good if you have to go home and apply to your bank. What you want is instant replacement. Furthermore, what do you do if you lose your cheques and money and have a day or more to travel to the replacement office? The answer is to keep an emergency cash-stash in a totally separate place. In that same place you should keep a record of the cheque serial numbers, proof of purchase slips and your passport number.

American Express makes considerable noise about 'instant replacement' of their cheques but a lot of people find out, to their cost, that without a number of precautions 'instantly' can take longer than you think. If you don't have the receipt you were given when you bought the cheques, rapid replacement will be difficult. Obviously the receipt should be kept separate from the cheques, and a photocopy in yet another location doesn't hurt either. Chances are you'll be able to get a limited amount of funds on the spot, and the rest will be available when the bank has verified your initial purchase of the cheques. American Express have a 24 hour number in Delhi (☎ (011) 687-5050) which you must ring within 24 hours of the theft.

> **WARNING**
> **Carbon-Monoxide Poisoning**
> Although there have been no reports of carbon-monoxide poisoning in Rajasthan, it is important to be aware of this danger if you intend travelling on to cold climates in India. Tragically, a number of people have died, including a young English couple in Darjeeling in 1996, of carbon-monoxide poisoning due to burning charcoal in their poorly ventilated hotel rooms. Avoid lighting charcoal-fuelled fires; ask the proprietor for more blankets if you need to get warm. If you do wish to light a fire, ensure that the room is well ventilated and that the fuel you use does not give off toxic fumes. ■

LEGAL MATTERS

If you find yourself in a sticky legal predicament, contact your embassy. You should carry your passport with you at all times.

In the Indian justice system it seems the burden of proof is on the accused, and proving one's innocence is virtually impossible. The police forces are often corrupt and will pay 'witnesses' to give evidence.

Drugs

For a long time India was a place where you could indulge in all sorts of illegal drugs (mostly grass and hashish) with relative ease – they were cheap, readily available and the risks were minimal. These days things have changed. Although dope is still widely available, the risks have certainly increased. Penalties for possession, use and trafficking in illegal drugs are strictly enforced. If convicted on a drugs-related charge, sentences are long (*minimum* of 10 years), even for minor offences, and there is no remission or parole.

So, if you partake in drugs, be aware of the risks.

BUSINESS HOURS

Government offices are open from 10 am to 5 pm, Monday to Saturday, and are closed every second Saturday. Banks are open 10 am to 2 pm Monday to Friday, and 10 am to noon on every second Saturday. Travellers' cheque transactions usually cease 30 minutes before the official bank closing time. In Jaipur, at least one bank opens for several hours in the afternoon when travellers' cheques can be exchanged. See that chapter for details. Shops and offices are usually closed on Sunday and public holidays. In popular tourist areas such as Jaisalmer and Pushkar, most shops open around 9 am, and close at around 7 pm. About half close on Sunday.

PUBLIC HOLIDAYS & SPECIAL EVENTS

Festivals in Rajasthan generally take one of three forms: purely religious festivals; tourist-oriented festivals; and *melas*, or fairs, such as the Pushkar Camel Fair, which provide opportunities for villagers from remote regions to trade livestock and socialise. In this last category, fairs can also have a religious element – villagers attending the Pushkar Camel Fair, for example, take advantage of their visit to

---

FESTIVALS OF RAJASTHAN

Festivals which are celebrated across the entire state of Rajasthan are given below. Many of these are nationwide celebrations.

February-March

Shivratri – This day of fasting is dedicated to Lord Shiva; his followers believe that it was on this day he danced the *tandava* (the Dance of Destruction). Processions to the temples are followed by the chanting of mantras and anointing of *lingams* (phallic symbols).

Holi – This is one of the most exuberant Hindu festivals, with people marking the end of winter by throwing coloured water and red powder known as *gulal* at one another. On the night before Holi, bonfires are built to symbolise the destruction of the evil demon Holika. Rajasthanis celebrate Holi with particular enthusiasm, and foreign visitors are considered fair game for a dousing with gulal. It's great fun, and your best bet is just to give yourself up to the revelry, wear your oldest clothes, and expect to look like a *gulaab jamun* (red sticky sweet) at the end of the day. Udaipur and Jaisalmer are both excellent places to celebrate Holi.

March-April

Gangaur – This festival is a celebration of love – that between Shiva and his consort, Gauri, or Parvati, to be precise – and is a favourite with the women of Rajasthan. At this time, unmarried girls pay homage to Gauri in the hope that they will be blessed with a good husband. Married women pray for the long life and health of their husbands. Images of Gauri are garbed in colourful vestments and carried through the streets in processions. Women perform the *ghoomer* dance at this time, and married women try to be at their husbands' sides during the festival. Jaipur, Bikaner, Jodhpur, Nathdwara and Jaisalmer all host colourful celebrations of Gangaur.

Ramanavami – In temples all over India the birth of Rama, an incarnation of Vishnu and hero of the *Ramayana*, is celebrated on this day. In the week leading up to Ramanavami, the *Ramayana* is widely read and performed.

April-May

Baisakhi – This Sikh festival commemorates the day that Guru Govind Singh founded the Khalsa, the Sikh brotherhood, which adopted the five *kakkars* (means by which Sikh men recognise each other) as part of their code of behaviour. The *Granth Sahib*, the Sikh holy book, is read through at *gurudwaras* (Sikh temples). Feasts and dancing follow in the evening.

July-August

Teej – Also known as the Festival of Swings, a reference to the flower-bedecked swings which are erected at this time, Teej celebrates the onset of the monsoon, and is held in honour of the marriage of Shiva and Parvati.

Naag Panchami – This festival is dedicated to Ananta, the serpent upon whose coils Vishnu rested between universes. Offerings are made to snake images, and snake charmers do a roaring trade.

Raksha Bandhan (Narial Purnima) – On the full-moon day of the Hindu month of Sravana, girls fix amulets known as *rakhis* to their brothers' wrists to protect them in the coming year. The brothers give their sisters gifts. A woman can gain the brotherly protection of a man who is not actually her brother by giving him a rakhi. Political expediency encouraged the maharani of Chittorgarh to

this holy village by bathing in the sacred lake and offering *pujas* (prayers) at the temples.

Hindu Lunar Months

The months of the Hindu lunar calendar *(vikram samvat)* and their Gregorian equivalents are as follows:

Chaitra	March-April
Vaishaka	April-May
Jyaistha	May-June
Asadha	June-July
Sravana	July-August
Bhadra	August-September
Asvina	September-October
Kartika	October-November
Aghan	November-December
Pausa	December-January
Magha	January-February
Phalguna	February-March

honour the Emperor Humayun in this manner. The emperor was then compelled to try to save the Chittorgarh Fort from the Sultan of Gujarat.

Janmashtami – The anniversary of Krishna's birth is celebrated with happy abandon in tune with Krishna's own mischievous moods.

Independence Day – This holiday on 15 August celebrates the anniversary of India's independence from Britain in 1947. The prime minister delivers an address from the ramparts of Delhi's Red Fort.

August-September

Ganesh Chaturthi – This festival, held on the fourth day of the Hindu month Bhadra, is dedicated to Ganesh, the god of wisdom and prosperity. It is considered to be the most auspicious day of the year, but to look at the moon on this day is considered unlucky.

Shravan Purnima – After a day long fast, high-caste Hindus replace the sacred thread which they always wear looped over their left shoulder.

September-October

Dussehra – Dussehra is celebrated by Hindus all over India in the month of Asvina. Kota, in southern Rajasthan, celebrates Dussehra with a large mela (festival). Dussehra celebrates the victory of Rama over the king of Lanka, Ravana.

Gandhi Jayanti – This is a solemn celebration of Mahatma Gandhi's birthday on 2 October.

October-November

Diwali (Deepavali) – This is the happiest festival of the Hindu calendar, celebrated on the 15th day of Kartika. At night countless oil lamps are lit to show Rama the way home from his period of exile. The festival runs over five days.

Govardhana Puja – This is a Hindu festival dedicated to that holiest of animals, the cow.

Nanak Jayanti – The birthday of Guru Nanak, the founder of the Sikh religion, is celebrated with prayer readings and processions.

November-December

Christmas Day – A holiday in India.

Muslim Holidays

The dates of the Muslim festivals are not fixed; they fall about 11 days earlier each year.

Ramadan
The most important Muslim festival is a 30 day dawn-to-dusk fast. It was during this month that the prophet Mohammed had the Koran revealed to him in Mecca. Ramadan starts around 10 January 1997, 31 December 1998, and 20 December 1999.

Id-ul-Fitr
This day celebrates the end of Ramadan.

Id-ul-Zuhara
This is a Muslim festival commemorating Abraham's attempt to sacrifice his son. It is celebrated with prayers and feasts.

Muharram
Muharram is a 10 day festival commemorating the martyrdom of Mohammed's grandson, Imam Hussain.

REGIONAL FESTIVAL CALENDAR

Descriptions of regional festivals are included at the beginning of individual chapters. The following is a quick reference for dates of regional fairs and festivals up to the year 2000.

Festival/Fair	Lunar Calendar	1996	1997	1998	1999	2000
Bikaner Camel Festival	Pausa 14	4-5 Jan	22-23 Jan	11-12 Jan	1-2 Jan	20-21 Jan
Nagaur Fair	Magha 7-10	26-30 Jan	13-16 Feb	3-6 Feb	24-27 Jan	12-15 Feb
Jaisalmer Desert Festival	Magha 13-15	2-4 Feb	20-22 Feb	9-11 Feb	29-31 Jan	17-19 Feb
Jaipur Elephant Festival	Phalguna 15	4 Mar	23 Mar	12 Mar	1 Mar	19 Mar
Gangaur Fair, Jaipur	Chaitra 3-4	22-23 Mar	10-11 Apr	30-31 Mar	20-21 Mar	7-8 Apr
Mewar Festival, Udaipur	Chaitra 3-4	22-23 Mar	10-11 Apr	30-31 Mar	20-21 Mar	7-8 Apr
Teej Fair, Jaipur	Sravana 3-4	17-18 Aug	6-7 Aug	26-27 Aug	14-15 Aug	2-3 Aug
Marwar Festival, Jodhpur	Asvina 14-15	25-26 Oct	15-16 Oct	4-5 Oct	23-24 Oct	12-13 Oct
Pushkar Camel Fair	Kartika 12-15	22-25 Nov	11-14 Nov	1-4 Nov	20-23 Nov	9-11 Nov
Dussehra Mela, Kota	Asvina 8-10	19-21 Oct	9-11 Oct	29 Sep-1 Oct	17-19 Oct	5-7 Oct
Chandrabhaga Fair, Jhalawar	Kartika 14	24-26 Nov	13-15 Nov	2-4 Nov	22-24 Nov	10-12 Nov

ACTIVITIES

Camel Safaris

It seems just about everyone in Rajasthan is offering camel safaris these days. An old favourite is in the environs of Jaisalmer, in western Rajasthan, where it's possible to take a safari lasting from one day up to a week or more. Prices vary according to what is provided, ranging from budget safaris which start at around Rs 150 per day, up to deluxe models which can cost up to Rs 800 per day. The environs of Pushkar are also popular for camel safaris, and a couple of operators in Shekhawati are now offering camel treks around those towns with the most interesting painted havelis of this semi-arid region. Several operators in Bikaner (western Rajasthan) also offer camel safaris. See the relevant chapters for more details.

Horse Safaris

Ghanerao Tours in Jaipur offers exclusive horse safaris mainly in southern Rajasthan, visiting historic monuments, temples and other attractions. At night you recharge your batteries by living like royalty at exotic castles, forts and havelis. Itineraries can be arranged to visitors' requirements. See under Other Tours in the Jaipur chapter for details.

Aravali Safari & Tours, also in Jaipur, can arrange horse safaris in southern Rajasthan

See under Travel Agencies and Other Tours in the Jaipur chapter for details.

Water Sports

The RTDC is developing water sports at Ramgarh Lake, 35 km north-east of Jaipur. These include rowing boats, pedal boats and motorboats. Unfortunately similar activities are planned for beautiful Lake Pichola at Udaipur. Rates will be around Rs 20 per person per hour for a pedal boat, and Rs 50 to Rs 100 per person per hour for a motor boat. In future the RTDC is planning to introduce parasailing, waterskiing, wind surfing and water scooters at both Ramgarh and Lake Pichola. See the relevant chapter for details.

Cycling

Ramesh Jangid (see under Nawalgarh in the Northern Rajasthan chapter) can organise cycling tours around the villages of Shekhawati, including informative commentaries on the remarkable paintings of this region.

Trekking

Various operators can organise treks in the Aravalli Range of Rajasthan. The busy Ramesh Jangid from Nawalgarh in the Shekhawati region organises treks including guide, all meals, transport and accommodation in village homes and *dharamsalas* (pilgrims' lodgings). See under Nawalgarh in the Northern Rajasthan chapter for details.

Aravali Safari & Tours in Jaipur can also organise treks in the Aravalli Range. Registhan Tours Pvt Ltd in Jaipur organises treks in the Udaipur region. See the Jaipur chapter for details.

Music, Dance & Drama

Few operators have taken advantage of the vast opportunities for cultural tourism in Rajasthan. Ramesh Jangid from Nawalgarh (see the Northern Rajasthan chapter) can organise ethnological tours around Rajasthan.

COURSES

Meditation Retreats

The Dhammathali Vispasana Meditation Centre near Jaipur runs free courses in meditation for both beginners and more advanced students throughout the year at its centre near the Galta (temple of the sun god), about three km east of Jaipur. See the Jaipur chapter for details.

The Brahma Kumaris Spiritual University is at Mt Abu, and has branches around the world. It is possible to attend introductory courses in raja yoga meditation here. Residential courses are also offered, but these need to be organised through one of the 4000 overseas branches of the university before arrival in India. See under Mt Abu in the Southern Rajasthan chapter for more details.

Ramesh Jangid, from Nawalgarh, in the Shekhawati region (Northern Rajasthan), can organise on request supervised yoga, meditation, nutrition and fasting courses for groups at his Apani Dhani (Eco Farm). See under Nawalgarh in the Northern Rajasthan chapter for Ramesh Jangid's contact details.

Polo & Horse Riding

It is possible to learn horse polo and other equestrian skills at the Royal Equestrian Polo Centre at the tiny village of Dundlod, in the Shekhawati region of northern Rajasthan. See that chapter for more details. The Pratap Country Inn, near Udaipur, offers horse riding lessons for beginners. See under Udaipur in the Southern Rajasthan chapter for details.

Music & Dance

It is possible to learn traditional music and dance at the Maharaja Sawai Mansingh Sangeet Mahavidyalaya in Jaipur. See the Jaipur chapter for details.

Painting

In Jhunjhunu, in the heart of the Shekhawati region, it's possible to learn traditional Shekhawati painting from a local artist. See the Northern Rajasthan chapter for details.

Tuition in miniature painting is available in Jaipur. See the Jaipur chapter for details.

VOLUNTARY WORK

Numerous charities and international aid agencies have branches in India and, although they're mostly staffed by locals, there are some opportunities for foreigners. It may be possible to find temporary volunteer work when you are in India. However, you'll probably be of more use to the charity concerned if you write in advance and, if they need you, stay for long enough to be of help.

For information on specific charities in India, contact the main branches in your own country. For long-term posts, the following organisations may be able to help or offer advice and further contacts:

Australian Volunteers Abroad: Overseas Service Bureau Programme
   PO Box 350, Fitzroy Vic 3065, Australia
   (☎ (03) 9279-1788; fax (03) 9416-1619)
Co-ordinating Committee for International Voluntary Service
   c/o UNESCO, 1 rue Miollis, F-75015 Paris, France (☎ (01) 45 68 27 31)
Council of International Programs (CIP)
   1101 Wilson Blvd Ste 1708, Arlington VA 22209, USA (☎ (703) 527-1160)
International Voluntary Service (IVS)
   St John's Church Centre, Edinburgh EH2 4BJ, UK (☎ (0131) 226-6722)
Peace Corps of the USA
   1990 K St NW, Washington DC 20526, USA (☎ (202) 606-3970; fax (202) 606-3110)
Voluntary Service Overseas (VSO)
   317 Putney Bridge Rd, London SW15 2PN, UK (☎ (0181) 780-2266; fax 780-1326)

Help in Suffering

Help in Suffering is an animal hospital in Jaipur funded by the World Society for the Protection of Animals (London) and Animaux Secours, Arthaz, France. The philosophy of Help in Suffering is to create a 'friendly, rabies-free healthy street dog population'.

It takes voluntary vets 20 minutes to desex dogs, at an average cost of Rs 300 per dog (which covers a collar, tattoo, overheads and the rabies vaccination). Qualified vets interested in working with Help in Suffering in a voluntary capacity should write to: Help in Suffering, Maharani Farm, Durgapura, Jaipur, Rajasthan 302018. Voluntary donations are gratefully accepted, and can be forwarded to: Help in Suffering, 12 Victoria Place, Paddington, NSW, Australia.

SOS Worldwide

SOS, which has its headquarters in Vienna, runs over 30 programmes across India and celebrated its 30th year in India in 1995. The society looks after orphaned, destitute and abandoned children, which are cared for by unmarried women, abandoned wives and widows. In Jaipur, SOS has a fine garden-surrounded property, and cares for over 144 children and young adults aged from birth to 25 years. Children live in 'families' of up to 10 children with a 'mother' in semi-detached

homes on the grounds, and are all provided with education.

Volunteers are welcome at the centre, to teach English, help the children with their homework and simply to join in their games. Monetary donations are also gratefully accepted, as are clothes in good condition, games, and sporting equipment. It is also possible to sponsor a child. Prospective sponsors should specify the age and sex of the child they would like to sponsor, and will receive details of the child, progress reports and a photograph. For more information on either voluntary work at SOS or child sponsorship, write to SOS Children's Village, Opposite Pital Factory, Jhotwara Rd, Jaipur 302016 (☎ 32-2393; fax 31-8140).

Les Amis du Shekhawati

The aim of the Friends of Shekhawati is to safeguard and preserve Shekhawati's rich artistic heritage including both the remarkable paintings of this region, and the havelis themselves. The society's work includes educating local villagers about the social and artistic importance of the paintings of Shekhawati, as well as undertaking restoration work and promoting the region. Ramesh Jangid (see under Nawalgarh in the Northern Rajasthan chapter) is the president of the association. He welcomes volunteers keen to preserve the paintings of Shekhawati. For more information, or to become a member of the society (FF 200), write to Les Amis du Shekhawati, 70 Rue Bonaparte, 75006 Paris.

Urmul Trust

This trust was founded by Mr Sanjay Gosh in 1986. The main aims of the trust are to provide primary health care and education to the people of the remote villages of the desert; raise awareness among the women of the desert of their rights and privileges in society; and promote the handicrafts of rural artisans and cut out middlemen and commissions, with profits going directly to artisans.

Those interested in volunteer work with the trust should contact the secretary at the Urmul Trust (☎ (0151) 52-3093), inside Urmul Dairy, Ganganagar Rd, Bikaner (adjacent to he bus station). There is work available in ocial welfare, teaching English, health care, nd other projects. Even if you don't have kills in these areas, Urmul may have positions n implementation and overseeing of projects. A high level of commitment is required. Donaions are also gratefully accepted.

ACCOMMODATION

There is accommodation in Rajasthan to suit ll budgets, from budget guest houses and notels at less than US$5 per night to some of ndia's most luxurious hotels, most of which nave been converted from forts and palaces.

In the desert village of Khuri, 40 km from aisalmer, it's possible to stay in a *jhonpa*, a raditional mud hut with a thatched roof; in Pushkar, one place is offering accommodaion to travellers in treehouses; or you can always sleep under the stars on the Sam sand dunes.

Tourist Bungalows

The Rajasthan Tourism Development Cororation (RTDC) has a good network of ourist bungalows throughout the state. Generally there is a non-veg restaurant on the premises, and sometimes a bar or 'beer hop'. Frequently the local tourist office is also on the same premises, which is handy or information. Prices for doubles range rom Rs 100 to Rs 700, and three types of ooms are usually available, all with attached bathroom: ordinary rooms (Rs 100 to Rs 300) nave ceiling fans and, in some instances, may only have cold water; deluxe rooms (Rs 300 o Rs 500) have air coolers; super-deluxe ooms (Rs 450 to Rs 700) are carpeted and nave air-conditioning. Most tourist bungaows also have dormitories with attached aths; beds cost Rs 50 per person.

Railway Retiring Rooms

Railway retiring rooms are just like regular notels or dormitories except they are at the ailway stations. To stay here you are generlly supposed to have a railway ticket or ndrail Pass. The rooms are extremely conenient if you have an early train departure, lthough they can be noisy if it is a busy station. They are often very cheap and in some places they are also excellent value. In Jaisalmer, the railway retiring rooms are in a cluster of small jhonpas, opposite the railway station.

Cheap Hotels

There are cheap hotels all over Rajasthan, ranging from filthy, uninhabitable dives (but with prices at rock bottom) up to quite reasonable places. Ceiling fans, mosquito nets on the beds, private toilets and bathrooms are all possibilities, even in rooms which cost Rs 120 or less per night for a double.

Although prices are generally quoted in this book for singles and doubles, most hotels will put an extra bed in a room to make a triple for about an extra 25%. In some smaller hotels it's often possible to bargain a little if you really want to. On the other hand, these places will often put their prices up if there's a shortage of accommodation.

Expensive Hotels

Rajasthan has a disproportionate number of expensive hotels, largely due to its tourist appeal. As well, many former maharajas have been compelled to convert their beautiful forts and palaces into swanky hotels to bring in the tourist dollars. (See under Palaces, Forts & Castles, following.) In Jaipur, there are also five star hotels belonging to the Holiday Inn and Sheraton groups.

Palaces, Forts & Castles

Rajasthan is famous for its delightful palace hotels. The most well known are the Lake Palace Hotel and Shiv Niwas Palace in Udaipur, the Rambagh Palace in Jaipur and the Umaid Bhawan Palace in Jodhpur (where the Maharani suite will set you back a mere US$850 *per night*). Standards and facilities at these places are world class.

You don't have to spend a fortune to stay in a palace, however. There are plenty of smaller ones which are more moderately priced. Throughout the state there are many finely appointed historical buildings which have been converted into tourist accommodation known as Heritage Hotels. These include havelis, forts and former royal hunting lodges. RTDC tourist offices have a brochure listing Heritage Hotels.

Homestays

Staying with an Indian family can be a real education. It's a change from dealing strictly with tourist-oriented people, and a good opportunity to experience everyday Indian life.

Rajasthan's homestay programme, known as the Paying Guest Scheme, operates in Jaipur, Jodhpur, Udaipur, Bundi, Jaisalmer, Bikaner, Ajmer and Pushkar. The cost is anything from Rs 50 per day upwards, depending on the level of facilities offered, but most places charge Rs 100 to Rs 200. Meals are available with prior notice.

The scheme is administered by the RTDC, and tourist offices have comprehensive lists of the families offering this service.

Geysers

Many places to stay have geysers as the source of water. These are simply small hot water tanks.

Taxes & Service Charges

The state government imposes a variety of taxes on hotel accommodation (and restaurants). At most rock-bottom hotels you won't have to pay any taxes. Once you get into the top end of budget places, and certainly for mid-range accommodation, you will have to pay something. As a general rule, you can assume that room rates over about Rs 250 will attract a 10% (sometimes just 5%) tax. Most mid-range and all luxury hotels attract a 10% loading.

Another common tax, which is additional to the above, is a service charge which is pegged at 10%. In some hotels, this is only levied on food, room service and use of telephones, not on the accommodation costs. At others, it's levied on the total bill. If you're trying to keep costs down, don't sign up meals or room service to your room bill and keep telephone use to a minimum if you know that service charge is levied on the total bill.

Rates quoted in this book are the basic rate only unless otherwise indicated. Taxes and service charges are extra.

Seasonal Variations

In the winter months (December to February) hoteliers crank up their prices by a factor of two to three times the low-season price.

Conversely, in the low season (May to August), prices at even normally expensive hotels can be surprisingly reasonable.

Touts

Hordes of accommodation touts operate in many towns in Rajasthan – Jaipur, Ajmer, Pushkar, Udaipur and Jaisalmer in particular – and at any international airport terminal. Very often they are the rickshaw-wallah who meet you at the bus or railway station. They earn a commission from hoteliers for taking you to their hotel. Some very good cheap hotels simply refuse to pay the tout and you'll then hear lots of stories about the hotel you want being 'full', 'closed for repairs', 'no good any more' or even 'burnt down'. On one occasion, a traveller was informed that the hotel of their choice had been bombed! (It hadn't.) Nine chances out of 10 they will be just that – stories.

Touts do have a use though – if you arrive in a town when some big festival is on, or during peak season, they will take you to a place where they know there are rooms available.

FOOD
Rajasthani Cuisine

Considering the paucity of fresh fruit and vegetables in the arid zones, Rajasthan has a surprising variety of regional dishes. Local restaurants, which are known elsewhere in the country as *dhabas*, are often known as *bhojanalyas* in Rajasthan, from *bhojan* (food or meal), and *alya* (place).

Vegetarian dishes include *govind gatta*, lentil paste with dried fruit and nuts which is rolled into a sausage shape, cut into slices and deep fried. *Papad ki sabzi* is simply papadam with vegetables and *masala* (mixed spices). *Alu mangori* is a ground lentil paste which is dried in the sun and then put in a curry with potatoes *(alu)*. Once rolled by hand, it is now often forced through a machine in the same way as macaroni. *Alu singade* are pastry cones stuffed with spicy potato.

Mogri mangori is also a curry. Mogri is a type of desert bean. A sweeter version is *methi mangori* – methi is the leaves of a green desert vegetable. Another type of desert bean is *sangri*. It forms part of the dish *kair sangri*; kair is a small round desert fruit which grows on a prickly shrub and is a particular favourite of camels. *Kachri* is a type of desert fruit which is made into a chutney. *Dana methi* consists of a preparation of a small pea-shaped vegetables *(dana)* and methi which are boiled and mixed with sugar, masala and dried fruit. *Cheelra ka saag* is a *gram* (legume) flour paste *chapati* (unleavened bread) which is chopped up, fried, and then added to a curry.

Hunting or *shikhar* was an important Rajput tradition and this introduced a variety of game to the dinner table, including venison, peacock, quail, duck and wild boar. Non-veg dishes include *sule*, which is barbecued meat (usually mutton), and *khade masala ka keema*, which is minced meat *(keema)* with whole spices *(khade)*. Some meat dishes are cooked in an earthenware pot known as a *handi*. *Hari mirch ka keema* is minced meat with green chillies. *Maas ke sule* is a type of kebab made from roasted or charcoal-grilled meat placed on skewers.

Cereal dishes include *kabooli Jodhpuri*, which has meat, vegetables such as cauliflower, cabbage and peas, and fried gram paste balls. *Khichri* is a mix of cereals including millet which is added to meat dishes. *Dalia ki khichri* is wheat porridge *(dalia)*, mixed with masala, a little *gur* (jaggery, or raw sugar) and *ghee* (clarified butter). *Ghaat* is a corn porridge served with yoghurt.

Breads *(roti)* include *sogra*, a millet chapati; *makki roti*, a delicious thick corn chapati; and *dhokla*, maize flour which is steamed and formed into cubes or balls and cooked with green coriander, spinach and mint, and eaten with chutney. A *purat roti* is a type of Rajasthani filo pastry. The roti is repeatedly coated with oil and folded so that when it is cooked it is light and fluffy. *Bati* is a popular Rajasthani bread, traditionally buried in the sand and left to bake in the scorching desert sun. Once cooked, a generous amount of ghee is applied. Today bati is usually baked in an oven. *Saadi bati* is a ball of wheat flour paste which is baked. *Bafle bati* is steamed wheat flour balls. *Cheelre* is a gram powder paste chapati. *Masala bati* is wheat balls stuffed with masala, peas and peanuts.

Pickles and chutneys, known as *achars*, include *goonde achar*; goonde is a green fruit that is boiled and mixed with mustard oil and masalas. *Kair achar* is a pickle which uses a desert bean as its base. *Lahsun achar* is an onion pickle. *Lal mirch* is a garlic-stuffed red chilli. *Kamrak ka achar* is a pickle with kamrak, a type of desert vegetable with a pungent, sour taste. *Bathua raita* is a raita (similar to Greek *tzatziki*) which has the leaves of a plant (bathua) which is used like spinach. It is boiled, rinsed, made into a paste and mixed with yoghurt.

Sweets include *lapsi*, which is jaggery with a wheat flour porridge; *kheer*, or rice pudding with cardamom and saffron, a favourite throughout north India; and *mal pua*, a small, sweet chapati made from wheat flour, turned into a paste, rolled in sugar and fried.

Badam ki barfi is a type of almond fudge made from sugar, powdered milk, almonds and ghee. *Chakki* is a small piece of *barfi* (a type of milk-based fudge) made from gram flour, sugar and milk cake. *Churma* is a sweet of gram flour, sugar, cardamom, ghee and dried fruits. *Ghewar* is a paste of *urad* cereal which is crushed, deep fried and then dipped in a sugar syrup. It is served hot. *Feeni* is a ball-shaped sweet made from threads of urad cereal, deep fried and then dipped in sugar syrup. *Sooji halwa* is semolina pudding. *Meetha chaval* is sweet boiled rice. *Alu ki jalebi*, or fried potato-paste sweets, are made from a mashed potato mixture, sugar, saffron and arrowroot. The mixture is made into spirals and fried in hot oil, then soaked in a warm sugar syrup. This popular sweet is usually served hot.

Paan

An Indian meal should properly be finished with *paan* – the name given to the collection of spices and condiments chewed with betel nut. Found throughout eastern Asia, betel is a mildly intoxicating and addictive nut, but by itself it is quite inedible. After a meal you chew paan as a mild digestive.

Paan sellers have a whole collection of little trays, boxes and containers in which they mix either *saadha* 'plain' or *mithaa* 'sweet' paans. The ingredients may include, apart from the betel nut itself, lime paste (the ash not the fruit), the powder known as *catachu*, various spices and even a dash of opium in a pricey paan. The whole concoction is folded up in a piece of edible leaf which you pop in your mouth and chew. When finished you spit the leftovers out and add another red blotch to the pavement. Over a long period of time, indulgence in paan will turn your teeth red-black and even addict you to the betel nut. Trying one occasionally won't do you any harm.

DRINKS
Non-Alcoholic Drinks

Tea & Coffee Surprisingly, tea is not the all-purpose and all-important drink in India that it is in Iran and Afghanistan. What's worse, the Indians, for all the tea they grow, make some of the most hideously over-sweetened, murkily-milky excuses for that fine beverage that you'll ever see. Still, many travellers like Indian *chai* (tea) and it is cheap. At railway stations it is often served in small clay pots, which you then smash on the ground when empty. Unfortunately, these days chai-wallahs are increasingly using plastic cups which are not nearly as environmentally friendly.

Better tea can be obtained if you ask for 'tray tea', which gives you the tea, the milk and the sugar separately and allows you to combine them as you see fit. Unless you specify otherwise, tea is 'mixed tea' or 'milk tea', which means it has been made by putting cold water, milk, sugar and tea into one pot and bringing the whole concoction to the boil, then letting it stew for a long time. The result can be imagined.

It's almost impossible to get a decent cup of coffee in the north. Even in an expensive restaurant instant coffee is almost always used. The branches of the Indian Coffee House (there's one in Jaipur) are one of the few places with decent coffee.

Water In the big cities, the water is chlorinated and safe to drink, although if you've just arrived in India, the change from what you are used to drinking is in itself enough to bring on a mild dose of the runs.

Outside the cities you're on your own. Some travellers drink the water everywhere and never get sick, others are more careful and still get hit with a bug. Basically, you should not drink the water in small towns unless you know it has been boiled, and definitely avoid the street vendors' carts everywhere. Even in the better class of hotel and restaurant, the water is usually only filtered and not boiled. The local water filters remove solids and do nothing towards removing any bacteria. Water is generally safer in the dry season than in the monsoon when it really can be dangerous.

See the Health section for further information.

Mineral Water Most travellers to India these days avoid tap water altogether and stick to mineral water. It is available virtually everywhere, and comes in one litre plastic bottles. The price ranges from Rs 12 to Rs 30, with Rs 18 being about the average. Brand names include Bisleri, India King, Officer's Choice, Honeydew and Aqua Safe.

Virtually all the so-called mineral water available is actually treated tap water. A recent reliable survey found that 65% of the available mineral waters were less than totally pure, and in some cases were worse than what comes out of the tap! Generally, though, if you stick to bottled water, any gut problems you might have will be from other sources – food, dirty utensils, dirty hands, etc. (See under Basic Rules in the Health section earlier.).

Soft Drinks Soft drinks are a safe substitute for water. Coca-Cola got the boot from India a number of years back for not co-operating with the government, but both they and Pepsi Cola are back with a vengeance. There are many similar indigenous brands with names like Campa Cola, Thums Up, Limca, Gold Spot or Double Seven. They are reasonably priced at around Rs 7 for a 250 ml bottle (more in restaurants). They're sickly sweet.

Juices & Other Drinks One very pleasant escape from the sickly sweet soft drinks is apple juice, sold for Rs 4 per glass from the Himachal fruit stands found at many railway stations. Also good are the small cardboard boxes of various fruit juices. For Rs 6 these are excellent, if a little sweet. Freshly squeezed orange juice is usually available at bus and train stations in Rajasthan.

Another alternative to soft drinks is soda water – Bisleri, Spencer's and other brands are widely available. Not only does it come in a larger bottle, but it is also cheaper – generally around Rs 3.50. With soda water you can get excellent, and safe, lemon squash sodas.

Falooda is a popular drink made with milk, nuts, cream and vermicelli strands. Finally there's *lassi*, that oh so cool, refreshing iced curd (yoghurt) drink. *Makhania lassi* is a delicious saffron-flavoured version.

Rajasthani Drinks *Chach* is a thin, salted lassi. *Jaljeera* is a mix of masalas and water. *Kairi chach* is unripe mango juice with water and salt. It is widely available in summer, and is allegedly a good remedy for sunstroke.

Alcohol
Alcohol is relatively expensive – a bottle of Indian beer can cost anything from Rs 23 up to Rs 160 in a flashy hotel; Rs 40 to Rs 60 is the usual price range. Indian beers have delightful names such as Golden Eagle, Rosy Pelican, Cannon Extra Strong, Bullet,

Black Label, Knock Out, Turbo, Kingfisher, Guru or Punjab.

Beer and other Indian interpretations of western alcoholic drinks are known as IMFL – Indian Made Foreign Liquor. They include imitations of whisky and brandy under a plethora of different brand names. The taste varies from hospital disinfectant to passable imitation whisky. Always buy the best brand.

With the continuing freeing up of the economy, it is likely that in the near future well known foreign brands of beer and spirits will be available.

Local drinks are known as country liquor and include *toddy*, a mildly alcoholic extract from the coconut palm flower, and *feni*, a distilled liquor produced from fermented cashew nuts or from coconuts. The two varieties taste quite different.

Arak is what the peasants (and bus drivers' best boys) drink to get blotto. It's a clear, distilled rice liquor and it creeps up on you without warning. Treat with caution and only ever drink it from a bottle produced in a government-controlled distillery. *Never, ever* drink it otherwise – hundreds of people die or are blinded every year in India as a result of drinking *arak* produced in illicit stills. You can assume it contains methyl alcohol (wood alcohol).

ENTERTAINMENT
The RTDC can often arrange cultural programmes for visitors. In Jaipur for example, they can put on a traditional Rajasthani banquet followed by performances of folk dances. While you're in Jaipur, it's also well worth seeing a film at the Raj Mandir cinema, which is decked out in 1920s style.

SPECTATOR SPORT
Cricket
In recent years, Jaipur's Mansingh Stadium (☎ (0141) 51-4732) has been the venue for several World Cup cricket matches (winter only). Tickets generally go on sale 10 days prior to the match, and matches are advertised in English-language papers. Telephone the stadium for details of forthcoming events.

Tennis

Some international tennis tournaments are held at the Jai Club, off MI Rd in Jaipur (near Panch Batti). Matches are generally well advertised, and tickets can often be obtained from sponsors. In 1996, the Bank of Baroda sponsored a Davis Cup match between India and the Netherlands.

Polo

Polo matches are played at the Polo Club (☎ (0141) 36-6492) in Jaipur, Bhawani Singh Rd, near the Rambagh Palace hotel, and at the polo ground in Jodhpur. The horse polo season is in March. During Jaipur's Elephant Festival, in March, matches of elephant polo are played. For more details, contact the tourist office.

THINGS TO BUY

Rajasthan really is one of the easiest places to spend money in India – there are so many colourful arts and crafts, busy bazaars, gorgeous fabrics, miniature paintings, and more. The cardinal rule when purchasing handicrafts is to bargain and bargain hard. You can get a good idea of what is reasonable in quality and price by visiting the Rajasthan state emporium, Rajasthali, in either New Delhi or Jaipur. Because prices are fixed, you will get an idea of how hard to bargain when you purchase similar items from regular dealers.

Be careful when buying items which include delivery to your home country. You may well be given assurances that the price includes home delivery and all customs and handling charges. Inevitably this is not the case, and you may find yourself having to collect the item yourself from your country's main port or airport, pay customs charges (which could be as much as 20% of the item's value) and handling charges levied by the airline or shipping company (which could be up to 10% of the value). If you can't collect the item promptly, or get someone to do it on your behalf, exorbitant storage charges may also be charged.

Unfortunately, the quality of Rajasthan's handicrafts is not always what it could be, particularly in paintings, which are produced in great numbers for tourist buyers. Sellers may claim that the paintings are antiques – they rarely are, but a proficient artist should be able to produce a good reproduction of an old miniature. Udaipur has some good shops specialising in modern reproductions which are copies of those painted in Mewar from the early 18th century. These are produced on many different surfaces such as cloth, paper and marble. Other good buys in Udaipur include jewellery, block-printed fabrics, *durries* (cotton rugs), lac bangles and wooden handicrafts.

Pushkar is lined with shops selling silver

Polo

Horse polo was very popular among the maharajas, especially during the British Raj. Maharajas often patronised this expensive game, providing polo ponies, facilities and training to talented players. Some of the Indian maharajas were among the top players in the world, such as Maharaja Man Singh of Jaipur, whose polo team was champion on the European polo circuit in the 1930s. The maharaja had a stable of some 40 ponies, who were shipped over to England. The team was accompanied by a carpenter (to keep them supplied with polo sticks). Man Singh actually died playing the sport he loved, at a polo match in England in 1970.

Emperor Akbar was believed to have been the first person to introduce rules to the game, but polo, as it is played today, was introduced by a British Cavalry Regiment stationed in India during the 1870s. A set of international rules was implemented after WWI.

The game flourished in India until Independence, when the level of patronage decreased and the game became less popular. Today there is a renewed interest in polo, and Rajasthan produces some of the nation's finest players. The Mewar (Udaipur) polo team has been one of the country's most successful both in India and abroad.

The Polo Bar at the Rambagh Palace hotel in Jaipur is dedicated to this sport of kings, and has photos of every great Indian polo player. ■

jewellery, much of it designed with western tastes in mind. Traditional silver folk jewellery, which is quite chunky, can be purchased in the bazaars of towns and cities, where jewellers sell items by weight. In Ajmer, you can buy other silver items such as cigarette and pill boxes. A good buy in Pushkar is painted and glass beads. Some travellers buy beads in large quantities which they make into attractive necklaces as gifts. Also in Pushkar you can buy attractive silk blouses with prices starting at around Rs 35. They're very light, so don't take up much space in your pack. But be warned: after several washes they tend to fray irreparably at the seams.

Another good buy in Pushkar is music cassettes featuring contemporary and classical Indian music. Prices are around Rs 50 per tape.

Durries can be good buys. Medium fine quality knotted carpets have between 150 to 160 knots per square inch, and cost somewhere in the vicinity of Rs 300 per square foot.

Jaipur is renowned for its blue-glazed pottery which features floral and geometric motifs. Its *meenakari* enamelwork, likewise, is beautifully crafted. Filigree animals and birds are richly coloured in ruby reds, blues, greens and whites. Also in Jaipur you can buy Sanganeri block-print fabrics which are produced in the nearby village of Sanganer. Other Rajasthani textiles can also be purchased in the bazaars of the pink city, such as *bandhani* tie and dye prints. It's worth visiting the Anokhi showroom in Jaipur (see that chapter), where printed fabrics in traditional and contemporary designs are made into fashionable western garments.

Kota is best known for its saris, while Mt Abu has a jumble of things to buy, including carpets, bronze Hindu deities and wooden items.

A Warning!

In touristy places such as Jaipur, take extreme care with the commission merchants – these guys hang around waiting to pick you up and cart you off to their favourite dealers where whatever you pay will have a hefty margin built into it to pay their commission. Stories about 'my family's place', 'my brother's shop' and 'special deal at my friend's place' are just stories and nothing more.

Whatever you might be told, if you are taken by a rickshaw driver or tout to a place, be it a hotel, craft shop, market or even restaurant, the price you pay will be inflated. This can be by as much as 50%, so try to visit these places on your own. And don't underestimate the persistence of these guys. I heard of one desperately ill traveller who virtually collapsed into a cycle-rickshaw in Agra and asked to be taken to a doctor – he ended up at a marble workshop, and the rickshaw insisted that, yes, indeed a doctor did work there!

Another trap which many foreigners fall into occurs when buying with a credit card. You may well be told that if you buy the goods, the merchant won't forward the credit slip for payment until you have received the goods, even if it is in three months time – this is total bullshit. No trader will be sending you as much as a postcard until he or she has received the money, in full, for the goods you are buying. What you'll find in fact is that within 48 hours of you signing the credit slip, the merchant has telexed the bank in Delhi and the money will have been credited to his or her account.

Also beware of any shop which takes your credit card out the back and comes back with the slip for you to sign. It has occurred that, while out of sight, the vendor will imprint a few more forms, forge your signature, and you'll be billed for items you haven't purchased. Get them to fill out the slip right in front of you.

If you believe any stories about buying anything in India to sell at a profit elsewhere, you'll simply be proving (once again) that old adage about separating fools from their money! Precious stones and carpets are favourites for this game. Merchants will tell you that you can sell the items in Australia, Europe or the USA for several times the purchase price, and will even give you the (often imaginary!) addresses of dealers who will buy them. You'll also be shown written statements, supposedly from other travellers, documenting the money they have supposedly made – it's all a scam. The stones or carpets you buy will be worth only a fraction of what you pay. Don't let greed cloud your judgement.

While it is certainly a minority of traders who are actually involved in dishonest schemes, virtually all are involved in the commission racket, so you need to shop with care – take your time, be firm and bargain hard. Good luck! ■

The tradition of fine quality embroidery
endures in Rajasthan.

(and neighbouring Gujarat) is famous, are popular buys. Pieces can range from small cushion-sized squares to bedspread-sized pieces. Prices range from a couple of hundred rupees up to several thousand for a large piece.

For more information on the handicrafts of Rajasthan, see the Arts section in the Facts about the Region chapter. Note that it is illegal to export ivory or any artefacts made from wild animals.

Antiques

In Jodhpur there are several showrooms specialising in antiques. Most of the good merchandise has been picked over by dealers, but they are still fascinating places to visit, and you can purchase some excellent antique reproduction furniture here, or have it made to order.

Articles over 100 years old are not allowed to be exported from India without an export clearance certificate. If you have doubts about any item and think it could be defined as an antique, you can check with:

Calcutta
    Superintending Archaeologist, Eastern Circle, Archaeological Survey of India, Narayani Bldg, Brabourne Rd
Delhi
    Director, Antiquities, Archaeological Survey of India, Janpath, New Delhi
Madras
    Superintending Archaeologist, Southern Circle, Archaeological Survey of India, Fort St George
Mumbai (Bombay)
    Superintending Archaeologist, Antiquities, Archaeological Survey of India, Sion Fort

Colourful wooden and papier-mâché puppets make excellent gifts, and are ridiculously cheap – only about Rs 40 to Rs 50.

Some travellers bring home a pair of *jootis*, the traditional leather shoes of Rajasthan, some of which feature embroidery and curled up toes.

Wall hangings made from segments of intricately embroidered fabric, some with the beautiful mirrorwork for which Rajasthan

Getting There & Away

No international airlines fly directly to Rajasthan, so getting there is a two part journey. Therefore, the first part of this chapter deals with travel from international destinations to India. Delhi and Mumbai (Bombay) are the two main entry points, and a selection of accommodation options is also provided. The second section concentrates on travel from Delhi and Mumbai to Rajasthan.

India

AIR

Your plane ticket will probably be the single most expensive item in your budget. Some of the cheapest tickets have to be bought months in advance, and some popular flights sell out early. Phone around travel agents for bargains. (Airlines can supply information on routes and timetables; however, except at times of inter-airline war, they do not supply the cheapest tickets.) Find out the fare, the route, the duration of the journey and any restrictions on the ticket. (See Restrictions in the Air Travel Glossary in this chapter.) Then sit back and decide which is best for you.

If you are travelling from the UK or the USA, you will probably find that the cheapest flights are being advertised by obscure

> **Warning: Reconfirmation**
> It is essential to reconfirm your return flight home at least 72 hours prior to departure. Some travellers have reported that failure to do so resulted in cancelled seats and several anxious days' waiting to try to secure new seats for their return journey – not a pleasant way to spend your last days in India! ■

bucket shops whose names haven't yet reached the telephone directory. Many such firms are honest and solvent, but there are a few rogues who will take your money and disappear, to reopen elsewhere a month or two later under a new name. If you feel suspicious about a firm, don't give them all the money at once – leave a deposit of 20% or so and pay the balance when you get the ticket. If they insist on cash in advance, go somewhere else. And once you have the ticket, ring the airline to confirm that you are actually booked on the flight.

You may decide to pay more than the rock-bottom fare by opting for the safety of a better-known travel agent. Firms such as STA Travel, who have offices worldwide, Council Travel in the USA or Travel CUTS in Canada are not going to disappear overnight, leaving you clutching a receipt for a nonexistent ticket, but they do offer good prices to most destinations.

> **Warning**
> The information in this chapter is particularly vulnerable to change: prices for international travel are volatile, routes are introduced and cancelled, schedules change, special deals come and go, and rules and visa requirements are amended. Airfares quoted here do not necessarily constitute a recommendation for the carrier. Airlines and governments seem to take a perverse pleasure in making price structures and regulations as complicated as possible. You should check directly with the airline or a travel agent to make sure you understand how a fare (and any ticket you may buy) works. In addition, the travel industry is highly competitive and there are many lurks and perks.
> The upshot of this is that you should get opinions, quotes and advice from as many airlines and travel agents as possible before you part with your hard-earned cash. The details given in this chapter should be regarded as pointers and are not a substitute for your own careful, up-to-date research. ■

Once you have your ticket, write down its number, together with the flight number and other details, and keep the information somewhere separate. If the ticket is lost or stolen, this will help you get a replacement.

It's sensible to buy travel insurance as early as possible. If you buy it the week before you fly, you may find, for example, that you're not covered for delays to your flight caused by industrial action.

International Airports

Delhi Delhi's somewhat chaotic, confusing and tatty Palam airport is now officially the Indira Gandhi international airport. The domestic terminal (Terminal I) is seven km from the centre, and the new international terminal (Terminal II) is nine km from the centre.

If you're arriving at Delhi airport from overseas, there's a 24 hour State Bank of India foreign exchange counter in the arrivals hall, before you go through customs and immigration. Once you've left the arrivals hall you won't be allowed back in. The service is fast and efficient.

Many international flights to Delhi arrive and depart in the small hours of the morning. Take special care if this is your first foray into India and you arrive exhausted and jet-lagged. If you're leaving Delhi in the early hours of the morning, book a taxi the afternoon before. They'll be hard to find at night.

For international flights the departure tax (Rs 300) must be paid at the State Bank of India counter in the departures hall before check-in.

Delhi Transport Corporation buses connect the international and domestic terminals for Rs 10. There is also the free IA/AI bus between the two terminals, although no one seems willing to admit such a service exists. The bus stop is just outside the domestic terminal. It only leaves every hour. EATS (see To/From the Airports in this section) will also take you between terminals on their roundabout route.

Places to Stay There are *retiring rooms* at both the domestic (Terminal I: ☎ (011) 329-5126) and international (Terminal II: ☎ (011) 545-2011) sections of the airport. You can use them if you have a confirmed departure within 24 hours, but you'll need to ring in advance, as demand far outstrips supply. At Terminal II, it costs Rs 175 for an air-con double and Rs 40 for a dorm bed. At Terminal 1, the cost is Rs 175 for an ordinary double and Rs 250 for an air-con double. The tourist information officer at the desk at the airport may insist that the retiring rooms are 'full' and try to direct you to a hotel where the officer gets the commission.

The bazaar known as Pahar Ganj, which is only a stone's throw from the New Delhi railway station, has dozens of cheap hotels. On Main Bazaar, the main street of Pahar Ganj, is the popular *Hotel Vivek* (☎ (011) 777-7062), which has singles/doubles from Rs 80/100, the *Hotel Vishal* (☎ (011) 753-2079), with rooms at Rs 120/150 and, next door, the *Hare Krishna Guest House*, which has clean rooms from Rs 125.

There are *retiring rooms* at both the Old Delhi and New Delhi railway stations. The YMCAs are also good mid-range options: The *YMCA Tourist Hotel* (☎ (011) 31-1915) is on Jai Singh Rd and has rooms from Rs 250/425. The *YWCA International Guest House* (☎ (011) 31-1561) at 10 Sansad Marg (Parliament St) has singles/doubles for Rs 300/500.

The five star *Hotel Maurya Sheraton* (☎ (011) 301-0101; fax 301-0908) is on Sardar Patel Marg, the road to the airport. Rooms start at Rs 5000/5800.

Mumbai Although Delhi is closer to Jaipur, the capital of Rajasthan, you may find that you fly into Mumbai, which is the main international gateway to India. The international terminal (Sahar) is about four km from the domestic terminal (Santa Cruz). They are 30 km and 26 km respectively from Nariman Point in central Mumbai.

Facilities at Sahar include a 24 hour State Bank foreign exchange counter, counters of the national (Government of India) and state (MTDC) tourist organisations, car rental kiosks, and a cafe and snack bar. The duty-free shop inside the departure lounge area has inflated prices and will accept only US dollars.

For all international flights the departure tax (Rs 300) must be paid at the counter opposite the check-in desks before you check in.

Indian Airlines, which flies both nationally and on local international routes, moved its office to the Army & Navy Building on MG Rd just north of Colaba after the Air India building was bombed in 1993. There is talk of them moving back to the Air India building – ask around before you leave. Indian Airlines also has a reservation desk at both the Taj Mahal and Centaur Juhu Beach hotels.

Places to Stay There are *retiring rooms* at the domestic airport which are reserved for transit passengers and cost Rs 160/320 for a single/double. Ask at the airport manager's office. There are a number of hotels in the suburb of Vile Parle (pronounced 'Veelay Parlay') close to the domestic terminal. The *Hotel Aircraft International* (☎ (022) 612-3667) at 179 Dayaldas Rd has ordinary/deluxe rooms at Rs 470/500 and super-deluxe rooms at Rs 580. The *Hotel Airport International* (☎ (022) 612-2883) and the *Hotel Avion* (☎ (022) 611-3220), both on Nehru Rd, have rooms for Rs 700/900. Off Nehru Rd, close to the five star Sun-n-Sand Hotel, is the *Hotel Transit* (☎ (022) 610-5812). It has rooms including breakfast for Rs 1060/1450 and suites for Rs 1500.

To/From the Airports

Delhi The EATS (Ex-Servicemen's Air Link Transport Service: ☎ 331-6530) has a regular bus service between both the international and domestic terminals and Connaught Place. The counter for the EATS bus is just to the right before you exit the international terminal. The fare is Rs 20, with an additional charge of Rs 5 for luggage. The driver will drop you off or pick you up at most of the major hotels en route if you ask. There is also an EATS city-to-airport service which departs regularly from opposite Palika Bazaar on Radial Rd 8 (Janpath) between 4 am and 11.30 pm.

A regular Delhi Transport Corporation bus service runs from the airport to the New Delhi railway station and the Interstate bus station; it costs Rs 20 and there is a Rs 5 charge for luggage. At New Delhi railway station, it uses the Ajmer Gate side. There is also a public bus service to the airport (No 780) from the Super Bazaar at Connaught Place, but it can get very crowded.

Just outside the international terminal is a prepaid taxi booth, and a taxi to the centre costs Rs 160 when booked here. This is an excellent way to get into town if you're at all unsure of how things work. From Connaught Place to the airport you'll be asked for anything from Rs 180 upwards. Auto-rickshaws will run out to the airport too, but you'll be covered in exhaust fumes by the time you get there. If you can find a driver willing to take you it should cost around Rs 60.

Mumbai The airport bus service operates between the Air India building at Nariman Point and Santa Cruz (domestic) and Sahar (international) airports. (The Air India building is at the junction of Madame Cama Rd and Marine Drive.) The journey to Santa Cruz takes about one hour and costs Rs 36. To Sahar it takes about 1½ hours and is Rs 44. Baggage costs Rs 7 per piece. From Nariman Point, departures are at 12.30, 4, 5 and 8.15 am, then hourly until 2.15 pm, and then at 3.45, 5.30, 7, 8, 9 and 11 pm. It would be wise to check these departure times, as they're subject to change. In peak hour the trip through Mumbai's horribly congested streets can take well over two hours, so don't cut things too fine. From the airports, there are departures hourly except between 1 and 4 am.

Tickets for the buses are bought either on the buses themselves, at the Air India building or at the terminals. Buses between the domestic and international terminals depart every 30 minutes and are free if you can show a ticket for a connecting flight, otherwise they cost Rs 15.

Air Travel Glossary

Apex Tickets Apex stands for Advance Purchase Excursion fare. These tickets are usually between 30% and 40% cheaper than the full economy fare, but there are restrictions. You must purchase the ticket at least 21 days in advance (sometimes more) and must be away for a minimum period (normally 14 days) and return within a maximum period (90 or 180 days). Stopovers are not allowed, and if you have to change your dates of travel or destination, there will be extra charges to pay. These tickets are not fully refundable – if you have to cancel your trip, the refund is often considerably less than what you paid for the ticket. Take out travel insurance to cover yourself in case you have to cancel your trip unexpectedly, for instance due to illness.

Baggage Allowance This will be written on your ticket; you are usually allowed one 20 kg item to go in the hold, plus one item of hand luggage. Some airlines which fly transpacific and transatlantic routes allow for two pieces of luggage (there are limits on their dimensions and weight).

Bucket Shops At certain times of the year and/or on certain routes, many airlines fly with empty seats. This isn't profitable and it's more cost-effective for them to fly full, even if that means having to sell a certain number of drastically discounted tickets. They do this by off-loading them onto bucket shops (UK) or consolidators (USA), travel agents who specialise in discounted fares. The agents, in turn, sell them to the public at reduced prices. These tickets are often the cheapest you'll find, but you can't purchase them directly from the airlines. Availability varies widely, so you'll not only have to be flexible in your travel plans, you'll also have to be quick off the mark as soon as an advertisement appears in the press.

Bucket-shop agents advertise in newspapers and magazines and there's a lot of competition – especially in places like Amsterdam and London which are crawling with them – so it's a good idea to telephone first to ascertain availability before rushing from shop to shop. Naturally, they'll advertise the cheapest available tickets, but by the time you get there, these may be sold out and you may be looking at something slightly more expensive.

Bumped Just because you have a confirmed seat doesn't mean you're going to get on the plane – see Overbooking.

Cancellation Penalties If you have to cancel or change an Apex or other discount ticket, there may be heavy penalties involved; insurance can sometimes be taken out against these penalties. Some airlines impose penalties on regular tickets as well, particularly against 'no show' passengers.

Check-In Airlines ask you to check in a certain time ahead of the flight departure (usually two hours on international flights). If you fail to check in on time and the flight is overbooked, the airline can cancel your booking and give your seat to somebody else.

Confirmation Having a ticket written out with the flight and date on it doesn't mean you have a seat until the agent has confirmed with the airline that your status is 'OK'. Prior to this confirmation, your status is 'on request'.

Courier Fares Businesses often need to send their urgent documents or freight securely and quickly. They do it through courier companies. These companies hire people to accompany the package through customs and, in return, offer a discount ticket which is sometimes a phenomenal bargain. In effect, what the courier companies do is ship their freight as your luggage on the regular commercial flights. This is a legitimate operation – all freight is completely legal. There are two shortcomings, however: the short turnaround time of the ticket, usually not longer than a month; and the limitation on your luggage allowance. You may be required to surrender all your baggage allowance for the use of the courier company, and be only allowed to take carry-on luggage.

Discounted Tickets There are two types of discounted fares – officially discounted (such as Apex – see Promotional Fares) and unofficially discounted (see Bucket Shops). The latter can save you more than money – you may be able to pay Apex prices without the associated Apex advance booking and other requirements. The lowest prices often impose drawbacks, such as flying with unpopular airlines, inconvenient schedules, or unpleasant routes and connections.

Economy-Class Tickets Economy-class tickets are usually not the cheapest way to go, though they do give you maximum flexibility and they are valid for 12 months. If you don't use them, most are fully refundable, as are unused sectors of a multiple ticket.

Full Fares Airlines traditionally offer first class (coded F), business class (coded J) and economy class (coded Y) tickets. These days there are so many promotional and discounted fares available that few passengers pay full fare.

Lost Tickets If you lose your airline ticket, an airline will usually treat it like a travellers' cheque and, after inquiries, issue you with a replacement. Legally, however, an airline is entitled to treat it like cash, so if you lose a ticket, it could be forever. Take good care of your tickets.

MCO An MCO (Miscellaneous Charges Order) is a voucher for a value of a given amount, which resembles an airline ticket and can be used to pay for a specific flight with any IATA (International Air Transport Association) airline. MCOs, which are more flexible than a regular ticket, may satisfy the irritating onward ticket requirement, but some countries are now reluctant to accept them. MCOs are fully refundable if unused.

No Shows No shows are passengers who fail to show up for their flight for whatever reason. Full-fare no shows are sometimes entitled to travel on a later flight. The rest of us are penalised (see Cancellation Penalties).

Open Jaw Tickets These are return tickets which allow you to fly to one place but return from another, and travel between the two 'jaws' by any means of transport at your own expense. If available, this can save you backtracking to your arrival point.

Overbooking Airlines hate to fly with empty seats, and since every flight has some passengers who fail to show up (see No Shows), they often book more passengers than they have seats available. Usually the excess passengers balance those who fail to show up, but occasionally somebody gets bumped. If this happens, guess who it is most likely to be? The passengers who check in late.

Promotional Fares These are officially discounted fares, such as Apex fares, which are available from travel agents or direct from the airline.

Reconfirmation You must contact the airline at least 72 hours prior to departure to 'reconfirm' that you intend to be on the flight. If you don't do this, the airline can delete your name from the passenger list and you could lose your seat.

Restrictions Discounted tickets often have various restrictions on them, such as necessity of advance purchase, limitations on the minimum and maximum period you must be away, restrictions on breaking the journey or changing the booking or route etc.

Round-the-World Tickets These tickets have become very popular in the last few years; basically, there are two types – airline tickets and agent tickets. An airline RTW ticket is issued by two or more airlines that have joined together to market a ticket which takes you around the world on their combined routes. It permits you to fly pretty well anywhere you choose using their combined routes as long as you don't backtrack, that is, keep moving in approximately the same direction east or west. Other restrictions are that you (usually) must book the first sector in advance and cancellation penalties then apply. There may be restrictions on how many stopovers you are permitted. The RTW tickets are usually valid for from 90 days up to a year.

Quite a few of these combined-airline RTW tickets go through India, including ones in combination with Air India which will allow you to make several stopovers within India. RTW tickets typically cost around A$1950 to A$2400, UK£560 to UK£940 and US$1250 to US$2500.

The other type of RTW ticket, the agent ticket, is a combination of cheap fares strung together by an enterprising travel agent. These may be cheaper than airline RTW tickets, but the choice of routes will be limited.

Standby This is a discounted ticket where you only fly if there is a seat free at the last moment. Standby fares are usually only available directly at the airport, but sometimes may also be handled by an airline's city office. To give yourself the best possible chance of getting on the flight you want, get there early and have your name placed on the waiting list. It's first come, first served.

Student Discounts Some airlines offer student-card holders 15% to 25% discounts on their tickets. The same often applies to anyone under the age of 26. These discounts are generally only available on ordinary economy-class fares. You wouldn't get one, for instance, on an Apex or an RTW ticket, since these are already discounted.

Tickets Out An entry requirement for many countries is that you have an onward or return ticket, in other words, a ticket out of the country. If you're not sure what you intend to do next, the easiest solution is to buy the cheapest onward ticket to a neighbouring country or a ticket from a reliable airline which can later be refunded if you do not use it.

Transferred Tickets Airline tickets cannot be transferred from one person to another. Travellers sometimes try to sell the return half of their ticket, but officials can ask you to prove that you are the person named on the ticket. This may not be checked on domestic flights, but on international flights tickets are usually compared with passports.

Travel Periods Some officially discounted fares, Apex fares in particular, vary with the time of year. There is often a low (off-peak) season and a high (peak) season. Sometimes there's an intermediate or shoulder season as well. At peak times, when everyone wants to fly, both officially and unofficially discounted fares will be higher, or there may simply be no discounted tickets available. Usually the fare depends on your outward flight – if you depart in the high season and return in the low season, you pay the high-season fare. ■

A taxi to the domestic airport on the meter costs about Rs 150 from Colaba and Rs 60 from Juhu, but they generally ask for more (Rs 170 and Rs 70 respectively). It's a bit further to the international airport. During rush hours you won't find anyone who's prepared to use the meter, so expect to pay even more.

From the international airport there's a prepaid taxi booth where you pay a set fare: Rs 93 to Juhu, Rs 113 to Dadar, Rs 138 to Bombay Central railway station and Rs 1187 to Churchgate, VT or Colaba. You're assigned to a taxi, you give the driver your slip and there's no further fuss. You do, however, pay a bit more than the meter fare.

International Airlines
Delhi Offices of international airlines in Delhi (telephone area code: 011) are as follows:

Aeroflot
    Cozy Travels, BMC House, 1st Floor, 1 N block, Connaught Place (☎ 331-2916)
Air France
    7 Atmaram Mansion, Connaught Place (☎ 331-0407; fax 372-2666; airport ☎ 565-2294)
Air India
    Jeevan Bharati Bldg, 124 Connaught Circus (☎ 331-1225)
Air Lanka
    Student Travel Information Centre, Imperial Hotel, Janpath (☎ 332-4789)
Alitalia
    19 Kasturba Gandhi Marg (☎ 331-1019)
British Airways
    DLF Bldg, Sansad Marg (Parliament St) (☎ 332-7428)
Iran Air
    Ashok Hotel, Chanakyapuri (☎ 60-4397)
Iraqi Airways
    Ansal Bhawan (☎ 331-8632)
Japan Airlines (JAL)
    Chandralok Bldg, 36 Janpath (☎ 332-3409)
KLM
    Tolstoy Marg (☎ 331-5841)
LOT (Polish Airways)
    G-55 Connaught Place (☎ 332-4308)
Lufthansa
    56 Janpath (☎ 332-3206)
Malaysian Airline System (MAS)
    G Block, Connaught Place (☎ 332-5786)
Pakistan International Airlines (PIA)
    Kailash Bldg, 26 Kasturba Gandhi Marg (☎ 331-6121)

Royal Nepal Airlines
    44 Janpath (☎ 332-0817)
SAS
    1 Block, Connaught Place (☎ 332-7503)
Syrian Arab Airlines
    GSA Delhi Express Travels, 13/90 Connaught Place (☎ 34-3218)
Thai Airways International
    Ambadeep Bldg, 14 Kasturba Gandhi Marg (☎ 332-9554; fax 372-4757)

Mumbai Most international airline offices in Mumbai are in the Nariman Point area between Maharshi Karve Rd and Marine Drive. Offices of international airlines in Mumbai (telephone area code: 022) are as follows:

Aeroflot
    241/242 Nirmal, Nariman Point (☎ 22-1682)
Air Canada
    Amarchand Mansion B1, Madame Cama Rd (☎ 202-1111)
Air France
    Maker Chambers VI (1st floor), Nariman Point (☎ 202-4818)
Air India
    Air India Bldg, Nariman Point (☎ 202-4142)
Air Lanka
    Mittal Towers (C Wing), Nariman Point (☎ 22-3299)
Air Mauritius
    Air India Bldg (ground floor), Nariman Point (☎ 202-8474)
Alitalia
    Industrial Assurance Bldg, Veer Nariman Rd, Churchgate (☎ 22-2144)
Biman Bangladesh Airlines
    199 J Tata Rd, Churchgate (☎ 22-4659)
British Airways
    Valcan Insurance Bldg, 202B Veer Nariman Rd, Churchgate (☎ 22-0888)
Cathay Pacific Airways
    Taj Mahal Hotel, Apollo Bunder, Colaba (☎ 202-9112)
Egypt Air
    Oriental House, 7 J Tata Rd, Churchgate (☎ 22-1415)
Ethiopian Airways
    Taj Mahal Hotel, Apollo Bunder, Colaba (☎ 202-8787)
Gulf Air
    Maker Chambers V, Nariman Point (☎ 202-4065)
Iraqi Airways
    Mayfair Bldg, 79 Veer Nariman Rd, Churchgate (☎ 22-1399)

Japan Airlines (JAL)
2 Raheja Centre (ground floor), Nariman Point
(☎ 287-4936)
Kenya Airways
Airlines Hotel, 199 J Tata Rd, Churchgate
(☎ 22-0064)
KLM
Khaitan Bhavan, 198 J Tata Rd, Churchgate
(☎ 283-3338)
Kuwait Airlines
2A Stadium House, 86 Veer Nariman Rd,
Churchgate (☎ 204-5351)
LOT (Polish Airways)
6 Maker Arcade, Cuffe Parade (☎ 218-5494)
Lufthansa
Express Towers (4th floor), Nariman Point
(☎ 202-3430)
Malaysian Airline System (MAS)
GSA Stic Travels & Tours, 6 Maker Arcade,
Cuffe Parade (☎ 218-1431)
Pakistan International Airlines (PIA)
7 Brabourne Stadium, Veer Nariman Rd,
Churchgate (☎ 202-1598)
Qantas
42 Sakhar Bhavan, Nariman Point (☎ 202-9297)
SAS
Podar House, 10 Marine Drive (☎ 202-7083)
Singapore Airlines
Taj Mahal Hotel, Apollo Bunder, Colaba
(☎ 287-0986)
Swissair
Maker Chambers VI, 220 Nariman Point
(☎ 287-2210)
Thai Airways International
Podar House, 10 Marine Drive (☎ 202-3284)
Zambia Airways
207 Maker Chambers V, Nariman Point
(☎ 202-6942)

Travellers with Special Needs

If you have special needs of any sort – you've broken a leg, you're vegetarian, travelling in a wheelchair, taking the baby, terrified of flying – you should let the airline know as soon as possible so that they can make arrangements accordingly. You should remind them when you reconfirm your booking (at least 72 hours before departure) and again when you check in at the airport. It may also be worth ringing around the airlines before you make your booking to find out how they can handle your particular needs.

Flying with Children Children under the age of two travel for 10% of the standard fare (or free, on some airlines), as long as they don't occupy a seat. They don't get a baggage allowance either. Bassinets should be provided by the airline if requested in advance; these will take a child weighing up to about 10 kg. Children between two and 12 can usually occupy a seat for half to two-thirds of the full fare, and do get a baggage allowance. Strollers can often be taken as hand luggage.

Cheap Tickets in India

Although you can get cheap tickets in Mumbai and Calcutta, it is in Delhi that the real wheeling and dealing goes on. There are a number of 'bucket shops' around Connaught Place, but enquire with other travellers about their trustworthiness.

Fares from Delhi to various European capitals cost around Rs 5000 to Rs 7000, a bit less from Mumbai. The cheapest flights to Europe are with airlines such as Aeroflot, LOT, Kuwait Airlines, Syrian Arab Airlines and Iraqi Airways. Delhi-Hong Kong-San Francisco costs around US$600.

Although Delhi is the best place for cheap tickets, many flights between Europe and South-East Asia or Australia pass through Mumbai; it's also the place for flights to East Africa. Furthermore, if you're heading east from India to Bangladesh, Myanmar (Burma) or Thailand you'll probably find much better prices in Calcutta than in Delhi, even though there are fewer agents.

Africa

There are plenty of flights between East Africa and Mumbai due to the large Indian population in Kenya. Typical fares from Mumbai to Nairobi are around US$440 return with Ethiopian Airways, Kenya Airways, Air India and Pakistan International Airlines (PIA, via Karachi).

Aeroflot operates a service between Delhi and Cairo (via Moscow).

Australia & New Zealand

Advance-purchase return fares from the east coast of Australia to India range from A$1250 to A$1500 depending on the season and the destination in India. Fares are slightly cheaper to Madras and Calcutta than to Mumbai or Delhi. From Australia, fares are cheaper from Darwin and Perth than from the east coast. The low travel period is from March to September; peak is from October to February.

Tickets from Australia to London or other European capitals with an Indian stopover range from A$1200 to A$1350 one way and A$2000 to A$2500 return, again depending on the season.

Return advance-purchase fares from New Zealand to India range from NZ$1799 to NZ$1889 depending on the season.

STA Travel and Flight Centres International are major dealers in cheap airfares in both Australia and New Zealand. Check the travel agents' ads in the Yellow Pages and ring around.

Bangladesh
Biman Bangladesh and Indian Airlines fly from Calcutta to Dhaka (US$32) and Chittagong (US$40) in Bangladesh. Many people use Biman from Calcutta through to Bangkok – partly because they're cheap and partly because they fly through Yangon (Rangoon) in Myanmar. Biman should put you up overnight in Dhaka on this route but be careful – it appears they will only do so if your ticket specifically endorses that you are entitled to a room. If not, tough luck – you can either camp out overnight in the hot transit lounge or make your way into Dhaka on your own, pay for transport and accommodation, and get hit for departure tax the next day.

Continental Europe
Fares from Continental Europe are mostly far more expensive than from London; see the UK section for comparison. At the rates listed below, it's obviously much cheaper to go to London and buy a flight ticket from there.

From Amsterdam to Mumbai/Delhi, return excursion fares are about DFL2400 (UK£900). To Calcutta, expect to pay around DFL2665 (UK£1000).

From Paris to Mumbai/Delhi, return excursion fares are from FFr7880 (UK£980; about one-third the standard return economy fare).

From Frankfurt to Mumbai/Delhi, return excursion fares are around DM1950 (UK£820).

Malaysia
Not many travellers fly between Malaysia and India because it is so much cheaper to fly from Thailand, but there are flights between Penang or Kuala Lumpur and Madras. You can generally pick up one-way tickets for the Malaysian Airline System (MAS) flight from Penang travel agents for around RM$780, which is rather cheaper than the regular fare. Other fares include Kuala Lumpur-Mumbai for RM$700 one way and RM$1275 return, and Kuala Lumpur-Delhi for RM$700 one way and RM$1070 return.

The Maldives
Thiruvananthapuram (Trivandrum) to Malé costs US$63. This is cheaper than flying to the Maldives from Colombo in Sri Lanka.

Myanmar
There are no land crossing points between Myanmar and India (or between Myanmar and any other country), so if you want to visit Myanmar your only choice is to fly there. Myanma Airways flies Calcutta-Yangon; Biman Bangladesh flies Dhaka-Yangon.

If you are coming from Bangkok via Myanmar, the one-way Bangkok-Yangon-Calcutta fare is around US$240 with Thai, or US$225 on Myanma Airways.

Nepal
Royal Nepal Airlines Corporation (RNAC) and Indian Airlines share routes between India and Kathmandu. Both airlines give a 25% discount to those under 30 years of age on flights between Kathmandu and India; no student card is needed.

Delhi is the main departure point for flights between India and Kathmandu. The daily one hour Delhi to Kathmandu flight costs US$142.

Other cities in India with direct air connections with Kathmandu are Mumbai (US$257),

Calcutta (US$96) and Varanasi (US$71). The flight from Varanasi is the last leg of the popular Delhi-Agra-Khajuraho-Varanasi-Kathmandu tourist flight.

If you want to see the mountains as you fly into Kathmandu from Delhi or Varanasi, you must sit on the left side.

Pakistan

Pakistan International Airlines (PIA) and Air India operate flights from Karachi to Delhi for US$75 and Lahore to Delhi for about US$140. Flights are also available between Karachi and Mumbai.

Singapore

Singapore is a great cheap-ticket centre and you can pick up Singapore-Delhi tickets for about S$900 return.

Sri Lanka

Because the ferry service is out of operation, flying to Sri Lanka is now the only way to get there. There are flights to and from Colombo (the capital of Sri Lanka) and Mumbai, Madras, Tiruchirappalli or Thiruvananthapuram (Trivandrum). Flights are most frequent on the Madras-Colombo route.

Thailand

Bangkok is the most popular departure point from South-East Asia into Asia proper because of the cheap flights from there to Calcutta, Yangon in Myanmar, Dhaka in Bangladesh or Kathmandu in Nepal. The popular Bangkok-Kathmandu flight is about US$220 one way and US$400 return. You can make a stopover in Myanmar on this route and do a circuit of that fascinating country. Bangkok-Calcutta via Myanmar is about US$270 one way.

The UK

Various excursion fares are available from London to India, but you can get better prices through London's many cheap-ticket specialists. Check the travel page ads in the *Times, Business Traveller* and the weekly 'what's on' magazine *Time Out*; or check give-away papers such as *TNT*. Two reliable London shops are Trailfinders, 194 High Street Kensington, London W8 7RG (☎ (0171) 938-3939), or 46 Earls Court Rd, London W8 (☎ (0171) 938-3366); and STA Travel, 74 Old Brompton Rd, London SW7 (☎ (0171) 937-9962), or 117 Euston Rd, London NW1. Also worth trying are Quest Worldwide (☎ (0181) 547-3322) at 29 Castle St, Kingston, Surrey KT11ST, and Bridge the World (☎ (0171) 911-0900) at 1-3 Ferdinand St, Camden Town, London NW1.

From London to Delhi, fares range from around UK£300/342 one way/return in the low season, or UK£409/493 one way/return in the high season – cheaper short-term fares are also available. The cheapest fares are usually with Middle Eastern or Eastern European airlines. You'll also find very competitive air fares to the subcontinent with Biman Bangladesh or Air Lanka. Thai International always seems to have competitive fares despite its high standards.

If you want to stop in India en route to Australia, expect to pay around UK£500 to UK£600. You might find fares via Karachi (Pakistan) or Colombo (Sri Lanka) slightly cheaper than fares via India.

Most British travel agents are registered with the Association of British Travel Agents (ABTA). If you have paid for your flight through an ABTA-registered agent who then goes out of business, ABTA will guarantee a refund or an alternative. Unregistered bucket shops are riskier but are also sometimes cheaper.

The USA & Canada

The cheapest return air fares from the US west coast to India are around US$1350. Another way of getting to India from the USA is to fly to Hong Kong and get a ticket from there. Tickets to Hong Kong cost about US$430 one way and around US$725 return from San Francisco or Los Angeles; in Hong Kong you can find one-way tickets to Mumbai for US$300 depending on the carrier. Alternatively, you can fly to Singapore for around US$595/845 one way/return, or to Bangkok for US$470/760 one way/return.

From the east coast you can find return tickets to Mumbai or Delhi for around US$950. The cheapest one-way tickets will be around US$660. An alternative way of getting to India from New York is to fly to London and buy a cheap fare from there.

Check the Sunday travel sections of papers such as the *New York Times, San Francisco Chronicle/Examiner* or *Los Angeles Times* for cheap fares. Good budget travel agents include the student travel chains STA Travel, and Council Travel, the travel division of the Council on International Education Exchange. The magazine *Travel Unlimited* (PO Box 1058, Allston, Mass 02134) publishes details of the cheapest air fares and courier possibilities for destinations all over the world from the USA.

Fares from Canada are similar to the USA fares. From Vancouver the route is like that from the US west coast, with the option of going via Hong Kong. From Toronto it is easier to travel via London.

The *Toronto Globe & Mail* and the *Vancouver Sun* carry travel agents' ads. The magazine *Great Expeditions* (PO Box 8000-411, Abbotsford BC V2S 6H1) is useful.

LAND

Drivers of cars and riders of motorcycles will need the vehicle's registration papers, liability insurance and an international driver's permit in addition to their domestic licence. Beware: there are two kinds of international permit, one of which is needed mostly for former British colonies. You will also need a *carnet de passage en douane*, which is effectively a passport for the vehicle, and acts as a temporary waiver of import duty. The carnet may also need to have listed any more-expensive spares that you're planning to carry with you, such as a gearbox. This is necessary when travelling in many countries in Asia, and is designed to prevent car import rackets. Contact your local automobile association for details about all documentation.

Liability insurance is not available in advance for many out-of-the-way countries, but has to be bought when crossing the border. The cost and quality of such local insurance vary widely, and you will find in some countries that you are effectively travelling uninsured.

Anyone who is planning to take their own vehicle with them needs to check in advance what spares and petrol are likely to be available. Lead-free fuel is not available in India, and neither is every little part for your car.

For more details on driving your own vehicle in India, or cycling in Rajasthan, see the Car, Motorcycle and Bicycle sections in the Getting Around chapter.

Bangladesh

Unfortunately most land entry and exit points are closed, so the choice is much more limited than a glance at the map would indicate.

The main crossings are at Benapol/Haridaspur on the Calcutta route and Chiliharti/Haldibari on the Darjeeling route. The Tamabil/Dauki border crossing, in the northeast corner on the Meghalaya route, opened in 1995.

No exit permit is required to leave Bangladesh. If border officials mention anything about a permit, remain steadfast. However, if you enter Bangladesh by air and exit via land, you do need a road permit, which can be obtained from the Passport & Immigration office, 2nd floor, 17/1 Segunbagicha Rd in Dhaka, and if you are driving from Bangladesh in your own vehicle, two permits are required: one from the Indian High Commission (☎ 504-897), House 120, Road 2, Dhanmondi in Dhaka, and one from the Bangladesh Ministry of Foreign Affairs (☎ 883-260), Pioneer Rd (facing the Supreme Court), Segun Bagicha in the centre of Dhaka.

We have received in recent years letters from travellers who have crossed at Bhurungamari (east of Haldibari)/Changrabandha (an alternative route from Darjeeling), Hili/ Balurghat and Godagari/ Lalgola, both north of Benapol/Haridaspur. These lesser crossings witness so few westerners that everyone assumes they're closed. Getting the truth from Indian and Bangladeshi officials is virtually impossible, so crossing the border on these lesser routes is never certain.

Dhaka to Calcutta The Dhaka to Calcutta route is the one used by the majority of land travellers between Bangladesh and India. Coming from Dhaka it's wise to book your seat on the bus at least a day in advance. The buses that operate overnight between Dhaka and the border are direct. Buses only depart from 8 to 11 pm; they reach Benapol (the Bangladeshi border town) at dawn. From Benapol to the border, it's about 10 minutes by cycle-rickshaw (Tk 5). There are no buses in the daytime between the border and Benapol. Crossing the border takes an hour or so with the usual filling in and stamping of forms. From the border at Haridaspur, on the Indian side, to Bangaon, it's about 10 km (Rs 10, 20 minutes by cycle-rickshaw, or Rs 50 by auto-rickshaw). It's possible to change money at Bangaon, and the rate is better than at the border.

Alternatively, you can take a Coaster (minibus) from Jessore to Benapol (Tk 12), from where you can proceed to the border and India.

Chiliharti to Darjeeling The Bangladesh border point is at Chiliharti, and this can be reached by train, although it's much quicker to take the bus. From Chiliharti to Haldibari (the Indian border checkpoint), it's a seven km walk along a disused railway line. The trip from Haldibari to New Jalpaiguri takes two hours and costs Rs 9 by train. From New Jalpaiguri to Darjeeling you can take the fast buses or the slower more picturesque toy train. Note that changing money in Chiliharti is virtually impossible. There are money-changers at Haldibari.

Sylhet to Shillong In the early 1970s, the route between Shillong in Meghalaya and Sylhet in Bangladesh was closed on the Indian side to both regional and international traffic because of problems in Assam caused by the influx of illegal immigrants from Bangladesh. In 1995, the permit requirement was dropped; it may take a while before crossing

here becomes problem free. If you're travelling by bus and border officials demand such a permit, you may have to educate them.

It takes 2½ hours to get to Tamabil from Sylhet by bus, and it's a 15 minute hike to the border. It is then a further 1.5 km walk to Dauki in India, from where buses run to Shillong, a 3½ hour trip. From Shillong, at an elevation of 1496m, if it's not cloudy the views over Bangladesh are superb.

Europe
The classic way of getting to India has always been overland. Sadly, events in the Middle East and Afghanistan have turned the cross-Asian flow into a trickle. Afghanistan is still off-limits but the trip through Turkey, Iran and into Pakistan is straightforward.

The Asia overland trip is certainly not the breeze it once was, but it is definitely possible. Many travellers combine travel to the subcontinent with the Middle East by flying from India or Pakistan to Amman in Jordan or one of the Gulf states. A number of the London-based overland companies operate their bus or truck trips across Asia on a regular basis. Check with Exodus (☎ (0181) 675-5550), 9 Weir Rd, London SW12 0LT; Encounter Overland (☎ (0171) 370-6951), 267 Old Brompton Rd, London SW5 9LA; or Top Deck Travel (☎ (0171) 370-4555) for more information.

For more detail on the Asian overland route see the Lonely Planet guides to Pakistan, Iran and Turkey.

Nepal
There are direct buses from Delhi to Kathmandu, but these generally get bad reports from travellers. It's cheaper and more satisfactory to organise this trip yourself.

The most popular routes are from Raxaul (near Muzaffarpur), Sunauli (near Gorakhpur) and Kakarbhitta (near Siliguri). If you are heading straight to Nepal from Delhi or elsewhere in western India then the Gorakhpur to Sunauli route is the most convenient. From Calcutta, Patna or most of eastern India, Raxaul to Birganj is the best entry point. From Darjeeling it's easiest to go to Kakarbhitta.

To give an idea of costs, a 2nd class rail ticket from Delhi to Gorakhpur costs US$6 and bus tickets from Gorakhpur to the border and then on to Kathmandu cost another US$6.

Via Sunauli Buses from Kathmandu to Sunauli travel along the Kathmandu-Pokhara (Prithvi) Highway to Mugling before joining the Siddhartha Highway for the beautiful trip south. The journey takes around nine hours, but unfortunately direct buses only run at night. The government-owned, blue Sajha Yatayat buses are faster and less crowded than most of the privately run buses.

Buses from Pokhara also travel via Mugling, and this trip also takes nine hours.

From Sunauli, frequent buses make the three hour trip to Gorakhpur. From Gorakhpur to Delhi involves an overnight rail journey.

Via Mahendranagar The border crossing at Mahendranagar is the most interesting option. It will take a while for things to start operating smoothly, but when they do, this will present an interesting alternative route to Delhi or some of the hill stations in northern Uttar Pradesh. When the Mahendra Highway is finally completed (some time this century would be nothing short of a miracle) the route will be open all year, but until then it is a dry season-only proposition, and strictly for the hardy.

There are buses from Banbassa, the nearest Indian village to the border, to New Delhi. Banbassa is also connected by rail to Bareilly, and by bus with the hill station Almora in India.

Direct buses from Kathmandu to Mahendranagar take a gruelling 25 hours. The countryside is beautiful and fascinating, so it's much better to do the whole trip during daylight and to break the journey at Nepalganj.

Pakistan

At present, due to the continuing unstable political situation between India and Pakistan, there's only one border crossing open.

There are no border crossings between Rajasthan and Pakistan.

Lahore to Amritsar The crossing at Attari is open daily to all traffic. It may be worth checking the situation in the Punjab with the Home Ministry in Delhi or the Indian High Commission in Islamabad, Pakistan, before you travel, as this could change if there's major problems either side of the border.

For the Lahore (Pakistan) to Amritsar (India) train you have to buy one ticket from Lahore to Attari, the Indian border town, and another from Attari to Amritsar. The train departs Lahore daily at 11.30 am and arrives in Amritsar at 3 pm after a couple of hours at the border passing through immigration and customs. Going the other way, you leave Amritsar at 9.30 am and arrive in Lahore at 1.35 pm. Pakistan immigration and customs are handled at Lahore station. Sometimes, however, border delays can make the trip much longer.

From Amritsar you cannot buy a ticket until the morning of departure and there are no seat reservations – arrive early and push. Moneychangers on the platform offer good rates for Pakistani rupees. Travellers have reported that whichever direction you're travelling, the exchange rate between Indian and Pakistan rupees is more advantageous to you on the Pakistan side of the border, but you can change Indian rupees to Pakistani rupees or vice versa at Wagah (the Pakistani border town) and in Amritsar – no matter what the Pakistanis may tell you!

Few travellers use the road link between India and Pakistan. It's mainly of interest to people with vehicles or those on overland buses. By public transport the trip from Lahore entails taking a bus to the border at Wagah between Lahore and Amritsar, walking across the border and then taking another bus or taxi into Amritsar.

From Lahore, buses and minibuses depart from near the general bus station on Badami Bagh. The border opens at 9.15 am and closes at 3.30 pm. If you're stuck on the Pakistan side you can stay at the *PTDC Motel*, where there are dorm beds and double rooms.

South-East Asia

In contrast to the difficulties of travelling overland in central Asia, the South-East Asian overland trip is still wide open and as popular as ever. From Australia the first step is to Indonesia – Timor, Bali or Jakarta. Although most people fly from an east-coast city or from Perth to Bali, there are also flights from Darwin and from Port Hedland in the north of Western Australia. The shortest route is the flight between Darwin and Kupang on the Indonesian island of Timor.

From Bali you head north through Java to Jakarta, from where you either travel by ship or fly to Singapore or continue north through Sumatra and then cross to Penang in Malaysia. After travelling around Malaysia, you can fly from Penang to Madras in India or, more popularly, continue north to Thailand and eventually fly out from Bangkok to India, perhaps with a stopover in Myanmar. Unfortunately, crossing by land from Myanmar to India (or indeed to any other country) is forbidden by the Myanmar government.

An interesting alternative route is to travel from Australia to Papua New Guinea and from there cross to Irian Jaya; then to Sulawesi in Indonesia. There are all sorts of travel variations possible in South-East Asia; the region is a delight to travel through, it's good value for money, the food is generally excellent and healthy, and all in all it's an area of the world not to be missed. For full details see the Lonely Planet guide *South-East Asia on a shoestring*.

SEA

The ferry service from Rameswaram in southern India to Talaimannar in Sri Lanka has been suspended for some years due to the unrest in Sri Lanka. This was a favourite route for shipping arms and equipment to the Tamil guerrilla forces in the north of the country.

The shipping services between Africa and India only carry freight (including vehicles), not passengers.

The service between Penang and Madras also ceased some years ago.

DEPARTURE TAX

For flights to neighbouring countries (Pakistan, Sri Lanka, Bangladesh, Nepal) the departure tax is Rs 100, but to other countries it's Rs 300. The airport tax applies to everybody, even to babies who do not occupy a seat. The method of collecting the tax varies but generally you have to pay it before you check in, so look out for an airport tax counter as you enter the check-in area.

INSURANCE

Regardless of how you plan to travel to India, it's worth taking out travel insurance. For more information, see Visas & Documents in the Facts for the Visitor chapter.

ORGANISED TOURS

There are numerous foreign eco-travel and adventure travel companies which can provide unusual and interesting trips in addition to companies that provide more standard tours. There are too many to include them all here; check newspapers and travel magazines for advertisements, and journals such as *Earth Journal* (USA) for listings. Several companies which have special-interest tours exclusively to Rajasthan are listed under Organised Tours in the Getting Around chapter. Companies that organise tours to various parts of India include the following:

Australasia

Peregrine Adventures
258 Lonsdale St, Melbourne 3000, Australia (☎ (03) 9663 8611). Also offices in Sydney, Brisbane, Adelaide, Perth and Hobart.

Venturetreks
164 Parnell Rd (PO Box 37610), Parnell, Auckland, New Zealand
(☎ (09) 379-9855; fax (09) 377-0320)

World Expeditions
3rd Floor, 441 Kent St, Sydney, NSW 2000, Australia (☎ (02) 9264-3366; fax (02) 9261-1974)
1st Floor, 393 Little Bourke St, Melbourne, Vic 3000, Australia
(☎ (03) 9670-8400; fax (03) 9670-7474)

The UK

Encounter Overland
267 Old Brompton Rd, London SW5 9JA
(☎ (0171) 370-6845)

Exodus Expeditions
    9 Weir Rd, London SW12 0LT
    (☎ (0181) 673-0859)

The USA
Adventure Center
    1311 63rd St, Suite 200, Emeryville, CA 94608
    (☎ (800) 227-8747)
All Adventure Travel, Inc.
    PO Box 4307, Boulder, CO 80306
    (☎ (303) 440-7924)

Rajasthan

AIR
With the deregulation of the Indian skies, Indian Airlines no longer has a monopoly on domestic air services, and at least half a dozen new airlines, known as Air Taxi Operators (ATOs), have started services, a number of which fly to Jaipur, Udaipur and Jodhpur in Rajasthan.

Jet Airways is planning to commence flights to Jaipur in late 1996. See the Getting There & Away section in the Jaipur chapter for fares and more details on domestic flights.

Domestic Airlines
Delhi The addresses in New Delhi (telephone area code: 011) of airlines serving Rajasthan are as follows:

Indian Airlines
    Malhotra Bldg, F Block, Connaught Place
    (☎ 331-0517; fax 462-4322; airport ☎ 141)
    PTI Bldg, Sansad Marg (☎ 371-9168)
Jagson Airlines
    12-E Vandana Bldg, 11 Tolstoy Marg
    (☎ 372-1593; fax 372-1594; airport ☎ 329-5126
    ext 2200)
Jet Airways
    3-E Hansalaya Bldg, 15 Barakhamba Rd
    (☎ 335-1352; fax 371-4867, 329-5402; airport
    ☎ 329-5404)
ModiLuft
    VIPPS Centre, ground floor (North Wing), 2
    Commercial Complex, Masjid Moth, Greater
    Kailash II
    (☎ 335-4446; fax 643-0929; airport ☎ 548-1351)

Sahara Airlines
    7th Floor, Ambadeep Bldg, 14 Kasturba Gandhi
    Marg
    (☎ 332-6851; fax 322-8868; airport ☎ 329-5234)
Skyline NEPC
    G-39, 4th Floor, Pawan House, Connaught Circus
    (☎ 332-2525; fax 332-9292; airport ☎ 329-557)
UP Airways
    A2 Defence Colony
    (☎ 403-8201; fax 463-6584; airport ☎ 329-5126, ext
    2389)

Mumbai The addresses/telephone numbers in Mumbai (telephone area code: 022) of domestic airlines serving Rajasthan are as follows:

Indian Airlines
    Army & Navy Bldg, MG Rd
    (☎ 202-2131; fax 283-0832; airport ☎ 611-4433)
Jet Airways
    Amarchand Mansion, Madame Cama Rd
    (☎ 285-5788; fax 821-5079; airport ☎ 610-2767)
ModiLuft
    Akash Ganga, 2nd Floor, 89 Bhulabhai Desai
    Marg, Cumballa Hill
    (☎ 363-5859; airport 610-3807)
Sahara
    (☎ 283-2466; fax 873-8824; airport ☎ 615-0948)
Skyline NEPC
    Lyka Labs, 77 Nehru Rd, Vile Parle (E)
    (☎ 610-7356; fax 610-7599)
    17 Nehru Rd, Vakola, Santa Cruz (E)
    (☎ 610-2525; fax 610-2544; airport ☎ 610-9726)

Domestic Air Services
There are regular domestic air services between Jaipur and the cities of Delhi, Mumbai, Aurangabad, Bangalore, Cochin, Goa, Ahmedabad, Patna, Varanasi and Calcutta. To Udaipur, there are flights from Delhi, Mumbai, Aurangabad and Goa. To Jodhpur, there are flights from both Delhi and Mumbai. See Getting There & Away under Jaipur, Udaipur and Jodhpur in their respective chapters for details.

Booking Flights
Indian Airlines has computerised booking at all but the smallest offices, so getting flight information and reservations is relatively simple – it's just getting to the head of the queue that takes the time. Nevertheless, all flights are still heavily booked and you need to plan as far in advance as possible.

The ATOs are all reasonably efficient, and most have computerised booking. In Jaipur, all of the ATOs are represented by two travel agencies which are conveniently located in Jaipur Towers on MI Rd. See the Jaipur chapter for details.

Buying Tickets

All Indian Airline tickets must be paid for with foreign currency or by credit card, or rupees backed up by encashment certificates. Change, where appropriate, is given in rupees.

Infants up to two years old travel at 10% of the adult fare, but only one infant per adult can travel at this fare. Children two to 12 years old travel at 50% of the adult fare. There is no student reduction for overseas visitors but there is a youth fare for people 12 to 29 years old. This allows a 25% reduction.

Refunds on adult tickets attract a charge of Rs 100 and can be made at any office. There are no refund charges on infant tickets. If a flight is delayed or cancelled, you cannot refund the ticket. If you fail to show up 30 minutes before the flight, this is regarded as a 'no-show' and you forfeit the full value of the ticket.

Indian Airlines accepts no responsibility if you lose your ticket. They absolutely will not refund lost tickets, but at their discretion may issue replacements.

Fares

Private airlines serving Rajasthan usually charge slightly more than Indian Airlines on the same routes.

Indian Airlines also has a 21 day 'Discover India' pass which costs US$500. This allows unlimited travel on their domestic routes; however, if you are only planning to travel to and within Rajasthan, it probably doesn't represent good value. If you are planning to travel elsewhere in India, then it can be reasonable value if you have limited time. There's also a 25% youth discount if you're under 30.

Check-In

The Indian Airlines check-in time is one hour. On some internal routes, as a security measure you are required to identify your checked-in baggage on the tarmac immediately prior to boarding. Don't forget to do this or it won't be loaded onto the plane.

BUS

Following are details on travelling by bus from the gateway cities of Delhi and Mumbai to Rajasthan. For more general information on travelling by bus in India, see Bus in the Getting Around chapter. There are also regular bus services between other major Indian cities and Rajasthan, such as Agra, Aurangabad and Ahmedabad.

Delhi

The main bus station is at the Interstate Bus Terminal (ISBT) at Kashmir Gate, north of the Old Delhi railway station. It has 24 hour left-luggage facilities, a State Bank of India branch, post office, pharmacy and Delhi Transport's Nagrik Restaurant. Bookings to Jaipur with the state government bus company, Rajasthan Roadways (☎ (011) 252-2246), can be made between 7 am and 9 pm. Express services to Jaipur take 5½ hours and cost Rs 68.

There is also a Rajasthan Roadways office (☎ 338-3469) in the same complex as the Rajasthan Tourist Reception Centre, Bikaner House, Pandara Rd, New Delhi. Deluxe (two seat by two seat) buses (Rs 125) and air-con (Rs 215) services leave approximately every hour between 6.30 am and 10.45 pm. The 261 km journey takes around five hours.

There are numerous travel agencies in the popular budget hotel area of Pahar Ganj. Quoted rates for luxury (2x2) buses to destinations in Rajasthan, and to Agra, were as follows: Jaipur, Rs 150; Pushkar, Rs 180; Udaipur, Rs 190; Jodhpur, Rs 190; Jaisalmer, Rs 220; and Agra, Rs 170.

Work is currently underway on the main highway between New Delhi and Jaipur, National Highway No 8. When this is completed, travel time between these two cities will be considerably reduced, to around four hours.

Mumbai

Long-distance buses depart from the state road transport terminal opposite Bombay Central railway station. It's fairly chaotic and there are almost no signs or information available in English.

There are no direct Rajasthan Roadways services between Mumbai and Jaipur. You will need to change buses at Udaipur. Numerous private travel agencies can book luxury services to Udaipur from Mumbai (16 hours, Rs 200), and there are regular services on to Jaipur (nine hours, Rs 105) and other centres such as Ajmer (for Pushkar), Kota and Jodhpur.

TRAIN

Comprehensive information on travelling in India by train is in the Getting Around chapter. This section includes information on train travel between Delhi and Mumbai and Rajasthan. For details on the *Palace on Wheels*, a luxury escorted train journey which departs from Delhi and takes in Agra and the major tourist sights of Rajasthan, see Organised Tours in the Getting Around chapter.

Delhi

There is a special foreign tourist booking office upstairs in the New Delhi railway station. It is open Monday to Saturday from 7.30 am to 5 pm. This is the place to go if you want a tourist-quota allocation, are the holder of an Indrail Pass or want to buy an Indrail Pass (for information on these passes, see the Getting Around chapter).

It gets very busy and crowded, and it can take up to an hour to get served. If you make bookings here tickets must be paid for in foreign currency (US dollars and pounds sterling only, and your change will be given in rupees), or with rupees backed up by bank exchange certificates.

The main ticket office is on Chelmsford Rd, between New Delhi railway station and Connaught Place. This place is well organised, but incredibly busy. Take a numbered ticket from the counter as you enter the building, and then wait at the allotted window. Even with 50 computerised terminals, it can take up to an hour to get served. It's best to arrive first thing in the morning, or when it reopens after lunch. The office is open Monday to Saturday from 7.45 am to 1.50 pm and 2 to 9 pm. On Sunday it's open until 1.50 pm only.

There are two main railway stations in Delhi – Delhi railway station in Old Delhi and New Delhi railway station at Pahar Ganj. New Delhi railway station is much closer to Connaught Place, and if you're departing

Trains from Delhi to Rajasthan

Train	Station*	Depart Delhi	Arrive Jaipur	Arrive Ajmer	Arrive Jodhpur	Arrive Udaipur
2413 *Delhi-Jaipur Superfast* 9966 *Garib Nawaz/*	OD	5.30 am	10.35 am	–	–	–
2901 *Pink City Express*	SR	6 am	12 pm	3.35 pm	–	–
2016 *Shatabdi Express*	ND	6.10 am	11 am	1.30 pm	–	–
9903 *Ahmedabad Express*	SR	9.20 am	5 pm	9.25 pm	–	–
9615 *Chetak Express*	SR	1.20 pm	8.30 pm	12.40 am	–	9.25 am
9760 *Intercity Express*	OD	4.40 pm	10 pm	–	–	–
2905 *Ashram Express*	SR	6 pm	–	2.30 am	–	–
2461 *Mandore Express*	OD	8 pm	1.30 am	–	–	–
4893 *Delhi-Jodhpur Mail*	SR	8.35 pm	–	5.40 am	11.40 am	–
9901 *Ahmedabad Mail* 2907 *Surya Nagri Express/*	SR	9.10 pm	4.30 am	9.10 am	–	–
9733 *Shekhawati Express*	SR	11.15 pm	11.10 am	–	9.05 pm	–

* SR = Sarai Rohilla; ND = New Delhi Railway Station; OD = Old Delhi Railway Station

rom the Old Delhi railway station you hould allow adequate time to wend your vay through the traffic snarls of Old Delhi. Between the Old Delhi and New Delhi ailway stations you can take the No 6 bus or just Rs 1. Recently some trains between Delhi and Jaipur, Jodhpur and Udaipur have been operating to and from Sarai Rohilla railway station – it's about 3.5 km north-west of Connaught Place on Guru Govind Singh Marg. They may still be, so check when you book your ticket. The exception is the Shatabdi Express to Jaipur, which operates from New Delhi railway station.

The table on page 126 is intended as a quick reference only; check all departure times carefully when you purchase your ticket. Not all of these trains depart daily.

Mumbai

There are no direct trains from Mumbai to Rajasthan; all trains are via Ahmedabad, the capital of Gujarat. Two railway systems operate out of Mumbai: Central Railways, which mostly handles services to the east and south; and Western Railways, which has services to the north from Churchgate and Central stations. Trains to Ahmedabad all leave from Bombay Central railway station. Bookings can be made at the Western Railways booking office (☎ (022) 203-8016, ext 4577) next to the Government of India tourist office opposite Churchgate, Monday to Saturday between 8 am and 8 pm (Sunday until 2 pm). Tourist-quota tickets are issued from here, but only between 9.30 am and 4.30 pm (Saturday from 9.30 am to 2.30 pm; closed Sunday). They can be paid in foreign currency, or in rupees if you can show a recent encashment certificate. Indrail passes can also be purchased here.

CAR & MOTORCYCLE

Few people bring their own vehicles to India. If you do decide to bring a car or motorcycle to India it must be brought in under a carnet (a customs document guaranteeing its removal at the end of your stay). Failing to do so will be very expensive.

Rental

Self-drive car rental in India is not widespread, but it is possible. Hertz maintains offices in Delhi, Mumbai and Jaipur, as well as several other Indian cities. Hertz also has chauffeur drive rates. Prices are available on application. Addresses of Hertz offices are listed on the following page.

Trains from Mumbai to Ahmedabad

Train	Depart Mumbai	Arrive Ahmedabad
9011 Gujarat Express	5.45 am	3.05 pm
2009 Shatabdi Express	6.25 am	1.15 pm
2933 Karnavati Express	1.40 pm	9.15 pm
9007 Ahmedabad Janata Express	7.35 pm	4.50 am
9005 Saurashtra Mail	8.10 pm	5.45 am
9101 Gujarat Mail	9.25 pm	6.30 am

Trains from Ahmedabad to Rajasthan

Train	Depart Ahmedabad	Arrive Abu Road	Arrive Jodhpur	Arrive Ajmer	Arrive Jaipur
9902 Delhi Mail	5.15 am	10.40 am	–	6.20 pm	10.40 pm
9932 Aravali Express	8.25 am	1.50 pm	–	9.40 pm	–
4828 Ranakpur Express	7.50 am	12.50 pm	8.20 pm	–	–
2906 Ashram Express	4.30 pm	8.15 pm	–	1.45 am	–
9904 Delhi Express	5 pm	10.10 pm	–	6.15 am	10.15 am
9965 Jodhpur Express	10 pm	–	10.50 am	–	–

Self-Drive Rates (in Rs) with Hertz

Model	24 hours/200 km	3-6 days (per day)	7+ days (per day)	Extra km	Extra hr
Maruti 800cc	900	850	800	3	45
Premier 118 NE	1350	1300	1250	6	65
Contessa Classic	1550	1500	1450	6.50	75
Maruti 1000cc	1750	1700	1650	7.50	85
Tata Estate	2200	2100	2000	10	100

Delhi
    Ansal Chambers-I, GF 29, No 3, Bhikaji Cama
    Place (☎ (011) 687-7188; fax 687-7206)
Jaipur
    Hotel Holiday Inn, Amber Rd
    (☎ 0141) 60-9000; fax 60-9090)
Mumbai (Bombay)
    Autoworld, 139 Tardeo Rd
    (☎ (022) 492-1429; fax 492-1172)

Fuel is in addition to the above rates, and you will be required to pay a deposit of at least Rs 1000 (returnable if there's no damage whatsoever to the car – a scratch constitutes 'damage').

If you don't feel confident about driving on Indian roads it is easy to hire a car and driver either from the Rajasthan Tourism Development Corporation or privately through your hotel. By western standards the cost is quite low, certainly cheaper than a rent-a-car (without driver) in the west. Almost any local taxi will quite happily set off on a long-distance trip in India; enquiring at a taxi rank is the easiest way to find a car – you can also ask your hotel to book one for you although this will cost more. For more information regarding car and motorcycle travel in India see the Getting Around chapter.

SANJAY SINGH BADNOR

RICHARD I'ANSON

SANJAY SINGH BADNOR

aipur
Top: The gateways to the 'pink city', the old city of Jaipur.
Middle: Jaipur street scene.
ottom: Jaipur's Jantar Mantar (observatory) built in the 18th century.

City Palace, Jaipur

Getting Around

AIR
Domestic Air Services
There are airports in Rajasthan at Jaipur, Jodhpur, Udaipur and Jaisalmer. In addition to flights serving Rajasthan from other Indian cities (see Air in the Getting There & Away chapter), there are several air services between the cities of Rajasthan. Information on booking domestic flights is in the Getting There & Away chapter.

There are daily flights between Jaipur and Jodhpur with either Indian Airlines (US$45), ModiLuft (US$46) or UP Airways (US$54). There are daily services between Udaipur and Jaipur with either Indian Airlines or UP Airways (both US$51), or ModiLuft (US$54).

Between Udaipur and Jodhpur there are daily flights with either Indian Airlines (US$41) or ModiLuft (US$43). Jagson Airlines has flights between Jodhpur and Jaisalmer on Tuesday, Thursday and Saturday (US$50).

Airfares Update
At the time of going to press, Indian Airlines announced that US$ sector fares will increase from 1 March 1997. It is expected that the other domestic airlines will follow suit. Increases should be no more than 16%. ∎

BUS
The state government bus service is called Rajasthan Roadways. There are also often privately owned local bus services, and luxury private coaches between major cities which can be booked with travel agencies.

Types
Generally bus travel is crowded, slow and uncomfortable.

Ordinary buses generally have five seats across, although if there are only five people sitting in them consider yourself lucky! There are usually mounds of baggage in the aisles, chickens under seats and in some more remote places there'll be people travelling 'upper class' (ie on the roof) as well. These buses tend to be frustratingly slow, are usually in an advanced state of decrepitude and stop frequently – often for seemingly no reason – and for long periods, and can take forever.

Express buses are a big improvement in that they stop far less often. They're still crowded, but at least you feel as though you're getting somewhere. The fare is usually a few rupees more than on an ordinary bus – well worth the extra.

Deluxe buses have only four seats across and these will usually recline. Super-deluxe buses offer even greater comfort and have air-conditioning.

Unlike state-operated bus companies, private operators are keen to maximise profits; therefore, maintenance is less and speed more – a dangerous combination.

If you're travelling overnight by bus, try to avoid video coaches, which generally screen macho garbage at full volume.

Getting a Seat
If there are two of you, work out a bus boarding plan where one of you can guard the gear while the other storms the bus in search of a seat. The other accepted method is to pass a newspaper or article of clothing through the open window and place it on an empty seat, or ask a passenger to do it for you. Having made your 'reservation' you can then board the bus after things have simmered down. This method rarely fails.

At many bus stations there is a separate women's queue. You may not notice this because the relevant sign (where it exists at all) will not be in English and there may not be any women queuing. Usually the same ticket window will handle the male and the female queue, taking turn about. What this means is that women can usually go straight up to the front of the queue (ie alongside the male queue) and get almost immediate service.

Baggage

Baggage is generally carried for free on the roof, so it's an idea to take a few precautions. Make sure it's tied on properly and that nobody dumps a tin trunk on top of your (relatively) fragile backpack.

Theft is sometimes a problem, so keep an eye on your bags at chai stops and carry your valuables on board with you. Having a large, heavy-duty bag into which your pack will fit can be a good idea, not only for bus travel but also for air travel.

If someone carries your bag onto the roof, expect to pay a few rupees for the service.

Toilet Stops

On long-distance bus trips, chai stops can be far too frequent or, conversely, agonisingly infrequent. Long-distance trips can be a real hassle for women travellers – toilet facilities are generally inadequate to say the least. Forget about modesty and do what the local women do – wander a few yards off or find a convenient bush.

TRAIN

The Indian Railways system is the world's fourth largest with a route length of over 60,000 km. Every single day over 7000 passenger trains run, carrying over 10.5 million passengers and connecting 7100 stations. It's also the world's largest single employer with a shade over 1.6 million employees!

The first step in coming to grips with Indian Railways is to get a timetable. *Trains at a Glance* is a handy guide covering all the main routes and trains. *Western Railways* covers, as you'd expect, the western half of India. Both cost Rs 15 and are usually available at major railway stations, and sometimes on newsstands in the larger cities.

The timetables indicate the km distance between major stations and a table in front shows the fares for distances from one km to 5000 km for the various train types. With this information it is very easy to calculate the fare between any two stations. Unless otherwise indicated, the fares quoted in this guide are based on the faster ('express' rather than 'passenger') trains.

Details of train services between Rajasthan and New Delhi/Mumbai (Bombay) are in the Getting There & Away chapter.

Classes

There are generally two classes – 1st and 2nd – but there are a number of subtle variations on this basic distinction. For a start there is 1st class and 1st class air-con. The air-con carriages only operate on the major trains and routes. The fare for 1st class air-con is more than double normal 1st class. A slightly cheaper air-con alternative is the air-con two tier sleeper, which costs about 25% more than 1st class. These carriages are a lot more common than 1st class air-con, but are still only found on the major routes.

Between 1st and 2nd class there are two more air-con options: the air-con three tier sleeper and air-con chair car. The former has three levels of berths rather than two, while the latter, as the name suggests, consists of carriages with aircraft-type layback seats. Once again, these carriages are only found on the major routes, and the latter only on day trains. The cost of air-con three tier is about 70% of the 1st class fare; air-con chair is about 55% of the 1st class fare.

Types

What you want is a mail or express train. What you do not want is a passenger train. No Indian train travels very fast, but at least the mail and express trains keep travelling more of the time.

Air-con 'superfast' express services operate on certain main routes, and because of tighter scheduling and fewer stops they are much faster. A separate fare structure applies to them as meals are included. The *Shatabdi Express*, which operates between Delhi and Jaipur, and Mumbai and Ahmedabad, is such a service.

Gauge

There are three gauge types in India: broad, metre and narrow, and what you want nearly as much as a mail or express train is broad gauge. In broad gauge the rails are 1.676m apart; metre gauge is, as it says, one metre wide; narrow gauge is either 0.762m (two feet six inches) or 0.610m (two feet).

Broad gauge has a major advantage – it is much faster. It also gives a smoother ride. The carriages are much the same between broad gauge and metre gauge, but on narrow gauge they are much, much narrower and the accommodation very cramped. In areas where there are no broad-gauge lines, it may be worth taking a bus, which will often be faster then the metre-gauge trains. Many of the narrow-gauge lines in Rajasthan are currently being converted to broad gauge, which means you may be subject to delays or cancellations on some services.

Life on Board
It's India for real on board the trains. In 2nd class, unreserved travel can be a nightmare since the trains are often hopelessly crowded. Combined with the crowds, the noise and the confusion there's the discomfort. Fans and lights have a habit of failing at prolonged stops when there's no air moving through the carriage, and toilets can get a bit rough towards the end of a long journey. Worst of all are the stops. Trains seem to stop often, interminably and for no apparent reason. Often it's because somebody has pulled the emergency stop cable because they are close to home – well, so it's said; some people deny this. Still, it's all part of life on the rails.

In 2nd class reserved it's a great deal better since, in theory, only four people share each bench. However, there's inevitably the fifth, and sometimes even the sixth, person who gets the others to bunch up so they can get at least part of their bum on the seat. This normally doesn't happen at night or in 1st class, where there are either two or four people to a compartment, and the compartment doors are lockable.

Costs
Fares operate on a distance basis. The time-tables indicate the distance in km between the stations and from this it is simple to calculate the cost between any two stations. If you have a ticket for at least 400 km, you can break your journey at the rate of one day per 200 km so long as you travel at least 300 km on the first sector. This can save a lot of hassle buying tickets and also, of course, results in a small saving.

Reservations
The cost of reservations is nominal – it's the time it takes which hurts, although even this is generally not too bad as computerised reservation becomes more widespread. At the moment it is limited to the major towns and cities only. There is a special counter for foreign tourists at the Jaipur reservation office.

Reservations can be made up to six months in advance and the longer in advance you make them the better. Your reservation ticket will indicate which carriage and berth you have, and when the train arrives you will find a sheet of paper fixed to each carriage listing passenger names beside their appropriate berth number. Usually this information is also posted on notice boards on the platform. It is Indian rail efficiency at its best.

As at many bus stations, there are separate women's queues, usually with a sign saying 'Ladies' Queue' (see Getting a Seat in the Bus section).

Reservation costs are Rs 25 in air-con 1st class, Rs 15 in 1st class and air-con chair class, Rs 10 in a 2nd class three tier sleeper, and Rs 5 in 2nd class sitting. There are very rarely any 2nd class sitting compartments with reservations. There are also some super-fast express trains that require a supplementary charge.

If the train you want is fully booked, it's often possible to get an RAC (Reservation Against Cancellation) ticket. This entitles you to board the train and have seating accommodation. Once the train is underway, the TTE (Travelling Ticket Examiner) will find a berth for you, but it may take an hour or more. This is different from a wait-listed ticket, as the latter does not give you the right to actually board the train (should you be so cheeky you can be 'detrained and fined'). The hassle with RAC tickets is that you will probably get split up if there are two or more of you.

If you've not had time to get a reservation or been unable to get one, it's worth just getting on the train in any reserved carriage. Although there's the risk of a small fine for 'ticketless travel', most TTEs are sympathetic. If there are spare berths/seats they'll allot you one, and charge the normal fare plus reservation fee. If all the berths/seats are already reserved, you'll simply be banished to the crush and confusion in the unreserved carriages. This trick only works well for day travel. At night sleepers are generally booked out well in advance, so if you can't get one (or an RAC ticket) then sitting up in 2nd class is your only choice.

If you plan your trip well ahead, you can avoid all the hassles by booking in advance from abroad. A good Indian travel agent will book and obtain tickets in advance and have them ready for you on arrival. As an alternative to buying tickets as you go along, it's possible to buy a ticket from A to Z with all the stops along the way prebooked. It might take a bit of time sitting down and working it out at the start, but if your time is limited and you can fix your schedule rigidly, this can be a good way to go.

Refunds

Booked tickets are refundable but cancellation fees apply. If you present the ticket more than one day in advance, a fee of Rs 10 to Rs 30 applies, depending on the class. Up to four hours before, you lose 25% of the ticket value; up to three to 12 hours after departure (depending on the distance of the ticketed journey) you lose 50%. Any later than that and you can keep the ticket as a souvenir.

Tickets for unreserved travel can be refunded up to three hours after the departure of the train, and the only penalty is a Rs 2 per passenger fee.

When presenting your ticket for a refund, you are officially entitled to go straight to the head of the queue (where there isn't a dedicated · window for refunds), the rationale being that the berth/seat you are surrendering may be just the one required by the next person in the queue.

Sleepers

There are 2nd class and 1st class sleepers, although by western standards even 1st class is not luxurious. Bedding is available, but only on certain 1st class and air-con two tier services, and then only if arranged when booking your ticket. First class sleepers are generally private compartments with two or four berths in them, sometimes with a toilet as well. Usually the sleeping berths fold up to make a sitting compartment during the day. First class air-con sleepers are more luxurious, and much more expensive, than regular 1st class sleepers.

Second class sleepers are known as three tier. Doorless compartments each contain six berths. During the day, the middle berth is lowered to make seats for six or eight. At night they are folded into position, everybody has to bed down at the same time, and a TTE ensures that nobody without a reservation gets into the carriage.

Broad-gauge, three tier sleeping carriages also have a row of narrow two tier (upper and lower) berths along the passage. These 'outside berths' are not only narrower than the 'inside' berths, but are about 20 cm shorter, so that for the average person, stretching right out is not possible. When reserving 2nd class berths, always write 'inside' on the 'Accommodation Preference' section of the booking form. Sleeping berths are only available between 9 pm and 6 am.

For any sleeper reservation, you should try to book at least several days ahead. There is usually a board or computer screen in each station indicating what is available or how long before the next free berth/seat comes up on the various routes. Once you've selected a particular train and date, you must fill in a reservation form. Do this before you get to the front of the queue. The forms are usually found in boxes around the reservation hall. The demand for 1st class sleepers is generally far less than for 2nd class.

Be warned that on timetables and state-of-reservation boards at railway stations, train names are often listed without destinations. This is where your *Trains at a Glance* comes in. If you don't have one, you'll have to ask and that's going to soak up time. Tourist offices can usually help by suggesting the best trains but there isn't always a tourist office. It's something you'll just have to come to terms with.

Getting a Space Despite Everything

If you want a sleeper and there are none left, then it's time to try and break into the quotas. Ask the stationmaster, often a helpful man who speaks English, if there is a tourist quota, station quota or if there is a VIP quota. The latter is often a good last bet because VIPs rarely turn up to use their quotas.

If all that fails then you're going to be travelling unreserved and that can be no fun at all. To ease the pain get yourself some expert help. For, say, Rs 10 baksheesh you can get a porter who will absolutely ensure you get a seat if it's humanly possible. If it's a train starting from your station, the key to success is to be on the train before it arrives at the departure platform. Your porter will do just that, so when it rolls up you simply stroll on board and take the seat he has warmed for you. If it's a through train then it can be a real free-for-all, and you can be certain he'll be better at it than you are – he'll also not be encumbered with baggage or backpacks.

Women can ask about the Ladies' Compartments which many trains have and which are often a refuge from the crowds in other compartments.

Left Luggage

Most stations have a left-luggage facility, quaintly called a cloak room, where backpacks can be left for Rs 2 per day. This is a very useful facility if you're visiting (but not staying in) a town, or if you want to find a place to stay, unencumbered by gear. The regulations state that any luggage left in a cloak room must be locked, although this is not strictly enforced.

Special Trains

The very special *Palace on Wheels* makes a regular circuit of Rajasthan. It is also possible to hire a former maharaja's private rail carriage, which can be connected to sched-

uled train services. See Organised Tours later in this chapter.

In August 1997 there are plans by the Royal Scotsman, leading tour operators of the UK, to run two luxury coach trains in India, one of which, the *Royal Indian*, will include Rajasthan in its itinerary. No further details were available at the time of writing.

Indrail Passes

Indrail passes permit unlimited travel on Indian trains for the period of their validity, but they are expensive and, overall, probably not worth the expense. In purely dollar terms, to get the full value out of any of the passes, you need to travel around 300 km per day; with the speed of Indian trains that's at least six hours travelling! If you are only planning to travel to and within Rajasthan, they're not worth considering.

The average visitor to India might cover around 3000 km in a month by rail. An air-con Indrail Pass for this costs US$500; to buy the tickets as you go along would cost around US$100 to US$160, depending on the number and length of the individual journeys; even if you did twice as many km, you still wouldn't even come close to getting your money's worth. It's the same story with the passes for other classes: a 2nd class, one month Indrail Pass costs US$110, the individual tickets for 3000 km of travel would cost around US$12 to US$25.

Children aged five to 12 years pay half-fare. Indrail passes can be bought overseas through some travel agents or in India at certain major railway offices. Payment in India can be made only in US dollars or pounds sterling (cash or travellers' cheques), or in rupees backed up with exchange certificates. Second class passes are not available outside India. Indrail passes cover all reservation and berth costs, and they can be extended if you wish to keep on travelling. The main offices in India which handle Indrail passes are:

Calcutta
    Railway Tourist Guide, Eastern Railway, Fairlie Place

Central Reservation Office, South-Eastern Railway, Esplanade Mansion

Delhi

Railway Tourist Guide, New Delhi Railway Station

Madras

Central Reservation Office, Southern Railway, Madras Central

Mumbai (Bombay)

Railway Tourist Guide, Western Railway, Churchgate

Railway Tourist Guide, Central Railway, Victoria Terminus

They are also available from the central reservation office of Jaipur railway station. See the Jaipur chapter for details.

S&K Enterprises Ltd (☎ (0181) 903-3411) is a UK company which specialises in Indrail passes. They sell the passes and can make reservations if given at least one month's notice. Their address is: 103 Wembley Park Drive, Wembley, Middlesex, HA9 8HG, UK. Second/1st class passes cost from £49/90 for seven days up to £145/320 for 90 days.

CAR
Renting
Hertz is the only car rental operator in Rajasthan which offers self-drive. See Car & Motorcycle in the Getting There & Away chapter for current rates.

An alternative to self-drive is to hire a car and driver. Numerous travel agencies or your hotel will be able to provide this service for you. The trick is to get a driver who can speak English and who is preferably knowledgeable about the areas you plan to travel to. For this, you will probably need to pay extra.

Official rates for a car and driver with the Rajasthan Tourism Development Corporation are Rs 4.30 per km for a non air-con car, and an expensive Rs 10 per km for an air-con car, with the usual 250 km minimum hire charge per day. More competitive rates are offered by some travel agencies in Jaipur. See Getting There & Away in the Jaipur chapter for details.

Buying
Buying a car is naturally expensive in India and not worth the effort unless you intend to stay for months.

Road Conditions
Because of the extreme congestion in th cities and the narrow bumpy roads in th country, driving is often a slow, stop-sta process – hard on you, the car and fue economy. Service is so-so in India, parts an tyres not always easy to obtain, though ther are plenty of puncture-repair places. All i all driving is no great pleasure except in rura areas where there's little traffic. Having sai that, some intrepid souls will try anythin once – a young German fellow recently trav elled around India at the wheel of a 48 seate bus!

Road Safety
In India there are 155 road deaths daily 56,000 or so a year – which is an astonishin total in relation to the number of vehicles o the road. In the USA, for instance, there ar 43,000 road fatalities per year, but it also ha more than 20 times the number of vehicles

The reasons for the high death rate in Indi are numerous and many of them fairl obvious – starting with the congestion on th roads and the equal congestion in vehicles When a bus runs off the road there are plent of people stuffed inside to get injured, an it's unlikely too many of them will be able t escape in a hurry. One newspaper articl stated that 'most accidents are caused b brake failure or the steering wheel gettin free'!

Many of those killed are pedestrian involved in hit-and-run accidents. The pro pensity to disappear after the incident is no wholly surprising – lynch mobs can assem ble remarkably quickly, even when the drive is not at fault!

Most accidents are caused by trucks, fo on Indian roads might is right and trucks ar the biggest, heaviest and mightiest. Yo either get out of their way or get run down As with so many Indian vehicles, they'r likely to be grossly overloaded and not in th best of condition. Trucks are actually license and taxed to carry a load 25% more than th maximum recommended by the manufacture It's staggering to see the number of truc wrecks by the sides of the national highways and these aren't old accidents, but ones which have obviously happened in the last 24 hours or so – if they haven't been killed, quite often the driver and crew will be sitting around, wondering what to do next.

If you are driving yourself, you need to be extremely vigilant at all times. At night there are unilluminated cars and ox carts, and in the daytime there are fearless cyclists and hordes of pedestrians. Day and night there are the crazy truck drivers to contend with. Indeed, at night, it's best to avoid driving at all along any major truck route unless you're prepared to get off the road completely every time a truck is coming in the opposite direction! The other thing you have to contend with at night is the eccentric way in which headlights are used – a combination of full beam and totally off (dipped beams are virtually unheard of). A loud horn definitely helps since the normal driving technique is to put your hand firmly on the horn, close your eyes and plough through regardless. Vehicles always have the right of way over pedestrians and bigger vehicles always have the right of way over smaller ones.

MOTORCYCLE

This section is based largely on information originally contributed by intrepid Britons Ken Twyford and Gerald Smewing, with updates from Jim & Lucy Amos.

Travelling around India by motorcycle has become increasingly popular in recent years. Motorcycling offers the freedom to go when and where you like – making it the ideal way to get to grips with the vastness that is India.

What to Bring

An International Driving Licence is not mandatory, but is handy to have. Regulations may change, but currently Indian motorcycle companies and traffic authorities need little, if any, evidence that you have a local or foreign licence for any vehicle, or that you can even ride a motorcycle.

In Delhi, helmets are required for all drivers (but not pillion passengers), but are rarely used. In Rajasthan, helmets are not compulsory (but are advisable). If required, leathers, gloves, boots, waterproofs and other protective gear should be brought from your home country.

A few small bags will be a lot easier to carry than one large rucksack.

It is always a good idea, and vital in remote areas, to carry spare tubes and chains. A tent and sleeping bag are handy where accommodation is scarce, and essential in areas where you may be caught in bad weather (which can happen at any time of the year in some parts).

Renting

Motorcycles can be rented from companies in Delhi for a negotiable price, including insurance, for about Rs 6000 per month, or from Rs 175 to Rs 250 per day. Rental companies will want a substantial bond of about US$500 – some unused travellers' cheques will probably do.

Buying & Selling

India does not have used-vehicle dealers, motorcycle magazines or weekend newspapers with pages of motorcycle classified advertisements. To purchase a second-hand machine one simply needs to enquire. A good place to start is with mechanics. They are likely to know somebody who is selling a bike. In Delhi, the area around Hari Singh Nalwa St, Karol Bagh, is full of places selling, buying and renting motorcycles. One place recommended by travellers is Inder Motors, 1744/55 Hari Singh Nalwa St (☎ (011) 572-5879).

To buy a new bike, you'll have to have a local address and be a resident foreign national. However, unless the dealer you are buying from is totally devoid of imagination and contacts, this presents few problems. When buying second-hand, all you need to do is give an address.

New bikes are generally purchased through a showroom. When buying second-hand, it is best to engage the services of an 'auto-consultant'. These people act as go-betweens to bring buyers and sellers together. They will usually be able to show you a number of machines to suit your price bracket. These agents can be found by enquiring, or may sometimes advertise on their shop fronts.

For around Rs 500, which usually covers a bribe to officials, they will assist you in transferring the ownership papers through the bureaucracy. Without their help this could take a couple of weeks.

The overall appearance of the bike doesn't seem to affect the price greatly. Dents and scratches don't reduce the cost much, and added extras don't increase it by much.

When the time comes to sell the bike, don't appear too anxious to get rid of it. Don't hang around in one town too long, as word gets around the autoconsultants and the offers will get smaller as the days go by. If you get a reasonable offer, grab it. Regardless of which bike it is, you'll be told it's the 'least popular in India' and other such tales.

Ownership Papers A needless hint perhaps, but do not part with your money until you have the ownership papers, receipt and affidavit signed by a magistrate authorising the owner (as recorded in the ownership papers) to sell the machine. Not to mention the keys to the bike and the bike itself!

Each state has a different set of ownership transfer formalities. Get assistance from the agent you're buying the machine through or from one of the many 'attorneys' hanging around under tin roofs by the Motor Vehicles Office. They will charge you a fee of up to Rs 300, which will consist largely of a bribe to expedite matters.

Alternatively you could go to one of the many typing clerk services and request them to type out the necessary forms, handling the matter cheaply yourself – but with no guarantee of a quick result.

Check that your name has been recorded in the ownership book and stamped and signed by the department head. If you intend to sell your motorcycle in another state, then you will need a 'No Objections Certificate'. This confirms your ownership and is issued by the Motor Vehicles Department in the state of purchase, so get it immediately when transferring ownership papers to your name.

The standard form can be typed up for a few rupees, or more speedily and expensively through one of the many attorneys. This document is vital if you are going to sell the bike in another state.

Insurance & Tax As in most countries, it is compulsory to have third party insurance. The New India Assurance Company or the National Insurance Company are just two of a number of companies who can provide it. The cost for fully comprehensive insurance is Rs 720 for 12 months, and this also covers you in Nepal.

Road tax is paid when the bike is bought new. This is valid for the life of the machine and is transferred to the new owner when the bike changes hands.

Helmets

Good-quality helmets are available in the big cities for Rs 500 to Rs 600. The cheaper ones should be avoided as they don't come up to standard.

Which Bike?

The big decision to make is whether to buy new or second-hand. Obviously cost is the main factor, but remember that with a new motorcycle you are less likely to get ripped off as the price is fixed, the cost will include free servicing and you know it will be reliable. Old motorcycles are obviously cheaper and you don't have to be a registered resident foreign national, but you are far more open to getting ripped off, either by paying too much or getting a dud bike.

Everyone is likely to have their own preferences, and so there is no one motorcycle which suits everybody. However, here is a rundown of what's readily available:

Mopeds These come with or without gears. As they are only 50cc capacity, they are really only useful around towns or for short distances.

Scooters There are the older design Bajaj and Vespa scooters, or the more modern Japanese designs by Honda-Kinetic and others. The older ones are 150cc. The Honda is 100cc and has no gears.

Scooters are inherently unstable creatures, largely due to the high centre of gravity and small wheels. On rough roads they're positively lethal.

On the plus side, they are economical to buy and run, are easy to ride, have a good resale value, and most have built-in lockable storage.

100cc Motorcycles The four main Japanese companies – Honda, Suzuki, Kawasaki and Yamaha – all have 100cc, two stroke machines, while Honda and Kawasaki also have four stroke models.

There's little to differentiate between these bikes; all are lightweight, easy to ride, very economical and reliable, with good resale value. They are suitable for intercity travel on reasonable roads, but they should not be laden down with too much gear. Spares and servicing are readily available. The cost of a new bike of this type is about Rs 32,000, plus the costs of getting it on the road.

Another competitor in this market is the Rajdoot 175 XLT, based on a very old Polish model. It lacks power but is a cheap option, costing around Rs 6000 to Rs 10,000 less than the Japanese bikes.

The Enfield Fury is a modern machine with a front disc brake. It's very unpopular, has a poor gearbox, spares are hard to come by and the resale value is low – avoid.

Bigger Bikes The Yezdi 250 Classic is a cheap and basic bike. It's a rugged machine, and one which you often see in rural areas.

The Enfield Bullet is the classic machine and is the one most favoured among foreigners. Attractions are the traditional design, thumping engine sound, and the price, which is not much more than the new 100cc Japanese bikes. It's a wonderfully durable bike, is easy to maintain, economical to run, but mechanically a bit 'hit and miss', largely because of poorly engineered parts and inferior materials – valves and tappets are the main problem areas. Another drawback is the lack of an effective front brake – the small drum brake is a joke, totally inadequate for what is quite a heavy machine. The Bullet is also available in a 500cc single cylinder version. It has a functional front brake and has 12 volt electrics which are superior to the 350's 6 volt. If you opt for a 350cc, consider paying the Rs 4000 extra to have the 500cc front wheel fitted.

If you are buying a new Enfield with the intention of shipping it back home, it's definitely worth opting for the 500cc, as it has features – such as folding rear footrest and longer exhaust pipe – which most other countries would require. The emission control regulations in some places, such as California, are so strict that there is no way these bikes would be legal. You may be able to get around this by buying an older bike, as the regulations often only apply to new machines. Make sure you check all this out before you go lashing out on a new Enfield, only to find it unregisterable at home. The price is around Rs 40,000 for the 350cc model, or Rs 45,000 for the 500cc.

The Rajdoot 350 is an imported Yamaha 350cc. It's well engineered, fast and has good brakes. Disadvantages are that it's relatively uneconomical to run, and spares are hard to come by. These bikes are also showing their age badly, as they haven't been made for some years now. They cost around Rs 12,000 to Rs 15,000.

On the Road

It must be said that, given the general road conditions, motorcycling is a reasonably hazardous endeavour, and one best undertaken by experienced riders only.

Route-finding can be very tricky. The directions people give you can be very interesting. It is invariably a 'straight road', although if pressed the person might also reveal that the said straight road actually involves taking two right turns, three left turns and the odd fork or two.

Parking the bike and getting things stolen from it seems not to be a problem. The biggest annoyance is that people seem to treat parked motorcycles as public utilities – handy for sitting on, using the mirror to do the hair, fiddling with the switches – but they don't deliberately do any damage. You'll just have to turn all the switches off and readjust the mirrors when you get back on!

Run-ins with the law are not a major problem. The best policy is to give a smile and a friendly wave to any police officers, even if you are doing the opposite of what is signalled.

In the event of an accident, call the police straight away, and don't move anything until the police have seen exactly where and how everything ended up. One foreigner reported spending three days in jail on suspicion of being involved in an accident, when all he'd done was taken a child to hospital from the scene of an accident.

Don't try to cover too much territory in one day. As such a high level of concentration is needed to survive, long days are tiring and dangerous. On the busy national highways, expect to average 50 km/h without stops; on smaller roads, where driving conditions are worse, 10 km/h is not an unrealistic average. On the whole you can expect to cover between 100 and 150 km in a day on good roads.

Night driving should be avoided at all costs. If you think driving in daylight is difficult, imagine what it's like at night when there's the added hazard of half the vehicles being inadequately lit (or not lit at all), not to mention the breakdowns in the middle of the road.

Putting the bike on a train for really long hauls can be a convenient option. You'll pay about as much as the 2nd class passenger fare for the bike. It can be wrapped in straw for protection if you like, and this is done at the parcels office at the station, which is also where you pay the fare for the bike. The petrol tank must be empty, and there should be a tag in an obvious place detailing name, destination, passport number and train details.

Repairs & Maintenance

Anyone who can handle a screwdriver and spanner in India can be called a mechanic, or *mistri*, so be careful. If you have any mechanical knowledge it may be better to buy your own tools and learn how to do your own repairs. This will save a lot of arguments over prices. If you are getting repairs done by someone, don't leave the premises while the work is being done or you may find that good parts have been ripped off your bike and replaced with bodgy old ones.

Original spare parts bought from an 'Authorised Dealer' can be rather expensive compared with the copies available from your spare-parts *wallah* (literally 'man').

If you buy an older machine you would do well to check and tighten all nuts and bolts every few days. Indian roads and engine vibration tend to work things loose and constant checking could save you rupees and trouble. Check the engine and gearbox oil level regularly. With the quality of oil, it is advisable to change it and clean the oil filter every couple of thousand km.

Punctures Chances are you'll be requiring the services of a puncture-wallah *(punkuche wallah* in Hindi) at least once a week. They are found everywhere, often in the most surprising places, but it's advisable to at least have tools sufficient to remove your own wheel and take it to the puncture-wallah.

Given the hassles of constant flat tyres, it's worth lashing out on new tyres if you buy a second-hand bike with worn tyres. A new rear tyre for an Enfield costs around Rs 500.

Fuel

Petrol is expensive relative to the west and when compared to the cost of living in India – Rs 18 per litre – but diesel is much cheaper at around Rs 7.50 per litre. Petrol is usually readily available in all larger towns and along the main roads, although if you're travelling in more remote areas, it might pay to carry spare fuel with you.

Should you run out, try flagging down a passing car (not a truck or bus since they use diesel) and beg for some. Most Indians are willing to let you have some if you have a hose or siphon and a container. Alternatively hitch a truck ride to the nearest petrol station.

Organised Motorcycle Tours

Classic Bike Adventure (☎ (030) 782-3315, fax 7879-2720), Haupstrasse 5, D 10827

Berlin, Germany, organises bike tours on well maintained Enfields with full insurance. Tours last two to three weeks and some itineraries include Rajasthan. Costs are from DM2800 to DM3820.

BICYCLE

The following cycling information comes from Ann Sorrel, with updates from various travellers.

Every day millions of Indians pedal along the country's roads. If they can do it, so can you. Nevertheless, long-distance cycling is not for the faint of heart or weak of knee. You'll need physical endurance to cope with the roads and the climate, plus you'll face cultural challenges – 'the people factor'. Cycling is a cheap, convenient, healthy, environmentally sound and above all fun way of travelling.

One note of caution: before you leave home, go over your bike with a fine-toothed comb and fill your repair kit with every imaginable spare. As with cars and motorcycles, you won't necessarily be able to buy that crucial gizmo for your machine when it breaks down somewhere in the back of beyond as the sun sets.

Useful Information

Before you set out, read some books on bicycle touring such as the Sierra Club's *The Bike Touring Manual* by Rob van de Plas (Bicycle Books, 1993). Cycling magazines provide useful information including listings for bicycle tour operators and the addresses of spare-parts suppliers. They're also good places to look for a riding companion.

For a real feel of the adventure of bike touring in strange places read Dervla Murphy's classic *Full Tilt – From Ireland to India on a Bike*, or Lloyd Sumner's *The Long Ride*, and *Riding the Mountains Down* (subtitled 'A Journey by Bicycle to Kathmandu') by Bettina Selby (Unwin Publications, 1984).

The International Bicycle Fund (IBF; (☎ (206) 628-9314), 4887 Columbia Drive South, Seattle, Washington 98108-1919, USA, has two publications which may help you prepare for your cycling adventure. These are *Selecting and Preparing a Bike for Travel in Remote Areas* and *Flying With Your Bike*. Each is US$2 plus postage and handling (in the USA: US$1 for first item and US$0.50 for each additional item; other countries: US$2 for first item and US$1 for each additional item).

The IBF is also happy to help prospective long-distance cyclists with information and advice.

Using Your Own Bicycle

If you are planning to tour Rajasthan by bicycle you will have to decide whether to use a lightweight touring bicycle or a mountain bike. If you are going to keep to sealed roads and already have a touring bike, by all means consider bringing it. Mountain bikes, however, are especially suited to countries such as India. Their smaller sturdier construction makes them more manoeuvrable, less prone to damage, and allows you to tackle rugged roads unsuitable for lighter machines.

Bringing your own bicycle does have disadvantages. Your machine is likely to be a real curiosity and subject to much pushing, pulling and probing. If you can't tolerate people touching your bicycle, don't bring it to India.

Spare Parts If you bring a bicycle to India, prepare for the contingencies of part replacement or repair. Bring spare tyres, tubes, patch kits, chassis, cables, freewheels and spokes. Ensure you have a working knowledge of your machine. Bring all necessary tools with you, as well as a compact bike manual with diagrams in case the worst happens and you need to fix a rear derailleur or some other strategic part. Indian mechanics can work wonders and illustrations help overcome the language barrier.

Most of all, be ready to make do and improvise.

Roads don't have paved shoulders and are very dusty, so keep your chain lubricated.

Although India is officially metricated, tools and bike parts follow 'standard' or 'imperial' measurements. Don't expect to find tyres for 700cc rims, although 27 x 1¼ tyres are produced in India by Dunlop and Sawney. Some mountain bike tyres are available but the quality is dubious. Indian bicycle pumps cater to a tube valve different from the Presta and Schraeder valves commonly used in the west. If you're travelling with Presta valves (most high-pressure 27 x 1¼ tubes) bring a Schraeder (car type) adaptor. In India you can buy a local pump adaptor, which means you'll have an adaptor on your adaptor. Bring your own pump as well; most Indian pumps require two or three people to get air down the leaky cable.

In major cities, Japanese tyres and parts (derailleurs, freewheels, chains) are available, but pricey – although so is postage, and transit time can be considerable. If you receive bike parts from abroad, beware of exorbitant customs charges. Say you want the goods as 'in transit' to avoid these charges. They may list the parts in your passport!

You may locate parts in Mumbai or Delhi. Try Metre Cycle, Kalba Devi Rd, Mumbai; or the cycle bazaar in the old city around Esplanade Rd, Delhi. Alternatively, take your bicycle to a cycle market and ask around – someone will know which shop is likely to have things for your 'special' cycle. Beware of Taiwanese imitations and do watch out for tyres which may have been collecting dust for years.

Luggage Your cycle luggage should be as strong, durable and waterproof as possible. I don't recommend a set with lots of zippers, as this makes pilfering easier. As you'll be frequently detaching luggage when taking your bike to your room, a set designed for easy removal from the racks is a must: the fewer the items, the better. *(Never* leave your cycle in the lobby or outside your hotel – take it to bed with you!)

Bike luggage that can easily be reassembled into a backpack is also available, just the thing when you want to park your bike and go by train or foot.

Theft If you're using an imported bike, try to avoid losing your pump (and the water bottle from your frame) – their novelty make them particularly attractive to thieves. Don leave anything on your bike that can easil be removed when it's unattended.

Don't be paranoid about theft – outside th major cities it would be well-nigh impossibl for a thief to resell your bike as it would stan out too much. And not many folk understan quick-release levers on wheels. Your bike probably safer in India than in western citie

Buying & Selling a Bicycle in India
Finding an Indian bike is no problem: ever town will have at least a couple of cycl shops. Shop around for prices and remembe to bargain. Try to get a few extras – bel stand, spare tube – thrown in. There are man brands of Indian clunkers – Hero, Atlas, BSA Raleigh, Bajaj, Avon – but they all follow th same basic, sturdy design. A few mountain bike lookalikes have recently come on th market, but they have no gears. Raleigh considered the finest quality, followed b BSA which has a big line of models includ ing some sporty jobs. Hero and Atlas bot claim to be the biggest seller. Look for th cheapest or the one with the snazziest plat label.

Once you've decided on a bike, you hav a choice of luggage carriers – mostly th rat-trap type varying only in size, price an strength. There's a wide range of saddle available but all are equally bum-breaking A stand is certainly a useful addition and bell or airhorn is a necessity. An advantag of buying a new bike is that the brakes actu ally work. Centre-pull and side-pull brake are also available but at extra cost and ma actually make the bike more difficult to sel The average Indian will prefer the standar model.

Sportier 'mountain bike' styles with straigh handlebars are popular in urban areas. It i also possible to find in big cities and tourist areas used touring bikes left by travellers Also check with diplomatic communit members for bikes.

Reselling the bike is no problem. Ask th proprietor of your lodge if they know anyon who is interested in buying a bike. Negotiate a price and do the deal personally or through the hotel. Most people will be only too willing to help you. Count on losing a couple of hundred rupees or about 30%, depending on local prices. Retail bike stores are not usually interested in buying or selling second-hand bikes. A better bet would be a bike-hire shop, which may be interested in expanding its fleet.

Spare Parts As there are so many repair 'shops' (some consist of a pump, a box of tools, a tube of rubber solution and a water pan under a tree) there is no need to carry spare parts, especially as you'll only own the bike for a few weeks or months. Just take a roll of tube-patch rubber, a tube of Dunlop patch glue, two tyre irons and the wonderful 'universal' Indian bike spanner, which fits all the nuts. There are plenty of puncture-wallahs in all towns and villages who will patch tubes for a couple of rupees, so chances are you won't have to fix a puncture yourself anyway. Besides, Indian tyres are pretty heavy duty, so with luck you won't get a flat.

Routes
You can go anywhere on a bike that you would on trains and buses with the added pleasure of seeing all the places in between.

While the major highways should be avoided, some national highways can be pleasant – often lonely country roads well marked with a stone every km. A basic knowledge of Hindi will help you to translate the signs, although at least one marker in five will be in English.

Another option is to follow canal and river paths. It's also possible in some areas to bike along railway tracks on maintenance roads. Do make enquiries before venturing off road.

I once travelled most of a day before discovering the reason I had not encountered any pedestrian traffic: a major railway bridge was down and no ferry in service to ford the raging waters!

Ann Sorrel

Crossing international borders with a bicycle is relatively uncomplicated. India has border crossings with Pakistan, Nepal and Bangladesh (see the Getting There & Away chapter). Unlike a car or motorcycle, papers need not be presented. Do not be surprised, however, if the bike is thoroughly inspected for contraband!

Distances
If you've never before cycled long distances, start with 20 to 40 km a day and increase this as you gain stamina and confidence. Cycling long distances is 80% determination and 20% perspiration. For an eight hour pedal, a serious cyclist and interested tourist will average 125 to 150 km a day on undulating plains, or 80 to 100 km in mountainous areas.

Accommodation
There's no need to bring a tent. Inexpensive lodges are widely available, and a tent pitched by the road would merely draw crowds. There's also no need to bring a stove and cooking kit (unless you cannot tolerate Indian food), as there are plenty of tea stalls and restaurants (called 'hotels'). When you want to eat, ask for a 'hotel'. When you want a room ask for a 'lodge'. On major highways stop at *dhabas*, the Indian version of a truck stop. The one with the most trucks parked in front generally has the best food (or serves alcohol). Dhabas have *charpoys* (string beds) to serve as tables and seats or as beds for weary cyclists. You should keep your cycle next to you throughout the night. There will be no bathroom or toilet facilities but plenty of road noise. Dhabas are not recommended for single women riders.

Directions
Asking directions can be a real frustration. Always ask three or four different people just to be certain, using traffic police only as a last resort. Try to be patient; be careful about 'left' and 'right' and be prepared for instructions like 'go straight and turn here and there'.

Transporting Your Bicycle
Sometimes you may want to quit pedalling. For sports bikes, air travel is easy. With luck,

airline staff may not be familiar with procedures, so use this to your advantage. Tell staff that the bike doesn't need to be dismantled and that you've never had to pay for it. You may have to remove the pedals and turn the handlebars sideways so that it takes up less space in the aircraft's hold; check all this with the airline well in advance, preferably before you pay for your ticket. Remove all luggage and accessories and let the tyres down a bit. You *can* take bikes to pieces and put them in a bike bag or box, but it's much easier simply to wheel your bike to the check-in desk, where it should be treated as a piece of baggage.

Bus travel with a bike varies from state to state in India. In Rajasthan, it generally goes for free on the roof. If it's a sports bike stress that it's lightweight. Secure it well to the roof rack, check it's in a place where it won't get damaged and take all your luggage inside.

Train travel is more complex – pedal up to the railway station, buy a ticket and explain you want to book a cycle for the journey. You'll be directed to the luggage offices (or officer) where a triplicate form is prepared. Note down your bike's serial number and provide a good description of it. Again leave only the bike, not luggage or accessories. Your bike gets decorated with one copy of the form, usually pasted on the seat, you get another, and God only knows what happens to the third. Produce your copy of the form to claim the bicycle from the luggage van at your destination. If you change trains en route, *personally* ensure the cycle changes too!

Organised Bicycle Tours

These are yet to take off in a big way. Currently the only person offering cycle tours is Ramesh Jangid in Nawalgarh, who can organise tours around the painted *havelis* (mansions) of Shekhawati (northern Rajasthan). See that chapter for details.

Final Words

Just how unusual is a cycle tourist in India? I'd venture to guess that currently 2000 foreign cyclists tour for a month or more

each year somewhere on the subcontinent. That number appears to be growing rapidly. Perhaps 5000 Indians tour as well – mostly young men and college students. 'Kashmir to Kanyakumari' or a pilgrimage to holy places are their most common goals.

If you're a serious cyclist or amateur racer and want to contact counterparts while in India there's the Cycle Federation of India; contact the Secretary, Yamun Velodrome, New Delhi. Last words of advice – make sure your rubber solution is gooey, all your winds are tailwinds and that you go straight and turn here and there.

HITCHING

Hitching is not a realistic option. There are not that many private cars streaking across India so you are likely to be onboard trucks. You are then stuck with the old quandaries of: 'Do they understand what I am doing?'; 'Should I be paying for this?'; 'Will the driver expect to be paid?'; 'Will they be unhappy if I don't offer to pay?'; 'Will they be unhappy if I offer or will they simply want too much?'. But it is possible.

However, it is a very bad idea for women to hitch. Remember India is a developing country with a patriarchal society far less sympathetic to rape victims than the west, and that's saying something. A woman in the cabin of a truck on a lonely road is perhaps tempting fate.

LOCAL TRANSPORT

Although there are comprehensive local bus networks in most major towns, unless you have time to familiarise yourself with the routes, you're better off sticking to taxis, auto-rickshaws, cycle-rickshaws and hiring bicycles. The buses are often so hopelessly overcrowded that you can only really use them if you get on at the starting point – and get off at the terminus!

A basic ground rule applies to any form of transport where the fare is not ticketed or fixed (unlike a bus or train), or metered – agree on the fare beforehand. If you fail to do that you can expect enormous arguments and hassles when you get to your destination.

And agree on the fare clearly – if there is more than one of you make sure it covers all of you. If you have baggage make sure there are no extra charges, or you may be asked for more at the end of the trip. If a driver refuses to use the meter, or insists on an extortionate rate, simply walk away – if he really wants the job the price will drop. If you can't agree on a reasonable fare, find another driver.

To/From the Airport

There are often official buses, operated by the government, Indian Airlines or some local co-operative, to most airports in India. Where there aren't any, there will be taxis or auto-rickshaws.

Taxi

There are taxis in most towns in Rajasthan, and most of them (certainly in the major cities) are metered. Getting a metered fare is rather a different situation. First of all the meter may be 'broken'. Threatening to get another taxi will usually fix it immediately, except during rush hours.

Secondly, the meter will almost certainly be out of date. Fares are adjusted upwards so much faster and more frequently than meters are recalibrated that drivers almost always have 'fare adjustment cards' indicating what you should pay compared to what the meter indicates. This is, of course, wide open to abuse. You have no idea if you're being shown the right card or if the taxi's meter has actually been recalibrated and you're being shown the card anyway.

The only answer to all this is to try and get an idea of what the fare should be before departure (ask at information desks at the airport or your hotel). You'll soon begin to develop a feel for what the meter says, what the cards say and what the two together should indicate.

Auto-Rickshaw

An auto-rickshaw is a noisy three wheel device powered by a two stroke motorcycle engine with a driver up front and seats for two (or sometimes more) passengers behind. They don't have doors and have just a canvas top. They are also known as scooters or autos.

They're generally about half the price of a taxi, usually metered and follow the same ground rules as taxis.

Because of their size, auto-rickshaws are often faster than taxis for short trips and their drivers are decidedly nuttier – hair-raising near-misses are guaranteed and glancing-blow collisions are not infrequent; thrill-seekers will love it!

Tempo

Somewhat like a large auto-rickshaw, these ungainly looking three wheel devices operate rather like minibuses or share-taxis along fixed routes. Unless you are spending large amounts of time in one city, it is generally impractical to try to find out what the routes are. You'll find it much easier and more convenient to go by auto-rickshaw.

Cycle-Rickshaw

This is effectively a three wheeler bicycle with a seat for two passengers behind the rider. Although they no longer operate in most of the big cities, you will find them in all the smaller cities and towns, where they're the basic means of transport.

Fares must always be agreed on in advance. Avoid situations where the driver says something like: 'As you like'. He's punting on the fact that you are not well acquainted with correct fares and will overpay. Invariably no matter what you pay in situations like this, it will be deemed too little and an unpleasant situation often develops. This is especially the case in heavily touristed places, such as Agra and Jaipur. Always settle the price beforehand.

In the well touristed places the riders are as talkative and opinionated as any New York cabby.

It's quite feasible to hire a rickshaw-wallah by time, not just for a straight trip. Hiring one for a day or even several days can make good sense. Ensure that your watches are synchronised before you set out!

Hassling over the fares is the biggest difficulty of cycle-rickshaw travel. They'll often go all out for a fare higher than it would cost you by taxi or auto-rickshaw. Nor does actually agreeing on a fare always make a difference; there is a greater possibility of a post-travel fare disagreement when you travel by cycle-rickshaw than by taxi or auto-rickshaw – metered or not.

Tonga

In some smaller regional towns, such as Nawalgarh in Shekhawati, you'll come across horse-drawn carriages known as tongas. Prices are generally comparable with cycle-rickshaws.

Bicycle

India is a country of bicycles – it's an ideal way of getting around the sights in a city or even for making longer trips – see the section on touring India by bicycle earlier in this chapter. Even in the smallest of towns there will be a shop which rents bicycles. They charge from around Rs 3 to Rs 5 per hour or Rs 10 to Rs 15 per day. In some places they may be unwilling to hire to you since you are a stranger, but you can generally get around this by offering some sort of ID card as security, or by paying a deposit – usually Rs 300 to Rs 500.

If you should be so unfortunate as to get a puncture, you'll soon spot men sitting under trees with puncture-repair outfits at the ready – it'll cost just a couple of rupees to fix it.

If you're travelling with small children and would like to use bikes a lot, consider getting a bicycle seat made. If you find a shop making cane furniture they'll quickly make up a child's bicycle seat from a sketch. Get it made to fit on a standard-size rear carrier and it can be securely attached with a few lengths of cord.

ORGANISED TOURS
RTDC Tours

In most of the larger cities and places of tourist interest in Rajasthan – Jaipur, Jodhpur, Udaipur, Jaisalmer and Bikaner – the RTDC operates city tours or tours to places of interest in the environs. These tours are usually excellent value, particularly where

the tourist sights are spread out over a wide area, such as in Jaipur.

The big drawback is that many of them try to cram far too much into too short a period of time. Nevertheless, they're normally very good value, and you can always return to places of interest at your leisure later on. It's also possible to arrange an English-speaking guide at most RTDC tourist offices. Official rates in Jaipur, for example, for a half day (four hour) tour for up to four people is Rs 80 (per person). In Jaipur, it's also possible to hire French, German, Italian, Japanese and Spanish-speaking guides for a small extra supplement.

The RTDC also offers a range of package tours. These include a six day Mewar tour which leaves Delhi every Saturday and takes in Jaipur, Chittorgarh, Udaipur, Ranakpur, Ajmer and Pushkar; a three day Golden Triangle tour, which leaves Delhi every Friday and takes in Siliserh, Sariska, Jaipur, Bharatpur, Fatehpur Sikri and Agra (approximately Rs 3500 to Rs 4000 per person); a three day Hawa Mahal tour, which leaves Delhi every Tuesday, and takes in Agra, Fatehpur Sikri, Bharatpur, Deeg, Sariska and Jaipur (approximately Rs 3500 to Rs 4000); the seven day desert circuit tour, which leaves Delhi every Monday and takes in Bikaner, Jaisalmer, Jodhpur, Ajmer and Pushkar; a Wildlife tour, which takes four days and leaves every Thursday, including Sariska, Ranthambhore and Keoladeo Ghana national parks; and the 15 day Rajasthan tour, which leaves on the first and third Thursday of every month and covers the entire state (Rs 8500 to Rs 9000). Approximate rates are based on twin or double share and include rail transfers from Delhi, but not meals.

RTDC can organise the rental of a former maharaja's rail carriage, which can be connected to scheduled train services. These carriages can accommodate up to 20 people and have private cabins and share bathroom facilities. Although air-conditioned or especially luxurious, they are certainly a novel way to tour around if you are in a large group. For more information contact the Rajasthan Tourism Development Corporation, Bikaner

House, Pandara Rd, Nr India Gate, New Delhi (☎ (011) 338-3837; fax 338-2823).

Other Tours

Indian Operators Jetair Tours (part of Jetair Ltd) (☎ (0141) 36-8640; fax 37-4242), 112/113 Jaipur Towers, MI Rd, Jaipur, books various tours, treks and safaris in Rajasthan (see the Jaipur chapter). They offer treks in the Aravalli Range (winter months only), visiting the tribal villages of Bhils, Garsia and other groups. Costs are around Rs 3000 per person per day and include meals, transport, tent accommodation and a guide. They also offer wildlife tours to Ranthambhore, Keoladeo Ghana and Sariska national parks staying in luxury hotels, and can organise car and driver for extended touring. Prices are based on a minimum of 250 km per day, at Rs 4.50 per km for a non air-con car, and Rs 6.50 per km for an air-con car.

Registhan Tours Pvt Ltd (☎ & fax (0141) 38-0824), E-141 Sadar Patal Marg (near the Rajmahal Palace Hotel), in Jaipur, arranges camel and horse safaris, treks in the Udaipur area, and jeep safaris. For more information, see Other Tours in the Jaipur chapter.

Aravali Safari & Tours (☎ (0141) 37-3124; fax 36-5345), opposite the Hotel Rajputana Palace Sheraton, Palace Rd, Jaipur, can book luxury camel treks in the environs of Jaisalmer and around Shekhawati, horse safaris in southern Rajasthan, and treks in the Aravalli Range.

Ghanerao Tours (☎ (0141) 31-1309), Jaipur, organises tailor-made horse safaris in southern Rajasthan. See Activities in the Facts for the Visitor chapter for more details.

Alternative Travels (☎ (01594) 22-129; fax 22-491), Apani Dhani, Nawalgarh, Shekhawati, is one of the few outfits in Rajasthan which promotes sustainable cultural tourism. Ramesh Jangid of Alternative Travels can organise

Palace on Wheels

The RTDC *Palace on Wheels* is a special tourist train service which operates weekly tours of Rajasthan, departing from Delhi every Wednesday from September to April. The itinerary takes in Jaipur, Chittorgarh, Udaipur, Sawai Madhopur (for Ranthambhore National Park), Jaisalmer, Jodhpur, Bharatpur (for the Keoladeo Ghana National Park) and Agra. It's a lot of ground to cover in a week, but most of the travelling is done at night.

Originally this train used carriages which once belonged to various maharajas, but these became so ancient that new carriages were refurbished to look like the originals. They were also fitted with air-conditioning. The result is a very luxurious mobile hotel and it can be a memorable way to travel if you have limited time and limitless resources. The train comes equipped with two dining cars and a well stocked bar. Each coach, which is attended by a splendidly costumed captain and attendant, contains four coupés (either double or twin share) which have attached bath with running hot and cold water.

The cost includes tours, entry fees, accommodation on the train plus all meals. Rates per person per day are US$240 for triple occupancy (the third person sleeps on a fold-away bed), US$300 for double occupancy and US$425 for single occupancy. It's a very popular service and bookings must be made in advance at the RTDC Tourist Reception Centre, Bikaner House, Pandara Rd, New Delhi (☎ (011) 338-1884; fax 338-2823), or at the Tourist Reception Centre, Office Annexe, Hotel Swagatam, Jaipur (☎ (0141) 31-9531; fax 31-6045). ■

SANJAY SINGH BADNOR

camel and cycling trips around the painted towns of Shekhawati, treks in the Aravalli Range and homestays with villagers.

Foreign Operators Voyageurs en Inde (☎ (01) 42 86 16 90; fax (01) 42 61 45 86), 55 rue Sainte Anne, 75002 Paris, is a French company which runs cultural tours to Rajasthan. A five day tour includes transfers to and from Delhi, accommodation at the Apani Dhani (Eco Farm) in Nawalgarh in the Shekhawati region (northern Rajasthan), excursions, all meals, guides and camel treks. Prices are available on application.

Another French outfit operating tours to Rajasthan is Nomade (☎ (01) 46 33 71 71; fax (01) 43 54 76 12), 49 rue de la Montagne Sainte Geneviève, 75005 Paris. This company previously specialised in trips to Africa, but has commenced cultural tours to India. Their 10 and 17 day Rajasthan tours include an excursion around the painted havelis of Shekhawati, a camel safari and trips to Jaisalmer and Pushkar.

Based in Germany is Nepal Reisen (☎ (030) 788-1313; fax 788-3035), Ebersstrasse 76, 10827 Berlin. This outfit operates 17 and 22 day tours to Rajasthan including trekking, wildlife safaris, homestays with villagers and tours of the Shekhawati region. Prices start at DM 3990 for the 17 day tour, and DM 4590 for the 22 day tour, and include return airfares.

Jaipur

*e na dekkhyo Jaipario
o kal menakar kya kario*
f one has not seen Jaipur, what is the point of having
een born?

Population: 1.7 million
Telephone Area Code: 0141

Jaipur, the capital of Rajasthan, rarely disap-
points the first-time visitor. It is a city of
contrasts, where camels wait at traffic lights
with auto-rickshaws and Ambassador cars.
And film hoardings depicting many times
larger-than-life mustachioed heroes, their
faces contorted into desperate grimaces as
they battle their adversaries, loom down over
luxury car showrooms, while artisans engage
in such traditional crafts as block-printing, gem
cutting and polishing, puppet making, and
durrie (carpet) weaving. Women resplendent
in iridescent lime green, hot pink, and sun-
lower coloured saris thread their way
through the crowded bazaars of the old city.
Providing stunning backdrops are the
ancient forts of Amber, Nahargarh, Jaigarh
and Moti Dungri, dramatic testaments to a
bygone era which lend a lingering romance
to this bustling, chaotic city.

Among Jaipur's highlights is the fascinating City Palace, which has an excellent
museum with priceless exhibits dating from
the successive reigns of the Kachhwaha
rulers. Nearby is the Jantar Mantar, the
observatory built by the founder of Jaipur,
Jai Singh II, in the second quarter of the 18th
century. It looks more like an outdoor exhibition of modern art than an observatory, but
astrologers and astronomers still consult the
strange devices here to make their celestial
calculations.

The old city is a fascinating place to
wander around, with its colourful bazaars
and artisans' quarters. As it is laid out on a
grid pattern, it's fairly easy to orient yourself
here. The *chaupars*, or three main squares in
the old city, are great places to be at sunset,
when the pink walls give off a rosy hue and

HIGHLIGHTS

- Jaipur's bazaars and emporiums, for
  handicrafts
- The City Palace complex, which has one
  of Rajasthan's best museums
- Amber Fort, 11 km from Jaipur
- Sanganer, a village outside of Jaipur,
  world famous for its block-printed fabrics

you can sit and watch the chaos unfold
around you as vendors make their way home.

Only 16 km south of the city is the village
of Sanganer, famous for its Sanganeri block
prints. The banks of the river which run
through the village are a riot of colour, with
thousands of sheets of printed cloth laid out
to dry in the sun.

History

The city of Jaipur is named after its founder,
the great warrior-astronomer Maharaja Jai
Singh II (1693-1743), who came to power at
the age of 12 upon the death of his father,
Maharaja Bishan Singh. The maharaja had
been informed by astrologers upon his son's
birth that the boy would achieve great things
in his lifetime, and Bishan Singh ensured that
he received the very best education in the
arts, sciences, philosophy and military affairs.

At 15 years old the prodigal prince match-
ed his wits against the Mughal emperor,
Aurangzeb, who summoned the lad to the
Mughal court to explain why he had failed
to report to the Deccan to fight the Marathas
as he had been ordered. When the emperor
grasped the lad's hand the youth retorted
that, as the emperor had extended the traditional gesture of protection offered by a
bridegroom to his new wife by taking his
hand, it was incumbent upon Aurangzeb to
protect the young ruler and his kingdom in a
similar fashion. Impressed by his wit and
pluck, Aurangzeb conferred on Jai Singh the
title 'Sawai', meaning 'one and a quarter', a

title which was proudly borne by all of Jai Singh's descendants.

Jai Singh could trace his lineage back to the Rajput clan of Kachhwahas, who consolidated their power around the 12th century and built the impressive Amber Fort which lies about 11 km to the north-east of present day Jaipur. The dominion of the Kachhwahas progressively spread, eventually encompassing a large area which abutted the kingdoms of Mewar (Udaipur region) and Marwar (Jodhpur region).

The Kachhwahas recognised the expediency of aligning themselves with the powerful Mughal empire, and enjoyed the patronage of the Mughal emperors. However, Jai Singh incurred the displeasure of Aurangzeb's successor, Bahadur Shah, who came to power following Aurangzeb's death in 1707.

Bahadur Shah's accession was contested by his younger brother, Azam Shah, and Jai Singh unfortunately supported the younger brother's bid for power. Bahadur Shah responded by demanding his removal from Amber Fort, installing Jai Singh's younger brother Vijay Singh in his place. This naturally rankled with Jai Singh, who eventually dislodged his brother. Soliciting the support of other large Rajput states, Jai Singh formed a formidable front against the Mughal ruler, and eventually reconsolidated his rule.

The wealth of the kingdom increased exponentially, and this, together with the need to accommodate the ever burgeoning population and a paucity of water at the old capital at Amber, prompted the maharaja in 1727 to commence work on a new city which he named after himself – Jaipur.

It was a collaborative endeavour, the synthesis of the vision of the maharaja and the impressive expertise of his chief architect, Vidyadhar. Jai Singh's strong grounding in the sciences is reflected in the precise symmetry of the new city which, as opposed to the other unplanned and labyrinthine cities which predominated in North India at the time, was laid out according to strict principles of town planning set down in the *Shilpa-Shastra*, an ancient Hindu treatise on architecture. The small villages which lay in

Maharaja Jai Singh II. This precocious maharaja came to power at the age of 12.

the vicinity were incorporated into the new city, which was dissected by wide boulevards flanked by stalls of equal size forming seven rectangles, called *mohallas*, of varying size.

The most central of the seven rectangles comprises the city palace complex, containing the palace itself, the administrative quarters, the Jantar Mantar (Jai Singh's remarkable observatory) and the *zenana mahals*, or women's palaces, where the maharaja's 2 wives and several concubines were installed – the maharaja held the dubious honour of maintaining more wives and concubines than any of his predecessors, although most of these alliances were motivated more by political expediency than by amorous compulsions.

The city was not just an aesthetic triumph; its stout walls served to protect its inhabitants from would-be invaders, encouraging merchants and tradespeople to flock here and further serving to enhance the city's growth and prosperity. Jai Singh's interest in the arts, sciences and religion fostered their development in Jaipur, and the royal court became a centre of intellectual and artistic endeavour.

Following Jai Singh's death in 1744, inevitable power struggles between his many offspring lay the kingdom open to invasion by neighbouring Rajput kingdoms, who encroached on and appropriated large tracts of territory. The kingdom maintained good relations with the British Raj, although the British gradually began to undermine the independence of the state, exercising greater control over its administration.

In 1876, Maharaja Ram Singh had the entire old city painted pink, traditionally a colour associated with hospitality, to welcome the Prince of Wales (later King Edward VII) to the city. This tradition has been maintained, and today all residents of the old city are compelled by law to preserve the pink facade. Maharaja Man Singh also built Ramgarh Lake to supply water to the ever-growing city.

During the 19th and 20th centuries, even the spacious and carefully planned city contained within Jai Singh's original city walls could not contain the burgeoning population, and the city began to spread beyond its walled perimeters.

In 1922, Man Singh II, Jaipur's last maharaja, ascended the throne following the death of his adoptive father, Sawai Madho Singh II. During his reign, civic buildings such as schools, hospitals and the vast Secretariat complex were built outside the original walls.

Following Independence in 1947, the status of the princely state was to change forever. In March 1949, Jaipur merged with the Rajput states of Jodhpur, Jaisalmer and Bikaner, becoming the Greater Rajasthan Union. Jaipur was honoured above the other former states when the title Rajpramukh, meaning head of state, was conferred on Man Singh II, who was invested with administrative supervision of the new province. The title was later revoked, and Man Singh II was posted as Indian ambassador to Spain. In 1956, Jaipur became the capital of the state of Rajasthan.

FESTIVALS OF JAIPUR DISTRICT

Several important festivals are unique to Jaipur and these are described below. For statewide and nationwide festivals, see Festivals of Rajasthan in the Facts for the Visitor chapter.

March-April

Gangaur – Women across the state celebrate the love between Shiva and his consort Parvati (Gauri) during this much loved festival. It commences on the day following Holi, and continues for 18 days. Wooden images of Gauri are bedecked in beautiful costumes and jewels and worshipped. An elaborately garbed image of Gauri is carried on a palanquin from the Tripolia, at the City Palace, through the streets of the old city.

Elephant Festival – Jaipur's elephant festival is held in early to mid-March (depending on the lunar calendar) and is actually part of the Holi Festival. Gaily caparisoned elephants lumber through the streets, and matches of elephant polo are held at the polo ground near the Rambagh Palace. One of the more bizarre spectacles of this festival is that afforded by a tug-of-war between elephants and men.

Sheetala Ashtami – This festival is held in honour of the goddess of smallpox, Sheetala Mata, at the village of Chaksu, near Jaipur. The goddess is propitiated with special prayers petitioning her to spare young children from smallpox.

July-August

Teej – This festival heralds the onset of the monsoon, and is celebrated across Rajasthan in honour of the marriage of Shiva and Parvati. It is a favourite with Rajasthani women. At this time, flower-bedecked swings are hung from trees, and songs celebrating love are sung by maidens.

The population has expanded from some 300,000 in 1950 to close to two million today, and while the city remains prosperous and retains vestiges of its former grandeur, unplanned urban sprawl has disfigured what was possibly one of the most beautiful cities in India. All of the seven original gates into the old city remain but, unfortunately, much of the wall itself has been torn down for building material. There is now a preservation order on the remainder.

Orientation

The walled 'pink city' is in the north-east of Jaipur, while the new parts have spread to the south and west. The city's main tourist attractions are in the old part of town. The principal shopping centre in the old city is Johari Bazaar, the jewellers' market. Unlike other shopping centres in narrow alleys in India and elsewhere in Asia, this one is broad and open.

There are three main interconnecting roads in the new part of town – Mirza Ismail Rd (MI Rd), Station Rd and Sansar Chandra Marg. Along or just off these roads are most of the budget and mid-range hotels and restaurants, the railway station, the bus terminal, the GPO, many of the banks and the modern shopping centre.

Information

Tourist Offices The main RTDC tourist office (☎ 31-5714) is on platform No 1 at the railway station. It's open daily from 6 am to 8 pm, and the staff here are friendly and helpful. You can obtain a good map of Jaipur here. There is also a new Tourist Reception Centre at the Jaipur Tourist Hotel on MI Rd. It's open daily except Sunday from 6 am until 8 pm. Also at the Jaipur Tourist Hotel are the offices of the Gujarat Tourism Development Corporation (no phone) and the Garhwal (northern Uttar Pradesh) Tourism Development Corporation (☎ 37-8892).

Bookings for RTDC hotels around Rajasthan, accommodation in the tourist village during the Pushkar Camel Fair, and reservations for the *Palace on Wheels* can be made at the Central Reservation Office (☎ 31-

0586; fax 31-6045), opposite the railway station in the Hotel Swagatam.

Money Thomas Cook (☎ 36-0940) is on the 1st floor of Jaipur Towers on MI Rd. It's open Monday to Saturday from 9.30 am to 6 pm. An encashment fee of Rs 20 is payable on travellers' cheques other than Thomas Cook.

The Central Bank of India (☎ 31-7419), Anand Bldg, Sansar Chandra Marg, can do immediate cash advances on MasterCard. The minimum amount is US$100, and no charge is levied. The Andhra Bank (☎ 36-9606), MI Rd, gives instant cash advances on MasterCard, Visa and JCB (Japanese Credit Bureau) cards. Your account must have a credit balance if you wish to use this facility. The State Bank of Bikaner & Jaipur, opposite the GPO, changes most travellers' cheques between 2 and 4 pm, Monday to Saturday.

The branch of the Bank of Baroda at Tripolia Bazaar changes most travellers' cheques.

Post & Communications The telegraph office is in the same building as the GPO on MI Rd. The fax number at the GPO is 36-2018, and the office will hold incoming faxes for up to 15 days. It costs Rs 10 to receive faxes (up to three pages).

There is a handy parcel packing service in the foyer of the post office and a speedy and efficient desk which handles parcel postage. It is also possible to have parcels packed at the garment shop near the Evergreen Guest House. Unfortunately, not all parcels sent from this post office reach their destination.

There is a local/long-distance/overseas telecom service at the Jaipur railway station, open between 7 am and 2 am.

DHL Worldwide Express (☎ 36-2826), in a small lane off MI Rd at C-scheme, G-7A Vinoba Marg, can arrange air freight around the world.

Travel Agencies Sita World Travels (☎ 36-8226; fax 32-1522), Station Rd, can book domestic and international air tickets, cars and drivers and hotels, arrange freight cargo (both air and sea), and make train reservations. See

Getting Around in this section for details of car and driver rates. Registhan Tours Pvt Ltd (☎ & fax 38-0824) is at E-141 Sadar Patel Marg (near the Rajmahal Palace). Registhan also has competitive car and driver rates.

Jetair Tours (☎ 36-8640; fax 37-4242), 112/113 Jaipur Towers, MI Rd, Jaipur books various tours, treks and safaris in Rajasthan. Jetair Tours is a part of Jetair Ltd which is an agency for many international and domestic airlines.

Amber Tours Pvt Ltd (☎ 38-1543) has a desk at the Rambagh Palace. They can arrange cars and drivers.

Aravali Safari & Tours (☎ 37-3124; fax 36-5345) is opposite the Rajputana Palace Sheraton, Palace Rd. This IATA accredited agency specialises in tours of Rajasthan and can also book cars, buses and accommodation.

Bookshops National English-language dailies and a good selection of books on India, with particular emphasis on Rajasthan, can be found at Book Corner, MI Rd, near Niro's restaurant. Here you will also find the monthly publication *Jaipur Vision*, a small booklet which details most of Jaipur's more scenic and historic sights. In the same block, heading towards the old city, is the Books & News Mart, which also has a fair selection of books on Rajasthan. There is an excellent selection of books on India, including an extensive collection of titles pertaining to Rajasthan, at the bookshop (☎ 38-1430) at the Rambagh Palace.

There is also a bookshop with a good selection of books on Rajasthan near the art gallery at the city palace. Second-hand books can be bought and exchanged at the Evergreen Guest House, Chameliwala Market, just off MI Rd.

Film & Photography For reliable film processing try Goyal Colour Lab or Star Colour Lab, both in Nehru Bazaar in the old city.

Medical Services The Sawai Mansingh Hospital (☎ 56-0291) is on Ram Singh Rd. The Santokba Durlabhji Hospital (☎ 56-6251) is on Bhawani Singh Rd.

Emergency Police: 100; Fire: 101; Ambulance: 102.

Old City (Pink City)

The old city is partially encircled by a crenellated wall pierced at intervals by gates – the major gates are Chandpol ('pol' means gate), Ajmeri and Sanganeri. Broad avenues, over 30m wide, divide the pink city into neat rectangles, each of which is the domain of a particular group of artisans or commercial activities.

Chandpol is the entrance to the bustling **Chandpol Bazaar**. This is crossed by Khajane Walon ka Rasta, where you can see Jaipur's marble workers. At the intersection of Chandpol Bazaar and Kishanpol Bazaar you will find the **Choti Chaupar**, where villagers from outlying regions come to sell and trade their produce. **Kishanpol Bazaar** is famous for textiles, particularly tie-dye cloth, and you can see the artisans engaged in their work here, producing two forms of tie-dye, *bandhani* and *loharia*.

Tie-Dye

In the bandhani form of tie-dye, a pale background is covered with large splotches. This effect is achieved by knotting the dyed cloth and then bleaching it, with the knotted sections retaining their colour. A worker in this form of tie-dye is known as a bandhej. The second form of tie-dye, called loharia, features diagonal motifs in contrasting colours. Loharia pieces are named according to the number of colours employed: *panchrangi* features five colours (from *panch*, meaning five), and *satrangi* features seven different colours. The cloth is worn as turbans and saris. ■

Continuing west beyond Choti Chaupar brings you to **Tripolia Bazaar**, also known as Maniharon ka Rasta. Here passers by are confronted by stall after stall crammed with domestic kitchen utensils, textiles, trinkets and ironware. The stalls are closed on Sunday.

On the north side of Tripolia Bazaar is the **Iswari Minar Swarga Sal** (Heaven Piercing

Minaret), an apt name as this is the highest structure in the old city. The minaret was erected by Iswari Singh, who succeeded Jai Singh. Lacking the military prowess and courage of his warrior father, Iswari Singh took his own life rather than confront the advancing Maratha army. His ignominious end was overshadowed by the sacrifice of his 21 wives and concubines, who performed *sati* by immolating themselves upon his funeral pyre.

A short distance further west is **Tripolia Gate**, the triple-arched gate after which the bazaar takes its name. This is the main entrance to the City Palace (described later in this section) and Jantar Mantar, but only the maharaja's family is permitted entrance via its portals. The public entrance to the palace complex is via the less ostentatious **Atishpol**, or Stable Gate, to the left. To the north of the City Palace is the **Govind Devji Temple**, surrounded by gardens. Here is an image of Govinda Deva which Jai Singh installed as the patron deity of his family.

Proceeding east along Tripolia Bazaar you will come to another major intersection. To the south, **Johari Bazaar** leads to the Sanganeri Gate. Johari Bazaar (closed for part of Sunday and Tuesday) and the small lane-ways which dissect it are where you will find Jaipur's jewellers and gold and silversmiths. Of particular interest are the artisans engaged in enamelling, or *meenakari*. This highly glazed and intricate work in shades of ruby, bottle green and royal blue is a speciality of Jaipur. On Johari Bazaar you can also find cotton merchants, with their bolts of white cloth. Interspersed with the uniform shop fronts are the grand *havelis* or homes of Jaipur's wealthy merchants. If you turn right before exiting the Sanganeri Gate you'll reach **Bapu Bazaar**, and further west, **Nehru Bazaar** (closed Tuesday), which extends between Chaura Rasta and Kishanpol Bazaar on the inside of the southern wall. Brightly coloured bolts of fabric, shoes of camel skin, trinkets and aromatic perfumes make this bazaar a favourite shopping destination for Jaipur's women.

The northern extension of Johari Bazaar, to the north of the large square known as

Badi Chaupar, is **Siredeori Bazaar**, also known as Hawa Mahal Bazaar. The latter name is derived from the extraordinary **Hawa Mahal**, or Palace of Winds (described later in this section), a short distance to the north along the bazaar on the left hand side.

Back on Tripolia Bazaar, if you proceed further east beyond **Ramganj Chaupar**, you'll pass through **Ramganj Bazaar**, where you can see shoemakers at work. Further east is **Surajpol Bazaar**. The area to the south is known as **Mahavaton ka Mohalla**, traditionally the quarters of elephants and their *mahoots* (elephant masters). Surajpol Bazaar leads to the Surajpol, the main exit from the old city in the eastern wall.

City Palace In the heart of the old city, the City Palace complex occupies a large area divided into a series of courtyards, gardens and buildings. The outer wall was built by Jai Singh, but other additions are more recent, some dating to the start of this century. Today the palace is a blend of Rajasthani and Mughal architecture. When he is in Rajasthan, the son of the last maharaja and his family still live in part of the palace, and at these times two flags can be seen flying over the palace. When the former prince resumes his duty as the Indian ambassador to Brunei, only one flag is raised.

Before the palace proper lies the **Mubarak Mahal**, or Welcome Palace, which was built in the late 19th century by Maharaja Sawai Madho Singh II as a reception centre for visiting dignitaries. It now forms part of the **Maharaja Sawai Mansingh II Museum**, containing a collection of royal costumes and superb shawls including Sanganeri block prints, royal shawls, Kashmiri *pashmina* (goats' wool) shawls, folk embroideries and Benares silk saris. One remarkable exhibit is a set of the voluminous clothes of Madho Singh II (reigned 1880-1922), who was over two metres tall, 1.2m wide and weighed 225 kg!

The **Maharani's Palace** (apartments of the queen) now houses a collection of weaponry. Note the extraordinary frescoes on the ceiling of this room: the colours were derived from semi-precious jewel dust and are beautifully preserved. The priceless collection of weapons dates back to the 15th century, and includes the notorious Rajput scissor-action daggers – when the dagger enters the body, the handles are released, causing the blades to spread. The dagger is then withdrawn, virtually disembowelling the hapless victim.

Other exhibits include swords with pistols attached to their blades; beautiful crystal, ivory and silver-handled daggers; armour of chain mail, one complete set of which can weigh up to 35 kg; and a ruby-encrusted sword presented by Queen Victoria to Maharaja Sawai Ram Singh, the ruler of Jaipur between 1835 and 1880. There is also an assortment of guns, including some which also serve as walking sticks, a gun the size of a small cannon for use on camel back, and double barrelled pistols which held bullets made of lead dipped in poison and packed with gunpowder.

Between the armoury and the art gallery is the **diwan-i-khas**, or hall of private audiences. In its marble-paved gallery stand two silver vessels which Maharaja Madho Singh II took to London filled with holy Ganges water. As a devout Hindu, the maharaja was reluctant to risk ritual pollution by imbibing English water. These enormous vessels each have a capacity of over 8000l, stand 160 cm tall, and are the largest sterling silver objects in the world.

The art gallery is housed in the former **diwan-i-am**, or hall of public audiences, beyond and to the right of the diwan-i-khas. It retains a beautifully preserved painted ceiling, on which the original semi-precious stone colours have barely faded and from which is suspended an enormous crystal chandelier. Exhibits include a copy of the entire *Bhagavad Gita*, handwritten in tiny script, and miniature copies of other holy Hindu scriptures which could be easily hidden from Aurangzeb in the event that he endeavoured to destroy the sacred texts. There are also beautiful handwritten books in Persian and Sanskrit; early manuscripts on palm leaf; miniature paintings of the Rajas-thani, Mughal and Persian schools depicting religious themes, most notably scenes from the *Ramayana*; various ornate howdahs (elephant saddles); and exquisitely detailed paper cuttings incised with a thumbnail.

The palace and museum are open between 9.30 am and 4.45 pm daily, except on public holidays. Entry is Rs 30, plus Rs 50 if you wish to take photos with a still camera, Rs 100 for a video.

Jantar Mantar Next to the entrance to the City Palace is the Jantar Mantar, or observatory (Jantar Mantar means instrument of calculation), begun by Jai Singh in 1728. Jai Singh's passion for astronomy was even more notable than his prowess as a warrior. Before commencing construction on the Jantar Mantar, he sent scholars abroad to study foreign observatories. The Jaipur observatory is the largest and the best preserved of the five he built, with 13 different instruments for calculating the movement of celestial bodies. It was restored in 1901. Others are in Delhi (the oldest, dating from 1724), Varanasi and Ujjain. The fifth observatory, at Mathura, has now disappeared.

At first glance, Jantar Mantar appears to be just a curious if somewhat compelling collection of sculptures. In fact, each construction has a specific purpose, for example measuring the positions of the stars, altitudes and azimuths, and calculating eclipses.

The most striking instrument is the **Brihat Samrat Yantra** sundial, an imposing edifice to the far left of the observatory complex which has a 27m high gnomon set at an angle of 27°. The shadow this casts moves up to four metres in an hour, and aids in the calculation of local and meridian pass time and various attributes of the heavenly bodies, including declination (the angular distance of a heavenly body from the celestial equator) and altitude. It is still used by astrologers today, and is the focus of a gathering of astrologers during the full moon days of June and July, when it is used to aid in the prediction of the monsoon rains, and subsequent success or failure of crops.

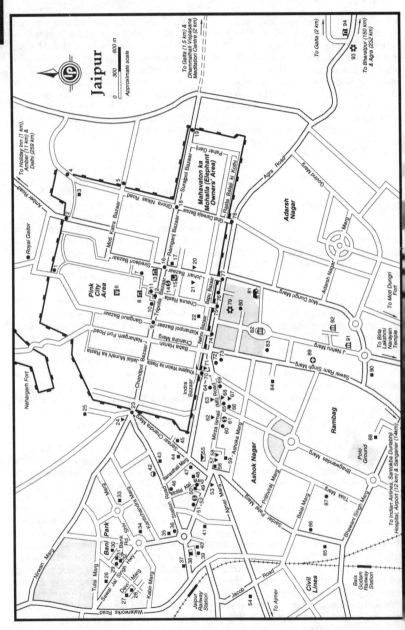

Jaipur

0   300   600 m

Approximate scale

Immediately to the left as you enter the compound is the **Laghu Samrat Yantra**, or small sundial. This does not measure as precisely as the Brihat Samrat Yantra, but also serves to calculate the declination of celestial bodies, and the shadow cast by its gnomon enables local time to be determined. Nearby is the **Dhruva Darshak Yantra**, an instrument which is used to determine the location of the Pole Star.

The large hemispherical shaped object nearby, known as the **Narivalaya Yantra**, is actually two small sundials. The two faces of the instrument represent the northern and southern hemispheres, and enable calculation of the time within a minute's accuracy.

The two large disks suspended from wooden beams nearby are the **Yantra Raj**, a multi-purpose instrument which, among other things, can help determine the positions of

PLACES TO STAY			85	Rajmahal Palace	18	Ramganj Chaupar
3	Samode Haveli		88	Rambagh Palace	19	Surajpol
17	Hotel Kailash		90	Narain Niwas Palace	23	Chandpol
22	Hotel Sweet Dream			Hotel	36	Sita World Travels
25	Hotels Bissau Palace				39	Aravali Safari &
	& Khetri House		**PLACES TO EAT**			Tours
26	Hotel Meghniwas		20	Royal's	42	Main Bus Terminal
27	Tirupati Guest House		21	LMB Hotel &	46	Polo Victory Cinema
28	Shahpura Guest			Restaurant	49	Cathay Pacific
	House		24	Bismiliah Restaurant	51	Alitalia, British
29	Madhuban Guest		53	Rainbow Restaurant		Airways & Air India
	House		57	Copper Chimney	52	Jaipur Towers
30	Umaid Bhawan &		58	Handi Restaurant &		(Thomas Cook &
	Sajjain Niwas			State Bank of		Airline Agents)
	Guest Houses			Bikaner & Jaipur	55	GPO
31	Marudhara Hotel		62	Chanakya	60	DHL Worldwide
32	Pipalda House			Restaurant		Express
33	Jaipur Inn		63	Lassiwala	61	Andhra Bank
34	RTDC Hotel Jaipur		67	Golden Dragon	64	Skyline NEPC
	Ashok			Chinese	65	Book Corner
35	Hotel Teej			Restaurant &	66	Raj Mandir Cinema
37	Hotel Swagatam			Bake Hut	69	Books & News Mart
	& Central		68	Niro's, Natraj, Surya	70	Singhpol
	Reservation Office			Mahal & Jai Mahal	72	Rajasthali Emporium
38	Rajputana Palace			Restaurants		& Rajasthan
	Sheraton		71	Indian Coffee House		Handloom House
40	Hotel Kaiser-I-Hind				73	UP Airways
41	RTDC Hotel Gangaur		**OTHER**		74	Ajmeri Gate
43	Jai Mangal Palace		1	Samrat Gate	75	New Gate
44	Hotel Mangal		2	Zorawar Gate	76	Lufthansa
45	Hotel Arya Niwas		4	Gangapol	77	Sanganeri Gate
47	Mansingh Hotel &		5	Char Gate	78	Ghat Gate
	Central Bank of		6	Govind Devji Temple	79	Ram Niwas Public
	India		7	Jantar Mantar		Gardens
48	Hotel Neelam & Karni			(Observatory)	80	Ravindra Rangmanch
	Niwas		8	City Palace &		Art Gallery
50	Atithi Guest House			Maharaja Sawai	81	Zoo
54	Jai Mahal Palace			Mansingh II	82	Central Museum
	Hotel			Museum		(Albert Hall)
56	Jaipur Tourist Hotel,		9	Choti Chaupar	83	Maharaja College
	Tourist Reception		10	Iswari Minar Swarga	86	Registhan Tours
	Centre & Handi			Sal	87	Anokhi Showroom
	Bamboo Hut		11	Dr. Vinod Shastri	89	Sawai Mansingh
	Restaurant			(Astrologer)		Hospital
59	Evergreen Guest		12	Tripolia Gate	91	Doll Museum
	House, Hotel Pink		13	Hawa Mahal	92	Museum of Indology
	Sun & Ashiyana		14	Bank of Baroda	93	Vidyadharji ka Bagh
	Guest House		15	Jama Masjid	94	Sisodia Rani Palace
84	Hotel Diggi Palace		16	Badi Chaupar		& Gardens

constellations. A similar looking instrument, the **Unnatansha Yantra**, lies in the north-eastern corner of the observatory complex. The disk is divided into segments by horizontal and vertical lines. A hole where these lines intersect, in the centre of the instrument, aids in the calculation of the altitude of celestial bodies.

Nearby is the **Dakhinovrith Bhitti Yantra**, which serves a similar function to the Unnatansha Yantra in helping to determine placement of heavenly bodies.

Near the southern wall of the observatory is a cluster of 12 instruments known as the **Rashi Yantras**. Each rashi, or individual instrument, represents one of the 12 zodiac signs. The gradient of each rashi differs in accordance with the particular sign represented and its position in relation to the ecliptic.

The two concave structures on a plinth in the western section of the observatory compound are the **Kapali Yantra**. The eastern Kapali Yantra is inscribed with lines to which astronomers refer in their deliberations; it is used more for graphical analysis than calculation, as opposed to the western Kapali Yantra, which is used to determine the position of a celestial body.

The **Jai Prakash Yantra** was the last instrument installed at the observatory and was invented by Jai Singh, after whom it is named. The two marble bowls which comprise the instrument aid not only in celestial observations, but can be used to verify the calculations determined with the other instruments at the observatory.

Two other impressive instruments are the **Ram Yantras**, which are formed from 12 upright slabs and 12 horizontal slabs. They are used in the calculation of the altitude and azimuth of celestial bodies. Another instrument which is used for calculating azimuth, particularly of the sun, is the **Digansha Yantra**. It can also be used to determine the time of sunrise and sunset.

The observatory is open 9 am to 4.30 pm. Admission is Rs 4 (free on Monday) and it costs Rs 50 to use a still camera.

Those interested in the theory behind the construction of these monumental instruments should buy a copy of *A Guide to the Jaipur Astronomical Observatory* by BL Dhama, which can be purchased on site.

Hawa Mahal Built in 1799, the Hawa Mahal, or Palace of the Winds, is one of Jaipur's major landmarks, although it is actually little more than a facade. This five storey building, which looks out over the main street of the old city, is a stunning example of Rajput artistry with its pink, delicately honey-combed sandstone windows, of which there are 953. It was originally built to enable ladies of the royal household to watch the everyday life and processions of the city. You can climb to the top of the Hawa Mahal for an excellent view over the city. The palace was built by Maharaja Sawaj Pratap Singh and is part of the City Palace complex. There's a small archaeological museum on the same site.

Entrance to the Hawa Mahal is from the rear of the building. To get there, go back to the intersection on your left as you face the Hawa Mahal, turn right and then take the first right again through an archway. It's sign-posted and open daily from 9 am to 4.30 pm. There's an entry fee of Rs 2, plus an additional Rs 50 if you want to use a still camera.

New City

By the mid-19th century it became obvious that even Jai Singh's well planned city could not accommodate the growing population. It was during the reign of Maharaja Ram Singh (reigned 1835-1880) that the city began to spread beyond the original city walls. Civic facilities such as a postal system and piped water were introduced, and the maharaja commissioned the landscaping of the **Ram Niwas Public Gardens**, on Jawaharlal Nehru Marg, and the construction in the gardens of the impressive **Albert Hall**, which now houses the Central Museum (described later in this section).

These civic improvements were continued by Jaipur's last maharaja, Man Singh II, who can be credited with the construction of the university, the Secretariat, residential colonies, schools, hospitals and colleges.

Unfortunately unplanned urban growth is now spoiling this once beautiful city, with private interests and political expediency now outweighing aesthetic considerations, and buildings are being constructed with little regard for Jaipur's rich architectural heritage.

There is a small **zoo** in the Ram Niwas Gardens with a collection of unhappy looking animals and a small crocodile breeding farm. Nearby, an old theatre houses Jaipur's modern **art gallery**, the Ravindra Rangmanch (free entry). A short distance away is the **Maharaja College**, which was founded in 1845 for the study of Urdu and Persian.

The **Museum of Indology** is an odd private collection of folk art objects and other bits and pieces of interest – there's everything from a map of India painted on a rice grain, to manuscripts (one written by Aurangzeb), jewellery, fossils, coins, old currency notes, clocks, watches and much more. The museum is in fact a private home (although the living quarters seem to have been swallowed up by the collection), and is signposted off J Nehru Marg, south of the Central Museum. It's open daily from 10 am to 5 pm. Entry is Rs 30.

Close to the Museum of Indology, also on J Nehru Marg, is the **Doll Museum**. The small collection includes dolls wearing traditional costumes from around India and the world. It's open daily from 9 am to 6 pm (entry Rs 2).

Further south down J Nehru Marg, looming above the road to the left, is the small and romantic fort of **Moti Dungri**. It has also served as a prison, but today remains in the possession of the erstwhile royal family, and entry is prohibited.

The **Birla Lakshmi Narayan Temple** is a large modern marble edifice at the foot of Moti Dungri fort. The wealthy industrialist Birla, who was born in Palani, Rajasthan, bought the land on which the temple now stands from the maharaja for a token Rs 1. Stained glass windows depict scenes from Hindu scriptures. Ganesh, the protector of households, is above the lintel, and the fine quality of the marble is evident when you enter the temple and look back at the entranceway – Ganesh can be made out *through* the marble, which is almost transparent. The images of Lakshmi and Narayan are carved from one piece of marble. Many of the deities of the Hindu pantheon are depicted inside the temple, and on the outside walls great historical personages and religious figures from other religions are shown, including Socrates, Zarathustra, Christ, Buddha and Confucius.

There is a small **museum** next to the temple which is open daily from 9 to 11.30 am and 2 to 6 pm (free). The collection includes household objects and clothing of the Birla family. English-speaking guides can explain aspects of the temple's architecture and of Hinduism free of charge.

About three km south-west of the old city is the **Rambagh Palace**, now maintained as one of India's most beautiful and prestigious hotels. Nowhere is the encroachment of the new city more evident than here – once maintained by Maharaja Ram Singh as a hunting lodge, well beyond the limits of the city centre, the Rambagh is now surrounded by sprawling suburbs. However, its spacious and beautifully maintained gardens still engender a sense of luxurious isolation. Man Singh, the last maharaja of Jaipur, converted the former lodge into a magnificent home for his third wife, Gayatri Devi, a glamorous princess from the small state of Cooch Bihar.

The Man Singhs were renowned for their lavish hospitality, and at Rambagh they entertained some of the world's rich and famous people, including Eleanor Roosevelt and Jackie Kennedy. It was a fairy tale romance and a fairy tale life, evocatively recounted by the former maharani in her autobiography, *A Princess Remembers*. Today Gayatri Devi retains residential quarters at the Rambagh Palace, which became a hotel (see Places to Stay in this section) in 1958.

Central Museum This dusty collection is housed in the architecturally impressive Albert Hall in the Ram Niwas Gardens, south of the old city. Entry to the museum is Rs 3, free on Monday. It is open daily (except

Friday) from 10 am to 4.30 pm. No photography is permitted.

Exhibits include a natural history collection, models of yogis adopting various positions, tribal ware, dioramas depicting various Rajasthani dances, and sections on the decorative arts, costumes, drawings, musical instruments and tribal costumes. On the upper parts of the outside walls are huge colour portraits of the maharajas of Jaipur.

To the right of the Albert Hall is the smaller **Durbar Hall**, which is generally closed, but the caretaker may open it on request (a little baksheesh may help). This hall houses an exquisite collection of old carpets, some 400 years old.

Beauty Parlours

Jaipur is renowned for its beauty parlours for women. These specialise in *kayakalp* treatments – a beauty therapy system using traditional ayurvedic (herbal) creams. Treatments include face packs, facial massages and henna designs for hands and feet. The creams are all prepared in Jaipur. Cost for a one hour treatment including a 20 minute facial massage is approximately Rs 150.

Astrology

It costs Rs 200 for a 30 minute consultation with Dr Vinod Shastri (☎ 43-338), the General Secretary of the Rajasthan Astrological Council & Research Institute. He can be found in his shop near the City Palace, Chandani Chowk, Tripolia Gate.

Meditation

The Dhammathali Vispasana Meditation Centre (☎ 49-520) runs free courses in meditation for both beginners and more advanced students throughout the year at its centre near the Galta (temple of the sun god), about three km east of the city centre. Accommodation is provided in single rooms and meals are available. Write in advance to Dhammathali Vispasana Meditation Centre, Near Galta, Jaipur 302015.

Music & Dance Classes

Music and dance are taught at the Maharaja Sawai Mansingh Sangeet Mahavidyalay (☎ (0141) 41-397), Chandani Chowk, behin Tripolia, City Palace complex in Jaipu Tuition is given in traditional Indian instru ments such as tabla, sitar and flute, as we as Rajasthani folk instruments. There is ind vidual and group tuition. It costs around F 100 per month in a small group for regul. students. Classes are held six days a week, : the morning from 7 to 10 am, and in th evening from 5 to 8 pm. Individual tuitic costs about Rs 500 per month. There is als tuition in classical Indian dance *(kathak)*, well as Rajasthani folk dances. Vocal tuitic can also be undertaken here.

Miniature Painting Classes

Mr Kripal Singh (☎ (0141) 31-1227), B- Shivamarg, Bani Park, Jaipur, offers lessons miniature painting of both the Mughal ar Rajput schools.

Organised Tours

It's possible to book approved governme day tours of the city and environs wit English speaking guides. The tours visit th Hawa Mahal, Amber Fort (see 'Aroun Jaipur' later in this section), Jantar Manta City Palace and the Central Museum (clos Friday). At the end of the tour there's th inevitable stop at a craft shop. Here the pr cesses of production are explained and the is often a small demonstration in a tradition. craft, such as block printing.

The half day tours are a little rushed b otherwise OK. Times are 8 am to 1 pm, 11.3 am to 4.30 pm and 1.30 to 6.30 pm. The fu day tours are from 9 am to 6 pm, including lunch break at the Nahagarh Fort. The ha day tour is Rs 60, and the full day tour is R 90. Tours depart daily from the railwa station throughout the year according demand, picking up additional passengers c route at RTDC hotels. Ring ☎ 37-5466 f more details. Bookings can be made either the tourist office at the railway station, or the Tourist Reception Centre at the Jaip Tourist Hotel, MI Rd, opposite the GPO.

Approved guides for local sightseeing ca be hired through the tourist officer, Touri

eception Centre, Jaipur Tourist Hotel. A
alf day (four hour) tour for up to four people
 Rs 80 per person. A full day (eight hour)
ur for up to four people is Rs 100 per
erson. An additional lunch allowance of Rs
0 is payable for the full day tour within
aipur, and Rs 60 outside the city. An addi-
onal fee of Rs 50 per person for the half day
ur and Rs 80 per person for the full day tour
 levied for French, German, Italian, Japan-
se or Spanish speaking guides.

ther Tours
or details of the following tour operators,
ee Travel Agencies earlier in this chapter.

 Sita World Travels books tours and excur-
ons including elephant and bicycle polo
atches.

 Registhan Tours can arrange camel and
orse safaris, trekking in the Udaipur area,
ep expeditions and tailor-made tours. Their
orse safaris start at Rs 3500 per day per
erson, including breakfast, dinner and tent
ccommodation. The camel safaris are run in
e Jaisalmer and Shekhawati districts.
round Jaisalmer, prices start at Rs 950 per
erson per day, and in Shekhawati, Rs 1250
er day. Transport to and from these districts
 extra. Amber Tours offers chauffeur driven
ay tours to Sariska and Ranthambhore wild-
fe sanctuaries. A day excursion to Sariska
osts Rs 1895 for an Ambassador (non air-
on), Rs 2350 for an air-con vehicle, and Rs
350 for a Contessa. To Ranthambhore, it's
s 2180 in an Ambassador, Rs 2900 in an
ir-con vehicle, and Rs 4090 in a Contessa.

 Aravali Safari & Tours has luxury camel
eks in the Jaisalmer and Shekhawati
gions, and horse safaris in the Udaipur
gion. They can also organise treks in the
ravalli Range.

 Ghanerao Tours (☎ 31-1309), B-11/302
amal Apartments, Bani Park, Jaipur 302012,
rganises tailor-made horse safaris in south-
rn Rajasthan. It costs Rs 5000 per day (per
erson) or Rs 4500 per day (per person) for
roups of five people or more. This price
cludes horses with grooms, riding equip-
ent, accommodation, all meals, refresh-
ents on safari and an English-speaking

escort/guide. You need to bring your own
riding boots and hat. The best time to ride is
during the cooler months (usually mid-
October to mid-March). Bookings should be
made in advance.

There are tours on demand to Nahargarh
Fort for Rs 100, including a vegetarian
dinner, run by RTDC. There are also RTDC
tours (on demand) leaving at 6 pm to
Nahargarh Fort (Rs 85) and Chokhi Dhani,
a rather kitsch restaurant near the airport
which has evening traditional folk performances and Rajasthani cuisine (Rs 100).
Check in advance to make sure these are
operating.

Places to Stay
Getting to the hotel of your choice in Jaipur
can be a problem. Auto-rickshaw drivers
besiege every traveller who arrives by train
(less so if you come by bus). If you don't
want to go to a hotel of their choice, they will
either refuse to take you at all or they'll
demand at least double the normal fare. If
you do go to the hotel of their choice, you'll
pay through the nose for accommodation
because the manager will be paying them a
commission of at least 30% of what you are
charged for a bed (and the charge won't go
down for subsequent nights). The way to get
around this 'Mafia' is to go straight to the
prepaid auto-rickshaw stands which have
been set up at both the bus and railway
stations, where rates are set by the government.

Most hotels give discounts of 25% to 40%
in the low season (April to September). The
tourist office has an extensive list of families
who have registered with the Paying Guest
Scheme in Jaipur. The office has over 240
families on its books.

Places to Stay – bottom end A popular
place with travellers is the squeaky clean
Atithi Guest House (☎ 37-8679), 1 Park
House Scheme, Motilal Atal Marg, between
MI and Station Rds. All rooms have attached
bath and are light and airy. Standard singles/
doubles are Rs 250/300 and deluxe rooms
are Rs 300/350. Another popular travellers'

hangout is the *Hotel Arya Niwas* (☎ 37-2456; fax 36-4376), behind Amber Tower, just off Sansar Chandra Marg. There are tiny singles/doubles for Rs 200/300, larger standard rooms for Rs 300/400, and deluxe rooms for Rs 400/500. Amenities include a travel desk, bike hire (Rs 20 per day), a laundry service and a bookshop. Within walking distance, close to the Polo Victory Cinema and in a lane behind the Hotel Neelam, is the small and friendly *Karni Niwas* (☎ 36-5433), at C-5 Motilal Atal Marg. It's a very clean place in a quiet location. Singles/doubles with fan are Rs 225/275, air-cooled rooms are Rs 300/350 and air-con rooms are Rs 500/600.

For more atmosphere try the *Hotel Diggi Palace* (☎ 37-3091; fax 37-0359), just off Sawai Ram Singh Marg less than a km south of Ajmeri Gate. Doubles with common bath (hot water free by the bucket) are Rs 100 and Rs 125. With attached bath and geyser, they're Rs 200; with air-cooler, Rs 300 and Rs 350; and with air-con, Rs 500 and Rs 600. There's a restaurant here, bikes can be hired for Rs 50 per day, and there's free horse-riding. The building is the former palace of the *thakur* (similar to a lord or baron) of Diggi. The part which has been turned into a hotel is the old women's quarters.

There's a small cluster of budget hotels just off MI Rd in the area known as Chameli-wala Market. A long time favourite is the *Evergreen Guest House* (☎ 36-3466), which is geared up for travellers, with a laundry service, small swimming pool, a very good and reasonably priced restaurant, a shop selling handicrafts and a kiosk. It costs Rs 50 in the rather shabby dorm; Rs 100/120, or Rs 120/150 for larger rooms, with attached bath (hot water by the bucket for Rs 5); and Rs 175/200 and Rs 200/250 for rooms with attached bath and geyser. Checkout is an ungenerous 10 am.

A few steps away is the relatively new *Hotel Pink Sun*, which has clean singles with common bath for Rs 100 (hot water free by the bucket), and doubles with attached bath and geyser for Rs 150. Nearby is the *Ashiyana Guest House* (☎ 37-5414), run by a

friendly and enthusiastic manager. It's a ne place, and rooms are spotless. Single doubles with common bath (which has geyser) are Rs 100/150, and with attach bath with geyser, Rs 150/200.

Another area with some good budg options is Bani Park, about one km north the railway station. The *Shahpura Gue House* (☎ 31-2293; fax 32-1494) at D-2 Devi Marg, is currently undergoing maj renovations and will have rooms from 250 to Rs 750 (the latter with air-co There's a restaurant and travel counter, a they offer camel safaris around Jaipur for 810 per person per day (minimum tw people), or horse-drawn carriage trips for 1000 total per day.

Also in Bani Park is *Pipalda House* (☎ 3 1925) at D-240A Bank Rd. Basic and rath shabby singles/doubles with attached ba (hot water by the bucket) are Rs 75/150, a air-cooled rooms with geysers are Rs 275/35 There's a rooftop restaurant. It's possible take horse and camel safaris from here Pipalda Fort, about 250 km from Jaipur.

Nearby is the *Marudhara Hotel* (☎ 32-191 D-250 Bani Park. It's run by Raju and Shob Singh, and offers basic rooms in a friend atmosphere. Singles with common bath (h water by the bucket) are Rs 70, and double with attached bath and geyser are Rs 125.

Another friendly place, run by the affab Manish Sharma, is the *Tirupati Guest Hous* D-152 Durga Marg, Bani Park. Single doubles with common bath are Rs 50/80, a doubles with attached bath are Rs 100. Bas veg meals are available, and there's a plea ant lawn area.

An old time favourite in the Bani Park are is the *Jaipur Inn* (☎ 31-6821) at B-17 (1 Shiv Marg, run by Wing Commander R Bhargava. Beds in the rather busy dorm a Rs 50, and it's possible to camp on the law (own tents required) for Rs 30 per perso with full use of bathroom facilities. Room range from very basic spartan single doubles for Rs 80/100 to larger rooms for F 350/400.

The *Hotel Mangal* (☎ 37-5126) on Sans Chandra Marg is not far from the bus stan

Rates are from Rs 175/225 for deluxe rooms to Rs 500/550 for air-con rooms. There's 24 hour room service, 24 hour checkout, a restaurant, bar and beauty parlour. It's a friendly place, and the cheaper rooms are good value.

Right opposite the bus stand is the *Jai Mangal Palace*. There's a swimming pool here (summer only), which non-guests are welcome to use for Rs 40, as well as a bar and restaurant. Standard singles/doubles/triples are Rs 200/250/300, air-cooled rooms are Rs 300/350/400, and air-con rooms are Rs 500/600/700. The rooms are OK, but nothing flash.

There are a few places to stay within the old city. Opposite the Jama Masjid is the budget priced *Hotel Kailash* (☎ 56-5372). It's nothing fancy but is friendly and clean, with tiny singles/doubles with common bath (with geyser) for Rs 90/100; with attached bath, Rs 135/160; and larger rooms for Rs 200/250 and Rs 245/295 at the front of the hotel. Checkout is 24 hours. In Nehru Bazaar, just inside the city walls, is *Hotel Sweet Dream* (☎ 31-4409). Apart from the super deluxe rooms, which are larger and have air-con and colour TV, all rooms are the same size, differing only in amenities provided. The ordinary rooms have attached bath with cold water for Rs 170/225. Deluxe air-cooled rooms are Rs 250/300, and have hot water. Standard air-con rooms are Rs 400/450, and the super deluxe rooms are Rs 500/550. Some of the ordinary rooms are better than others, with balconies, so ask to see several rooms. There's a vegetarian rooftop restaurant here.

Outside the Chandpol, to the north-west of the old city, is the extraordinary *Hotel Khetri House* (no phone), built for the Maharaja of Khetri and now in a state of dusty decay. Some people will love this place and some will find it downright spooky. Rooms are enormous, with tatty old Art Deco furniture and claw-feet baths, and the otherworldly atmosphere is enhanced by a creaky caretaker. All rooms have air-coolers and running hot water, and range from Rs 200/300 to Rs 500/600 for the suites. Meals are available.

Dating from 1882, the *Hotel Kaiser-I-Hind* (☎ 31-0195), on Palace Rd near the Rajputana Palace Sheraton hotel, is extremely run down, covered in a centuries' old patina of dust. Mark Twain stayed in room No 6, Henry Ford was another guest, and Mussolini's brother-in-law was kept here as a prisoner of war. Rooms with enormous attached bathrooms with claw-feet baths are Rs 150/300, and hot water is free by the bucket.

There are reasonable *retiring rooms* at the railway station. Singles/doubles with common bath are Rs 60/100, with attached bath, Rs 80/150, and an air-con double is Rs 300. There is a dorm (men only) for Rs 35.

RTDC Places The *Jaipur Tourist Hotel* (☎ 36-0238) has a certain faded appeal, although it's looking quite shabby these days. The dorm is equipped with beds on the floor for Rs 50 per person. Ordinary singles/doubles/triples with attached bath and geysers are Rs 125/175/250, and the deluxe air-cooled rooms are Rs 200/275/375. There's a bar, and very basic meals can be provided on request. It's possible to book day tours here; see under Organised Tours, earlier.

Possibly a better choice is the *Hotel Swagatam*, at the west end of MI Rd near the railway station. The ordinary rooms are clean but spartan and cost Rs 155/235. Deluxe rooms with air-cooling are Rs 280/410, and there are dorm beds for Rs 50. All rooms have attached baths with hot water, and the rates include breakfast and bed tea.

Places to Stay – middle At the bottom end of this category, and very good value, is the *Madhuban Guest House* (☎ 31-9033), about one km north of the railway station, and run by the friendly Mahaveer Singh Rathore. The address is D-237 Bihari Marg, Bani Park. All rooms have attached bath with hot water. Standard rooms are Rs 250/300/400, deluxe singles/doubles are Rs 350/400, super deluxe rooms are Rs 500/550/700, and there are air-con single/double rooms for Rs 600/700. It's a lovely quiet and tranquil place, and the more expensive rooms have fine antique furnishings. A 25% discount is offered in May and June.

Another charming place to stay in Bani Park is the *Hotel Meghniwas* (☎ 32-2661; fax 32-1420) at C-9 Sawai Jai Singh Hwy. It's a gracious old white building with a pleasant lawn area and a pool. Air-cooled rooms are Rs 650/700, air-con rooms are Rs 750/800, and air-con suites are Rs 945/995.

Also in Bani Park, at the end of a quiet road, is the friendly family-run *Umaid Bhawan Guest House* (☎ 31-6184) at D1-2A, behind the Collectorate via Bank Rd. The guest house is an extraordinary egg-shell blue confection with orange trims. Rooms range from Rs 350/450 to the deluxe suite for Rs 1100. Next door is the *Sajjain Niwas Guest House* (☎ 31-1444), which is currently under construction and will have rooms from Rs 250 to Rs 750.

If you want to stay in an old palace but can't afford the Rambagh and its ilk, the *Hotel Bissau Palace* (☎ 30-4391; fax 30-4628) is a good option. There's a swimming pool, tennis court, library and restaurant, and the more expensive rooms have fine antique furnishings. The hotel was built by Rawal Raghubir Singh, the Maharaja of Bissau (in Shekhawati), and has fine old touches such as the lovely wood-panelled library and gracious dining room. Air-cooled singles/doubles are Rs 495/660, and air-con rooms are Rs 660/900 and Rs 900/1320. The cheaper rooms are very good value.

In the old city is the *LMB Hotel* (☎ 56-5844; fax 56-2176) above the popular restaurant of the same name in Johari Bazaar. Standard singles/doubles are Rs 725/925, and deluxe doubles are Rs 1275. The standard rooms are comfortable if a little tatty, and the larger deluxe rooms each have good views and a mini-fridge.

Near the Polo Victory Cinema is the *Hotel Neelam* (☎ 37-2215; fax 36-7808), at A-3 Motilal Atal Marg. Pleasant if somewhat dark standard singles/doubles start at Rs 350/400, and air-con rooms start at Rs 550/650. There's a vegetarian restaurant here.

The *Narain Niwas Palace Hotel* (☎ 56-1291; fax 56-3448) is a good choice. It's in Kanota Bagh, in the south of the city on Narain Singh Rd. The air-con standard rooms are in a new annexe which has been decorated in traditional style reminiscent of a coach house, with antique furnishings. The beautifully appointed air-cooled suites have four-poster beds, settees and other opulent touches, and the dining room, which is dripping with priceless antiques, has to be seen to be believed. Standard rooms are Rs 845/1125, and suites are Rs 1195/1495. There's a daily puppet show, and a swimming pool (summer only).

John Singh, convenor of INTACH, a trust formed to promote the conservation and preservation of Rajasthan's heritage buildings, is planning to provide cottage accommodation at *Anokhi Farm*, 15 minutes from Jaipur near Jagatpura. The accommodation will be part of the proposed Anokhi Craft Village, where artisans can be seen engaged in traditional crafts. Plans include a health food restaurant, and John is keen to promote eco-friendly tourism with innovations such as the use of solar energy and drip irrigation. Contact John at Anokhi (☎ 38-1619; fax 38-1654), 2 Tilak Marg, Jaipur, for more details.

RTDC Places The *Hotel Gangaur* (☎ 36-1233) is just off MI Rd. All singles/doubles have attached bath with hot water. Ordinary rooms are Rs 250/300, deluxe air-cooled rooms are Rs 375/425, and super deluxe rooms are Rs 500/600. There's a very good non-veg restaurant here, as well as a coffee shop.

The *Hotel Teej* (☎ 32-2538) is opposite the Moti Mahal cinema on Collectorate Rd in the area to the north of the railway station known as Bani Park. It's an old fashioned place, but well maintained. Dorm beds are Rs 50, deluxe air-cooled rooms are Rs 300/425/525, and air-con super deluxe rooms are Rs 500/550/675.

Places to Stay – top end A great choice in this category is the superb *Samode Haveli* (☎ 60-2407; fax 60-2370) in the north-east corner of the old city. This 200 year old building was once the town house of the awal (nobleman) of Samode, who was also the prime minister of Jaipur. It has a beautiful open terrace area, a stunning painted dining room, and a couple of amazing rooms. Ordinary rooms are cool and spacious, adorned with paintings of Hindu deities and antique furniture. Several of the suites are truly astonishing, featuring intricate mirrorwork, ornate paintings, tiny alcoves and recesses and soaring arches. Ordinary singles/doubles are Rs 1195/1400, and deluxe rooms are Rs 1195/2100. All rooms are air-cooled. There are puppet performances daily.

For sheer opulence you can't beat the *Rambagh Palace* (☎ 38-1919; fax 38-1098), Bhawani Singh Marg. It was previously the palace of Maharaja Man Singh II of Jaipur, and the Maharani still lives in separate quarters on the hotel grounds. There are all the luxurious appointments you would expect of a world class hotel, in addition to beautiful grounds. Standard singles/doubles are US$155/175, superior rooms are US$180/200, Royal rooms are US$275, the Maharaja suite is US$525, and the Royal suite is US$675. Non-guests are welcome to dine in the restaurant with advance notice or take tea on the verandah without notice. Breakfast is Rs 210 plus 22% tax, lunch is Rs 350 plus tax, and dinner is Rs 400 plus tax.

Also with fine gardens and offering gracious hospitality is the *Jai Mahal Palace Hotel* (☎ 37-1616; fax 36-5237), on the corner of Jacob Rd and Ajmer Marg, south of the railway station. Standard singles/doubles are US$130/150, and suites are US$350/450. There are the usual amenities you would expect of a hotel in this category, including beautiful swimming pool.

A more modest edifice than either the Rambagh or Jai Mahal is the *Rajmahal Palace* (☎ 38-1676; fax 38-1887) on Sardar Patel Marg in the south of the city. There are 13 finely appointed rooms and suites, as well as a good restaurant, badminton courts, swimming pool and jogging track. This was formerly the British Residency, and was also temporarily the home of Maharaja Man Singh II and the Maharani after their residence, the Rambagh Palace, was converted

into a luxury hotel. Standard singles/doubles are US$70/90 and a suite is US$300.

The five star *Mansingh Hotel* (☎ 37-8771; fax 37-7582), off Sansar Chandra Marg in the centre of town, has nicely appointed rooms for Rs 1195/2390, and large two bedroom suites for Rs 6500. There are two restaurants featuring veg and non-veg cuisine, a bar, swimming pool, spa and health club.

The *Holiday Inn* (☎ 60-9000; fax 60-9090) is in bleak surroundings about one km north of the old city on Amber Rd. Comfortably appointed standard rooms are US$60/70, executive suites are US$85, and deluxe suites are US$100. These rates include a buffet breakfast. There's a swimming pool, coffee shop, bar, restaurants, car hire desk and foreign exchange, and musicians play traditional Rajasthani folk music all day in the courtyard.

The swanky *Rajputana Palace Sheraton* (☎ 36-0011; fax 36-7848) is between Station and Palace Rds, conveniently located close to the railway station. The entrance is on Palace Rd. Amenities include three expensive restaurants, a swimming pool, health club, 24 hour coffee shop and a shopping arcade. Deluxe rooms are US$120/140, executive rooms are US$180/200, and suites are US$290 and US$400.

About 10 km south of the town centre is the *Hotel Clarks Amer* (☎ 55-0616), which has comfortably appointed rooms for US$100/110. There's a swimming pool, coffee shop, sauna and restaurant.

RTDC Places The *Hotel Jaipur Ashok* (☎ 32-0091; fax 32-2999) is at Jai Singh Circle, Bani Park, about one km north of the railway station. It's not as glitzy as some of its more modern competitors, but is nicely appointed with air-con rooms for Rs 1195/2200. There's a pool (non-guests welcome for Rs 100), a coffee shop, restaurant, bar and 24 hour room service.

Places to Eat
The rather shabby *Handi Bamboo Hut Restaurant*, out the front of the Jaipur Tourist Hotel on MI Rd, has veg and non-veg cuisine

JAIPUR

and Continental dishes such as 'scrummelled eggs'! It shouldn't be confused with the much more salubrious *Handi Restaurant*, a short distance to the east on MI Rd, tucked away at the back of the Maya Mansions building. The latter is quite reasonably priced, with non-veg dishes from Rs 50 to Rs 80, and in the evenings, it's possible to get cheap and tasty takeaway kebabs at the entrance to the restaurant.

A short distance to the east, right opposite the post office, is the excellent *Copper Chimney* restaurant, which was formerly part of the nationwide Kwality chain of restaurants. It has both veg and non-veg cuisine, with veg dishes from Rs 40 to Rs 70, and non-veg from Rs 80 to Rs 115. The food is great, and the service attentive. Try the Rajasthani dish lal maas – mutton in a thick spicy gravy – for Rs 80. Also on MI Rd, a block or two to the west, is the pure-veg *Rainbow Restaurant*, opposite the new Ganpati Plaza. It specialises in Indian, Continental and Chinese cuisine, and prices are reasonable. Try the Rainbow Special – a vegetable sizzler – for Rs 50.

Further east up MI Rd towards the old city is a cluster of mid-range places to eat. The air-con vegetarian *Natraj Restaurant* has an extensive menu featuring North Indian and Chinese cuisine. The house special, Bombay curry, is Rs 55, and there are delicious sweets to take away. Nearby is the fancy *Niro's* restaurant, which has both veg and non-veg cuisine. Prices for main courses range from Rs 40 to around Rs 110, and the staff are very attentive.

Less upmarket is the reasonably priced *Surya Mahal*, nearby. It's a popular place with a range of South Indian dishes, as well as some specials such as the delicious makki ki roti sarson ka saag (Rs 43). There are also pizzas and tandoori cuisine. Next door is *Jai Mahal's*, a takeaway ice-cream parlour which also has espresso coffee (Rs 8) and Italian thickshakes (Rs 12 to Rs 16). Down a lane next to Niro's is the *Golden Dragon Chinese Restaurant*. It specialises in Chinese dishes, but also serves Indian and some Japanese dishes (such as the delicious and filling chicken

sukiyaki – Rs 100). Most non-veg mains are around Rs 70. A few doors north is the *Bake Hut*, with freshly baked fare such as croissant (Rs 9), chocolate donuts (Rs 5) and variou delicious cakes (plum, date and walnut, and black forest) to take away.

On MI Rd, on the opposite side to Niro's is *Lassiwala*, a veritable institution, where you will probably have to queue for delicious thick, creamy lassis served in terracotta cup (Rs 10 for the small size, Rs 18 for the jumb cup).

Further west down MI Rd, on the opposit side to Niro's, is the very pleasant *Chanaky Restaurant*. The service is excellent at thi pure veg restaurant, and the food delicious The staff will helpfully explain the variou dishes. Continental dishes range from Rs 7 to Rs 120, and Indian cuisine ranges from R 40 to Rs 85.

Just outside the Chandpol is the *Bismilia Restaurant*, a basic but clean and cheap plac serving veg and non-veg dishes. Wort trying is the fish curry (the fish market i right next door), for Rs 26.

The *Indian Coffee House* is on MI Rd close to Ajmeri Gate. It has the usual dark all male and somewhat seedy ambience tha is found in this chain of coffee houses al over India, but it has good, cheap Sout Indian dishes and excellent coffee. It's dow a lane beside Arrow men's wear.

The *LMB* is a *sattvik* (pure vegetarian air-con restaurant in Johari Bazaar, near th centre of the old city, which has been goin strong since 1954. The food is tasty, althoug the 50s decor is looking slightly jaded thes days. Main dishes range from Rs 35 to Rs 70 the paneer tikka – cubes of grilled panee (cheese) stuffed with fennel-scented min chutney – is excellent (Rs 65). There is liv classical music each evening from 7 pm.

Diagonally opposite the LMB is *Royal's* which has good value vegetarian fast foo and specialises in South Indian cuisine.

Entertainment

It's well worth visiting the **Raj Mandir** cinema just off MI Rd on Bhagwandas Marg. Thi opulent and extremely well kept cinema is

Jaipur tourist attraction in its own right and is always full, despite its immense size. Tickets range from Rs 15 to Rs 24 per session.

Spectator Sport

Maharaja Man Singh indulged his passion for polo by building an enormous **polo ground** next to the Rambagh Palace, which is still the site of polo matches today. The royal team, led by their flamboyant maharaja, sailed for England in 1933 accompanied by 39 horses and their own personal carpenter (to keep the team in a constant supply of polo sticks), and stunned the opposition players and spectators with their equestrian flair, winning every important match in the tournament. Sadly the maharaja's passion was to prove fatal, and he died during a polo match in England in 1970. The polo season extends over winter, with the most important matches played during March. During Jaipur's elephant festival in March it is even possible to watch elephant polo matches at the ground. Telephone the Polo Club on ☎ 36-6492 for details.

Things to Buy

The state government emporium, Rajasthali, is opposite Ajmeri Gate on MI Rd. There's a good selection of artefacts and crafts from all over the state, including enamel work, embroidery, pottery, woodwork, jewellery, puppets, block-printed sheets, miniatures, brassware, mirrorwork and more. Next door is Rajasthan Handloom House, where there's an excellent selection of the state's textiles.

It's well worth visiting the Anokhi showroom at 2 Tilak Marg, near the Secretariat. Here you'll find top quality representative examples of arts and crafts from across Rajasthan including block-printed garments, jewellery, bed covers, printed fabrics, handmade paper products, bags, belts, scarves, *jootis* (handmade leather shoes) and blue ceramics.

The cutting, polishing and selling of precious and semi-precious stones is centred around the Muslim area of Pahar Ganj, in the Surajpol Bazaar area. Silver jewellery is also made here. There are numerous factories and showrooms strung along the length of Amber Road between Zorawar Gate and the Holiday Inn. Here you'll find hand-block prints, blue pottery, carpets and antiques.

Getting There & Away

Air Many of the international airlines which serve India are represented by two agencies based at the conveniently located Jaipur Towers building on MI Rd (in the same building as Thomas Cook). Jetair Ltd (☎ 37-7051; fax 37-4242) is open Monday to Friday from 9.30 am to 1 pm and 2 to 5 pm and Saturday from 9.30 am to 1 pm. It represents Air France, Royal Jordanian Airlines, Singapore Airlines, Gulf Airways, Air Canada, Biman Bangladesh and Jet Airways. Interglobe Air Transport (☎ 36-1487; fax 36-1886) is in the same building, and is open Monday to Saturday from 9 am to 1 pm and 2 to 5.30 pm. It represents United Airlines, South African Airways, SAS, Thai, Syrian Airways, Pakistan International Airlines (PIA), Tarom, Canadian Pacific, Ansett Australia, Air New Zealand, Varig and Alliance airlines.

Airlines flying to and between destinations in Rajasthan are: Indian Airlines, Skyline NEPC (formerly Damania Airways), ModiLuft, UP Airways and Sahara Indian Airlines. All domestic airlines can be booked through Satyam Travels & Tours (☎ 37-4490; fax 37-0843), ground floor, Jaipur Towers. Satyam has a computer link with Indian Airlines, so there's no need to visit the Indian Airlines office, which is some distance from the centre of the city on Tonk Rd. Satyam is open Monday to Saturday from 10 am to 6 pm.

Addresses of airlines in Jaipur are as follows:

Alitalia
    opposite HMT Showroom, MI Rd (☎ 36-9120)
Air India
    opposite All India Radio, MI Rd (☎ 36-8569)
British Airways
    near All India Radio, MI Rd (☎ 37-0374)

Jaipur Air Services

Flight	Service	Departs	Arrives	Cost (US$)*
Indian Airlines				
Delhi-Jaipur IC491	Wed, Thurs, Sat, Sun	7.15 am	7.55 am	38
Jaipur-Delhi IC492	as above	12.35 pm	1.15 pm	38
Delhi-Jaipur IC493	Mon, Wed, Fri, Sat	5.05 pm	5.45 pm	38
Jaipur-Delhi IC494	as above	8.05 pm	8.45 pm	38
Jaipur-Aurangabad IC491	Wed, Thurs, Sat, Sun	6.55 am	9.15 am	86
Jaipur-Mumbai	daily	–	–	102
Jaipur-Jodhpur	Mon, Wed, Fri, Sat	–	–	45
Jaipur-Udaipur	daily (except Tues)	–	–	51
ModiLuft				
Jaipur-Mumbai	daily	–	–	123
Jaipur-Bangalore (via Mumbai)	daily	–	–	203
Jaipur-Cochin (via Mumbai)	daily	–	–	226
Jaipur-Goa (via Mumbai)	daily	–	–	179
Jaipur-Delhi	daily	–	–	46
Jaipur-Jodhpur	daily	–	–	46
Jaipur-Udaipur	daily	–	–	54
Sahara				
Jaipur-Ahmedabad	daily (except Wed & Sun)	–	–	90
Jaipur-Delhi	as above	–	–	45
Jaipur-Patna	as above	–	–	122
Jaipur-Varanasi	as above	–	–	108
Jaipur-Calcutta	Mon, Tues, Thurs, Fri	–	–	157
UP Airways				
Jaipur-Delhi	daily	–	–	43
Jaipur-Udaipur	as above	–	–	51
Jaipur-Jodhpur	Tues, Thurs, Sat	–	–	54
Skyline NEPC				
Jaipur-Mumbai	Wed, Fri, Sun	–	–	123

* It is expected that all airfares will increase in 1997. See Airfares Update on page 129.

Cathay Pacific
  opposite Hotel Neelam, Motilal Atal Marg
  (☎ 37-5625)
Indian Airlines
  Nehru Place, Tonk Rd (☎ 41-4407)
Kuwait Airways
  Jaipur Towers, MI Rd (☎ 37-2896)
Lufthansa
  126-7 Sarogi Mansion, MI Rd (☎ 56-1360)
ModiLuft
  Navee Javan Chambers, Vinoba Marg, MI Rd
  (☎ 36-9693)
Sahara Airlines
  Shalimar Complex, Church Rd
  (☎ & fax 36-5741)
Skyline NEPC
  1st Floor, Ganesham, MI Rd (☎ 36-5118)
UP Airways
  Anukampa Bldg, Phase 2, MI Rd (☎ 37-8206)

Private Bus Services from Jaipur

Destination	Duration (hours)	Cost (Rs)
Agra	5	80
Ahmedabad	12-14	150
Ajmer	3	60
Bhopal	14	180
Bikaner	7	80
Delhi	6	90
Gwalior	10	130
Indore	14	180
Jhansi	12	140
Jodhpur	7	80
Kanpur	14	180
Kota	4	70
Mt Abu	12	159
Surat	18	250
Udaipur	9	100

Bus Rajasthan State Transport Corporation (RSTC) buses all leave from the main bus terminal (☎ 36-3277) on Station Rd. Some services are deluxe (essentially non-stop). There is a left-luggage office at the terminal. The deluxe buses all leave from platform No 3, which is tucked away in the right-hand corner of the bus terminal. These buses should be booked in advance, and the booking office, open from 8 am to 10 pm, is also at platform 3. 'Express service' is a bit of a misnomer, as these are essentially ordinary three seat by two seat buses, generally crowded, and stop at every little burgh en route to their specified destination.

There are no direct RSTC services to Mumbai or Baroda; you need to change at Udaipur. Numerous private agencies operate direct services to these cities; see below. There is one direct RSTC service to Ahmedabad at 5 pm.

There are numerous private travel agencies in Jaipur which book deluxe (two seat by two seat) services to major cities (generally services run overnight). There's a cluster along Motilal Atal Marg, near the Polo Victory Cinema.

Train The efficient computerised railway reservation office (☎ 13-1133) is to your right as you exit the railway station. It's open Monday to Saturday from 8 am to 2 pm and 2.15 to 8 pm, and Sunday from 8 am to 2 pm, and is for advance reservations only. Join the queue for 'Freedom Fighters and Foreign Tourists'. For same-day travel, you'll need to buy your ticket

---

RSTC Bus Services from Jaipur

Destination	Duration (hours)	Express	Cost (Rs) Deluxe	Air-Con
Abu Road	12	–	147 (dep. 8 pm)	–
Agra	5	62.50	76	–
Ajmer	2½	34	43	–
Alwar	4	40	–	–
Bharatpur	4½	46	76 (Agra service)	–
Bikaner	8	90 (dep. 9 pm)	–	–
Chittorgarh	7	81	–	–
Delhi	5½	68	125	215
Jaisalmer	15	161 (dep. 5 am)	–	–
	13	187 (dep. 10 pm)	–	–
Jodhpur	7	85	102	–
Kota	5	64	75	–
Udaipur	10	105	120	–
Mt Abu	–	123	–	–
	13	–	157	–
Pushkar	3½	91	–	–
Sawai Madhopur*	4½	46 (dep. 5.30 pm)	–	–
Tonk**	2½	28	–	–
Shekhawati District				
Sikar	2	30	37	–
Nawalgarh	3	38	46	–
Jhunjhunu	6	46	57	–
Pilani	7½	59	71	–
Churu	6	54	64	–
(via Sikar & Mandawa)				

There are regular services throughout the day to all destinations listed above, except where departure time is specified.

*Bus connections to Sawai Madhopur can be made at Tonk.
**Buses for Tonk leave from both the bus stand and near Ghat Gate.

Jaipur Train Services

Train & Service	Departs	Arrives	Cost (Rs)			
			2nd Class	1st Class	Chair	Air-con
2015 Shatabdi Express						
New Delhi-Jaipur	6.10 am	11.00 am		620 (air-con)	315 (air-con)	
Jaipur-New Delhi (via Alwar)	5.35 pm	10.15 pm	195	375	–	–
Jaipur-Ajmer	11.15 am	1.30 pm	–	–	–	–
2413 Delhi-Jaipur Superfast						
Delhi Junction-Jaipur	5.30 am	10.45 am	–	–	87	451
Jaipur-Delhi Junction	4.30 pm	9.50 pm	–	–	87	451
Intercity Express						
Old Delhi-Jaipur	4.40 pm	10.00 pm	–	198	82	–
Jaipur-Old Delhi (via Alwar)	6.30 am	11.30 am	–	198	82	–
9615 Chetak Express						
Jaipur-Udaipur	10.00 pm	9.30 am	109	423	–	–
Udaipur-Jaipur	6.30 pm	6.00 am	109	423	–	–
2915 Pink City Express						
Jaipur-Udaipur (via Ajmer)	12.20 pm	10.00 pm	109	388	–	–
Udaipur-Jaipur	5.30 am	4.30 pm	109	388	–	–
2465 Intercity Express						
Jaipur-Jodhpur	5.30 pm	10 pm	89	214	–	–
Jodhpur-Jaipur	6.30 am	10.30 am	89	214	–	–
2461 Mandore Express						
Jaipur-Jodhpur	1.45 am	7.30 am	118	–	–	470 (sleeper)
Jodhpur-Jaipur	5.30 pm	11.30 pm	118	–	–	470 (sleeper)
2308 Howrah Jodhpur Express						
Jaipur-Agra	11.15 pm	6.00 am	124	–	–	460 (sleeper)
Agra-Jaipur	8.10 pm	4.00 am	124	–	–	460 (sleeper)
Jaipur-Jodhpur	4.15 am	10.00 am	–	–	–	–
9901 Ahmedabad Mail						
Jaipur-Abu Road	4.50 am	4.10 pm	133	388	–	–
Abu Road-Ahmedabad	4.20 pm	9.55 pm	78	210	–	–
9902 Sarai Rohilla Mail						
Ahmedabad-Jaipur (via Abu Road)	5.15 am	10.40 am	170	505	–	–
2956 Bombay Superfast						
Jaipur-Kota	3.50 pm	5.00 pm	97	–	–	390
Kota-Jaipur	8.00 am	12.20 pm	97	–	–	390
Kota-Mumbai	5.00 pm	7.30 am	–	–	–	–
Mumbai-Kota	7.00 pm	8.00 am	–	–	–	–
Jaipur-Mumbai	3.50 am	7.30 am	253	–	–	1056
Regular Passenger Services						
Jaipur-Kota			72	229	–	–
Jaipur-Sawai Madhopur	6.00 am	9.30 am	40	–	–	–
	5.15 pm	8.30 pm	40	–	–	–
2468 Intercity Express						
Jaipur-Bikaner	2.55 pm	9.30 pm	104 (no reservation in 2nd class)			310
Bikaner-Jaipur	6.00 am	noon	104 (no reservation in 2nd class)			310
4737 Bikaner Express						
Jaipur-Bikaner	9.05 pm	7.00 am	83	–	–	477 (sleeper)
Bikaner-Jaipur	8.25 pm	7.00 am	83	–	–	477 (sleeper)
9736 Intercity Express						
Jaipur-Sikar	1.30 pm	4.30 pm	29	135	–	–
9734 Shekhawati Express						
Jaipur-Sikar	6.05 pm	8.05 pm	29	135	–	–

at the railway station. For metre-gauge trains, the booking office is on platform No 6.

Many of the lines into Jaipur have been converted to broad gauge. As other parts of the state's railway are converted expect disruptions to services.

Car Cars and drivers can be hired through numerous travel agencies, including Sita World Travels. Costs at Sita are Rs 4 per km (minimum 250 km per day) for a non air-con car, Rs 7 for an air-con car; the overnight charge is Rs 100 per day extra. Registhan Tours has very competitive car and driver rates. Non air-con vehicles are Rs 3.50 per km, with a minimum charge of Rs 250 per day. Air-con cars are Rs 6 per km. Rates with the RTDC are Rs 4.30 per km for a non air-con car, and an expensive Rs 10 per km for an air-con car, with the usual 250 km minimum per day. The only place where you can hire self-drive rental cars is at the Hertz office (☎ 60-9000; fax 60-9090), which has a desk at the Holiday Inn on Amber Road. See the Getting There & Away chapter under Car & Motorcycle for self-drive rates.

Getting Around

To/From the Airport There is currently no scheduled bus service between the airport and the city. A taxi will cost at least Rs 150 for the 15 km journey into the city centre.

Auto-Rickshaw There are prepaid auto-rickshaw stands at the bus and railway stations. Rates are fixed by the government.

Bicycle Bicycles can be hired from most bike shops, including that to the right as you exit the railway station, a few steps past the reservation terminal.

Around Jaipur

Jaipur is an excellent base from which to visit some of the ancient sites and interesting towns and villages in the precincts. A comprehensive network of local buses makes getting to these regions relatively simple, or it's possible to join an organised tour run by the RTDC which includes a commentary on the various sites visited. See under Organised Tours earlier in this section for more details.

Amber

Situated about 11 km out of Jaipur on the Delhi to Jaipur road, Amber was once the ancient capital of Jaipur state. The Kachhwahas originally hailed from Gwalior, in present day Madhya Pradesh, where they reigned for over 800 years. A marital alliance between a Kachhwaha prince, Taj Karan, and a Rajput princess, resulted in the granting of the region of Daosa, close to Amber, to the prince by the princess' father.

Taj Karan's descendants coveted the hilltop on which Amber Fort was later built, recognising its virtue as a potential military stronghold. The site was eventually prised from its original inhabitants, the Susawat Minas, and the Minas were granted guardianship of the Kachhwahas' treasury in perpetuity.

The Kachhwahas, despite being devout Hindus belonging to the Kshatriya (warrior) caste, recognised the expediency of aligning themselves with the powerful Mughal empire. They paid homage at the Mughal court, and cemented the relationship with marital alliances. They were handsomely rewarded for their bravery defending the Mughals in their various skirmishes. With war booty they were able to finance construction of the fortress-palace at Amber, which was begun in 1592 by Maharaja Man Singh, the Rajput commander of Akbar's army. It was later extended and completed by the Jai Singhs before the move to Jaipur on the plains below. The fort is a superb example of Rajput architecture, stunningly situated on a hillside and overlooking a lake which reflects its terraces and ramparts.

You can climb up to the fort from the road in 10 minutes, and cold drinks are available within the palace if the climb is a hot one. A seat in a jeep up to the fort costs Rs 15 return. Riding up on elephants is popular, though daylight robbery at Rs 250 per elephant one way (each can carry up to four people). A quick ride around the palace courtyard costs about Rs 20.

An imposing stairway leads to the **diwan-i-am**, or hall of public audiences, with a double row of columns, each topped by a capital in the shape of an elephant, and latticed galleries above. Here the maharaja received the petitions of his subjects.

Steps to the right lead to the small **Kali Temple**, where every day from the 16th century until 1980 (when the government banned the practice) a goat was sacrificed. It's a beautiful temple, entered by gorgeous silver doors featuring repoussé work. Before the image of Kali lie two silver lions. According to tradition, Maharaja Man Singh prayed to the goddess for victory in a battle with the ruler of Bengal. The goddess came to the maharaja in a dream advising that if he won the battle he should retrieve her image which was lying at the bottom of the sea. After vanquishing his foes, the maharaja recovered the statue and installed it in the temple as Shila Devi. *Shila* means slab, and the image is carved from one piece of stone. Above the lintel of the temple is the usual image of Ganesh, this one carved from a single piece of coral.

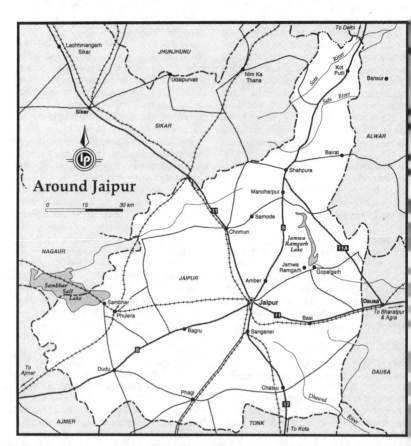

Around Jaipur

0   15   30 km

The maharaja's apartments are on the higher terrace – you enter through a gateway decorated with mosaics and sculptures. The **Jai Mandir**, or Hall of Victory, is noted for its inlaid panels and glittering mirror ceiling. Regrettably, much of this was allowed to deteriorate during the 1970s and 1980s but restoration proceeds.

Opposite the Jai Mandir is the **Sukh Niwas**, or Hall of Pleasure, with an ivory-inlaid sandalwood door and a channel running right through the room which once carried cooling water, acting as an ingenious early air-cooling system. Not a single drop of water was wasted, with the overflow passing through conduits to the palace gardens. From the Jai Mandir you can enjoy the fine views from the palace ramparts over the lake below.

The zenana, or **women's apartments**, are to the rear of the complex. The rooms have been cleverly designed so that the maharaja could embark on his nocturnal visits to their respective chambers without the knowledge of the other wives and concubines, as the chambers are all independent of each other but open onto a common corridor.

Amber Palace is open from 9 am to 4.30 pm and entry costs Rs 4. To use a still camera costs Rs 50, and a video camera is Rs 100. If you find your own way to the fort, as opposed to joining one of the RTDC city tours, it's possible to hire a RTDC guide at the fort who can explain the salient features. It costs Rs 12 for a two hour excursion (up to three people), Rs 15 for a half day excursion, and Rs 24 for a full day.

Getting There & Away There are regular buses from both the railway station and near the Hawa Mahal in the old city (20 minutes, Rs 2.50).

Nahargarh Fort

The Nahargarh Fort, also known as the Tiger Fort, overlooks the city from a sheer ridge to the north and is floodlit at night. The fort was built in 1734 by Jai Singh and extended in 1868. An eight km road runs up through the hills from Jaipur, and the fort can be reached along a zigzagging two km path which starts

This inlay stonework is typical of that at the Amber Fort.

from the north-west of the old city. The views fully justify the effort, and the entry fee is only Rs 2.

The small restaurant at the fort is popular at sunset, which is the best place to watch the sun going down and see the lights over Jaipur. There is one double room with common bath here where guests can stay (Rs 275). Reservations should be made with the tourist office in Jaipur.

Jaigarh Fort

The imposing Jaigarh Fort, built in 1726 by Jai Singh, was only opened to the public in mid-1983. It's within walking distance of Amber and offers a great view over the plains from the Diwa Burj watchtower. The fort served as the treasury of the Kachhwahas, and some people are convinced that at least part of the royal treasure is still secreted somewhere among its corridors. It's a remarkable feat of military architecture, in a fine state of preservation. The fort, with its water reservoirs, residential areas, puppet theatre and enormous cannon, Jaya Vana, is open from 9 am to 4.30 pm.

Royal Gaitor

This beautiful, peaceful place is just outside the city walls, accessible via the Zorawar or Samrat gates in the northern wall of the old city. It contains the cenotaphs of the maharajas of Jaipur, from Jai Singh II, the founder of Jaipur, to that of the last maharaja, Man Singh II. The more ancient cenotaphs, including that of Jai Singh, are in a walled compound to the rear of the complex. A caretaker may be required to open the gate here. Behind Maharaja Madho Singh II's beautifully carved cenotaph is a cenotaph commemorating his 13 sons who died of malaria. Beside the entrance to the Royal Gaitor, steps lead in 20 minutes to a Ganesh temple.

The cenotaphs of the maharanis of Jaipur are on Amber Rd, midway between Jaipur and Amber. Further north is the **Jal Mahal** (Water Palace), in the middle of a lake and reached by a causeway. Or at least it was in the middle of the lake; the water is now all but squeezed out by the insidious weed, water hyacinth.

Sisodia Rani Palace & Gardens & Vidyadharji ka Bagh

Six km from the city on Agra Rd (leave Jaipur by the Ghat Gate), and surrounded by terraced gardens, this palace was built for Maharaja Jai Singh's second wife, the Sisodia princess. The outer walls are decorated with murals depicting hunting scenes and the Krishna legend.

Vidyadharji ka Bagh, a garden built in honour of Jai Singh's chief architect and town planner, Vidyadhar, is about 500m before Sisodia Rani Palace on Agra Rd.

Getting There & Away Regular local buses leave from out the front of the railway station and from Ghat Gate for the Sisodia Rani Palace (10 minutes, Rs 2). You could ask the bus driver to drop you at the Vidyadharji ka Bagh, and then continue on to the palace. Entry to the palace gardens costs Rs 2 (open daily from 10 am to 6 pm). It's possible to get a good view out over the gardens without entering the complex by continuing along the road past the entrance and driving to the back of the gardens. This road continues to the temple of the sun god at Galta (see below). Above the palace, a steep zigzag staircase leads to a Jain temple.

Galta

The temple of the sun god at Galta is 100m above Jaipur to the east, a 2½ km climb from Surajpol. A deep temple-studded gorge stands behind the temple and there are fine views over the surrounding plains. Very heavy rains in 1991 destroyed many of the original frescoes. Restoration is currently underway, although unfortunately the new work has little of the artistic skill of the original frescoes. In the temple are images of Brahma, Vishnu, Garlo Rishi, Shankaracharya, Parvati and Ganesh. The temple is fronted by pools into which some daring souls jump from the adjacent cliffs. The water is claimed to be 'several elephants deep'.

There are some original frescoes in reasonable condition in the chamber at the end of the bottom pool, including those depicting athletic feats, the maharaja playing polo, and the exploits of Krishna and the *gopis* (milk maids). On the ceiling are swirl motifs, and it is possible to make out faces which are not initially evident on first viewing. Galta is perched between the cliff faces of a rocky valley, and is a fairly desolate and barren, if somewhat evocative, place.

Sanganer & Bagru

The small town of Sanganer is 16 km south of Jaipur and is entered through the ruins of two *tripolias*, or triple gateways. In addition to its ruined palace, Sanganer has a group of Jain temples with fine carvings to which entry is restricted. The town is noted for its handmade paper and block printing, and a highlight of a visit here is to walk down to the riverbank (on the right as you enter the town), to see the brightly coloured fabric drying in the sun.

About 20 km to the west of Sanganer is the small village of Bagru, also notable as a centre for block-printing, particularly of bold and colourful designs featuring circular motifs.

Getting There & Away Buses to Sanganer leave from out the front of the railway station, near the reservation hall (30 minutes, Rs 5). Alternatively, tempos leave from the Ajmeri Gate for Sanganer every two minutes (30 minutes, Rs 3).

Samode

The small village of Samode is nestled among rugged hills about 50 km north of Jaipur, via Chomu. The only reason to visit is if you can afford to stay at the beautiful **Samode Palace** (although strictly speaking it's not actually a palace, as it wasn't owned by a ruler, but by one of his noblemen). Like the Samode Haveli in Jaipur, this building was owned by the Rawal of Samode. It's a beautiful building built on three levels, each with its own courtyard. The highlight of the building is the absolutely exquisite diwan-i-khas, which is completely covered with original paintings and mirrorwork, and is probably the finest example of its kind in the country. Unfortunately the palace is open only to guests, and public transport requires a change in Chomu.

To stay in the palace will cost Rs 1195/2100, or Rs 1195/2500 for the deluxe rooms. Breakfast is Rs 150, and lunch and dinner are Rs 260.

Getting There & Away Buses leave from near the Chandpol for Chomu (one hour, Rs 6), from where it's necessary to get another bus for the 30 minute trip to Samode (Rs 3).

Bairat

Continuing beyond Amber, 52 km north of Jaipur and a short distance to the east of the main Jaipur-Delhi road, is the ancient Buddhist centre of Viratnagar, or Bairat. Archaeological evidence in the form of ancient coins, the remains of a Buddhist monastery, and several rock-cut edicts, a legacy of the great 3rd century BC Buddhist convert Ashoka, indicate that this was once an important centre of Buddhism.

Balaji

The Hindu exorcism temple of Balaji is about 1½ km off the Jaipur to Agra road, about 1½ hours by bus from Bharatpur. The exorcisms are sometimes very violent and those being exorcised don't hesitate to discuss their experiences.

Getting There & Away Express (but not luxury) buses to Agra from Jaipur make the short detour to Balaji.

Eastern Rajasthan

The sites and cities of eastern Rajasthan are all easily accessible from Jaipur, and this region hosts a vast array of attractions for visitors. For those who wish to steep themselves in history, there are beautiful palace complexes at Alwar and Deeg, and fine fortresses at Bharatpur and Ranthambhore. Wildlife and bird enthusiasts are well catered for, with tiger spotting possibilities at both Ranthambhore National Park and the Sariska Tiger Reserve, both of which are administered by Project Tiger. Keoladeo Ghana National Park is India's premier bird sanctuary, with an astonishing population of resident and migratory birds in a beautiful wetland setting.

The holy Hindu pilgrimage town of Pushkar, set around a small lake, is one of the most popular travellers' centres in India. You can stay in one of the dozens of tiny whitewashed guest houses here, dine in any one of numerous vegetarian restaurants, have a priest perform a *puja* on your behalf, or shop in the fascinating market where you'll find colourful clothes designed to western tastes. Pushkar is most famous for the Camel Fair that it hosts annually in October/November. Ajmer, close to Pushkar, is an important pilgrimage centre for Muslims, who pay homage at the Dargah, a tomb to the Sufi saint, Khwaja Muin-ud-din Chishti. Ajmer is also the site of the prestigious Mayo College, where many of Rajasthan's young princes were educated.

HISTORY

The erstwhile state of Alwar, in north-eastern Rajasthan, is possibly the oldest kingdom in kingdom-studded Rajasthan. In 1500 BC it formed part of the Matsya territories of Viratnagar (present-day Bairat), which also encompassed Bharatpur, Dholpur and Karauli.

History becomes inextricably bound with mythology, as it was here in the ancient kingdom of Matsya that the Kauravas embarked on the cattle-rustling mission

---

HIGHLIGHTS

- Ranthambhore National Park and Sariska Tiger Reserve for tiger and wildlife spotting
- Keoladeo Ghana National Park, a World Heritage bird sanctuary
- Pushkar, a peaceful and sacred town; the Pushkar Camel Fair in October/November
- The palace complexes at Alwar and Deeg
- The Dargah in Ajmer, tomb of an important Muslim Sufi

---

which precipitated the war between them and their kinsfolk, the Pandavas. This great battle forms the basis of the *Mahabharata*. The city of Alwar is believed to have been founded by a member of the Kachhwaha family who hailed from Amber, but control was wrested from the Kachhwahas by the Nikumbhas. They in turn lost the city to the Bada Gurjara Rajputs of Machari. It then passed to the Khanzadas, under Bahadura Nahara of Mewat, who converted from Hinduism to Islam to win the favour of Emperor Tughlaq of Delhi. At this time, Alwar and Tijara were part of the kingdom of Mewat.

Descendants of Bahadura Nahara bravely defended the Alwar fort against the Muslims in 1427. Alwar's fortunes were inextricably bound with those of Mewat, which was contiguous with Delhi. Although the Mewati leader professed the Muslim faith, he chose to ally himself with the Rajputs as opposed to the Muslims in Delhi. As Alwar was located on the strategic south-western frontier of Delhi, this of course rankled with the Mughals, who mounted numerous military forays into the region, only conquering it after great difficulty. Alwar was later granted to Sawai Jai Singh of Jaipur by Aurangzeb, only to be retaken when the emperor visited the city and noted the great strategical virtues of its fortress.

The Jats of Bharatpur then threw their hat into the ring, briefly overrunning the region, and installing themselves in the Alwar fort. They were evicted by the Lalawat Narukas (descendants of the Kachhwaha prince of Amber, Naru) between 1775 and 1782 under the leadership of the Naruka *thakur* (noble) Pratap Singh. His descendants were great patrons of the arts, commissioning the transcription of numerous sacred and scholarly texts and encouraging painters and artisans to visit the Alwar court.

In 1803, the British invested the Alwar thakur with the title of maharaja as thanks for their support in a battle against the Marathas. This friendly alliance was short-lived, however, with the maharaja of Alwar strongly resenting British interference in governance when a British Resident was installed in the city.

Following Independence, Alwar was merged with the other princely states of Bharatpur, Karauli and Dholpur, forming the United State of Matsya, a name which reflected the fact that these states all comprised the ancient Matsya kingdom. In 1949, Matsya was merged with the state of Rajasthan.

Another large ancient city of eastern Rajasthan is Bharatpur, which is traditionally the home of the Jats, who were well settled in this region before the emergence of the Rajputs. The relationship between the Jats, tillers of the soil, and the warrior Rajputs was at best an uneasy one. Marital alliances between the two groups went some way to reducing the friction, but territorial encroachments on the part of both parties led to inevitable confrontations. There simmered through the centuries, only being overcome when both groups turned to face the mutual threat posed by the Mughals. One of the Jats' strongest leaders was Badan Singh, who ruled in the mid-18th century. He expanded Jat territory far beyond its original boundaries, and was awarded by the maharaja of Amber with the title of Brij-Raj.

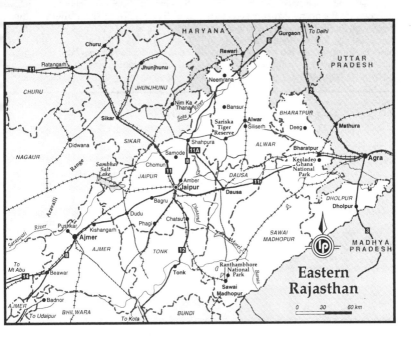

Eastern Rajasthan

It was the Jat leader Suraj Mahl who built the beautiful palace and gardens at Deeg and commenced work on the Bharatpur Fort, which was completed in the late 18th century after nearly 60 years of work. Evidently this was time well spent, as the British unsuccessfully besieged the fort for nearly half a year, finally conceding defeat after substantial losses. The rulers of Bharatpur were the first to enter into an agreement with the East India Company.

The massive fort at Ranthambhore predates that at Bharatpur by many centuries, having been founded in the 10th century by the Chauhan Rajputs. Ranthambhore was held in great reverence by the Jains, and several temples here were considered sites of great spiritual importance. Over the centuries Ranthambhore was subjected to numerous assaults by the Muslims, and in the 14th century, the first *jauhar*, or collective sacrifice, was declared in Rajasthan when the women of Rajasthan heard word that their ruler, Hammir Deva, had died on the battlefield.

The Mughal emperor Akbar negotiated a treaty with Surjana Hada, a Bundi ruler who purchased the fort of Ranthambhore from Jhunjhar Khan, and the fort passed to Jagannatha, under whose leadership the Jain

religion flourished. The fort was taken by the Mughals under Aurangzeb, with whom it remained until the 18th century, when it was granted to the Maharaja of Jaipur.

Ajmer was also founded by the Chauhans, three centuries earlier than Ranthambhore. In the late 12th century it passed to Mohammed of Ghori, and remained a possession of the Sultanate of Delhi until the second decade of the 14th century. Fought over by various neighbouring states over subsequent centuries, it later passed to the Mughals, briefly taken by the Rajput Rathores, was restored to the Mughals under Akbar, later passed to the Scindias, and came under direct British rule in 1818.

BHARATPUR & KEOLADEO GHANA NATIONAL PARK
Population: 1,646,501
Telephone Area Code: 05644

Bharatpur is famous for its World Heritage-listed bird sanctuary, the Keoladeo Ghana National Park, the main entrance to which lies five km from the railway station. According to a recent report, 354 species of birds have been identified at the park. Keoladeo Ghana National Park is described later in this section.

FESTIVALS OF EASTERN RAJASTHAN

Eastern Rajasthan hosts the state's most colourful and lively fair, the Pushkar Camel Fair, as well as an important Jain festival. For statewide and nationwide festivals, see Festivals of Rajasthan in the Facts for the Visitor chapter.

February-March
Brij Festival – This festival takes place in Bharatpur over several days prior to Holi, and is held in honour of Krishna. At this time the *Rasalila* dance is performed.

March-April
Shri Mahavirji Fair – This fair is held in honour of Mahavir, the 24th and last of the Jain *tirthankars*, or teachers, at the village of Chandangaon in Sawai Madhopur district. Thousands of Jains congregate on the banks of the Gambhir River, to which an image of Mahavir is carried on a golden palanquin.

November
Pushkar Camel Fair – Possibly the most well known regional festival in India, the Pushkar Camel Fair attracts tens of thousands of visitors, both from around Rajasthan and neighbouring states. Many travellers time their visit to this beautiful town to correspond with the fair. More detail is given in a boxed section under Pushkar in this chapter.

In the 17th and 18th centuries, Bharatpur was an important Jat stronghold. Before the arrival of the Rajputs, the Jats inhabited this area and were able to maintain a high degree of autonomy, both because of their prowess in battle and because of their chiefs' marriage alliances with Rajput nobility. They successfully opposed the Mughals on more than one occasion and their fort at Bharatpur, constructed in the 18th century, withstood an attack by the British in 1805 and a long siege in 1825. This siege eventually led to the signing of the first treaty of friendship between the states of north-west India and the East India Company.

The town itself, which was once surrounded by an 11 km long wall (now demolished), is of little interest. Bring mosquito repellent with you as mosquitoes can be a problem.

Orientation & Information

The Keoladeo National Park lies five km to the south of the city centre, and is easily accessed by cycle-rickshaw. There is a good selection of hotels both in the town centre and closer to the park.

The tourist office (☎ 22-542) is at the RTDC Hotel Saras Bharatpur, about 700m from the park entrance. It's open Monday to Saturday from 10 am to 5 pm (closed for lunch between 1.30 and 2 pm).

There are currency exchange facilities at the State Bank of Bikaner & Jaipur, near the Binarayan Gate.

The GPO is the main post office.

There is a bookshop at the checkpoint, 1½ km from the main gate, inside the park, which has a good selection of titles on Indian animal and birdlife.

Lohargarh Fort

The Lohargarh Fort, also known as the Iron Fort, was built in the early 18th century and took its name from its supposedly impregnable defences. Maharaja Suraj Mahl, the fort's constructor and the founder of Bharatpur, built two towers within the ramparts, the Jawahar Burj and Fateh Burj, to commemorate his victories over the Mughals and the British.

The fort occupies an entire small artificial island in the centre of the town, and the three palaces within its precincts are in an advanced state of decay. In fact, the entire fort has a forlorn, derelict feel, and is in need of restoration. The main entrance is the **Austdhatu Gate**. *Austdhatu* means 'eight metals', a reference to the spikes on the gate which are reputedly made of eight different metals.

Museum The government museum is housed in the former *durbar* (maharaja's meeting hall) in the fort. There's a display of sculpture which spans the ages, some pieces dating from the 2nd century AD. There's a well preserved 7th century carving of Shiva and Parvati which was recovered from Kama (near Deeg), and a fine carving of Shiva as Nataraja, the cosmic dancer, dating from the 10th century. In a separate hall, but also part of the museum's collection, is a gallery featuring portraits and old photographs of the maharajas of Bharatpur. Other exhibits include weaponry and an assortment of stuffed beasts, including a couple of pitiful baby bear cubs. The museum is open from 10 am to 4.30 pm daily except Friday. Entry is Rs 2.

Jawaharbij This viewing point is a short walk to the north-east of the museum along a steep path. It was from here that the maharajas surveyed their city. It's a nice place capturing the cool breezes in a series of pavilions, the ceilings of which feature badly deteriorating frescoes – scenes of elephants and chariots can be made out. As you would expect, the views down over the city are superlative.

Nehru Park From the museum to Nehru Park is a five minute walk. Nehru Park is between the museum and the main gate (Austdhatu Gate) of the fort. There are pleasant lawns and flower beds, as well as the Madhuban cafeteria.

Ganga Temple

Just outside the Lohiya Gate is this temple dedicated to the goddess Ganga. On the laneway leading up to the temple, vendors sell mattress stuffing made of Punjabi wool. Construction of the temple commenced in 1845 during the reign of Maharaja Balwant Singh, but it was not completed until 1937, during the reign of Maharaja Brijendra Sawai. The two storey temple, made of sandstone, features a black and white chequered floor and ornately carved arches. Pujas are performed here at 5 am and 5 pm. Note that the edges of the terrace on which the temple stands, overlooking the busy streets below, are not stable, and you should not approach them too closely.

Keoladeo Ghana National Park

The sanctuary, which has now been denoted a national park, came into being in the 18th century. Maharaja Suraj Mahl of Bharatpur converted what was essentially a low-lying swamp formed by the confluence of the Gambhir and Banganga rivers into a reservoir, the Ajun Bund. Flooding during subsequent monsoons soon inundated the surrounding region, creating a shallow wetland ecosystem, the perfect habitat for an astonishing variety of birds.

The maharaja was compelled not by conservationist motives, but by the desire to have a ready supply of waterfowl, affording fine shooting (and dining) possibilities. Indeed, Keoladeo continued to supply the maharajas' tables until as late as 1965. An inscription on a pillar near the small temple in the park bears testimony to the maharajas' penchant for hunting. It reveals that on one day alone, over 5000 ducks were shot.

A fence was built around the forests of the wetlands in the latter part of the 19th century to stop feral cattle from roaming through the area. Between 1944 and 1964, afforestation policies were pursued, with the plantation of stands of acacias.

The post-Independence period was one of great turmoil. Local communities were keen to divert the canals which feed the swamplands for irrigation, and to convert the wetlands into croplands. Fortunately, the conservationists won the day, and in 1956 the region was declared a sanctuary. In 1982, it was denoted a national park, encompassing a small area of some 29 sq km, of which one third is submerged during the annual monsoon.

Today Keoladeo is recognised as one of

Siberian Cranes

Park authorities at Keoladeo were concerned when the endangered Siberian crane (*Grus leucogeranus*) failed to appear during two successive winter seasons in 1994 and 1995. In 1996, on the first day of winter, ornithologists around the world heaved a collective sigh of relief when four of these magnificent birds flew into the park, nearly two months after their usual arrival.

It is believed that the total population of Siberian cranes wintering in Iran and India is only 15; an estimated 100 of these birds have perished over the last 12 years during their 5000 km long journey from the Orb river basin in Siberia over inhospitable terrain. There are two other populations of Siberian cranes which hail from the Orb River. The most substantial population, numbering almost 3000, winters at the Yangtze River in China. A small population of about a dozen flies to winter grounds along the south coast of Iran's Caspian Sea. The tiny remaining population makes its annual winter journey to India, and it is this group that is hosted at Keoladeo. About 30 years ago more than 200 sibes, as they are known, wintered at Keoladeo, and this sharp drop in numbers raises grave fears about their survival as a species. They have been termed 'critically endangered' by the International Union of Conservation of Nature.

Tragically, it is not the natural rigours of the long migration which are blamed for the critical depletion of sibe numbers, but the Afghanistan war, with sibes being slaughtered for meat by Afghanis. They are also believed to fall prey to hunters in Pakistan, who shoot them for sport. Unfortunately, efforts to install a transmitter on one of the sibes which arrived at Keoladeo in 1996 failed, due to various problems, including bureaucratic delays. The transmitter would have provided conservationists and scientists with invaluable information about the birds' migratory route, habitats and breeding range. The transmitter would have sent signals through the Argos satellite launched jointly by the USA and France. Conservationists can now only wait and hope that these brave journeyers will return to their winter grounds, hopefully in replenished numbers, in future seasons. ■

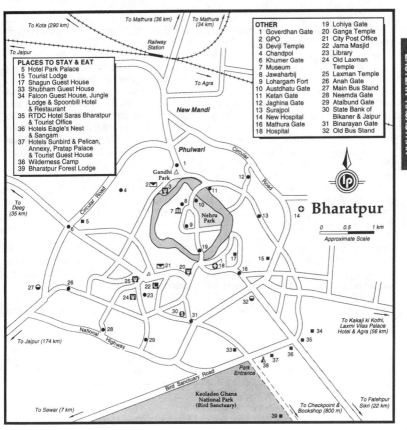

the most important bird breeding and feeding grounds in the world.

Keoladeo Fauna During the monsoon period (July to August), and for a month or so following the monsoon, the park is home to vast colonies of birds which come here to breed and feed on the wetland's rich aquatic species. Some of the numerous species which nest at this time include storks, moorhens, herons, egrets and cormorants. Around October the park's bird population increases with the arrival of wintering migratory birds who stay until around the end of February.

Among these birds is the highly endangered Siberian crane, which is found in India only at this park (see the boxed information in this section). This is the best time to visit the sanctuary.

The migratory birds have mostly left by the end of March. At the beginning of April, when the waters begin to recede, there is still a substantial population of birds of prey (vultures), some kingfishers, and smaller birds such as robins, wagtails, and mynas. Many of these birds feed at the few pools, teeming with fish, that remain in the park during the dry summer months. During the height of summer, when the waters have all but disappeared, the sanctuary is carpeted in dry grasslands which afford habitat to a variety of fauna such as deer (spotted, sambar, bluebull), jackal, jungle cat and mongoose.

Visiting the Park The park is open from 6 am to 6 pm daily. Only one sealed road goes through the park, but a series of raised embankments thread their way between the shallow wetlands. Walking or cycling along these embankments affords unique opportunities to observe the rich birdlife at close quarters.

Entry to the park costs Rs 25 per person. A still camera is Rs 10, and it costs Rs 100 to bring a video camera into the park. There's also an entry fee for cycles (Rs 3), scooters (Rs 10) and cycle-rickshaws (Rs 5). Motorised vehicles are prohibited beyond the checkpoint, 1½ km beyond the main gate, inside the park, so the only way of getting around is by foot, bicycle or cycle-rickshaw.

Only those cycle-rickshaws authorised by the government (recognisable by the yellow plate bolted onto the front) are allowed inside the park – beware of anyone who tells you otherwise! Although you don't pay entry fees for the drivers of these cycle-rickshaws, you'll be up for Rs 25 per hour if you take one and they'll expect a tip on top of that. It's definitely worthwhile hiring one of these government-approved rickshaw-wallahs, who have been trained in bird identification – it was one of these wallahs, Runghu Singh, who first observed the four Siberian cranes which thrilled ornithologists with their return to the park after two years absence in 1996. Not only are you encouraging local employment, but these fellows really do know their birds. If you wish to hire an experienced ornithologist, this will cost around Rs 40 per hour or Rs 300 a day.

Boats can be hired for Rs 60 per hour. They are a very good way of getting close to the wildlife in this park. Binoculars are Rs 10 per hour. Guides can be organised at the park entrance. Official government prices are Rs 35 for one to five people per hour, and Rs 75 for five to 10 people. Government guides can be hired at the main gate to the national park. A horse-drawn tonga costs Rs 50 per hour.

After your initial visit to the park with a rickshaw-wallah or trained guide, a good way to see the park on subsequent visits is to hire a bicycle. These can be hired at the park entrance for Rs 10 per day. Having a bike allows you to easily avoid the bottlenecks, which inevitably occur at the nesting sites of the larger birds. It's just about the only way you'll be able to watch the numerous kingfishers at close quarters – noise or human activity frightens them away.

Some of the hotels rent bicycles (see Places to Stay below). If you plan to visit the national park at dawn (one of the best times to see the birds), you'll have to hire a bicycle the day before.

The southern reaches of the park are virtually devoid of *humanus touristicus*, and so are much better than the northern part for serious bird-watching.

There's a small snack bar and drinks kiosk about halfway through the park, next to the tiny Keoladeo Temple.

There is a small informative display at the main entrance to the park which has a range of stuffed birds, nests of various species, examples of aquatic species found in the park's lakes and a good photographic display. Entry is free.

Places to Stay & Eat – Bharatpur

Close to the Mathura Gate and near the old bus stand is the *Tourist Lodge* (☎ 23-742), a pleasant enough place which is popular with travellers. Rooms are cheap at Rs 30/40 for singles/doubles with common bath, and Rs 50/60 and Rs 80/100 with attached bath. Meals are available and there's a good balcony area. Bikes and binoculars are on hire for Rs 30 each per day.

Another popular and friendly place to stay is the *Shagun Guest House*. There are primitive grass huts for Rs 46/66 which have mosquito nets and lights, singles/doubles with common bath for Rs 52/80, and with attached bath and hot water Rs 68/86. Bike hire is Rs 24, and electric fans are available.

You can get basic meals here, and the owner, Rajeev, is friendly and helpful and has a wealth of knowledge on the park and Bharatpur. The guest house is down a laneway just inside the Mathura Gate.

About equidistant between the national park and the town centre is the *Laxmi Vilas Palace Hotel* (☎ 23-523; fax 25-259), which is at Kakaji ki Kothi on the old Agra road. There are no single rates. Standard doubles are Rs 750, deluxe rooms are Rs 1000, super deluxe are Rs 1600, and suites are Rs 2200. The hotel was originally built for the younger son of Maharaja Jaswant Singh and is now operated by the Heritage group. The standard rooms are in a new annexe and are nothing special, and the deluxe rooms are small and also not good value. The suites are enormous – cool, spacious oases with antique furniture and original wall paintings, and the super deluxe rooms also feature fine antique furniture.

A good choice is the *Hotel Park Palace* (☎ 23-783), which is the closest hotel to the bus stand, close to the Khumer Gate. This well run place has clean budget rooms for Rs 150/200, air-cooled rooms for Rs 200/250, deluxe rooms for Rs 400/450 and air-con rooms for Rs 500/550. All rooms have attached bath with hot water, and the manager is very helpful. There's a restaurant here.

Places to Stay & Eat – Park Precincts

The following places are all within easy walking distance of the main entrance to the national park – none are over one km from the entrance. The RTDC *Hotel Saras Bharatpur*, at the junction of Fatehpur Sikri and Bird Sanctuary Rds, has ordinary singles/ doubles for Rs 250/275 with attached bath and geyser. Deluxe air-cooled singles/ doubles/triples are Rs 400/450/550, and the super deluxe rooms, with air-con and TV, cost Rs 500/600/725. Dorm beds cost Rs 50. There's a restaurant (but no bar) which has a wide selection of veg meals and a few token non-veg dishes.

Just behind the Hotel Saras is the *Spoonbill Hotel & Restaurant* (☎ 23-571), which has rooms with common bath for Rs 80/100,

or with attached bath (hot water by the bucket for Rs 5) for Rs 100/150. There are also dorm beds for Rs 40. Good discounts are offered in the off season, and the restaurant features both veg and non-veg cuisine including Rajasthani dishes such as churma, the royal dish of Rajasthan – sugar, cheese and dried fruit fried in butter. There is also a variety of thalis from Rs 35 to Rs 50. There's a campfire in winter, bike hire is Rs 20 per day, binoculars are Rs 30 per day, and there's a bird spotter's guide available for loan for Rs 10 per day.

Nearby is the *Falcon Guest House* (☎ 23-815), which has good sized singles/doubles for Rs 150/200 and Rs 250/300, all with attached bath and 24 hour hot water. Bikes are available for hire here. Possibly an even better choice is the *Jungle Lodge* (☎ 25-622) nearby, which has small but comfortable rooms with attached bath and hot water for Rs 125/150 which open onto a shady verandah. There are also larger rooms for Rs 200/250, as well as a nice lawn area. Discounts of up to 50% are offered in the off season, and there's a lending library here.

Directly opposite the Saras, on Fatehpur Sikri Rd, is the *Hotel Sangam* (☎ 25-616). Ordinary singles/doubles downstairs with cold water are Rs 150/200, and upstairs fairly plain rooms with hot water cost Rs 250/300. There's a veg and non-veg restaurant which has some Continental dishes such as spaghetti and a variety of pancakes.

Nearby on Bird Sanctuary Rd is the *Hotel Eagle's Nest* (☎ 25-144). Rooms with fan and hot water by the bucket are Rs 150/300 and Rs 200/400. Air-cooled rooms with geyser are Rs 400/600. This is a clean, comfortable and reasonably quiet place, and a 25% discount is offered between mid-April and mid-September. There's a non-veg restaurant here.

A short distance further down this road, heading towards the sanctuary, is the *Hotel Sunbird* (☎ 25-701). Downstairs rooms with geyser are Rs 200/300, and upstairs rooms, also with geyser, are Rs 300/450. The *Flamingo Restaurant* here features Chinese, Continental and Indian cuisine. New bikes are available for hire at Rs 50 per day between sunrise and sunset. This is a popular place, and there's a pleasant garden area.

Nearby on the same road is the *Hotel Pelican* (☎ 24-221). Tiny but light and airy singles/doubles with common bath (hot water by the bucket for Rs 3) are Rs 60/100. With attached bath, rooms cost Rs 150/200. Rooms with attached bath and air-coolers cost Rs 200/300, and the restaurant, which has Continental, Indian and Chinese cuisine, can provide a packed lunch. Bike hire and binoculars cost Rs 30 each for 24 hours.

Further towards the park gates is the *Annexy* (no phone), which is only open between November and February. It costs Rs 75/100 for rooms with common bath, and has a popular outdoor restaurant. Next door in a eucalyptus grove is the overpriced *Wilderness Camp* (no phone), which has tiny two person tents for Rs 200 and larger double deluxe tents with *charpoys* (string beds), a light and heater for Rs 400. Mattresses and sleeping bags are provided. The campsite is open from 15 October to 15 February. Bring mosquito repellent if you're planning to stay here, as the mozzies are a real hassle.

Also close to the park entrance, on Bird Sanctuary Rd, is the new *Hotel Pratap Palace* (☎ 24-245). Ordinary singles/doubles with attached bath and geyser are Rs 150/250, carpeted deluxe rooms are Rs 500/650, and deluxe air-con rooms with TV are Rs 700/850. Breakfast costs Rs 65, and lunch and dinner are Rs 150. There are also rooms with common bath (with hot water) for Rs 100/150. The cheaper rooms aren't bad value, but the more expensive ones are a bit overpriced. A 30% discount is offered between mid-April and mid-September.

The *Tourist Guest House* (no phone), on Bird Sanctuary Rd, has large spartan singles/doubles for Rs 150/200 with attached bath and hot water. There is a small dorm with beds for Rs 50.

You have to pay for the privilege of staying in the national park itself. The ITDC (Indian Tourism Development Corporation) *Bharatpur Forest Lodge* (☎ 22-760; fax 22-864) is about one km beyond the entrance

gate and eight km from the Bharatpur railway station. Rooms are comfortably appointed, if not luxurious, with lovely old prints of birds. Singles/doubles/triples cost Rs 1195/2200/2450; breakfast is Rs 130, and lunch and dinner cost Rs 275 each. There is a bank and postal facilities here.

A short distance up the road opposite the park entrance is the *Shubham Guest House* (no phone), at B-173 Jawahar Nagar. It's not bad value at Rs 125/150 for singles/doubles with attached bath with hot water, and is in a handy location close to the park.

Getting There & Away

Bus There are buses to Deeg (one hour, Rs 10), to Jaipur (4½ hours, Rs 46) and to Agra (1½ hours, Rs 17), every 30 minutes. There are also regular services to Fatehpur Sikri between 7 am and 4 pm (one hour, Rs 7), and to Ajmer (Rs 80). These buses all leave from the main bus stand.

There are no direct buses to Sawai Madhopur (for Ranthambhore National Park). All services require a change at Dausa. The train is a far better option.

Train Bharatpur is on the Delhi to Mumbai broad-gauge line. A good service between Delhi and Bharatpur is the 9024 *Firozpur Janta Express*. It leaves New Delhi station at 1.50 pm, arriving into Bharatpur at 5.47 pm. The 175 km trip costs Rs 46/184 in 2nd/1st class. It leaves Bharatpur at 8.12 am, arriving into the capital at 1.10 pm. There are several good services to Sawai Madhopur (182 km, Rs 52/193), which continue on to Kota (290 km, Rs 66/270) and Mumbai (1210 km, Rs 235/796 in a 2nd class/1st class sleeper).

The metre-gauge line between Jaipur and Agra is currently being converted to broad gauge, and there are currently no rail services between these centres and Bharatpur.

DEEG
Population: 38,000

Very few travellers ever make it to Deeg, about 36 km north of Bharatpur. This is a shame, because this small town with its massive fortifications, stunningly beautiful palace and busy market is much more interesting than Bharatpur itself. It's an easy day trip from Bharatpur, or from Agra or Mathura, both in the adjacent state of Uttar Pradesh.

Built by Suraj Mahl in the mid-18th century, Deeg was formerly the second capital of Bharatpur state. The Bharatpur maharajas ruled from both Bharatpur and Deeg. At Deeg, the maharaja's forces successfully withstood a combined Mughal and Maratha army of some 80,000 men. Eight years later, the maharaja even had the temerity to attack the Red Fort in Delhi! The booty he carried off included an entire marble building which can still be seen.

Suraj Mahl's Palace

Suraj Mahl's Palace, the **Gopal Bhavan**, built by Maharaja Suraj Mahl between 1756 and 1763, has to be one of India's most beautiful and delicately proportioned buildings. Built in a combination of Rajput and Mughal architectural styles, it is in an excellent state of repair and, as it was used by the maharajas until the early 1970s, most of the rooms still contain their original furnishings. These include chaise longes, plenty of antiques, a stuffed tiger which was shot by a maharaja, elephant feet stands, and exquisite china from China and France.

The mostly two storey palace is three and four storeys high in places. The eastern facade is fronted by imposing arches to take full advantage of the early morning light. On either side of the palace are two exquisite pavilions. In the northern pavilion is a throne of black marble, while that in the southern pavilion is of white marble. In an upstairs room at the rear of the palace is an Indian style dining table – a raised, horse-shoe shaped affair, on both sides of which guests sat. In the maharaja's bedroom is an enormous, stadium sized (3.6 by 2.4m) bed.

The palace is flanked by two tanks, to the east the **Gopal Sagar**, and to the west the **Rup Sagar**. The magnificently maintained gardens and flowerbeds are fed by water from these reservoirs. In the gardens is the **Keshav Bhavan**, or Summer Pavilion, a single storey edifice with five arches along each side. An arcade runs around the interior of the pavilion over a type of canal, in which are hundreds of fountains, many of which are still functional, though only turned on for local festivals.

On the north side of the palace grounds is the **Nand Bhavan**, an oblong hall enclosed by a grand arcade. The eaves have fallen, and this building is currently undergoing restoration.

The palace is open daily from 8 am to noon and 1 to 7 pm; admission is free. Deeg's massive walls (up to 28m high) and 12 bastions, some with their cannons still in place, are also worth exploring.

Laxmi Mandir

This very old temple is presided over by a *mataji*, or female priest. There are alcoves on three sides enshrining images of Durga, Hanuman and Gada, and a small shrine to Shiva to one side. The temple is on Batchu Marg, about 20 minutes walk from the palace.

Places to Stay & Eat

There are only two choices for accommodation, both within five minutes walk of the bus stand and the palace, to the right on the Bharatpur side of the bridge before you enter the town centre. The *Dak Bungalow* is dilapidated and dirty, although it was evidently once a grand building, with enormous high ceilings. Obviously few dignitaries now make their way to Deeg, as the bungalow is in a shocking state of disrepair. Double rooms are Rs 100.

A far better choice is the new RTDC *Midway Deeg* (no phone), on the same road. It has clean rooms with attached bath with hot water for Rs 225/275/325, and meals are available.

There is only one restaurant in Deeg, the *Damolia Restaurant*, which is on Batchu Marg, near the Laxmi Mandir. It's about a 20 minute walk from the palace. Ask for directions to the temple.

Getting There & Away

There are numerous buses between Deeg and Alwar from 6 am to 8.30 pm (2½ hours, Rs

20). Buses for Bharatpur leave every 30 minutes (one hour, Rs 10). From Agra, you may need to change buses at Mathura or Bharatpur.

ALWAR
Population: 235,000
Telephone Area Code: 0144

Alwar was once an important Rajput state, which gained pre-eminence in the 18th century under Pratap Singh, who pushed back the rulers of Jaipur to the south and the Jats of Bharatpur to the east, and who successfully resisted the Marathas. It was one of the first Rajput states to ally itself with the fledgling British Empire, although British interference in Alwar's internal affairs meant that this partnership was not always amicable. Beautiful palace buildings, hunting lodges at Sariska, and the extraordinary collection of *objets d'art* in the government museum at the palace bear testament to the wealth of this erstwhile state.

Alwar has several small, pleasant gardens, a feature of which appear to be topiary animals – there are immaculately clipped and maintained rampant lions, elephants and other beasts, set incongruously among the rose bushes.

Orientation & Information

The city palace and museum are in the northwest of the city, about one km north of the bus stand. There is a collection of budget hotels a short distance to the east of the bus stand. The GPO is about midway between the bus stand and the railway station, the latter on the eastern edge of the town.

The tourist office (☎ 21-868) is opposite Company Garden, Nehru Bal Vihar. It's open daily except Sunday from 10 am to 5 pm (lunch from 1.30 to 2 pm). The State Bank of Bikaner & Jaipur, near the bus stand, changes travellers' cheques.

English-language newspapers can be obtained at the bus stand.

Bala Quila

This huge fort, with its five km of ramparts, stands 300m above the city. Predating the time of Pratap Singh, it's one of the very few forts in Rajasthan constructed before the rise of the Mughals. Unfortunately, because the fort now houses a radio transmitter station, it can only be visited with special permission.

Palace Complex

Below the fort is the large and imposing city palace complex, its massive gates and tank lined by a beautifully symmetrical chain of *ghats* with four pavilions on each side and two at each end. Today, most of the complex is occupied by government offices, but there is a museum (see below), housed in the former city palace. To gain access to the tank and its ghats, take the steps on the far left hand side when facing the palace.

Cenotaph of Maharaja Bakhtawar Singh

This double storey edifice resting on a platform of sandstone was built in 1815 by Maharaja Viney Singh in memory of his father. The cenotaph is also known as the Chhatri of Moosi Rani, as one of the wives of Bakhtawar Singh performed *sati* (self-immolation) on his funeral pyre. Every day women can be seen paying homage to the maharani at the cenotaph by pouring holy water over raised sculpted footprints of the deceased royal couple. There is fine carving on the interior of the cenotaph (shoes should be removed), but unfortunately the frescoes on the ceiling are almost indiscernible.

Museum The excellent and comprehensive collection housed here includes royal vestments in beautiful brocades; stuffed animals, including an enormous bear; Kashmiri lacquer work; and stone sculptures including an 11th century sculpture of Vishnu. There are some extraordinary exhibits testifying to the wealth of the maharajas of Alwar, including a pair of ivory slippers and a silver dining table with lions' feet legs. Other exhibits include miniature models depicting various themes; one shows two red-haired British men in negotiation with the maharaja. There are also tiny potters, *chai-wallahs* and fruit vendors.

There's a fine collection of traditional instruments, including a sitar in the shape of a peacock, and a standard of the Alwar royal house presented to Maharao Raja Mangal Singh by Queen Victoria (whose bust stands nearby).

A separate exhibition hall has a collection of paintings including a lovely depiction of Krishna and Radha featuring gold leaf, and miniatures on ivory. There is a copy of *Gulistan (A Rose Garden)* by Shekh Muslihuddin-Sadi, originally written in 1258. This copy was commissioned by Maharaja Vinaya Singh of Alwar in 1858, and the scribes spent over 12 years meticulously copying the text which features beautiful calligraphy. There is also a painting of a seated Christ, and scrolls of the *Bhagavad Gita* and *Mahabharata* in miniature script. The armoury section has a stunning collection of weapons and armour.

This government museum is open daily except Friday from 10 am to 4.30 pm; entry is Rs 2.

Places to Stay

Finding a budget place to stay is not a problem in Alwar. About 500m east of the

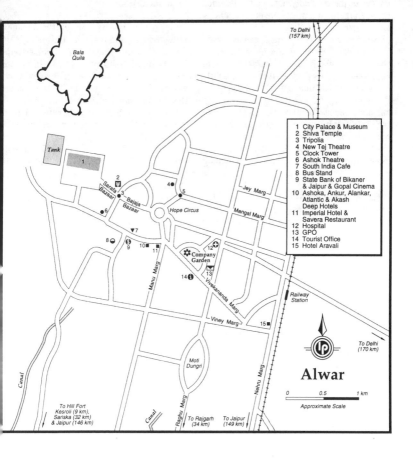

1 City Palace & Museum
2 Shiva Temple
3 Tripolia
4 New Tej Theatre
5 Clock Tower
6 Ashok Theatre
7 South India Cafe
8 Bus Stand
9 State Bank of Bikaner & Jaipur & Gopal Cinema
10 Ashoka, Ankur, Alankar, Atlantic & Akash Deep Hotels
11 Imperial Hotel & Savera Restaurant
12 Hospital
13 GPO
14 Tourist Office
15 Hotel Aravali

Alwar

bus stand, set back from Manu Marg, is a cluster of five cheap hotels which all face each other around a central courtyard. The hotels are each owned by one of five brothers, and each hotel begins with the letter 'A': there's the *Ankur* (☎ 33-3025); *Alankar* (☎ 20-027); *Atlantic* (☎ 21-581); *Akash Deep* (☎ 22-912); and the *Ashoka* (☎ 21-780)! Without wishing to upset any of the brothers, the Ashoka seems to be the best of the lot, with singles/doubles with attached bath (hot water by the bucket) for Rs 75/100 and Rs 100/150, with geyser, Rs 150/200, and doubles with air-con for Rs 400. However, there's really not much difference between them, and prices are comparable at all the hotels.

Nearby, at the start of the laneway which leads to the five As, is the *Imperial Hotel* (☎ 21-438), which has singles/doubles with air-cooler from Rs 80/150. It could be a little noisy, as it fronts the busy Manu Marg.

A good choice if you have an early morning rail departure is the two star *Hotel Aravali* (☎ 33-2883). It has ordinary singles/doubles with fan and attached bath for Rs 200/250, air-cooled rooms for Rs 500/550, and air-con rooms from Rs 700/750. There's a swimming pool (summer only), a good restaurant and a bar.

Eleven km from Alwar is Kesroli, which boasts a 14th century fort. It has been recently converted into a hotel, the *Hill Fort Kesroli* (☎ 81-312; Delhi (011) 461-6145), and has 10 double rooms which cost Rs 1200 and Rs 1600.

Beds in the railway *retiring rooms* cost Rs 40 per person.

Places to Eat

There's a fairly good restaurant at the *Hotel Aravali*, near the railway station. Vegetarian dishes are from Rs 28 to Rs 50, and non-veg dishes start at Rs 40.

The *Savera Restaurant*, attached to the Imperial Hotel on Manu Marg, has vegetarian dishes and specialises in South Indian cuisine. Most dishes are under Rs 30, and the special thali is Rs 45.

Opposite the Gopal Cinema, on the road leading to the bus stand, is the *South India Cafe*, which has cheap and good dishes such as masala dosas (Rs 14).

Getting There & Away

Bus From the bus stand, buses for Sariska leave every 30 minutes throughout the day (one hour, Rs 9). There are also buses every 30 minutes to Jaipur (four hours, Rs 40), and numerous buses to Delhi between 5.10 am and 5 pm (four hours, Rs 37). There are regular buses to Deeg (2½ hours, Rs 20), and to Bharatpur (for Keoladeo Ghana National Park; 3½ hours express, Rs 30; 4½ hour local, Rs 25).

Train Alwar boasts one of the cleanest railway stations in India. To Delhi, the 2013 *Shatabdi Express* leaves at 7.32 pm, arriving into Delhi at 10.15 pm (Rs 214 in air-con chair car). The 9760 *Intercity* leaves Alwar at 8.50 am, arriving into Delhi at 11.30 am (Rs 47 in second class; no first class). To Jaipur the 2015 *Shatabdi Express* departs Alwar at 8.48 am, arriving into Jaipur at 1 am (Rs 195 in air-con chair car), and Ajmer at 1.30 pm (Rs 300). The 9759 *Intercity* leaves at 7.33 pm, arriving into Jaipur at 10 pm (Rs 41). There is also a service to Jaipur at 11 pm which continues through to Jodhpur (Rs 149).

Getting Around

Rickshaw-wallahs in Alwar are not nearly as rapacious as they seem to be in other more touristed parts of Rajasthan, and Rs 5 will get you just about anywhere in the town centre.

AROUND ALWAR
Neemrana

This small village lies 76 km north of Alwar on the main Delhi-Jaipur highway, a short distance to the south of the Haryana border. There's not much of interest in the village itself, but lying two km distant is the recently restored fortress palace. Dating from 1464 it was from here that the Rajput maharaja Prithviraj Chaudan III reigned. In usual Rajasthan style, it has been converted into a luxury hotel, the *Neemrana Fort Palace*

☎ (01494) 6005; fax (011) 462-1112). Singles/doubles start at Rs 1000/1500, andfor Rs 2500 you get fine views and air-conditioning. The restaurant serves Rajasthani cuisine. Camel rides are available for Rs 250 per camel or camel cart per hour. Every weekend between October and March there is a Rajasthani folk music programme, and to complete the picture, the hotel has its own helipad.

Buses on the main Delhi-Jaipur route generally stop at Behror, 14 km from Neemrana, and a further two km from the hotel. A taxi from Behror to the hotel will cost Rs 200.

Siliserh

At Siliserh, which lies 20 km south-west of Alwar off the road to Sariska Tiger Reserve, is a restored palace which was built by the Alwar maharaja Vinaya Singh, and overlooks a tranquil lake. Inevitably, it is now a hotel, the RTDC *Hotel Lake Palace* (☎ 22-991). If you're on a budget but want to stay at a genuine Rajasthani palace, it's not bad value. There are dorm beds for Rs 50, deluxe (air-cooled) singles/doubles are Rs 275/355, and air-con rooms are Rs 500/600. There's a bar and restaurant here, and a 10% discount is offered between April and July.

SARISKA TIGER RESERVE & NATIONAL PARK
Telephone Area Code: 0144

Situated 107 km from Jaipur and 200 km from Delhi, the sanctuary is in a wooded valley surrounded by barren hills. It covers 800 sq km (including a core area of 498 sq km) and has bluebulls, sambar, spotted deer, wild boar and, of course, tigers. Project Tiger has been in charge of the sanctuary since 1979.

Like Ranthambhore National Park, this park contains ruined temples as well as a fort, pavilions and a palace (now a fine hotel) built by the maharaja of Alwar. The sanctuary can be visited year round, although during July and August your chance of spotting wildlife is minimal, as the animals move to higher ground. The best time is between November and June. The park is closed only during the twice-yearly census, which usually takes

place around May. The last census was in May 1995, and numbers of tigers were determined by pug marks (like fingerprints, each pug mark is different). According to the census, there are more than 25 tigers in the park. During this census, the rusty spotted cat (*Poionailusrus rubiginosus*) was identified for the first time at Sariska. There are over 300 species of birds in the park.

You'll see most wildlife in the evening, though tiger sightings are becoming more common during the day.

Wildlife Safaris

While it is possible to take private cars into the park, they are limited to sealed roads only, minimising the chances of spotting wildlife. The best way to visit the park is by jeep. Petrol jeeps cost Rs 400 per jeep, and can take up to five people. There's an entry fee of Rs 75 per jeep, and an additional park entry fee of Rs 25 per person for three hours. A still camera costs Rs 10, and a video camera is Rs 100.

Diesel jeeps cost Rs 300 per jeep and can also take up to five people. The entry fee for diesel jeeps is Rs 100 – these cost more than petrol jeeps, as they are noisier and more polluting.

Bookings can be made at the Forest Reception Office (☎ 41-333) on Jaipur Rd (the state highway), which is where buses will drop you. The park is open in winter (October to the end of February) from 7 am to 4 pm, and during the rest of the year from 6 am to 5 pm.

Places to Stay & Eat

There are three double rooms at the *Forest Rest House*. Bookings should be made through the Chief Wildlife Warden at 1 Van Bhawan, Jaipur. The guest house is next door to the Forest Reception Office.

Nearby is the RTDC *Tiger Den Sariska* (☎ 41-342). It has a six bed dorm for Rs 50, deluxe air-cooled singles/doubles for Rs 375/500, air-con rooms for Rs 600/675 and a suite for Rs 850. There's a bar (beer is Rs 45) and restaurant. Breakfast costs Rs 80, and lunch and dinner are Rs 100 for the veg menu and Rs 120 for the non-veg menu.

There's a small shop here selling chocolate and similar fare.

The beautiful and imposing *Hotel Sariska Palace* (☎ 41-322) is at the end of a long sweeping driveway directly opposite the Forest Reception Office. This was the former hunting lodge of the maharajas of Alwar. This gracious and well maintained hotel, which is over 100 years old, is set on 37 hectares. The Aravalli Range affords a fine backdrop, and the grounds are traversed by the Ruparail River. It is possible to take short horse and camel rides around the grounds. The drawing room has an assortment of stuffed beasts, and the dining room is replete with antiques. There's a lending library, music and cultural programmes at night, and a campfire is lit in winter. The standard rooms are enormous and have lovely views out over the grounds.

Singles/doubles cost US$33/53, and suites are US$70. Meals cost US$5 for breakfast and US$10 for lunch and dinner. Non-guests are welcome to dine here with one hour's advance notice.

Getting There & Away

Sariska is 35 km from Alwar, which is a convenient town from which to approach the sanctuary. There are direct buses to Alwar from Delhi and Jaipur. Though some people attempt to visit Sariska on a day trip from Jaipur, this option is expensive and largely a waste of time. There are numerous buses between Sariska and both Jaipur and Alwar. It takes one hour to Alwar (Rs 9) and about three hours to Jaipur. Buses stop out the front of the Forest Reception Office.

AJMER
Population: 447,000
Telephone Area Code: 0145

South-west of Jaipur is Ajmer, a green oasis on the shore of the Ana Sagar, hemmed in by barren hills. Situated in a valley, Ajmer is a major religious centre for Muslim pilgrims during the fast of Ramadan, and has some superb examples of early Muslim architecture. It is famous for the tomb of Khwaja Muin-ud-din Chishti, a venerated Sufi saint

who founded the Chishtiya order, which i still the prime Sufi order in India today.

The British selected Ajmer as the site fc Mayo College (see the boxed text in thi section), a school opened in 1875 exclusivel for Indian princes. Today it is open to all boy (who can afford the fees). Other monumen which stand as reminders of Ajmer's colonia past are the Edward Memorial Hall, Ajme Club and Jubilee Clock Tower.

The main streets of Ajmer are cramme with traffic, pedestrians and busy bazaars There's even a street that sells nothing bu silver items. But Ajmer doesn't really hav the same rustic charm or panache as man other Rajasthani towns and it is more of pilgrimage centre than a tourist destination This is reflected in the lack of good accom modation and eating places.

Although it does have some impressiv architecture, an ancient fort overlooking th town, and is an important religious centre Ajmer is really just a stepping stone t nearby Pushkar for most travellers. If you ar unable to get accommodation in Pushkar which is often the case during the Came Fair, Ajmer makes a good base.

History

The town of Ajmer, which has always ha great strategic importance due to its secur position, protected by the Aravalli Range and its location on the major trade rout between Delhi and the ports of Gujarat, wa founded by Ajaipal Chauhan in the 7t century. Ajaipal constructed a hill fort her and named the place Ajaimeru, or invincibl hill. Ajmer was ruled by the Chauhans unt the late 12th century, when Prithvira Chauhan lost it to Mohammed of Ghori. became part of the Sultanate in Delhi an remained so until 1326. After that Ajmer wa continually fought over by surroundin states including the sultans of Delhi an Gujarat and the rulers of Mewar and Marwar

Later, Ajmer became a favourite residenc of the great Mughals. One of the first con tacts between the Mughals and the Britis occurred in Ajmer when Sir Thomas Roe me with Emperor Jehangir here in 1616.

The city was subsequently taken by the Scindias and, in 1818, was handed over to the British, becoming one of the few places in Rajasthan controlled directly by the British rather than being part of a princely state.

Orientation

The main bus stand is close to the Hotel Khadim Tourist Bungalow on the east side of town. The railway station and most of the hotels are on the west side of town. North of the GPO is Naya Bazaar and Agra Gate. Further north is the large artificial lake Ana Sagar.

Information

Tourist office The tourist office (☎ 52-426) is in the Hotel Khadim Tourist Bungalow and has a good range of literature. It's open Monday to Saturday from 8 am to noon, 3 to 6 pm. Posted outside the office are bus and train timetables, as well as telephone numbers of paying guest houses. This is useful if you get here when the office is closed. There's also a small tourist information counter at the railway station.

Money You can change money at the State Bank of India, opposite the Collectorate, but

PLACES TO STAY
1 RTDC Hotel Khidmat
5 Mansingh Palace
10 Bhola Hotel
13 Hotel Samrat
18 Hotel Ashoka & Sirtaj Hotel
19 KEM Rest House, Nagpal Tourist Hotel & Honeydew Restaurant
24 RTDC Hotel Khadim Tourist Bungalow, Tourist Office & Aravali Holiday Resort

PLACES TO EAT
12 Gangaur Fast Food
27 Tandoor Restaurant

OTHER
2 Adhai-din-ka-Jhonpra
3 Dargah
4 Agra Gate
6 Circuit House
7 JLN Hospital
8 College
9 Nasiyan (Red) Temple
11 Church
14 Bank of Baroda
15 Akbar's Palace (Ajmer Museum)
16 GPO
17 Pushkar Buses
20 Kaisar Ganj
21 Government College
22 Super Bazaar
23 Collectorate
25 State Bank of India
26 Bus Stand

Ana Sagar

Subash Bagh & Dault Bagh

Ajmer

To Taragarh
To Foy Sagar (3 km)
To Pushkar (11 km)
Circular Road
Dargah Bazaar
Naya Bazaar
Nalla Bazaar
Digoi Bazaar
Madar Gate
Prithviraj Marg
Station Road
Kutchery Road
Jaipur Road
Railway Station
Patel Ground
Nasirabad Road
Railway Colony
To Udaipur (270 km) & Badnor (80 km)
To Nasirabad (23 km)
To Phulera
To Mayo College & Mahabodhi Mission
To Jaipur (135 km) & Kishangarh (27 km)

0 250 500 m

they don't do cash advances on credit cards. The Bank of Baroda on Prithviraj Marg, opposite the GPO, does issue cash advances on credit cards and also changes money.

Ana Sagar

Flanked by hills, this artificial lake was created in the 12th century by damming the River Luni. On its bank is a fine park, the **Dault Bagh**, which has a series of marble pavilions erected in 1637 by Emperor Shah Jahan. It's a popular place for an evening stroll. At the Ana Sagar jetty, paddle boats are available for hire every day from 9 am to 5 pm. They cost Rs 40 for 30 minutes or Rs 80 for one hour.

The lake tends to dry up if the monsoon is poor, so the city's water supply is taken from Foy Sagar, three km further up the valley. There are good views from the hill beside the Dault Bagh.

Dargah

Situated at the foot of a barren hill in the old part of town, this is one of India's most important places for Muslim pilgrims. The Dargah is the tomb of a Sufi saint, Khwaja Muin-ud-din Chishti, who came to Ajmer from Persia in 1192 and died here in 1236. Construction of the shrine was completed by Humayun and the gate was added by the Nizam of Hyderabad. Akbar used to make the pilgrimage to the Dargah from Agra once a year.

You have to cover your head in certain parts of the shrine, so remember to take a scarf or cap. There are plenty for sale at the colourful bazaar leading to the shrine.

As you enter the courtyard, removing your shoes at the gateway, a mosque constructed by Akbar is on the right. The enormous iron cauldrons are for offerings which are customarily shared by families involved in the shrine's upkeep. In an inner court there is another mosque built by Shah Jahan. Constructed of white marble, it has 11 arches and a Persian inscription running the full length of the building.

The saint's tomb is in the centre of the second court. It has a marble dome and the actual tomb inside is surrounded by a silver platform. The horseshoes nailed to the shrine doors are offerings from successful horse dealers! Beware of 'guides' hassling for donations around the Dargah using the standard fake donation books. Don't be bullied into signing any books or 'visitors registers' which mean you'll have to make a hefty donation.

This shrine is a hive of activity and you can really get a sense of how deeply significant it is to the Muslim people. The tomb attracts hundreds of thousands of pilgrims every year on the anniversary of the saint's death, the Urs, in the seventh month of the lunar calendar, Jyaistha (May/June). It's an interesting festival that's worth attending if you're in the area. As well as the pilgrims, Sufis from all over India converge on Ajmer. You may even get to see a whirling or howling dervish.

Adhai-din-ka-Jhonpra & Taragarh

Beyond the Dargah, on the very outskirts of town, are the ruins of the Adhai-din-ka-Jhonpra mosque. According to legend its construction, in 1153, took just 2½ days, as its name indicates (Adhai-din-ka-Jhonpra translates as 'the 2½ day building'). Others believe that it was named after a festival that lasted for 2½ days. It was originally built as a Sanskrit college, but in 1198 Mohammed of Ghori took Ajmer and converted the building into a mosque by adding a seven arched wall covered with Islamic calligraphy in front of the pillared hall.

Although the mosque is now in need of repair, it is a particularly fine piece of architecture – the pillars are all different and the arched 'screen', with its damaged minarets, is noteworthy.

Three km and a steep 1½ hour climb beyond the mosque, the Taragarh, or Star Fort, commands an excellent view over the city. It was built by Ajaipal Chauhan, the town's founder. A road is currently being constructed so cars will be able to go to the fort, making the trip faster and less tiring. The fort was the site of much military activity during Mughal times and was later used as a sanatorium by the British.

Akbar's Palace

Back in the city, near the railway station, this imposing building was constructed by Akbar in 1570 and today houses the Ajmer Museum, which is really not worth the bother. It is open daily, except Friday, from 10 am to 4.30 pm. There's a small admission fee.

Nasiyan (Red) Temple

The Red Temple on Prithviraj Marg is a Jain temple built in 1865. Its double storey hall contains a series of large, gilt wooden figures from Jain mythology which depict the Jain concept of the ancient world. The hall is decorated with gold, silver and precious stones. It's unlike any other temple in Rajasthan and is definitely worth a visit. A sign in the temple warns that 'Smoking and chewing of beatles is prohibited'! The temple is open daily from 8.30 am to 4.30 pm and entry costs Rs 2.

Places to Stay

Most of Ajmer's budget hotels are typical Indian boarding houses of similar standard.

Mayo College

The very first pupil to attend Ajmer's Mayo College was the Maharaja of Alwar, who arrived in grand style in 1875 on an elephant, accompanied by a huge entourage of servants, trumpeters, horses, camels and other elaborate trimmings. This prestigious primary and secondary school was founded by Lord Mayo, a viceroy of India, and was open only to the sons of Indian aristocracy. The school premises were certainly fit for a king, with well maintained gardens and beautiful buildings. Some princes even had their own lavish house built on the extensive school compound, named after the state ruled by their family.

SANJAY SINGH BADNOR

The Mayo coat of arms was designed by Rudyard Kipling's father and this 'Eton of the East' was based on the English public school system. At Mayo, the young and impressionable Indian princes were groomed to be proper gentlemen, and possibly continue to Oxford or Cambridge universities in England for tertiary studies. These elite English institutions have been paramount in educating the sons of nobility and continue to be so today.

Destined to one day become rulers of a kingdom, for many of the princes academic results were not high on their list of priorities. Education was simply considered as a fashionable accessory for their future role as king, not as a means of improving their chances of finding a good job.

In the past, royalty did not have to work as they predominantly derived their wealth from the taxation of land. Many royal families had other sources of revenue too. Of course this all changed after Independence in 1947, when the princes merged their states with the Indian Union.

Today Mayo College is no longer exclusively for the sons of kings. It has opened its gates to boys from all walks of life (if, of course, their parents can afford the school fees). Mayo is one of India's leading educational institutions and is geared towards academic excellence. After graduating from Mayo, most students pursue tertiary studies and enter a range of vocations from medicine to commerce.

The school has retained its old-world charm and still takes great pride in its illustrious history. Even though British rule ended in India almost five decades ago, a flavour of the British Raj still lingers at Mayo. The walls proudly display austere portraits of former English headmasters and British lords once on the school's governing council. ■

They offer basic essentials and are OK for a night, but those in Pushkar are far preferable. Many of the hotels cater to the large number of Muslim pilgrims that visit Ajmer each year. When leaving the railway station you'll be accosted by cycle and auto-rickshaw drivers all keen to take you 'anywhere' for Rs 5 or less – unfortunately 'anywhere' usually means to a hotel where they get commission.

A good and often cheaper alternative to hotels are paying guest houses, which give you the opportunity to live with an Indian family. Rates range from Rs 50 to Rs 400 depending on the facilities provided. The tourist office has details about these paying guest houses, right down to the languages spoken by the host family and the profession of the breadwinner.

To the left as you exit the railway station is the huge *King Edward Memorial Rest House* (☎ 20-936), Station Rd, known locally as 'KEM'. Don't let the grand name fool you. This place is run down and has lax service. Very few travellers seem to stay here and it's mainly used by Muslim pilgrims. Rooms range from Rs 40 for a basic '2nd class' single to Rs 60/100 for '1st class' singles/doubles and Rs 80/140 for deluxe rooms. Close by is the recommended *Nagpal Tourist Hotel* (☎ 21-603). Clean singles/doubles with private bath range from Rs 100/200 to Rs 225/350. Although this hotel is more expensive than the King Edward Memorial Rest House, it's definitely a much better choice.

Not far away is the cheap *Hotel Ashoka* (☎ 24-729), with basic singles/doubles off a balcony that overlooks the noisy fruit and vegetable market for Rs 60/80 with common bath. Hindi signs in each room warn that 'Consumption of meat and alcohol are prohibited'. The nearby Sikh-run *Sirtaj Hotel* (☎ 20-096) has rooms around a court-yard for Rs 50/150 with private bath. There's also a restaurant serving Punjabi food.

There are more budget hotels along Prithviraj Marg, between the GPO and the Red Temple. Opposite the church near Agra Gate is the *Bhola Hotel* (☎ 23-844) with good singles/doubles for Rs 100/150 with private bath. Self-service buckets of hot water are available from the geyser on the outside terrace. There's a good vegetarian restaurant here.

The RTDC *Hotel Khadim Tourist Bungalow* (☎ 52-490) is not far from the bus stand. There's a range of rooms with private bath priced from Rs 200/250 to Rs 250/375 with air-con. Dorm beds are available for Rs 50. Next door is the *Aravali Holiday Resort* (☎ 52-089) which has cheap singles/doubles for Rs 75/100 with attached bath and hot water by the bucket. Dorm beds will soon be available for Rs 25.

There's a newer RTDC place, the *Hotel Khidmat* (☎ 52-705), east of the lake on Circular Rd. It offers good singles/doubles for Rs 175/225 with attached bath. Dorm beds cost Rs 50. Although this place is a bit remote, it's better value than the Hotel Khadim.

On Kutchery Rd, just a few minutes walk from the railway station, is the *Hotel Samrat* (☎ 31-805). The rooms are small but it's very convenient for early morning departures with the private bus companies, as they have their offices just across the road. Singles/doubles cost Rs 150/250 or Rs 450/550 with air-con. All rooms have satellite TV.

The only top-end hotel in Ajmer is the *Mansingh Palace* (☎ 42-5702), Circular Rd, overlooking Ana Sagar. While it looks OK, closer inspection reveals poor maintenance and lack of attention to detail. The position is ideal but it's distinctly overpriced at Rs 1195/2000 for singles/doubles or Rs 2500 for a suite. There's also a bar and restaurant here.

Places to Eat

Ajmer has a limited selection of restaurants. The vegetarian restaurant at the *Bhola Hotel* is very good and well maintained. There are delicious thalis for Rs 30, and a good range of other dishes.

The *Honeydew Restaurant* near the KEM Rest House has reasonably priced Indian and Chinese dishes. There's also a variety of fast food such as hot dogs, pizzas (Rs 30), milkshakes and espresso coffee. A favourite with travellers is the banana lassi. There's seating indoors and outdoors. *Gangaur Fast Food*

SANJAY SINGH BADNOR

SANJAY SINGH BADNOR

ADAM MCCROW

astern Rajasthan

Top: Crowds at the Pushkar Fair.
Middle: The whitewashed town of Pushkar with the holy lake in the foreground.
ottom: Mural featuring the Hindu deities, Pushkar.

SANJAY SINGH BADNOR

SANJAY SINGH BADNOR

SANJAY SINGH BADNOR

Southern Rajasthan

Top Left: Tower of Fame, Chittorgarh Fort.
Top Right: View of the Nakki Lake from Toad Rock, Mt Abu.
Bottom: City Palace ghats on Lake Pichola, Udaipur.

off Kutchery Rd serves the usual selection of fast food including burgers, pizzas (Rs 35) and ice-cream sodas. There are also Indian and Chinese dishes.

A little out of town on Jaipur Rd is the slightly expensive *Tandoor Restaurant*. It specialises in tandoori food and offers a wide selection of veg and non-veg dishes; a tandoori chicken costs Rs 70. There's seating indoors and outdoors.

The top restaurant in town is the *Sheesh Mahal*, at the Mansingh Palace. It's expensive though, with main dishes ranging from Rs 65 to Rs 150 for a tandoori chicken.

Getting There & Away

Bus There are buses from Jaipur to Ajmer every 15 minutes, some non-stop. The 131 km trip costs Rs 34 and takes 2½ hours. From Delhi, there are state transport buses which run daily in either direction at a cost of Rs 110.

Buses leave every few minutes throughout the day for Pushkar from the bus stand near the railway station (30 minutes, Rs 4).

State transport buses also go to Jodhpur (210 km, Rs 64), Udaipur (303 km via Chittorgarh, Rs 75), Chittorgarh (191 km, Rs 44), Kota (200 km, Rs 62), Bundi (165 km, Rs 53), Ranakpur (237 km, Rs 54), Bharatpur (305 km, Rs 80), Mt Abu (383 km, Rs 91) and Bikaner (277 km, Rs 71). In addition, buses leave for Agra (385 km, Rs 95) and for Jaisalmer (490 km, Rs 125). These buses leave from the bus stand on Jaipur Rd.

Also available are private deluxe buses to Ahmedabad, Udaipur, Jodhpur, Jaipur, Mt Abu, Jaisalmer, Bikaner, Delhi and Mumbai. Most of the companies have offices on Kutchery Rd. If you book your ticket to one of these destinations through an agency in Pushkar, they will provide a free jeep transfer to Ajmer to commence your journey.

Train Ajmer is on the Delhi-Jaipur-Marwar-Ahmedabad line and most trains stop at Ajmer. The 135 km journey from Jaipur costs Rs 35/177 in 2nd/1st class. The *Pink City Express* takes about the same time as the buses to cover the distance.

To Udaipur, the fastest express takes 7½ hours. The comfortable *Shatabdi Express* travels daily, except Thursday, between Ajmer and Delhi (Rs 395/770 in ordinary/executive class) via Jaipur (Rs 195/375 in ordinary/executive class). Refreshments and meals are served, which are inclusive of the ticket price. The train leaves Delhi at 6.15 am and arrives in Ajmer at 1.30 pm. Going in the other direction, the train leaves Ajmer at 3.10 pm and arrives in Delhi at 10.15 pm.

Getting Around

Ajmer is a relatively small town and easy enough to get around on foot, but there are plenty of auto and cycle-rickshaws, as well as some tongas.

AROUND AJMER
Kishangarh

Kishangarh is 27 km from Ajmer and was founded in the early 17th century by Kishan Singh, a Rathore prince. Since the 18th century, Kishangarh has had one of India's most famous schools of miniature painting. One of the most renowned paintings is that of Krishna's consort, Radha, who is depicted as a beautiful woman with enchanting almond-shaped eyes. Today local artists are trying to revive this magnificent school of painting by making copies of the originals on various surfaces such as wood, stone and cloth. The original paintings were done on paper.

Kishangarh town is divided into the old city, which still has an old-world charm, and the new city, which is mainly commercial. Pollution is steadily increasing largely due to the growing number of marble factories and textile mills.

Places to Stay Twenty-five km out of town is *Roopangarh Fort* which has recently been converted into a delightful hotel by the maharaja and maharani of Kishangarh. Roopangarh was the capital of this province for about 100 years and was never conquered despite being repeatedly attacked by neighbouring states. The fort was founded in 1653 by Maharaja Roop Singh, the fifth ruler of Kishangarh. He was inspired to make this site his capital after watching a mother sheep gallantly protect her lambs from a pack of hungry wolves.

Today this impregnable fort has singles/doubles for Rs 1100/1350 and Rs 2500 for a suite; all rooms have private bath and hot water. There are a total of 16 rooms in this unique hotel, all with different themes, and there's also a restaurant serving traditional Rajasthani food. The road to the fort passes through an interesting little village where you can get a glimpse of everyday life as it would have been long ago. The hotel can arrange village tours, bird watching and camel, horse or jeep safaris. Hotel reservations should be made by phoning Delhi (☎ (011) 66-5021) or through travel agents. It's also worth keeping an eye on the *Phool Mahal Palace* in Kishangarh, which the maharaja is in the process of converting into another upmarket hotel.

Badnor

About 80 km south-west of Ajmer is Badnor, best known for its imposing fort which is more than 500 years old. Badnor is a small fortified town surrounded by 10 lakes that fill during the monsoon. Badnor's historic fort was home to a former feudal family until 1962. Today it belongs to the government and is unfortunately poorly maintained. There are good views of the town and surrounding countryside from the fort, which is on an elevated site. This sleepy little town, off the beaten track, seems to belong to a bygone era. It's a good place to go if you want to visit a small rural community that encounters very few tourists and is virtually untouched by modernisation. To arrange a visit to the fort you need to contact the descendants of the former feudal owners, the Singh family, in Ajmer (☎ (0145) 52-579).

PUSHKAR
Population: 12,000
Telephone Area Code: 0145

Like Goa or Dharamsala, the mellow, quiet and enchanting town of Pushkar is one of those travellers' centres where people go for respite from the hardships of life on the

Indian road. It's a welcoming little town with friendly people and an easy-going atmosphere. Situated right on the edge of the desert, it's only 11 km north-west of Ajmer but separated from it by Nag Pahar, the Snake Mountain.

Pushkar is a very important pilgrimage centre and devout Hindus should visit it at least once in their lifetime. The town also attracts a large number of *sadhus* (individuals on a spiritual search) who mainly congregate around the lake and temples. Unfortunately after a poor monsoon the lake doesn't get refilled and can be almost empty. This is a great pity, as it is a big factor in the town's appeal and is of great religious importance. Many tourists who visit Pushkar fall so deeply in love with the place that they stay for weeks, even years, longer than they originally planned.

Pushkar is also world famous for the huge colourful Camel Fair which takes place here each October/November in the Hindu lunar month of Kartika. At this time, the town is jam-packed with tribal people from all over Rajasthan, pilgrims from all over India and film-makers and tourists from all over the world. And of course there are camels – thousands of them. If you're anywhere within striking distance at the time, it's an event not to be missed. Camel rides are however, available year round from a number of operators around the town. Camel safaris lasting several days are also possible.

Being a holy place, alcohol, meat and even eggs are banned. Drugs are prohibited and there are stiff penalties for offenders.

It is unknown how old Pushkar actually is. According to legend, the sacred lake of Pushkar sprang up at the spot where Brahma dropped a lotus flower from the sky. Brahma, Lord of Creation, wanted to perform a *yagna*, or holy sacrifice, at the lake on a full moon night. Since his wife, Savitri, did not attend, he impetuously married another woman named Gayatri. Savitri felt terribly betrayed when she found out and bitterly vowed that Brahma would not be worshipped anywhere other than Pushkar. Since then, this temple has remained one of the only ones in the world dedicated to Brahma. On two hills near Pushkar Lake are temples, one dedicated to Savitri and the other to Gayatri.

Orientation

The desert town clings to the side of the small but beautiful Pushkar Lake with its many bathing ghats and temples. Pushkar town is a maze of narrow streets filled with interesting little shops, food stalls, hotels and temples. Fortunately there's virtually no traffic in the main bazaar, making it a pleasurable place to explore at leisure. The town is very tourist friendly and most people speak English to some degree, so you'll have no problem finding your way around. There are a plethora of guest houses, hotels and eating places to suit all budgets.

Information

As Pushkar is a small town, everything you need is in easy walking distance. You can change money at the State Bank of Bikaner

---

Camel Fair

The exact date on which the Camel Fair is held depends on the lunar calendar but, in Hindu chronology, it falls on the full moon of Kartik Purnima, when devotees cleanse away their sins by bathing in the holy lake. Each year, up to 200,000 people flock to Pushkar for the Camel Fair, bringing with them some 50,000 camels and cattle for several days of pilgrimage, livestock trading, and spirited festivities. There are camel races, street theatre and a variety of stalls selling everything from colourful skirts to tribal trinkets. The place becomes a flurry of activity with jugglers, musicians, comedians, tourists, traders, animals and devotees all converging on the small town. It's truly a feast for the eyes, so don't forget to bring your camera and plenty of film. Rajasthani folk music plays well into the night and the air is aromatic with Indian food.

Although the place is transformed into somewhat of a carnival, the Camel Fair is taken very seriously by livestock owners, who come from all over the country with the sole intent of trading. A good camel can fetch tens of thousands of rupees and is a vital source of income for many villagers.

This fair is the only one of its kind in the world and has featured in numerous magazines, travel shows and films. The Rajasthan tourist office has promoted the fair as an international attraction by adding Rajasthan dance programmes and other cultural events, and by putting up a huge tent city for Indian and foreign visitors. It's one of India's biggest, most colourful festivals and is definitely worth attending.

Dates of the fair in forthcoming years are as follows:

1996	22 to 25 November
1997	11 to 14 November
1998	1 to 4 November
1999	20 to 23 November

EASTERN RAJASTHAN

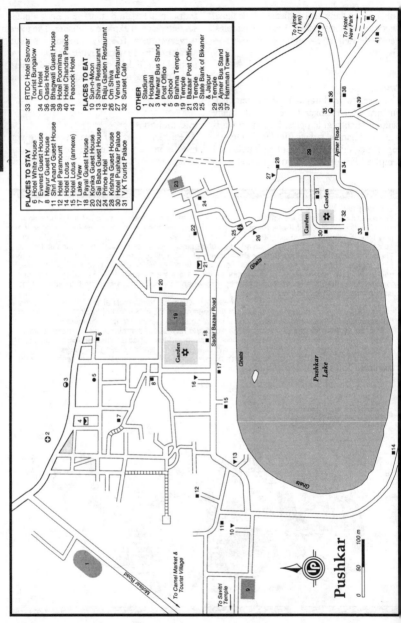

PLACES TO STAY
6 Hotel White House
7 Everest Guest House
8 Mayur Guest House
11 Shri Anand Guest House
12 Hotel Paramount
14 Hotel Lotus
15 Hotel Lotus (annexe)
17 Lake View
18 Payal Guest House
20 Konika Guest House
24 Sai Baba Guest House
28 Prince Hotel
30 Krishna Guest House
30 Hotel Pushkar Palace
31 V K Tourist Palace

33 RTDC Hotel Sarovar
Tourist Bungalow
34 Om Hotel
36 Oasis Hotel
38 Bhagwati Guest House
39 Hotel Poornima
40 Hotel Chandra Palace
41 Peacock Hotel

PLACES TO EAT
10 Sun-n-Moon
13 Shiva Restaurant
16 Raju Garden Restaurant
26 Om Shiva
27 Venus Restaurant
32 Sunset Cafe

OTHER
1 Stadium
2 Hospital
3 Marwar Bus Stand
4 Post Office
5 School
9 Brahma Temple
19 Temple
21 Bazaar Post Office
23 Temple
25 State Bank of Bikaner
& Jaipur
29 Temple
35 Ajmer Bus Stand
37 Hamman Tower

Pushkar

and Jaipur. There is no tourist office in Pushkar, but there are quite a number of travel agencies.

Temples

Pushkar boasts temples, though few are as ancient as you might expect at such an important pilgrimage site, since many were destroyed by Aurangzeb in the 17th century and subsequently rebuilt. The most famous is the **Brahma Temple**, said to be the only temple in India dedicated to this deity. It's marked by a red spire, and over the entrance gateway is the *hans*, or goose symbol, of Brahma, who is said to have personally chosen Pushkar as the temple's site.

The one hour trek up to the hilltop **Savitri Temple** overlooking the lake is best made early in the morning; the view is magnificent.

Ghats

Numerous ghats run down to the lake and pilgrims are constantly bathing in the lake's holy waters. If you wish to join them, do it with respect – remove your shoes, don't smoke and don't take photographs. This is not Varanasi and the pilgrims here can be very touchy about insensitive intrusions by non-Hindus.

Camel Safaris

There are quite a few people in Pushkar who conduct camel rides and safaris. It's best to ask your hotel or a travel agent to recommend somebody who organises good safaris, or speak to other travellers. The usual price is Rs 25 per hour or Rs 200 per day, but you may even be able to bargain these down. Most organisers are happy to tailor-make a safari for you and have good suggestions about places of interest in and around Pushkar. Camel safaris are a great way of taking in the sights and experiencing the rugged beauty of the desert. If it's your first time on a camel, take it easy and avoid galloping!

Places to Stay

Pushkar is such a small but popular town that it can be difficult to find accommodation, especially if you arrive late in the day. Most of the available hotels are cheap but very basic, and rooms have just a bed, common bathroom facilities and no hot water. Some have only charpoys (string beds) with no mattresses or sheets. On the other hand, rooms are generally clean and freshly whitewashed. You should ask to see a few rooms before deciding on one, as many have a cell-like atmosphere due to the small or nonexistent windows. Mosquitoes come with most rooms, so bring insect repellent. During the Camel Fair when demand for rooms is high, some hotels hike up their rates. Unfortunately there isn't much that you can do about this, as it's usually a case of get what you can before it's all gone.

With thousands of tourists visiting Pushkar each year, the town has been exposed to the 'wicked ways of the west' and many hotels display prominent signs warning: 'In Pushkar, holding hands or kissing in public are not permitted'; 'ladies and men should dress appropriately'; 'drugs, alcohol and meat are not permitted'.

Pushkar Passports

You can tell a traveller who's been to the ghats in Pushkar by the red ribbon (the 'Pushkar Passport') tied round their wrist. Getting one can be an expensive procedure if you allow yourself to be talked into a more generous donation than you might otherwise have wanted to give. Priests, some genuine, some not, will approach you near the ghats and offer to do a puja. At some point during the prayers they'll ask you to tell Brahma how much you're going to give him, Rs 100 to Rs 300 being the suggested figure. Don't fall for this emotional blackmail – if you want to give just a few rupees, that's fine, although the 'priest' will tell you it's not enough and doesn't even cover the cost of his 'materials'. ■

The most popular and luxurious place to stay is the *Hotel Pushkar Palace* (☎ 72-001; fax 72-226), an upmarket hotel that also has 14 budget rooms at Rs 100/150 with common bath. These are small and a little dark but in a superb position right by the lake. Smart rooms with air-cooling, attached bath and hot water cost Rs 350/450 or Rs 650/750 with air-con. The best rooms with excellent views over the lake cost Rs 950/1050. There's also a pleasant sitting area overlooking the lake and a very good, though slightly pricey, restaurant serving Rajasthani and Continental food.

Next to the Hotel Pushkar Palace, but approached from a different entrance, is the RTDC *Hotel Sarovar Tourist Bungalow* (☎ 72-040), set in its own spacious grounds at the far eastern end of the lake and with a restaurant. It's better value than the Tourist Bungalow in Ajmer, and has ordinary singles/doubles for Rs 100/125 with common bath, Rs 175/225 with attached bath, and air-cooled deluxe rooms for Rs 225/275. The best rooms overlooking the lake cost Rs 275/350. Dorm beds are available for Rs 50.

Other hotels in this area include the *VK Tourist Palace* (☎ 72-174), a popular cheapie with rooms from Rs 50/80 with common bath, Rs 80/150 with attached bath. There's also a good rooftop restaurant. In the same area is the *Krishna Guest House* (☎ 72-091) which has cheap rooms with common bath for Rs 60/80 or Rs 100/150 with private bath. The nearby *Om Hotel* is similarly priced.

There are several options around the Ajmer bus stand. The *Hotel Poornima* (☎ 72-254) is good value. Built around a little courtyard, it has rooms with attached bath for Rs 60/80. The *Bhagwati Guest House* (☎ 72-423) has very cheap rooms with common bath for just Rs 40/60. Large deluxe doubles with attached bath cost Rs 100. Across the road is the *Oasis Hotel* (☎ 72-100) with a friendly owner who offers discounts for long-staying guests. Comfortable singles/doubles with attached bath cost Rs 125/150. Deluxe rooms with views over the town cost Rs 175/200 and super deluxe rooms cost Rs

225/250. There's a swimming pool and the rooftop terrace is popular for sunbaking.

On the eastern outskirts of town, to the south-east of the Ajmer bus stand, is the *Peacock Hotel* (☎ 72-093), with clean rooms set around a leafy courtyard. Although a little far from the lake, it is peaceful and has a pool and spa (unfilled during winter). Ordinary singles/doubles with private bath cost Rs 100/150 and deluxe rooms are Rs 450/750. Nearby is the *Hotel Chandra Palace* with basic double rooms from Rs 100 with attached bath. Not far from here is *Hotel New Park* (☎ 72-464), surrounded by tranquil flower gardens and wheat fields. Clean singles/doubles with attached bath cost Rs 200/300 or Rs 350/450 for deluxe rooms. There's a swimming pool and restaurant.

The *Prince Hotel*, closer to the lake, has a small courtyard and basic singles/doubles for Rs 50/80 with common bath. In the same area is the basic *Sai Baba Guest House* with rooms from Rs 30. The *Konika Guest House* is not far from here and has clean doubles with private bath for Rs 80.

North of the lake is the *Hotel White House* (☎ 72-147) run by a friendly Brahmin family. Singles/doubles with common bath cost Rs 50/100, Rs 125/150 with attached bath. There are good views from the rooftop restaurant, which serves a wide variety of reasonably priced Indian and Continental food including pancakes and sizzlers. Their mango tea is delicious.

The popular *Everest Guest House* (☎ 72-080) is good value even though it's a warren of a place. Dorm beds are Rs 15, while small singles/doubles cost Rs 30/50 with common bath and Rs 60/80 with bath attached. There's also a small restaurant. Nearby is the *Mayur Guest House* (☎ 72-302) with large rooms for Rs 80/100 with attached bath, Rs 30/50 without.

The very popular *Payal Guest House* (☎ 72-163), right in the middle of the main bazaar, has singles/doubles starting from Rs 40/75 with common bath and Rs 100/125 with attached bath. There's a pleasant banana tree shaded courtyard and the place is more like a home than a hotel. Across the street, the *Lake View* (☎ 72-106) does have good views of the lake and is also popular. Rooms with common bath are Rs 40/80.

One of Pushkar's first guest houses was the *Shri Anand Guest House*, run by a charming mother and daughter. Rooms cost Rs 40/60, or Rs 80/100 with attached bath. Nearby, and with excellent views over the lake, is the *Hotel Paramount* (☎ 72-428). Rooms cost Rs 80 with common bath. The best rooms here are Nos 107 and 111, each with a small balcony and an attached bath for Rs 200.

On the south side of the lake is the serene *Hotel Lotus*, set under a large banyan tree. The rooms are rather small and grubby, but cheap at Rs 30/60 with common bath. There's a quiet outdoor sitting area overlooking the lake.

About two km from the centre of town is *JP's Tourist Village Resort* (☎ 72-067), set in a fragrant garden. Comfortable rooms range from Rs 90 to Rs 400. For those who want to relive their childhood, small treehouse accommodation is available for Rs 45 per person. There's also a restaurant, swimming pool, free bikes and jeeps for hire.

Tourist Village During the Camel Fair, the RTDC sets up a tented 'Tourist Village' (☎ 72-074) on the *mela* (fair) ground right next to the Camel Fair, with accommodation for up to 2000 people. It's a self-contained village with a dining hall, coffee shop, toilets, bathrooms (bucket hot water), foreign exchange facilities, post office, medical centre, safe deposit, shopping arcade and tourist information counter.

Accommodation is very expensive due to the heavy demand at fair time. There are five dormitory tents, each with 60 beds, at Rs 200 per person, 150 deluxe tents with singles/doubles for Rs 2000/2500 including all meals. An extra bed costs Rs 1000. Swiss cottages (super deluxe tents) cost Rs 3000/3500, Rs 1150 for an extra bed. There are also 30 huts which cost Rs 3500/4000 for singles/doubles including meals. These huts are in fact open all year round, and are available for just Rs 175/225 when the fair is not on.

Demand for tent accommodation can be high so, if you want to be sure of a bed, contact the General Manager (☎ Jaipur (0141) 31-0586 or 31-9531; fax 31-6045), RTDC, Hotel Swagatam Campus, Nr Railway Station, Jaipur, well in advance. Full payment must be received 45 days in advance if you want to be sure of accommodation. It is advisable to make reservations as far as one year ahead to avoid disappointment.

Another tented village is the *Royal Desert Camp*. Deluxe tents cost Rs 2800 and Swiss cottages cost Rs 3795 for singles/doubles. Prices include all meals and a 'camel shuttle service' to and from the fair. Bookings can be made through the Hotel Pushkar Palace. Again, it is strongly recommended to make reservations well in advance.

The maharaja of Jodhpur offers 'royal tents' during the fair. Singles/doubles cost Rs 1190/2390. Breakfast costs Rs 175, lunch is Rs 275 and dinner costs Rs 325. Bookings should be made through the Umaid Bhawan Palace in Jodhpur (☎ (0291) 33-316; fax 35-373).

Places to Eat

Pushkar is one of those towns in which everyone has a favourite restaurant, and there's plenty to choose from. There are quite a few rooftop and garden restaurants. Strict vegetarianism that forbids even eggs rather limits the range of ingredients, but the cooks make up for this with imagination. You can get an eggless omelette in some places!

Buffet meals seem to have taken off here in a big way, with many places offering all-you-can-eat meals for Rs 20 to Rs 30 – breakfast, lunch or dinner. It's safest to eat buffet meals at the busiest places where the food is more likely to be freshly cooked for each meal, rather than reheated. The *Shiva Restaurant* on the western edge of the lake was the original buffet specialist, but these days the *Om Shiva* (with the 'Om' written in Hindi to try and cash in on the original Shiva Restaurant's popularity), near the State Bank of Bikaner & Jaipur, on the north-east side of the lake, is better. The rooftop restaurant at the *VK Tourist Palace* also does a good buffet. An Indian or Continental dinner costs just Rs 27.

There are some pleasant and popular garden restaurants in Pushkar. The *Venus Restaurant*, near the Krishna Guest House, serves reasonably priced Indian, Chinese, Italian and Continental food. A vegetarian thali costs Rs 20. There's a big garden and a rooftop terrace here. The *Sun-n-Moon* has tables arranged under a large bo tree, and offers a variety of western dishes including pizzas and apple pie. *Raju Garden Restaurant* has western food including tasty oven-baked pizzas (Rs 40) and baked potatoes, as well as Indian and Chinese food. There are enough jars of Marmite here to last well into the next century.

The best buffet is at the *Hotel Pushkar Palace*. It costs Rs 75 and the menu is posted up each evening. There's a good selection of dishes and you can eat indoors or outdoors. The nearby *Sunset Cafe* is very popular, especially at sunset. Western music is usually playing at this little place by the lake shore, which has seating indoors and outdoors. Although the cleanliness and service are variable, there's a good range of pastries including brownies (Rs 15), croissants (Rs 5), breads, cinnamon rolls and sandwiches. Indian and Tibetan food is also available.

Things to Buy
Pushkar has a wide selection of handicraft shops all along the main bazaar and it's hard to resist buying something. It's especially good for embroidered fabrics such as wall hangings, bed covers, cushion covers and shoulder bags. There are also many shops selling trinkets and souvenirs. A lot of what is stocked here actually comes from the Barmer district south of Jaisalmer and other tribal areas of Rajasthan. There's something to suit all tastes and pockets, though you'll have to haggle over prices. The shopkeepers here have been exposed to tourists with plenty of money and not much time, so there's the usual nonsense about 'last price' quotes which aren't negotiable. Take your

time and visit a few shops. In between these shops are the inevitable clothing shops catering to styles which were in vogue in Goa and Kathmandu at the end of the '60s. You may find occasional timeless items, but most of it is pretty clichéd.

The music shops (selling tapes and records), on the other hand, are well worth a visit if you're interested in picking up some examples of traditional or contemporary classical Indian music. The shops here don't seem to stock the usual banal current film-score rages.

There are a number of bookshops in the main bazaar selling second-hand novels in various languages, and they'll buy them back for 50% of what you pay.

Getting There & Away
To Pushkar, buses depart Ajmer frequently from the stop near the railway station for the Rs 4 trip (although it's only Rs 3 when going *from* Pushkar *to* Ajmer – because of the road toll). It's a spectacular climb up and over the hills – if you can see out of the window.

It is possible to continue straight on from Pushkar to Jodhpur without having to backtrack to Ajmer, but the buses go there via Merta and can take eight hours. It's much faster to go to Ajmer and take the 4½ hour express bus.

There are a couple of travel agencies in Pushkar offering tickets for private buses to various destinations. These buses all leave from Ajmer, but the agencies provide you with free transport to Ajmer in time for the departures. See the Ajmer section for destinations. Some travel agencies will also book rail tickets for services ex-Ajmer for an additional booking fee, which saves the hassle of going down to Ajmer station.

Getting Around
There are no rickshaws in town, but it's easy to get around by foot. Alternatively, there are lots of bicycles for hire around town which cost Rs 3 per hour or Rs 20 per day. It's possible to get a wallah to carry your luggage on a hand-drawn cart to or from the bus stand for a small fee.

TONK

You may well find yourself in this town, 95 km to the south of Jaipur, en route to Sawai Madhopur, gateway to the Ranthambhore National Park. To the north of the modern new town is the original walled city, which was built in the mid-17th century. Tonk was originally ruled by a tribe of Afghani Pathans, and their prosperous Muslim descendants have left a legacy of fine mansions, a testament to the wealth they accumulated when they ruled as nawabs from this region. Tonk also served as an important administrative centre during the era of the Raj, and the British have left behind some well preserved colonial buildings.

Getting There & Away

There are many buses from Jaipur's main bus stand which pass through Tonk (2½ hours, Rs 28) en route to Kota. There are numerous buses between Tonk and Sawai Madhopur (for Ranthambhore National Park; two hours, Rs 15).

SAWAI MADHOPUR & RANTHAMBHORE NATIONAL PARK
Telephone Area Code: 074621

Situated near the town of Sawai Madhopur, midway between Bharatpur and Kota, Ranthambhore National Park is one of the prime examples of Project Tiger's conservation efforts in Rajasthan. Sadly, it also demonstrates the programme's overall failure; for it was in this park that government officials were implicated in the poaching of tigers for the Chinese folk medicine trade.

Not only tigers, but all species of the cat family inhabiting the park are threatened, as well as several other animals such as the ratel, or honey badger *(Mellivora capensis)*, a nocturnal beast which is a member of the weasel family.

Prior to Independence, the park was the preserve of Jaipur's maharajas, who mounted elaborate big game shoots, or *shikhars*, here. The Queen and Prince Philip were the special guests of Maharaja Man Singh in 1960. They stayed in the luxuriously appointed shooting lodge (now a hotel, the Castle Jhoomar Baori – see under Places to Stay), and the Duke of Edinburgh proved himself as a hunter, bagging a large tiger.

In 1955 the game park was declared a wildlife sanctuary, and in 1973 was one of nine sanctuaries selected as part of the Project Tiger programme (see Where Have All the Tigers Gone? in this section). It was designated as a national park in 1980, and in 1984 the forests to the south and north-east of the original park were declared as the Sawai Man Singh and Keladevi sanctuaries respectively. In 1991, Project Tiger extended its coverage at Ranthambhore to include the Keladevi Sanctuary. The park now covers 1334 sq km.

According to the most recent census, conducted in 1995, there are 27 tigers in the park, including three cubs. The previous census was in 1993, when the count was 25 tigers, and this small increase in numbers offers some encouragement to conservationists. Other animals inhabiting Ranthambhore include the endangered caracal, also a member of the cat family, the leopard and jungle cat, several members of the dog family, such as hyena, fox and jackal, the sloth bear and a variety of deer, including the chital (spotted) deer and the sambar, India's largest deer. There are also two species of antelope: the chinkara (Indian gazelle) and nilgai (bluebull).

In addition to its animal population, Ranthambhore boasts over 270 species of birds, including a number of migratory birds which visit the park either in winter or during the monsoon. Birdlife includes various types of owl, such as the brown fish owl and the great Indian horned owl, and other birds of prey such as Bonelli's eagle and the crested serpent eagle. There are also migratory populations of kingfishers, geese and storks.

The vegetation of the park is primarily deciduous forest, with the dominant species being the hardy dhok *(Anogeissus pendula)*, the leaves of which are used for animal fodder. In April, the brilliant flame of the forest blooms, creating a spectacular vision of fiery red across the park precincts. Around the four lakes of Ranthambhore can be seen various tree species including gurjan (*Lannea coromandelica*), with its grey trunk, gums (*Sterculia urens*) and salar (*Boswellia serrata*).

Villagers compete with all these species for land in both the national park and its buffer zones. Villagers need land both for cultivation and wood-felling. There are between 150 and 200 villages in the buffer areas, and four villages within the national park. The four villages will eventually be relocated with government assistance. Between 150 and 200 villages are directly dependent on the park for fodder and fuel, representing a population of some 100,000 people and an equal number of cattle. Although it is illegal to graze stock within the core national park area, villagers have been compelled to break the law. As overgrazing in the park precincts has resulted in some villages having no grazing grounds at all.

Orientation

The main bazaar in Sawai Madhopur runs roughly east-west, about 100m north of the railway station. Most of the cheaper hotels are strung along the eastern end of the bazaar (turn right when you reach the bazaar from the railway station), except for the Hotel Pink Palace.

It's 10 km from Sawai Madhopur to the first park gate, where you pay the entry fees, and a further three km to the main gate and the Ranthambhore Fort. There is mid-range and top-end accommodation strung all the way along the road from Sawai Madhopur to the park. Advance booking is essential during the busy Christmas and New Year periods.

Information

Tourist Office The tourist office (☎ 20-808) is open daily except Sunday from 10 am to 5 pm (lunch from 1.30 to 2 pm). It's about 1½ km from the railway station; follow the road to the west, walk over the overpass and turn left. The tourist office is about 100m down this road on the left. For information about safari timings, and to make bookings, you'll need to go to the Project Tiger office (see following).

Ranthambhore Revival

In the last three or four years, eco-development work has been initiated on the park peripheries, including the establishment of fodder production plots and fuel-wood plantations – some 90% of which are acacias. The viability of the project will become more evident when the forests are ready for harvesting, which will be eight to 10 years after planting. Veterinary services are provided free to villages, including artificial insemination and vaccination. The goal is to vaccinate 100% of the cattle, as diseased cattle can potentially contaminate water sources which are vital to the animal inhabitants of the national park.

Much of this conservation work is due to the commitment of workers and volunteers of the Ranthambhore Foundation, which was inaugurated in 1987 as a non-profit society for the creation of natural integration and harmony between the park's human dwellers, vegetation and wildlife. Programmes implemented by the foundation include the dissemination of knowledge at the village level regarding health, medicine and family planning; the revival of traditional arts and crafts, which provide alternative forms of income for villagers; the introduction of stall-fed cattle, such as buffaloes, to reduce the negative impacts of grazing; the establishment of nurseries and seed collection as part of a regreening initiative; education focused on environmental awareness; research into animal habitat, including a study of water resources; the establishment of 'green groups' in villages to raise environmental awareness; introduction and research into alternative forms of energy, such as biogas in place of firewood; facilitating the relocation of villages from sensitive park areas and aiding villagers in this relocation; and integrating traditional wisdom with modern science in regenerating the park's ecosystem and ensuring a healthy habitat for its animal dwellers.

For more information on the work of the foundation, write to: Ranthambhore Foundation, 19 Kautilya Marg, Chanakyapuri, New Delhi, 110021 (☎ 301-6261; fax 301-9457); or Ranthambhore Foundation, 10 Bal Mandir Colony, Maintown, Sawai Madhopur, Rajasthan, 322001 (☎ (07462) 20-286). ∎

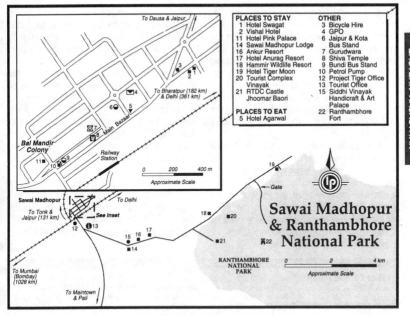

PLACES TO STAY
1 Hotel Swagat
2 Vishal Hotel
11 Hotel Pink Palace
14 Sawai Madhopur Lodge
16 Ankur Resort
17 Hotel Anurag Resort
18 Hammir Wildlife Resort
19 Hotel Tiger Moon
20 Tourist Complex
    Vinayak
21 RTDC Castle
    Jhoomar Baori

PLACES TO EAT
5 Hotel Agarwal

OTHER
3 Bicycle Hire
4 GPO
6 Jaipur & Kota
    Bus Stand
7 Gurudwara
8 Shiva Temple
9 Bundi Bus Stand
10 Petrol Pump
12 Project Tiger Office
13 Tourist Office
15 Siddhi Vinayak
    Handicraft & Art
    Palace
22 Ranthambhore
    Fort

Project Tiger Office The Project Tiger information office (☎ 20-223) is tucked away half a km west of the railway station. Just follow the tracks (don't go along the road) west from the station, through the overpass, and the office is on the left, just before the cinema, which is on the other side of the tracks. The office is open daily except Sunday from 10 am to 5 pm (closed for lunch between 1 and 2 pm).

Post Office The GPO is on the street which runs parallel to and north of the main bazaar.

Money It may be possible to change money at banks in Maintown, Sawai Madhopur City, which is four km south of the main bazaar.

Bookshops Siddhi Vinayak Handicraft & Art Palace, on the Ranthambhore road near the Sawai Madhopur Lodge, has a small collection of books on Indian birds and wildlife, with particular emphasis on Ranthambhore. English-language newspapers are available at the railway station.

Wildlife Safaris

The best time to visit the park is between October and April, and the park is actually closed during the monsoon from 1 June to 1 October. Early morning and late afternoon are the best times to view wildlife.

There's a reasonable chance of spotting a tiger, but you should plan on two or three safaris. Other game, especially the larger and smaller herbivores, are more numerous. Even if you don't see a tiger, it's worth the effort for the scenery alone: in India it's not often you get the chance to visit such a large area of virgin bush.

A good network of four gravel tracks crisscrosses the park and on each safari two or three jeeps take each trail. There are also large trucks (open-topped) called canters, which seat 22 people, but they're limited to only two of the trails. Safaris are undertaken in open-sided jeeps driven by a ranger. If you've ever been on safari in Africa, you might think this is an unduly risky venture but the tigers appear unconcerned by jeep loads of garrulous tourists touting cameras only metres away from where they're lying. No-one has been mauled or eaten – yet!

If you are taking photos, it's worthwhile bringing some 400 or 800 ASA film, as the undergrowth is dense and surprisingly dark in places.

There's a Rs 25 entry fee to the park, plus Rs 10 for a camera. You'll also have to pay the entry fee of Rs 75 per jeep (the entry fee for canters is included in the ticket price). Jeeps and canters must be booked at the Project Tiger office. A seat in a canter costs Rs 60, and you can arrange to be picked up if your hotel is on the road between the town and the park. Jeeps cost Rs 500 per trip and this can be shared by up to five people. This includes all km charges, so if you're staying further from the park entrance, the trip isn't going to cost more.

A maximum of 10 jeeps is permitted in the park at any one time. Five of these can be booked one month in advance, and the remaining five can be booked either on the evening before or the morning of the day of the safari. Bookings for morning trips can be made between 6 and 7 pm on the evening prior, and between 10.30 am and 2 pm for the afternoon safari.

Some travellers have reported that a few local entrepreneurial types are involved in a scam with the Project Tiger office whereby they buy all the jeeps and canters available for hire each day and offer these vehicles to

---

Where Have All the Tigers Gone?

The first mention of tigers in India is found in scriptures dating from the Vedic era (1500-1200 BC). It is believed that they migrated to India from China and Burma, first entering the country at Bengal, giving rise to the name 'Bengal tiger'. The tigers gradually drove out the pre-existing population of lions, and today lions are found in India only in the Gir National Park, in Gujarat.

It has been estimated that at the turn of the century, there may have been as many as 40,000 tigers in India. However, it was not until 1972 that the first official all-India census was conducted. This was a direct result of the General Assembly of International Union for Conservation of Nature and Natural Resources held in Delhi in 1969, which led to a national ban being imposed on tiger hunting in 1970. The survey confirmed what conservationists had feared: tiger numbers were seriously depleted, with a total of only 1827 tigers recorded in the survey. In 1972, the Wildlife (Protection) Act was implemented.

A number of factors had contributed to the reduction of the tiger population. Requisitioning of land for agriculture by an ever-increasing population began to take its toll towards the end of the last century, and the tiger's habitat was severely reduced. Problems were exacerbated by organised hunting expeditions mounted by Indian princes. Following independence, formerly private forests were appropriated for agriculture and fuel requirements, and where hunting had once been only for the rich and privileged, it now became a means of supplementing the livelihood of the poorer members of society. The hunting of smaller animals on which the tigers preyed resulted in tigers turning to domestic livestock for food. This in turn led to the hunting and poisoning of tigers.

In 1973-74, Project Tiger was implemented. This programme was aimed at establishing a number of protected reserves across India. The programme was formally inaugurated in Corbett National Park, in the Siwalik hills of Uttar Pradesh, in 1973. The project's aims are to establish sanctuaries consisting of a core area for the exclusive use of animals, free from human exploitation and disturbance and a buffer zone in which limited human activity was permitted within strict conservation guidelines. Other aims include restoring habitat to pre human-disturbance levels and conducting research into habitat conservation.

The project is a joint central and state government initiative, and nine sanctuaries have so far been established, each one administered by Project Tiger. Naturally the aims of the project ran counter to other vested interests, resulting in sometimes bloody altercations between poachers, villagers and conservationists. Today there are 17 reserves operated across India by Project Tiger.

During the first decade of the project's implementation, tiger numbers increased in sanctuaries falling under Project Tiger from some 268, according to the census undertaken at the project's inception, to 854 in 1983. However, it is an uphill battle, with the goals of conservationists needing to be balanced with the needs of villagers living in national park zones, and the greed of poachers eroding the successes of the project. ■

the high-end hotel guests for two to four times the normal price. Although this was not this author's experience, it is a good idea to be prepared for any eventuality.

In winter (October to February), both canters and jeeps leave at 7 am and 2.30 pm; the safari takes three hours. In summer (March to June), they leave at 6.30 am and 3.30 pm. A guide costs Rs 55; Saleem Ali is a young guide who, like his namesake, the famous Indian ornithologist, Salim Ali, is good at spotting wildlife.

Ranthambhore Fort

The ancient Ranthambhore Fort, in the heart of the national park, is believed to have been built by the Chauhan Rajputs in the 10th century AD, only a few years before the invasion of India by Mohammed Ghori. According to tradition, the fort was erected over the site at which two princes were engaged in a boar hunt. The boar eluded the princes and dived into a lake. Not to be thwarted, the princes prayed to Shiva to restore the boar. This Shiva deigned to do, on condition that the princes build a fort in his honour at the spot.

However, it is Ganesh who is most revered at the fort, and a temple in his honour can be found overlooking its southern ramparts. Traditionally when a marriage is to take place, invitations are forwarded to Lord Ganesh before any other guests. The temple at the fort receives hundreds of letters each week addressed to the elephant god, some of which include money to enable him to pay for his fare to the marriage celebration!

The fort is believed to be the site at which the first jauhar (collective suicide) in Rajput history was performed. In the early 14th century, the ruler of the fort, Hammir Deva, was engaged in a protracted battle with the Muslim forces. Although Hammir repulsed the Muslim invaders, the women who were installed in the fort for their safety heard word that the brave Rajput had succumbed on the battle field. In usual Rajput style, preferring death to dishonour, they committed mass suicide, much to the dismay of the returning victorious Hammir. Hammir re-solved to kill himself when confronted with the grisly news, and beheaded himself before the image of Shiva in the temple at the fort.

From a distance, the fort is not an imposing edifice, being almost indiscernible on its hilltop looking out over the lake of Padam Talab. However, it affords very fine views from the disintegrating walls of the Badal Mahal, on its north side, and its seven enormous gateways are still intact. Inside the fort are three Hindu temples, dedicated to Ganesh, Shiva and Ramlalaji, as well as a Jain temple. They date from the 12th and 13th centuries and are constructed of impressive blocks of red Karauli stone. Constructed of the same stone are a number of cenotaphs which can be seen in the precincts of the fort.

Places to Stay & Eat – Sawai Madhopur

The *Vishal Hotel* (☎ 20-504), main bazaar, has a range of clean rooms, some with balconies. Singles/doubles with attached bath (hot water free by the bucket) downstairs are Rs 50/60. The larger upstairs rooms are Rs 70/80 and Rs 80/90. Checkout is 24 hours after check in.

A few doors further east is the *Hotel Swagat* (☎ 20-601), which has quite basic rooms with attached bath (hot water by the bucket) for Rs 60/80 and Rs 80/100.

On the west side of the overpass, at plot A1, Bal Mandir Colony, is the popular *Hotel Pink Palace* (☎ 20-722). It has clean, basic rooms for Rs 125/150 with attached bath (hot water by the bucket), or Rs 175/200 with geyser. Rooms with common bath are Rs 100 for singles and doubles, and meals are available here.

There are *retiring rooms* at the railway station at Rs 95 for a double with attached bath with hot water. Dorm beds are Rs 35.

The *Hotel Agarwal* is a small dhaba on main bazaar which has a good variety of cheap vegetarian dishes.

Places to Stay & Eat – Ranthambhore Road

All of the places below offer fixed priced meals, and some also offer an a la carte selection.

The first place to stay on the Ranthambhore road (coming from Sawai Madhopur) is the Taj Group's *Sawai Madhopur Lodge* (☎ 20-541), which is three km from the railway station. The lodge formerly belonged to the Maharaja of Jaipur, and is suitably luxurious, with a bar, restaurant, pool and beautiful garden. Rooms are US$95/130 per night, and a suite is US$160. Non-guests are welcome to dine at the restaurant here with advance notice; lunch is Rs 240 plus 10% tax, and dinner is Rs 280 plus tax.

The next place to stay, heading towards the national park, is the *Ankur Resort* (☎ 20-792). Rooms are cool and spotless, and there's a pleasant garden area. Singles/doubles are Rs 400/550 with attached bath and 24 hour hot water. There are also cottages for Rs 500/550. A 50% discount is offered between May and September. It costs Rs 70 for vegetarian meals, and Rs 125 for non-veg meals.

Four km from the railway station is the *Hotel Anurag Resort* (☎ 20-451). Ordinary singles/doubles are Rs 300/400, and deluxe rooms are Rs 400/500. Dorm beds are Rs 50, and it's possible to camp here (in your own tent) for Rs 50 per campsite, which includes access to toilets and bathroom facilities. Breakfast is Rs 40, lunch is Rs 70 (veg) and Rs 90 (non-veg), and dinner is Rs 80 (veg) and Rs 100 (non-veg). There is also an a la carte menu. From 1 April to 30 June a 25% discount is offered on room prices, and from 30 June to 30 September there's a 50% discount. All rooms have running hot water.

Six km from the railway station is a turnoff which leads in one km to the RTDC *Castle Jhoomar Baori* (☎ 20-495). This former royal hunting lodge, in a fine position perched on a hilltop, has 12 well furnished and spacious rooms which have modern toilet and bathroom facilities with hot water. There's also a beautiful lounge, as well as open rooftop areas and a bar. Deluxe air-cooled rooms are Rs 400/500, the air-con Panther Suite is Rs 600/725, and the Tiger and Leopard suites, also with air-con, are Rs 725/900. Fixed price non-veg Continental lunch and dinners are Rs 155, and veg meals

are Rs 125. There are also veg thalis for Rs 55, and non-veg thalis for Rs 65. Breakfast is Rs 85, and there is also a la carte. This is a lovely place to stay, and the staff are friendly and helpful.

Seven km from the railway station is the *Hammir Wildlife Resort* (☎ 20-562). Rooms are comfortable, if a little tatty, and there's a good lawn area. Singles/doubles are Rs 400/500, and cottages are Rs 700 for a double. The 'Jungle Plan' includes accommodation and all meals, as well as two safaris, park entry fees and transfer to and from Sawai Madhopur railway station. It costs Rs 1225/2150 for ordinary singles/doubles, and Rs 2350 for cottages.

Also seven km from the railway station is the RTDC *Tourist Complex Vinayak*. Comfortable carpeted and well furnished rooms are Rs 375/450/550, all with air-cooling, and there's 24 hour hot water. A camp fire is lit in winter.

At the end of Ranthambhore road, 11 km from the railway station, is the swish *Hotel Tiger Moon* (Mumbai ☎ (022) 643-3622; fax 640-6399; Sawai Madhopur ☎ 6842; fax 21-212), which is US$51 per person per night including all meals. There is also a 'Jungle Plan', which includes accommodation, meals and a morning and evening safari, for US$83 per person. There's a pool here, and railway station transfer can be provided for an additional cost.

Getting There & Away

Bus There are buses every hour to Jaipur via Dausa between 5.30 am and 3.30 pm. They take four hours and cost Rs 33. There's one daily service to Kota, leaving at 1.30 pm (four hours, Rs 35). To get to Bharatpur you need to change at Dausa (three hours from Sawai Madhopur), from where there are many buses on to Bharatpur. All these buses leave from the main bus stand, which is about two minutes walk north of the main bazaar. Buses to Bundi leave from the Bundi bus stand, which is at the west end of the main bazaar. They leave at 6 and 8.30 am, 1, 2 and 3.10 pm. The trip takes two hours and costs Rs 28 on the ordinary service and Rs 34 on the express (3.10 pm) service.

Train Sawai Madhopur is on the main Delhi to Bombay broad-gauge railway line and, as most trains stop here, there's a wide range to choose from. To Kota, the *Agra-Kota Passenger* leaves at 2.50 pm, arriving into Kota at 7 pm. The fare is Rs 19/135 in 2nd/1st class. The 2904 *Frontier Mail* is an express service leaving Sawai Madhopur at 1.20 pm, arriving into Kota at 4 pm (Rs 24 in 2nd class). The 5063 *Aved Express* leaves Sawai Madhopur at 9.47 am, arriving into Kota at 12.30 pm (Rs 29/122).

To Agra, the *Kota-Agra Passenger* leaves at 11.20 pm, arriving into Agra the following morning at 7 am (Rs 30/226 for a 2nd/1st class sleeper). There's also a day service, the *Agra-Kota Passenger*, which leaves Sawai Madhopur at 10.50 am, arriving into Agra at 7 pm (Rs 30/226).

Trains to Delhi are via Bharatpur. The 4005 *Indore Nijumaddin Express* leaves Sawai Madhopur at 12.10 am, arriving into Delhi at 6 am (Rs 82/334). There's a second overnight service, the 2471 *Bombay-Jammu Superfast*, which leaves Sawai Madhopur at 11.10 pm, arriving into Delhi at 6 am (Rs 87/334). The 2953 *Agasgranti-Rajdhani Express* leaves Sawai Madhopur at 6.20 am, arriving into the capital at 10 am (Rs 370/650). The 2903 *Frontier Mail* leaves Sawai Madhopur at 12.50 pm, arrives into

Bharatpur (Rs 52) at 4 pm, and Delhi at 8 pm (Rs 87 in 2nd class; no first class).

Sawai Madhopur is also the junction of the metre-gauge spur to Jaipur and Bikaner, but this may soon be converted to broad gauge. The 2955 *Bombay Superfast* leaves Sawai Madhopur for Jaipur at 10 am, arriving into the pink city at 12.30 pm (Rs 40 in second class; there's no first class). There's also the 191 *Kota-Jodhpur Passenger* which leaves Sawai Madhopur at 7.10 am, arriving into Jaipur at 9.30 am (Rs 21). Services to Bikaner require a change at Jaipur.

Getting Around
You can hire bikes for Rs 10 per day at the shops just outside the main entrance to the railway station, and at the east end of the main bazaar.

DHOLPUR
Situated almost midway between Agra (Uttar Pradesh) and Gwalior (Madhya Pradesh), on an eastward thrusting spur of Rajasthan, is Dholpur. It was near here that Aurangzeb's sons fought a pitched battle to determine who would succeed him as emperor of the rapidly declining Mughal Empire. The Shergarh Fort in Dholpur is very old and is now in ruins.

Dholpur, located on National Highway 3, is most easily reached from either Agra or Gwalior, and there are regular rail and bus connections from both of these cities.

Southern Rajasthan

Bordering Gujarat and Madhya Pradesh, southern Rajasthan is one of the state's most fertile regions. It has a varied topography, with rolling hills, lush valleys and desolate plains. The region is also dotted with many lakes, including Jaisamand, one of the biggest artificial lakes in Asia. The south boasts some of Rajasthan's most important forts, including the huge hilltop Chittorgarh Fort. This sprawling fort occupies a paramount place in the annals of Rajput valour, for this was where tens of thousands of Rajput men and women perished in the name of honour. The imposing 15th century Kumbhalgarh Fort is the second most significant in the Mewar (Udaipur) region, after Chittorgarh.

Southern Rajasthan has one of the best known palace-hotels in India: the breathtaking Lake Palace Hotel in Udaipur. Superbly situated in the middle of a lake, this enchanting palace once served as the royal summer residence. It has an incomparable location, regal heritage, lavish interior and beautiful architecture.

Kota is one of the state's major industrial centres and has seen an increasing rate of industrialisation and pollution. This trend is not limited to Kota: over the past decade, many cities and towns in southern Rajasthan have experienced a rising level of pollution, largely because of industrial growth and urban sprawl. Marble mining has burgeoned in the south and contributed to denuding the landscape of vegetation; it's not unusual to see quarries and piles of rubble strewn across the countryside. Although the government has taken measures to curtail industrial waste, a handful of historic monuments are believed to have already been adversely affected by pollution.

An increasingly popular way of exploring the smaller forts, palaces and other sights of this region is on horseback. Horse safaris provide an opportunity to experience the rugged beauty of the countryside and to visit

places that are off the beaten track. It's advisable to have some riding experience if you intend to take a longer horse trek.

Southern Rajasthan has the state's only hill station, Mt Abu. Situated along a 1200m high plateau, the locals throng here during summer to escape the sweltering Indian heat. Like many other hill stations in the country, Mt Abu is very popular with Indian honeymooners and young families. The Brahma Kumaris Spiritual University is located here and attracts a large number of devotees from all around the world; it accounts for most of the foreigners seen in Mt Abu. Also located at this hill station are the superb Dilwara Temples, which are an important Jain pilgrimage centre. These temples have some of the most amazing marble carvings in Rajasthan, if not India. Another impressive and important Jain temple at Ranakpur is renowned for its 1444 exquisite pillars, no two of which are alike.

This part of the state is rich in antiquities and many potentially remain undiscovered. Jhalawar, for instance, is an archaeologist's heaven, with a seemingly endless number of historic relics being continually unearthed. Jhalawar has a rare assortment of ancient sites, including extraordinary Buddhist caves and stupas atop a hill.

Historically, Rajasthan has been a flourishing centre of art and culture, and produced some of India's finest schools of miniature painting. Many former rulers were great patrons of the arts and employed local artists to develop unique styles of painting. In southern Rajasthan, prominent schools in Bundi, Kota, Udaipur and Nathdwara produced some of the finest miniature paintings in the state. The famous Bundi school of painting had Mughal influences and specialised in hunting and palace scenes. Kota was once surrounded by dense forests which were popular hunting grounds for the local nobility; the miniature paintings produced here in the early 19th century are particularly acclaimed for their eloquent depictions of hunting scenes and have featured at many international exhibitions.

Mewar also developed its own style of painting and was especially known for its highly detailed court scenes. Created from the early 18th century for the Mewar rulers, some of these paintings can be seen at the City Palace Museum in Udaipur. Also noteworthy are the vivid Nathdwara *pichwai* paintings, which were produced in the 17th century after the image of Vishnu was brought to this town from Mathura. Other small towns, predominantly those with royal connections, had their own school of painting.

Many traditional tribal folk dances and songs have survived from southern Rajasthan's colourful past. A prime example is that of the Bhil tribal people, who are concentrated in southern Rajasthan. These tribal people often perform their vibrant dances during special festivals, such as Holi.

There are a handful of wildlife reserves in southern Rajasthan and an abundance of birdlife around the many lakes, particularly at Udaipur, Jaisamand, Dungarpur and Deogarh.

HISTORY

Southern Rajasthan's history is dominated by the region of Mewar, which was wracked with bloodshed and acts of astounding valour. The events at Chittorgarh, the former capital of Mewar, were undoubtedly the most catastrophic and poignant in all of Rajasthan, for it was here that countless Rajput men, women and children chose death over defeat. Chittorgarh was sacked three times in its history and each defeat ended in immense carnage. While the men died in

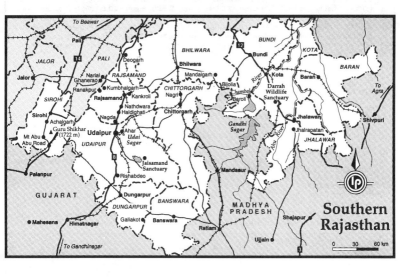

Southern Rajasthan

battle, the women committed *jauhar* (collective sacrifice) by throwing themselves into the flames of huge pyres to avoid the infamy of capture. The first defeat took place in 1303, after a Pathan king of Delhi seized the fort in a desperate attempt to possess Chittorgarh's beautiful noblewoman, Padmini. His relentless quest resulted in the tragic deaths of thousands of Rajput men and women: the men gallantly fought a far stronger enemy

FESTIVALS OF SOUTHERN RAJASTHAN

Several colourful festivals are celebrated in southern Rajasthan. For statewide and nationwide festivals, see Festivals of Rajasthan in the Facts for the Visitor chapter.

January-February

Baneshwar Fair – This festival is celebrated by thousands of Bhil people at the confluence of the Mahi and Som rivers at Baneshwar, in Dungarpur district. It is in honour of Vishnu who is worshipped as Kalki. Festivities include acrobatic performances and cultural programmes, and a silver image of Kalki is paraded through the village on horseback.

February-March

Holi – Holi is celebrated across India in late February/early March, and Udaipur is one of the best places in Rajasthan to be during this happy celebration. The festival heralds the end of winter and the beginning of spring. It symbolises the victory of divine power over demonic strength. Holi is also known as the festival of colours, because of the exuberant throwing of coloured powder and water on the last day of this festival.

The Udaipur royal family hosts an elaborate function at the City Palace to celebrate Holi. In the evening, there's a regal procession with decorated horses, a band, local nobility decked out in traditional attire and, of course, the royal family. After performing an ancient religious ceremony, the royal family lights a huge sacred fire which signifies the triumph of good over evil. Tribal people then commence a traditional dance around the blazing fire. Afterwards, you get the chance to rub shoulders with nobility at a reception held in the *Zenana Mahal* at the City Palace. Tickets for this unique event cost US$25 per person or US$35 per couple, and can be obtained at the Shiv Niwas Palace Hotel (☎ (0294) 52-8016; fax 52-8006) in Udaipur.

March-April

Gangaur – This festival is celebrated by women across Rajasthan: wives pray for their spouses and unmarried women pray for good husbands. Essentially a festival for women, it is dedicated to the goddess Gauri (Parvati). The Garasia tribes of the Mt Abu region add an interesting element to the festivities: they celebrate Gangaur for an entire month, and the image of Gangaur is carried aloft from village to village. Young unmarried youths and maidens are able to meet without social sanctioning and select their marriage partners, with whom they elope. In Bundi, Kota and Jhalawar, unmarried girls collect poppies from the fields which are made into wreaths for the goddess.

Mewar Festival – In late March/early April, Udaipur hosts its own colourful version of the Gangaur Festival. People dressed in traditional costumes sing and dance in a lively procession which goes through the town to Gangaur Ghat at Lake Pichola. Idols of Gauri and Lord Shiva, who represent the perfect couple, are carried in the procession. There are also cultural programmes, fireworks and boat races on Lake Pichola.

June

Summer Festival This festival takes place in Mt Abu, which registers the coolest temperatures in the state at this scorching time of the year, so is not a bad place to be. The festival takes place over three days and includes classical and traditional folk cultural programmes.

August-September

Kajli Teej – This festival heralding the onset of the monsoon commences eight days before Janmashtami, Lord Krishna's birthday.

October-November

Chandrabhaga Cattle Fair This large cattle fair takes place on the last day of the Hindu month of Kartika on the banks of the Chandrabhaga River near Jhalrapatan, attracting villagers from around Rajasthan and neighbouring states. It includes livestock trading and colourful stalls, and also has a religious element – pilgrims at this time bathe in a sacred part of the river known as Chandrawati.

and the women, including Padmini, committed jauhar. The same grim outcome occurred in 1535, when the Sultan of Gujarat besieged the fort, and finally in 1568, when Chittorgarh was seized by the Mughal emperor, Akbar. After the third attack, Mewar's ruler, Maharana Udai Singh II, decided to leave Chittorgarh and establish his new capital in Udaipur.

Geographically, Udaipur was shielded by thick forests and the Aravalli Range, and was therefore far less vulnerable than the exposed Chittorgarh. But this did not stop invaders from trying to lay siege to the new capital of Mewar, and Udaipur also had its share of battles. These power struggles ended in the early 19th century when the British signed an alliance pledging to protect the Mewar rulers.

Historically, the rulers of the Mewar region have occupied the top of the Rajput hierarchy, making this an important part of Rajasthan. This dynasty is believed to be one of the oldest in the world, reigning in unbroken succession for over 1400 years. The rulers of Mewar come from the illustrious Sisodia Rajput clan, which traces its descent from the sun. They staunchly defied foreign domination of any kind and were the only Hindu princes who refused to intermarry with the once influential Mughal emperors. For them, honour, heritage and independence were of paramount importance, even if they meant deprivation and suffering.

Other princely states in southern Rajasthan, such as Kota and Bundi, were formed long after the region of Mewar. For example, the remote princely state of Jhalawar was only created in 1838.

KOTA
Population: 596,000
Telephone Area Code: 0744

Kota is one of Rajasthan's less inspiring cities and today serves as an army headquarters. It is also Rajasthan's prime industrial centre (mainly chemicals), powered by the hydroelectric plants on the Chambal River – the only permanent river in Rajasthan – and

a nearby nuclear plant. The latter made headlines in 1992 when it was revealed that levels of radioactivity in the area were way above 'safe' levels. Kota also has one of Asia's largest fertiliser plants.

Growing industrialisation has led to an increasing level of pollution in Kota and black smoke billows into the air from two huge chimneys across the river. Fortunately, there are a handful of leafy parks scattered throughout the town and there's also an artificial lake with an enchanting palace on a little island in the middle.

Kota is well known for its saris, which are woven at the nearby village of Kaithoon. Known as *Kota doria* saris, they are made of cotton or silk in an assortment of colours, many with delicate golden thread designs. The Kota miniature paintings are also noteworthy, particularly the hunting scenes. These present a vivid and detailed portrayal of hunting expeditions in the once thickly wooded forests in and around Kota.

Very few tourists visit Kota, which is surprising because the fort and part of the palace complex are open to the public and the Rao Madho Singh Museum has to be one of the best in Rajasthan.

History
Following the Rajput conquest of this area of Rajasthan in the 12th century, Bundi was chosen as the capital, with Kota as the land grant of the ruler's eldest son. In 1624 Kota became a separate state and remained so until it was integrated into Rajasthan after Independence.

Building of the city began in 1264 following the defeat of Koteya, a Bhil chieftain. He was beheaded and on that very spot the foundation stone of the fort was laid. Kota didn't reach its present size until well into the 17th century, when Rao Madho Singh, a son of the ruler of Bundi, was made ruler of Kota by the Mughal emperor, Jehangir. Subsequent rulers have all added to the fort and palaces which stand here today, and each also contributed to making Kota a flourishing centre of art and culture.

SOUTHERN RAJASTHAN

Orientation & Information

Kota is strung out along the east bank of the Chambal River. The railway station is well to the north; the Hotel Chambal Tourist Bungalow, a number of other hotels and the bus stand are in the middle; and Chambal Gardens, the fort and the Kota Barrage are to the south.

The tourist office (☎ 27-695) is at the Hotel Chambal Tourist Bungalow. The staff here are keen and a range of leaflets is available. It's open Monday to Saturday from 8 am to noon and 3 to 6 pm.

City Palace & Fort

Standing beside the Kota Barrage and overlooking the Chambal River, the City Palace and Fort is one of the largest such complexes in Rajasthan. The palace itself was the former residence of the Kota rulers and used to be the centre of power. The treasury, courts, arsenal, soldiers and various state offices were all located here. Some of its buildings are now occupied by schools but most of the complex is open to the public. Entry is from the south side through the **Naya Darwaza**, or New Gate.

The **Rao Madho Singh Museum**, in the City Palace, is superb. It's on the right-hand side of the complex's huge central courtyard and is entered through a gateway topped by rampant elephants like those at the Bundi Fort. Inside, there are displays of weapons, clothing and some of the best preserved murals in Rajasthan. There's also a collection of animal trophies and portraits of past rulers. Indeed, everything about this former palace is colourful. The pieces are well displayed and it's an enjoyable place to take in the history of the region. The museum is open daily, except Friday, from 11 am to 5 pm. Admission costs Rs 40 for foreigners, Rs 7 for Indians, plus Rs 35 for a camera or Rs 75 for a video camera.

After visiting the museum, it's worth wandering around the rest of the complex just to

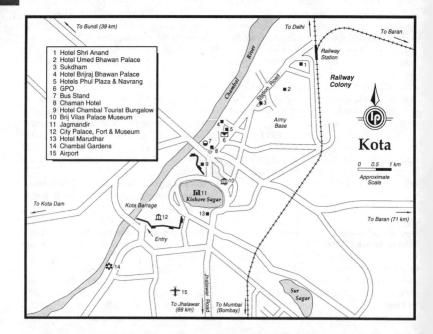

Kota

1 Hotel Shri Anand
2 Hotel Umed Bhawan Palace
3 Sukhdham
4 Hotel Brijraj Bhawan Palace
5 Hotels Phul Plaza & Navrang
6 GPO
7 Bus Stand
8 Chaman Hotel
9 Hotel Chambal Tourist Bungalow
10 Brij Vilas Palace Museum
11 Jagmandir
12 City Palace, Fort & Museum
13 Hotel Marudhar
14 Chambal Gardens
15 Airport

To Bundi (39 km)
To Delhi
To Baran
Railway Station
Railway Colony
Chambal River
Station Road
Army Base
To Kota Dam
Kota Barrage
Kishore Sagar
To Baran (71 km)
Entry
Jhalawar Road
Sur Sagar
To Jhalawar (88 km)
To Mumbai (Bombay)

0   0.5   1 km
Approximate Scale

appreciate how magnificent it must have been in its heyday. Unfortunately, a lot of it is falling into disrepair and the gardens are no more, but there are some excellent views over the old city, the river and the large industrial complex across the river. Pollution is believed to be contributing to the deterioration of the fort. Some of the exterior murals are gradually fading, which is a great pity.

Jagmandir

Between the City Palace and the Hotel Chambal Tourist Bungalow is the picturesque artificial tank of Kishore Sagar, constructed in 1346. Right in the middle of the tank, on a small island, is the beguiling little palace of Jagmandir. Built in 1740 by one of the maharanis of Kota, it's best seen early in the morning but is exquisite at any time of day. It's not currently open to the public but you could get a close look by renting one of the RTDC paddle boats. They cost Rs 20 for 15 minutes or Rs 40 for 30 minutes.

Brij Vilas Palace Museum

The government museum is in a small, plain palace near the Kishore Sagar. It has a collection of stone idols and other such fragments, mainly from the archaeological sites at Baroli and Jhalawar. There are also some weapons, paintings and old manuscripts. Neither the museum nor the palace are of great interest, though. The museum is open daily, except Friday, from 10 am to 4.30 pm; entry is Rs 2. Photography is not allowed.

Gardens

There are several well maintained, peaceful gardens in Kota which provide a splash of colour to this fairly drab town. The **Chambal Gardens** are on the banks of the Chambal River, south of the fort. They're a popular place for picnics and there's a cafe here, as well as a small children's park with rides. The centrepiece is a murky pond well stocked with crocodiles. Once common all along the river, by the middle of this century crocodiles had been virtually exterminated by

hunting. There are also some rare gharials (thin-snouted, fish-eating crocodiles).

Just beside the Hotel Chambal Tourist Bungalow are the **Chhattar Bilas Gardens**, a curious collection of somewhat neglected but impressive royal tombs, or *chhatris*.

Organised Tours

A three hour tour starts at the Hotel Chambal Tourist Bungalow at 9 am daily. It costs Rs 50 and covers all of the major city sites.

Frequent half hour boat cruises up the Chambal River depart every day from the Chambal Gardens. Tickets cost Rs 5 and are available from where the boat departs.

Places to Stay

Serving more as a commercial centre than as a tourist destination, Kota has few interesting hotels. Although there are a number of reasonable hotels close to the busy railway station, few people choose to stay such a long way from the centre of things. A good place here is the *Hotel Shri Anand* (☎ 21-773), 100m along the street opposite the station. The rooms are small and noisy but cheap, and all have satellite TV. Ordinary singles with a common bath cost Rs 50 and singles/doubles with private bath are Rs 100/130. Dorm beds cost Rs 30. Vegetarian meals are available here.

The *Hotel Marudhar* (☎ 26-186), Jhalawar Rd, is between the fort and Kishore Sagar. Small and somewhat gloomy air-cooled doubles with attached bath and B&W TV cost Rs 165; an extra Rs 35 gets you colour TV. Air-con rooms cost Rs 300/350 and deluxe rooms are Rs 400/450. Veg and non-veg food is available. There are several other similarly priced hotels in this area.

The RTDC *Hotel Chambal Tourist Bungalow* (☎ 26-527) is set in scrubby gardens near Kishore Sagar. The mosquitoes are tenacious, but this is a problem common to most hotels here. Small and rather dirty air-cooled rooms cost Rs 225/275 or Rs 400/450 for air-con. It's not great value, but all rooms have attached bath with constant hot water. Dorm beds cost Rs 50. There's a small restaurant which serves Indian and Continental food. A vegetarian thali costs Rs 37. For something much cheaper, head for the *Chaman Hotel* (☎ 23-377), closer to the bus stand, on Station Rd. It's one of the cheapest hotels in town, but be prepared for grubby sheets and rooms the size of cupboards. It's a noisy place and some rooms share a common ceiling, so you'll be able to hear everything happening in the room next door. Prices are blatantly painted above the door of each room (just in case you forget) and start at just Rs 35 with common bath and water by the bucket. Women travelling alone should perhaps think twice about staying here.

The *Hotel Phul Plaza* (☎ 22-356), near the GPO, has ordinary singles/doubles with attached bath and air-cooling for Rs 220/270 or Rs 380/450 with air-con. Suites cost Rs 900/975. There's also a good vegetarian restaurant, but it's definitely better to stay next door at the delightful *Hotel Navrang* (☎ 23-294). Don't be deceived by the front of the hotel, which looks rather run down. The rooms are well furnished and arranged around an open air courtyard. Spacious and clean singles/doubles cost Rs 220/330 with air-cooling or Rs 385/495 with air-con; all rooms have an attached bath. There's also a reasonably priced restaurant.

Undoubtedly one of the best hotels in Kota is the *Hotel Brijraj Bhawan Palace* (☎ 45-0529; fax 45-0057), once a palace of the maharaos of Kota and also the former British Residency. Situated on an elevated site overlooking the Chambal River, the hotel was named after the current Maharao of Kota, Brijraj Singh, who converted this serene place into a hotel in 1964. Today the maharao and his family live in one portion of the palace, while the rest is an upmarket hotel replete with the trimmings of India's royal past. There are well maintained gardens, a tennis court and an elegantly furnished lounge filled with pictures of former rulers and various dignitaries. The dining room is equally stylish. Rooms open onto a large verandah and are furnished with antiques, armchairs and a writing table. They cost Rs 750/980, or Rs 1200 for a magnificent suite.

Since there's only one single and six doubles try to make reservations in advance.

The *Hotel Umed Bhawan Palace* (☎ 25-262), in the north of the town, has recently been converted into an upmarket hotel by the Welcomgroup chain. Surrounded by sprawling gardens, this gracious palace is tastefully furnished and has many original pieces. There's a restaurant, bar and plush billiard room. A single room is expected to cost around Rs 1500. Nearby, another new upmarket hotel worth checking out is the *Sukdham* (☎ 28-001). The building is over 100 years old and used to be the home of the British resident's surgeon. Rates are yet to be confirmed.

Places to Eat

Virtually all the cheap restaurants are around the railway station; there are very few around the Hotel Chambal Tourist Bungalow or the bus stand. The best places to eat are in the hotels.

On the footpath outside the GPO, many omelette stalls and other small food places set up in the early evening. This can be a cheap alternative, but if you do eat here remember to avoid a possible tummy upset by selecting food that has been freshly cooked, not reheated.

The *Hotel Phul Plaza* has a good vegetarian restaurant with main dishes for about Rs 35. The similarly priced *Hotel Navrang* offers a wide range of veg and non-veg Indian, Chinese and Continental food.

If you're staying at the *Hotel Brijraj Bhawan Palace*, you'd be mad to eat anywhere else – it's certainly an experience. The intimate royal dining room offers excellent Indian or Continental food at reasonable prices. Unlike most other palaces in Rajasthan, the dining room here is homely rather than grand. Unfortunately, it is not open to non-guests.

Getting There & Away

Air There used to be flights to and from Kota, but these have recently been discontinued. Flights may be rescheduled in the future, so ask a travel agent or at any airport.

Bus There are bus connections to Ajmer (ordinary/deluxe Rs 53/62), Chittorgarh (Rs 54/60), Jaipur (Rs 64/75), Udaipur (Rs 74/85) and other centres in Rajasthan. Buses leave for Bundi every hour, usually on the half hour, from around 6.30 am to 10.30 pm. The fare for the 50 minute journey is Rs 10. If you're heading into Madhya Pradesh, several buses a day go to such places as Gwalior, Ujjain and Indore. None of the timetables at the bus stand are in English.

Train Kota is on the main broad gauge Mumbai (Bombay) to Delhi line via Sawai Madhopur, the gateway to the Ranthambhore National Park, so there are plenty of trains to choose from. For Sawai Madhopur, the 108 km journey takes a bit over two hours at a cost of Rs 29/122 in 2nd/1st class. To Agra Fort it's 343 km at a cost of Rs 77/291 in 2nd/1st class. Trains to Jaipur cost Rs 72/229 in 2nd/1st class. To Delhi it costs Rs 124/404 in 2nd/1st class. There's a broad gauge line linking Kota with Chittorgarh via Bundi. The daily train departs at 7.30 am.

Getting Around

Minibuses link the railway station and bus stand (Rs 1.50). An auto-rickshaw should cost Rs 12 for this journey, although naturally you'll be asked for more. A cheaper alternative is to take a cycle-rickshaw.

AROUND KOTA
Wildlife Sanctuaries

The 250 sq km **Darrah Wildlife Sanctuary** is located about 50 km from Kota. Here there are spotted deer, wild boars, bears, sambars, leopards, panthers and antelopes. The sanctuary is open daily from sunrise to sunset, but is closed during the monsoon (usually from early July to mid-September). You need to get permission to visit the sanctuary from the local forest ranger, or ask at the tourist office in Kota. Entry costs Rs 10 for foreigners, Rs 2 for Indians, plus Rs 50 per jeep. Photography is not allowed. Also accessible from Kota is the **National Chambal Wildlife Sanctuary**, which extends into neighbouring Madhya Pradesh. This 549 sq km reserve is best known for its gharials, which inhabit the Chambal River, but blackbuck, chinkara, wolves and the very rarely seen caracal can also be found here.

About 45 km east of Kota, flanking the main canal of the Chambal and Parvan rivers, are the **Sorsan grasslands**. Covering 35 sq km, these grasslands are rich in insects during the monsoon and attract a good variety of resident and migratory birds, including the great Indian bustard, a reluctant flier which is more commonly seen stalking through the grasslands on its sturdy legs. Other birds of Sorsan include mynas, orioles, quails, partridges, flycatchers, bulbuls, chats, drongos, shrikes, larks, robins and weavers. Flocks of migrants, such as warblers, flycatchers, larks, starlings and rosy pastors, winter at Sorsan between October and March. Indian rollers can be seen in early winter. The nearby canal and lakes attract waterfowl, such as bar-headed and greylag geese, common pochards, common teal and pintails.

Baroli

One of Rajasthan's oldest temple complexes is at Baroli, 56 km from Kota on the way to Pratap Sagar. Set in a peaceful area, many of these 9th century temples were vandalised by Muslim armies but much remains and it warrants a visit. The main temple is the **Ghateshvara Temple**, which features impressive columns and figures of gods and goddesses. Although it is one of the best preserved temples here, some of the figures have been damaged. Many of the sculptures from the temples are displayed in the government museum in Kota. There are hourly buses from Kota.

Bhainsrodgarh

Not far from Baroli is the picturesque Bhainsrodgarh Fort. Perched on a cliff-top overlooking the Chambal River, it is still occupied by descendants of a feudal family. You must get permission to visit the fort – ask at the tourist office in Kota.

JHALAWAR

Situated 87 km south of Kota, at the centre of an opium-producing region, Jhalawar was the capital of a small princely state created in 1838. This town is well off the main tourist circuit, and only attracts a small number of travellers, but there are many historic sites to be seen and ancient relics are continually being discovered. During winter, many of the fields are carpeted with picturesque pink and white poppies.

In the centre of town is the **Jhalawar Fort**, built by Maharaja Madan Singh in 1838. Today it houses the government offices and is run down. There's also the small **Government Museum** which has a collection of 8th century sculptures, gold coins, weapons and old paintings. It's open every day, except Friday, from 10 am to 4.30 pm and entry is free.

The annual **Chandrabhaga Cattle Fair** is held on the banks of the Chandrabhaga River, just outside Jhalrapatan (see the Jhalrapatan section below). The fair takes place in the Hindu lunar month of Kartika (in October/November), when thousands of devotees take a holy dip. It's a colourful event and worth attending if you're in the area: apart from the cattle trading, numerous little shops and food stalls are set up for the festival.

Places to Stay & Eat

Accommodation and restaurants are very limited in Jhalawar. The best places to eat are in the hotels. The RTDC *Hotel Chandrawati* (☎ (07432) 30-015), on Jhalrapatan Rd, has ordinary rooms for Rs 125/150 and deluxe rooms for Rs 225/275, all with attached bath. There's also a small restaurant. The **tourist office** is located in this hotel and is open Monday to Saturday from 10 am to 5 pm. In the same area, the *Hotel Dwarika* (☎ (07432) 2626) has ordinary rooms for Rs 130/150 with attached bath and bucket hot water. Deluxe rooms with constant hot water cost Rs 160/180. Dorm beds are Rs 50 and there's also a vegetarian restaurant.

Not far away, near the clock tower, is the quaint *Purvaj Hotel* (☎ (07432) 30-951), a *haveli* (mansion) once owned by a feudal family. The rooms are basic but cheap and the friendly owner offers off-season discounts. This place has a lot more character than the other hotels. Ordinary singles with attached bath cost Rs 60, plus Rs 40 for an extra bed. Deluxe doubles with views over the town cost Rs 150. Dorm beds are just Rs 30.

Getting There & Away

There are hourly buses from Kota to Jhalawar and the 2½ hour journey costs Rs 25. From Jhalawar, buses travel to most major towns in Rajasthan, including Jaipur, Udaipur, Ajmer, Jodhpur and Alwar.

The nearest railway station to Jhalawar is 25 km away and a taxi to/from the station costs Rs 150.

Getting Around

To travel anywhere in town by auto-rickshaw should cost around Rs 10. If you plan to visit the historic sites out of town, it's best to hire a jeep because the roads are in poor condition. Enquire at your hotel or at the tourist office (both can usually arrange jeep hire).

AROUND JHALAWAR
Jhalrapatan

Seven km south of Jhalawar on the Kota road is Jhalrapatan or the 'city of temple bells'. This walled town once had more than 100 temples, although far fewer remain. The best known is the huge, 10th century **Surya Temple**, which contains magnificent sculptures as well as one of the best preserved idols of Surya (the sun god) in the whole of India.

There's also the 12th century **Shantinath Jain Temple**, a colourful and well maintained temple with intricately carved statues and two huge stone elephants. Just outside Jhalrapatan, the 7th century **Chandrabhaga Temple** is set in quiet gardens on the banks of the Chandrabhaga River. There's also a small *baori* (stepwell) here.

Gagron Fort

While you're in this area, you should also take a look at the impressive Gagron Fort, 10 km from Jhalawar. Very few tourists even suspect its existence and if you like to explore in peace and quiet this place is perfect. Within the fort walls there's a small village and the shrine of the Sufi saint, Mitthesah. From the ramparts there are good views of the surrounding countryside. Though perhaps not as famous as others like Chittorgarh, Jodhpur and Jaisalmer, the huge fort occupies a prominent place in the annals of Rajput chivalry and has been fought over for centuries.

Gagron Fort is open daily from sunrise to sunset and admission is free. There are local buses from Jhalawar every hour. The fort is close to (and visible from) the road between Kota and Ujjain and Indore.

Other Attractions

Jhalawar's other attractions are further out of town and are difficult to reach without transport. About 54 km from Jhalawar at **Dalhanpur** are some temple ruins believed to be hundreds of years old. Located near the Chhapi River, this small collection of ruins includes some carved pillars with erotic figures. Take care not to damage the fragments of pillars and statues that have fallen to the ground. About 11 km from Dalhanpur, at **Kakuni**, are the ruins of an old township. There's also a small 18th century temple with a huge orange idol of Lord Ganesh. Beyond Kakuni is the large **Fort of Manohar Thana**, once of great strategic importance. There are several small temples within its walls and a reforestation programme has filled the compound with vegetation and birdlife.

There are ancient Buddhist caves and stupas on top of a desolate hill near the town of **Kolvi**, about 90 km from Jhalawar. It's a short climb to the top, where you'll find several enormous figures of Buddha. A narrow path winds past large stupas and numerous meditation chambers. These remarkable caves are believed to date back to the 5th century and some contain weathered sculptures of Buddha; unfortunately, they are neglected and slowly deteriorating.

BUNDI

Population: 72,000
Telephone Area Code: 0747

Visiting Bundi is like stepping back in time. Located only 39 km north-west of Kota, it's a picturesque and captivating little town which has more or less retained a mediaeval atmosphere. Bundi is off the beaten track, so there are very few tourists here. In the evening, people throng to the colourful and bustling markets that meander through the town's lanes. There are very few shops that cater exclusively for tourists, and unlike many places in Rajasthan, you won't be tormented by persistent shopkeepers. This is part of Bundi's appeal.

The Rajput legacy is well preserved in the shape of the massive Taragarh Fort, which broods over the town in the narrow valley below, and the huge palace which stands beneath it. In this palace are found the famous Bundi murals – similar to those in the Rao Madho Singh Museum in Kota. Bundi is well known for its school of painting – especially its hunting and palace scenes, which are regarded as some of the finest in the country.

History

Conquered in 1241 by Rao Deva Hara, Bundi was the capital of a major princely state during the heyday of the Rajputs. Kota was part of Bundi, deemed as the land grant of the ruler's eldest son. But in 1624, Kota was made into a separate state at the instigation of the Mughal emperor, Jehangir. Although Bundi's importance dwindled with the rise of Kota during Mughal times, it maintained its independence until its incorporation into the state of Rajasthan after Independence.

Orientation

It's relatively easy to find your way to the palace on foot through the bazaar – once you pass through the city gate, there are only two main roads through town and the palace is visible from many points.

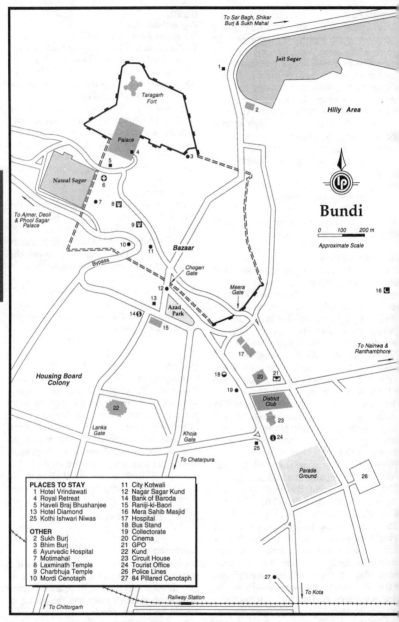

Bundi

0   100   200 m

Approximate Scale

PLACES TO STAY
1 Hotel Vrindawati
4 Royal Retreat
5 Haveli Braj Bhushanjee
13 Hotel Diamond
25 Kothi Ishwari Niwas

OTHER
2 Sukh Burj
3 Bhim Burj
6 Ayurvedic Hospital
7 Motimahal
8 Laxminath Temple
9 Charbhuja Temple
10 Mordi Cenotaph

11 City Kotwali
12 Nagar Sagar Kund
14 Bank of Baroda
15 Raniji-ki-Baori
16 Mera Sahib Masjid
17 Hospital
18 Bus Stand
19 Collectorate
20 Cinema
21 GPO
22 Kund
23 Circuit House
24 Tourist Office
26 Police Lines
27 84 Pillared Cenotaph

nformation

Many people visit Bundi on a day trip from Kota, but it's worth spending a night or two here. There's a small, helpful tourist office (☎ 22-697) in the grounds of the Circuit House. It's open Monday to Saturday from 10 am to 5 pm. Make sure you're carrying enough rupees with you, as it can be difficult to change foreign currency in Bundi.

Taragarh Fort

Also known as the Star Fort, Taragarh was built in 1354. It is reached by a steep road leading up the hillside to an enormous gateway topped by rampant elephants. Inside are huge reservoirs carved out of solid rock and the Bhim Burj, the largest of the battlements, on which is mounted a famous cannon. The views over the town and surrounding countryside are excellent. It's just a pity that the national broadcaster, Doordarshan, decided to build a huge concrete transmission tower right next to the fort – it's a real eyesore.

Palace

The palace itself is reached from the northwestern end of the bazaar, through a huge wooden gateway and up a steep cobbled ramp. Only two parts of the outer perimeter of the palace, known variously as the Chittra Shala and Ummed Mahal, are generally open to the public. Some of the famous Bundi murals can be seen on the upper level. Photography is prohibited.

The rest of the palace, which houses the bulk of the superb Bundi murals, can only be visited with special permission. It was closed to the public, mainly because of a dispute between the current maharaja and his sister. It seems that the maharaja sold all of the family properties (Taragarh Fort, this palace and the Phool Sagar Palace) to the Oberoi hotel chain, but his sister is now claiming her share of the proceeds. Until the dispute is settled (if it is in fact settled), it seems likely the palace will remain closed. What is more, maintenance seems to be nonexistent and the palace is already rapidly deteriorating, which is tragic.

Nawal Sagar

Visible from the fort is the square artificial lake of Nawal Sagar. In the centre is a temple to Varuna, the Aryan god of water.

Baoris

Bundi has a couple of beautiful baoris right in the centre of town. The very impressive **Raniji-ki-Baori** is 46m deep and has some superb carving. It is one of the largest of its kind and was built in 1699 by Rani Nathavatji. The **Nagar Sagar Kund** is a pair of matching stepwells just outside the Chogan Gate to the old city, right in the centre of the town.

Other Attractions

Bundi's other attractions are all out of town and are difficult to reach without transport. The modern palace, known as the **Phool Sagar Palace**, has a charming artificial tank and gardens, and is several km out of town on the Ajmer road. It is closed to the public but you can glimpse it over the brick wall.

There's another palace, the smaller **Sukh Mahal**, closer to town on the edge of Jait Sagar, where Rudyard Kipling once stayed. It's now the Irrigation Rest House. The nearby, rather neglected **Sar Bagh** has a collection of royal cenotaphs, some with beautifully carved statues. **Shikar Burj** is a small hunting lodge and picnic spot on the road which runs along the north side of Jait Sagar.

There are paddle boats for hire from the jetty at Jait Sagar. They cost Rs 40 for 30 minutes.

South of town is the magnificent 84 Pillared Cenotaph. It's set among well maintained gardens, and this architecturally impressive monument is definitely worth visiting.

Places to Stay & Eat

Bundi has only a few good hotels and restaurants. Many auto-rickshaw drivers will try to bully you into staying at a hotel of their choice (usually not the best place) where they get commission.

Bundi has recently started the Paying Guest Scheme which offers accommodation with a local family for Rs 50 to Rs 350. Contact the tourist office for details.

There is really only one hotel worth staying at in Bundi, and that is the homely *Haveli Braj Bhushanjee* (☎ 32-322; fax 32-142), just below the palace. It's part of the Bundi Cafe Crafts shop, and is run by the very friendly and helpful Braj Bhushanjee family. The shop and rooms are housed in the family's 150 year old haveli, and the views from the rooftop terrace are excellent, especially at night when the palace is illuminated. The haveli is decorated with pictures of former rulers, paintings and colourful village crafts. Clean rooms with attached bath start at Rs 200/300, or Rs 350 for a deluxe double; super deluxe doubles cost Rs 950. In the cheaper rooms hot water comes by the bucket. There's a good, though expensive, vegetarian restaurant. If you arrive after hours, when the shop is closed, just ring the doorbell. This place is popular with travellers, so it's a good idea to make bookings ahead. In the same area is the new *Royal Retreat* situated in the palace compound. It's a small, comfortable place, but the rooms are expensive at Rs 475/575 with attached bath. There's also a vegetarian restaurant.

In the noisy and bustling bazaar area there are several basic but cheap hotels. The *Hotel Diamond* (☎ 22-656) has rather grubby singles/doubles for Rs 50/100 with attached bath and hot water by the bucket. Deluxe doubles with constant hot water, softer mattresses and a balcony cost Rs 150. The restaurant is OK; main dishes are around Rs 25 (veg only).

Opposite the tourist office is the run-down *Kothi Ishwari Niwas* (☎ 32-414). Although it has royal associations it lacks character and is poorly maintained. Singles/doubles with private bath cost Rs 150/250 or Rs 400 for a deluxe room. The only other option is the two room RTDC *Hotel Vrindawati* (☎ 32-473) out by Jait Sagar. Rooms cost Rs 200/275. Meals are available.

Things to Buy
The Bundi Cafe Crafts shop, at the Haveli Braj Bhushanjee, has a good and interesting range of local souvenirs, including miniatures, jewellery and scarves. And just so you know what you're missing, ask to see their photos of the Bundi murals which were taken inside the closed part of the palace.

Although there is nothing really special to buy in town, it's worthwhile taking a stroll through the interesting little markets, just to get a taste of local life.

Getting There & Away
It takes about five hours by bus from Ajmer to Bundi (Rs 53). From Kota, it's only 50 minutes to Bundi (Rs 10). Buses also go from Bundi to Jaipur, Sawai Madhopur and Udaipur. For Chittorgarh, the morning train is much faster than the bus.

Getting Around
The bus stand is at the Kota (south-east) end of town. Auto-rickshaws are also available and can be hired for Rs 10 from outside the bus stand. Bikes can be rented near the City Kotwali for Rs 8 per day.

CHITTORGARH (Chittor)
Population: 79,000
Telephone Area Code: 01472
The massive hilltop fort of Chittorgarh is one of the most historically significant in Rajasthan and epitomises the whole romantic doomed ideal of Rajput chivalry. Three times in its long history, Chittor was sacked by a stronger enemy and, on each occasion, the end came in textbook Rajput fashion: jauhar was declared in the face of impossible odds. The men donned the saffron robes of martyrdom and rode out from the fort to certain death, while the women immolated themselves on a huge funeral pyre. Honour was always more important than death and Chittor still holds a special place in the hearts of many Rajputs.

The only real reason to come to Chittor is to see the fort – the town itself is quite crowded and does not really have anything of much interest. In and around Chittorgarh today there are an increasing number of industries, some of which can be seen from the fort. Hopefully the pollution that usually comes with industrial growth will not affect this fort, as it has some other historic monuments in Rajasthan.

Despite the rugged fort's impressive location and colourful history, Chittor is well and truly off the main tourist circuit and sees surprisingly few visitors. Many people go to Chittor on a day trip from Udaipur. It's well worth the detour.

History

Chittor's first defeat occurred in 1303 when Ala-ud-din Khilji, the Pathan King of Delhi, besieged the fort in order to capture the beautiful Padmini, wife of the Rana's uncle, Bhim Singh. When defeat was inevitable the Rajput noblewomen, including Padmini, committed jauhar and Bhim Singh led the orange-clad noblemen out to their deaths.

In 1535 Bahadur Shah, the Sultan of Gujarat, besieged the fort and, once again, the mediaeval dictates of chivalry determined the outcome. This time, the carnage was immense. It is said that 13,000 Rajput women and 32,000 Rajput warriors died following the declaration of jauhar.

The final sack of Chittor came just 33 years later, in 1568, when the Mughal emperor, Akbar, took the town. The fort was defended heroically, but once again the odds were overwhelming; the women performed jauhar, the fort gates were flung open and 8000 orange-robed warriors rode out to their deaths. On this occasion, Maharana Udai Singh II fled Chittor for Udaipur, where he re-established his capital. In 1616, Jehangir returned Chittor to the Rajputs but there was no attempt at resettlement.

Orientation & Information

The fort stands on a 280 hectare site on top of a 180m high hill which rises abruptly from the surrounding plain. Until 1568 the town of Chittor was also on the hilltop, within the fort walls, but today's modern town, known as the Lower Town, sprawls to the west of the hill. A river separates it from the bus stand, railway line and the rest of the town.

The Tourist Reception Centre (☎ 41-089) is near the railway station and has a good range of literature. It's open Monday to Saturday from 10 am to 5 pm.

Fort

According to legend, Bhim, one of the Pandava heroes of the *Mahabharata*, is credited with the fort's original construction. All of Chittor's attractions are within the fort. A zigzag ascent of over one km leads through seven gateways to the main gate on the western side, the **Rampol** ('pol' means gate).

On the climb, you pass two **chhatris**, memorials marking spots where Jaimal and Kalla, heroes of the 1568 siege, fell during the struggle against Akbar. The main gate on the eastern side of the fort is the **Surajpol**. Within the fort, a circular road runs around the ruins and there's a **deer park** at the southern end.

There are good views over the town, countryside and the huge cement factory from the western end of the fort; there's even a small village located here.

Today, the fort of Chittor is a virtually deserted ruin, but impressive reminders of its grandeur still stand. The main sites can all be seen in half a day (assuming you're not walking) but, if you like the atmosphere of ancient sites, then it's worth spending longer as this is a very mellow place and there are no hassles whatsoever.

Entry to the fort is free. English-speaking guides are usually available inside the fort at the Rana Kumbha Palace (see below) and charge Rs 200 for one to four people. Make sure you get a government approved guide (they carry a guide licence).

Rana Kumbha Palace Entering the fort and turning right, you come almost immediately to the ruins of this 15th century palace. It contains elephant and horse stables and a Shiva temple. One of the jauhars is said to have taken place in a vaulted cellar. Across from the palace is the **archaeological office** and **museum**, and the **treasury building** or Nau Lakha Bhandar. Close by is the **Singa Chowri Temple**.

Fateh Prakash Palace Just beyond the Rana Kumbha Palace, this palace is much more modern (Maharana Fateh Singh died in 1930). It houses a small and poorly lit

SOUTHERN RAJASTHAN

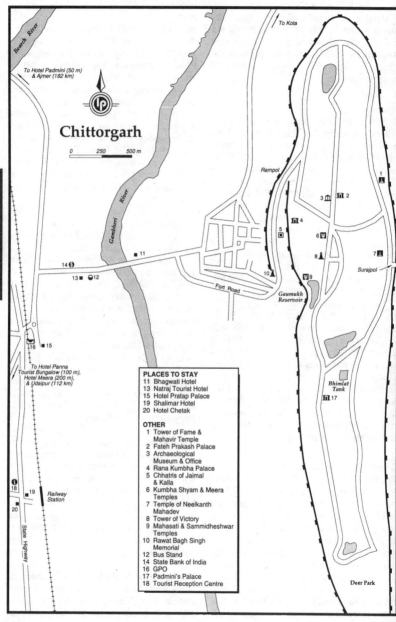

Chittorgarh

0   250   500 m

To Hotel Padmini (50 m)
& Ajmer (182 km)

Beach River

Gambheri River

To Kota

Rampol

Surajpol

Fort Road

Gaumukh Reservoir

Bhimlat Tank

Deer Park

To Hotel Panna
Tourist Bungalow (100 m),
Hotel Meera (200 m),
& Udaipur (112 km)

Railway Station

State Highway

SOUTHERN RAJASTHAN

PLACES TO STAY
11 Bhagwati Hotel
13 Natraj Tourist Hotel
15 Hotel Pratap Palace
19 Shalimar Hotel
20 Hotel Chetak

OTHER
1 Tower of Fame &
   Mahavir Temple
2 Fateh Prakash Palace
3 Archaeological
   Museum & Office
4 Rana Kumbha Palace
5 Chhatris of Jaimal
   & Kalla
6 Kumbha Shyam & Meera
   Temples
7 Temple of Neelkanth
   Mahadev
8 Tower of Victory
9 Mahasati & Sammidheshwar
   Temples
10 Rawat Bagh Singh
   Memorial
12 Bus Stand
14 State Bank of India
16 GPO
17 Padmini's Palace
18 Tourist Reception Centre

museum, and the rest of the building is closed. The museum is open daily except Friday from 10 am to 4 pm. Entry costs Rs 2.

Tower of Victory The Jaya Stambh, or Tower of Victory, was erected by Rana Kumbha between 1458 and 1468 to commemorate his victory over Mahmud Khilji of Malwa in 1440. It rises 37m in nine storeys and you can climb the narrow stairs to the eighth storey. Entry is Rs 0.50; free on Friday. Watch your head on the lintels! Hindu sculptures adorn the outside of the tower, but the dome was damaged by lightning and repaired during the last century.

Close to the tower is the **Mahasati**, an area where the ranas were cremated during Chittorgarh's period as the Mewar capital. There are many *sati* stones (stones to commemorate women who committed sati, by throwing themselves on their husbands' funeral pyres) here. The **Sammidheshwar Temple** stands in the same area.

Gaumukh Reservoir Walk down beyond the temple and, at the very edge of the cliff, you'll see this deep tank. The reservoir takes its name from a spring which feeds the tank from a cow's mouth carved in the cliff-side. The opening here leads to the cave in which Padmini and her compatriots are said to have committed jauhar.

Padmini's Palace Continuing south, you come to Padmini's Palace, built beside a large lotus pool with a pavilion in its centre. Legend relates that, as Padmini sat in this pavilion, Ala-ud-din was permitted to see her reflection in a mirror in the palace. This glimpse was the spark that convinced him to destroy Chittor in order to possess her.

The bronze gates in this pavilion were carried off by Akbar and can now be seen in the fort at Agra. Near Padmini's Palace is a small prison where captured invaders were kept and a sultan of Malwa and a sultan of Gujarat were once locked up. Not far away are the former military training grounds for Rajput soldiers, today used as a helipad for visiting dignitaries. Continuing round the circular road, you pass the deer park, the **Bhimlat Tank**, the **Adhbudhnath Shiva Temple**, the **Surajpol** and the **Neelkanth Mahadev Jain Temple** before reaching the Tower of Fame.

Tower of Fame Chittor's other famous tower, the Kirti Stambha, or Tower of Fame, is older (probably built around the 12th century) and smaller (22m high) than the Tower of Victory. Built by a Jain merchant, it is dedicated to Adinath, the first Jain *tirthankar* (prophet), and is decorated with naked figures of the various tirthankars, thus indicating that it is a Digambara, or 'sky clad', monument. A narrow stairway leads through the seven storeys to the top.

Other Buildings Close to the Fateh Prakash Palace is the **Meera Temple**, built during the reign of Rana Kumbha in the ornate Indo-Aryan style and associated with the mystic-poetess Meerabai. The larger temple in this same compound is the 15th century **Kumbha Shyam Temple**, or Temple of Varah.

Across from Padmini's Palace is the **Kalika Mata Temple**, an 8th century temple originally dedicated to Surya, but later converted to a temple to the goddess Kali. At the northern tip of the fort is another gate, the **Lokhota Bari**, while at the southern end is a small opening from which criminals and traitors were hurled into the abyss.

Places to Stay & Eat
Accommodation possibilities in Chittor are limited. At the railway station, *retiring rooms* cost Rs 55 for an ordinary double or Rs 170 for an air-con room.

There are several other places around the station. The *Shalimar Hotel* (☎ 40-842) has singles/doubles for Rs 60/80 with common bath, Rs 80/100 with bath attached. Deluxe air-cooled singles/doubles cost Rs 150/175. All rooms have hot water by the bucket. The nearby *Hotel Chetak* (☎ 41-588) is better, with rooms from Rs 150/225 – hot water in the mornings only. Deluxe rooms cost Rs 200/275 or Rs 250/350 with air-con and colour TV. There's a restaurant serving Indian, South

Indian and Chinese food. A vegetarian thali costs Rs 32.

By the bus stand there's the very basic *Natraj Tourist Hotel*. Small, dark rooms with common bath cost Rs 30/50, Rs 60/90 with bath; but you'll probably have to get them to change the sheets. Just over the river is the *Bhagwati Hotel* (☎ 42-275), where basic and noisy rooms with common bath cost Rs 40/50, Rs 50/70 with attached bath and bucket hot water. Deluxe air-cooled rooms with constant hot water cost Rs 150. There are also dorm beds for just Rs 20.

Closer to the town centre (ie further away from the fort) is the RTDC *Hotel Panna Tourist Bungalow* (☎ 41-238). Unlike many other RTDC hotels, this place is surprisingly well kept. Singles/doubles with cold water in the attached bathrooms are Rs 100/150, better rooms with constant hot water are Rs 200/275 and air-con rooms cost Rs 400/500. Dorm beds are available for Rs 50. The hotel has a bar and good meals are available in the restaurant. A whole roast chicken costs Rs 100, and there are set meals for Rs 67 (veg) and Rs 83 (non-veg). In the same area is the *Hotel Meera* (☎ 40-266), a modern building with comfortable rooms. Ordinary singles/doubles with private bath and bucket hot water cost Rs 120/170 or Rs 250/300 with constant hot water. Deluxe rooms with air-con and colour TV cost Rs 425/500. Dorm beds are Rs 60. There's also a bar and reasonably priced restaurant here.

A good place to stay is the *Hotel Pratap Palace* (☎ 40-099; fax 41-042), between the bus stand and the Hotel Panna Tourist Bungalow. Clean air-cooled rooms with attached bath cost Rs 330/380 or Rs 430/480 with air-con. There's a small bar and very good restaurant near a pleasant garden. A tasty half tandoori chicken costs Rs 60; set meals are Rs 130.

A little out of town near the Bearch River is the overpriced *Hotel Padmini* (☎ 41-718) with rooms at Rs 600/700. The vegetarian restaurant has main dishes for around Rs 25.

Getting There & Away

Chittor is on the main bus and rail routes. By road, it's 182 km from Ajmer, 158 km from Bundi and 112 km from Udaipur. There are frequent connections to these places, and all the Kota buses (ordinary Rs 54, deluxe Rs 60, 4½ hours) go via Bundi.

It's possible to take an early bus from Udaipur to Chittorgarh (Rs 30, three hours) spend about three hours visiting the fort (by auto-rickshaw or tonga), and then take a late afternoon bus to Ajmer, but this is definitely pushing it.

Chittorgarh also has rail links with Ahmedabad, Udaipur, Ajmer, Jaipur and Delhi. The broad gauge line to Kota and Bundi would be convenient, except that the only passenger train on this route leaves Chittor at 2.50 pm reaching Bundi at 6 pm and Kota at 7.15 pm.

Getting Around

It's six km from the railway station to the fort, less from the bus stand, and seven km around the fort itself, not including the long southern loop out to the deer park. Auto-rickshaws charge around Rs 80 from either the bus or railway station, and this includes waiting time at the various sites. Bicycles can also be rented near the railway station (Rs 2 per hour or Rs 15 per day) to visit the fort but, as Indian bicycles rarely have gears, you'll have to push the machine to the top. Still, they're great on the top and for the journey back down.

AROUND CHITTORGARH
Bijaipur

The 16th century palace in this village, 40 km south of Chittor, is now a delightful hotel, the *Castle Bijaipur*. Singles/doubles in this peaceful palace cost Rs 800/850, all rooms with private bath. There's a pleasant garden courtyard and an airy restaurant serving Rajasthani food – the set dinner is Rs 175.

There are some good walks in the quiet countryside around the castle. The friendly owners can arrange horse and jeep safaris to places of interest around Bijaipur, such as the nearby Bhil tribal village. Or you can see local craftspeople at work in **Bassi** village, 12 km from Bijaipur – they specialise in wooden handicrafts. Tribal folk singing and

TRADITIONAL DRESS

Although it is not unusual these days to see Rajasthani women in saris, the traditional dress consists of a full, often brightly coloured, ankle-length skirt known as a *lehanga* or *ghaghara*, which is worn with a short blouse called a *choli* or *kanchali*. A looser blouse called a *kurti* or *angarkhi* is worn over the choli. As well, a head scarf *(odhni)* of a bold, vibrant fabric, either plain or patterned, and often with a fancy border in silver thread is worn. Sometimes odhnis are also adorned with mirrorwork, beads and shells. If the woman is a widow, the odhni is not brightly coloured. The leather shoes worn by men and women are called *jootis* or *mojdis*. Women's jootis have no heel.

For special occasions such as weddings and festivals, women decorate their palms, feet and fingers with intricate henna designs known as *mehndi*. The lehanga, traditionally worn by a bride, is generally a Sanganeri or Jaipur printed fabric, and the odhni is always red.

SANJAY SINGH BADNOR

SANJAY SINGH BADNOR

SARA-JANE CLELAND

Top Left: A woman of the Garasia tribe, Mt Abu.

Top Right: A Rajput groom with traditional sword stands along-side his veiled bride at Deogarh.

Bottom: Tribal women, Pushkar Camel Fair.

SANJAY SINGH BADNOR

SANJAY SINGH BANDOR

Left: A tailor near the Jagdish Temple in Udaipur.

Right: The Indian man's prêt-à-porter – the dhoti.

Everyday wear for men consists of a long shirt with either a short upright collar or no collar, which is known as a *kurta*. It is worn over a *dhoti*, which is simply a long piece of material drawn up between the legs. Today Rajasthani men have adopted the Jodhpuri, a buttoned coat which is the official judicial dress of Rajasthan's courts. Men's jootis curl up at the toes. The turban (see Rajasthani Turbans following) is worn by men of most classes. It can be either plain or vividly coloured, and is tied in various ways according to the class of the wearer. Men also take pride in their moustaches. Rajputs are renowned for their long, bushy moustaches, which are supposed to suggest chivalry. As with turbans, the way the moustache is worn varies from region to region.

Bridegrooms traditionally carry a sword which is known as a *dalwar*

JEWELLERY

Rajasthani women, most notably in the villages, bedeck themselves in heavy and ornate jewellery, generally of silver, the lavishness and extent of which symbolises the relative affluence of their husbands. Even the poorest families ensure that their daughters are married appropriately adorned in silver ornaments, which form part of their dowries.

The ornament which is worn by women on their forehead is known as a *bor*, *tikka* or *rakhadi*. Ear ornaments have various names, such as *jhela, bhujali*, or *bali*. Not just worn for decorative purposes, the manipulation of an earring is believed to restore equilibrium to internal organs. Nose pins and rings are known as *nathdis*, *laonghs* and *bhanvatiyas*, and are sometimes connected to earrings by silver chains.

Necklaces are known as *timania* and *galsadi*, among other names. They may be just a simple thread upon which a small token is hung, a beautiful and elaborate locket, or a heavy and chunky neckpiece of silver.

Bangles, which cover the entire arm, increasing in diameter from the wrist to just below the shoulder, are called *chudas*. Today, poorer women may wear chudas of plastic, while their richer sisters adorn their arms with ivory chudas. A chuda may also consist of a single ornament, often of silver, which covers the entire upper arm. Toe rings, known as *bichiyas*, are only worn by married women. The silver anklets worn by women are called *payal*. Silver ornaments worn on the back of the hand, and connected to four rings, one on each finger, are known as *hathphool*, from *phool*, meaning flower, and *hath*, for hand – literally, hand flower.

Left: The bor, or forehead ornament, is commonly worn by Rajasthani women.

Right: Jewellery, such as nose rings, necklaces and bangles, are part of the Rajasthani village woman's everyday attire.

MICHELLE COXALL

MICHELLE COXALL

RAJASTHANI TURBANS

The turbans of Rajasthan are perhaps the most colourful and impressive in the whole of India. Known as a *safa*, *paag* or *pagri*, the turban is a prominent and important part of a Rajput man's dress. In the past, the turban was worn in battle to protect the head against weapons such as swords and axes. A saffron-coloured turban signified chivalry, and was thus often worn by warriors. The exchange of turbans symbolises a bond of friendship and honour. There are a number of instances of wives burning themselves to death along with their husband's turban, the husband having fallen on a battlefield far from home. A male heir will don his deceased father's turban, a symbol of his assumption of duties as the head of the household.

An average turban is about nine metres long, but it can be much longer – up to 20m! It is possible to identify which part of Rajasthan a man comes from and his social class according to the way his turban is tied. Safa-style turbans are favoured by Rajputs, while businessmen prefer the pagri style. Today, not only is it traditional to wear a turban, but it also serves as protection from the harsh desert sun.

The versatile turban has a wide variety of other practical uses. It can be used as a pillow or sheet at night, a rope to draw water from a well or as protective headgear in case the wearer falls over or is hit on the head!

Today many young men, particularly those in the larger cities such as Jaipur and Jodhpur, are rejecting the turban as a symbol of rural parochialism, although the turban is always worn by the groom at a marriage celebration.

Left: Porter, Jaipur railway station.

Right: Turban tying is a time-honoured art, as shown by this man in Salawas village, near Jodhpur.

MICHELLE COXALL

MICHELLE COXALL

dancing can also be organised at the castle with advance notice. Bookings for this hotel should be made through the Hotel Pratap Palace (☎ (01472) 40-099; fax 41-042) in Chittorgarh. Frequent buses travel daily to Bijaipur from Chittorgarh for Rs 10.

Menal & Bijolia

Lying on the Bundi to Chittorgarh road, 48 km from Bundi, Menal is a complex of Shiva temples built in the Gupta period. After a good monsoon, there's a waterfall in this area that is also a big attraction.

Bijolia, 16 km from Menal, was once a group of 100 temples. Most of these were destroyed by Mughal invaders and today only three are left standing, one of which has a huge figure of Ganesh.

Mandalgarh

A detour between Menal and Bijolia takes you to Mandalgarh. It is the third fort of Mewar built by Rana Kumbha – the others are the great fort of Chittorgarh and the fort at Kumbhalgarh.

Nagri

One of the oldest towns in Rajasthan, Nagri is 17 km north of Chittor. Hindu and Buddhist remains from the Mauryan to the Gupta periods have been found here. Many old copper coins and sculptures discovered in Nagri are now at museums in Chittorgarh and Udaipur.

Jagat

At this small town, 20 km south of the road between Udaipur and Chittorgarh, is a small 10th century **Durga Temple**. There are some fine carvings, including a couple of small erotic carvings which have inspired some people to call the town the 'Khajuraho of Rajasthan'. (This is total nonsense.)

UDAIPUR
Population: 342,500
Telephone Area Code: 0294

Possibly no city in Rajasthan is quite as romantic as Udaipur, even though the state is replete with fantastic hilltop forts, grandi-

ose palaces and gripping legends of chivalry and heroism. The French Impressionist painters, let alone the Brothers Grimm, would have loved this place and it's not without justification that Udaipur has been called the 'Venice of the East'. Indeed, with its bewitching palaces surrounded by tranquil lakes and rolling hills, Udaipur looks as though it has been lifted straight from the pages of a fairy tale book.

No trip to Rajasthan is complete without a visit to Udaipur. This 'oasis' in the desert has become a jewel of India's tourism industry and thousands of people flock here each year. Consequently, Udaipur has no dearth of hotels – there are places to suit all tastes and pockets, from simple guest houses to incredible palaces. And this town would have to have more rooftop restaurants than any other place in India. They're the perfect place to sit back, relax and take in the picturesque views.

Udaipur is the kind of place that people keep coming back to. Getting married in Udaipur is a new phenomenon that's really taken off with foreigners – many have even travelled thousands of miles to come back here and tie the knot! And what could be more romantic than pledging your vows of eternal love at a royal palace in the middle of a lake?

Udaipur rivals any of the world-famous creations of the Mughals with superbly crafted elegance and the Rajput love of the whimsical. The Lake Palace is certainly the best late example of this cultural explosion, but Udaipur is full of palaces, temples and havelis ranging from the modest to the extravagant. And, since water is relatively plentiful in this part of the state (in between the periodic droughts), there are plenty of parks and gardens, many of which line the lake shores.

Udaipur is proud of its heritage as a centre for crafts and the performing arts, and its school of miniature painting is noteworthy. These paintings were produced for the maharanas of Udaipur from the early 18th to the mid-20th centuries and many superb examples can be seen at the City Palace Museum.

SOUTHERN RAJASTHAN

Until recently the higher, uninhabited parts of the city were covered in forests; as elsewhere in India, most of these have inevitably been turned into firewood, but there is a movement afoot to reverse this process. The city was once surrounded by a wall and, although the gates and much of the wall over the higher crags remain, a great deal of it has disappeared. It's sad that this fate should have befallen such a historic place, but its essence remains.

In common with all Indian cities, Udaipur's urban and industrial sprawl goes beyond the city's original boundaries and pollution of various kinds can be discouraging. This will be your first impression of Udaipur if you arrive at the railway or bus stations. Ignore it and head for the old city, where a different world is waiting for you.

History

Udaipur was founded in 1568 by Maharana Udai Singh II following the final sacking of Chittorgarh by the Mughal emperor, Akbar. According to legend, Udai Singh II found the site of his new capital some years before the last assault on Chittor, after coming across a holy man meditating on a hill near Lake Pichola. The old man advised the maharana to establish his capital on that very spot and that's how Udaipur came into existence. Surrounded by forests, lakes and the protective Aravalli Range, the new capital of Mewar was certainly in a less vulnerable location than Chittor.

Maharana Udai Singh II died in 1572 and was succeeded by his son, Pratap, who bravely defended Udaipur from subsequent Mughal attacks, and gallantly fought at the battle of Haldighati in 1576 (see the North of Udaipur section). Unlike many other rulers in Rajasthan, the rulers of Mewar refused to be controlled by foreign invaders, even though they were constantly attacked. After struggling against the Mughals, Udaipur was later attacked by the Marathas.

An end to bloody battles and instability came with British intervention in the early 19th century, when a treaty was signed which pledged to protect Udaipur from invaders.

This umbrella of protection ended when India gained independence from the British. Along with all the other princely states, Udaipur surrendered its sovereignty and became part of a united India.

Orientation

The old city, bounded by the remains of a city wall, is on the east side of Lake Pichola. The railway station and bus stand are both just outside the city wall to the south-east.

Information

Tourist Office The Tourist Reception Centre (☎ 41-1535) is located in the Fateh Memorial Building near Surajpol, less than a km from the bus stand. The office is open Monday to Saturday from 10 am to 1.30 pm and 2 to 5 pm. There are also smaller tourist information counters at the railway station and airport.

Post & Communications The GPO is directly north of the old city, at Chetak Circle but poste restante is at the post office at the junction of Hospital Rd and the road north from Delhi Gate, close to the Hotel Kajri Tourist Bungalow.

Lake Pichola

The beautiful Lake Pichola was enlarged by Maharana Udai Singh II after he founded the city. He built a masonry dam, known as the Badipol, and the lake is now four km long and three km wide. Nevertheless, it remains fairly shallow and can actually dry up in severe droughts. At these times, you can walk to the island palaces from the shore. Fortunately, this doesn't happen often. A handful of crocodiles are believed to live in the more remote parts of the lake near uninhabited sections of the shore.

The City Palace extends a considerable distance along the east bank. South of the palace, a pleasant garden runs down to the shore. North of the palace, you can wander along to some interesting bathing and *dhobi* (laundry) ghats.

Out in the lake are two islands – Jagniwas and Jagmandir. Boat rides, which leave reg ularly from the City Palace jetty (known as Bansi Ghat), are enjoyable and cost Rs 45 for 30 minutes, Rs 90 for an hour. The popular sunset cruise is Rs 110.

Jagniwas Island (Lake Palace Hotel) Jagniwas, the Lake Palace island, is about 1.5 hectares in size. The palace was built by Maharana Jagat Singh II in 1754 and covers the whole island. Once the royal summer palace, it was converted into a hotel in the 1960s by Maharana Bhagwat Singh. It is the ultimate in luxury hotels, with courtyards, fountains, gardens, restaurants and even a swimming pool. The gleaming white Lake Palace Hotel was largely responsible for putting Udaipur on the international tourist map. Its unparalleled location, majestic interior, deluxe service and exquisite architecture have placed it among the top hotels in the world today.

It's a magical place but casual visitors are discouraged. It used to be possible to visit the palace for afternoon tea, but now non-guests can only come over for lunch or dinner – and then only if the hotel is not full, which it often is. Hotel launches cross to the island from the City Palace jetty. The Lake Palace and two other palaces in Udaipur, the Shiv Niwas Palace and the Monsoon Palace, appeared in the James Bond film *Octopussy*.

Behind Jagniwas is a much smaller island called **Arsi Vilas**. It was built by a former maharana of Udaipur to watch the sunset. There's a landing attached to this island, which is occasionally used as a helipad.

Jagmandir Island The other island palace, Jagmandir, was commenced by Maharana Karan Singh, but takes its name from Maharana Jagat Singh (1628-52), who made a number of additions to it. It is said that the Mughal emperor, Shah Jahan, derived some of his ideas and inspiration for the Taj Mahal from this palace after staying here in 1623-4 while leading a revolt against his father, Jehangir. The island has some beautiful stone carvings, including a row of huge elephants that look as though they are guarding the island. An intricately carved chhatri made of grey-blue stone is also impressive. There are trees, flowers and courtyards on this ancient island palace, which has recently served as the venue for several moonlight piano concerts and other special events, including weddings. The view across the lake from the southern end, with the city and its great palace rising up behind the island palaces, is a scene of rare beauty.

City Palace & Museums
The huge City Palace, towering over the lake, is the largest palace complex in Rajasthan. Actually a conglomeration of buildings added by various maharanas, the palace manages to retain a surprising uniformity of design. Building was started by Maharana Udai Singh II. The palace is surmounted by balconies, towers and cupolas and there are wonderful views over the lake and the city from the upper terraces.

The palace is entered from the northern end through the Baripol of 1600 and the Tripolia Gate of 1725, with its eight carved marble arches. It was once a custom for maharanas to be weighed under the gate and their weight in gold or silver distributed to the populace.

The main part of the palace is now preserved as a museum with a large and varied collection. The museum includes the **Mor Chowk** with its beautiful mosaics of peacocks, the favourite Rajasthani bird. The **Manak** (or Ruby) **Mahal** has glass and porcelain figures while **Krishna Vilas** has a remarkable collection of miniatures. In the **Bari Mahal** there is a fine central garden. More paintings can be seen in the **Zenana Mahal**. The **Moti Mahal** has beautiful mirrorwork and the **Chini Mahal** is covered in ornamental tiles.

Enter the **City Palace Museum** through the Ganesh Deori, which leads to the Rai Angam, or Royal Courtyard. The museum is open from 9.30 am to 4.30 pm and entry is Rs 15, plus Rs 30 for a camera. A guide (Rs 45) is worthwhile. There's a Rajasthani art school in the museum complex where you can see live demonstrations of miniature painting. There's also a **government museum**

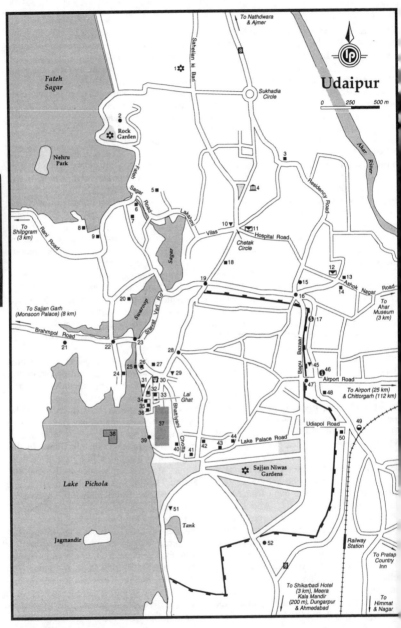

SOUTHERN RAJASTHAN

Udaipur

0   250   500 m

Fateh Sagar

To Nathdwara & Ajmer

Sukhadia Circle

1

8

2

Rock Garden

Nehru Park

3

Fateh Sagar Road

5

4

Residency Road

6

7

Lakshmi Vilas

10

11

Chetak Circle

Hospital Road

8

9

Sagar

To Shilpgram (3 km)

Rani Road

18

12

13

14

Ashok Nagar Road

19

15

To Sajjan Garh (Monsoon Palace) (8 km)

20

Swaroop

Silawat Vari Rd

16

17

Bapu Bazaar

To Ahar Museum (3 km)

Brahmpol Road

21

22

23

28

26 27

29

45

46

Airport Road

To Airport (25 km) & Chittorgarh (112 km)

24

25

31

34
35
36

32

30

33

Lal Ghat

Bhattiyani Chotta

47

48

37

49

38

39

40

41 42 43

44

Lake Palace Road

Udaipol Road

50

Lake Pichola

Sajjan Niwas Gardens

51

Jagmandir

Tank

52

Railway Station

To Pratap Country Inn

To Shikarbadi Hotel (3 km), Meera Kala Mandir (200 m), Dungarpur & Ahmedabad

To Himmat & Nagar

Ahar River

(Rs 2) within the palace complex which exhibits a collection of sculptures and paintings, plus a stuffed kangaroo that's coming apart at the legs, a fierce-looking stuffed monkey holding a small lamp, and a Siamese-twin deer. The large rectangular courtyard outside the City Palace Museum has some shops selling expensive handicrafts, a small cafe selling soft drinks and snacks and several places where you can pick up film for your camera.

The other part of the palace is up against the lake shore and, like the Lake Palace, has been converted into two luxury hotels known as the Shiv Niwas Palace and the Fateh Prakash Palace hotels.

Jagdish Temple

Located only 150m north of the entrance to the City Palace, this fine Indo-Aryan temple was built by Maharana Jagat Singh in 1651 and enshrines a black stone image of Vishnu as Jagannath, Lord of the Universe. There is a brass image of the Garuda in a shrine in front of the temple and the steps up to the temple are flanked by elephants.

Fateh Sagar

North of Lake Pichola, this lake is over-looked by a number of hills and parks. It was originally built in 1678 by Maharana Jai Singh, but reconstructed by Maharana Fateh Singh after heavy rains destroyed the dam. A pleasant drive winds along the east bank and in the middle is Nehru Park, a popular garden island with a boat-shaped cafe. You can get there by boat from near the bottom of Moti Magri for Rs 3. Pedal boats (Rs 40 for 30 minutes) are also available.

Pratap Samak

Atop the Moti Magri, or Pearl Hill, overlooking Fateh Sagar, is a **statue** of the Rajput hero Maharana Pratap, who frequently defied the Mughals. The path to the top traverses elegant **gardens**, including a Japanese rock garden. The park is open from 9 am to 6 pm and admission is Rs 5.

SOUTHERN RAJASTHAN

PLACES TO STAY
3 Mewar Inn
5 Laxmi Vilas Palace Hotel & Hotel Anand Bhawan
6 Gulab Niwas
7 Hotel Hilltop Palace
8 Hotel Lakend
9 Hotel Ram Pratap Palace
13 Hotel Kajri Tourist Bungalow
14 Prince, Alka & Ashok Hotels
18 Ajanta Hotel
20 Hotel Natural
24 Lake Pichola & Lake Shore Hotels
25 Jheel Guest House
26 Hotel Gangaur Palace
27 Hotel Badi Haveli, Anjani Hotel & Lehar Guest House
31 Hotel Caravanserai, Lalghat & Evergreen Guest Houses & Restaurant Natural View
32 Lake Ghat & Ratan Palace Guest Houses
33 Centre View & Shri Karni Guest Houses
34 Jagat Niwas Palace Hotel & Rainbow Guest House
35 Hotel Sai-Niwas & Shiva Guest House
36 Lake Corner Soni Paying Guest House
38 Jagniwas (Lake Palace Hotel)
40 Hotel Raj Palace
41 Rang Niwas Palace Hotel
42 Ranjit Niwas Hotel
43 Hotel Mahendra Prakash
44 Haveli Hotel
48 Hotel Apsara
50 Hotel Welcome

PLACES TO EAT
10 Berry's Restaurant
29 Mayur Cafe
45 Park View
51 Cafe Hill Park

OTHER
1 Saheliyon ki Bari
2 Moti Magri
4 Bhartiya Lok Kala Museum
11 GPO
12 Poste Restante
15 Indian Airlines
16 Delhi Gate
17 Bank of Baroda
19 Hathi Gate
21 Brahmpol
22 Amba Gate
23 Chandpol
28 Clock Tower
30 Jagdish Temple
37 City Palace, Museums, Shiv Niwas Palace & Fateh Prakash Hotels
39 Bansi Ghat
46 Tourist Reception Centre
47 Surajpol
49 Bus Stand
52 Kishan Gate

Bhartiya Lok Kala Museum

The interesting collection exhibited by this small museum and foundation for the preservation and promotion of local folk arts includes dresses, turbans, dolls, masks, musical instruments, paintings and – its high point – puppets. It's definitely worth visiting. The museum is open daily from 9 am to 6 pm and admission costs Rs 7, plus Rs 10 for a camera and Rs 50 for a video camera. Regular 15 minute puppet shows are held daily (usually every half hour) and are included in the admission charge. From 6 to 7 pm there's a Rajasthani dance and puppet show for Rs 20. Call ☎ 52-9296 for details.

Saheliyon ki Bari

The Saheliyon ki Bari, or Garden of the Maids of Honour, is in the north of the city. This small ornamental garden is well maintained, and has fountains, kiosks, marble elephants and a delightful lotus pool. It's open from 9 am to 6 pm and entry is Rs 2. They sometimes ask for Rs 2 to turn the fountains on.

Shilpgram

Shilpgram, a crafts village three km west of Fateh Sagar, was inaugurated by Rajiv Gandhi in 1989. It's an interesting place with traditional houses from four states – Rajasthan, Gujarat, Goa and Maharashtra – and there are daily demonstrations by musicians, dancers or artisans from the various states. Although it's much more animated during festival times (usually in early December, but check with the Tourist Reception Centre for details), there's usually something happening.

The site covers 80 hectares, but most buildings are in a fairly compact area. Camel or horse rides are available here. It's open daily from 9 am to 6 pm and entry is Rs 2.

The open air Shilpi Restaurant next to the site serves snacks and good Indian and Chinese food. It also has a swimming pool (Rs 100), open from 11 am to 4 pm. There's no public transport to Shilpgram, so you'll have to rent a bicycle, or take an auto-rickshaw or taxi.

Ahar Museum

Three km east of Udaipur are the remains of an ancient city. Here, you'll find a small museum housing old earthen pottery, sculptures and other archaeological finds. The museum is open daily, except Friday, from 9.30 am to 4.30 pm and entry is free. Nearby are a cluster of cenotaphs of the maharanas of Mewar.

Other Attractions

The huge **fountain** in the centre of Patel or Sukhadia Circle, north of the city, is illuminated at night. **Sajjan Niwas Gardens** has pleasant lawns and a zoo. Beside it is the Rose Garden, or **Gulab Bagh**. Don't confuse the **Nehru Park** opposite Bapu Bazaar with the island park of the same name in Fateh Sagar. The city park has some strange topiary work, a giant cement teapot and children's slides incorporating an elephant and a camel.

Not to be missed is the breathtaking **Crystal Gallery** at the Hotel Fateh Prakash Palace in the City Palace complex. This rare collection of Osler's crystal, manufactured by an English company, was ordered by Maharana Sajjan Singh in 1877, although the maharana was unable to see the crystal because of his untimely death. Items include crystal dressing tables, chairs, crockery, table fountains and even beds. The Crystal Gallery looks onto the huge **Durbar Hall**, once the royal hall of audience, which is filled with historical paintings, large portraits of former rulers of Mewar and amazing chandeliers.

On the distant mountain range, visible from the city, is the former maharana's **Monsoon Palace**, also known as Sajjan Garh. It was built by Maharana Sajjan Singh. This deserted and run-down palace is today owned by the government and closed to the public, although there are sensational views from the mountain on which it is sited. The round trip takes about one hour by rickshaw or car. At night this palace is illuminated and can be seen from most parts of town.

Festivals

Both Holi and Gangaur are celebrated with much pageantry and colour in Udaipur. See the section on festivals at the beginning of this chapter for more details.

Organised Tours
A five hour tour starts at the Hotel Kajri Tourist Bungalow at 8 am each day. It costs Rs 40 and takes in all the main city sights. An afternoon tour (2 to 7 pm) which goes to Eklingji, Haldighati and Nathdwara (see the North of Udaipur section) costs Rs 70. Contact the Tourist Reception Centre for details.

Places to Stay – homestays
Udaipur pioneered the Paying Guest Scheme in Rajasthan, and there are now over 200 families participating. Expect to pay Rs 100 to Rs 500 per night, depending on the level of comfort and facilities you want. The

Tourist Reception Centre has a list detailing all the places and the services offered.

Places to Stay – bottom end
There are four main clusters of budget hotels in Udaipur, but those around the Jagdish Temple are definitely preferable to the others. Next best are those between the City Palace and the bus stand, along Lake Palace Rd and Bhattiyani Chotta. The third cluster is along the main road between the bus stand and Delhi Gate. This is a very noisy and polluted road, and you'd have to be desperate or totally lacking in imagination to stay here. The last cluster is around the Hotel Kajri Tourist Bungalow and, although it's better than staying on the main road, it's somewhat inconvenient.

Watch out for check-out times, which vary

Durbar Hall
Many palaces in India have a durbar hall, or hall of audience. Historically, the durbar hall was used by India's rulers for official occasions such as state banquets. It was also used to hold formal or informal meetings.

The recently restored durbar hall at the City Palace in Udaipur is undoubtedly one of India's most impressive, with a lavish interior boasting some of the largest chandeliers in the country. The walls display numerous old paintings, royal weapons and grand portraits of former maharanas of Mewar. The illustrious Mewar rulers come from what is believed to be the oldest ruling dynasty in the world, spanning 76 generations.

The foundation stone of the durbar hall was laid in 1909 by Lord Minto, the Viceroy of India, during the reign of Maharana Fateh Singh. As a mark of honour to Lord Minto, it was originally named the Minto Hall. The top floor of this high-ceilinged hall is surrounded by viewing galleries, where ladies of the palace could watch in veiled seclusion what was happening below.

Today, the durbar hall in Udaipur is open to visitors. It still has the capacity to hold hundreds of people and can even be hired for special functions, such as conferences or social gatherings. ■

COURTESY OF THE CITY PALACE, UDAIPUR

greatly in Udaipur, and note that many places whack a 10% service charge on the room rates they advertise.

Jagdish Temple Area You'll pay more for a hotel in this area, but there is no traffic noise, most places have fantastic views over the lake and the central location is ideal. As it's the most popular area to stay in, you get a lot of the 'yes have a look change money buy something' from the touts and shop owners, but this is not Agra.

The *Hotel Badi Haveli* (☎ 41-2588) has small rooms for Rs 80/120 with common bath, Rs 150 with attached bath or Rs 200 for the best room at the top. This little labyrinth has narrow staircases, terraces, a courtyard and two rooftops with great views over the lake and old city. There's a vegetarian restaurant with thalis for Rs 25. The nearby *Anjani Hotel* (☎ 52-7670) has clean rooms with private bath from Rs 100. There's a reasonably priced rooftop restaurant. The *Lehar Guest House* is in the same area and has good doubles with attached bath for Rs 80, or Rs 150 for a better view over the town. There's a small rooftop restaurant, with good views, which serves Indian and Continental food. If nobody is at reception when you get here, just go up to the restaurant.

The well established *Lalghat Guest House* (☎ 52-5301) is very popular with travellers. Right by the lake, it has a large courtyard with tables and chairs, rooftop areas with excellent views over the lake and a back terrace which overlooks the ghats. A variety of rooms are available, ranging from dorm beds for Rs 50, small rooms with common bath for Rs 75/100, larger rooms for Rs 150, or Rs 200 with attached bath, and for Rs 250 you also get a lake view. All the rooms have fans and mosquito nets. There are facilities for self caterers and a small shop. The rooftop terrace is popular for sunbaking (remember to slap on the sunscreen lotion).

Next door, the small *Evergreen Guest House* (☎ 27-823) has clean rooms around a small courtyard, soft beds and the Restaurant Natural View on the roof. The management is friendly and hot water is available by the bucket at no extra charge. Rooms cost Rs 60/80 with common bath, or Rs 100/150 with attached bath. The nearby *Rainbow Guest House* has just three rooms (all doubles): one with common bath for Rs 100 and two with private bath for Rs 150 (with cold water) or Rs 200 with hot water.

Across the road from the Lalghat Guest House, the *Lake Ghat Guest House* (☎ 52-1636) is another popular place. There's a wide range of accommodation, although none of the rooms here have a view. Singles/doubles without bath cost Rs 60/100 and doubles with bath go for Rs 125 to Rs 200. There's also a good restaurant and terrace area.

Opposite the Lake Ghat Guest House is the cheap *Centre View Guest House* (☎ 52-0039) with just a few rooms, all with common bath, for Rs 40/60. There are no views but the family who runs it is very friendly. Another cheapie in the same area is the *Shri Karni Guest House*. It has one single room with attached bath for Rs 70 and doubles with common bath for Rs 60, or Rs 100 with own bath.

In the Lal Ghat area, the *Lake Corner Soni Paying Guest House* has basic rooms set around a small courtyard. Charges are Rs 60/80 for rooms with common bath, Rs 100 for a double with bath attached. Meals are available, there are excellent views from the rooftop and it's run by a lovely elderly couple. Nearby is the similarly priced *Shiva Guest House*.

The *Jheel Guest House* (☎ 28-321) is right at the bottom of the hill, by the ghat. It is housed in an old haveli and has a good deal of character and charm. Doubles cost Rs 100 with common bath, or Rs 200 in a larger room with bath attached and a view. Pleasant rooms with private balcony and superb views over the lake and ghats cost Rs 550; the best room is No 201. There's also a good rooftop restaurant here. Nearby is the *Hotel Gangaur Palace* (☎ 23-451), where large, clean doubles with attached bath range from Rs 150, to Rs 350 for lake view rooms. The rooftop restaurant serves Indian and Continental food.

If you want to escape the bustle and the touts, try the *Lake Shore Hotel*, next to the Lake Pichola Hotel, about a 10 minute walk across the Chandpol bridge from the Jagdish Temple. It's fairly basic, with just a few rooms (all doubles), but it's very peaceful and there's a fine terrace with views back across to Lal Ghat. Rooms are Rs 80 with common bath or Rs 150 with a lake view; Rs 300 gets you a larger room with a lake view and private bath. Discounts are offered if you stay at least three nights.

Further away, and even more peaceful, is the *Hotel Natural* (☎ 52-7879), run by a very friendly family. It's right by the water and a delightful place to stay. The rooms are basic but clean and many are decorated with colourful wall paintings. Singles with bucket hot water cost Rs 60 or, with constant hot water and a balcony, Rs 80. Doubles with constant hot water cost Rs 100, or Rs 150 with balcony; all rooms have attached baths. Tasty food is available at the rooftop restaurant.

Lake Palace Rd Area There are numerous places to stay in this area. The *Haveli Hotel* (☎ 28-294) is small, with a little garden, but the comfortable rooms range from Rs 100 to Rs 250, all with attached bath. The *Hotel Mahendra Prakash* (☎ 52-9370) is a modern building with rooms arranged around a courtyard. There are clean doubles with attached bath from Rs 100, or Rs 300 for a bigger room. Meals are available; a vegetarian thali costs Rs 30. From the rooftop terrace, there are very good views of the City Palace, especially when it is lit up at night.

The *Ranjit Niwas Hotel* (☎ 52-5774) is a small, family-run guest house in quite a good location. Dorm beds cost Rs 40, while basic single/double rooms with common bath are Rs 70/100, or Rs 150/175 with attached bath and air-cooling. Deluxe rooms cost Rs 200/225. There's a discount if you stay for three days or more. Meals are available and there's a small garden courtyard.

Tourist Bungalow Area Like many of the RTDC operations, the *Hotel Kajri Tourist Bungalow* (☎ 41-0501), at the traffic circle on Ashok Nagar Rd, has seen better days. With so many more interesting and better located hotels in Udaipur, there's little reason to stay here. There are dorm beds for Rs 50, and dull rooms with attached bath from Rs 200/250 to Rs 500/600.

Across the road there are some cheaper places. The *Prince Hotel* (☎ 41-4355) offers ordinary singles/doubles for Rs 60/80 and rooms with TV, attached bath and constant hot water for Rs 100/200. The *Alka Hotel* (☎ 41-4611) is a very large place with little character. Singles/doubles cost Rs 70/120 or Rs 120/200; the more expensive rooms are air-cooled and have constant hot water. Reasonably priced vegetarian meals are served; a thali costs Rs 22. The nearby *Ashok Hotel* (☎ 41-1925) has dorm beds for just Rs 25 and rooms with common bath for Rs 45/75. Doubles with attached bath go for Rs 160.

Bus Stand Area There are a number of choices for those who don't mind the noise and pollution of the main road. Best of the group is the *Hotel Apsara* (☎ 52-3400), a huge place set back from the road. The rooms front onto an internal courtyard, making them relatively quiet. There are dorm beds for Rs 35 and rooms range from Rs 75/100 to Rs 250, all with private bath. The more expensive rooms have constant hot water and air-cooling.

There are several hotels opposite the bus stand. The best of these is the *Hotel Welcome* (☎ 48-5375), with basic singles/doubles with attached bath for Rs 95/125. Deluxe rooms cost Rs 250/300 and there's also a vegetarian restaurant.

Elsewhere The *Mewar Inn* (☎ 52-2090), north of town on Residency Rd, is a real bargain. It's an exceptionally cheap and friendly hotel well away from the centre. The rickshaw drivers detest this place (because they get no commission), and you'll have difficulty persuading one to take you there. Dorm beds go for an astonishingly low Rs 12. Small, basic rooms with common bath cost Rs 28/37, bigger rooms with private bath and hot water cost Rs 59 to Rs 79, and a discount is given to YHA members. There's a rooftop vegetarian restaurant that serves Indian and Continental food and plays funky western music. The slightly inconvenient location is no great disadvantage as there are bicycles for hire (Rs 8).

The *Ajanta Hotel* (☎ 52-8914) is set around a very pleasant courtyard between Chetak Circle and Hathi Gate. The well kept rooms are good value, ranging from Rs 125/200 to Rs 175/350, all with private bath and hot water.

There's a relaxing country retreat at Titadha village, seven to eight km outside Udaipur – the *Pratap Country Inn* (☎ 58-3138; fax 58-3058). Away from the hustle and bustle of town, this place specialises in horse safaris. Double rooms with attached bath range from Rs 200 to Rs 800 and there's also a restaurant. Short horse rides are available and they also organise longer safaris – from Rs 3500 per person per day. People who stay here for more than one night get a free two hour horse ride. For learners, there are riding lessons for Rs 75 per day. Auto-rickshaws from Udaipur cost Rs 30 and there are city buses from Bapu Bazaar to Titadha, from where it's a short walk. Alternatively, you could ride out here on a bike.

Places to Stay – middle

Right on the lake shore in the Lal Ghat area is the delightful *Jagat Niwas Palace Hotel* (☎ 29-728), a converted haveli. There are courtyards, cool marble floors and a very pleasant open-air restaurant with magnificent views across to the Lake Palace. Rooms with common bath range from Rs 150 to Rs 300; with attached bath they cost from Rs 450 to Rs 750. The hotel also has a horse-riding club out of town. Rides cost Rs 300 per hour or Rs 1500 per day. Free transport to and from the club is provided if you book at least two hours of riding.

The *Rang Niwas Palace Hotel* (☎ 52-3891), Lake Palace Rd, is one of the best mid-range options. Set in peaceful gardens, with a marble swimming pool, it's a very relaxing place to stay. There's accommoda-

tion in the old building, formerly a royal guest house, and good rooms in the tastefully designed new building. Rooms with common bath start at Rs 150/200, and doubles with attached bathroom range from Rs 350 to Rs 880. It's all very clean and well run, and there's also a good restaurant.

Also very highly recommended is the homely *Hotel Sai-Niwas* (☎ 52-4909), just down the hill towards the ghat from the City Palace entrance. There are just seven double rooms, all with attached bath. Each room has been imaginatively decorated with vibrant wall paintings – even the toilet has been transformed into a groovy work of art! Rooms range from Rs 550 to Rs 850 and the more expensive rooms have balconies with a lake view. There's a peaceful restaurant with a menu that includes Continental food 'for those feeling homesick or suffering from the Amoeba blues'. Very good value is the *Ratan Palace Guest House* (☎ 56-1153), near the Hotel Sai-Niwas. Spotlessly clean rooms with private bath cost from Rs 200 to Rs 450. There are lake views from the terrace and excellent food is available.

Near the Evergreen Guest House is the new *Hotel Caravanserai* (☎ 41-1103), a more upmarket place with comfortable singles/doubles with attached bath for Rs 675/700. Rooms on the top floors have the best lake view. The slightly pricey rooftop restaurant has good views over the lake and a puppet show is staged here each evening at 7 pm.

Midway along Bhattiyani Chotta down from the Jagdish Temple, is the *Hotel Raj Palace* (☎ 52-3092) with rooms from Rs 150 to Rs 600 with private bath. There's an open-air restaurant with views of the city side of the City Palace and a lush courtyard with chairs and tables.

There are other options away from this area. The *Gulab Niwas* (☎ 52-3644) is a small guest house in an attractive old lodge near Fateh Sagar, with a pleasant garden to relax in. There are air-cooled rooms with attached bath from Rs 575/675 and Rs 675/775 with air-con. Not far away, off Rani Rd, is the enormous *Hotel Lakend* (☎ 23-841) an 85 room place with a helpful owner.

Good singles/doubles cost Rs 500/700, or Rs 800/1100 for air-con deluxe rooms. There's a swimming pool, table tennis, bar, restaurant and a garden running down to Fateh Sagar. Nearby is the serene and highly recommended *Hotel Ram Pratap Palace* (☎ 52-8700; fax 52-0168), an elegant modern haveli with a homely ambience. It's excellent value with pleasant air-cooled singles/doubles for Rs 350/450, or Rs 625/850 with air-con; all rooms have attached bath. The mattresses are soft and most rooms have a balcony and lake view. There's also a very good restaurant and fine views from the rooftop terrace.

To the north of the Hotel Ram Pratap Palace is the *Hotel Anand Bhawan* (☎ 52-3256), where rooms start from Rs 500/650 with attached bath. The restaurant serves veg and non-veg food.

Places to Stay – top end

Undoubtedly, the best of the lower priced top-range hotels is the popular *Lake Pichola Hotel* (☎ 29-387), Chandpol, in an excellent location which looks out across to the ghats, the Jagdish Temple and the northern end of the City Palace. It's a modern building, in the traditional style, which is well maintained and managed. The very friendly and helpful owner can give you some good tips on what to see in and around Udaipur. Comfortable rooms with private bath cost Rs 975/1000; most rooms have a balcony and lake view. There's also a good bar and restaurant and the rooftop terrace has some of the best views in all Udaipur.

Up on the hill between Pichola and Fateh Sagar lakes, is the ITDC *Laxmi Vilas Palace Hotel* (☎ 52-9711), a four star place where air-con rooms cost US$90/120. There's a lovely garden with views of the lakes, and a swimming pool, bar and restaurant.

The *Hotel Hilltop Palace* (☎ 56-1765) is a modern hotel atop another hill in the same area. Clean rooms start at Rs 1175/1600 and there's also a bar and restaurant. Although it is rather lacking in character, its rooftop terrace is probably the best place in town to see a 360° view of Udaipur, and nobody seems to mind if you come here just for the views.

If you want to escape from the rest of the world, head for the tranquil *Shikarbadi Hotel* (☎ 58-3200), three km out of town on the Ahmedabad road. Bookings can also be made through the Shiv Niwas Palace Hotel (☎ 52-8016; fax 52-8006) in the City Palace complex. Once a royal hunting lodge, it is set in wilderness and has a swimming pool, pleasant gardens, small lake and deer park. Delightful rooms with a jungle theme cost US$35/60; all rooms have a private bath. Deluxe tents are also available for US$30 each. There's a quiet bar and three restaurants including the open-air Risala, which serves barbecued Mewari food. On the extensive compound is a stud farm which offers 45 minute horse rides for Rs 125 or a one day horse safari with lunch for Rs 1250.

At the very top end of the scale are two of India's most luxurious hotels, facing each other across Lake Pichola. The incomparable *Lake Palace Hotel* (☎ 52-7961; fax 52-7974) looks like something out of a romantic novel. It's the very image of what a maharaja's palace should be like and most people with sufficient money to spend would not pass up an opportunity to stay here. This white palace offers every conceivable comfort, including a small mango tree-shaded swimming pool, shopping arcade, bar and restaurant. The cheapest rooms are US$160/180, while suites cost US$280 to US$600. Needless to say, you need to book well in advance.

The equally luxurious *Shiv Niwas Palace Hotel* (☎ 52-8016; fax 52-8006) forms part of the City Palace complex. It's a good deal cheaper at US$65 for tastefully decorated air-con rooms, most with a lake view. Suites range from US$175, to US$400 for the sumptuous Imperial suite where Queen Elizabeth II of England once stayed. There's also heavy demand for rooms here, so it's wise to book ahead. Most rooms overlook a peaceful courtyard with tables and chairs arranged around a marble swimming pool. Refreshments and meals are available and it's the ideal place to relax with a good book.

The hotel also has a luxurious bar and restaurant. Each evening, a small bagpipe band performs for about 45 minutes in a courtyard near the hotel lobby. In the same complex is the intimate and highly recommended *Hotel Fateh Prakash Palace* (☎ 52-8016; fax 52-8006), built in the early 1900s during the reign of Maharana Fateh Singh. It has just nine rooms ranging from US$100, to US$150/200 for lavish suites; most have a lake view. There are two restaurants (one on the rooftop), with superb views.

Places to Eat

There's quite a reasonable range of restaurants in Udaipur, from rooftop cafes in the Lal Ghat area catering for travellers to excellent restaurants at the top hotels.

The little *Mayur Cafe*, by the Jagdish Temple, has long been popular. It serves good South Indian dishes as well as western alternatives, such as macaroni with cheese (Rs 25), milkshakes (Rs 20) and apple pie (Rs 25). This was one of the first places to start a nightly video showing of *Octopussy* (partly filmed in Udaipur). Several other restaurants now try to attract customers with showings of this James Bond movie as you eat.

Above the Evergreen Guest House, the rooftop *Restaurant Natural View* has great views over Lake Pichola. It serves pizzas from Rs 25, baked potatoes from Rs 20 and has a good range of Chinese and Indian dishes; one of their specialities is delicious local cheese flavoured with garlic. Other popular places in this area include the *Gokul Restaurant*, the *Four Seasons Restaurant* and the *Relish Roof Top Restaurant*.

Just round the corner from the Rang Niwas Palace Hotel, facing the City Palace, the *Roof Garden Cafe* has the appearance of a Hanging Gardens of Babylon. There's Indian, Chinese and Continental food, including 'spegati Napolitance' for Rs 30. The food here is slightly more expensive, but there's a good menu and live folk music most nights during the week. The pleasant, dimly lit *Mayur Roof Top Restaurant* in the same area has reasonable Indian, Chinese and Continental food, including Rajasthani pizzas (Rs 28) and pistachio shakes (Rs 15); it screens *Octopussy* on request.

There are several places to eat around the Hotel Natural, a 15 minute walk from the Jagdish Temple on the other side of the northern arm of Lake Pichola. The popular rooftop restaurant at the *Hotel Natural* offers cheap vegetarian food. It's run by Ritu, who is keen to please and cooks a variety of dishes, including a wicked chocolate cake and a delicious chapati stuffed with onion, tomato and garlic cheese. From 8 am to noon, there's a buffet breakfast for Rs 30. Although rather plain inside, the small *Natural Attic* next door has an extensive menu featuring Mexican, Chinese, western, Indian and Tibetan food. There's a free puppet show most evenings at 7.30 pm. Their branch in Lal Ghat is not as good.

South of the Sajjan Niwas Gardens, on the hill overlooking Lake Pichola, is the *Cafe Hill Park*, worth a visit just for the views. They offer snacks, South Indian and Chinese food; main dishes are around Rs 35. There's seating indoors and outdoors.

For excellent North Indian food, go to the *Park View*. It's opposite the park in the main part of town but there's absolutely no view. There's also South Indian and Chinese dishes. Prices are reasonable – a half tandoori chicken costs Rs 43 – and it's often packed with middle-class Indian families. *Berry's Restaurant* on Chetak Circle is more expensive and rather lacking in character, but has a wide range of mainly Indian food. Opposite is a branch of *Kwality* which offers the usual selection.

The restaurant at the *Jagat Niwas Palace Hotel* is recommended for a minor splurge and its position – right above the water and overlooking the Lake Palace – is superb. Western non-veg dishes are expensive (around Rs 85) but Indian food is cheaper. The *Shiv Niwas Palace Hotel* (in the City Palace complex) is more expensive but an excellent place to eat, with seating indoors or out by the pool. Their Indian food is best, and they do delicious mango and strawberry ice cream. Indian classical music is performed by the poolside each evening, setting the perfect mood for a memorable dining experience.

For something really special, try the intimate *Gallery Restaurant* at the Hotel Fateh Prakash Palace. This small, elegant restaurant has dreamy views over Lake Pichola and serves very good Continental food. There's also a popular 'afternoon cream tea' served from 3 to 5 pm. A full cream tea – cakes, scones with jam and cream and a pot of tea – costs Rs 100. Alternatively, there's a choice of sandwiches, or home-made biscuits and cakes. This place oozes style and character and musicians perform Indian classical music here every evening. On the rooftop in the same complex there's a new restaurant that's open for afternoon tea and dinner. It has sensational views over Lake Pichola and the old city.

The ultimate dining experience is, of course, at the *Lake Palace Hotel* (☎ 52-7961). While the food gets mixed reports, and the dining room is not the most impressive room in the palace, it's nevertheless well worth it just to see this beautiful hotel. There's live sitar music to accompany the buffet dinner, service is attentive, and before your meal you can take a drink in the pleasant bar and watch the folk dances. There's no guarantee that you'll be able to get in, though, since it's only possible to eat here when the hotel is not full. Reservations are necessary and you usually have to book on the same day you intend to go. Reasonably tidy dress is expected. The buffet dinner (7.30 to 10.30 pm) costs Rs 550, and there's also a buffet lunch for Rs 450 (12.30 to 2.30 pm). Charges include the boat crossing.

Entertainment

From August to April there are one hour Rajasthani folk dance and music performances daily (except Sunday) at 7 pm at the Meera Kala Mandir (☎ 58 -3176), Sector 11, Hiran Magari, near the Pars Theatre. It costs Rs 30 per head and is well worth attending. You can expect to see not only a whole range of tribal dances, but also some more spectacular acts which involve balancing numerous pots on top of the head while dancing on broken glass or unsheathed sabres. An autorickshaw to the auditorium from the City Palace area costs around Rs 20.

Some hotels around town stage their own special shows which can also be very good. Puppet shows and Indian music performances are put on by some of the topnotch hotels during the peak tourist season.

Things to Buy

Udaipur has countless small shops and many interesting local crafts, particularly miniature paintings in the Rajput-Mughal style. The miniatures are executed on cloth, marble, wood, paper and even leaves. You can also buy jewellery, carpets, block-printed fabrics, marble items, wooden figures and papier mâché. There's a good cluster of shops on Lake Palace Rd, next to the Rang Niwas Palace Hotel, and others around the Jagdish Temple.

Shops in Udaipur are accustomed to tourists with lots of money to spend, so make sure you bargain hard. Most shops are open daily from 9.30 am to 7.30 pm. *Manglam Arts* at Sukhadia Circle has a wide and interesting range of ethnic Rajasthani handicrafts. Although slightly pricey, it's a great place just to browse, and you can also watch artists at work.

Getting There & Away

Air Indian Airlines has at least one flight a day to Delhi (US$74), Jaipur (US$51) and Mumbai (Bombay; US$88), and flights five times a week to Jodhpur (US$41) and Aurangabad (US$71). The direct flight between Udaipur and Aurangabad can save a great deal of bus or train time. The Indian Airlines office (☎ 41-0999) at Delhi Gate is open every day from 10 am to 1 pm and 2 to 5 pm.

ModiLuft (☎ 52-6374) has daily flights to Mumbai (US$93), Goa (US$152), Delhi (US$78) and Jaipur (US$54). UP Airways (☎ 52-4388) has daily flights to Delhi (US$74), Mumbai (US$88) and Jaipur (US$51).

It's advisable to make flight bookings well in advance as they can get very heavily booked.

Bus Frequent RSTC buses run from Udaipur to other regional centres, as well as to Delhi and Ahmedabad. If you use these buses, make sure you take an express since the ordinary buses take forever, make innumerable detours to various towns off the main route and can be very uncomfortable. For long-distance travel, it's best to use private buses.

Destinations served by express bus include Jaipur (Rs 105, 10 hours, nine daily), Ajmer (Rs 75, eight hours, 11 daily), Kota/Bundi (Rs 85, six hours, six daily), Mt Abu (Rs 50, seven hours), Jodhpur (Rs 80, eight to 10 hours, 12 daily), Nathdwara (Rs 15, one hour, two daily) and Chittorgarh (Rs 30, three hours, eight daily). Express and deluxe buses should be booked in advance.

There are quite a few private bus companies which operate to such places as Ahmedabad (Rs 80, six hours), Vadodara (Rs 150, eight hours), Mumbai (Rs 200, 16 hours), Delhi (Rs 160, 14 hours), Indore (Rs 140, 10 hours), Jaipur (Rs 100, nine hours), Jodhpur (Rs 70, nine hours), Kota (Rs 70, six hours) and Mt Abu (Rs 60, five hours). Most have their offices along the main road from the bus stand to Delhi Gate. Book at least one day in advance.

Train Lines into Udaipur are currently metre gauge only. As the city is not high on the list for conversion to broad gauge, rail travel to and from Udaipur is likely to become less convenient as other places in Rajasthan are linked to the wider gauge.

The best train between Delhi and Udaipur is the *Pink City/Garib Nawaz Express*, which covers the 739 km trip in 15½ hours and goes via Jaipur (Rs 109/423 in 2nd/1st class), Ajmer (Rs 87/324 in 1st/2nd class) and Chittorgarh (Rs 52/220 in 2nd/1st class). It currently leaves Delhi's Sarai Rohilla station daily except Sunday (daily except Saturday in the other direction), but you may need to change trains at Rewari (83 km from Delhi) since the Delhi end of this metre-gauge route is being converted to broad gauge. Fares for the trip are Rs 151/603 in 2nd/1st class. This train operates during the day and reaches its destination in the late evening. If you'd rather do the journey overnight and arrive at a more civilised hour, the *Chetak Express* does the trip, but takes 20 hours; it costs Rs 188/588 in 2nd/1st class.

There's currently still a metre-gauge link, the *Jodhpur-Udaipur Passenger*, between Udaipur and Jodhpur (Rs 49/262 in 2nd/1st class).

Taxi If you want to rent a taxi to tour this area of Rajasthan the drivers will show you a list of 'official' rates to places like Mt Abu and Jodhpur. Shop around – you can often get a better price from travel companies, of which there are many around town. Remember that taxis usually charge return trip fares even if you're only going one way.

Getting Around
The Airport The airport is 25 km from the city. There's no airport bus; a taxi costs around Rs 125.

Local Transport Udaipur has a reasonably good city bus service. Auto-rickshaws and taxis are unmetered, so you must agree on a fare before setting off. The standard fare for tourists anywhere within the city appears to be Rs 15, and you'll be very lucky to get it for less since there are too many tourists around who pay the first price asked.

Owing to cut-throat hotel competition, the commission system is in place with a vengeance. Rickshaw drivers will try to take you to a place of their choice rather than yours, especially if you want to go to the Lal Ghat area. Some really tenacious drivers may even claim that the hotel you wish to go to has suddenly closed or burned down! If that's the case, just ask for the Jagdish Temple, as all the guest houses in that area are within easy walking distance of the temple.

Udaipur is small enough and the vehicle traffic is slow enough to make getting around on a bicycle quite enjoyable. You can hire bicycles all over town for around Rs 3 an hour or Rs 15 per day. Rates tend to be higher at the places right by the tourist hotels.

NORTH OF UDAIPUR
Eklingji & Nagda

The interesting little village of Eklingji – only 22 km and a short bus ride north of Udaipur – has a number of ancient **temples**. The Shiva temple in the village itself was originally built in 734, although its present form dates from the rule of Maharana Raimal between 1473 and 1509. The walled complex includes an elaborately pillared hall under a large pyramidal roof and features a four faced Shiva image of black marble. The temple is open daily at rather odd hours – 4.15 to 6.45 am, 10.30 am to 1.30 pm and 5.15 to 7.45 pm. Photography is not permitted. It's best to avoid the temple on Mondays, an auspicious day when people flock here to worship Shiva.

At Nagda, about a km off the road and a km before Eklingji, are three 10th century temples. The Jain **temple of Adbudji** is essentially ruined, but its architecture is interesting. The nearby **Sas Bahu**, or Mother and Daughter-in-Law group, has very fine and intricate carvings including some erotic figures. You can reach these temples most conveniently by hiring a bicycle in Eklingji itself. There are also some small temples submerged in a nearby lake.

Getting There & Away Buses run from Udaipur to Eklingji every hour from 5 am onwards and cost Rs 7. There's a small guest house in the village if you want to stay overnight.

Haldighati

This site, 40 km from Udaipur, is where Maharana Pratap valiantly defied the superior Mughal forces of Akbar in 1576. The site is a battlefield and the only thing to see is the small chhatri to the warrior's horse, Chetak, a few km away. Although badly wounded and exhausted, this brave horse carried Maharana Pratap to safety before collapsing and dying. It is for this loyalty and courage that Chetak is honoured. The site has a beautiful courtyard and is in a peaceful setting, which makes a change from most other tourist attractions in Rajasthan.

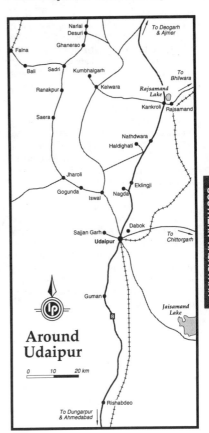

Around Udaipur

0   10   20 km

SOUTHERN RAJASTHAN

Nathdwara

The important 18th century Vishnu temple of **Sri Nathji** stands here, 48 km from Udaipur, and it's an important shrine for Vaishnavites. The black stone Vishnu image was brought here from Mathura in 1669 to protect it from Aurangzeb's destructive impulses. According to legend, when an attempt was later made to move the image, the getaway vehicle, a wagon, sank into the ground up to the axles, indicating that the image preferred to stay where it was!

Attendants treat the image like a delicate child, getting it up in the morning, washing it, putting its clothes on, offering it specially prepared meals, putting it down to sleep etc. It's a very popular pilgrimage site, and the temple opens and closes around the image's daily routine. It gets very crowded around 4.30 to 5 pm when Vishnu gets up after a siesta.

Nathdwara is also well known for its pichwai paintings, which were produced after the image of Vishnu was brought to the town. These bright paintings, with their rather static images, were usually done on hand-spun fabric. As with many other schools of painting, numerous inferior reproductions of the pichwai paintings are created specifically for the lucrative tourist trade.

The RTDC *Hotel Gokul Tourist Bungalow* (☎ (02953) 30-917) offers air-cooled rooms for Rs 225/275, and dorm beds for Rs 50. There's also a bar, and a restaurant where vegetarian thalis cost Rs 42.

There are RSTC buses from Udaipur to Nathdwara every hour from 5 am onwards for Rs 15.

Kankroli & Rajsamand Lake

At Kankroli, Dwarkadhish (an incarnation of Vishnu) has a **temple** similar to the temple at Nathdwara, and opening hours here are similarly erratic.

Nearby is the large Rajsamand Lake, created by a dam constructed in 1660 by Maharana Raj Singh. There are many ornamental arches, and picturesque chhatris along the huge *bund* (embankment). It also has several old inscriptions.

There are frequent RSTC buses from Udaipur for Rs 24.

Kumbhalgarh Fort

This is the most important fort in the Mewar region after Chittorgarh. It's an isolated and fascinating place 84 km from Udaipur, built by Maharana Kumbha in the 15th century. Because of its inaccessibility – at 1100m on top of the Aravalli Range – it was taken only once in its history. Even then, it took the combined armies of the Mughal emperor, Akbar, and of Amber and Marwar to breach its defences. It was here that the rulers of

Mewar retreated in times of danger. The thick walls of the fort stretch some 36 km and enclose many temples, palaces, gardens and water storage facilities. This mighty fort was renovated in the last century by Maharana Fateh Singh. It's worth taking a leisurely walk in the large compound, which has some interesting ruins and is very peaceful. The fort is open daily and entry is free.

There's also a large **sanctuary** here, known for its wolves. The scarcity of water holes between March and June makes this the best time to see animals. Other wildlife includes chowsingha (four horned antelope), leopard, panther and sloth bear. This is one of the few sanctuaries that allows people to enter on horseback. The Aodhi Hotel (see Places to Stay & Eat) can organise horse hire and jeeps for guests. Jeeps can also be hired in Udaipur, or at the Ghanerao Royal Castle at Ghanerao (see Ghanerao later in this section).

Entry costs Rs 10 for foreigners, Rs 5 for Indians, plus Rs 50 for cameras. Jeep entry is Rs 100 and for horses it's Rs 20. You need to get permission to enter the reserve from the forest department in nearby Kelwara, or from the Deputy Chief Wildlife Warden in Udaipur (☎ (0294) 28-413), but if you're staying at the Aodhi Hotel, they will organise it for you.

Places to Stay & Eat Without a doubt the best place to stay here is at the extremely peaceful and delightful *Aodhi Hotel* (☎ (02954) 4222, or bookings through Shiv Niwas Palace Hotel in Udaipur; ☎ (0294) 52-8016; fax 52-8006). Designed to blend in with the rugged surroundings, this would have to be one of the best retreats in Rajasthan. Built on the side of a hill, rooms are decorated in a wilderness theme and cost US$35/55; all rooms have attached bath and constant hot water. Suites are US$75. There's also a cosy bar, restaurant and swimming pool. It's a short walk from the hotel to the fort and horse safaris are available. Visits to nearby tribal villages can also be arranged.

A little far from the fort is the cheaper *Hotel Ratandeep* (☎ (02954) 4217) in Kelwara. Clean double rooms with attached bath start from Rs 350 and dorm beds cost Rs 100. There's also a small restaurant. The *Thandiberi Forest Guest House* is in the sanctuary. Bookings need to be made through the Deputy Chief Wildlife Warden in Udaipur (☎ (0294) 28-413).

Getting There & Away There are four RSTC buses a day from Udaipur (Rs 15, three hours), but not all leave from the bus stand – some go from Chetak Circle. Private buses are also available. It's a pleasant two to three km walk from where the bus drops you to the fort. If you want to hire a jeep, it's a good idea to come here as part of a small group and share the cost.

Ranakpur

One of the biggest and most important Jain temples in India, the extremely beautiful Ranakpur complex is well worth seeing. It lies in a remote and quiet valley of the Aravalli Range 60 km from Udaipur.

The main temple is the **Chaumukha Temple**, or Four Faced Temple, dedicated to Adinath, the first tirthankar. Built in 1439, this huge, beautifully crafted and well kept marble temple has 29 halls supported by 1444 pillars, no two of which are alike. Within the complex are two other Jain temples – to **Neminath** and **Parasnath** – and, a little distance away, a **Sun Temple**. The **Amba Mata Temple** is one km from the main complex.

The temple complex is open to non-Jains from noon to 5 pm. Shoes and all leather articles must be left at the entrance. Admission to the temple is free, but there's a Rs 20 camera charge, or Rs 100 for a video camera.

Places to Stay & Eat Staying overnight at Ranakpur breaks up the long trip between Udaipur and Jodhpur, but accommodation options are limited.

The poorly run RTDC *Hotel Shilpi Tourist Bungalow* (☎ (02934) 3674) has ordinary singles/doubles for Rs 150/175, deluxe rooms for Rs 225/275, and dorm beds for Rs 50. Overpriced vegetarian thalis are available in the dining room. The *dhaba* (basic restaurant) at the bus stand is far better value and has tasty veg dishes with rice and chapatis.

For a donation, you can stay at the *dharamsala* (pilgrims' lodgings) within the temple complex. If you arrive at meal time you can get a good thali in the dining hall, just inside the main entrance to the complex on your left, again for a small donation.

The *Maharani Bagh Orchard Retreat* (☎ (02934) 3705; or bookings through Umaid Bhawan Palace in Jodhpur, ☎ (0291) 33-316; fax 35-373) is situated in a mango orchard four km from Ranakpur. It offers accommodation in 18 cottage rooms for Rs 675/975, with bathrooms attached. There's also a rather small swimming pool. Meals are available; lunch or dinner cost Rs 190. Nearby is *The Castle* (☎ (02934) 3733), set in large grounds. Singles/doubles with private bath cost Rs 500/600 and there's also a restaurant.

Getting There & Away Ranakpur is 39 km from Falna Junction on the Ajmer to Mt Abu rail and road routes. From Udaipur (Rs 24, 3½ to 4½ hours), there are five RSTC express buses per day, leaving in the morning. Although it's just possible to travel through from Ranakpur to Jodhpur or Mt Abu on the same day, it's hardly worth it since you'll arrive well after dark. It's better to stay for the night and continue the next day. There's also a daily bus from Mt Abu which terminates at Sadri, only seven km from Ranakpur.

Ghanerao

Ghanerao is a small place not far from Ranakpur and Kumbhalgarh. The tranquil *Ghanerao Royal Castle* (☎ (02934) 7335) has 20 rooms for Rs 650/850 with private bath and hot water by the bucket. Meals are also available. This hotel is currently a little run down and there are mixed reports about the service, but renovations are planned. The owners can arrange walking treks and jeep excursions. There's a pavilion in a central courtyard of the castle where palace musicians used to perform. Near the castle are the cenotaphs of former rulers.

There are frequent RSTC buses from Udaipur to Ghanerao for Rs 28.

Narlai

Narlai is located just seven km from Ghanerao and can make a good base for exploring the various attractions around Udaipur. The best place to stay in Narlai is at the *Rawla Narlai* (bookings at the Ajit Bhawan Palace Hotel in Jodhpur, ☎ (0291) 37-410; fax 37-774). This 17th century fortress has 12 pleasant rooms with attached bath and hot water for Rs 1190/1495. Don't miss the groovy bedside lamps made from chain armour helmets. Meals are available and the hotel can organise tribal shows with advance notice. Opposite the hotel is a mammoth single granite rock with a small temple on top. There's also a good **baori** in Narlai, several old temples and lots of quiet walks.

Deogarh

The attractive little town of Deogarh, or 'castle of the gods', is 135 km north of Udaipur and is unknown to most tourists. Surrounded by lakes, hills and rugged countryside, it's an ideal place to take a break from the rigours of travelling on the Indian roads. It makes a good stopover if you're on your way from Udaipur to Ajmer or Jodhpur.

Deogarh has lots of pleasant walks and is popular for horse safaris. It's also known for its school of miniature painting. While here, you should visit **Anjaneshwar Mahadev**, a small cave temple dedicated to Lord Shiva. It's believed to be around 2000 years old and is unusually situated on the side of a hill. From the top of this hill there are good views of the countryside. There's also the **Raj Mahal**, a 17th century castle overlooking the town which is in the process of being converted into a hotel. The castle is reached through a small bazaar which has a huge idol of Lord Ganesh.

The best place to stay here is at the homely *Gokal Vilas* (☎ (02904) 52-017), a small guest house belonging to the royal family. It overlooks a picturesque lake that is home to a multitude of birdlife. This place is really more like a home than a hotel, with just four rooms for Rs 1000/1200, all with private bath. Meals are available with prior notice. Opposite the guest house, across the lake, are cenotaphs of former rulers and nearby there's a war fort atop a hill.

SOUTH OF UDAIPUR
Rishabdeo

A 15th century Jain temple of Lord Rishabdeo is in this village, located about 65 km south of Udaipur. Lord Rishabdeo was a reincarnation of Mahavir, the 24th and last of the Jain prophets, who founded Jainism around 500 BC. The temple has an image of Lord Rishabdeo, who is also worshipped as a reincarnation of Vishnu. There are also some beautiful carvings and two large black stone elephants at the temple's entrance. A short walk through a lane lined with small shops gets you to the temple, which is an important pilgrimage centre.

There are irregular buses to Rishabdeo from Udaipur.

Dungarpur

About 110 km south of Udaipur is the serene little town of Dungarpur. Unknown to most tourists, it has a very impressive palace which has partly been converted into a hotel by the Maharaj Kumar (prince) of Dungarpur. The tranquil *Udai Bilas Palace* (☎ (02964) 30-808; fax 31-008) is ideally located near Gaibsagar Lake, which is a good place for birdwatching. On the lake is a small temple. Singles/doubles with large bathrooms cost Rs 1100/1400 and many rooms are decorated in Art-Deco style. Rooms open onto a verandah and some have a private balcony with lake views. There are also suites so big you could get lost in them! These cost Rs 2400. Meals are available with prior notice. Made from grey-blue stone, the palace has retained an old-world charm and has lots of ornate balconies and pleasant gardens. There's a formal banquet room with a big collection of animal trophies. A feature of this palace is the Ek Thambia Mahal (one pillared palace), a large, exquisitely carved building in the middle of an inner courtyard.

The hotel can arrange a visit to the **Juna Mahal**, a palace built in the 13th century and now deserted. This seven storey palace has old frescoes, miniature paintings and colourful glass inlay work. The Aam Khas, or main living room, has some particularly impressive mirrorwork and glass inlays. The former royal hunting lodge, on a nearby hilltop, has excellent views over the town and its many temples.

There are regular daily buses from Udaipur to Dungarpur for Rs 28.

Galiakot

About 50 km south-east of Dungarpur is an important Muslim pilgrimage centre at Galiakot. This town is famous for the tomb of Saint Fakruddin, who spread the word of Mohammed in the 10th century. Each year, thousands of local and international Bohra Muslim pilgrims flock here to pay homage to the saint.

Baneshwar

Around January/February each year, the **Baneshwar Festival** is held at the Baneshwar Temple, about 70 km south-east of Dungarpur. It is one of the biggest Bhil festivals in Rajasthan and attracts thousands of tribal people from all over India.

Jaisamand Lake

Located in a stunning site 48 km south-east of Udaipur, Jaisamand Lake is one of the largest artificial lakes in Asia. It was built by Maharana Jai Singh in the 17th century and created by damming the Gomti River; today it measures 14 km long and nine km wide. There are beautiful marble chhatris around the embankment, each with an elephant in front. The summer palaces of the Udaipur maharanis are also here. The lake features a variety of birdlife and a nearby **wildlife sanctuary** is home to leopards, deer, wild boar and crocodiles. The sanctuary is open daily and entry is free.

There's a *Tourist Bungalow* on the shores of the lake. The *Jaisamand Island Resort*

(☎ (02906) 2222; or bookings through the Hotel Lakend in Udaipur, ☎ (0294) 23-841) is a modern hotel in an isolated position 20 minutes by boat across the lake. Comfortable singles/doubles cost Rs 1100/2000, all with views over the water. Meals are available. The hotel can also arrange visits to nearby tribal villages. There is also a *forest guest house* at Jaisamand. Contact the Deputy Chief Wildlife Warden, Udaipur (☎ (0294) 28-413) for reservations.

Hourly RSTC buses from Udaipur run from 5.30 am onwards for Rs 15.

MT ABU
Population: 17,000
Telephone Area Code: 02974

Rajasthan's only hill station sprawls along a 1200m high plateau in the south of the state, close to the Gujarat border. It's a pleasant hot season retreat from the plains of both Rajasthan and Gujarat, but you won't find many western travellers here – apart from those who come to study at the Brahma Kumaris Spiritual University. Indian visitors include many Gujarati families and starry-eyed honeymooners who come here to enjoy the pleasant climate and easy pace. Like most other hill stations in India, it's best to avoid Mt Abu in summer, when people throng here to escape the heat. Mt Abu's climate is not as cool as it used to be, believed to be due to increased development, predominantly for tourism. Vegetation has been cleared to make space for the many hotels that continue to spring up.

Apart from being a popular holiday resort, Mt Abu also has a number of important temples, particularly the Dilwara group of Jain temples, five km away. This is an important pilgrimage centre for Jains and the temples' superb marble carvings are among the best in Rajasthan. Also, like some other hill stations in India, Mt Abu has its own lake.

Nobody really seems to know when or how Mt Abu came into existence. Its history is fraught with myths and legends. According to one legend, Mt Abu is believed to be as old as the Himalaya. It was named after

Arbuda, a mighty serpent who saved Lord Shiva's revered bull, Nandi, from plunging into an abyss. Another relates that in Mt Abu, the four Rajput fire clans, the Chauhans, Solankis, Pramaras and Pratiharas, were created from a fire pit by Brahmin priests.

Orientation & Information

Mt Abu is on a hilly plateau about 22 km long by six km wide, 27 km from the nearest railway station, Abu Road. The main part of the town extends along the road in from Abu Road, down to Nakki Lake.

The tourist office (☎ 3151) is opposite the bus stand and is open Monday to Saturday from 10 am to 1.30 pm and 2 to 5 pm. The GPO is on Raj Bhavan Rd, opposite the art gallery and museum. Several banks change money, including the Bank of Baroda near the southern part of the polo ground. A number of top-end hotels also change money.

Nakki Lake

Virtually in the centre of Mt Abu, legend has it this small lake was scooped out by a god using only his nails, or *nakh*. Some Hindus thus believe it to be a holy lake. The lake is surrounded by hills, several parks and some

strange **rock formations**. The best known, Toad Rock, looks just like a toad about to hop into the lake. Others, like Nun Rock, Nandi Rock or Camel Rock, require more imagination. The 14th century **Raghunath Temple** stands beside the lake. It's a short and easy stroll around the lake. A number of maharajas built lavish summer houses around Nakki Lake; the maharaja of Jaipur's former summer palace is perched on a hill overlooking the water.

Nakki Lake is really the heart of all activity in Mt Abu. Near the lake there are lots of juice stalls, ice-cream parlours, balloon vendors, restaurants and small shops. You'll probably have to plough through persistent photographers, all eager to take a happy snap of you by the water. The lake is also popular with honeymooners and young couples are likely to be approached by innovative sellers offering a range of unusual aphrodisiacs that 'make big difference'.

A one hour horse ride around Nakki Lake costs Rs 80. From 8 am to 7 pm daily, you can hire your own boat (Rs 25 for 30 minutes), or be rowed (Rs 4 per person).

Viewpoints

Of the various viewpoints around town, **Sunset Point** is the most popular. Hordes stroll out here every evening to catch the setting sun, the food stalls and all the usual entertainment. Other popular spots include **Honeymoon Point**, which also offers a view of the sunset, **The Crags** and **Robert's Spur**. You can follow the white arrows along a rather overgrown path up to the summit of **Shanti Shikhar**, west of Adhar Devi Temple, where there are superb panoramic views.

For a good view over the lake the best point is probably the terrace of the maharaja of Jaipur's former **summer palace**. No-one seems to mind if you climb up here for the view and a photo.

Museum & Art Gallery

Although it's not very interesting and poorly kept, the museum, opposite the GPO, has some items from archaeological excavations which date from the 8th to 12th centuries, as well as Jain bronzes, carvings, brasswork and local textiles. 'Art gallery' is hardly an accurate description of the handful of pictures here. The museum is open daily, except Friday, from 10 am to 4.30 pm, and admission is free.

Adhar Devi Temple

Three km to the north of the town, around 200 steep steps lead to this ancient Durga temple built in a natural cleft in the rock. You have to stoop to get through the low entrance to the temple. There are good views over Mt Abu from up here.

Brahma Kumaris Spiritual University & Museum

The Brahma Kumaris teach that all religions lead to God and so are equally valid, and the principles of each should be studied. The university's stated aim is the establishment of universal peace through 'the impartation of spiritual knowledge and training of easy raja yoga meditation'. There are over 4000 branches in 60 countries around the world and followers come to Mt Abu to attend courses at the spiritual university. To attend one of these residential courses you need to contact your local branch and arrange things in advance. You can, however, arrange for someone here to give you an introductory course (seven lessons) while you're in Mt Abu; this would take a minimum of three days. There's no charge – the organisation is entirely supported by donations.

There's a museum (free) in the town outlining the university's teachings and offering meditation sessions. It's open daily from 8 am to 8 pm.

Dilwara Temples

These Jain temples are Mt Abu's main attraction and among the finest examples of Jain architecture in India. The complex includes two temples in which the art of carving marble reached unsurpassed heights.

The older of the temples is the **Vimal Vasahi**, built in 1031 and dedicated to the first tirthankar, Adinath. The central shrine has an image of Adinath, while around the

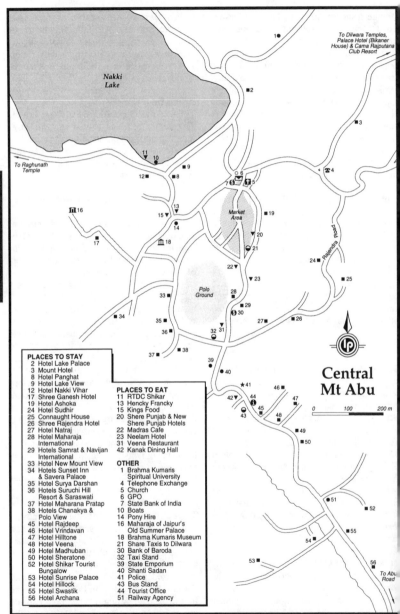

Central Mt Abu

0   100   200 m

To Dilwara Temples,
Palace Hotel (Bikaner
House) & Cama Rajputana
Club Resort

*Nakki
Lake*

To Raghunath
Temple

Market
Area

Rajendra Road

Polo
Ground

To Abu
Road

PLACES TO STAY
2 Hotel Lake Palace
3 Mount Hotel
8 Hotel Panghat
9 Hotel Lake View
12 Hotel Nakki Vihar
17 Shree Ganesh Hotel
19 Hotel Ashoka
24 Hotel Sudhir
25 Connaught House
26 Shree Rajendra Hotel
27 Hotel Natraj
28 Hotel Maharana
   International
29 Hotels Samrat & Navijan
   International
33 Hotel New Mount View
34 Hotels Sunset Inn
   & Savera Palace
35 Hotel Surya Darshan
36 Hotels Suruchi Hill
   Resort & Saraswati
37 Hotel Maharana Pratap
38 Hotels Chanakya &
   Polo View
45 Hotel Rajdeep
46 Hotel Vrindavan
47 Hotel Hilltone
48 Hotel Veena
49 Hotel Madhuban
50 Hotel Sheratone
52 Hotel Shikar Tourist
   Bungalow
53 Hotel Sunrise Palace
54 Hotel Hillock
55 Hotel Swastik
56 Hotel Archana

PLACES TO EAT
11 RTDC Shikar
13 Hencky Francky
15 Kings Food
20 Shere Punjab & New
   Shere Punjab Hotels
22 Madras Cafe
23 Neelam Hotel
31 Veena Restaurant
42 Kanak Dining Hall

OTHER
1 Brahma Kumaris
   Spiritual University
4 Telephone Exchange
5 Church
6 GPO
7 State Bank of India
10 Boats
14 Pony Hire
16 Maharaja of Jaipur's
   Old Summer Palace
18 Brahma Kumaris Museum
21 Share Taxis to Dilwara
30 Bank of Baroda
32 Taxi Stand
39 State Emporium
40 Shanti Sadan
41 Police
43 Bus Stand
44 Tourist Office
51 Railway Agency

courtyard are 52 identical cells, each with a Buddha-like cross-legged image. Forty-eight elegantly carved pillars form the entrance to the courtyard. In front of the temple stands the **House of Elephants**, with figures of elephants marching in procession to the temple entrance.

The later **Tejpal Temple** is dedicated to Neminath, the 22nd tirthankar, and was built in 1230 by the brothers Tejpal and Vastupal. Like Vimal, they were ministers in the government of the ruler of Gujarat. Although the Tejpal Temple is important as an extremely old and complete example of a Jain temple, its most notable feature is the fantastic intricacy and delicacy of the marble carving. The carving is so fine that, in places, the marble becomes almost transparent. In particular, the lotus flower which hangs from the centre of the dome is an incredible piece of work. It's difficult to believe that this huge lace-like filigree actually started as a solid block of marble. The temple employs several full-time stone carvers to maintain and restore the work. There are three other temples in the enclosure, but they all pale beside the Tejpal and Vimal Vasahi.

The complex is open from noon to 6 pm. Photography is not allowed, and bags are thoroughly searched to prevent cameras being taken in. As at other Jain temples, all articles of leather (including belts) have to be left at the entrance. You must also observe a number of other regulations which include 'bags, shoes, umbrellas, firearms not allowed' and 'moving hand-in-hand, hand on shoulders or waist is strictly prohibited'. There's also a dire warning for women: 'Entry of ladies in monthly course is strictly prohibited. Any lady in monthly course if enters any of the temples she may suffer'.

You can stroll out to Dilwara from the town in less than an hour, or take a share taxi for Rs 2 from opposite the Madras Cafe in the centre of town.

Organised Tours
The RTDC offers daily tours of all the main sites. They leave from the tourist office and cost Rs 30 plus all entry and camera fees. Tour times are 8.30 am to 1.15 pm and 1.30 to 6 pm (later in summer). The afternoon tour finishes at Sunset Point, and a notice warns that sunset is only included in the afternoon tour!

Places to Stay
There are plenty of hotels to choose from, with new ones being opened all the time. Most are along or just off the main road through to Nakki Lake. The high season lasts from mid-March to mid-November. As most hotel owners raise prices to whatever the market will bear at those times, Mt Abu can be an expensive place to stay. The real peak time is late April to mid-June and a room of any kind for less than Rs 200 is very hard to find. During the five days of Diwali (November), rooms are virtually unobtainable without advance booking. Avoid the place at this time.

In the low season (with the exception of Christmas and New Year), discounts of up to 50% are available and mid-range accommodation can be an absolute bargain. Most places are definitely open to a bit of bargaining, and the rates get cheaper the longer you stay. The hotels usually have a 9 am check-out time and many also levy a 10% tax.

At all times of the year there are plenty of touts working the bus and taxi stands. In the low season you can safely ignore them; at peak times they can save you a lot of legwork as they'll know exactly where the last available room is.

Mt Abu has recently started the Paying Guest Scheme and you can live with a local family for Rs 100 to Rs 300. Contact the tourist office for details.

Places to Stay – bottom end
The popular *Hotel Lake View* (☎ 3659) overlooks picturesque Nakki Lake but, although the views are certainly good, it's really only an average hotel. In winter, doubles with attached bath range from Rs 150 to Rs 250. Hot water is available between 6 and 11 am, and there's a pleasant terrace.

Close by and better value is the *Hotel Panghat* (☎ 3386). There are rooms with a lake view, attached bathroom and TV for Rs 100. Hot water is available from 7 to 9 am. Also in this lakeside area is the similarly priced *Hotel Nakki Vihar* (☎ 3481). Some rooms have a lake view.

A recommended place is the *Shree Ganesh Hotel* (☎ 3591), up the hill towards the maharaja of Jaipur's old summer palace. The location is certainly quiet. The rooms are clean and well kept, although some lack windows, and there are good views from the rooftop terrace. As this place is a little further from the centre of things, the high season rates tend to be a little more sensible than elsewhere, and bargaining is possible. Low-season rates are around Rs 100 for a double with bath, while high-season rates are Rs 350.

Another place that's very cheap is the *Hotel Ashoka* (☎ 3559), just east of the market area. Doubles with private bath start from Rs 60.

The *Hotel Rajdeep* (☎ 3525) is right opposite the bus stand. It's an old building and some of the rooms are good value. A large double with attached bath is Rs 100 in winter. There's a small restaurant at the front of this hotel which doubles as reception. The similarly priced, rather grubby *Hotel Veena* is nearby. There's not really a view of anything much from here, and while the main road is generally quiet by Indian standards, the noise can be annoying.

If you take the right-hand fork going up the hill opposite the taxi stand and polo ground, you'll find several other budget hotels. The *Hotel Natraj* (☎ 3532) has reasonable double rooms from Rs 100, all with private bath. Right across the road, the *Shree Rajendra Hotel* (☎ 3174) is one of the cheapest places here, with rooms from Rs 80 to Rs 250, all with attached bath. Bucket hot water costs Rs 4. There's a large restaurant serving Gujarati vegetarian thalis for Rs 25. In the same area is the *Hotel Sudhir* (☎ 3311). Basic doubles with attached bath and bucket hot water cost Rs 100 and better rooms with constant hot water cost Rs 500. There are good views from the terrace.

Further away from the lake is the *Hotel Swastik* (☎ 3752) which has clean doubles with attached bath for Rs 200 and family rooms (four beds) for Rs 350. There's an Indian vegetarian restaurant with thalis for Rs 35. Nearby, the *Hotel Archana* (☎ 3444) has small doubles for Rs 250 with attached bath and hot water. Meals are available.

The 80 room RTDC *Hotel Shikhar Tourist Bungalow* (☎ 3129), back from the main road and up a steepish path, is one of the biggest places in Mt Abu. Although fairly popular, it's certainly not the best value in town and the service is unenthusiastic. All rooms have attached bath; ordinary singles/ doubles cost Rs 125/200 (with bucket hot water), deluxe rooms are Rs 270/350, and cottages cost Rs 650. These are the year-round prices. There's a somewhat indifferent restaurant which serves Indian food.

On the far side of the polo ground there's a string of hotels, which are definitely mid-range in the high season, but offer quite good rates in the low season. The *Hotel Chanakya* (☎ 3438) charges Rs 225 in the low season for a comfortable double with attached bath and constant hot water. In the high season it's Rs 450. Nearby, the *Hotel Polo View* (☎ 3487) and the *Hotel Surya Darshan* (☎ 3165) both charge around Rs 250 for a room with attached bath, and hot water from 6.30 to 11 am.

Also in this price range, the *Hotel New Mount View* (☎ 38-279) is an older building and the rooms on the 1st floor have a terrace and good views. Doubles cost Rs 150 with private bath and hot water from 6.30 to 10 am.

Nearby, the *Hotel Saraswati* (☎ 3237) is very good value. There are clean doubles for Rs 80 with attached bath and bucket hot water, and a range of other rooms from Rs 100 to Rs 250 with hot water from 7 to 11 am. It's well run and a recommended place to stay, but the lilac and pink paint job is a bit radical. There's a vegetarian restaurant that serves Gujarati thalis for Rs 35.

Places to Stay – middle

In a peaceful location along the road to the Dilwara temples, the *Mount Hotel* (☎ 3150) once belonged to a British army officer and has changed little since those days, except for a lick of paint and upgraded bathrooms. It's surrounded by large gardens and is a homely place. There are only a few rooms, and these cost Rs 250/300. Vegetarian meals (Rs 60) are available with advance notice. The owner and his dog, Spots, are very friendly.

The *Hotel Lake Palace* (☎ 3254) makes the most of its excellent location – just across from Nakki Lake – with high prices. Singles/doubles/triples with attached bath are Rs 400/600/800 in the high season; bargain hard in the low season and you should be able to get at least 30% off these prices. Meals are available.

The *Hotel Sunset Inn* (☎ 3194) on the western edge of Mt Abu is a modern hotel that's well run. There are good doubles with attached bath from Rs 500, triples from Rs 600 and a 30% low-season discount. There's a restaurant serving Punjabi and Gujarati food. The nearby *Hotel Savera Palace* (☎ 3354) is similarly priced but not as good. Musty singles/doubles cost Rs 600/700 with private bath. There's also a restaurant and swimming pool. At the bottom end of the polo ground is the *Hotel Suruchi Hill Resort* (☎ 3577). Singles/doubles with attached bath cost Rs 490/690 in the high season, and there's a 50% low-season discount. It has an Indian restaurant. At the end of this road is the *Hotel Maharana Pratap* (☎ 3667), a smart, new place with rooms from Rs 750.

There are numerous other hotels in this price bracket. The *Hotel Vrindavan* (☎ 3147) is a pleasant place near the bus stand with comfortable rooms from Rs 400 with attached bath. There's a vegetarian restaurant with thalis for Rs 32. In the same area is the *Hotel Sheratone* (☎ 3544), with large, airy double rooms with private bath for Rs 750 and honeymoon suites with a bathtub for Rs 1250. It has good views from the rooftop terrace and there's an Indian restaurant. Nearby is the *Hotel Madhuban* (☎ 3122) which has doubles ranging from Rs 750 to Rs 1250; all rooms have attached bath and hot water from 7 to 11 am. There are only snacks available here.

The *Hotel Samrat* (☎ 3153) and *Hotel Navijan International* (☎ 3173), on the main street, are basically the same hotel, although they appear to be separate. Off-season rates in the Samrat start from Rs 250/550 for rooms with bath, and hot water from 7 am to noon; the Navijan is a little cheaper. Prices double in the high season. The *Hotel Maharaja International* (☎ 3161), directly opposite, is a little more upmarket. Doubles cost Rs 390 with attached bath.

Places to Stay – top end

The delightful *Palace Hotel* (Bikaner House; ☎ 3121; fax 3674) is a worthwhile treat and a very relaxing place to stay. The hotel was once the summer residence of the maharaja of Bikaner and is now managed by the maharaja's very amiable and helpful son-in-law. The hotel is in a picturesque location near the Dilwara temples and has well laid-out gardens, a private lake, two tennis courts, a billiard room and pony rides by arrangement. There are 38 very comfortable rooms and seven magnificent suites. The cost is a very reasonable Rs 850/1025 or Rs 1300 for suites, all year round. Excellent meals are available in the spacious dining room. Nearby is the new *Cama Rajputana Club Resort* (☎ 3163), once a private club but now a large hotel. Set in pleasant gardens, ordinary singles/doubles cost Rs 1190/1490 and deluxe rooms cost Rs 1390/1690; there are off-season discounts. There's a good restaurant serving Chinese, Continental and Punjabi food. A buffet lunch or dinner costs Rs 175.

If you want a quiet and homely atmosphere, try *Connaught House* (☎ 3439; or bookings through Umaid Bhawan Palace in Jodhpur, ☎ (0291) 33-316; fax 35-373), which belongs to the maharaja of Jodhpur. It's more like an English cottage than a hotel and is set in shady gardens. As well as rooms in the charming old building there's also a new wing of airy rooms. Comfortable singles/doubles with attached bath and constant hot water are Rs 850/1150. Meals are available but should be ordered in advance.

At the southern end of Mt Abu is the *Hotel Sunrise Palace* (☎ 3573), yet another former summer residence of a Rajput maharaja (this time the maharaja of Bharatpur). Although it lacks the style of the above two places, it's a very tranquil hotel with fabulous views. The rooms are well furnished and have attached bath, and range from Rs 600 to Rs 1150. The restaurant has excellent views.

If you want a modern hotel, the *Hotel Hilltone* (☎ 3112) is centrally located and is quite a good choice. Within the complex there's a swimming pool, restaurant, bar, sauna and bookshop. Singles/doubles cost Rs 750/ 950; cottages go for Rs 1800. There's a 20 to 30% discount in the low season. Near the Hotel Shikar Tourist Bungalow, the *Hotel Hillock* (☎ 3277) is a swanky place – large, spotlessly clean and well decorated. The comfortable rooms cost Rs 990 to Rs 1300. There's a restaurant serving Indian, Chinese and Continental food, as well as a bar, swimming pool and pleasant gardens.

Places to Eat

Near the bus stand, the *Kanak Dining Hall* is a good place to eat. It's very clean and the excellent South Indian vegetarian dishes and tasty thalis for Rs 35 make this a popular place at lunchtime. There are also masala dosas for Rs 15 and seating is available indoors or outdoors.

Further uphill, next to the junction at the bottom end of the polo ground, are several restaurants. The *Veena Restaurant* has very good Gujarati thalis (among the best in town) for Rs 30, with plenty of refills. It's open from 7 am to 3 pm and 6 pm to midnight. The nearby *Shanti Restaurant* is particularly recommended for its breakfasts.

In the bazaar area, there's strong competition between the *Shere Punjab Hotel* and the *New Shere Punjab Hotel*. The former has an excellent reputation, but the latter is a bit cheaper. Rivalry between the two restaurants is fierce and each pours scorn on the other's catering abilities. Both serve tandoori dishes, veg and non-veg.

The *Madras Cafe*, also in this area, is pure veg. There's some outdoor seating and the menu includes pizzas (Rs 20) and masala dosas (Rs 15). It's a reasonable place. Nearby,

the *Neelam Hotel* does non-veg as well as veg dishes.

At the top of the road leading down to the lake there's a cluster of restaurants. *King Food* has the usual have-a-go-at-anything menu and a good, fresh-juice stand. Behind it is the *Haveli Punjabi*, a pure veg restaurant. The amazingly named *Hencky Franck* used to be a fast food place, but is now an ice-cream parlour. From here down to the lake are a number of small snack places. On the lake itself there's a large dilapidated concrete 'boat' restaurant, the RTDC *Shikhar*, a tea shop that's closed in the low season.

For a splurge, go to a hotel restaurant. Lunch or dinner at the *Palace Hotel (Bikaner House)* costs Rs 175 for veg, Rs 225 for non-veg. The food is great and it's a good idea to make an advance booking.

Things to Buy

Most shops are located on the roads leading down to the lake. There are a variety of jewellery, clothing and craft shops, as well as places selling cheap souvenirs and knick-knacks. It's fun to take a stroll through the shop-lined town streets, which really come to life in the evening. Most shops are open until 9 pm.

Getting There & Away

As you enter Mt Abu, there's a toll gate where bus and car passengers are charged Rs 5, plus Rs 5 for a car. If you're travelling by bus this can be an irritating hold up, as you have to wait until the collector has gathered the toll from every passenger.

Bus From 6 am onwards, regular buses make the 27 km climb from Abu Road up to Mt Abu (Rs 10, one hour). Some RSTC buses go all the way to Mt Abu, while others terminate at Abu Road, so make sure you get the one you want.

The bus schedule from Mt Abu is extensive and, to many destinations, you will find a direct bus faster and more convenient than going down to Abu Road and waiting for a train. To Udaipur, RSTC buses take seven hours at a cost of Rs 50. To Ajmer (Rs 91 eight hours) and Jaipur (Rs 123, 11 hours) there's one departure daily. For Ahmedabad there are many departures (Rs 60, seven hours).

Deluxe and private buses are more expensive, but definitely preferable to state transport buses and there's plenty of choice. There are seemingly many companies with offices on the main street, but most are just ticketing agents; Shobha is one that operates its own buses. Buses to Udaipur take five hours and cost Rs 65. Other destinations served include Ajmer (Rs 120) and Jaipur (Rs 159).

Train Abu Road, the railhead for Mt Abu, is on the metre-gauge line between Delhi and Ahmedabad via Jaipur and Ajmer.

In Mt Abu there's a railway agency at the HP service station near the Hotel Shikar Tourist Bungalow, and it has quotas on most of the express trains out of Abu Road. It is open daily from 9 am to 1 pm and 2 to 4 pm (only until noon on Sunday).

There's a variety of trains; the best is the daily superfast Delhi to Ahmedabad *Ashram Express*. Fares for the five hour, 187 km journey from Ahmedabad are Rs 78/210 in 2nd/1st class.

Direct trains also run from Abu Road to Ajmer, Jodhpur and Agra. For Bhuj and the rest of the Kathiawar Peninsula in Gujarat, change trains at Palanpur, 53 km south of Abu Road.

Taxi A taxi, which you can share with up to five people, costs Rs 130 from Abu Road. If you want to hire a jeep and driver for sightseeing in and around Mt Abu, it costs Rs 600 per day but you may be able to bargain this down to Rs 500. Many hotels can organise jeeps or you can usually find jeeps for hire in the town centre.

Getting Around
Buses from the bus stand go to the various sites in Mt Abu, but it takes a little planning to get out and back without too much hanging around. Some buses only go to Dilwara, while others will take you out to Achalgarh (see below), so which you decide

to visit first will depend on the schedule. For Dilwara it's easier to take a share taxi and these leave when full from opposite the Madras Cafe in the centre of town; the fare is Rs 2. There are plenty of taxis with posted fares to anywhere you care to mention.

There are no auto-rickshaws in Mt Abu, but it's pretty easy to get around on foot. Porters with pram-like trolleys can transport your luggage for a small charge – they will even transport you in their trolley if you wish!

AROUND MT ABU
Achalgarh
The Shiva temple of **Achaleshwar Mahandeva**, 11 km north of Mt Abu, has a number of interesting features, including a toe of Shiva, a brass Nandi and, where the Shiva *lingam* would normally be, a deep hole said to extend all the way to the underworld.

Outside, by the car park, is a tank beside which stand three stone buffaloes and the figure of a king shooting them with a bow and arrows. A legend states that the tank was once filled with ghee, but demons in the form of buffaloes came down and drank each night, until the king shot them. A path leads up the hillside to a group of colourful **Jain temples** with fine views out over the plains.

Guru Shikhar
At the end of the plateau, 15 km from Mt Abu, is Guru Shikhar, the highest point in Rajasthan at 1721m. A road goes almost all the way to the summit. At the top is the **Atri Rishi Temple**, complete with a priest and good views all around.

Below the temple is a cafe selling soft drinks and snacks.

Mt Abu Wildlife Sanctuary
This 290 sq km wildlife sanctuary, eight km north-east of Mt Abu, is home to panthers, bears, sambars, fox, wild boar and birds. It spreads through forested hills, including 1721m high Guru Shikhar. In the sanctuary is **Trevor's Tank**, a small reservoir which was built and named after an English engineer. A sign at the sanctuary gives the

following advice: 'Use your eyes to observe the plants, birds and animals, use your ears to hear birds and animals call, use your legs to walk – the more you walk the more you see and hear'. The sanctuary is open daily from 8 am to 5 pm. Entry costs Rs 10, plus Rs 10 for cameras. Vehicles cost Rs 75 for petrol cars or jeeps, Rs 100 for diesel vehicles and Rs 10 for motorbikes. Taxis and jeeps can he hired in Udaipur.

Gaumukh Temple

Down on the Abu Road side of Mt Abu, a small stream flows from the mouth of a marble cow, giving the shrine its name. There is also a marble figure of the bull Nandi, Shiva's vehicle. The tank here, Agni Kund, is said to be the site of the sacrificial fire, made by the sage Vasishta, from which four of the great Rajput clans were born. An image of Vasishta is flanked by figures o Rama and Krishna.

ABU ROAD

This station down on the plains is the rai junction for Mt Abu. The railway station an bus stand are right next to each other on th edge of town. Although there are RSTC buses from Abu Road to other cities such a Jodhpur, Ajmer, Jaipur, Udaipur an Ahmedabad, there's little point in catching them here as they're all available from M Abu itself. Buses operated by private companies also run from Mt Abu.

There are lots of cheap hotels in Abu Road and many are only a short walk from the railway station. These places are OK for a night, but those in Mt Abu are far preferable The railway station has *retiring rooms* for a small charge.

Northern Rajasthan (Shekhawati)

The semi-desert Shekhawati region lies in the triangular area between Delhi, Jaipur and Bikaner. Starting around the 14th century, a number of Muslim clans moved into the area and the towns which developed became important trading posts on the caravan routes emanating from the ports of Gujarat. The name of the region and its inhabitants can be traced to a 15th century Rajput Kachhwaha chieftain by the name of Rao Shekha.

Although the towns have long since lost whatever importance they once had, they have not lost the amazing painted havelis built by the merchants of the region. Most of the buildings date from the 18th century to early this century, and such is their splendour that the area has been dubbed by some as the 'open air gallery of Rajasthan'. There are also the obligatory (for Rajasthan) forts, a couple of minor castles, distinctive wells, *baoris* (stepwells), *chhatris* (cenotaphs) and a handful of mosques.

The major towns of interest in the region are Nawalgarh, Fatehpur, Mandawa, Ramgarh and Jhunjhunu, although at least a few havelis survive in virtually every town.

HISTORY

As the Mughal Empire fell into decline after the death of Aurangzeb in 1707, the descendants of Rao Shekha, who had already

installed themselves in areas to the east of the Aravalli Range, began to encroach on the regions to the north and west. Covering an area of some 30,000 sq km, today this region encompasses the administrative districts of Churu, Jhunjhunu and Sikar, and is known as Shekhawati.

The chieftains of the region retained a nominal loyalty to the Rajput states of Jaipur and Amber, who in turn honoured them with hereditary titles known as *tazimi sardars*. It was probably exposure to the courts of Jaipur and Amber which encouraged the chieftains, who were known as *thakurs*, or barons, to commission the first of the thousands of murals which decorated their *havelis*, or mansions.

By 1732, two of these chieftains, Sardul Singh and Shiv Singh, had overthrown the nawabs of Fatehpur and Jhunjhunu and

FESTIVALS OF NORTHERN RAJASTHAN

Festivals peculiar to the Shekhawati region are given below. For statewide and nationwide festivals, see Festivals of Rajasthan in the Facts for the Visitor chapter.

March
Nawalgarh Fair – This fair is a relatively recent innovation promoted by the RTDC. Frankly, it's not wildly exciting: it features sports matches and displays on civic accomplishments with captions in Hindi. Given Rajasthan's propensity for spectacle, it may become more colourful in time.

September-October
Bissau Festival – Ten days before the festival of Dussehra, Bissau hosts dramatic performances of the *Ramayana*. The actors wear costumes and masks made locally, and the performance takes place in the bazaar at twilight.

In 1945, at the age of 12, Rao Shekha ruled over a number of villages. By 1471 he ruled the entire Shekhawati region.

NORTHERN RAJASTHAN

British ports at Bombay and Calcutta were able to handle a much greater volume of trade than those at Gujarat. Pressure by the British East India Company compelled Jaipur state to drastically reduce its levies, and it became no longer necessary for traders to travel via Shekhawati. However, the Shekhawat merchants had received a good grounding in the practices and principles of trade, and were reluctant to relinquish what was obviously a lucrative source of income.

Towards the end of the 19th century, the menfolk began to emigrate en masse from their desert homes to the thriving trading centres emerging on the ports of the Ganges. Their business acumen was unparalleled, and some of the richest merchants of Calcutta hailed from the tiny region of Shekhawati on the other side of India. Some of India's richest industrialists of the 20th century, such as the Birlas, were originally Marwaris (as the people from Shekhawati came to be known).

carved their territories up between them. Their descendants, particularly the sons of Sardul Singh, installed themselves in surrounding villages, where they commanded the allegiance and respect of the villagers. Their coffers were filled by heavy taxes imposed on the poor farmers of the area and duties levied on the caravans carrying goods from the ports of Gujarat overland to northern India and the countries bordering India to the north, north-west and north-east. Financial incentives prompted the merchants to travel via Shekhawati because the Rajput royal states on either side imposed even greater levies on traders than those of the Shekhawats. The arid region of Shekhawati thus saw a great deal of transit trading activity, encouraging merchants to establish themselves here.

The rise of the British Raj following the eclipse of the Mughal Empire could have sounded the death knell for Shekhawati. The

THE HAVELIS

With large amounts of money coming from trade, the merchants of Shekhawati were keen to build mansions on a grand scale. The merchants themselves lived frugally in their adopted homes, sending the bulk of the profits back to their families in Shekhawati. Their vast fortunes were used to commission the construction of grand havelis commensurate with their new stations in life: symbols of their success and increasing prosperity. Merchants competed with one another to build ever more grand edifices – homes, temples, wells – and these were richly decorated, both inside and out, with thousands of painted murals.

Many of the artists and masons were commissioned from beyond Shekhawati – particularly from Jaipur, where they had been employed decorating the palaces of the new capital – and others flooded into the region to offer their skills. There was a cross-pollination of ideas and techniques, with local artists learning from the new arrivals and adopting many of their designs.

The Buildings

They employed masons who were known as *chajeras*. The popular design was a building which from the outside was relatively unremarkable; rather the focus was on one or more internal courtyards which provided security and privacy for the women and offered some relief from the fierce heat which grips the area in summer. The plain exteriors also made the houses easy to defend.

The main entrance is a large wooden gate, which is usually locked. In this gate is a smaller doorway which gives access to a small outer courtyard. Often an enormous ramp leads to the entrance, up which a prospective groom could ascend in appropriate grandeur on horse or, in some cases, elephant back. Above the entrance can usually be seen one or more small shield-shaped devices called *torans*. These are generally wrought of wood and silver, and often feature a parrot – the bird of love. In a mock show of conquest, the groom was required to pierce the toran with his sword before claiming his bride. Each toran represents the marriage of a female from the household.

To one side of the outer courtyard is the

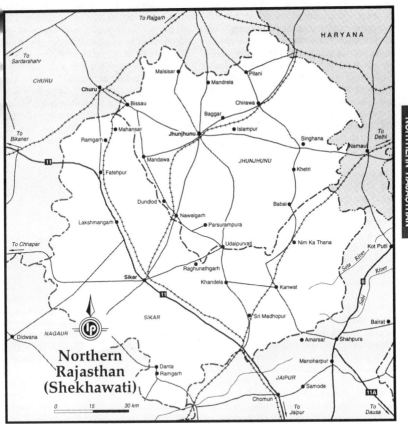

baithak, or salon, in which the merchant could receive guests. In order to impress visitors, this room was generally the most elaborately crafted and often featured marble or mock marble walls. Here the merchant and his guests reclined against bolsters as they discussed the business of the day.

Between the outer and inner courtyard is a type of vestibule, traversed by a blank wall in which is a small window. Through this window the women of the household, who were kept in strict *purdah* (isolation), could peep at prospective guests. Entry into the inner courtyard behind the blank wall – the domain of the womenfolk – was restricted to women, members of the family and, very occasionally, privileged guests. Access was gained on either side of the partitioning wall. That this courtyard was the main domestic arena is evident in the smoke-stained walls, the residue left by countless kitchen fires. Rooms off this courtyard served as bedrooms or store rooms, and staircases led to upper levels, the rooms of which mostly comprised bedrooms. The largest of the mansions had as many as four courtyards and were up to six storeys high.

The Paintings

The early Mughal influence, manifested in floral arabesques and geometric designs – according to the dictates of their religion, the Mughals never created a representation of an animal or human – gave way to influences from the Rajput royal courts. Later the walls were embellished with paintings of the new British technological marvels to which the Shekhawat merchants were exposed in centres such as Calcutta. Many of the pictures of motor cars and steam trains which adorn the buildings of Shekhawati were painted by artisans who had probably never even seen a motorised vehicle!

Originally the colours used in the murals were all ochre-based, but in the 1860s artificial pigments were introduced from Germany. The predominant colours are blue and maroon, but other colours such as yellow, green and indigo are also featured.

The major themes employed by artists, who were known as *chiteras*, were scenes from Hindu mythology, history, folk tales, eroticism (many of these works have been defaced or destroyed), and – among the most interesting – foreigners and their modern inventions, such as trains, planes, telephones, gramophones and bicycles. Animals and landscapes were also popular. The colourful paintings were often a response to the arid landscape, and served both an educational and entertainment purpose. Religious themes mostly featured the legends of lords Krishna and Rama, and were used as moral teachings where good prevailed over evil.

The paintings also served as social documents depicting the concerns of the day. The advent of photography and exposure to European art had a dramatic influence on the execution of art in Shekhawati. Previously, subjects were depicted two dimensionally, and there was little emphasis on anatomical accuracy or the use of shade for perspective. With the influence of photography, artists sought a more faithful rendering of their subjects. Before photography, there was far more emphasis on the imagination.

The paintings of Shekhawati are thus an extraordinary synthesis of eastern and western influences. An haveli in Fatehpur perfectly illustrates this cultural collision: in one painting, Krishna is depicted playing a gramophone for his consort Radha. Some of the paintings of the early 20th century exhibit an extraordinary technical expertise; others are florid, grotesque and executed in lurid colours. But all are interesting.

RESPONSIBLE TRAVEL

The tourist boom has still not caught up with Shekhawati, but with so much to see, and some interesting places to stay, it's an area well worth exploring. The best plan is to just wander at random through these small, dusty towns. There's no chance of getting lost, and there are surprises around every corner. While tourism can play a positive role in promoting interest in Shekhawati's great legacy of beautifully painted buildings, therefore generating the political will to preserve

NORTHERN RAJASTHAN

ARCHITECTURE

TEMPLES

Temples in south-eastern Rajasthan bear architectural influences of the Gupta Empire, which held sway over northern India from the 4th to the 6th centuries. Examples include those at Darrah and the Sheetaleshvara Temple at Jhalrapatan.

Around the 8th and 9th centuries, a new style of temple architecture emerged with the consolidation of the Gurjara Pratihara dynasty of Mandore. Temples built at this time include those at Chittorgarh and the exquisitely carved temples at Osiyan, in western Rajasthan, many of which feature magnificent sculptural work, such as that evident in the Laxminarayan Temple. A usual feature of these temples is a single *shikhara*, or spire, and a sculpted *mandapa*, or outer chamber, before the inner sanctum. In several cases, the main temple is surrounded by a series of small and finely sculpted shrines. Well preserved examples are the Kalika Mata and Kumbha Shyama temples in Chittorgarh Fort.

There is a fine temple group at Kiradu, to the west of Barmer, which conforms to the architectural style known as Solanki. The most inspiring of the five temples here is the Someshvara Temple, which has a fine sculpted frieze and a multi-tiered spire.

The 10th century saw the construction of many fine Jain temples. One of the most impressive and well known groups is the Dilwara group at Mt Abu, renowned for its remarkable and exquisite carving. The Mahavira Temple near Ghanerao in southern Rajasthan is also of note.

Of the later temples, the 15th century temples at Ranakpur, 40 km from Udaipur, are the finest. The most important of these is the Chaumukha Temple. It features a series of mandapas adorned with fine carving, and achieves a breathtaking symmetry. The beautiful group of Jain temples in Jaisalmer Fort are also noteworthy. Entrance to the mandapas of some of these temples is through beautifully carved *toranas*, or gateways.

MICHELLE COXALL

The small Laxminarayan Temple is situated alongside the main Sachiya Mata Temple in Osiyan. It is one of a series of small shrine-like temples which are remarkable for their beautiful sculptural detail.

FORTS & PALACES

Secular architecture is no less inspiring than religious architecture, as is evident in the massive and beautiful forts and/or palaces of Chittorgarh, Jodhpur, Jaisalmer, Bikaner, Bundi, Kota, Amber, Jaipur, Alwar, Deeg, Bharatpur, Ranthambhore, Nagaur and Udaipur. These encompass *mahals* (palaces), *zenanas* (women's quarters), *diwan-i-am* (public audience halls) *diwan-i-khas* (private audience halls), *sals* (galleries), *mandirs* (temples) and *baghs* (gardens). The palaces and forts of Rajasthan are the last word in opulence. Sometimes the beauty of the royal edifice was reflected in an artificial pool, or tank, as is evident at Deeg and Alwar. In the later palaces, the Rajputs often borrowed architectural inspiration from the Mughals. The *sheesh mahal*, or mirror palace, which is found in some of the palaces of Rajasthan, is a Mughal innovation.

Amber Fort was the capital of the Kachhwaha dynasty prior to the foundation of Jaipur. This magnificent fort, dating from the late 16th century, features exquisite tilework, which is evident in many of its chambers. The tradition of fine architecture was maintained when the capital was shifted to Jaipur, evident in the soaring Hawa Mahal, or Palace of the Winds, an impressive edifice which is in fact little more than a facade with hundreds of windows, from which the women of the royal court could watch passing processions. Nearby is the vast City Palace complex, construction of which commenced during the reign of Jai Singh II, founder of Jaipur. Jai Singh II, known as the warrior astronomer, also built the Jantar Mantar, an observatory with a series of huge and amazing devices for observing the celestial bodies and their movements, such as the Samrat Yantra, the largest sundial in the world.

Below: Detail of the facade of the Palace of the Winds, Jaipur.

Top Right: The awe-inspiring Meherangarh Fort dominates the skyline of Jodhpur. The fort encompasses magnificent palaces and numerous courtyards.

Bottom Right: The Ganeshpol at Amber Fort features elaborate inlay.

SARA-JANE CLELAND

ADAM MCCROW

RICHARD I'ANSON

HAVELIS

The merchants of Rajasthan built fine mansions, known as *havelis*, and commissioned masons and artists to ensure that these buildings were constructed and decorated in a manner befitting the importance and prosperity of their owners. The Shekhawati district is riddled with havelis, most of which are comprehensively covered, inside and out, with extraordinarily vibrant murals. The merchants also commissioned the construction of civic buildings such as wells, which benefited the entire community. There are also beautiful havelis in Jaisalmer, constructed of sandstone, featuring the fine work of the renowned *silavats* (stone-carvers) of Jaisalmer.

MICHELLE COXALL

WELLS & TANKS

Given the importance of water in a predominantly desert-covered state such as Rajasthan, it is not surprising that wells and reservoirs, often known as tanks or *sagars* (lakes), were frequently beautiful and elaborate edifices. The Mertani *baori*, or stepwell (a well in which a series of steps leads down to the water table), at Jhunjhunu, built in the 18th century, is architecturally a very impressive structure, with a series of chambers built into the side walls, supported by pillars. Also in Jhunjhunu is the beautiful Ajit Sagar, with ornate pavilions around its edges, some featuring painted murals in the domes. In Jaisalmer, in the arid western region of the state, is the fine Gadi Sagar, which supplied water to the city prior to the construction of the Indira Gandhi Canal. It features beautiful freestanding pavilions in the lake centre, and a series of *ghats* (steps) leading down to the water's edge. In southern Rajasthan, there are some very good baoris at Bundi and Ghanerao.

MICHELLE COXALL

Top: Fine detail on the back section of the Aath havelis, Shekhawati.

Bottom: The picturesque Gadi Sagar, in Jaisalmer, was once the lifeblood of this desert town. It is surrounded by temples and shrines.

CHHATRIS

Rajasthan's architectural heritage is also evident in the chhatris, o cenotaphs, built to commemorate maharajas, and, as is the case in the Shekhawati district, wealthy merchants such as the Poddars and Goenkas. In rare instances, chhatris also commemorate women, such as the Chhatri of Moosi Rani at Alwar. Although built in honour of Maharaja Bakhtawar Singh, his wife is also commemorated here as she earned herself a degree of immortality by performing the highest sacrifice – committing herself to the flames of her husband's funeral pyre in an act of *sati* (self-immolation). Chhatri translates as 'umbrella', a reference to the pillared domes of the cenotaphs.

MICHELLE COXALL

There is a series of beautiful chhatris of the Rathore Rajputs at Mandore, the ancient capital of Marwar before Jodhpur was founded. Chhatris generally comprise a central dome, supported by a series of pillars on a raised platform, with a series of small pavilions on the corners and sides. In the Shekhawati district, it is not unusual for the inside of the dome to be completely covered with paintings, such as that in the Chhatri of Thakur Sardul Singh at Parsurampura, which features battle scenes from the *Ramayana*. Fine chhatris can also be found in the villages of Dundlod and Ramgarh. Excellent royal chhatris may be seen in Jaipur and flanking Jaisamand Lake, near Udaipur.

MICHELLE COXALL

Top: The Chhatri of Moosi Rani, Alwar.

Bottom: Detail of the paintings that cover the Chhatri of Thakur Sardul Singh at Parsurampura. The fine paintings date from the mid-18th century.

BUILDING CONSERVATION

The Indian National Trust for Art & Cultural Heritage (INTACH) is a voluntary organisation that works to conserve and restore Rajasthan's historic monuments. Visitors can help the trust by writing to the chief minister of the Rajasthan state government to advise that the work carried out by INTACH is appreciated. For more information, write to Dharmendar Kanwar, INTACH, 2 Tilak Marg, Jaipur 302 001 (☎ (0141) 38-1619; fax 38-1654).

them, it should be borne in mind that this is both an ecologically and culturally sensitive region. While there is a basic infrastructure in place to accommodate the increasing number of foreign visitors to Shekhawati, tourism here is still in its infancy. There is only one RTDC guest house in the entire region – at Fatehpur – although there are some excellent places to stay in some of the villages, including beautiful converted fortresses at Dundlod and Mandawa, and fine guest houses at Nawalgarh and Jhunjhunu.

Camel safaris are an increasingly popular way to visit the villages of Shekhawati. Visitors can help minimise the potentially destructive nature of these expeditions by ensuring that all rubbish is carried out and insisting on kerosene fires instead of using the already beleaguered sources of wood upon which locals depend. It is also possible to stay in village homes: Ramesh Jangid from Nawalgarh has some excellent homestay programmes; visitors are kept to manageable numbers so that the experience is rewarding both for the hosts and their guests. Ramesh is a terrific source of information on the havelis of Shekhawati, and visitors interested in learning more about preservation

and conservation programmes in this region are encouraged to contact him.

Ramesh Jangid is the president of Les Amis du Shekhawati (The Friends of Shekhawati) – for more information about the society and its endeavours to protect the paintings of Shekhawati, see under Voluntary Work in the Facts for the Visitor chapter. He has initiated some visionary conservation measures at his Eco Farm in Nawalgarh, including experiments in solar water heating, organic toilets and biogas. Another excellent source of information on the painted havelis of Shekhawati is Laxmi Kant Jangid, at the Hotel Shiv Shekhawati in Jhunjhunu.

These days most of the havelis are not inhabited by their owners, who find that the small towns in rural Rajasthan have little appeal. Many are occupied just by a single *chowkidar* (caretaker), while others may be home to a local family. None are open as museums or for display, and consequently many are either totally or partially locked up. While locals seem fairly tolerant of strangers wandering into their front courtyard, be aware that these are private places, so tact and discretion should be used – don't just blunder in as though you own the place.

NORTHERN RAJASTHAN

The Legend of Dhola Maru

One of the most popular paintings to be seen on the walls of Shekhawati havelis depicts the legend of Dhola Maru, the Shekhawati equivalent of Romeo and Juliet.

The princess Maru hailed from Pugal, near Bikaner, and Dhola was a young prince from Gwalior. When Maru was two years old, there was a bad drought in Pugal, so her father, who was the maharaja, shifted to Gwalior, where his friend, the maharaja, and father of Dhola, ruled. He stayed for three years, returning to Pugal when he learned that the drought there had broken. Before he left, as a token of friendship between the two rulers, a marriage alliance was contracted between their children. However, after 20 years the promise had been forgotten and Maru was contracted to marry a man by the name of Umra.

Wedding plans would have proceeded apace, but a bard, who had travelled from Pugal to Gwalior, sang at the royal court of the childhood marriage of Dhola and Maru. In this way Dhola came to hear of the beautiful Maru, with whom he immediately fell in love after simply hearing her virtues described, and resolved to meet her. Of course, when Maru laid eyes on her champion she fell in love with him, and they decided to flee together. Her betrothed, Umra, heard of the flight of the lovers, and set chase with his brother, Sumra. They pursued the camel-borne lovers on horseback, and the brave Maru fired at them with arrows, which proved of little use against the brothers, who had guns. They were able to temporarily elude the brothers and took shelter in a forest. However, Dhola was bitten by a snake and succumbed on the spot. Maru, thus thwarted by death, proceeded to weep for her lost lover, and her lamentations were heard by Shiva and Parvati who were walking nearby. Parvati beseeched Shiva to restore the dead Dhola to life and the couple were reunited. ■

Local custom dictates that shoes should be removed when entering the inner courtyard of an haveli.

One unfortunate aspect of the tourist trade is also beginning to manifest itself here – the desire for antiques. A couple of towns have antique shops chock-a-block with items ripped from the havelis – particularly doors and window frames, but anything that can be carted away is fair game. Investing in these antiques is tantamount to condoning this desecration.

One last note: flashes from cameras can damage the paintings. You may not be forbidden to use them, but don't!

GUIDEBOOKS

For a full rundown on the history, people, towns and buildings of the area, it's well worth investing in a copy of *The Guide to the Painted Towns of Shekhawati*, by Ilay Cooper. Although it's a little expensive at Rs 450, it gives details of buildings of interest in each town, precise locations of interesting paintings and fine sketch maps of the larger tours of the area. Another excellent general reference to the region is *Shekhawati: Rajasthan's Painted Homes* by Pankaj Rakesh (text) and Karoki Lewis (photographer).

GETTING THERE & AWAY

Access to the region is easiest from Jaipur or Bikaner. The towns of Sikar (gateway to the region, but with no notable havelis) and Fatehpur are on the main Jaipur to Bikaner road and are served by many buses. Churu is on the main Delhi to Bikaner railway line, while Sikar, Nawalgarh and Jhunjhunu have several daily passenger train links with Jaipur and Delhi. Shekhawati is also easily accessible by train from Delhi. For more details on getting to this region, see the relevant sections throughout this chapter.

GETTING AROUND

The Shekhawati region is crisscrossed by narrow bitumen roads and all towns are well served by government or private buses. The local services to the smaller towns can get very crowded and riding 'upper class' (on the roof!) is quite acceptable – and often necessary.

If you have a group of four or five people, it is worth hiring a taxi for the day to take you around the area. It's easy to arrange in the towns which have accommodation, although finding a driver who speaks English is more of a problem. The official rate for a taxi is Rs 3 per km with a minimum of 300 km per day. There is an Ambassador taxi stand near the bus stand in Sikar, or taxis can be arranged at the Hotel Shiv Shekhawati and the bus stand in Jhunjhunu.

A number of operators are now offering camel safaris in the Shekhawati region. See Organised Tours under Nawalgarh and Dundlod for details.

NAWALGARH

Telephone Area Code: 01594

Nawalgarh was founded in 1737 by Nawal Singh, one of the five sons of the Rajput ruler Sardul Singh. The arrival of merchants from Jaipur increased the town's prosperity, and some of India's most successful merchants hailed from Nawalgarh, including the wealthy Goenka family, who built many havelis in this region. Nawalgarh has some of the best preserved havelis in Shekhawati. The township is built in a depression where a number of rivers terminate. The accumulated silt carried by these rivers was used in the bricks used to construct the havelis.

Information

The best source of information on Nawalgarh and its painted havelis is Ramesh Jangid at the Ramesh Jangid Tourist Pension (☎ 22-129; fax 22-491). Ramesh is actively involved in the preservation of Shekhawati's havelis, and has initiated educational programmes to raise local awareness about the rich cultural legacy they represent.

Travellers' cheques can be changed at the Bank of Baroda and the State Bank of Bikaner and Jaipur, both in the same building in the old fort.

Things to See

Bala Qila The main building in this town is the fort, founded in 1737. Today it is largely disfigured by modern accretions. It houses government offices and two banks (see under Information, earlier). One room in the south-eastern quarter of the fort retains paintings on its ceiling which depict street scenes of both Jaipur and Nawalgarh from the mid-19th century.

The Havelis To the south-west of the Bala Qila is a group of six havelis known as the **Aath Havelis**. The incongruous name – *aath* means 'eight' – refers to the fact that originally eight havelis were planned, although only six were completed. The paintings are not technically as proficient as some others in this town, but they illustrate the transition in painting styles over the decades. As you approach the group from the road, the first haveli to the left is a case in point: there are older paintings on the front of the side external wall, while newer paintings, evidenced by the synthetic colours, are at the rear of this wall. The front section of the side wall depicts a steam locomotive, while the back section has monumental pictures of elephants, horses and camels.

Opposite this group of havelis is the **Murarka Haveli**, which has some very fine paintings including, above the entrance, miniatures depicting the Krishna legends. The haveli is no longer inhabited, but is hired for marriage celebrations. Unfortunately, unless a marriage is taking place, the richly painted inner courtyard is usually locked.

About 10 minutes walk to the north is the **Hem Raj Kulwal Haveli**, which was built in 1931. Above the entrance are portraits of members of the Kulwal family, as well as portraits of Gandhi and Nehru. Very colourful architraves surround the windows and an ornate silver door leads to the inner courtyard. This features paintings depicting mostly religious themes. Opposite the haveli is a guest house with distinct European architecture in which guests of the Kulwal family were accommodated.

Nearby is the **Khedwal Bhavan**, which features beautiful mirrorwork above the entrance to the inner courtyard, and fine blue tilework. A locomotive is depicted above the archway and a frieze along the north wall

shows the Teej Festival: note the women on swings. On the west wall is a large locomotive crossing a bridge and underneath are portraits of English people. On the outside north wall is the story of Dhola Maru in two frames. In the first frame, soldiers chase the fleeing camel-borne lovers. Maru fires arrows at the assailants while Dhola urges the camel on. Above can be seen a smaller painting of an English woman with an infant.

To the east of the Baori Gate is the **Bhagton ki Haveli**. On the external west wall is a locomotive and a steam ship. On the wall above, *gopis* (milkmaids) with the bodies of elephants dance, and adjacent, women perform the Ginder dance during the festival of Holi.

Above the doorway to the inner courtyard is a very detailed picture of the marriage of Rukmani. Krishna cheated the groom Sisupal of his prospective wife by touching the *toran* (shield-shaped device above the doorway) first, thus claiming her for himself. The walls of the salon are reminiscent of marble – the wall is first painted black then decorative incisions are executed. The inner chamber upstairs contains the family quarters. The rooms are also elaborately painted. A room on the west side has a picture of a European man with a cane and pipe and a small dog on his shoulder. Adjacent, a melancholy English woman plays an accordion.

On Dharni Dharka Rd is the **Parsurampura Haveli**, which dates from early this century and belongs to a merchant from Parsurampura. The paintings are very grand, and almost *too* perfect – the European influence on their execution is evident. Themes include both the religious and secular.

In the street behind this haveli is the **Dharni Dharka Haveli**, which dates from 1930. There is an ornate painted carving above the arches and portraits of Gandhi, Nehru in an automobile, and Krishna and Radha on a swing.

A short distance to the south of the fort is the **Chhauchharia Haveli**, with paintings dating from the last decade of the 19th century. Some of the more interesting pictures include those of a hot air balloon being inflated by several Europeans blowing vigorously through pipes, and a man who on first glance appears to be, well, exposing himself – closer examination reveals that he is holding out his finger! There are very elaborate floral motifs over the enormous doorway and, in the outer court, intricate geometric and floral designs and inlaid mirrors above scalloped archways.

To the south-west of the fort is the **Shankar Lal Haveli**, which is famous for its different representations of cars on an external wall. Other pictures include an English couple sitting stiffly on a bench and a tractor with a tip tray – a new invention.

A short distance to the north is the **Geevrajka Haveli**, which has very fine paintings

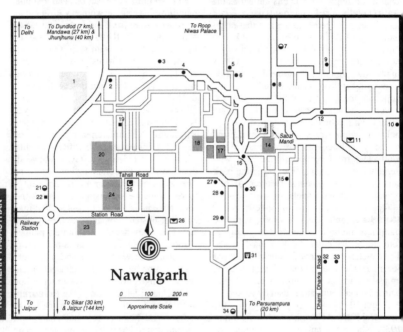

Nawalgarh

PLACES TO STAY	7	Dundlod Bus Stand	20	Maur Hospital
1 Apani Dhani (Eco Farm)	8	Baori Gate	21	Main Bus Stand
13 Hotel Natraj	9	Bhagton ki Haveli	23	Poddar College
19 Ramesh Jangid Tourist Pension	10	Ananda Lal Poddar Haveli	24	Eye Hospital
22 Nawal Hotel	11	Central Post Office	25	Mosque
	12	Poddar Gate	26	Post Office
OTHER	14	Bala Qila, Bank of Baroda & State Bank of Bikaner & Jaipur	27	Jhunjhunuwala Haveli
2 Bicycle Hire			28	Geevrajka Haveli
3 Well	15	Chhauchharia Haveli	29	Shankar Lal Haveli
4 Mandi Gate	16	Nansa Gate	30	Bicycle Hire
5 Hem Raj Kulwal Haveli	17	Aath Haveli	31	Ganga Mai Temple
6 Khedwal Bhavan	18	Murarka Haveli	32	Parsurampura Haveli
			33	Dharni Dharka Haveli
			34	Parsurampura Bus Stand

on the ceiling of the entrance, including various Hindu deities.

On the right as you enter the town centre from Tahsil Rd is the **Jhunjhunuwala Haveli**, which is an unfortunate example of the lack of will to conserve the havelis. The main courtyard of this building has been destroyed with the construction of six shops. The side wall retains a fine procession frieze – a train, horses, camels and soldiers carrying a palanquin.

The **Anandi Lal Poddar Haveli**, which dates from 1920, is now a secondary school. The paintings of this haveli are some of the few in Nawalgarh which have been restored. A side wall retains the paintings in their deteriorated condition, which are in stark contrast to the paintings across the front facade. In the first courtyard close to the entrance is a tiny picture of Christ.

Ganga Mai Temple Several hundred metres to the south of the Nansa Gate is the Ganga Mai Temple, which, as its name suggests, is dedicated to the Goddess Ganga. There is fine mirrorwork around the inner sanctum. The courtyard is surrounded by four aisles formed by five archways, above each of which are floral motifs. There are some good, small paintings above the *mandapa* (courtyard before the inner sanctum). The temple was built by the wealthy Chhauchha-ria merchants in 1868.

Organised Tours

Ramesh Jangid and his son Rajesh are keen to promote rural tourism, which entails staying with families in small villages in the Shekhawati region. Numbers are kept to a minimum (a maximum of two couples only per host family) and an English-speaking interpreter is provided. They can also organise three day treks in the Aravalli Range, camel safaris around Rajasthan, and informative guided tours around the painted havelis of Shekhawati, including trips by bicycle.

Costs of treks are from Rs 1250 per person per day for up to two people, Rs 1000 per

person up to three people, and Rs 850 for up to four people.

Prices for jeep tours to the villages of Shekhawati from Nawalgarh are as follows: three hour trip taking in Dundlod and Parsurampura, Rs 600 for up to four people; five hour trip taking in Mandawa, Dundlod and Fatehpur, Rs 800 for up to four people; seven to eight hour trip visiting Mandawa, Fatehpur, Ramgarh and Mahansar, Rs 1050. See under Information earlier in this section for Ramesh Jangid's contact details.

The Roop Niwas Palace hotel can provide English-speaking guides for walking tours around the painted walls of Nawalgarh for Rs 50 for a half day, Rs 100 for a full day.

Places to Stay

The cheapest place to stay is the *Hotel Natraj* (☎ 22-404), overlooking the Sabzi Mandi (vegetable market), right outside the entrance to the fort. Very basic singles/doubles with common bath are Rs 50/80 and you can get basic meals here.

The *Nawal Hotel* (☎ 22-155) is right on the bus stand, about one km from the town centre. It costs Rs 60 for a double with attached bath and there are doubles for Rs 100, Rs 150 and Rs 200, all with attached bath. Meals are available here.

The *Roop Niwas Palace* (☎ Jaipur (0141) 62-2949) is on the northern edge of town, about one km from the fort. It has comfortable air-cooled singles/doubles for Rs 700/900, although the décor is somewhat eclectic. There are also suites for Rs 1500. This was the residence of the thakur of Nawalgarh, Nawal Singh (1880-1926).

An excellent choice is the *Ramesh Jangid Tourist Pension* (☎ 22-129; fax 22-491), within easy walking distance of some of Nawalgarh's best havelis. Very comfortable rooms are Rs 200/250 with attached bath, or the upstairs rooms, which open onto a sunny terrace, are Rs 120/150 with attached bath. Pure veg meals are available here, including a veg thali for Rs 40.

Ramesh has a second place to stay, on the west side of the main Jaipur road, called *Apani Dhani*, or Eco Farm. Here Ramesh has implemented his various experiments in alternative energy, such as solar water heaters, biogas and solar cookers. Rooms are decorated in traditional style and have thatched roofs and mud plaster. They cost Rs 500/600 for singles/doubles with attached bath. The farm has buffaloes, cows and goats, the manure from which is used on the vegie garden and to produce biogas for cooking. Fresh vegies from the garden make up the bulk of the pure veg meals available here.

Getting There & Away

Bus There are buses every 30 minutes between Nawalgarh and Jaipur (express 3½ hours, Rs 38; deluxe three hours, Rs 46), and several services each day to Delhi (eight hours, Rs 70). There is also an overnight service to Delhi.

There are two buses during the day and two night buses to Jodhpur (nine hours).

Buses for destinations in Shekhawati leave every few minutes and share jeeps leave according to demand; prices are as follows: Sikar, Rs 8; Jhunjhunu, Rs 10; Fatehpur, Rs 9.

There is a daily deluxe service to Ahmedabad (18 hours, Rs 180) via Ajmer (six hours, Rs 150) and Udaipur (14 hours, Rs 150).

Train The 9734 *Shekhawati Express* leaves Nawalgarh at 10 pm, arriving at Delhi's Sarai Rohilla station at 5.30 am (Rs 89/267). To Jaipur, the *Shekhawati Express* leaves Nawalgarh at 7 am, reaching Jaipur at 10.30 am (Rs 35/105).

Getting Around

Bicycles can be hired near Nansa Gate and at Ramesh Jangid Tourist Pension for Rs 10 to Rs 15 per day.

A share auto-rickshaw from the railway or bus station to the fort is Rs 2, and you can wave it down anywhere along this route. To hire an auto-rickshaw or horse-drawn tonga from either the bus or railway station to the fort costs Rs 16.

PARSURAMPURA

This tiny village, 20 km south-east of Nawalgarh, has some of the best preserved and oldest paintings in the Shekhawati region. The fine paintings on the interior of the dome of the **Chhatri of Thakur Sardul Singh** date from the mid-18th century. The very fine and detailed work here is reminiscent of miniature painting. The antiquity of the painting is evident in the muted, russet colour employed. Pictures include those of the thakur and his five sons, graphic battle scenes from the *Ramayana*, and the love story of Dhola Maru, a common theme employed by the painters of Shekhawati. To visit the cenotaph you must obtain the key from the caretaker, Sri Banwari Lal (nicknamed Maharaj), who lives in the Shamji Sharaf Haveli. Maharaj is a Brahmin priest and it is almost entirely through his endeavours that the chhatri is so well maintained. Maharaj is also responsible for the pretty flowerbeds of roses and jasmine which surround the chhatri. He is more than happy to explain the various paintings and a small donation would not be unwelcome – it will be put to good use to maintain the chhatri and its garden.

The **Shamji Sharaf Haveli** dates from the end of the 18th century. Pictures include a grandmother having her hair dressed, an Indian woman spinning and an English woman in shiny patent leather shoes carrying a parasol. A frieze shows a celebration, probably of a marriage, and on one side is a frame showing a priest presiding over the ceremony. The opposite wall depicts Europeans in a car. Above the lintel are some very well preserved portraits, and below, portrayals of Ganesh, Vishnu, Krishna and Radha. Saraswati is riding a peacock in the right hand corner.

Also in Parsurampura is the small **Gopinathji Mandir**, on the left just before you leave the village on the road to Nawalgarh. The temple was built by Sardul Singh in 1742 and it is believed that the same artist responsible for the paintings on the Chhatri of Sardul Singh executed the fine paintings in the temple. According to local lore, the artist had half completed the work in the temple when the son of Sardul Singh chopped his hands off because he wanted the artist's work to be exclusive to his father's chhatri. Not to be deterred, the valiant artist completed the work with his feet!

Getting There & Away

There are numerous buses throughout the day to Parsurampura from Nawalgarh. You'll have to fight for a seat (or roof space!), and it's a dusty, corrugated road which crosses a dry river bed just before the village.

DUNDLOD

Telephone Area Code: 015945

Dundlod is a tiny village lying about seven km north of Nawalgarh. Its small fort was built in 1750 by Keshri Singh, the fifth and youngest son of Sardul Singh. Major additions were made in the early 19th century by his descendant Sheo Singh, who resettled in the region despite attempts on his life by Shyam Singh of Bissau, who murdered his father and brother in an endeavour to claim the region for himself. Members of the wealthy Goenka merchant family also settled at Dundlod, and their prosperity is evident in their richly painted havelis here.

Things to See

The **Dundlod Fort** dates from 1750 and features a blend of the Rajputana and Mughal styles of art and architecture. The *diwan-i-khas*, or Private Audience Hall, has stained glass windows, fine Louis XIV antiques and an impressive collection of rare books. Above the diwan-i-khas is the *duchatta*, or women's gallery, from where the women in purdah could view the proceedings below. The *zenana*, or women's quarters, features walls of duck egg blue, and opens onto the reading room of the *thakurani* (noblewoman), which has a hand-carved wooden writing table bearing oriental motifs in the form of dragons. Above the entrance to the ladies' quarters can be seen 10 torans, indicating that 10 daughters from the Singh family of the fort were married.

Only one room retains paintings, which can be seen on the ceiling of a small alcove. Unfortunately, they are irreparably damaged, although Krishna can still be made out.

The beautiful **Chhatri of Ram Dutt Goenka** and the adjacent well were both built by Ram Chandra Goenka in 1888. They lie about five minutes walk to the south-east of the fort. The interior of the dome has floral motifs extending in banners down from its centre. The dome is encircled by a frieze depicting Krishna dancing with the gopis, interspersed with peacocks and musicians. The dominant colours are blue, red, yellow, turquoise and brown. Paintings around the inner base of the dome show a battle scene from the *Mahabharata*, a marriage celebration and Vishnu reclining on a snake.

The **Tuganram Goenka Haveli** is often locked, but you can see fine mirrorwork above the windows on the upper walls of the courtyard. Finely preserved paintings under the eaves mostly comprise portraits in round frames. The haveli opposite is interesting, as the work has not been completed, and it is possible to see how the artist sketched the drawings before adding colour. Pictures include those of an elephant, camel and rider, and a horse.

In a small square to the right just before the fort entrance is the **Satyanarayan Temple**, which was built by a member of the Goenka family in 1911. On the west wall of the temple is a long frieze showing Europeans on bicycles, in cars, and a long train, above which electricity lines extend. The portraits under the eaves show various nobles engaged in leisure pursuits, such as smelling flowers and reading. One fine mustachioed and turquoise-turbaned fellow has a bird in his hand, and another painting shows a woman admiring herself in a mirror.

A short distance to the south of the temple is a **Goenka Haveli** built by Arjun Dass Goenka in 1875. Above the window arches, mirrors are arranged in florets. Better preserved paintings can be seen on the east wall of the nearby **Jagathia Haveli**. There is a good railway station scene – in one carriage, a man appears to be in a passionate embrace with his wife, but closer inspection reveals his angry expression and that he is in fact beating her. A man hurries along on a bicycle parallel to the train, pursued by a dog.

Organised Tours

The Dera Dundlod Kila hotel (see below) can organise horse safaris around the Shekhawati area: a five day safari is Rs 4000 per person, including meals, tent accommodation and horse. There is also an eight day trip which takes in Bikaner and Jaipur for Rs 4500. It's also possible to hire a camel and an English-speaking guide to visit the havelis of Dundlod (Rs 250 per hour). You can also learn equestrian skills, including polo, at the Royal Equestrian Polo Centre at the hotel. Lessons are for two or more days, and prices are available on application.

Places to Stay

The *Dera Dundlod Kila* (☎ 2519; Jaipur ☎ & fax (0141) 36-6276), at the fort, is still in the family of Dundlod's founder, being now run by Raghuvendra Singh, the second son of the last thakur of Dundlod. It has air-cooled standard rooms for Rs 750/900 and suites for Rs 1500. Each room is different, and while not luxurious, they are certainly cosy and comfortable. Breakfast is Rs 80, lunch is Rs 160 and dinner is Rs 180, and there's a bar here.

There is a second place to stay at the fort, the *Castle Dundlod Ford* (☎ 52-180). Rooms here are Rs 900/1300.

Getting There & Away

It's possible to walk from Nawalgarh to Dundlod, although it's a hot walk along a busy, dusty road. There are local buses between these two towns every few minutes. From Nawalgarh, you can either catch a bus from the main bus stand, or from the Dundlod stand, just outside the Baori Gate.

JHUNJHUNU

Telephone Area Code: 01592

Jhunjhunu lies 245 km from Delhi and 180 km from Jaipur, and is one of the largest towns of Shekhawati. It is currently the district headquarters of the region. It has some of the region's most beautiful buildings, and should not be missed.

The town was founded by the Kaimkhani nawabs in the middle of the 15th century, and remained under their control until it was taken by the Rajput ruler Sardul Singh in 1730. It was in Jhunjhunu that the British based their Shekhawati Brigade, a troop raised locally in the 1830s to try to halt the activities of *dacoits* (bandits). The dacoits were largely local petty rulers who had decided it was easier to become wealthy by pinching other peoples' money than by earning their own.

In Jhunjhunu you can see tiny donkeys pulling enormous loads on heavy carts.

Information

The RTDC tourist office (☎ 32-909) is at the Hotel Shiv Shekhawati (see Places to Stay). It's open Monday to Friday and every second Saturday from 10 am to 5 pm (lunch between 1.30 and 2 pm). You can arrange guides here for visits to the havelis of Jhunjhunu. Official Government of India rates for a four hour tour are Rs 200 for up to four people and Rs 300 for five to 15 people. A full day tour is Rs 300 for up to four people and Rs 400 for five to 15 people.

The Bank of Baroda can exchange travellers' cheques. English-language newspapers are available at the bus stand.

Things to See

On the north-west side of the town is the **Badani Chand Well**. The well is surmounted by four imposing minarets (two minarets generally symbolise the presence of a stepwell). Because water is such a precious commodity in the desert, wells were treated almost like temples, and in fact it is not unusual to see a temple at a well – there is a small temple at this well which is sacred to Hanuman. Wells were often decorated in rich paintings, and there are often one or two pavilions erected nearby at which women could gather and exchange news – the local village well served as an important social centre. As at this well, you will often find a neem tree nearby, the twigs from which are used to clean the teeth.

Unfortunately, the paintings on the minarets at this well have faded. Near the well on its west side is an old inn at which caravans would once have halted.

A few km further north is the picturesque artificial **Ajit Sagar**, built by Jitmal Khaitan in 1902. The lake is fed by rainwater which runs down from the sides of nearby Moda Pahar *(pahar* means 'hill') and very rarely dries up. There are pavilions on each corner of the lake, some of which retain paintings beneath their domes. Livestock drink from the tank on the north side of the lake.

The **Mertani Baori** is to the north-west of the fort, and is named after the woman who commissioned it – Mertani, the widow of Sardul Singh. It was built in 1783 and has recently been restored. The stepwell is approximately 30m deep, and its sulphuric waters are said to cure skin diseases. On either side of the well steps give access to a series of cool rooms in which visitors could rest. Stepwells were often used by visitors who didn't want to carry the rope necessary for normal wells. A series of steps gives access to the water table.

To the south of Kana Pahar is the **Dargah of Kamaruddin Shah**. A ramp leads up to the imposing entrance and there is a very good view from the top down over the town (steps lead to the rooftop from the inside courtyard). To the east is **Kali Pahadi** (Black Hill), at which there is a village of the same name. To the north can be seen **Kana Pahar**, and to the north-east, **Badal Fort**. The older **Shyamsingh Fort** can be seen behind the complex to the north.

The Dargah of Kamaruddin Shah complex consists of a *madrassa* (Islamic college), a mosque and a *mehfilkhana*, at which religious songs are sung. Fragments of paintings depicting floral motifs remain around the courtyard, particularly on the east and north sides, although many have been whitewashed. Blue is the predominant colour used and is a favourite colour of the Muslims.

A series of small laneways lead to the **Khetri Mahal**, considered by some people to be one of the finest buildings in Shekhawati. The palace dates from around 1770 and is

believed to have been built by Bhopal Singh, who founded Khetri. The lime plaster has not been painted, and has a rosy cast. There are no doors or windows as such in the palace, but an intricate series of arches and columns lend an elegant symmetry to the building. The palace has been compared to the Palace of the Winds at Fatehpur Sikri.

In the private chamber of the thakur are two small alcoves which retain fragments of paintings in natural earth pigments. The various levels of the palace are connected by a series of ramps along which the thakur and thakurani could be pulled – the thakur could reach the rooftop, where he could gaze down over his subjects, without having to take a single step! Unfortunately, the palace is in a sad state of disrepair, and has a desolate, forlorn atmosphere. There are good views over the town from the rooftop.

Near the Khetri Mahal are two havelis opposite each other which are known as the **Modi Havelis**. The haveli on the east side has a painting of a woman in a blue sari sitting before a gramophone, and a frieze depicts a train, alongside which soldiers race on horses. The spaces between the brackets above show the Krishna legends, and above this are floral arabesques. Part of the facade of the haveli on the east side of the road has been painted over. Still remaining, however, are numerous portrayals of rabbits which are quite lifelike; rabbits were introduced by the British. The enormous ramp enabled the bridegroom to ride into the haveli on elephant back to claim his bride.

The haveli on the west side has pictures with an almost comic appeal – the facial expressions are remarkable. Note the different styles and colours of turbans on the inside of the archway between the outer and inner courtyard of this haveli. Some of the subjects have enormous bushy moustaches and others have perky little pencil moustaches.

A short distance to the north-west of the Jorawargarh Fort is the fine **Bihariji Temple**, which dates from approximately 1776 and is dedicated to Lord Shiva. As you would expect, most of the paintings depict religious themes, but there is also a painting of Sardul

NORTHERN RAJASTHAN

Singh and his five sons. On the left corner of the east wall, Sardul Singh reclines against a bolster while his five sons kneel before him. Krishna and the gopis are portrayed on the inside of the dome, and are rendered in natural pigments. The circular form of domes makes the dance of Krishna and the gopis, called the *rasalila*, a popular theme here.

On the south wall, the battle from the *Ramayana* is shown. The multi-headed, multi-armed Ravana can be seen. These paintings were executed with natural pigments on wet plaster, which posed a challenge for the artist because the paintings

had to be completed before the plaster dried. Close to the temple, gold and silversmiths weigh their merchandise on tiny scales.

A short distance away is the **Kaniram Narsinghdas Tibrewala Haveli**, fronted by a vegetable market. On the west wall of the first courtyard there is a frieze of two trains approaching each other. That on the left is a passenger train and on the right is a goods train whose carriages contain livestock. The artist had probably never actually seen a real train and used his imagination. On the north wall, a man ties his turban while another holds a looking glass in front of him. Close

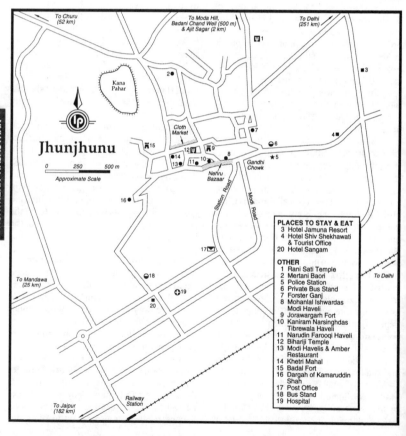

Jhunjhunu

0   250   500 m

Approximate Scale

PLACES TO STAY & EAT
3 Hotel Jamuna Resort
4 Hotel Shiv Shekhawati
   & Tourist Office
20 Hotel Sangam

OTHER
1 Rani Sati Temple
2 Mertani Baori
5 Police Station
6 Private Bus Stand
7 Forster Ganj
8 Mohanlal Ishwardas
   Modi Haveli
9 Jorawargarh Fort
10 Kaniram Narsinghdas
   Tibrewala Haveli
11 Narudin Farooqi Haveli
12 Bihariji Temple
13 Modi Havelis & Amber
   Restaurant
14 Khetri Mahal
15 Badal Fort
16 Dargah of Kamaruddin
   Shah
17 Post Office
18 Bus Stand
19 Hospital

by, a man and woman pass a child between them.

A short distance to the west is the **Narudin Farooqi Haveli**, close to the Noor Mosque. In usual Muslim style, only floral motifs are depicted – there are no animal or human representations – and blue is the dominant colour. Unfortunately, the arches leading to the salons off the first courtyard have been sealed off with concrete.

On the north side of Nehru Bazaar is the **Mohanlal Ishwardas Modi Haveli**, which dates from 1896. There is the inevitable train on the front facade. Above the entrance to the outer courtyard are scenes from the legend of Krishna, including, in the centre, Krishna stealing the clothes of the gopis, who stand waist deep in water. Krishna has secreted himself up a tree with the gopis' saris arrayed around him. On a smaller, adjacent arch can be seen British imperial figures, including monarchs and judges in robes. On the opposite side are Indian rulers, including maharajas and nawabs.

Around the archway between the inner and outer courtyard can be seen portrait miniatures framed behind glass. There is also fine mirror and glass tile work. In the second half of the antechamber, Krishna dances with the gopis while angels fly overhead. This is very fine work. In the inner courtyard, the hierarchy of the universe is shown, with deities depicted in the upper frieze, human portraits in the middle band, and animal and floral motifs below.

Close by is **Forster Ganj**, which was the headquarters of the Shekhawati Brigade and the home of Henry Forster. There's a plaque on the gate with an inscription in both English and Hindi.

In the north-east corner of town is the enormous **Rani Sati Temple**. It's fronted by two courtyards, around which 300 rooms offer shelter to pilgrims. This temple receives the second highest number of donations in India and is particularly revered by the wealthy merchant class. The temple is of marble with elaborate silver repoussé work before the inner sanctum.

A tile and mirror mosaic on the ceiling of the mandapa depicts a merchant's wife who committed *sati* (self-immolation for the sake of honour) in 1595, and to whom the temple is dedicated, while Shiva, Ganesh and Durga watch over her. A relief frieze on the north wall depicts her story. Her husband was killed by the nawab's army, and after battling the soldiers (one of whom has been decapitated), Rani Sati can be seen ascending the funeral pyre; a later panel shows her being consumed by flames. Durga can be seen sending Rani power to withstand the pain. In the next panel Rani commands a chariot driver to place her ashes on a horse, and to build a temple over the spot where the horse halts. The final panel shows the ostentatious temple built in her honour. Rani Sati is the patron goddess of the merchant class, who is believed to hold 60% of the wealth in India and control all the major newspapers.

Painting Classes

For tuition in traditional Shekhawati painting, contact Laxmi Kant Jangid at the Hotel Shiv Shekhawati (☎ 32-651; fax 32-603), Jhunjhunu. Laxmi can organise lessons with a local artist in traditional Shekhawati painting, and offers a 50% discount on accommodation at the Hotel Shiv Shekhawati for students who stay for 10 or more days.

Organised Tours

Camel and jeep safaris or camel cart excursions can be arranged at the Hotel Shiv Shekhawati (see Places to Stay below).

Places to Stay

Conveniently located behind the bus stand is the *Hotel Sangam* (☎ 32-544), which has budget singles/doubles with common bath for Rs 50/65 and Rs 60/75; singles/doubles with geyser for Rs 150/175, and semi-deluxe rooms with geyser for Rs 250/300. There are no meals here. This is a large hotel: the budget rooms are at the front and could be a bit noisy, but the rooms are spotless.

A great place to stay is the *Hotel Shiv Shekhawati* (☎ 32-651; fax 32-603); it is two km from the bus stand in a quiet area on the eastern edge of town, but still close to the centre. Spotless rooms with common bath (fresh towels, soap and toilet paper are provided) are Rs 100/150. Rooms with attached bath (with geyser) and air-cooler are Rs 350/400, and deluxe air-con rooms are Rs 600/800. Breakfast is Rs 50, the veg lunch or dinner is Rs 120, and non-veg is Rs 150. The owner, Laxmi Kant Jangid, is a wealth of knowledge on the villages of Shekhawati, and is friendly and helpful.

Also run by Laxmi Kant Jangid is the *Hotel Jamuna Resort* (☎ 32-871), about one km distant. Traditionally decorated air-cooled cottages featuring mirrorwork are Rs 700/800. There's a swimming pool (summer only) and badminton, and a guide is available. Non-guests can use the swimming pool for Rs 50.

Places to Eat
There are only a few restaurants in Jhunjhunu, but you can get good veg and non-veg meals at the *Hotel Shiv Shekhawati*. The *Amber Restaurant* near the Modi Haveli has basic veg dishes. The *Natraj Restaurant*, near the Sangam Hotel (close to the bus stand), has cheap veg dishes including palak paneer.

Getting There & Away
There are regular buses between Jhunjhunu and Jaipur between 5 am and 7 pm (six hours, Rs 57 deluxe, Rs 46 express). Buses leave for Delhi every 30 minutes from 5 am (six hours, Rs 61).

To Churu there are buses every hour from 6 am (1¾ hours, Rs 14) which travel via Bissau (40 minutes, Rs 8). There are numerous buses to Mandawa from 6.30 am (one hour, Rs 5) and Nawalgarh (one hour, Rs 10).

There are several daily passenger trains between Jaipur and Jhunjhunu (Rs 46/184 in 2nd/1st class).

BISSAU
The small town of Bissau lies 32 km to the north-west of Jhunjhunu. Old 1950s round-snouted Tata Mercedes buses ply this route, with turbaned villagers hanging precariously to their rooftops. Bissau was founded in 1746 by the last of Sardul Singh's sons, Keshri Singh. The town prospered under Keshri Singh, but fell into brigandry during the rule of his grandson Shyam Singh. According to local lore, this malcontent inherited the disapprobation of the merchants of Bissau who had been encouraged to set up in the town by his grandfather. Shyam Singh extracted vast sums of money from them and the merchants promptly packed up and left town. The thakur then resorted to brigandry, embarking on raids with dacoits to neighbouring regions. The British called on the Shekhawati Brigade to restore order in the anarchic town, although by the time the expedition was mounted, Shyam Singh had expired and his heir, Hammir Singh, had driven out the brigands and encouraged the merchants to return. The British were impressed by the town's prosperity and left without a shot being fired.

In October each year, 10 days before the festival of Dussehra, Bissau hosts dramatic performances of the *Ramayana*. The local actors wear costumes and masks made in the town and the performance takes place in the bazaar at twilight.

Things to See
On the facade of the **Chhatri of Hammir Singh**, which is near the bus stand and dates from 1875, can be seen British folk being drawn in various fancy carriages, including one in the shape of a lion and another in the form of a hybrid lion-elephant. The chhatri is now a primary school and some of the rooms are used to store fodder. On the external back wall is a portrayal of Dhola Maru, and unusually, the bard who features in the love story is also depicted. On the south wall, a man on a horse dispatches a lion with a sword. The paintings on the four corner pavilions are badly deteriorated.

If you walk north from the bus stand and take the first street to the left, on the right hand side at the next intersection is the **Haveli of Girdarilal Sigtia**. The paintings on the external walls have been destroyed, but the rooms retain some vibrant paintings predominantly executed in bright oranges, blues, reds and greens. A room in the north-east corner of the haveli shows Shiva, who is unusually depicted with a moustache, with the Ganges flowing from his hair. There is also a painting of a woman nursing a tiny child. Note the orange handprints on the outer courtyard wall, signifying the birth in the family of a boy child. The handprints are a peculiarly Shekhawati custom.

On the opposite side of this lane is the **Motiram Jasraj Sigtia Haveli**, which is now a junior school. On the north wall, Krishna has stolen the gopis' clothes. The maidens have been modestly covered by the artist in the coils of snakes, although one reptile can be seen emerging from between a gopi's legs!

Getting There & Away
There are buses from Bissau to Jhunjhunu every 30 minutes (40 minutes, Rs 8), to Fatehpur (30 minutes, Rs 9) and to Mahansar (15 minutes, Rs 2).

Getting Around
Bicycles can be hired for a modest charge from the shops near the Chhatri of Hammir Singh. They are an excellent way to tour this region, and are particularly good for the six km trip to Mahansar (see below).

MAHANSAR
A turn-off to the left as you leave Bissau on the Churu road, leads six km to the tiny village of Mahansar. This is a dusty little place, where donkeys easily outnumber motorised vehicles. There is not an over-abundance of painted havelis, although the wealthy Poddar clan have left a legacy of very fine paintings in those that can be seen. It's peaceful, and a good place to break a journey.

Mahansar was founded by Nawal Singh in 1768, and the town prospered for several decades until one of the Poddars lost his livelihood when two shiploads of opium sunk without trace.

Things to See
The **Raghunath Temple**, in the town centre, dates from the mid-19th century. It has fine

floral arabesques beneath the arches on either side of the courtyard and a very fine facade.

A short distance to the north-east of the Raghunath Temple is the **Sona ki Dukan Haveli**, which, unusually for Shekhawati, incorporates gold leaf in its painting, particularly around the alcoves in the first chamber. The scenes from the *Ramayana* in the southern section of the ceiling in the first chamber are particularly fine and detailed. The lower walls are richly adorned with floral and bird motifs, creating an almost utopian fantasy with butterflies, trees laden with fruit, and flowers. Painted in gold script on panels on the west wall of this chamber are the names of the gods. Carved wooden beams divide the ceiling into three sections: on the north side, the life of Krishna is portrayed. A golden river connects the holy cities of Vrindavan, where Krishna spent his childhood, and Mathura, where he lived as a king. There is an entry charge of Rs 10, plus Rs 50 for a still camera.

About 10 minutes walk from the bus stand past the fort on the right hand side of Ramgarh Rd is the **Sahaj Ram Poddar Chhatri**. Unfortunately, some of the archways have been bricked in, but there are still some well preserved paintings on the lower walls, and this is a well proportioned and attractive building.

Places to Stay & Eat
The only place to stay is the *Narayan Niwas Castle* (no phone yet), in the old fort, about 100m north of the bus stand. Singles/doubles have attached bath (hot water by the bucket), and cost Rs 600/800. Breakfast is Rs 65, and lunch and dinner are each Rs 150. Some of the rooms have exquisite antique furniture and one room is completely covered in paintings. Ask to see several rooms before checking in, as some are better than others.

Getting There & Away
There are regular bus services between Mahansar and Ramgarh (Rs 2) and Bissau (Rs 2), with connections at these towns through to Jhunjhunu and Fatehpur.

RAMGARH

Sixteen km south of Churu and 20 km north of Fatehpur is Ramgarh, which was founded by a disaffected group from the wealthy Poddar family in 1791. The Poddars defected from nearby Churu after the thakur of that town imposed an extortionate wool levy on the merchants. The town prospered until the late 19th century, but is today a fairly quiet place. It retains a rich legacy of painted buildings.

The town is easy to explore on foot. The bus stand is at the western edge of town. In the northern section, about 600m from the bus stand, there is a concentration of havelis, as well as the main Shani Temple and the Ganga Temple. There's a smaller Shani Temple beyond the Fatehpur Gate, the southern entrance to the town, about 400m from the bus stand via the busy bazaar. There is nowhere to stay in Ramgarh.

Things to See

The imposing **Ram Gopal Poddar Chhatri**, just to the north of the bus stand, was built in 1872. The main dome of the chhatri is encompassed by a series of smaller domes. On the west side of the outer rim of the main dome, one of the projecting braces bears a picture of a naked woman stepping into her *lehanga* (skirt), while another woman shields her from the eyes of a man by holding the hem of her own skirt before her. The drum of the main dome is very brightly painted and has well preserved paintings in blues and reds depicting the battle from the *Ramayana*. The building on the north side of the chhatri was where family members paying homage to their dead ancestor could rest. Unfortunately the chhatri is in a sorry state – the north-east corner of the building is badly water damaged. To enter the compound, you will need to get the key from the little kiosk to the left of the main gate.

Just a short distance to the north of the Churu Gate, on the east side of the road, is the fine **Ganga Temple**, which is now a junior school. The temple was built by one of the Poddar clan in 1845, and is an imposing building with large elephant murals on its facade. The right side of the facade is

deteriorating – the foundations are crumbling and eroded. The temple is open only for morning and evening *pujas* (prayers). Other paintings depict religious themes, including some of Krishna.

About 20m further north on the left hand side is a **Ganesh Temple**. It has a densely painted forecourt and a series of interesting paintings between the brackets under the eaves, mostly featuring birds and religious themes.

If you pass back through the Churu Gate and immediately turn left, a road flanked by antique dealers leads to a second exit through the town wall. Pass through this gate and turn right, and you'll reach the beautiful and tiny **Shani Mandir** (Saturn Temple). The temple was built in 1840, and features some crude paintings on the facade. However, the exterior belies the richly ornate interior, which is completely covered in fantastic mirrorwork. There are some fine murals in the chamber before the inner sanctum, incorporating gold paint, and the overall effect is dazzling. Scenes from the *Mahabharata* are featured here, as well as depictions of Krishna and Radha. To the south (left) of the inner sanctum is a painting on the ceiling featuring the marriage of Shiva and Parvati. Unfortunately, the ceiling in the chamber on the right hand side of the inner sanctum is badly damaged, apparently by damp.

If you retrace your steps back to the Churu Gate, and continue past the gate for about 50m then turn left, you'll come to a group of **Poddar havelis**. Popular motifs include soldiers, trains, and an unusual design, peculiar to Ramgarh, which features three fish arranged in a circle with their faces touching each other. One haveli has a painting depicting women carrying water in pitchers on their heads, and there is an interesting portrayal of the Dhola Maru legend on the west wall of one building: while Maru fires at the advancing assailants, Dhola nonchalantly smokes a hookah!

There is a second, less well known, **Shani Mandir** on the south side of town on the left as you approach the post office from the Fatehpur Gate. It also features exquisite mirrorwork, and the chamber fronting the inner sanctum has some fine paintings interspersed with large mirrors on the ceiling and in the ante-chambers on either side. The floors of these two chambers are also painted. The temple is presided over by a friendly *mataji* (female priest) and its plain blue exterior belies the rich work within.

Getting There & Away

Ramgarh is on the narrow gauge line which runs between Sikar and Churu, and there are daily services connecting these towns, as well as numerous bus services throughout the day. The bus to Churu costs Rs 4, and to Fatehpur, Rs 5.

FATEHPUR
Telephone Area Code: 01571

Fatehpur was established in 1451 as a capital for Muslim nawabs, but it was taken by the Shekhawat Rajputs in the 18th century. The relative wealth of the community of merchants here, who counted among their numbers the rich Poddar, Choudhari and Ganeriwala families, is evident in the many vibrantly painted havelis and fine chhatris. Unfortunately, the best of these are generally locked, which is rather disappointing if you've travelled here to see them. The town does, however, serve as a good base for visiting the nearby villages of Mandawa and Lakshmangarh.

Things to See

On the right of the Mandawa road, about 50m east of the main intersection with the Churu-Sikar road, is the badly deteriorating **Choudharia Haveli** – exercise extreme caution if you visit this haveli, as the entire edifice looks as if it will soon be a great heap of rubble. Poor drainage has caused water damage and is responsible for the haveli's sorry state. On the eastern wall is an interesting erotic painting. A woman embraces a man with one hand and holds a glass in the other while she is ravished, as a servant stands by. It's possible to take the stairs to the second floor, but be extremely careful. The front room upstairs overlooking the street is colourfully painted, with fragments of stain-ed glass still in the window spaces and a large carved wooden beam overhead. Unfortunately, these are practically all that remain of the original architectural embellishments, most of which have been stripped by antique dealers. On the north wall of an upstairs room on the east side of the building, the baby Ganesh takes milk through his trunk from his mother's (Parvati's) breast.

On the western side of Mandawa road, about 50m west of the Churu-Sikar road, and on the left hand side past the lac bangle vendors, is the **Geori Shankar Haveli**. There are very good mirror mosaics on the ceiling of the antechamber. You'll probably be asked for a donation to enter this haveli.

Nearby on the same road is the **Mahavir Prasad Goenka Haveli**, which is considered by some to have the very best paintings of Shekhawati, combining a perfect synthesis of colour and design. Unfortunately it is usually locked.

At the first intersection to the north past the Mandawa road and Churu-Sikar road intersection, if you turn right, on the right hand side after a short distance is the **Nand Lal Devra Haveli**. The facade retains some paintings, predominantly in tones of red and blue. Above the window frames are silhouettes of various creatures against a red background. There is a finely carved lintel over the centre of which Ganesh is sculpted (Ganesh, the protector of households, is often seen here). Fifty metres south of this haveli is the small **Chauhan Well**, which dates from the early 18th century. There is some uninspiring painting around the windows and a couple of the pavilions, and the minarets retain fragments of geometric and floral designs.

Return to the Nand Lal Devra Haveli, and from there retrace your steps to the main Churu-Sikar road. Cross this and continue along the same road, and after a short distance, on the right hand side, is the **Jagannath Singhania Haveli**. It is often locked, but has some interesting paintings on the facade, including those of Krishna and Radha framed by four elephants, and above this, some British men with guns.

In the north-west of the town (take the turn to the left off the Churu-Sikar road opposite the large Jagannath Singhania Chhatri) are **two large havelis** which were built by the Barthia family, and are still inhabited by members of this family. The paintings are not exceptional, but are excellently preserved and maintained. These havelis are reminiscent of Victorian-era theatres.

The **Jagannath Singhania Chhatri**, on the east side of the Churu-Sikar road (enter through a gateway behind the chhatri), has very pretty and well tended gardens. This is an imposing building, although not very comprehensively painted. Paintings, some of which appear to be unfinished, include hunting scenes. There is a small Shiva shrine in the basement of the chhatri at which villagers still pay homage.

Near the private bus stand is a large **baori** which was built by Sheikh Mohammed of Nagaur in 1614. There's a path to the baori from a lane opposite the private bus stand. Unfortunately, the baori is in a shocking state of disrepair. In fact, it's downright dangerous, and you shouldn't approach the edges too closely. It was obviously a feat of some magnitude to dig to this depth, and around the sides are a series of arched galleries, most of which have collapsed. The baori is now used as a rubbish dump. On the south side an haveli has half fallen into the well, and its courtyard paintings are exposed. Two ornate columns hang poised precariously over the abyss. The baori's minarets still stand as a testament to its obvious former grandeur.

Diagonally opposite the baori, on the south side of the private bus stand, the **Harikrishnan Das Saraogi Haveli** features a colourful facade with iron lacework on the upper verandahs and shops at street level. There's a vibrantly coloured outer courtyard. In one picture, a woman appears to be smoking a hookah. The inner courtyard has an interesting juxtaposition: a camel-drawn cart next to a motorcar.

Adjacent to this haveli (to the south) is the **Vishnunath Keria Haveli**. The outer courtyard has interesting pictures on either side of the door to the inner courtyard. Radha and Krishna can be seen in strange gondola-type flying contraptions, one with an animal's head, the other with the front portion of a vintage car, and both featuring angel-type wings. On the north wall of the outer courtyard is a portrait of King George and Queen Victoria with an Indian-inspired backdrop. The paintings in the south-east corner of the inner courtyard have been badly smoked by the kitchen fire. In this courtyard, the sun god Surya can be seen being drawn by horses in a carriage. On the southern external wall, pictures include Queen Victoria, a train, a

Fatehpur

0   100   200 m

To Churu (38 km)

To Mandawa (19 km)

To Fort

To Hotel Haveli (300 m), Lakshmangarh (20 km) & Sikar (52 km)

1 Barthia Haveli
2 Barthia Haveli
3 Jagannath Singhania Chhatri
4 Jagannath Singhania Haveli
5 Nand Lal Devra Haveli
6 Chauhan Well
7 Choudharia Haveli
8 Mahavir Prasad Goenka Haveli
9 Geori Shankar Haveli
10 Post Office
11 Baori
12 Private Bus Stand
13 Harikrishnan Das Sarogi Haveli
14 Vishnunath Keria Haveli
15 Bike Hire
16 Roadways Bus Stand
17 TGH Guest House

NORTHERN RAJASTHAN

holy man and Krishna playing a gramophone for Radha's listening enjoyment!

Places to Stay & Eat
The best place to stay is RTDC's *Hotel Haveli* (☎ 20-293), about 500m south of the bus stand on the Churu-Sikar road. Ordinary singles/doubles are Rs 175/275 with attached bath and hot water, and air-con rooms are Rs 350/450. Beds in the four bed dorm cost Rs 50. Good meals are available here. The manager also has rooms at Barwasi village, 10 km from Nawalgarh; ask him for more details.

If you're really strapped for cash, you could spend the night at the *TGH Guest House*, which has some fairly primitive rooms with *charpoys* (string beds) for Rs 20 (common bath with cold water only). It's right behind the Roadways bus stand.

Getting There & Away
From the private bus stand, on the Churu-Sikar road, buses leave for Jhunjhunu (one hour, Rs 10), Mandawa (30 minutes, Rs 7), Churu (one hour, Rs 14), Ramgarh (30 minutes, Rs 5), Mahansar (50 minutes, Rs 5) and Sikar (two hours, Rs 14).

From the Roadways bus stand, which is further south down this road, buses leave for Jaipur between 6 am and 9 pm (four hours, Rs 50); Delhi between 8 am and 10.30 pm (six hours, Rs 68); and Bikaner between 8 am and 9 pm (four hours, Rs 48).

Jeeps depart from outside the Roadways bus stand when full for Ramgarh (Rs 5), Lakshmangarh (Rs 5) and Churu (Rs 10).

Getting Around
Bicycles can be hired from the north side of the Roadways bus stand.

MANDAWA
Telephone Area Code: 01592
The compact and busy little market town of Mandawa, 19 km north-east of Fatehpur, was settled in the 18th century and fortified by the dominant merchant families. It has some fine painted havelis and is becoming increasingly popular among travellers, which would

account for the alarming number of antique shops cropping up along the main drag.

Information
The State Bank of Bikaner & Jaipur, on the north side of the Fatehpur-Jhunjhunu road, exchanges travellers' cheques. The shop opposite the bank sells English-language newspapers. Arvind Sharma, who drew the maps for Ilay Cooper's definitive guide to the paintings of Shekhawati, *The Painted Towns of Shekhawati*, is currently producing a guide to Mandawa which will be published in French, English and German. Check at the Hotel Castle Mandawa (see Places to Stay) for details.

Things to See
To the left of the main Fatehpur-Jhunjhunu road, about 50m before the bus stand, are several havelis belonging to the Goenka family. To the right of the entrance to the **Hanuman Prasad Goenka Haveli** is an unusual composite picture which depicts either Lord Indra on an elephant, or Lord Shiva on his vehicle the bull, depending on which way you look at it. Nearby is the **Goenka Double Haveli** which has two entrance gates and monumental pictures, including elephants and horses, on the facade. The paintings on the haveli to the left are rather badly deteriorated.

Adjacent is the **Nand Lal Murmuria Haveli**. From the sandy courtyard in front of this haveli, you can get a good view of the southern external wall of the adjacent double haveli: it features a long frieze of a train with a crow flying above the engine and much activity at the railway crossing. The Nand Lal Murmuria Haveli also reflects a strong European influence in its paintings. Nehru is depicted on horseback holding the Indian flag. Above the arches on the south side of the courtyard are two paintings depicting gondolas on the canals of Venice.

The **Binsidhar Newatia Haveli**, on the north side of the Fatehpur-Jhunjhunu road, is now the premises of the State Bank of Bikaner & Jaipur. The interior paintings have been whitewashed, but there are still some interesting paintings on the external eastern wall (accessible through the bank). These include a European woman in a car driven by a chauffeur; a man on a bicycle; the Wright brothers evoking much excitement in their aeroplane as women in saris, among others, point with astonishment; a boy on a telephone; and a bird man flying by in a winged device. The paintings date from the 1920s.

Unfortunately, many of the erotic images on the **Gulab Rai Ladia Haveli**, to the south-west of the fort, have been systematically defaced by prudish souls who have had their tender sensibilities offended. In the last pair of brackets on the first half of the southern wall a woman can be seen giving birth, attended by maidservants. There is an erotic image in the fifth niche from the end on this wall, but don't draw too much attention to it, or it might suffer the same fate as the other erotic art on this building. There is also something untoward happening in a train

carriage on this wall. The presence of a shop selling curios in this haveli suggests its popular appeal.

About 150m past this haveli to the south is the **Chokhani Double Haveli**. The pictures are not that special, but the building is rather grand. Paintings inside include floral arabesques and peacocks above the archways, as well as the Krishna legends.

Behind the Gulab Rai Ladia Haveli is the **Lakshminarayan Ladia Haveli**. On the west wall is a faded picture of a man enjoying a hookah, and a good procession frieze. Between the wall brackets, gopis emerge from the tentacles of a sea monster upon whose head Krishna dances. Other pictures include that of Rama slaying Ravana.

About 30m further north (continue along the road at the back of the Lakshminarayan Ladia Haveli) is the **Mohan Lal Saraf Haveli**. On the south wall, a maharaja grooms his fine bushy moustache. There is fine mirror and mosaic work around the door to the inner

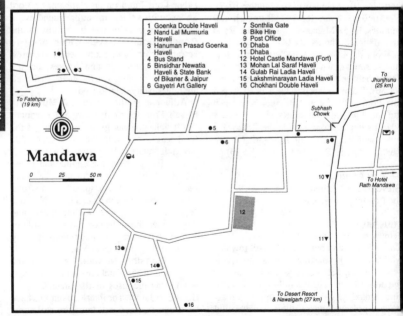

Mandawa

1 Goenka Double Haveli
2 Nand Lal Murmuria Haveli
3 Hanuman Prasad Goenka Haveli
4 Bus Stand
5 Binsidhar Newatia Haveli & State Bank of Bikaner & Jaipur
6 Gayetri Art Gallery
7 Sonthlia Gate
8 Bike Hire
9 Post Office
10 Dhaba
11 Dhaba
12 Hotel Castle Mandawa (Fort)
13 Mohan Lal Saraf Haveli
14 Gulab Rai Ladia Haveli
15 Lakshminarayan Ladia Haveli
16 Chokhani Double Haveli

To Fatehpur (19 km)

To Jhunjhunu (25 km)

Subhash Chowk

To Hotel Rath Mandawa

To Desert Resort & Nawalgarh (27 km)

0 25 50 m

courtyard and Surya, the sun god, can be seen over the lintel.

Organised Tours
It's possible to organise camel and horse rides at the Hotel Castle Mandawa (see below). A one hour camel ride is Rs 250, a half day trip is Rs 400, and a full day trip is Rs 600.

Places to Stay
The *Hotel Castle Mandawa* (☎ 23-124; fax 23-171) is *the* place to stay. Every room is individually furnished; some of the more interesting and beautiful rooms include No 210 – a lovely room with low cushions, old paintings and an antique bed; room No 309, with twin antique beds; room No 308, a suite with air-con and stained glass windows; and room No 312, which is also a suite, in one of the fort's towers; the stairs grandly sweep up to the sleeping area, and in the separate sitting area below are swing chairs and plenty of cushioned bolsters. Air-cooled singles/doubles are Rs 1100/1200, deluxe rooms with air-con are Rs 1150/1500, and suites are Rs 2390. All rooms have attached bathrooms with running hot water. Breakfast costs Rs 125, lunch is Rs 225 and dinner is Rs 250.

Run by the same people, but a little way out of town on the road to Mukundgarh, is the *Desert Resort*, which has a swimming pool. Rates for rooms and meals are the same as at the Hotel Castle Mandawa.

For budget accommodation, it is possible to stay in the *Lakshminarayan Ladia Haveli*. Rooms range from Rs 50 to Rs 100, and hot water is available in buckets. The paintings are faded and chipped in the rooms, but there are fine arches and carved pillars, and this is an opportunity to stay in a real haveli. Contact Shyam Singh at the Gayetri Art Gallery, near the veg market outside the Hotel Castle Mandawa.

On Dhingal Rd, about 1½ km from Sonthlia Gate, is the *Hotel Rath Mandawa*, which has ordinary rooms for Rs 250/325, deluxe rooms for Rs 355/465, and luxury rooms for Rs 445/465. Meals are available here. It's nothing special, and not really in a good location, but the staff are friendly.

Places to Eat
There are two *dhabas* (snack bars) near the turn-off to the Hotel Rath Mandawa on the Nawalgarh road, about two km from the town centre, which serve the long-distance truck drivers with very basic veg fare.

Getting There & Away
Buses for Nawalgarh leave between 6 am and 6 pm (one hour, Rs 7). There are buses to Fatehpur until 8 pm (30 minutes, Rs 7) and direct buses to Jaipur at 6 and 8 am (four hours, Rs 50). If you miss either of these, you'll need to change at Nawalgarh. There are direct buses to Bikaner at 8 am 2, 4 and 6 pm (four hours, Rs 55). A taxi between Mandawa and Fatehpur costs Rs 200.

Getting Around
Bikes can be hired from Subhash Chowk, at the eastern end of the Jhunjhunu-Fatehpur road, for Rs 3 per hour.

LAKSHMANGARH
The most imposing building in this town, which lies only 20 km south of Fatehpur, is its small fortress, which looms over the well laid out township on its west side. The fort was built by Lakshman Singh, the Raja of Sikar, in the early 19th century after the prosperous town was besieged by Kan Singh Saledhi. Unlike some of the other towns of Shekhawati, it is very easy to find your way around Lakshmangarh, as it is laid out on a grid pattern, with a main north-south oriented bazaar dissected at intervals by three busy squares, or *chaupars*. The villagers here are unfamiliar with tourist hordes. The children can be a little tiresome – even downright aggressive!

Things to See
About 50m north of the bus stand through the busy bazaar, a wide cobblestone path wends its way up the east side of the **fort**. There's a sign advising that the fort is private property, but there's a good view from the top of the ramp before the main entrance. From here you can see the layout of the double Char Chowk Haveli, below and to the

north-east. Head for this haveli when you descend the ramp.

Beneath the eave on the northern external wall of the **Char Chowk Haveli** is a picture of a bird standing on an elephant with another elephant in its beak. The large paintings on the facade of the northern face have mostly faded, and the paintings in the outer downstairs courtyard are covered by blue wash. The paintings in the inner courtyard are fairly well preserved. The walls and ceiling of a small upstairs room on the east side of the northern haveli are completely covered with paintings. It has some explicit erotic images, but is very badly illuminated, so although they're well preserved you'll need a flashlight to examine them properly.

In the same building, a room in the north-west corner retains floral swirls and motifs on the ceiling with scenes from the Krishna legends interspersed with inlaid mirrors. The black and white rectangular designs on the lower walls create a marbled effect. No one now lives in the haveli, but there may be someone around who will open it for you (for a small fee). The front facade is in very poor condition at the lower levels, with the plaster crumbling and the bricks exposed. The southern haveli is still inhabited.

About 50m east of this haveli is the large **Radhi Murlimanohar Temple**, which dates from 1845. It retains a few paintings beneath the eaves and some sculptures of deities around the external walls. To the south of this temple is the busy bazaar, flanked by a series of uniform shops whose overhanging balconies have three scalloped open arches flanked by two blank arches with lattice friezes. The shops were constructed in the mid-19th century by a branch of the Poddar family known as Ganeriwala, who hailed from the village of Ganeri.

If you turn left at the first intersection south of the temple, on the corner of the first laneway on the left is the **Chetram Sanganeeria Haveli**. The lower paintings on the west wall are badly damaged: the plaster has peeled away and concrete rendering has been applied. Paintings on this wall include a woman in a swing suspended from a tree; a

woman spinning; a man dancing on a pole balancing knives; people enjoying a ride on a Ferris wheel; a man ploughing fields with oxen; and men sawing timber.

On the north-east corner of the clock tower square, which is about 100m south of the temple via the busy bazaar, is the **Rathi Family Haveli**. On the west wall, a European woman in a smart red frock sews on a treadle machine. The European influence is very much in evidence here, with painted roses and a Grecian column effect. On the south side of this haveli are ostentatious flourishes and the British crown flanked by unicorns. On the east side is depicted a railway station (a painted sign reads 'A Railway Station', in case you weren't sure!), and some blue eyed British soldiers. There is a busy set of *chai* (tea) stalls on the west side of the haveli, and this is a good place to sit and admire these extraordinarily over-the-top paintings.

Behind this haveli, a short distance to the east, is the **Shyonarayan Kyal Haveli** which dates from around 1900. Under the eaves on the east wall, a man and woman engage in an intimate tryst while a maidservant stands by with a glass of wine at the ready. Other pictures include those of a woman admiring herself in a mirror and Europeans being drawn by horses with a tiny coachman at the reins.

Getting There & Away
There are many jeeps and buses between Lakshmangarh and both Sikar and Fatehpur (both 30 minutes, Rs 5).

Getting Around
A bicycle shop just to the south of the Radh Murlimanohar Temple hires bikes for Rs 4 per hour.

CHURU
Telephone Area Code: 01562
Churu is not technically part of Shekhawati falling within the administrative district of Bikaner. However, it is usually included in a discussion of the painted walls, as it was also a centre of trade and commerce, and many rich merchant families that hailed from here

left a legacy of fine painted havelis. About 95 km to the south-west of Churu is the small Tal Chhapar Sanctuary, home to a substantial population of blackbucks, together with other mammals and birds.

Things to See

You'll need assistance to find the **Malji ka Kamra**, which is to the north of the bus stand, down a lane on the west side of the main bazaar. It's well worth the effort to find this place: it's an extraordinary edifice covered in pale blue stucco and perched on green pillars like some baroque travesty of a wedding cake. This once grand building is now home to pigeons and rubbish-grazing cows. Statues on the facade include a bored-looking woman in a sari with a handbag and wings, turbaned men and angels. It was built in 1925, but its days of glory are long gone.

A short distance to the north-west (within easy walking distance) is the **Surana Double Haveli**. This five storey edifice with hundreds of windows achieves something of a Georgian effect. On the lower levels of the west wall are fragments of paintings, including processions and peacocks. The haveli is beyond an archway at the end of a narrow laneway.

A further 100m to the north-west is the **Surajmal Banthia Haveli**, which was built in the 1920s. It is best known for its infamous picture of Christ with a cigar on the external north wall, who is rather incongruously juxtaposed between two British ladies. Across the lane to the north is an haveli with what may be the most bizarre paintings on any of the havelis of Shekhawati – beneath the eaves of the facade is a series of paintings of naked men fondling rabbits!

Places to Stay & Eat

Directly opposite the private bus stand is the *Hotel Deluxe* (☎ 51-114). It's a green and

yellow building and the sign out the front is in Hindi. It has rooms with attached bath and hot water by the bucket for Rs 140/170, and there's a restaurant downstairs.

Getting There & Away

The Roadways bus stand is 500m south of the private bus stand. There are regular services to destinations in Shekhawati from the private bus stand, and to Delhi, Bikaner and Jaipur from the Roadways stand.

The railway station is 100m north of the private bus stand. To Bikaner, trains leave at 2.30, 4 and 6.30 am and 3 pm (approximately 4½ hours, Rs 47/193 in 2nd/1st class). There are trains to Delhi at 10 and 11.30 pm (about seven hours, Rs 65/270), and to Jaipur at 2.30 and 12.30 am (six hours, Rs 49/202).

AROUND CHURU
Tal Chhapar Sanctuary

This small grassland sanctuary, lying about 95 km south-west of Churu and 210 km north-west of Jaipur, covers 70 sq km and has healthy populations of blackbuck, as well as chinkara (Indian gazelle) and smaller mammals, such as desert foxes. The sanctuary lies on the migration route of a number of bird species, most notably harriers, which descend here during September. Other birds include various types of eagle (tawny, imperial, short-toed), which migrate here in winter, and the demoiselle crane, which also descends in large numbers in the winter months (early September to late March). Throughout the year there are populations of crested larks, ring and brown doves and skylarks.

The sanctuary is best visited between September and March. There is a *forest rest house* at Chhapar. Contact the Deputy Conservator of Forests (Wildlife), Jodhpur (☎ (0291) 44-371).

Western Rajasthan

Encompassing a vast area, including the districts of Jodhpur, Jaisalmer, Bikaner and Barmer, this desolate and arid land was believed to have been created by the falling of an arrow fired by Rama, hero of the *Ramayana*. The arrow was destined for the sea god who inhabited the straits between India and Lanka (Sri Lanka). However, when the sea god apologised to Rama for opposing his desire to cross the straits, Rama fired the arrow to the north-west, rendering this region a desolate wasteland.

Western Rajasthan includes the vast Thar Desert, which extends through the adjacent states of Punjab, Haryana, Gujarat and into Pakistan, and is the world's most populous arid zone. It has been the scene of bloody conflicts over the ages, as feudal kings fought both with each other and against external invaders such as the Muslims.

Western Rajasthan has two of the most stunning palace-fortress complexes in India at Jodhpur and Jaisalmer. Nothing rivals the Meherangarh Fort at Jodhpur for sheer awe-inspiring majesty, while the Jaisalmer Fort is romance incarnate, an extraordinary edifice in yellow sandstone which rises from the desert landscape. It is a tribute to the valour of the Bhatti Rajputs, who ruled here for centuries. Enormous balls of rock can still be seen perched precariously across the battlements; they were intended for the heads of advancing enemies, and those who escaped these missiles would then have to dodge the cauldrons of boiling oil poured from the ramparts.

Bikaner's Junagarh Fort is only slightly less impressive, and you can lose yourself for hours in the colourful bazaars of its old walled city, which also encompasses two exquisitely beautiful Jain temples.

Ancient Osiyan, north-west of Jodhpur, also has some ancient Jain temples, and between September and March at nearby Khichan you can see hundreds of graceful demoiselle cranes which descend morning and evening

on the fields surrounding this village to feed on grain distributed by villagers.

HISTORY

The district of Jodhpur was, until comparatively recent times, known as the ancient kingdom of Marwar, the largest kingdom in Rajputana and the third largest of the Indian kingdoms, after Kashmir and Hyderabad.

Little historical evidence remains of the period prior to the 3rd century BC. In 231 BC, Chandragupta Maurya's empire came to power, extending its dominion across northern India from its capital at present-day Patna, in Bihar. The indigenous inhabitants were subjugated by the Aryans during their invasion of northern India between 1500 and 200 BC. In subsequent centuries, the region fell to the Kushanas, the Hunas and the Guhilas. However, it was the Rajput Rathores, who hailed from Kanauj in present-day Uttar Pradesh, who consolidated themselves in this region, ousting the local tribal leaders, and from whom historians can more accurately trace the emergence of the state of Marwar. The Rathores originally settled at Pali, south-east of present-day Jodhpur, but in 1381 shifted their capital to Mandore. In 1459 the Rathore leader, Rao Jodha, shifted the capital nine km to the south and founded the city of Jodhpur.

Meanwhile the Muslims were entrenched at Nagaur, after Mohammad Bahlim, the governor of Sind, erected a fort here in 1122 upon subduing the local Hindu chief, Ajayaraja. Subsequently, rule of Nagaur fell variously to Ajayaraja (again), the Sultanate of Delhi, the Rathores, an independent local dynasty led by Shams Khan Dandani, the Lodi sultans of Delhi and the Mughals under Akbar. In 1572, Akbar granted it to the chief of Bikaner, Raisimha. In the early 18th century, Nagaur was acquired by the maharaja of Jodhpur.

The desert city of Bikaner was founded by one of the sons of Rao Jodha, founder of Jodhpur, following a schism in the ruling Rathore family.

JODHPUR
Population: 720,600
Telephone Area Code: 0291

Jodhpur stands at the edge of the Thar Desert and is the largest city in Rajasthan after Jaipur. The city is dominated by a massive fort, topping a sheer rocky ridge which rises right in the middle of the town.

The old city of Jodhpur is surrounded by a 10 km long wall, built about a century after

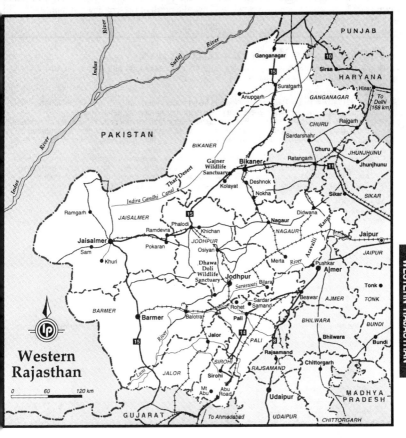

Western Rajasthan

WESTERN RAJASTHAN

the city was founded. From the fort, you can clearly see where the old city ends and the new one begins. It's fascinating to wander around the jumble of winding streets in the old city, out of which eight gates lead. It's one of India's more interesting cities and, yes, it was from here that those baggy-tight horse-riding trousers, jodhpurs, took their name.

There's plenty to see and do in Jodhpur, including wandering around the old city, visiting the fort (you could spend almost an entire day here), browsing through the antique shops or simply soaking up the ambience of this chaotic, bustling Indian desert city.

History

Founded in 1459 by Rao Jodha, a chief of the Rajput clan known as the Rathores, Jodhpur was the capital of the Rathore kingdom once known as Marwar, the Land of Death. The Rathores were driven from their homeland of Kanauj by Afghans serving Mohammed of Ghori, and fled west to the region around Pali, a short distance to the south of Jodhpur. An expedient marriage alliance between the Rathore Siahaji and the sister of a local prince enabled the Rathores to consolidate themselves in this region. In fact, they prospered to such a degree that they managed to oust the Pratiharas of Mandore, nine km to the north of present-day Jodhpur.

FESTIVALS OF WESTERN RAJASTHAN

Below are festivals celebrated in western Rajasthan. For statewide and nationwide festivals, see Festivals of Rajasthan in the Facts for the Visitor chapter.

January-February

Bikaner Camel Festival – This colourful festival takes place in January, with gaily caparisoned camels proudly displayed by their owners in a procession through the streets of Bikaner.

Nagaur Cattle Fair – This week-long cattle fair takes place in late January or early February and attracts thousands of rural people from far and wide. As at Pushkar, the fair includes camel races and various cultural entertainment programmes. There is very little in the way of accommodation here, however.

Jaisalmer Desert Festival – This annual festival includes camel races and dances, folk music, desert ballads and puppeteers. It's fairly touristy, with tugs-of-war between turbaned locals and foreigners. The RTDC sets up a special 'Tourist Village' at this time, similar to the one in Pushkar. The festival takes place over three days between late January and mid-February.

March-April

Barmer Cattle Fair – This fair is held at nearby Tilwara over a fortnight in March-April.

Barmer Thar Festival – This festival, organised by the tourist office (☎ (02982) 20-168), is held in early March.

April-May

Karni Mata Fair – Devotees throng to the Karni Mata Temple in Deshnok, near Bikaner, where rats are worshipped as the incarnations of storytellers, for this fair which is celebrated twice yearly, in April-May and October-November.

August-September

Ramdevra Fair – The Ramdev Temple in the village of Ramdevra, near Pokaran, is the focus of this fair, which takes place each year in either August or September, and is celebrated by both Hindus and Muslims. At this time, devotees place small embroidered horses in Ramdev's temple in honour of the holy man's trusty steed, who carried him to villages where he administered to the poor. Female performers, who have 13 small cymbals attached to their costumes, dance the *terahtal* (a traditional dance), while balancing pitchers of water on their heads.

October

Marwar Festival – This festival in Jodhpur celebrates the rich cultural legacy of Marwar (Jodhpur), with traditional dance and drama from the region. It is held over two days, one of which corresponds with the full moon.

By 1459, it became evident that a more secure headquarters was required. The high rocky ridge nine km to the south of Mandore was an obvious choice for the new city of Jodhpur, with the natural fortifications afforded by its steep flanks enhanced by a fortress of staggering proportions, and to which Rao Jodha's successors added over the centuries.

Orientation
The tourist office, railway stations and bus stand are all outside the old city. High Court Rd runs from the Raika Bagh railway station, past the Umaid Gardens, the RTDC Hotel Ghoomar and tourist office, and round beside the city wall towards the main (Jodphur) station and the GPO. Most trains from the east stop at the Raika Bagh station before the main station – handy if you want to stay at the hotels on the eastern side of town.

Information
Tourist Offices The RTDC tourist office (☎ 45-083) is adjacent to the RTDC Hotel Ghoomar, on High Court Rd. It's open Monday to Saturday from 10 am to 6 pm (lunch from 1 to 1.30 pm).

At the Mohanpura Overbridge is the Rajasthan Travel Service (RTS) (☎ 38-785), which can make hotel bookings, organise local sightseeing with English, French and German-speaking guides (Rs 500 for a half day city tour including guide and car, excluding entrance fees), and can book long-distance cars and drivers (Rs 2.75 per km, minimum 300 km).

At the main railway station is an International Tourists Bureau (☎ 39-052), which provides help for foreign passengers. There are comfortable armchairs and a shower and toilet here. Unattended luggage must be deposited in the railway station cloak room (Rs 3 per piece for 24 hours). It's possible to book day tours of Jodhpur at the railway station tourist bureau. A half day tour leaving at 9 am and returning at 1 pm, or leaving at 2 pm and returning at 6 pm, costs Rs 50. You can also book a car and driver here (Rs 2.50 per km, minimum of 300 km per day), as well as hotels.

Money You can change travellers' cheques at the Bank of Baroda, next to the Hotel Arun on Ratanada Rd.

Bookshops Just off Station Rd, opposite the Ranchodji Temple, is the Sarvodaya Bookstall. It has English-language newspapers, a good range of books on India and a limited selection of western novels. There is also a reasonable selection of books on India at the bookshop at the RTDC Hotel Ghoomar, on High Court Rd. There's a good bookshop just inside the entrance to the Meherangarh Fort.

Meherangarh Fort
Still run by the former maharaja of Jodhpur, the Majestic Fort is just that. Sprawled across a 125m high hill, this is the most impressive fort in fort-studded Rajasthan. It has been added to over the centuries by reigning Jodhpur maharajas, but the original fort was built in 1459 by Maharaja Rao Jodha, after whom the city takes its name. A winding road leads up to the entrance from the city, five km below. The first gate is still scarred by cannonball hits, indicating that this was a fort which earned its keep. To the right, just beyond the ticket office, is the **Chhatri of Kiratsingh Sodha**. This cenotaph was built over the site where a soldier fell defending Jodhpur against the invading Jaipurians in 1806.

The gates, of which there are seven, include the **Jayapol** (*pol* means gate) built by Maharaja Man Singh in 1806 following his victory over the armies of Jaipur and Bikaner. This is the main entrance to the fort. The **Fatehpol**, or Victory Gate, at the southwest side of the fort, was erected by Maharaja Ajit Singh to commemorate his defeat of the Mughals.

The final gate into the fort proper is the **Lahapol**, or Iron Gate, beside which are 15 handprints, the *'sati'* (self-immolation) marks

WESTERN RAJASTHAN

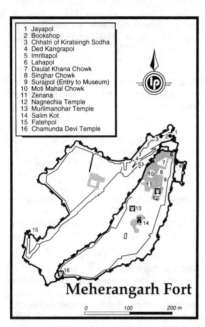

1 Jayapol
2 Bookshop
3 Chhatri of Kiratsingh Sodha
4 Ded Kangrapol
5 Imritiapol
6 Lahapol
7 Daulat Khana Chowk
8 Singhar Chowk
9 Surajpol (Entry to Museum)
10 Moti Mahal Chowk
11 Zenana
12 Nagnechia Temple
13 Murlimanohar Temple
14 Salim Kot
15 Fatehpol
16 Chamunda Devi Temple

Meherangarh Fort

0   100   200 m

17th to the 19th centuries, is an assortment of deadly weapons, each of which is a remarkable work of art. Note the amazing small cannon in the shape of a dog.

Beyond the armoury is the **Umaid Mahal**, which has representative miniatures from all the schools of art which flourished in Rajasthan under the Rajputs. The paintings depict various themes, including those of hunts, festivals, polo matches and, of course, religious themes. Suspended above this room is a finely embroidered canopy which was used by the maharajas during *shikhars*, or hunting expeditions. Off the north side of this room is a glass palace which was a place of prayer. It is covered with glass tiles and extraordinary modern Christmas ball-like decorations suspended from the ceiling.

Upstairs is the **Phool Mahal**, in which traditional dances were performed. The fine paintings adorning the walls of this palace were executed by a single artist, and took over 10 years to complete. In fact, the artist died before the work was finished, evident in the bare patch to the left of the hallway. The gold ceiling is embellished with over 80 kg of gold plate, and around the ceiling, the various maharajas of Jodhpur are depicted. The stained glass in this room further accentuates the room's opulence.

The next room you come to is the private chamber of Maharaja Thakhat Singh (reigned 1843-73), who had no less than 35 maharanis. There's a beautiful sandalwood ceiling adorned with lac painting. Nearby in the **Zhanki Mahal** are the cradles of infant princes, including that of the current maharaja. In the **Moti Mahal** are five alcoves along the west wall from where five maharanis watched proceedings below. The tiny alcoves around the wall were for oil lamps. The ceiling is of fragrant sandalwood, embellished with glass tiles and gold paint.

At the southern end of the fort, old cannons are on the ramparts overlooking the sheer drop to the old town beneath. There's no guard rail and you can clearly hear voices and city sounds carried up by the air currents from the houses far below. As Aldous Huxley wrote:

of Maharaja Man Singh's widows who threw themselves upon his funeral pyre in 1843. They still attract devotional attention and the sati marks are usually covered in red powder.

Inside the fort is a series of courtyards and palaces. The **palace apartments** have evocative names like the Moti Mahal, or Pearl Palace, the Sukh Mahal, or Pleasure Palace and the Phool Mahal, or Flower Palace. They now house one of the most fascinating collections of artefacts in Rajasthan, in the **Jodhpur Museum**. Entry to the museum is via the Surajpol. To the right, just beyond the entrance, is a collection of the maharajas' palanquins, including covered palanquins for the ladies in *purdah* (seclusion). Some of the howdahs feature exquisite repoussé silverwork, with designs such as rampant lions.

The **zenana**, or women's apartments, are adorned with fine latticework screens, featuring over 150 different designs. In the **armoury**, which has exhibits dating from the

From the bastions of the Jodhpur Fort one hears as the Gods must hear from Olympus – the Gods to whom each separate word uttered in the innumerable peopled world below, comes up distinct and individual to be recorded in the books of omniscience.

The views from these ramparts are nothing less than magical. From here, you can also see the many houses painted blue to distinguish them as those of Brahmins. The **Chamunda Devi Temple**, dedicated to Durga in her wrathful aspect, stands at this end of the fort.

The fort is open daily from 9 am to 1 pm and 2.30 to 5 pm. There's an elevator for mobility-impaired visitors. It costs Rs 50 to enter, Rs 50 to bring a still camera in, and Rs 100 for a video. The fee includes a guided tour of the museum, but the guides generally expect a small tip at the end. A group of musicians usually sits outside the cafe near the museum entrance and strikes up a merry Rajasthani number to herald your arrival – it helps set the mood and they, too, appreciate a tip.

The tours operated by the RTDC only give you an hour at the fort, so if you want to stay here longer (there's plenty to see), get here under your own steam. There is a restaurant at the fort, just before the museum on the right. It has veg and non-veg dishes, with most main meals under Rs 40.

Jaswant Thanda

This white marble memorial to Maharaja Jaswant Singh II is about 400m north-east of the fort, just off the fort road. The cenotaph, built in 1899, was followed by the royal crematorium and three later cenotaphs which stand nearby. There is marble *jali* (lattice) work over the windows and carved wooden doors. Good views are afforded from the terrace in front of the cenotaph, which is fronted by a little garden of flowering shrubs. Swimming in the Devakund, just a short distance to the west of the cenotaph is prohibited and strongly discouraged – it's infested by crocodiles during the rainy season!

Clock Tower & Markets

The clock tower is a popular landmark in the old city. The colourful Sadar Market is close to the tower, and narrow alleys lead from here to bazaars selling textiles, silver and handicrafts.

Umaid Gardens & Government Museum

The Umaid Gardens contain the government museum, the library and the zoo. The museum has a small and fairly uninteresting collection. There is the usual collection of moth-eaten stuffed animals, including a number of almost featherless desert birds in two glass cases. The military section includes cumbersome wooden biplane models and an extraordinary brass battleship. The museum is open daily except Friday from 10 am to 4.30 pm; entry is Rs 2.

Umaid Bhawan Palace

Constructed of marble and red sandstone, this immense palace is also known as the Chhittar Palace because of the local Chhittar sandstone used. Begun in 1927, it was designed by the president of the British Royal Institute of Architects for Maharaja Umaid Singh, and took 15 years to complete.

Probably the most surprising thing about this grandiose palace is that it was built so close to Independence, after which the maharajas, princely states and the grand extravagances common to this class would soon be a thing of the past. It has been suggested that the palace was built as some sort of royal job creation programme, but the fact that the project did provide employment for several thousand local people during a time of severe drought is probably coincidental.

Maharaja Umaid Singh died in 1947, four years after the palace was completed; his successor still lives in part of the building. The rest has been turned into a hotel – and what a hotel! While it lacks the charm of Udaipur's palace hotels, it certainly makes up for it in spacious grandeur (see Places to Stay – top end). Unfortunately, the palace is not open to non-guests, unless you want to pay the visiting fee of Rs 330, which is deducted from any food or drink you might purchase. Also unfortunately, the snooty staff won't allow non-guests to visit the hotel's bookshop.

Museum The museum is open to everyone and is well worth a visit. It has the usual assortment of beautifully crafted weapons; an array of stuffed leopards; an enormous banner presented by Queen Victoria to Maharaja Jaswant Singh Bahadur in 1877; human-sized Chinese urns and other fine china; and a fantastic clock collection, including specimens shaped like windmills and lighthouses. The ballroom is extra-ordinary in its opulence, with vaulted ceilings and three chandeliers.

Organised Tours & Village Safaris

The RTDC operates daily tours of Jodhpur from 9 am to 1 pm and 2 to 6 pm. These take in all the main sites including the Umaid Bhawan Palace, Meherangarh Fort, Jaswant Thanda, the Mandore Gardens and the government museum. The tours start from the RTDC tourist office, although they can also be booked at the International Tourists Bureau at the main railway station, and cost Rs 60.

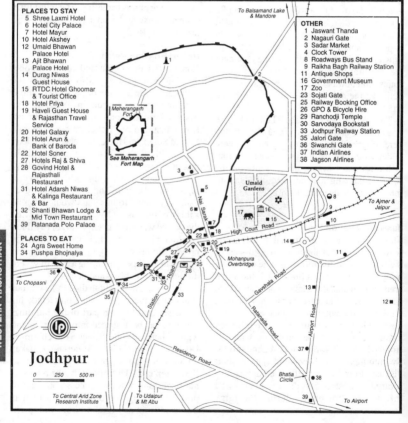

PLACES TO STAY
5 Shree Laxmi Hotel
6 Hotel City Palace
7 Hotel Mayur
10 Hotel Akshey
12 Umaid Bhawan Palace Hotel
13 Ajit Bhawan Palace Hotel
14 Durag Niwas Guest House
15 RTDC Hotel Ghoomar & Tourist Office
18 Hotel Priya
19 Haveli Guest House & Rajasthan Travel Service
20 Hotel Galaxy
21 Hotel Arun & Bank of Baroda
22 Hotel Soner
27 Hotels Raj & Shiva
28 Govind Hotel & Rajasthali Restaurant
31 Hotel Adarsh Niwas & Kalinga Restaurant & Bar
32 Shanti Bhawan Lodge & Mid Town Restaurant
39 Ratanada Polo Palace

PLACES TO EAT
24 Agra Sweet Home
34 Pushpa Bhojnalya

OTHER
1 Jaswant Thanda
2 Nagauri Gate
3 Sadar Market
4 Clock Tower
8 Roadways Bus Stand
9 Raikha Bagh Railway Station
11 Antique Shops
16 Government Museum
17 Zoo
23 Sojati Gate
25 Railway Booking Office
26 GPO & Bicycle Hire
29 Ranchodji Temple
30 Sarvodaya Bookstall
33 Jodhpur Railway Station
35 Jalori Gate
36 Siwanchi Gate
37 Indian Airlines
38 Jagson Airlines

Jodhpur

0   250   500 m

It's also possible at the RTDC tourist office to book safaris to the Bishnoi villages around Jodhpur. (See the Around Jodhpur section.) Bishnoi village safaris can also be booked at the Ajit Bhawan Palace Hotel (see Places to Stay – top end). They cost Rs 400 per person (four people required), including lunch, and take five hours. The Durag Niwas Guest House also runs tours to the Bishnoi villages at competitive prices.

Places to Stay – homestays

There are a number of families registered with the homestay Paying Guest Scheme. Costs per night range from Rs 90 to Rs 695. Enquire at the RTDC tourist office adjacent to the RTDC Hotel Ghoomar on High Court Rd.

Places to Stay – bottom end

One of the best budget places is the *Govind Hotel* (☎ 22-758), run by the friendly and helpful Jagdish Sadarangani. It's directly opposite the post office, only five minutes walk north (turn right when you exit) of the main railway station. Singles are Rs 60 and Rs 90 with common bath, and better singles/doubles are Rs 125/150 and Rs 150/175. The rooms at Rs 175/250 have attached bath and TV. There is also a dorm with lockers for Rs 40 with an attached bath. Hot water is free in buckets, and towels and soap are provided. The rooms at the back are quieter than those at the front, although some have no external window, so are a little dark. Jagdish is also keen to promote the *Blue House*, a 500 year old Brahmin home beneath the fort which has been converted into a guest house, at Brahm Puri Chuna ki Choki. Ask Jagdish for details.

Another excellent choice is the *Durag Niwas Guest House* (☎ 39-092), a very friendly place at 1 Old Public Park. Good rooms are Rs 150/200, all with attached bath and geyser. Surender Singh Rathore here can organise camel and Bishnoi village safaris on request. The *Durag Vilas*, next door, is cashing in on the Durag Niwas' popularity, but may be worth checking out.

Very pleasant, clean and fresh rooms can be found at the *Haveli Guest House* (☎ 27-374), at 7 Jagannath Bldg, Mohanpura Overbridge. There's one room with common bath (with geyser) for Rs 150/200, and rooms with attached bath cost Rs 250/300. Air-con is an extra Rs 50. This place is brand new, and is good value. Breakfast is available. It's directly opposite a small pink sandstone Shiva temple.

In the laneway near the Govind Hotel is the *Hotel Raj* (☎ 28-447), which has spotless rooms for Rs 100/125 with common bath (no external window), and Rs 100/125 with attached bath (hot water by the bucket).

Nearby is the *Hotel Shiva* (☎ 24-774), which has rooms with attached bath and air-cooler for Rs 150/250 (hot water free in buckets). Rooms open off a courtyard and are a bit dark and pokey, but clean.

In the street which runs directly opposite (ie away from) the railway station is the *Shanti Bhawan Lodge* (☎ 37-001). Rooms are spartan and a little scruffy, and the bathrooms could be cleaner. Rates are Rs 50/100 with common bath, Rs 90/150 with attached bath, and Rs 225 for a double with geyser. An air-cooler costs an extra Rs 50.

There are a couple of places close to Sojati Gate, about 10 minutes walk north of the railway station. The *Hotel Arun* (☎ 20-238) has singles/doubles with common bath for Rs 95/135, and with attached bath for Rs 140/200. There's a restaurant here. The *Hotel Galaxy* (☎ 25-098) has less than salubrious rooms from Rs 90/160 to Rs 340, all with attached bath.

At 181 Nai Sarak, Sojati Gate, is the *Hotel Priya* (☎ 47-463), which has air-cooled singles/doubles with shared bath for Rs 150/200, and air-con rooms with geyser for Rs 400/500.

Also in this area is the *Hotel Soner* (☎ 25-732), which has rooms with common bath for Rs 75/125, and with attached bath for Rs 100/200. Air-con doubles are Rs 375. Rooms are all much the same, apart from the cooling system provided, and clean.

Further north, at 132-133 Nai Sarak, is the *Shree Laxmi Hotel* (☎ 47-047), a well maintained place which has very clean rooms, some with balcony, for Rs 150/200 with attached bath and geyser. There are cheaper rooms with common bath for Rs 100/150. The singles are tiny, but adequate.

Also on Nai Sarak, at No 10, is the *Hotel Mayur* (☎ 47-411). It's nothing fancy, and the singles with common bath at Rs 70 are dark and pokey. Better rooms with attached bath cost Rs 80/150, and there's 24 hour check-out.

RTDC's *Hotel Ghoomar* (☎ 48-010) is on High Court Rd. It's not a bad choice, with ordinary rooms for Rs 175/250, rooms with air-cooling for Rs 375/425, and with air-con for Rs 500/600. Dorm beds are Rs 50. There's a reasonable non-veg restaurant and a bar. The tourist office is in an adjacent building. It's possible to book Roadways buses to Jaisalmer, Udaipur and Jaipur at the hotel, and no booking fee is levied.

Opposite the Raika Bagh railway station is the *Hotel Akshey* (☎ 37-327), which has dorm beds for Rs 30, ordinary rooms with geyser and TV for Rs 125/175, air-cooled rooms with hot shower for Rs 225/275, and air-con rooms for Rs 350/400. Meals are available here. This place is traveller friendly, with a pleasant small garden and a free cloak room.

The *retiring rooms* at the main railway station cost Rs 90 for an ordinary double room with attached bath and geyser, or Rs 300 for a double with air-con.

Places to Stay – middle

In the street directly opposite the main railway station is the two star *Hotel Adarsh Niwas* (☎ 23-658). Air-cooled rooms cost Rs 400/550/675 and Rs 500/650/800, or with air-con for Rs 600/800/1000. All rooms have geysers and Star TV. The cheaper rooms are clean and comfortable, but have no external windows.

A good choice near Sojati Gate is the new two star *Hotel City Palace* (☎ 31-933; fax 39-033), at 32 Nai Sarak. There's an indoor swimming pool, health club and laundry facilities, as well as the Gossip rooftop vegetarian restaurant and bar. Air-con rooms are

Rs 790/990. Non-guests can use the pool for Rs 150.

Places to Stay – top end

Jodhpur's finest hotel is the *Umaid Bhawan Palace Hotel* (☎ 33-316; fax 35-373), the residence of the former maharaja of Jodhpur. The hotel has everything from an indoor swimming pool, to golf, badminton, tennis and croquet facilities, a billiard room, endless manicured lawns, a vast dining room, countless tigers' heads hanging from the walls and every other conceivable service. Rooms range from US$145/160 per night to US$820/850 for the Maharani Suite. Non guests are welcome at the dining room, which is probably as close as most people will get to enjoying the facilities at this place. See Places to Eat for details.

An excellent choice in the top-end range is the *Ajit Bhawan Palace Hotel* (☎ 37-410; fax 37-774), which was the residence of the last maharaja's brother. Rooms consist of a series of modern stone cottages arranged around a garden and pools. There's a popular buffet dinner here (see Places to Eat), and amenities include a swimming pool, bookshop and gift shop. Cottages cost Rs 1075/1175, and suites are Rs 1199/2195.

Another option, but with less atmosphere, is the *Ratanada Polo Palace* (☎ 31-973; fax 33-118), on Residency Rd. It has a swimming pool and veg and non-veg restaurant, and rooms for Rs 2150/3000.

Places to Eat

While you're in Jodhpur, try makhania lassi, a delicious and filling saffron-flavoured variety of that most refreshing of drinks. The *Agra Sweet Home* opposite Sojati Gate is so popular they claim to sell over 1500 lassis a day in summer. A thick creamy glassful is Rs 8. The espresso coffee (Rs 5) here is also good. Other popular dessert specialities in Jodhpur include mawa ladoo and the baklava-like mawa kachori. Dhhod fini is a cereal dish consisting of fine threads of wheat in a bowl with milk and sugar.

The *Mid Town* restaurant, next to the Shanti Bhawan Lodge in the street opposite he main railway station, is popular. Most mains cost between Rs 30 and Rs 50, and there are Rajasthani specials such as chakki-ka-sagh and roti (wheat sponge cooked in rich gravy – a speciality of Jodhpur), or bajara-ki-roti pachkuta (bajara wheat roti with local dry vegetables). A Gujarati or Rajasthani thali is Rs 30, and the Rajasthani Maharaja thali is Rs 70.

Close by is the *Kalinga Restaurant & Bar*. It's popular in the evenings, and serves Indian and Continental dishes. A half tandoori chicken is Rs 70. You can get hearty Continental breakfasts here including sausage, eggs, toast, juice and coffee for Rs 75.

A great place to eat is the tiny *Pushpa Bhojnalya*, close to Jalori Gate and about 10 minutes walk from the railway station. This is the place to try authentic Rajasthani cuisine such as churma (Rs 8).

On Station Rd is the rooftop *Rajasthali Restaurant*, which has good views and veg and non-veg dishes. A beer here costs Rs 50.

Surprisingly one of the best places to eat is the non-veg *refreshment room* on the first floor of the main railway station. It's a cool, quiet haven, and the food is cheap and quite good. The veg thali is Rs 13, or non-veg is Rs 18. Chicken curry is Rs 28. It's open from 6 am to 10.30 pm.

At the *Govind Hotel* there's a pleasant rooftop veg restaurant which has excellent views of the palace and fort. In season (winter) you can get a refreshing chikku shake here for Rs 15.

It's possible to dine at the swish *Umaid Bhawan Palace*. It's a buffet set-up, and non-guests pay Rs 330 for the privilege of being waited on by turbaned and cummerbunded waiters. No advance reservation is required. There's also a buffet at the *Ajit Bhawan Palace Hotel*, although the food gets mixed reports. It costs Rs 196 for the veg and non-veg lunch and dinner. Ring to make a reservation.

Things to Buy

Jodhpur specialises in antiques, with the greatest concentration of antique shops along the road connecting the Ajit Bhawan with the Umaid Bhawan palace hotels. These shops are well known to western antique dealers who come here with wallets stuffed with plastic cards. As a result, you'll be hard pressed to find any bargains. The trade in antique architectural fixtures is contributing towards the desecration of India's cultural heritage and as such is not condoned by Lonely Planet. Most of these huge warehouse-sized showrooms also deal in antique reproductions, catering to a growing number of overseas export houses. They're fascinating places to wander around.

Certain restrictions apply to the export of Indian items over 100 years old – see under Antiques in the Things to Buy section of the Facts for the Visitor chapter.

Getting There & Away

Air ModiLuft (☎ 48-333) has an office at the RTDC Hotel Ghoomar. Indian Airlines (☎ 28-600) has an office south of the centre on Airport Rd: open daily from 10 am to 1.15 pm and 2 to 4.30 pm. Jagson Airlines (☎ 433-813) is at Bhatia Circle, in front of the VV John Memorial School.

ModiLuft has daily flights to Delhi (US$80), Jaipur (US$46) and Udaipur (US$43). Indian Airlines has flights to Mumbai (Bombay) on Monday, Wednesday, Friday and Saturday (US$94), and to Jaipur (US$45), Delhi (US$63) and Udaipur (US$41) on the same days. UP Airways has flights between Jodhpur and Jaipur on Tuesday, Thursday and Saturday (US$54). Jagson has flights to Delhi on Tuesday, Thursday and Saturday (US$94) and to Jaisalmer on the same days (US$50).

The telephone number of Jodhpur airport is ☎ 36-757.

Bus RSTC buses leave from the Roadways bus stand (☎ 44-686; 44-989).

There are a number of private bus companies opposite the railway station. Quoted rates are: Ahmedabad (nine hours, Rs 120); Delhi (12 hours, Rs 130); Jaipur (seven hours, Rs 60); Ajmer (four hours, Rs 50); Udaipur (nine hours, Rs 70); Jaisalmer (five hours, Rs 60); Mumbai (22 hours, Rs 350); and Pune (26 hours, Rs 350). These are all

RSTC Bus Services from Jodhpur

Destination	Duration (hours)	Departure Time	Cost (Rs)
Abu Road	6½ (deluxe)*	throughout the day	84
	6½ (express)*	throughout the day	66
Ajmer	–	regularly throughout the day	64
Barmer	5 (deluxe)	regular departures 5.00 am - 10.30 pm	78
	6 (express)	regular departures 5.30 am - 10.30 pm	66
Bikaner	6	regular departures 5.30 am - 10.30 pm	66
Delhi	12 (deluxe)	4 pm	226
	13 (express)	5.15, 9, 11.45 am, 3.30, 7.30 pm	154
Jaipur	6 (deluxe)	regularly throughout the day	102
	7 (express)	regularly throughout the day	85
Jaisalmer	5 (deluxe)	6 am	88
	5½ (express)	5.30, 8.30, 10.15 am, 1.30 pm	60
Osiyan	1½ (express)	every 30 minutes 5.30 am - 6pm	16
Udaipur	7 (deluxe)	throughout the day	81
	8 (express)	throughout the day	80

* The 10.30 pm service to Abu Road continues to Mt Abu.

Train Services from Jodhpur

Destination &Train	Depart	Arrive	Cost (Rs) 2nd Class	Cost (Rs) 1st Class
Ahmedabad (overnight) 9966 *Ahmedabad Express*	3.25 pm	5.45 am	137	421
Barmer 4807 *Jodhpur-Barmer Express*	7.10 am	11.40 am	54	208
Bikaner 394 *Jodhpur-Bikaner Passenger*	4.50 pm	10.30 pm	35	240
Delhi (overnight) 4894 *Delhi Mail*	3.10 pm	5.20 am	170	505
2452 *Mandore Express*	6.30 pm	5.30 am	–	–
Jaipur (overnight) 2466 *Intercity*	6.00 am	10.30 pm	89	214 (air-con) chair
Jaisalmer *IJPJ Passenger**	11.15 am	6 .00pm	67	–
Kalka via Bikaner (overnight) 4588 *Jodhpur-Kalka Express*	11.30 am	6.50 am	199	640
Kota 192 *Jodhpur-Kota Passenger*	7.20 am	10.30 pm	52	–
Lucknow (overnight) *Marudhar Express*	4.30 pm	10.55 am	–	223
Udaipur *Jodhpur-Udaipur Passenger*	10.15 am	10.15 pm	49	262
251 *Jodhpur-Udaipur Passenger* (overnight)	10.00 pm	10.10 am	49	262

*Note that a night train service to Jaisalmer is planned. As the only stop en route is at Phalodi, it's a good idea to bring water with you.

MICHELLE COXALL

MICHELLE COXALL

MICHELLE COXALL

MICHELLE COXALL

Northern Rajasthan (Shekhawati)
Top Left: Haveli and owner, Mandawa.
Top Right: Ajit Sagar, Jhunjhunu.
Bottom Left: Chai break, Lakshmangarh.
Bottom Right: Caretaker, Sigtia family haveli, Bissau.

SANJAY SINGH BADNOR

SANJAY SINGH BADNOR

MICHELLE COXALL

Western Rajasthan

Top: Jodhpur is known as the blue city because of its blue houses.

Middle: The main gate of the Umaid Bhawan Palace displays the coat of arms bearing the insignia of the royal family of Jodhpur.

Bottom: Jaisalmer Fort.

deluxe buses with 2x2 (two seat by two seat) pushback seats.

The main highway between Jodhpur and Jaisalmer is via Agolai, Shaitrawa and Pokaran, but it's more interesting to go on the less frequently travelled route via Osiyan and Phalodi (for Khichan), which meets the main route at Pokaran.

The best bus to Jaisalmer is the super-deluxe which departs from the RTDC Hotel Ghoomar at 6 am daily, arriving at 11.30 am (Rs 86).

Train The booking office is on Station Rd, between the railway station and Sojati Gate. Demand for tickets is heavy, so come here soon after you arrive in Jodhpur. There's a tourist quota and the office is open daily from 8 am to 8 pm, to 1.45 pm on Sunday.

Taxi A taxi to Jaisalmer will cost around Rs 1350 one way, and to Jaipur, Rs 1600 to Rs 1700 one way.

Getting Around
The Airport The airport is only five km from the centre. It costs about Rs 30 in an auto-rickshaw and Rs 100 in a taxi, less when travelling from the city to the airport.

Taxi There is a taxi stand to the right as you exit the main railway station. To Mandore a taxi costs Rs 100 including one hour at the cenotaphs. To Osiyan is Rs 400 return including a one hour stay there.

Bicycle Bikes can be hired from the bike repair shops near the GPO on Station Rd.

AROUND JODHPUR
Maha Mandir & Balsamand Lake
Two km north-east of the city is the Maha Mandir (Great Temple). It's built around a 100 pillared Shiva temple but is not of great interest. Five km further north is Balsamand Lake, a popular excursion spot. A palace, built in 1936, stands by the lake.

Mandore
Nine km to the north of Jodhpur, Mandore was the capital of Marwar prior to the foundation of Jodhpur. It was founded in the 6th century, and passed to the Rathore Rajputs in 1381 following a marriage alliance between a princess of the original founders, the Prati-haras, and the Rathore raja, Rao Chandor.

Today its extensive gardens with high rock terraces make it a popular local attraction. The gardens also contain the chhatris of the Rathore rulers. One of the most imposing is the **Chhatri of Maharaja Dhiraj Ajit Singh**, an enormous edifice with elephant acroteria, *amalaka* (disk-shaped flourishes with fluted edges), a pillared forechamber and fine sculpture. Opposite is the 17th century **Chhatri of Maharaja Dhiraj Jaswant Singh**, an enormous octagonal pavilion with a vast dome and huge pillars. It achieves a remarkable symmetry, with a gallery supported by pillars and sculptures of Krishna and the *gopis* (milkmaids).

At the rear of the complex, to the right, is the **Hall of Heroes**, which contains 15 figures carved out of a rock wall. The brightly painted figures represent Hindu deities or local Rajput heroes on horseback. The work was commissioned by Maharaja Dhiraj Ajit Singh (reigned 1707-24), but not finished until the reign of his successor, Maharaja Abhay Singh (reigned 1724-49). The **Shrine of 33 Crore** (330 million) **Gods** is painted with figures of deities and spirits.

There is a small **museum** here, open daily except Friday from 10 am to 4.30 pm.

Getting There & Away There are numerous buses throughout the day between Jodhpur and Mandore, which is on the main road between Jodhpur and Nagaur. Mandore is also included on the RTDC city tours (see Organised Tours & Village Safaris in the Jodhpur section earlier).

Bishnoi Villages
The Bishnoi are renowned for their conservationist philosophies, and hold all animal life as sacred, in particular the blackbuck, or Indian antelope, which thrives in large

numbers in Bishnoi regions. The Bishnoi cult was established in the late 15th century by Guru Jambhoji, who outlined 29 conservation principles *(bishnoi* translates as '29'). The Bishnoi can be considered as early conservationist martyrs – in 1730, a Bishnoi woman, Amritdevi, clung to a tree which had been marked for felling to provide timber for the maharaja. She was killed, as were the 362 other villagers who followed her example by clinging to trees destined for the axe. This collective sacrifice is commemorated each September at Khejadali village, where there is a memorial to the victims fronted by a small grove of khejri trees.

At **Guda Bishnoi**, locals are traditionally engaged in animal husbandry; there is a small artificial lake here where migratory birds and mammals such as blackbuck and chinkara can be seen, particularly at dusk, when they feed at the lake. The lake is full only during the monsoon (July and August). There are plans to shift Jodhpur airport here within the next decade.

Salawas is traditionally a centre for the weaving of *durries* (carpets). A four foot by six foot durrie can take about one month to complete, depending on the intricacy of the design and the number of colours used, and costs from Rs 2500 to Rs 3000, with all profits going to the artisan. These days, chemical rather than natural dyes are used. Durries are usually of cotton, but sometimes camel or goat hair, or silk, are used. After the weaving is completed, the durries are sometimes stonewashed to give an antique effect. Also in Salawas, several families, mostly of the Muslim community, are engaged in blockprinting. The hand-woven, block-printed cloth is known as *fetia*. A single bed sheet costs Rs 550, and a double sheet is Rs 650.

At the villages of **Zhalamand** and **Kakani**, potters can be seen at work using hand-turned wheels. **Guda Mogra** is a tiny desert village where the inhabitants live in thatched huts, and a tour here often includes lunch at a family home.

Getting There & Away The Bishnoi villages are strung along and off the Pali road, to the south-east of Jodhpur. Various operators, including the RTDC in Jodhpur, conduct jeep safaris to the villages. A tour is essential to visit this region: some of these villages are tiny, along tracks which can be barely made out in the sand, and which you will be hard pressed to find on any maps. See Organised Tours & Village Safaris in the Jodhpur section.

Rohet
In this village, 40 km south of Jodhpur, the former local ruler has converted his 350 year old house into a heritage hotel. Rooms at the *Rohet Garh* (☎ (02932) 66-231) cost around Rs 800. The place seems to attract travel writers: Bruce Chatwin wrote *The Songlines* here and William Dalrymple began *City of Djinns* in the same room – No 14.

Sardar Samand Lake
The route to this wildlife centre, 66 km south-east of Jodhpur off the Jodhpur to Pali route, passes through a number of colourful villages. There's upmarket accommodation at the maharaja's stylish Art-Deco summer palace, the *Sadarsamand Lake Resort* (book through the Umaid Bhawan Palace in Jodhpur: ☎ (0291) 33-316; fax 35-373), which overlooks the lake. There's a lakeside swimming pool, and singles/doubles cost Rs 1190/2400.

Dhawa Doli Wildlife Sanctuary
This sanctuary is about 40 km south-west of Jodhpur, on the road to Barmer. There is no accommodation here, but it is possible to take a half day tour from Jodhpur (Rs 500; check at the RTDC tourist office in Jodhpur). Animals and birds which can be seen here include blackbuck, partridges, desert fox and nilgai.

NAGAUR
Nagaur lies about midway between Jodhpur and Bikaner, 135 km to the north-east of Jodhpur. It has an historic **fort** protected by massive double walls which encompass a richly painted **palace**. Within the walls of the

old city are several **mosques**, including one commissioned by Akbar for a disciple of the Sufi saint Khwaja Muin-ud-din Chishti, who roamed India in the 13th century.

Nagaur also hosts the Nagaur Cattle Fair, a smaller version of Pushkar's Camel Fair, which takes place in late January or early February. See the Festival aside earlier in this chapter for more details.

Getting There & Away

Nagaur is on the main route between Jodhpur and Bikaner, and there are numerous buses throughout the day connecting it with these cities.

JODHPUR TO JAISALMER (NORTHERN ROUTE)

The most direct route by road to Jaisalmer is via Shergarh, Dechhu and Pokaran; however, there are some interesting places to visit on the lesser travelled northern route via Osiyan and Phalodi, which meets the main route at Pokaran. The exquisite Jain temples at Osiyan, the feeding grounds of the demoiselle cranes at Khichan and the important pilgrimage site of Ramdevra all lie on or just off this route, along which numerous buses ply each day.

Osiyan

The ancient Thar Desert town of Osiyan, 65 km north of Jodhpur, was a great trading centre between the 8th and 12th centuries when it was dominated by the Jains, and was known as Upkeshpur. The wealth of Osiyan's mediaeval inhabitants enabled them to build lavish and beautifully sculpted temples. The stone from which these temples were built was extracted from local quarries, and has managed for the most part to withstand the ravages of time. The village of Osiyan is inhabited mostly by Brahmins, as evidenced by the number of blue-painted houses.

Temples The temples of Osiyan rival the Hoysala temples of Karnataka and the Sun Temple of Konark in Orissa. About 200m

north of the bus stand is the **Sachiya Mata Temple** (Sachiya Mata is the ninth, and last, incarnation of the goddess Durga). In the forechamber before the *mandapa* (chamber before the inner sanctum), and beyond the impressive *torana* (gateway) are sandstone statues of various incarnations of Durga which were excavated by archaeologists and installed here. The main temple is flanked by nine smaller temples, each dedicated to an incarnation of the goddess, and built only in the last decade. Abutting the sides of the main temple is a series of ancient temples contemporary with the Sachiya Mata Temple.

The drum of the mandapa is elaborately carved, featuring 16 sculptures of dancing *apsaras* (maidens) who welcome the goddess to her temple. The mirrorwork which can be seen here is modern. The image of Sachiya Mata enshrined in the inner sanctum is of stone and, according to legend, was recovered from the ground where it was buried by a maharaja. The pillars flanking the sanctum are encircled by lions' heads.

Abutting the sanctum to the right is a small temple to Surya, the sun god, which has a dancing snake motif on the ceiling of the mandapa, and in the centre are Krishna and Radha. On the top left-hand corner of the lintel a sculpture over 1000 years old depicts a woman applying lip rouge with the aid of a mirror.

Outside the main temple (right-hand side), a small temple dedicated to Laxminarayan has some very tame erotic sculptures. In the top left-hand corner of the lintel is a lovely little sculpture of Ganesh with his consort, Chandrika, who is sitting on his knee. Around the external walls of this small temple is a series of extraordinary sculptures depicting men and women battling monster-like beasts. There are good views out over Osiyan from the platform adjacent to this temple. To the south-west can be seen the oldest temple in Osiyan, dedicated to Surya. To the west is the Jain Mahavira Temple. The sandstone temples immediately to the south are dedicated to Harihara (Shiva and Parvati).

On the north side of the small Surya Temple, which flanks the Sachiya Mata Temple, is a very rare statue of Harihara. It

WESTERN RAJASTHAN

is depicted with one breast, and Shiva's vehicle, the Nandi bull, is shown.

To the left of the Sachiya Mata temple are two small temples dedicated to Ganesh and Shiva respectively. The lintels are completely covered in sculptures depicting erotic contortions, particularly notable on the Shiva Temple.

Five minutes walk from the Sachiya Mata Temple is the **Mahavira Temple**, dedicated to the last of the Jain *tirthankars* (prophets). This is a more spacious temple than the Sachiya Mata Temple, with an open-air pavilion-type mandapa supported by carved pillars. As at the Sachiya Mata Temple, the drum of the dome features sculptures of apsaras. There is a beautiful torana before the temple, with very intricate sculptural work.

The image of Mahavira is difficult to make out in the dimly lit inner sanctum. According to legend it is over 2000 years old, and is made of sand and milk and coated in gold. On either side of the mandapa are identical marble statues of Adinath, the first Jain tirthankar. Fortunately, the garish mirrors which can be seen in the Sachiya Mata Temple have been removed from this temple, and you are able to appreciate it in its original state. In the right-hand corner is an ancient frieze which retains fragments of colour.

The four temples on two sides of the main temple are dedicated to eight of the 24 tirthankars. Behind the temple are fragments of sculpture retrieved from the precincts which were thrown down by the Mughals.

Among the other temples in Osiyan are those dedicated to Surya, Shiva and Harihara, but they are in poor condition and are being restored. There is also a badly deteriorating *baori* (stepwell).

Places to Stay & Eat Bhanu Prakash Sharma (☎ (02922) 4232), a Brahmin priest, has started a small *guest house* in Osiyan. It costs Rs 70 per person and includes meals. He is also an excellent guide to the temples and their wealth of beautiful sculptures. Ask any of the village children, who will happily track him down for you.

Getting There & Away Few people travel to Osiyan. Buses to Jodhpur depart every 30 minutes or so, take 1½ hours and cost Rs 16. To Phalodi, it's two hours and Rs 16.

Phalodi

Phalodi is a fairly nondescript large town lying about midway between Jodhpur and Jaisalmer. The main attraction here is the tiny village of **Khichan**, about 10 km east of Phalodi, and a feeding ground during the winter months for the beautiful demoiselle crane. Khichan also has some beautiful red sandstone *havelis* (mansions), some around 100 years old and many featuring fine carvings. A series of sand dunes affords a stunning desert panorama.

Places to Stay & Eat There's only one place to stay in Phalodi, the *Hotel Sunrise* (☎ 02925) 2257), which is directly opposite the Roadways bus stand. It costs Rs 100/150 for spotless rooms with attached bath and free bucket hot water. There's no food here. A small *dhaba* (food stall) serves very basic but filling veg food about 20m from the hotel in the evenings.

Visitors can stay in some of Khichan's havelis with advance notice. Very basic accommodation is available for Rs 50 per person per day, and meals can be provided for Rs 50 per day. Contact Prakash Jain (see The Demoiselle Cranes of Khichan on the next page) to advise of your visit.

Getting There & Away Phalodi is about 135 km from Jodhpur, 165 km from Jaisalmer and 150 km from Bikaner. There are numerous buses from the Roadways bus stand to Jodhpur from 6 am (Rs 30). The last bus, at 7 pm, leaves from the railway station bus stand at the other end of town. Buses for Bikaner leave between 6.30 am and 6.30 pm. The local bus takes 4½ hours and costs Rs 37; the express (not much of an improvement, but faster) takes 3½ hours and costs Rs 45).

Buses to Jaisalmer are via Pokaran (one hour, Rs 13) and leave between 7.30 am and 4 pm (local: five hours, Rs 35, express: four hours, Rs 43).

Phalodi is on the broad gauge line and has rail connections with both Jodhpur and Jaisalmer.

Getting Around There are buses between Phalodi and Khichan (15 minutes, Rs 1) at 6.30, 8, 10, 11 and 11.30 am, and 1, 3 and 5 pm, as well as a local taxi (Rs 2) which has

to be seen to be believed. The windscreen is so badly scratched that it is now opaque, and the innovative driver has used a glass cutter to shear a square foot hole through which he peers – disconcerting to say the least. The share taxi leaves when full from opposite the railway station. An auto-rickshaw will cost Rs 50 to Khichan.

Ramdevra

This tiny, desolate and windswept desert village lies 10 km north of Pokaran and,

---

The Demoiselle Cranes of Khichan

From the last week of August or the first week of September until the last week of March, over 7000 demoiselle cranes *(Anthropoides virgo)* fly every morning and evening to the fields around Khichan to feed on the grain which has been spread around the fields by villagers. The cranes, which are known locally as *kurjas*, appear in traditional Marwari songs, in which women beseech them to bring back messages from their loved ones when the birds return from distant lands. The cranes consume a phenomenal 600 kg of grain each day, all of which is funded by donations (donations to help pay for the grain are welcome).

Prakash Jain (☎ (02925) 2294) of Khichan has a great love for these majestic birds. He established the Kurja Sanrakshan Vikas Sansthan (Demoiselle Crane Protection & Development Organisation) in 1980, and the work of the organisation has recently come to the attention of the International Crane Foundation (ICF) based in the USA. Scientists and ornithologists from the ICF have travelled to Khichan to study the cranes.

The practice of feeding the cranes dates back some 150 years, and the numbers of cranes is increasing by about 10% to 15% each year. The grain is spread at night, ready for the birds to feed on at sunrise (about 6.30 am), and at around 1 pm, in time for the birds' return between 3 and 5 pm. The sight of these wonderful birds in such large numbers descending on the fields is truly awe-inspiring, and shouldn't be missed if you're in the area.

The demoiselle crane stands about 76 cm high and is a brown-grey colour with a black chest and throat. It has a long neck and sharp beak. Prakash Jain is a keen photographer and has some magnificent pictures of the birds silhouetted against the sun, which he is happy to show visitors.

The migration route of the demoiselle cranes has not yet been established, and two theories have been proposed as to their path. The ICF believes the birds originate from Mongolia, flying over China and Tibet to India. Locals believe that the birds originate from central Africa, and fly across central Asia, including Afghanistan, Pakistan and then India.

Visitors can only visit the feeding grounds if they are accompanied by a member of the Demoiselle Crane Protection & Development Organisation, and must stay some distance away so as not to disturb the feeding birds. Visitors should inform the organisation as far in advance as possible if they are planning to visit Khichan. Write to Prakash Jain, PO Khichan, 342308, District Jodhpur, Rajasthan. It is possible to stay in an haveli in Khichan; see Places to Stay & Eat in this section.

For more information about the demoiselle cranes and the feeding programme at Khichan, write to the International Crane Foundation, World Centre for the Study and Preservation of Cranes, E-11316 Shady Lane Rd, PO Box 447, Baraboo, WI 53913-0447, USA (☎ 608 356 9462; fax 608 356 9465). ∎

WESTERN RAJASTHAN

while it's probably not the most salubrious place to stay overnight, it has a very important temple dedicated to a deified local hero Ramdev, who lived in the Middle Ages. Ramdev was born in the village of Tanwar to a Rajput family and was opposed to all forms of untouchability, believing that all human beings are equal.

The **Ramdev Mandir** itself, with its brightly coloured facade, is not architecturally of great interest, but the devotional activities of the hundreds of pilgrims who pay homage at this shrine certainly are. The temple is full of statues of horses, including two life-sized silver horses featuring fine repoussé work. These commemorate the trusty horse of Ramdev, who accompanied him as he walked from village to village, helping ailing villagers. There are also elaborately regaled wooden horses covered with finely embroidered silk cloths. Pilgrims leave tiny models of horses at the temple – there must be hundreds of these embroidered horses here, like the ones you can buy all over Rajasthan. The silver image of Ramdev is fronted by a sacred fire at which priests anoint pilgrims' foreheads with *tikkas* (dots) and give *prasaad* (sacred food).

You'll be constantly assailed by people with receipt books demanding donations, both as you enter the temple complex, at the temple itself, and even by men who 'guard' your shoes! A festival is held in Ramdevji's honour at the temples in August/September.

Places to Stay & Eat There is a new hotel, the *Hotel Poonam Palace* (☎ (02996) 3742), which is on the right-hand side of the main road through the village if you're coming from Jodhpur, about 400m before the temple. Singles/doubles cost Rs 150, and hot water by the bucket costs Rs 4. There's a restaurant here; a veg lunch or dinner is Rs 40.

Getting There & Away All buses between Phalodi and Pokaran pass through Ramdevra. Share taxis leave when full along the main street for Pokaran (20 minutes, Rs 5).

Pokaran

At the junction of the Jaisalmer, Jodhpur and Bikaner roads, 110 km from Jaisalmer, is this desert town, site of another fortress, although not of the formidable dimensions of the Jodhpur and Jaisalmer forts. The railway station and bus stand lie at opposite ends of the town, four km apart. The bus stand is on the Jodhpur road at the southern edge of town. The fort is 1.5 km to the north-east of the bus stand. The post office is on the left-hand side on the road leading up to the fort. There is nowhere to change money in Pokaran.

Pokaran Fort & Museum The Pokaran Fort is an evocative place, although it has a rather desolate and abandoned atmosphere. The museum is nothing special, with an assortment of weaponry, brocaded clothes, old wooden printing blocks and various games of the maharajas of Pokaran, including dice and dominoes. There is a small shrine to Durga here.

The fort is open Monday to Saturday from 7 am to 6 pm; entry is Rs 15 and it costs Rs 10 to bring a camera or video with you.

Places to Stay & Eat The accommodation afforded at the *Hotel Pokaran* (☎ (02996) 22-274), in the fort, is not nearly as grand as that offered in some of Rajasthan's other amazing fort and palace complexes. However, it's quite comfortable, although not really great value at Rs 750/850 for singles/doubles with geyser and air-cooling. Breakfast is Rs 80, the veg lunch or dinner is Rs 150, and non-veg is Rs 175.

The *Hotel Monica*, opposite the share jeep stand at the old railway station, has overpriced and shabby rooms for Rs 100 with common bath. It's above a busy dhaba where you can get basic fare.

Three km west of the bus stand is the RTDC *Hotel Midway* (☎ (02994) 222), which has six air-cooled rooms with geyser for Rs 200/300. The veg lunch or dinner is Rs 100, and non-veg is Rs 130.

A popular place to eat is the *New Rajasthan*

Restaurant, a veg place on the Jaisalmer road.

Getting There & Away There are regular buses to Jaisalmer between 7 am and 5.30 pm (2½ hours, Rs 61). To Bikaner, there are buses at 7, 8.30 (express) and 11 am, noon, and 2.30 and 5 pm (express: Rs 61; local: Rs 50). To Jodhpur, there are local services regularly between 7 am and 6 pm (four hours, Rs 38) and a deluxe service at 7 pm (three hours, Rs 52).

There are rail services to Jaisalmer and Jodhpur.

JAISALMER
Population: 43,400
Telephone Area Code: 02992

Nothing else in India is remotely similar to Jaisalmer. Jodhpur certainly has one of the country's most spectacular fortress-palace complexes, and both Chittorgarh and Kumbhalgarh far surpass Jaisalmer in fame and sheer size. Yet this desert fortress is straight out of *Tales of the Arabian Nights* and you could easily be forgiven for imagining you've somehow been transported back to mediaeval Afghanistan. The vision of this massive fortress thrusting heavenwards out of the barren desertscape is unforgettable, and the magic doesn't diminish as you approach its walls and bastions, and lose yourself in its labyrinthine streets and bazaars. This incomparably romantic city has been dubbed the 'Golden City' because of the colour imparted to its stone ramparts by the setting sun. No-one who makes the effort to get to this remote city leaves disappointed.

History

There is some speculation as to the actual date of the foundation of the city and fort. Most historians place the date at around 1156, when the Bhatti Rajput ruler Jaisala moved the city from the vulnerable former capital of Lodhruva, 15 km to the south-east. Subsequent history has been derived from the tales and songs of the bards. The succession of maharajas of Jaisalmer trace their lineage back to a ruler of the Bhatti Rajput clan, Jaitasimha.

In the 13th century, the emperor of Delhi, Ala-ud-din Khilji, mounted an expedition to Jaisalmer to retrieve treasure which the Bhattis had carried off from a caravan train en route to the imperial capital, and he laid siege to Jaisalmer Fort for nine years. When defeat was imminent, *jauhar* (collective sacrifice) was declared, the women of Jaisalmer committing themselves to the flames while the men donned saffron robes and rode out to certain death. Later the Rathores of Mallani mounted an unsuccessful raid on Jaisalmer, but were vanquished by Jaitasimha's son Duda. Duda perished in a later attack on the fort led by Ala-ud-din.

Duda's descendants continued to rule over the desert kingdom, and in 1541, Lunakarna of Jaisalmer fought against Humayun when he passed through Jaisalmer en route to Ajmer. The relationship between the Jaisalmer rulers and the Mughal Empire was not always hostile, and various marriages were contracted between the two parties to cement their alliance. Later Jaisalmer notables include Sabala Simha, who won the patronage of the Muslim emperor Shah Jahan (reigned 1627-58), when he fought with distinction in a campaign at Peshawar. Although not the legitimate heir to the Jaisalmer *gaddi*, or throne, Shah Jahan invested Sabala Simha with the power to rule Jaisalmer, and during his reign he annexed many areas which now fall within the administrative districts of Bikaner and Jodhpur.

The Jaisalmer rulers lined their coffers with illicit gains won through cattle rustling and by more orthodox methods such as imposing levies on the caravans which passed through the kingdom to Delhi. They were renowned both for their valour in battle and their treachery, as they fought to enlarge and secure their territories.

Religion and the fine arts flourished under the rulers of Jaisalmer, and although professing Hinduism, they were tolerant of Jainism, encouraging the construction of the beautiful temples which now grace the old city within the fort walls. Sculptural depictions of both

Hindu and Jain deities and holy men stand side by side on the walls of these fine edifices. The visionary rulers commissioned scholars to copy precious sacred manuscripts and books of ancient learning which may otherwise have been lost during Muslim raids.

Jaisalmer's strategic position on the camel train routes between India and central Asia brought it great wealth. The merchants and townspeople built magnificent houses and mansions, all exquisitely carved from wood and from golden-yellow sandstone. These havelis can be found elsewhere in Rajasthan (notably in Shekhawati), but nowhere are they quite as exotic as in Jaisalmer. Even the humblest of shops and houses displays something of the Rajput love of the decorative arts in its most whimsical form. It's likely to remain that way too, since the city planners are keen to ensure that all new buildings blend in with the old.

The rise of shipping trade and the port of Bombay saw the decline of Jaisalmer. At Independence, partition and the cutting of the trade routes through Pakistan seemingly sealed the city's fate, and water shortages could have meant its death sentence. However, the 1965 and 1971 Indo-Pakistan wars revealed Jaisalmer's strategic importance, and the Indira Gandhi Canal to the north is beginning to restore life to the desert. Paved roads and a railway, recently converted from metre to broad gauge, link Jaisalmer to the rest of Rajasthan. There are flights to Delhi and Jodhpur several times a week, and luxury buses now ply between these cities.

Today, tourism rivals the military base as the pillar of the city's economy. The presence of the Border Security Force hardly impinges at all on the life of the old city and only the occasional sound of war planes landing or taking off in the distance disturbs the tranquillity of this desert gem.

Orientation

Jaisalmer is a great place to simply wander around. The streets within the old city walls are a tangled maze, but it's small enough not to matter. You simply head off in what seems like the right direction and you'll get somewhere eventually.

The old city was once completely surrounded by an extensive wall, much of which has sadly been torn down in recent years for building material. Some of it remains, however, including the city gates and, inside them, the massive fort which rises above the city and is the essence of Jaisalmer. The fort itself, which is entered via the First Fort Gate, is a warren of narrow, paved streets complete with Jain temples and the old palace of the former ruler, still flying his standard.

The main market, Bhatia Market, is directly below the hill, while the banks, the new palace and several other shops and offices are near the Amar Sagar Gate to the west. Continue outside the walled city in this direction and you'll soon come to the turn-off to the RTDC Hotel Moomal Tourist Bungalow.

Information

Tourist Office The Tourist Information Bureau (☎ 52-406) is on Gadi Sagar Rd, about two km south-east of the First Fort Gate. It's open daily except Sunday from 8 am to noon and 3 to 6 pm. It is possible to organise homestays here under the Paying Guest Scheme, as well as guides, tours of the city and to the Sam sand dunes, and to see cultural programmes.

Money There is nowhere to change money within the fort. The State Bank of India, near the Hotel Nachana Haveli, changes travellers' cheques, as does the Bank of Baroda, nearby at Gandhi Chowk. This bank also gives cash advances on Visa and Master-Card; the transaction takes 20 minutes. Below the Trio Restaurant is the State Bank of Bikaner & Jaipur, which changes all travellers' cheques. If the banks are closed, the Hotel Fort View will change travellers' cheques.

Bookshops Day-old newspapers can be bought at Bhatia News Agency, in Bhatia Market. There is also a good selection of new books here, as well as some second-hand books which can be bought or swapped. There's a good bookstore, the Students' Book Store, near the 8 July Restaurant in the fort. It has a good selection of new books, and a 50% refund if you return them. There are also books in German, French and Spanish. Also in Bhatia Market is Vyas & Co, where you can buy fresh slide and print film and batteries for still and movie cameras.

Medical Service The hospital here is a nightmare – it's dirty, overcrowded, there's often no running water and the staff are overworked.

Jaisalmer Fort

Built in 1156 by the Bhatti Rajput ruler Jaisala, and reinforced by subsequent rulers, the fort crowns the 80m high Trikuta Hill. Over the centuries it was the focus of a number of battles between the Bhattis, the Mughals of Delhi and the Rathores of Jodhpur. About a quarter of the old city's population resides within the fort walls, which have 99 bastions around their circumference. The fortress is protected by three walls. The lower wall is of solid stone blocks which reinforce the loose rubble of which Trikuta Hill is composed. The second wall snakes around the fort, and between this and the third, or inner, wall, the warrior Rajputs hurled boiling oil and water, and massive round missiles on their unwitting enemies below. Above the fort flies the Jaisalmer standard, featuring a *chhatri*, or umbrella-shaped device, against a red and yellow background.

It's fascinating to wander around this place. Nothing has changed here for centuries. It's packed with houses, temples and palaces, and honeycombed with narrow, winding lanes, all of them paved in stone and with a remarkably efficient drainage system keeping them free of effluent. It's also quiet – vehicles are not allowed up here and even building materials have to be carried up by camel cart. The fort walls provide superb views over the old city and surrounding desert. Strolling around the outer fort ramparts is a popular activity at sunset.

The fort is entered from the First Fort Gate through a forbidding series of massive gates via an enormous stone-paved ramp, which leads to a large courtyard. The former maharaja's seven storey palace fronts onto this.

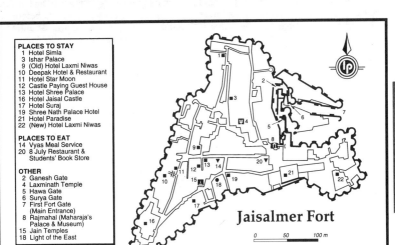

PLACES TO STAY
1 Hotel Simla
3 Ishar Palace
9 (Old) Hotel Laxmi Niwas
10 Deepak Hotel & Restaurant
11 Hotel Star Moon
12 Castle Paying Guest House
13 Hotel Shree Palace
16 Hotel Jaisal Castle
17 Hotel Suraj
19 Shree Nath Palace Hotel
21 Hotel Paradise
22 (New) Hotel Laxmi Niwas

PLACES TO EAT
14 Vyas Meal Service
20 8 July Restaurant &
   Students' Book Store

OTHER
2 Ganesh Gate
4 Laxminath Temple
5 Hawa Gate
6 Surya Gate
7 First Fort Gate
   (Main Entrance)
8 Rajmahal (Maharaja's
   Palace & Museum)
15 Jain Temples
18 Light of the East

Jaisalmer Fort

0   50   100 m

WESTERN RAJASTHAN

The square was formerly used to review troops, hear petitions and present extravagant entertainment for important visitors.

Jain Temples Within the fort walls are a group of beautifully carved Jain temples built between the 12th and 15th centuries. There are seven temples in the complex, including very fine temples dedicated to Rikhabdev and Sambhavanth. They are all connected by a series of corridors and walkways, and are open daily from 8 am to noon. It is free to enter the complex, but costs Rs 25 if you wish to take a camera inside, Rs 50 for a video.

The first temple you come to is that dedicated to **Chandraprabhu**, the eighth tirthankar, or Jain prophet. It was built in 1509 and features fine sculpture in sandstone in the mandapa. Around the inside of the drum are 12 statues of Ganesh, and around the hall which encompasses the inner sanctum are numerous statues of tirthankars. The mandapa is supported by elaborately sculpted pillars which form a series of toranas. No mortar was used in the construction of this temple; blocks of masonry are held together by iron staples. Around the upper gallery are 108 marble images of Parasnath, the 22nd tirthankar. In the inner sanctum is an image of Chandraprabhu. Note that the statue is unclothed. This is typical of Jain statues, and contrasts with those of Hindu deities, which are always elaborately garbed.

A few steps behind this temple is that dedicated to **Parasnath**. Entry is via an enormous and beautifully carved torana culminating in an image of the Jain tirthankar at its apex. There is a voluptuous carving of a sinuous dancing woman balancing sets of balls on her raised forearm. The spacious mandapa is supported by fine pillars, and in the drum of the dome the sculptures are painted. They represent dancing figures interspersed with musicians, who welcome the gods.

A door on the south side of the temple leads to the small **Shitalnath Temple**, dedicated to the 10th tirthankar, and only recently opened to visitors. The image of Shitalnath enshrined here is composed of eight precious metals. A door in the north wall leads to the beautiful **Sambhavanth Temple**. In the courtyard before this temple, Jain priests grind sandalwood in mortars for devotional use in the temples. As with the Parasnath Temple, the drum of the dome here has sculpted dancing figures. The statues flanking the wall are of Jaisalmer sandstone, but have been so highly polished they resemble marble. On either side of the inner sanctum, carved Jain saints stand with their heads hooded by cobras.

Steps in the courtyard of this temple lead to the **Gyan Bhandar**, a library founded in 1500 by Acharya Maharaj Jin Bhadra Suri. This small underground vault houses priceless ancient illustrated manuscripts, some dating from the 11th century. Other exhibits include astrological charts and the Jain version of the Christian's Shroud of Turin: the Shroud of Gindhasuri, a Jain hermit and holy man who died in Ajmer. When his body was placed on the funeral pyre, the shroud was miraculously unsinged. In a small locked cabinet are images of Parasnath made of various precious stones, including emerald, crystal and ivory. The Gyan Bhandar is open daily, but only between 10 and 11 am.

Steps lead from the courtyard before the Sambhavanth Temple to the **Shantinath Temple**, which was built in 1536. Curiously, the image enshrined here, which is made of eight different metals, is oriented to the north, rather than to the east as is customary. The enclosed gallery around this temple is flanked by hundreds of images of saints, some of marble, and some of Jaisalmer sandstone. Steps lead below this temple to the **Kunthunath Temple**, which was also built in 1536.

To the right of the Chandraprabhu Temple is the **Rikhabdev Temple**. There are some fine sculptures around the walls protected by glass cabinets, and the pillars are beautifully sculpted. This temple has a lovely, tranquil atmosphere. On the south side of the inner sanctum, a beautiful carving depicts a mother holding a child which stretches up to reach fruit she is holding just out of its reach.

Behind the sanctum is a depiction of the Hindu goddess Kali, flanked by a Jain sculpture of a woman, unclothed. Here it is possible to compare the elaborately garbed Hindu statue with its typically unadorned Jain equivalent.

Laxminath Temple This Hindu temple, in the centre of the fort, is simpler than the Jain temples, although there are some interesting paintings in the drum of the dome. Devotees offer grain which is distributed before the temple. There is a repoussé silver architrave around the entrance to the inner sanctum, and a heavily garlanded image enshrined within.

Rajmahal Part of this palace is open to the public, although there's really not much to see here – it's certainly not comparable to the museum housed within the palaces at the Meherangarh Fort at Jodhpur. The entrance to the palace is to the right just after you pass through the last gate into the fort proper. It's open daily from 8 am to 5 pm, and entry costs Rs 5.

On the eastern wall can be seen a sculpted pavilion-type balcony. Here drummers raised the alarm when the fort was under siege. The doorways connecting the rooms of the palace are quite low – this is not a reflection upon the stature of the Rajputs, but forced those walking beneath them to adopt a humble, stooped position, which was appropriate in case the room in which they were entering contained the maharaja.

A room on the east side of the palace affords fine views out over the entrance ramp to the fort and over the town spread beneath it. From here you can clearly see the numerous round stones piled on top of the battlements, ready to roll onto advancing enemies. There is a small *diwan-i-am* (public audience hall) with the lower walls lined with porcelain tiles. The adjacent room is lined with blue and white tiles. Upstairs, in a room close to the maharaja's private chamber on the east side of the palace, is a room which has some exquisitely carved stone panel friezes, which on first glance appear to be carved from wood. A door leads from the maharaja's

chamber to the maharanis' chambers. There are very fine paintings in a room off this passage, but unfortunately it and the passage are closed to visitors. The views from the top of the palace are superb.

The Havelis

There are several beautiful havelis in Jaisalmer which were built by wealthy merchants, and some are in excellent condition. There are no entry fees to most of the havelis, but some people are keen to get you to buy stone carvings and the like – there's some fine material to choose from.

Patwon ki Haveli This most elaborate and magnificent of all the Jaisalmer havelis stands in a narrow lane. It's divided into six apartments, two owned by the Archaeological Survey of India, two private homes, and two containing craftshops, including that of Kojraj Borawat, which was the first handicraft shop in Jaisalmer. The havelis were originally built between 1800 and 1860 by five Jain brothers who made their fortunes in trading jewellery and fine brocades. The havelis retain remnants of paintings in vibrant reds and gold, as well as fine mirrorwork.

Salim Singh ki Haveli This haveli was built about 300 years ago and part of it is still occupied. Salim Singh was the prime minister when Jaisalmer was the capital of a princely state, and his mansion has a beautifully arched roof with superb carved brackets in the form of peacocks. The stone elephants before the haveli are traditionally erected before the homes of prime ministers. The mansion is just below the hill and, it is said, once had two additional wooden storeys in an attempt to make it as high as the maharaja's palace, but the maharaja had the upper storeys torn down! There is a Rs 15 entry charge at this haveli, and it's open between 8 am and 6 pm.

Nathmal ki Haveli This late 19th century haveli was also a prime minister's house. The left and right wings of the building were

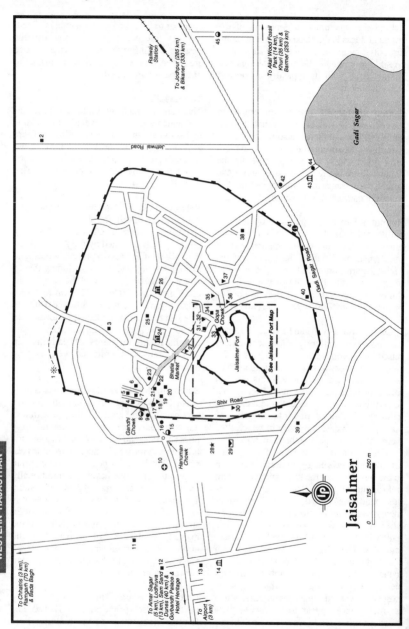

Jaisalmer

WESTERN RAJASTHAN

carved by brothers and are very similar, but not identical. Yellow sandstone elephants guard the building, and even the front door is a work of art.

Gadi Sagar Tank

This tank, south of the city walls, was once the water supply of the city, and befitting its importance in providing precious water to the inhabitants of this arid city, it is surrounded by small temples and shrines. A wide variety of waterfowl flock here in winter. The tank took advantage of a natural declivity which already retained some water, and was built in 1367 by Maharaja Gadsi Singh.

The beautiful yellow sandstone gateway which arches across the road down to the tank is known as the **Tilon ki Pol**, and is said to have been built by a famous prostitute, Tilon. When she offered to pay to have this gateway constructed, the maharaja refused permission on the grounds that he would have to pass under it to go down to the tank,

and he felt that this would be beneath his dignity. While he was away, she built the gate anyway, adding a Krishna temple on top so that the king could not tear it down.

Today, Jaisalmer's water is supplied by the Indira Gandhi Canal, which means that the Gadi Sagar tank retains water throughout the year.

It's possible to hire pedal boats on the lake (Rs 30 for 30 minutes).

On the right-hand side of the road leading down to the lake is the **Jaisalmer Folklore Museum** (open daily between 9 am and 6 pm). The well captioned exhibits include textiles, coins, fossils, photographic displays and traditional Rajasthani musical instruments. There's also a little bookshop here.

Government Museum

Close to the RTDC Hotel Moomal is this small museum (open daily from 10 am to 4.30 pm; entry free), which has a dusty although not uninteresting collection of fossils, some of which date back to the Jurassic era (160 to 180 million years ago!), and other artefacts. Other exhibits include well labelled examples of ancient script, coins, religious sculptures (some dating from the 11th century),

puppets and textiles. There is even a stuffed great Indian bustard, the state bird of Rajasthan which thrives in the Thar Desert but is declining in numbers elsewhere.

Camel Safaris Around Jaisalmer

The most interesting means of exploring the desert around Jaisalmer is on a camel safari and virtually everyone who comes here goes on one. October to February is the best time.

Competition between safari organisers is cut-throat and standards vary considerably. This has resulted in many complaints when promises have been made and not kept. Touts will begin to hassle you even before you get off the bus or train; and, at the budget end of the market, hotel rooms can be as little as Rs 10 – providing you take the hotel's safari. Try to talk to other travellers for feedback on who is currently offering good, reliable and honest service, and don't be pressured by agents who tell you that if you don't go on the trip leaving tomorrow there won't be another until next week. Naturally they all offer *the* best safari and spare no invective in pouring scorn on their rivals.

The truth is more mundane. None of the hotels have their own camels – these are all independently owned – so the hoteliers and the travel agents are just go-betweens, though the hotels often organise the food and drink supplies. You need to consider a few things before jumping at what appears to be a bargain. Hotel owners typically pay the camel drivers around Rs 80 per camel per day to hire them, so if you're offered a safari at Rs 120 per day, this leaves only a small margin for food and the agent's profit. It's obvious that you can't possibly expect three reasonable meals a day on these margins, but this is frequently what is promised. As a result, a lot of travellers feel they've been ripped off when the food isn't what was offered.

The realistic minimum price for a basic safari is Rs 150 to Rs 200 per person per day. For this you can expect a breakfast of porridge, tea and toast, and a lunch and dinner of rice, dhal and chapatis – pretty unexciting stuff. Blankets are also supplied. For Rs 250 you should also get fruit, and some relief from the rice-dhal-chapati tedium. You must bring your own mineral water. Of course you can pay still more for greater levels of comfort – tents, stretcher beds, better food, beer etc.

Two camel safari agents that are not linked to any hotels have been recommended. Sahara Travels (☎ 52-609), by the fort gate, is run by Mr Bissa, alias Mr Desert. If you think you've seen his face before it's because he's India's Marlboro Man – the model in the Jaisalmer cigarette ads. His basic tours cost Rs 250 a day for two to four days, or Rs 350 with a greater range of meals. Tented safaris start at Rs 500. Thar Safari (☎ 52-722; fax 52-259), at Gandhi Chowk by the Trio Restaurant, organises basic safaris including camel, linen, mattress (no tent; you sleep out in the open), meals and Continental breakfast for Rs 450 per person per day. The deluxe safari includes tented accommodation, and costs Rs 750 per day. Whoever you book your safari through, insist that all rubbish is carried back to Jaisalmer, and not left at the Sam sand dunes or in remote villages where the wind will carry it across the desert.

Every evening at 5.30 pm, camel drivers congregate near First Fort Gate and you may be able to negotiate a cheaper safari direct with them, thereby cutting out the middle man. You would of course have to obtain your own food, bedding and water.

However much you decide to spend, make sure you know exactly what is being provided and make sure it's there before you leave Jaisalmer. You should also make sure you know where they're going to take you. Attempting to get a refund for services not provided is a waste of time.

Most safaris last three to four days and, if you want to get to the most interesting places, this is a bare minimum. Bring something very comfortable to sit on – many travellers fail to do this and come back with very sore legs and/or backsides! A wide-brimmed hat (or Rajput-style turban), sun cream and a personal water bottle are also essential. It gets very cold at night, so if you have a sleeping bag bring it along even if you're told that lots of blankets will be supplied. Women should consider wearing a sports bra, as the trotting momentum of the camels can cause some discomfort after even just a few hours.

If you're on your own it's worth getting a group of at least four people together before looking for a safari. Organisers will make up groups but four days is a long time to spend with people you might not get on with. Usually each person is assigned their own camel, but check this, as some agencies might try to save money by hiring fewer camels, meaning you'll find yourself sharing your camel with a camel driver or cook, which is not nearly as much fun. The reins are fastened to the camel's nose peg, so the animals are easily steered. At resting points, the camels are completely unsaddled and hobbled. They limp away to browse on nearby shrubs while the cameleers brew sweet chai or prepare food. The whole crew rests in the shade of thorn trees by a tank or well.

Organised Tours

The RTDC has morning and evening city sightseeing tours for Rs 40 per person, and sunset tours to the Sam sand dunes for Rs 70 per person. Bookings can be made at the RTDC Hotel Moomal Tourist Bungalow. The tours to Sam may stop at Kanoi, five km before the dunes, from where it's possible to

A camel safari is a great way to see the desert, which is surprisingly well populated and sprinkled with ruins. You constantly come across tiny fields of millet, girls picking berries or boys herding flocks of sheep or goats. The latter are always fitted with tinkling neck bells and, in the desert silence, it's music to the ears. Unfortunately the same cannot be said for the noises emitted by the notoriously flatulent camels! Camping out at night in the Sam sand dunes, huddling around a tiny fire beneath the stars and listening to the camel drivers' yarns can be quite romantic. The camel drivers will expect a tip or gift at the end of the trip. Don't neglect to do this.

Take care of your possessions, particularly on the return journey. A current scam involves the drivers suggesting that you walk to some nearby ruins while they stay with the camels and keep an eye on your bags. The police station in Jaisalmer receives numerous reports of items missing from luggage but seems unwilling to help.

The usual circuit takes in such places as Amar Sagar, Lodhruva, Mool Sagar, Bada Bagh and Sam, as well as various abandoned villages along the way. It's not possible to ride by camel to the Sam sand dunes in one day; in 1½ days you could get a jeep to Sam, stay there overnight, and take a camel from there to either Khaba, Dedeha, Jajiya and Kuldehra (then a jeep back to Jaisalmer) or to Kanoi (and catch a jeep from there to Jaisalmer).

In 2½ days you could travel by camel to Lodhruva, spend the second night at the Sam sand dunes, and return the following day to Jaisalmer by jeep. Alternatively, you could travel to Sam via Bada Bagh, Ramkund, Lodhruva, Amar Sagar, Damodra and Kanoi by jeep, and return to Jaisalmer by camel, staying overnight at Kuldehra. If you have more time, obviously you can travel at a more leisurely pace through these regions and forgo the jeep component. ■

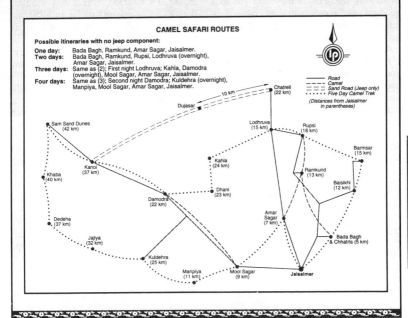

CAMEL SAFARI ROUTES

Possible itineraries with no jeep component:

One day: Bada Bagh, Ramkund, Amar Sagar, Jaisalmer.
Two days: Bada Bagh, Ramkund, Rupsi, Lodhruva (overnight), Amar Sagar, Jaisalmer.
Three days: Same as (2); First night Lodhruva; Kahla, Damodra (overnight), Mool Sagar, Amar Sagar, Jaisalmer.
Four days: Same as (3); Second night Damodra; Kuldehra (overnight), Manpiya, Mool Sagar, Amar Sagar, Jaisalmer.

Road
Camel
Sand Road (Jeep only)
Five Day Camel Trek
(Distances from Jaisalmer in parentheses)

Chatrell (22 km)
Dujasar — 10 km
Sam Sand Dunes (42 km)
Lodhruva (15 km)
Rupsi (18 km)
Barmsar (15 km)
Kahla (24 km)
Khaba (40 km)
Kanoi (37 km)
Ramkund (13 km)
Baisikhi (12 km)
Dhani (23 km)
Damodra (22 km)
Dedeha (37 km)
Amar Sagar (7 km)
Jajiya (32 km)
Bada Bagh & Chhatris (5 km)
Kuldehra (25 km)
Manpiya (11 km)
Mool Sagar (9 km)
Jaisalmer

get a camel to the dunes in time for the sunset (Rs 50).

Thar Safari (☎ 52-722; fax 52-259), at Gandhi Chowk by the Trio Restaurant, can organise jeep safaris to desert villages for Rs 900 for a half day (up to four people) and Rs 1200 for a full day. They also offer trips to the Sam sand dunes, and camel safaris (see Camel Safaris Around Jaisalmer in this section).

Places to Stay

Jaisalmer is a very popular place, and many hotels, both cheap and not so cheap, have sprung up to meet the demand. More than anywhere else you'll notice the number of touts swarming around the railway and bus stations, trying to grab the new arrivals. Unfortunately, some of them are less than honest – don't believe *anyone* who offers to take you 'anywhere you like' for Rs 2, and take with a grain of salt claims that the hotel you want to stay in is 'full', 'closed', 'no good any more' or has suffered some other inglorious fate. They'll only lead you to a succession of hotels, where of course they get commission if you stay. If you still insist on staying where *you* want, you'll be dropped unceremoniously outside the main fort gate, from where you'll have to walk. If you just want a lift into the centre, these people may be of use, but be prepared for the roundabout tour and pressure to stay in a particular place.

The touting situation has reached such proportions that the district magistrate has set up a Tourist Protection Squad, to keep the touts at a distance. Their aims are very laudable – it's just a pity they are totally ineffective.

Many of the popular budget hotels send a vehicle to meet the bus or train. They display their own sign and offer free transport; otherwise you can take an auto-rickshaw.

Unfortunately, quite a few of the cheap places are into the high-pressure selling of camel safaris and the situation can get quite ugly if you book a safari through someone else. Not only will they refuse to hold your baggage, but in many cases they'll actually evict you!

Staying at one of the hotels within the fort itself is the most imaginative choice, but there are equally good hotels outside the fort walls. Motorised traffic is not permitted within the fort at most times, which means you'll have to lug your backpack up the steep ramp and cart it around with you while you check out the options. A better plan is to spend the first night in a guest house outside the fort walls, and check out the places to stay within the fort for subsequent nights unencumbered by your pack.

As is so often the case in Rajasthani towns, if there's a festival on, prices skyrocket and accommodation of any kind can be hard to get.

Places to Stay – bottom end

Town Area There's a good choice of budget hotels along the two streets than run parallel to each other north of the Trio Restaurant, about five minutes walk east of the city bus stand. These include the *Peacock Guest House* (☎ 40-039), which has singles/doubles with common bath for Rs 30/50, and with attached bath from Rs 50/80 to Rs 60/100. Hot water is available free by the bucket. Check-out is 9 am, and there's no restaurant here. There's also a very gloomy dorm with beds for Rs 10.

Opposite is the *Hotel Swastika* (☎ 52-483), which has singles/doubles with common bath for Rs 100/150, and with attached bath for Rs 150/220 and Rs 220/250. Beds in the dorm are Rs 60. It costs a steep Rs 20 per day to store luggage here if you take a camel safari, unless you book it through the hotel, when it's free.

Nearby is the *Hotel Renuka* (☎ 52-757), which has rooms with common bath from Rs 60 to Rs 100, and with attached bath for Rs 80 to Rs 140. There's a roof terrace here with fantastic fort views, and a rooftop restaurant. Another place close by is the *Ringo Guest House* (☎ 53-027), which has rooms at similar rates and similarly fine views from the rooftop.

Also in this area is the *Hotel Pleasure* (☎ 52-323), which has singles with common bath for Rs 40, doubles for Rs 60 and Rs 80, and with attached bath for Rs 85/120. There's 24 hour hot water in the common bathroom. Further along this street is the very basic *Hotel Pushkar Palace*, with comparable rates and amenities.

A great choice is the *Hotel Golden City* (☎ 53-064), which is in the southern section of the walled city, just off Gadi Sagar Rd. It's a very laid back, no-hassle place, with good clean rooms with attached bath and hot water for Rs 30/60 and a rooftop restaurant serving veg food.

Across the other side of the old town is another group of budget hotels, close to the entrance to the fort. The *Hotel Fort View* here is popular. It has singles/doubles with attached bath for Rs 44/77 on the ground floor, and with attached bath with hot showers on the 1st floor for Rs 77/88. On the top floor, rooms with attached bath and hot water cost Rs 88/99. There are also rooms with fort views. A double with attached bath and hot water costs Rs 150, and there are triples for Rs 250 and Rs 300. Train, bus and air bookings can be made here, and there's a popular restaurant on the top floor.

Next door is the *Hotel City View* (☎ 52-804), which has good clean rooms starting from Rs 30/40 with attached bath, up to Rs 70/80. The more expensive rooms have good fort views from the balcony. Hot water is free by the bucket.

Also in this area is the *Hotel Flamingo* (☎ 52-889), which has rooms with attached bath for Rs 80/120. Hot water by the bucket costs Rs 3. There's no restaurant here.

A little bit further west (towards Bhatia Market) is the *Hotel Shree Giriraj Palace* (☎ 52-268). This is a terrific place with clean, comfortable rooms and friendly staff. Prices range from Rs 70 to Rs 150, all with attached bath, and there are three rooms with common shower for Rs 50 a double. There's a good restaurant upstairs.

Near the Patwon ki Haveli is the *Hotel Rajdhani* (☎ 52-746), which has small, spartan but clean rooms with common bath for Rs 50/100, and air-cooled rooms with attached bath for Rs 150/200. There are pleasant rooms with balcony and air-cooling

for Rs 250. There are good views of the fort from the roof.

Directly opposite is the *Hotel Jag Palace* (☎ 40-438), which has clean rooms with common bath for Rs 60/100 and with attached bath and hot water for Rs 150/200. Vegetarian meals are available on the roof terrace.

For somewhere a little different try the *Hotel Pooja*, inside the city walls to the east of the fort. It's an atmospheric little guest house, with very spartan rooms from Rs 20 with common bath. You can also sleep on the roof here (Rs 5), there's a dorm (Rs 10), free hot water and free bed tea.

There are very good *retiring rooms* at the railway station. Doubles are Rs 50 and Rs 90, and there are also thatched huts for Rs 80, which are in a cluster set back from the station, so should be very quiet. All rooms have geysers.

Fort The *Deepak Hotel & Restaurant* (☎ 40-202) is a popular place run by a friendly Brahmin family with rooms ranging from basic with common bath for Rs 30/60, to rooms with attached bath, hot shower and balcony for Rs 200/300. The hotel is actually part of the fort wall, so the views from some rooms are stunning, as are those from the rooftop. Both rooms No 2 and 16 are in old circular bastions (Rs 125/175, with common bath). There are also dorm beds for Rs 20.

Nearby is the *Hotel Star Moon* (☎ 40-363). Rooms are a little dank and musty, and cost from Rs 40/60 with common bath to Rs 250/450 with attached bath and west-facing windows. Run by the same people, and a much better choice, is the *Hotel Simla* (no phone). Rooms with common bath are Rs 60/100 and Rs 150/200. With attached bath (cold water; hot water by the bucket free) rooms are Rs 250/350, and a very pretty room with an alcove and balcony is Rs 300/450. It's possible to sleep on the roof for Rs 15, which includes blanket, mattress and a great view. The manager, Jora, is a friendly fellow.

Near the Laxminath Temple is the new *Ishar Palace* (no phone). Rooms are spartan but clean, and cost Rs 30 for a single with common bath, Rs 50/60 for singles/doubles with common bath, and a better room, also with common bath, is Rs 75. It costs Rs 15 to sleep on the roof. This was the home of a 19th century prime minister, Ishar Singh, as evidenced by the statues of elephants before the building.

Close to the Jain Temples is the *Hotel Shree Palace* (no phone). It's a little expensive, with doubles with common bath for Rs 150, and with attached bath from Rs 200 to Rs 400. There are no single rates. It's lacking atmosphere, but there are good views of the Jain Temples from the roof.

Of a similar standard is the nearby *Castle Paying Guest House* (☎ 52-988). There are no single rates; doubles with common bath are Rs 100, and with attached bath Rs 200. There are also rooms with balconies for Rs 300. Rooms are a little shabby but OK. In the same area is the (old) *Hotel Laxmi Niwas* (☎ 52-758). Very small rooms with common bath are Rs 50/100/150 (the common shower is a bit primitive, and the toilet is tiny). Doubles with attached bath are Rs 200 and Rs 300.

The *Hotel Paradise* (☎ 52-674) is a very popular place. You'll see it on the far side of the main square from the palace as you come through the last gate into the fort. It's a kind of haveli, with 18 rooms arranged around a leafy courtyard and has excellent views from the roof. Singles/doubles with common bath are Rs 60/150, and there's also a double with common bath for Rs 200. With attached bath, doubles cost from Rs 250 to Rs 650. The more expensive rooms hare running hot water and good views from the balconies. It's possible to sleep on the roof for Rs 30 – a blanket and mattress are provided.

In the south-east corner of the fort is the (new) *Hotel Laxmi Niwas* (☎ 53-065). It has only six rooms, ranging from Rs 50/100 with common bath to Rs 300/500 for rooms with attached bath (cold water) and a balcony. Rooms are OK, but nothing special.

Places to Stay – middle
Town Area Near the Amar Sagar Gate is the *Hotel Nachana Haveli* (☎ 52-110). This 280 year old haveli has recently been converted into a hotel, with rooms set around a courtyard. Ordinary air-cooled rooms are Rs 500/600, and deluxe air-cooled rooms are Rs 1000/1200, all with running hot water. The ordinary rooms are large and clean with stone floors and a few old effects. The deluxe rooms are reasonably comfortable with some antique furnishings.

Nearby is the *Hotel Jaisal Palace* (☎ 52-717), a clean and well run place which has rooms from Rs 250/350 (with no external window) to Rs 390/440/660 (with balcony). All rooms have attached bath with hot water, and there's a roof terrace with terrific views over the town, and a veg restaurant.

The RTDC *Hotel Moomal Tourist Bungalow* (☎ 52-392) is reasonable value, although it's set outside the walled city. In the grounds are air-cooled thatched huts for Rs 375/500. In the main complex, ordinary rooms are Rs 250/300, and air-con rooms are Rs 600. Beds in the dorm cost Rs 50. There's a restaurant serving both veg and non-veg fare, a beer shop. Check-out is at noon.

Just inside the town walls at Gandhi Chowk is the *Hotel Mandir Palace* (☎ 52-788; fax 52-778), a royal palace in part of which the erstwhile royal family still lives. Frankly it's a little bit run-down, but is still quite atmospheric. Ordinary rooms cost Rs 550/750, and deluxe suites are Rs 900/1050. The ordinary rooms are definitely not palatial, and those downstairs off the reception area are dark and stuffy. Those upstairs feature pretty tiles and black and white tiled bathrooms. The suites are better.

Also outside the town walls, south-west of the fort, is the *Hotel Neeraj* (☎ 52-442), which has clean, carpeted but otherwise unremarkable rooms for Rs 550/850 with air-cooling.

Inside the town walls, to the north of the fort, is the *Hotel Shri Narayan Vilas* (☎ 52-283). It has rooms for Rs 475/500, but it's better to pay a bit extra for the more comfortable and better appointed air-cooled rooms at Rs 475/600. Meals are available here.

The *Jawahar Niwas Palace* (☎ 52-208), which once belonged to Maharaja Jawahar

Singh, stands rather forlornly in its own sandy grounds about one km west of the fort. Rooms are spacious and comfortable, and have air-cooling in summer. They cost Rs 800/850, and meals are available here. There are stunning views of the fort from the hotel grounds.

Further out on the Sam road, about 2.5 km west of the fort, is the brand new *Gorbandh Palace* (☎ 53-111; fax 52-749). It's owned by the Maharani of Udaipur, and is replete with facilities such as (Jaisalmer's only) swimming pool, coffee shop, bar, travel counter and bakery. Built of Jaisalmer sandstone, the stone friezes around the hotel were sculpted by local artisans. Standard aircon rooms cost Rs 700/1000, deluxe air-con rooms are Rs 1195/1850, and enormous and luxurious suites are Rs 1195/2395. The deluxe rooms are comfortable, and the standard rooms are of a similar standard, but in a fairly nondescript block quite a distance behind the main building. Non-guests can use the magnificent swimming pool (rates on application), and are welcome to dine in the restaurant (see Places to Eat).

Fort Close to the Jain Temples is the *Shree Nath Palace Hotel* (☎ 52-907), a family-run establishment in a beautiful old haveli. The rooms reek with atmosphere with little alcoves and balconies, and some have windows which afford magnificent sunset views over the temple. Omjee, the owner, claims descent from one of Jaisalmer's past prime ministers. Rooms cost Rs 250/300, and hot water is available free by the bucket.

Nearby is the *Hotel Suraj* (☎ 53-023), another old haveli which features fine sculpture on the facade and good views from the roof. Each room is different, and they all have attached bath with hot shower for Rs 250/300. The restaurant serves basic fare.

The *Hotel Jaisal Castle* (☎ 52-362; fax 52-101) is another restored haveli, this one in the south-west corner of the fort. It's biggest attraction is its position, high on the ramparts overlooking the desert. Pleasant large air-cooled rooms cost Rs 500/650, and both veg and non-veg meals are available.

This is also the only place in the fort where you can get a beer (Rs 66).

Places to Stay – top end
The three star *Hotel Heritage* (☎ 52-769; fax 53-038) is on the Sam road, about 2.5 km west of the fort, next to the new Gorbandh Palace. Pleasant split level air-con rooms set around a landscaped garden are Rs 1100/1300, and air-con suites are Rs 2500.

The *Hotel Himmatgarh Palace* (☎ 52-002; fax 52-005) is about two km from First Fort Gate at 1 Ramgarh Rd. Comfortable air-cooled rooms in the main block are Rs 1195/1900, and air-con cottages are Rs 1195/2350.

Closer to the fort, and counting among its former guests Britain's Princess Anne, is the well run *Hotel Narayan Niwas Palace* (☎ 52-408; fax 52-101), which has deluxe air-con rooms for Rs 1175/1475 and suites for Rs 1800. The hotel has been designed to simulate the atmosphere of a Rajput ruler's desert camp, but there has been no compromise in comfort. Every evening there is a cultural programme including traditional Rajasthani dancing, and non-guests are welcome to attend (Rs 250).

An excellent choice in this category is the impeccable *Hotel Dhola Maru* (☎ 52-863; fax 52-761), on Jethwai Rd to the north-east of the walled city, about four km from the fort entrance. The location is not great, but this is more than compensated for by the service and the comfortable rooms. Air-con rooms are Rs 1190/1500, and suites are Rs 2000. There's an extraordinary bar, which has incorporated tree roots into its décor, and a restaurant. If there are enough people (minimum 10), the hotel can arrange dinner and a cultural show at the Sam sand dunes (Rs 600 per person).

Places to Eat
An excellent and friendly place to eat in the fort is the *Vyas Meal Service*, near the Jain Temples. This family-run veg restaurant has traditional cuisine from Jaisalmer. The Rajasthani thali includes dhal, bread, rice, papad and chutney, and costs Rs 50. The

WESTERN RAJASTHAN

more elaborate royal thali includes a fruit and nut biryani, curd and puri, and costs Rs 100.

A popular place to eat inside the fort is the *8 July Restaurant*, a veg place with a good terrace for watching the world go by. It caters to western tastes with (veg) hot dogs, pizza, apple pie, spaghetti and chow mein. There is a second 8 July Restaurant outside the fort, near the Mid Town Restaurant.

Outside the fort, near the entrance, are several rooftop restaurants which are popular, especially in the evenings. The vegetarian *Mid Town*, Gopa Chowk, has a Rajasthani special thali for Rs 40, and most main meals are under Rs 50. The food is OK, but nothing special. A short distance away is the *Monica Restaurant*, which is very popular in the early morning and evening. A few minutes walk down from the Monica is the *Natraj Restaurant*, which has attentive service and tasty food. Chicken curry is Rs 40, tandoori chicken is Rs 65, and a beer will set you back Rs 60. The open-air top floor has an excellent view of the upper part of the Salim Singh ki Haveli next door, and away to the south of town.

Opposite the Natraj is the *Seema Restaurant*, with comparable prices and a range of veg and non-veg dishes.

There is another group of restaurants near the Amar Sagar Gate, about 10 minutes walk north-west of the fort entrance. The best of these is the long-running *Trio Restaurant*. It's a bit pricier than its neighbours, but the food is excellent, and musicians play in the evening. The Saagwala mutton (with creamed spinach) for Rs 60 is excellent. Also in this area is the *Top Deck*, which has Indian, Chinese and Continental cuisine, the last of these including pizzas and sizzlers. Beneath the Top Deck is the *Sharma Lodge*, which has a filling Indian thali for Rs 20.

Non-guests are welcome at the restaurant at the *Gorbandh Palace*. The buffet costs Rs 175 for breakfast, Rs 275 for lunch, and Rs 400 for dinner. It looked delicious! There's also á la carte dining.

Not in a really convenient location, but serving fresh and tasty vegetarian food is the *Jain Restaurant* on Shiv Rd. All dishes are under Rs 20, and everything is freshly prepared, so might take a little longer than at some other places. This place sees very few westerners, but is popular with locals and Indian visitors.

For refreshing fruit juice and lassis, try *Mohan Juice Centre*, Bhatia Market.

Things to Buy

Jaisalmer is famous for embroidery, Rajasthani mirrorwork, rugs, blankets, old stonework and antiques. Tie and dye and other fabrics are made at the Kadi Bundar, north of the city. One traveller reports that you should watch out for silver items bought in Jaisalmer as the metal may be adulterated with bronze.

On the laneway leading up to the Jain Temples within the fort is a small shop, Light of the East, which sells crystals and rare mineral specimens, including zeolite, which can fetch up to Rs 5000 depending on the quality.

There is a branch of Rajasthali, the government handicraft emporium, just outside Amar Sagar Gate.

Getting There & Away

Air The ticketing agency for Jagson Airlines is Thar Safari (☎ 52-722; fax 52-259), near the Trio Restaurant at Gandhi Chowk. Jagson has flights between Jaisalmer and Jodhpur on Tuesday, Thursday and Saturday (US$50), which connect with flights through to Delhi (US$150).

Bus The private bus stand is near Gandhi Chowk. From here you can buy tickets for buses to Sam (noon, 3 and 5 pm, 1½ hours, Rs 10); Khuri (9 am, 3 and 5.30 pm, two hours, Rs 10); and Lodhruva via Amar Sagar (1, 3 and 8 pm, one hour, Rs 6).

The main Roadways bus stand (☎ 53-141) is some distance from the centre of town, near the railway station. Fortunately, all buses start from Gandhi Chowk, near Amar Sagar Gate, and then call at the main bus stand. Reservations are really only needed on the night buses, and these should be made at the main bus stand. Times given are for departures from the city stand; add 30 minutes for departures from the main stand.

To Jodhpur there are buses at 6.30 and 11.30 am, 12.30 (deluxe), 2.30, 4 and 5 pm (5 pm is deluxe 2x2; it continues to Jaipur; 13 hours, Rs 187). The ordinary express service takes 5½ hours and costs Rs 60; deluxe is five hours and Rs 88.

To Bikaner there are services at 6 and 8 am, noon, 2.30, 4.30 (deluxe), 8 and 9.30 (deluxe) pm. It takes 6½ hours by deluxe, and costs Rs 88; on the express, it takes 7½ hours and costs Rs 69.

To Barmer there's a service at 5.30 am which continues to Mt Abu (12 hours, Rs 118). There are regular express and deluxe departures throughout the day until 5.30 pm. This last service continues on to Ahmedabad (12 hours, Rs 126). To Barmer, the deluxe service takes three hours and costs Rs 40; express takes four hours and costs Rs 33.

It's possible to book luxury bus trips through most of the travel agencies. Quoted rates were: Udaipur, Rs 150; Jaipur, Rs 160; Delhi, Rs 240; Ajmer, Rs 140; Bikaner, Rs 90; and Jodhpur, Rs 70.

Train The reservation office at the railway station is open from 10 am to 4 pm. It's computerised, so it's possible to book trains here to anywhere in India. There is a waiting room here with a cold shower, and plans are underway to open a tourist office. The refreshment room was closed at the time of writing.

The *IJPJ Passenger* leaves Jaisalmer daily at 7.25 am, arriving at Jodhpur at 3 pm. It costs Rs 67 in 2nd class; 1st class is not available, but will cost around Rs 280 when this service resumes. A night service is also planned.

Jeep It's possible to hire jeeps from the stand on Gandhi Chowk. To Khuri expect to pay Rs 300 return with a one hour wait. For Lodhruva, you'll pay Rs 200 return with a one hour wait.

Getting Around
An auto-rickshaw to the Gadi Sagar Tank costs Rs 15 one way from the fort entrance,

or Rs 60 return with a 30 minute wait at the tank.

AROUND JAISALMER
There are some fascinating places to see in the area around Jaisalmer, although it soon fades out into a barren sand dune desert which stretches across the lonely border into Pakistan.

Due to the troubles in Punjab and alleged arms smuggling across the border from Pakistan, most of Rajasthan west of National Highway No 15 is a restricted area. Special permission is required from the Collector's office (☎ 52-201) in Jaisalmer if you want to go there, and this is only issued in exceptional circumstances. The only places exempted are Amar Sagar, Bada Bagh, Lodhruva, Kuldhara, Akal, Sam, Ramkund, Khuri and Mool Sagar.

Bada Bagh & Chhatris
About five km north of Jaisalmer, Bada Bagh is a fertile oasis with a huge old dam. It was built by Maharaja Jai Singh II and completed after his death by his son. Much of the city's fruit and vegetables are grown here and carried into the town each day by colourfully dressed women.

Above the gardens are royal chhatris with beautifully carved ceilings and equestrian statues of former rulers. In recent years some have fallen into disrepair, but they are currently being restored by the Archaeological Department.

Amar Sagar
Seven km north-west of Jaisalmer, this once pleasant formal garden has now fallen into ruin. The lake here dries up several months into the dry season. According to locals, the stepwells here were built by prostitutes.

Nearby is a finely carved Jain temple. Restoration commenced in the 1970s with craftspeople brought in from Agra in Uttar Pradesh. When the temple is complete, an image of Adinath, the first tirthankar, will be installed in the inner sanctum. There is some very fine sculpture here. It is free to enter the temple, but costs Rs 25 for a camera and Rs 50 for a video.

WESTERN RAJASTHAN

Lodhruva

Further out beyond Amar Sagar, 15 km north-west of Jaisalmer, are the deserted ruins of Lodhruva which was the ancient capital before the move to Jaisalmer. It was probably founded by the Lodra Rajputs, and passed to the ruler of Devagarh, Bhatti Devaraja, in the 10th century. In 1025, Mahmud of Ghazni lay siege to the town, and it was sacked various times over subsequent decades, prompting Jaisala to shift the capital to a new location, resulting in the foundation of Jaisalmer in 1156.

The **Jain Temples**, rebuilt in the late 1970s, are the only reminder of the city's former magnificence. The temple enshrines an image of Parasnath, the 23rd tirthankar, and is finely wrought in silver, and surrounded by fine sculptures. The temple has its own resident cobra, which is said to be 1.5m long and over 400 years old. It lives in a hole on the north side of the main temple. It's supposed to be very auspicious to see the cobra, but probably as close as you'll get is viewing the photograph of it which is housed inside the temple.

The small sculptures around the lower course of the inner sanctum are badly damaged, and still bear the scars of Muslim raids. Behind the inner sanctum is a 200 year old carved Jaisalmer stone slab which bears carvings of the tirthankars' feet in miniature. The ornate rosette in the centre of the drum of the dome over the mandapa was carved from a single piece of stone, and before the temple is a beautiful torana.

The small temple to the right of the main temple is dedicated to Adinath, the first tirthankar.

There is nowhere to stay in Lodhruva – the *dharamsala* (pilgrims' lodging) beside the temple is for Jains only. There is a cold drink stall opposite the entrance to the temple. It's free to enter the temple. To bring a camera in costs Rs 25, and a video camera is Rs 50.

Mool Sagar

Nine km directly west of Jaisalmer, this is another pleasant small garden and tank. It belongs to the maharaja of Jaisalmer.

Kuldehra

Twenty five km west of Jaisalmer is this small village. Around 400 years ago, all the villagers left after a dispute with the prime minister. However, according to legend, they couldn't carry all their gold and silver, so they buried it. Several years ago some westerners arrived at Kuldehra on motorcycles armed with gold detectors and found hundreds of gold and silver coins. However, local villagers became suspicious and called the police, and the treasure hunters were apprehended and divested of their booty! Kuldehra is included on some of the extended camel treks.

Khuri

Khuri is a small village 40 km south-west of Jaisalmer, out in the desert, in the touchy area near the Pakistan border. It's a delightfully peaceful place with houses of mud and straw decorated like the patterns on Persian carpets. There are, thankfully, no craft-shop lined streets or banana pancake restaurants. The attraction out here is the desert solitude and the brilliant star-studded sky at night.

Places to Stay & Eat There are few places to stay, and you won't get any bargains out here; basically you're paying for the peace and quiet, rather than the facilities, which are minimal. *Mama's Guest House* (☎ (02992) 8423) consists of various clusters of thatched huts. The cheapest cost Rs 350 per night, which includes meals and free bucket hot water in the common bath. These cost Rs 200 in the off season, but would be hellishly hot. The huts are set in a semi-circle around a campfire. There is a group of huts for Rs 450 each, which have a greater number of common bathrooms, and are better thatched, so will be cooler. The top-of-the-range huts are Rs 750, and include electric fan. There are only two huts in this group, so it's very private. It's also possible to stay in a conventional room (but not nearly so romantic!) for Rs 300 with common bath. Local musicians often give evening performances for an additional cost, and you can book camel safaris in the region for Rs 250 per day.

On the left of the main road as you enter the village is the new *Khuri Guest House* (☎ 8444). It's run by a friendly fellow and has five rooms with common bath which cost a reasonable Rs 125/250, including all meals. It's also possible to sleep on sand brought from a nearby dune for free. Huts with attached bath are planned, and should cost Rs 250. Camel safaris are Rs 225 per person per day, including meals, blankets and boiled water.

Getting There & Away There are three buses daily to Khuri from Jaisalmer's private bus stand, at 9 am, 3 and 5.30 pm. They return at 8 am, noon and 5 pm (two hours, Rs 10).

Sam Sand Dunes

The Desert National Park & Sanctuary has been established in the Thar Desert near Sam village. One of the most popular excursions is to the sand dunes on the edge of the park, 42 km from Jaisalmer along a very good sealed road (which is maintained by the Indian army).

This is the nearest real Sahara-like desert to Jaisalmer. It's best to be here at sunrise or sunset, and many camel safaris spend a night at the dunes. Just before sunset jeep loads of trippers arrive from Jaisalmer to be chased across the sands by persistent camel owners offering short rides.

Despite the tourist hype, it's a magical place, and it's still possible to frame pictures of solitary camels against lonely dunes. One tragic consequence of the increasing number of visitors to the dunes is the debris and rubbish lying at their base. Visitors are now charged Rs 2 to visit the dunes, money which could be put to good use to clean them up, but is more likely lining the pocket of some local official. If you feel strongly about the rubbish here, a letter to the Chief Tourism Officer, RTDC Tourism, Swagatam Hotel, Jaipur 302015, might have some effect. For further information, contact the Deputy Director, Desert National Park, Jaisalmer.

Places to Stay & Eat There's only one place to stay at the dunes, the RTDC *Sam Tourist Dhani* (no phone) which has eight rooms for Rs 125/172 with attached bath and fan, and dorm beds for Rs 50. Veg meals are available here. Bookings can be made through the RTDC Hotel Moomal (☎ 52-392) in Jaisalmer. There is currently no power at the Tourist Dhani, but it will be connected soon.

Akal Wood Fossil Park

Three km off the road to Barmer, 16 km from Jaisalmer, are the fossilised remains of a 180 million year old forest. To the untrained eye it's not particularly interesting.

BARMER
Telephone Area Code: 02982

Barmer is a centre for woodcarving, carpets, embroidery, block-printing and other handicrafts and its products are famous throughout Rajasthan. The centre for embroidery is Sadar Bazaar and various crafts are for sale on Station Rd at more reasonable prices than you'll find elsewhere in Rajasthan. Otherwise this desert town, 153 km from Jaisalmer and 220 km from Jodhpur, isn't very interesting. There's no fortress here and the most interesting part is probably the journey to Barmer through small villages, their mud-walled houses decorated with geometric designs. Barmer district hosts two festivals; see the Festival section earlier in this chapter.

Places to Stay & Eat

There are a couple of reasonable places to stay, including the *Krishna Hotel* (☎ 20-785), on Station Rd, which has air-cooled rooms for Rs 200/250, better rooms for Rs 250/300 and air-con rooms for Rs 400/450. It's very clean and has a 24 hour check-out. There's no restaurant here.

Further down Station Rd, away from the station and on the opposite side of the road, is the *Kailash Sarover Hotel* (☎ 20-730), which has cheaper rooms, starting at Rs 60/85 for those with common bath, air-cooled rooms with attached bath for Rs 175/250, and with air-con, geyser and TV, Rs 400/450.

The *Raj Restaurant*, on Station Rd between the railway station and the Krishna Hotel, has veg dishes.

WESTERN RAJASTHAN

Getting There & Away

Buses to Jodhpur depart every 30 minutes from 5.30 am onwards (deluxe: five hours, Rs 78; express: six hours, Rs 66) from out the front of the railway station. To Jaisalmer, there are buses at 6, 8 and 11 am, and 2 and 4 pm (deluxe: three hours, Rs 40; express: four hours, Rs 33). They leave from the main bus stand, which is about one km north of the railway station.

To Jodhpur, there are daily trains at 6 am, 4.20 and 10.30 pm (Rs 54/208 in 2nd/1st class).

AROUND BARMER

About 35 km from Barmer, the **Kiradu Temples** feature very fine sculpture. The temples conform to a style of architecture known as Solanki, and the most impressive of the five temples here is the **Someshvara Temple**, which has a multi-turreted spire and beautiful sculpture. However, you'll need permission from the District Magistrate and Superintendent of Police to visit it, as it's on the border road towards Pakistan. Buses will take you as far as Hathma (one hour, Rs 7), from where it is one km to the temple.

BIKANER

Population: 461,500
Telephone Area Code: 0151

This desert town in the north of the state was founded in 1488 by Rao Bika, a descendant of Jodha, the founder of Jodhpur. Like many others in Rajasthan, the old city is surrounded by a high crenellated wall and, like Jaisalmer, it was once an important staging post on the great caravan trade routes. The Gang Canal, built between 1925 and 1927, irrigates a large area of previously arid land around Bikaner.

Although it's less impressive than Jaisalmer, Bikaner is still an interesting place to visit, but not many travellers stop here. There's a superb fort, a government camel breeding farm just outside the town, and 30 km to the south is the Karni Mata Temple, where thousands of holy rats are worshipped.

Orientation

The old city is encircled by a seven km long city wall with five entrance gates, constructed in the 18th century. The fort and palace, built of the same reddish-pink sandstone as Jaipur's famous buildings, are outside the city walls.

Information

Tourist Offices The Tourist Reception Centre is at the RTDC Hotel Dhola Maru (☎ 28-621), about one km from the city centre on Pooran Singh Circle. The tourist officer, Ashok Kumar Vyas, is extremely helpful and informative. He paints miniatures and teaches painting to disabled children. Ask to see his work.

Money Travellers' cheques can be changed at the State Bank of Bikaner & Jaipur, near the Thar Hotel, PBM Hospital Rd.

Bookshops English-language newspapers are available from the railway station after noon.

Junagarh Fort

The Junagarh Fort was constructed between 1588 and 1593 by Raja Rai Singh, a general in the army of the Mughal emperor Akbar, with embellishments in the form of palaces and luxurious suites added by subsequent maharajas. It has a 986m long wall with 37 bastions, a moat and two entrances. The **Surajpol**, or Sun Gate, is the main entrance. The palaces within the fort are on the southern side and make a picturesque ensemble of courtyards, balconies, kiosks, towers and windows. A major feature of the fort and palaces is the superb quality of the stone carving.

Despite the fact that Junagarh doesn't command a hilltop position, as do some of Rajasthan's other grand fortresses, it is no less imposing and – a credit to its planners and architects – has never been conquered.

The fort is open daily from 10 am to 5 pm. Entry is Rs 30. You'll be besieged by 'guides' offering their services before you arrive at the ticket counter. Unless you want an indi-

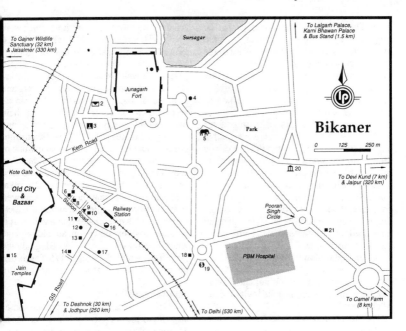

vidual tour, this is unnecessary, as the ticket price includes a tour with a group and official guide. It costs Rs 20 to bring a still camera into the fort, Rs 50 for a video camera.

The gold-painted ceiling of the beautiful **diwan-i-khas** (private audience hall) was executed in 1631, and the silver gaddi of the maharajas can still be seen here. Before the Anup Mahal (see below) is a fine courtyard, paved with Italian tiles. Through the lattice screens around the courtyard the ladies of the zenana could watch the activities below. In the **Phul Mahal**, or Flower Palace, which was built during the reign of Maharaja Gaj Singh, is a marble statue of Surya, the sun god, and around the upper edges of the walls, paintings depict scenes from the *Ramayana*.

The beautiful **Anup Mahal** was commissioned by Maharaja Karan Singh (1631-69). According to local lore, the maharaja was camping at Golkonda, in southern India, in his capacity as a general in the Mughal army, when an artist showed him fine works in

PLACES TO STAY
6 Hotel Deluxe & Restaurant
7 Hotel Akashdeep, Amit Hotel, Delight Guest House & Deluxe Rest House
8 Evergreen Hotel
10 Hotel Joshi
13 Hotel Shri Shanti Niwas
14 Indre Lodge
15 Hotel Bhanwar Niwas
18 Thar Hotel
21 Hotel Dhola Maru & Tourist Reception Centre

PLACES TO EAT
9 Joshi Misthan Bhandar Restaurant & Chhotu Motu Joshi Sweet Shop
11 Amber Restaurant

OTHER
1 Urmul Trust Shop
2 GPO
3 Ratan Behari Temple & Garden
4 Courts
5 Zoo
12 Bike Hire
16 Taxi Stand & Clock Tower
17 Victor Travels & Tours
19 State Bank of Bikaner & Jaipur
20 Ganga Golden Jubilee Museum

gold. The artist told the maharaja that he originally hailed from Jaisalmer, but had migrated to southern India when a famine swept over his homeland. The maharaja was inspired by the proficiency and great beauty of the work he had been shown, and invited the artist to return to Bikaner where he was given royal patronage.

It is the work of this artist and of his students which features in the Karan Mahal and Anup Mahal. Three types of work can be seen here: the *sonakin* style features white plaster which is decorated with delicate patterns and painted with gold leaf; the *jangali sunthari* style features plaster with a green background depicting floral motifs; and the *manovat* style features a pillar of clay embossed on plaster and the entire work painted with gold leaf.

In the **Badal Mahal**, or Cloud Palace, the walls are painted with blue cloud motifs and there is a statue here of Vishnu and Laxmi. The large pillars were installed with the aid of elephants nearly 400 years ago.

The **Gaj Mandir** was the private chambers of Maharaja Gaj Singh. The maharani's chamber is decorated with mirror tiles and gold painting, and on the ceiling is wooden lac painting. The maharaja's chamber has a beautiful painted wood ceiling featuring florets and geometric motifs, and carved ivory doors.

In the **Hawa Mahal**, or Summer Palace, is an ingenious device which alerted the maharaja to potential enemies: a mirror positioned over the bed enabled Maharaja Dunga Singh to see reflections of those people walking across the courtyard below – or at least this is the purpose of the mirror according to the official fort guides! The ceiling features floral arabesques and scenes of Krishna dancing. The blue tiles were imported from both Europe and China.

The handprints which can be seen close to the **Daulatpol** commemorate the wives of Rajput soldiers lost in battles who committed sati on their husbands' funeral pyres.

Museum This interesting exhibition is housed in several rooms at the fort. In the armoury are enormous bore guns which were used for shooting from the backs of camels as well as the usual collection of sinister looking pistols and swords.

In the diwan-i-khas of Ganga Singh are three massive arches, intricately carved, and a throne of sandalwood. Here also can be seen a 56 kg suit of armour, including chain mail, and sculptures of Krishna dancing and stealing the clothes of the gopis. Beautiful if deadly weapons, each an exquisite work of art – swords with ivory and crystal handles, some in the shape of lions – can also be seen here. In a separate chamber are the royal vestments of Maharaja Ganga Singh, as well as items from his office including a paperweight and his briefcase. From a gallery it is possible to look down on an old biplane which was presented to Ganga Singh by the British government during WWI. This is one of only two models of this plane in the world

Jain Temples

Two Jain temples can be found in the south east end of the walled city. The **Bhandasar Jain Temple** is dedicated to the fifth tirthankar, Sumtinath, and the building was commissioned in 1468 by a wealthy Jain merchant, Bhandasa Oswal. It was not completed until after his death, in 1514.

The interior of the temple is stunning with, unusually for a Jain temple, a series of vibrant paintings. The pillars bear floral arabesques and stories which depict the lives of the 24 Jain tirthankars. It is said that 40,000 kg of ghee was used instead of water in the mortar, which locals insist seeps through the walls on hot days.

There are fine carvings on either side of the inner sanctum, which is also decorated with English tiles. The floor is covered in Italian marble, and the foundation stones were transported from Jaipur. In each corner around the inner sanctum are elaborate carvings depicting the 24 tirthankars. The inner sanctum enshrines an image of Sumtinath and the altar is covered in gold gilding and mirrorwork.

On the 1st floor of the three storey temple are beautifully executed miniatures of the sentries of the gods. There are fine views out over the city from the 3rd floor, with the desert stretching behind it to the west. Photography is permitted inside the temple.

The second Jain temple here is the **Sandeshwar Temple**. It is smaller than the Bhandasar Temple, and has good carving around the door architraves and columns, and ornately carved painted pillars. Inside the drum of the *shikhara* (spire) are almost ethereal paintings, and the sanctum itself has a marble image of Sandeshwar flanked by smaller marble statues of other Jain tirthankars.

Lakshminath Temple Behind the Bhandasar Temple, to the right, is the Hindu Lakshminath Temple. It was built during the reign of Rao Lunkaran between 1505 and 1526. Lakshminath was the patron god of the rulers of Bikaner, and during major religious festivals a royal procession led by the maharaja paid homage at the temple. The elaborate edifice was maintained with tributes received from five villages and several shops which were granted to the temple by Maharaja Ganga Singh (1887-1943).

Lalgarh Palace
Three km north of the city centre, this red sandstone palace was built by Maharaja Ganga Singh in memory of his father Maharaja Lal Singh. Although it's an imposing building with overhanging balconies and delicate latticework, it's not the most beautiful of Rajasthani royal residences.

The **Shri Sadul Museum** covers the entire 1st floor of the palace. The museum was established in 1976 and is open daily except Wednesday from 10 am to 5 pm. Entry is Rs 5. There is a reasonable collection of artefacts and personal possessions of the Bikaner maharajas, reflecting the privileged lifestyles of these rulers, including (empty!) wine and sherry bottles and a brass vessel known as a *tokna* used to collect revenue which was transported by camel to the Bikaner state treasury. Other more pedestrian exhibits include Maharaja Karni Singh's golf tees, an electric toothbrush, and even his earplugs and sneakers! There is also a somewhat disturbing pictorial display of tiger carnage, including a shot of the five tigers shot in three minutes by Maharaja Ganga Singh in 1937.

In front of the palace is a carriage from the maharaja's royal train.

Ganga Golden Jubilee Museum
This interesting museum is on the Jaipur road and is open daily except Friday from 10 am to 4.30 pm. Entry is Rs 2. Exhibits include terracotta ware from the Gupta period, a range of Rajasthani traditional musical instruments, miniature wooden models of the Gajner and Lalgarh palaces and a miniature of the Royal Bikaner train with the roof folded back to reveal its comfortable amenities. There is a separate exhibition hall with antique carpets and royal vestments. Other interesting exhibits include decrees issued by the Mughals to the maharajas of Bikaner, including one advising Rai Singh to proceed to Delhi 'without any delay and with utmost expedition and speed, travelling over as great a distance as possible during the day time as well as by night' as 'Emperor Akbar is dying'. It was issued by Crown Prince (shortly to be emperor) Jehangir.

There are also some fine oil paintings, including one entitled 'Maharaja Padam Singh avenging...the death of his brother, Maharaja Mohan Singhji by killing the Emperor's brother-in-law...He drew his sword, rushed upon his enemy...and severed him in two with a blow which also left a mark upon the pillar'!

The sculptures include a beautiful and voluptuous image of Devi, and a marble Jain sculpture of Saraswati which dates from the 11th century.

Organised Tours
It's possible to book tours at the Tourist Reception Centre (see under Information) to Deshnok (for the Karni Mata Temple), and to the Gajner Wildlife Sanctuary (both Rs 350). An auto-rickshaw tour of the old city

with an English-speaking guide costs Rs 150 for 2½ hours.

For camel safaris, contact Shri Kamel (!) Vyas at Victor Travels & Tours (☎ 52-4117), Victor Tyre Re-Treading Company, Transport Line, GS Rd. Rajasthan Tours (☎ 24-834), which has an office at Junagarh Fort, can arrange a car and chauffeur (Rs 4 per km), camel safaris and guides, and can make hotel, train and bus reservations. Quoted rates for a chauffeur driven car to Jaisalmer are Rs 2915, and to Jaipur Rs 2215 (one way). Camel safaris ex Bikaner start at Rs 1400 per person per day and include all meals, tent accommodation, guide, camel and camel cart.

Places to Stay – homestays

The Tourist Reception Centre at the RTDC Hotel Dhola Maru (☎ 28-621) has a list of families registered with the Paying Guest Scheme. It costs from Rs 75 to Rs 750 for a double per night.

Places to Stay – bottom end

There are numerous budget options near the railway station. Station Rd is an amazingly busy thoroughfare, so the noise level in any room fronting it can be diabolical – choose carefully. The *Evergreen Hotel* (☎ 23-396) is not a bad choice, although it does front Station Rd. Rooms are clean, and there is 24 hour check-out. Singles/doubles with common bath (free hot water by the bucket) are Rs 60/90, or with attached bath (with cold water) are Rs 80/125/160 for singles/doubles/triples.

The nearby *Hotel Deluxe* may be a slightly better option, with a friendly manager and a veg restaurant downstairs. Singles/doubles are Rs 60/80, or Rs 80/100 and Rs 120 (for a double) with TV, all with attached bath. An air-cooler is available for an extra Rs 20 per night. Some rooms open onto a balcony.

Behind the Deluxe is the *Hotel Akashdeep* (☎ 26-024), which has rooms with attached bath for Rs 60/100 and free hot water by the bucket.

In the laneway behind the Deluxe is also the *Delight Guest House* (☎ 24-966). This is a shabby, grubby flophouse, but rooms are cheap at Rs 40/60 with common bath, and Rs 55/75 with attached bath. The rooms with attached bath are in the annexe on the opposite side of the laneway. Hot water is available in buckets for Rs 3.

Also in this laneway is the *Amit Hotel* (☎ 28-064). The impressive looking marble lobby is deceptive – rooms are shabby and tatty, and cost Rs 100/125, or Rs 125/150 with attached bath (hot water in buckets).

In the same laneway is the *Deluxe Rest House* (☎ 25-614), not to be confused with the Hotel Deluxe. It is even cheaper, but is the same dilapidated standard as the Delight, with singles/doubles with common bath for Rs 35/50, and with attached bath for Rs 40/65.

There are several budget places on the road directly opposite the railway station. The *Hotel Shri Shanti Niwas* has shabby but clean rooms at Rs 45/70 with common bath, and Rs 60/100 with attached bath. Deluxe air-cooled rooms are Rs 125/200.

About 10m further down this road, a laneway leads to the right. Down here you'll find the *Indre Lodge*, with has singles/doubles with attached bath for Rs 55/90 and large doubles for Rs 110.

It costs Rs 45/90 in the railway station *retiring rooms* for rooms with attached bath and hot water in buckets. Air-con rooms are Rs 105/135, and there's a dorm with beds for Rs 30.

Places to Stay – middle

The *Hotel Joshi* (☎ 52-7700; fax 52-1213) is on Station Rd, close to the railway station. It's a much more salubrious option that the budget flophouses further north, with air-cooled rooms for Rs 225/290, and carpeted air-con rooms for Rs 425/525. Better doubles are Rs 675. It's a well maintained place, and there's a veg restaurant here. There's running hot water in all rooms in winter only.

The RTDC *Hotel Dhola Maru* (☎ 28-621) is on Pooran Singh Circle, about one km from the centre of the city. Dorm beds are Rs 50, ordinary rooms with attached bath are Rs 125/175, air-cooled deluxe rooms are Rs

225/275 and air-con rooms are Rs 400/450. There's a non-veg restaurant here, and a place to buy takeaway beer. The tourist office is located in the same building.

There is a cluster of mid-range places on the road leading up to the Lalgarh Palace, and more under construction. It's hard to imagine why you would want to stay out here. The closest hotel to the palace is the *Hotel Palace View* (☎ 52-7072). There are, as you would expect, good views of the palace, and this is a quiet and well run place. Rooms are a little expensive at Rs 600/700/825 for singles/doubles/triples. There are also smaller rooms at Rs 400/500 for singles/doubles.

Nearby is the *Hotel Sagar* (☎ 52-0677). It's the first place to the left of the driveway as you approach the palace. Rooms cost Rs 900/1100, but the little thatched huts at this rate are way overpriced. Opposite the Sagar, on the right-hand side of the road, is the *Hotel Kalinga* (no phone), which has new but spartan rooms for Rs 300/400.

On PBM Hospital Rd is the *Thar Hotel* (☎ 27-180), which has deluxe rooms for Rs 350/470, and air-cooled rooms with TV for Rs 470/600. All rooms have attached bath and 24 hour hot water. There's a non-veg restaurant here.

Places to Stay – top end

The best place to stay in this category is the beautiful *Hotel Bhanwar Niwas* (☎ & fax 61-880), in the Rampuri Haveli in the old city. It's on Jail Rd near Kotwali police station. If you turn left at the Kote Gate, this road will take you straight to the haveli, about 500m distant. The hotel is close to a community of kite-makers, who can be seen practising their craft. It's a beautiful pink sandstone building, with rooms set around a courtyard. There's a finely appointed and elegant drawing room with gold-plated chairs, a hand-painted ceiling and gold floral motifs on the walls. A second smaller sitting room is riddled with European antiques. Singles/doubles are Rs 1175/2350. One room has a stadium-sized four-poster bed which is ascended by three steps. The single

rooms are also lovely, with antique dressers and other fine furniture.

The haveli still belongs to the Rampura family and was completed in 1927 for Seth Bhanwarlal Rampura, heir to a textile and real estate fortune. In the foyer is a stunning 1927 blue Buick with a silver horn in the shape of a dragon, and an immaculate 1942 Indian Ambassador.

Well appointed rooms at the *Hotel Lalgarh Palace* (☎ 52-3963; fax 52-2253) cost US$42/85. Rooms are enormous and are replete with antique furnishings and old prints. The hotel is part of the maharaja's modern palace. You can listen to live sitar and tabla music in the inner courtyard. There's a resident masseur (Rs 100 for 30 minutes) and a consultation with the resident astrologer, including the casting of your horoscope, is Rs 600.

About 800m east of the Hotel Lalgarh Palace, in Gandhi Colony, is the *Karni Bhawan Palace* (☎ 24-887; fax 52-2408). This was briefly the residence of Maharaja Karni Singh, and is a strange and somewhat ugly building in need of restoration, with rather dreary rooms furnished in Art Deco style. Rooms cost Rs 1150/2250, and meals are available.

Places to Eat

The vegetarian *Deluxe Restaurant* at the hotel of the same name on Station Rd features South Indian and Chinese cuisine. All dishes are under Rs 30, and you can get ice cream here.

Diagonally opposite the Deluxe is the popular vegetarian *Amber Restaurant*. Most dishes are under Rs 40, and there are some Continental dishes such as baked macaroni (Rs 32). South Indian snacks are available between 8 am and 7 pm, and there's a tasty variety of sweets.

Non-guests are welcome to dine in the vegetarian dining room at the *Hotel Bhanwar Niwas*. Breakfast is Rs 120, lunch is Rs 200 and dinner is Rs 220. Non-guests can also dine, with advance notice, at the restaurant at the *Hotel Lalgarh Palace*. Breakfast is US$6, lunch is US$9 and dinner is US$10.

On Station Rd near the railway station is the *Joshi Misthan Bhandar Restaurant*. There are Indian snacks and a range of sweets, but not much else. Next door is the very busy *Chhotu Motu Joshi Sweet Shop*, which has a range of sweets including the milk-based rasmalai and kesar cham cham, the latter a sausage-shaped sticky confection of milk, sugar and saffron which, when bitten, oozes a sweet sugar syrup. Fresh samosas are available out the front in the mornings.

Things to Buy

On the right-hand side as you enter the fort is an excellent craft shop, run by the Urmul Trust. Items sold here are of high quality and made by people from surrounding villages. Proceeds go directly to health and education projects in these villages. You can browse here without the usual constant hassles to buy.

If you are part of a guided group going to the fort, your guide might try to steer you away from this shop to a place where he receives commission. It's worth insisting that you be given five minutes at least to wander through the shop at your leisure. *Pattus*, lovely thick handloom shawls, cost from Rs 200 to Rs 860. Cushion covers are from Rs 65 to Rs 860, and the traditional folding chairs known as *pidas* cost Rs 740 for a single seat, and Rs 1110 for a double seat. There are also hand-printed cotton garments, puppets and more. For more information on the good work of the Urmul Trust, see the Voluntary Work section in the Facts for the Visitor chapter.

The shop is open daily from 9 am to 6 pm.

Getting There & Away

Bus The bus stand is in the north of the city, almost opposite the road leading up to Lalgarh Palace. The Roadways inquiry number is ☎ 52-3800.

There are numerous buses to Jodhpur between 5 am and 10.30 pm. Express buses cost Rs 66 and take six hours. The 2x2 semi-deluxe buses are faster and cost Rs 78. Some of these buses travel via Nagaur (three hours, Rs 31). There are also plenty of buses between these hours to Jaisalmer (deluxe: 6½ hours, Rs 88; express: 7½ hours, Rs 69). Buses for Jaipur leave between 7.45 am and 10 pm. The deluxe service costs Rs 106 and takes six hours. The express service is Rs 90 and takes eight hours.

There are numerous buses to Delhi up to 8.45 pm. The trip takes 11 hours and costs Rs 115. For Shekhawati, take any bus to Fatehpur (four hours, Rs 48), and change there.

Plenty of buses travel to Ajmer between 6 am and 11.30 pm (eight hours, Rs 71). Buses for Deshnok, home of the Karni Mata Temple, leave every 15 minutes between 5 am and 9 pm, take 30 minutes and cost Rs 7.

Other services include Udaipur (6.30 pm; 12 hours, Rs 144) and Barmer via Pokaran (5 and 9.15 am and 10.30 pm; 11 hours, Rs 128).

Train To Jodhpur, there is a service departing at 4 am, arriving at 10.40 am (Rs 35/240), and another departing at 11.25 pm, arriving at 4.30 am (Rs 65/264).

To Jaipur, there are services at 2.40 pm, arriving at 11.10 pm (Rs 42/477), and at 8.25 pm, arriving at 7 am (Rs 83/477). The 2467 *Intercity* departs at 6 am, arriving at Jaipur at noon (Rs 104/310).

To Delhi, trains depart at 8.35 am, arriving at 7.05 pm; the 4710 *Link* departs at 5.50 pm, arriving at 5.05 am; and the 4792 *Mail* departs at 7.45 pm, arriving at 6.25 am. Fares on all these services are Rs 99/404.

The reservation building is on the right as you approach the station. Bookings can be made between 8 am and 8 pm from Monday to Saturday, and 8 am to 2 pm on Sunday.

Getting Around

A cycle-rickshaw to the palace will cost Rs 15. It's possible to hire bicycles at Dau Cycle Shop, opposite the police station on Station Rd, for Rs 2 per hour, Rs 10 per day.

AROUND BIKANER

Camel Breeding Farm

This government-managed camel breeding station, eight km from Bikaner, is probably unique in Asia. There are hundreds of camels here and it's a great sight in the late afternoon as the camels come back from grazing. The British army had a camel corps drawn from Bikaner during WWI.

The farm is open Monday to Friday and every second Saturday from 3 to 5 pm; entry is free. It costs Rs 25 for a 25 minute camel ride. Cameras are theoretically prohibited, but this doesn't seem to be policed (although a little baksheesh might help).

Getting There & Away Half the auto-rickshaw and taxi drivers in Bikaner appear to be on the lookout for tourists to take to the farm, but you need to bargain hard with them. For the round trip including a half hour wait at the farm, you'll pay around Rs 40 for an auto-rickshaw, or Rs 100 for a taxi.

Devi Kund

Eight km east of Bikaner, this is the site of the royal chhatris of many of the Bika dynasty rulers. The white marble chhatri of Maharaja Surat Singh is among the most imposing.

Gajner Wildlife Sanctuary

The lake and forested hills of this reserve, 32 km from Bikaner on the Jaisalmer road, are inhabited by wildfowl and a number of deer and antelope including blackbuck and bluebull. There are also desert foxes. Imperial sand grouse migrate here in winter. It is possible to enter the park from Golari village free of charge. If, however, you enter via Gajner village, the Gajner Palace Hotel levies an arbitrary Rs 100 entry fee. There are no authorised guides at the sanctuary, and apart from the Gajner Palace Hotel, no accommodation or infrastructure for visitors.

A new sanctuary, to be called the Bikaner Bird Sanctuary, is proposed 15 km north of Bikaner on the Ganganagar road. The sanctuary will encompass a lake which is fed by the Indira Gandhi Canal. No further details were available at the time of writing.

Places to Stay The old red sandstone royal summer palace, on the banks of the lake, is now the *Gajner Palace Hotel* (☎ (01534) 5039). Rooms cost Rs 1150/2250, and bookings can be made through the Karni Bhawan Palace hotel (see the Bikaner section).

Getting There & Away There are many buses to Galari, on the outskirts of the park,

---

Get to Know your Camel

There are 270 camels at the Bikaner camel breeding farm, and three different breeds are reared here: the long-haired camels with hair in their ears are local camels from the Bikaner district. They are renowned for their strength. The light-coloured camels are from the Jaisalmer district, and are renowned for their speed (up to 22 km/h!). The dark-coloured camels are from Gujarat, and the females are renowned for the quantity of milk they produce: up to seven or eight litres at each milking. The milk tastes a little salty and is reputedly good for the liver. If you have a cup of chai in a small desert village, you're quite possibly drinking camel milk. The stout of heart might even like to try fresh, warm camel milk at the farm. The camels are crossbred, so in theory, camels from this farm should be the strongest, fastest and best milk-producing camels you'll find just about anywhere! Breeding season is December to March, and at this time the male camels froth disconcertingly at the mouth.

This is also a stud farm: locals bring their female camels here which are serviced free of charge. Female camels give birth every two to three years depending on their age and health, following a long (13 month) gestation period. A male camel can inseminate up to three cows per day.

When camels are five years old they go to 'camel school' at the farm for six months to learn basic commands such as 'sit', 'stand', 'left' and 'right'. On graduation, they are rewarded with a pin through the nose to which reins are attached. Adult camels consume 20 kg of fodder in summer, and drink 70L of water per day. In winter, they drink about 40L per day. In winter, a camel can work up to one month without food or water, and in summer, up to one week. ∎

WESTERN RAJASTHAN

from Bikaner (50 minutes, Rs 12). Unless you are staying at the Gajner Palace Hotel, it's best to continue past the Gajner turn-off (Gajner is 10 km off the Bikaner-Jaisalmer road) and disembark at Galari.

Deshnok

A visit to the fascinating temple of Karni Mata, an incarnation of Durga, at this village 30 km south of Bikaner along the Jodhpur road, is not for the squeamish. Here rats are considered to be incarnations of storytellers, and the holy rodents run riot all over the temple complex.

Karni Mata, who lived in the 14th century, asked the god of death, Yama, to restore to life the son of a grieving storyteller. When Yama refused, Karni Mata reincarnated all dead storytellers as rats in order to deprive Yama of human souls, which were later incarnated as human beings.

The temple is an important place of pilgrimage, with pilgrims being disgorged every few minutes from buses. Once at the village, they buy prasaad in the form of sugar balls to feed to the rats. The pilgrims are anointed with a tikka in the form of ash from a holy fire in the inner sanctum, while the objects of their devotion run over their toes (sorry, no shoes permitted!). Before the temple is a beautiful marble facade with solid silver doors- donated by Maharaja Ganga Singh. Across the doorway to the inner sanctum are repoussé silver doors – one panel shows the goddess with her holy charges at her feet. An image of the goddess is enshrined in the inner sanctum. There are special holes around the side of the temple courtyard to facilitate the rats' movements and a wire grille has been placed over the courtyard to prevent birds of prey and other predators consuming the holy rodents.

The rats are known as *kabas*, and it is considered highly auspicious to have one run across your feet – you'll find you'll be inadvertently graced in this manner numerous times whether you want it or not! White kabas are quite rare, although there are one or two at the temple, and sighting one augers well for your spiritual progress. Frankly the holy charges here are a rather moth-eaten assortment, who engage in decidedly unholy behaviour as they fight each other to get the best position around the enormous bowls of milk which are constantly replenished by the temple priests.

The temple is open from 4 am to 10 pm. It costs Rs 10 to bring a still camera into the complex, Rs 25 for a video camera.

There used to be a RTDC tourist bungalow near Deshnok, but it has closed. There is nowhere to stay in the village.

Getting There & Away Buses from the bus stand in Bikaner depart every 15 minutes for Deshnok (30 minutes, Rs 7). You'll have to bargain hard for a taxi, as the Bikaner drivers don't seem too keen to do this run. Rs 150 is not unreasonable. Ensure this leaves you at least 30 minutes at the temple.

Agra

Population: 1,050,500
Telephone Area Code: 0562

Although not in Rajasthan, falling in the state of Uttar Pradesh, Agra with its stunning Taj Mahal can be visited en route to or from Rajasthan.

At the time of the Mughals, in the 16th and 17th centuries, Agra was the capital of India, and its superb monuments date from that era. Agra has a magnificent fort and the building which many people come to India solely to see – the Taj Mahal. Nearby is the deserted city Fatehpur Sikri, which is not to be missed on a trip to Agra.

Agra became the capital of Sikandar Lodi in 1501, but was soon passed on to the Mughals, and both Babur and Humayun made some early Mughal constructions here. It was under Akbar that Agra first aspired to its heights of magnificence. From 1570 to 1585 he ruled from nearby Fatehpur Sikri. When he abandoned that city he moved to Lahore (now in Pakistan), but returned to Agra in 1599 and remained there until his death in 1605.

Emperor Shah Jahan (reigned 1627-58) built the Jama Masjid, most of the palace buildings inside the Agra Fort and, of course, the Taj Mahal. In 1638, a new capital – complete with a Red Fort and Jama Masjid – were started in Delhi and the capital was moved there in 1648.

In 1761, Agra fell to the Jats who did much damage to the city and its monuments, even going so far as to pillage the Taj Mahal. It was taken by the Marathas in 1770 and went through several more changes before the British took control in 1803. There was much fighting around the fort during the Mutiny in 1857.

Orientation

Agra is on the west bank of the Yamuna River, 204 km south of Delhi. The old part of the town, where you'll find the main marketplace in a narrow street (Kinari Bazaar), is north of the fort. The cantonment area to the

HIGHLIGHTS
• The Taj Mahal – one of the world's most beautiful architectural feats
• Agra Fort, an enormous complex to explore, just across the river from the Taj
• Itimad-ud-daulah, another impressive piece of Mughal architecture
• Fatehpur Sikri, the so-called deserted city, 40 km from Agra – a testimony to the wealth and power of the Mughal emperors

south is the modern part of town, known as Sadar Bazaar. On The Mall are the tourist office and the GPO. In this area you will also find handicraft shops, restaurants and many moderately priced hotels.

There are some lower priced hotels and the Uttar Pradesh (UP) Tourist Bungalow near the Raja Mandi railway station, but this area is rather inconveniently located, being from the Taj and the main hotel and restaurant area. Immediately south of the Taj in an area known as Taj Ganj is a tightly packed area of narrow alleys where you can find some popular rock-bottom hotels.

Agra's main railway station is Agra Cantonment; trains from New Delhi railway station arrive here. The main bus terminal for cities in Rajasthan, Delhi and for Fatehpur Sikri is Idgah. Agra airport is seven km out of town.

Information

The Government of India tourist office (☎ 36-3377) is at 191 The Mall. It's open from 9 am to 5.30 pm weekdays, 9 am to 1 pm Saturday, and is closed on Sunday. The UP tourist office (☎ 36-0517) is on Taj Rd, near the Clarks Shiraz Hotel. There's also a tourist information counter at the Agra Cantonment railway station.

The post office (with an inefficient poste restante service) is on The Mall, opposite the tourist office.

AGRA

Taj Mahal

This most famous Mughal monument was constructed by Emperor Shah Jahan in memory of his wife Mumtaz Mahal. It has been described as the most extravagant monument ever built for love, for the emperor was heartbroken when Mumtaz, to whom he had been married for 17 years, died in 1631 in childbirth, after producing 14 children.

Construction of the Taj began in the same year and was not completed until 1653. Workers were recruited not only from all over India but also from central Asia; in total, 20,000 people worked on the building. Experts were even brought from as far away as Europe – the Frenchman Austin of Bordeaux and the Italian Veroneo of Venice had a hand in its decoration. The main architect was Isa Khan, who came from Shiraz in Iran.

Dawn is a magical time to see the Taj, as it's virtually deserted. Fridays tend to be impossibly crowded and noisy – not very conducive to calm enjoyment of this most serene of buildings.

Shan Jahan, who ruled from 1627 to 1658, had a passion for building. The Taj Mahal is his most stunning achievement.

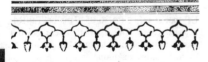

Intricate marble inlay is a feature of the exquisite Taj.

The main entrance to the Taj is on the western side, open from 6 to 8 am, 8.30 am to 4 pm and 5 to 7 pm. Entry costs Rs 100 for the early morning and evening opening times, Rs 10.50 during the day. You can also enter through the south and east gates, but they're open only between 8.30 am and 5 pm. There's no entry charge on Friday.

Twin red sandstone buildings frame the Taj when viewed from the river; the building on the west side is a mosque, the identical one on the east side is purely for symmetry. It cannot be used as a mosque, as it faces the wrong direction. The **tombs** of Mumtaz Mahal and Shah Jahan are in a basement room of the Taj. Above them in the main chamber are false tombs, a common practice in mausoleums of this type. Light is admitted into the central chamber by finely cut marble screens.

Although the Taj is amazingly graceful from almost any angle, it's the close-up detail which is really astounding. Semiprecious stones are inlaid into the marble in beautiful patterns and with superb craft in a process known as *pietra dura*.

Agra Fort

Construction of the massive Agra Fort was begun by Emperor Akbar in 1565, and additions were made up until the time of his grandson Shah Jahan. It's open from sunrise to sunset and admission is Rs 10.50 except on Friday when there's no charge.

Diwan-i-Am Shah Jahan's predecessors had a hand in the construction of this hall of public audiences, but the throne room, with its typical inlaid marble work, indisputably bears Shah Jahan's influence. Beside the diwan-i-am is the small **Nagina Masjid** or Gem Mosque and the Ladies' Bazaar where merchants came to display and sell goods to the ladies of the Mughal court.

Diwan-i-Khas The hall of private audiences was also built by Shah Jahan between 1636 and 1637. The famous Peacock Throne was kept here before being moved to Delhi by Aurangzeb. It was later carted off to Iran and its remains are now in Tehran.

Octagonal Tower The Musamman Burj, or Octagonal Tower, stands close to the diwan-i-khas and the small, private Mina Masjid. Also known as the Saman Burj, this tower was built by Shah Jahan for Mumtaz Mahal. It was here, with its views along the Yamuna to the Taj, that Shah Jahan died in 1666, after seven years' imprisonment.

Jehangir's Palace Akbar is believed to have built this palace, the largest private residence in the fort, for his son. The palace is interesting for its blend of Hindu and central Asian architectural styles – a contrast to the unique Mughal style which had developed by the time of Shah Jahan.

In front of Jehangir's Palace is the **Hauz-i-Jehangri**, a huge 'bath' carved out of a single block of stone – by whom and for what purpose is a subject of conjecture.

Jama Masjid

Across the railway tracks from the Delhi Gate of Agra Fort, the Jama Masjid was built by Shah Jahan in 1648. An inscription over

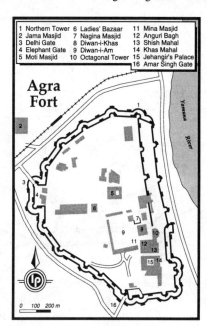

1 Northern Tower	6 Ladies' Bazaar	11 Mina Masjid
2 Jama Masjid	7 Nagina Masjid	12 Anguri Bagh
3 Delhi Gate	8 Diwan-i-Khas	13 Shish Mahal
4 Elephant Gate	9 Diwan-i-Am	14 Khas Mahal
5 Moti Masjid	10 Octagonal Tower	15 Jehangir's Palace
		16 Amar Singh Gate

the main gate indicates that it was built in the name of Jahanara, Shah Jahan's daughter, who was imprisoned with Shah Jahan by Aurangzeb.

Itimad-ud-Daulah

North of the fort and on the opposite bank of the Yamuna is the exquisite Itimad-ud-daulah – the tomb of Mirza Ghiyas Beg. This Persian gentleman was Jehangir's *wazir*, or chief minister, and his beautiful daughter later married the emperor. She then became known as Nur Jahan, the Light of the World, and her niece was Mumtaz Mahal, Chosen of the Palace. The tomb was constructed by Nur Jahan between 1622 and 1628 and is very similar to the tomb she constructed for her husband, Jehangir, near Lahore.

The tomb is of particular interest since many of its design elements foreshadow the Taj, construction of which started only a few years later.

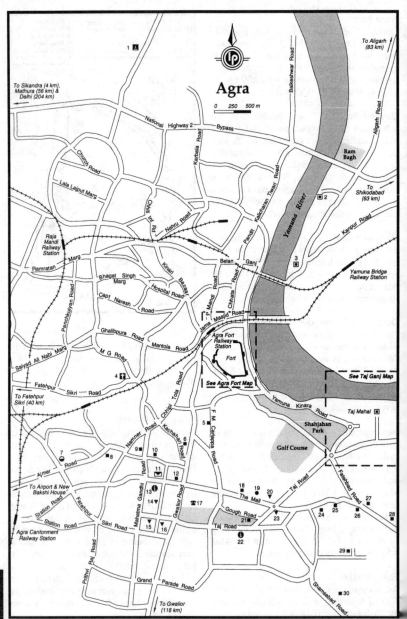

Agra

To Aligarh
(83 km)

Balkeshwar Road

To Sikandra (4 km),
Mathura (56 km) &
Delhi (204 km)

Aligarh Road

National Highway 2
Bypass

Karbala Road

Ram
Bagh

Church Road

Lala Lajpat Marg

Kachoharan Tiwari Road

Yamuna River

To
Shikodabad
(63 km)

Chhil Int Rd

Nehru Road

Kanpur Road

Raja
Mandi
Railway
Station

Ramratan Marg

Pandit

Belan Ganj

Yamuna Bridge
Railway Station

Panchkuyian Road

Bhagat Singh Marg

Kinari Bazaar

Hospital Road

Chhata Road

Capt Naresh Road

Ghalibpura Road

Mantola Road

Jama Masjid Road

P Mandi Road

Agra Fort
Railway
Station

Salyad Ali Nabi Marg

M G Road

Fort

Fatehpur Sikri Road

See Taj Ganj Map

See Agra Fort Map

To Fatehpur
Sikri (40 km)

Yamuna Kinara Road

Taj Mahal

Shahjahan
Park

Namner Road

Chhipi Tola Road

Kachahari Road

F. M. Cariappa Road

Golf Course

Ajmer Road

To Airport & New
Bakshi House

Mahatma Gandhi Road

Gwalior Road

Taj Road

Fatehpr Sikri Road

Station House

Station Road

The Mall

Gough Road

Fatehabad Road

Agra Cantonment
Railway Station

Prithvi Raj Road

Grand Parade Road

Taj Road

To Gwalior
(118 km)

Shamsabad Road

The Itimad-ud-daulah is open from sunrise to sunset and admission is Rs 5.50; free on Friday.

Other Attractions

The **Kinari Bazaar**, or old marketplace, is a fascinating area to wander around. It's in the old part of Agra, near the fort, and the narrow alleys of the market start near the Jama Masjid. There are several market areas, or *mandis*, in Agra with names left over from the Mughal days, although they bear no relation to what is sold there today. The Loha Mandi (Iron Market) and Sabji Mandi (Vegetable Market) are still used, but the Nai Ki Mandi (Barber's Market) is now famous for textiles. In the Malka Bazaar women beckon to passing men from the upstairs balconies.

Organised Tours

Tours commence from Agra Cantonment railway station and tickets are sometimes sold on the *Taj Express* or *Shatabdi Express* trains. These tours last all day and include the Taj, the fort and Fatehpur Sikri. Tickets cost Rs 100.

You can book the tours (and get picked up) from the tourist office in The Mall, or from the tourist information counter at Agra Cantonment railway station.

Places to Stay – bottom end

Taj Ganj Area The *Hotel Kamal* (☎ 36-0926) has views of the Taj from the rooftop.

There are singles with common bath for Rs 50, and doubles/triples with attached bath from Rs 80/100. The rooms are clean but a little dark. The other place with a Taj view is the *Shanti Lodge* (☎ 36-1644). Rooms are Rs 60/80 for singles/doubles with common bath, Rs 80/100 with attached bath.

Another good hotel is the *Hotel Siddhartha* (☎ 26-4711), not far from the western gate. Rooms range from Rs 60/80 to Rs 80/175, all with attached bathroom (bucket hot water in the cheaper rooms).

By the eastern gate, the friendly *Hotel Pink* (☎ 36-0677) has rooms with attached bath from Rs 40/70 with a bucket shower, to Rs 120/150 for a double/triple with running hot water.

On the road leading from the eastern gate is UP Tourism's *Hotel Taj Khema* (☎ 36-0140). There are rooms with common bath for Rs 100/125, but the semi-deluxe rooms with attached bath and water heater are much better value at Rs 150/175. There are excellent views of the Taj from the artificial hill in the garden.

South of Taj Ganj The *Paradise Guest House* (☎ 36-9199) hardly lives up to its name, but one advantage of this place is that it has a generator – Agra has chronic power problems, with blackouts virtually every night. Singles/doubles cost Rs 120/150 with attached bath. South of here is the popular *Hotel Safari* (☎ 36-0013) on Shamsabad Rd.

AGRA

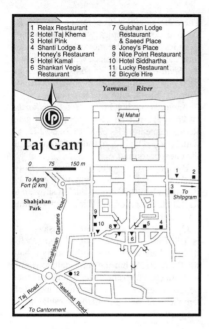

1 Relax Restaurant	7 Gulshan Lodge
2 Hotel Taj Khema	Restaurant
3 Hotel Pink	& Saeed Place
4 Shanti Lodge &	8 Joney's Place
Honey's Restaurant	9 Nice Point Restaurant
5 Hotel Kamal	10 Hotel Siddhartha
6 Shankari Vegis	11 Lucky Restaurant
Restaurant	12 Bicycle Hire

Yamuna River

Taj Ganj

0   75   150 m

Taj Mahal

To Agra Fort (2 km)

Shahjahan Park

Shahjahan Gardens Road

To Shilpgram

Taj Road

Fatehbad Road

To Cantonment

It's clean and good value with rooms at Rs 75/120 with air-cooling and hot-water bath. The Taj is visible from the rooftop.

On a quiet residential street just to the east of this area is the very pleasant *Upadyay's Mumtaz Guest House* (☎ 36-0865), 3/7 Vibhav Nagar. Singles/doubles with attached bath are Rs 75/150, or Rs 200 for a deluxe double with bathtub. There's a small garden and sun terrace on the roof.

Sadar The *Tourist Rest House* (☎ 36-3961) is on Kachahari Rd, not far from The Mall. Basic singles/doubles start at Rs 55/65. They don't give commissions, so rickshaws may be unwilling to take you there.

Down the scale a bit is the friendly *Deepak Lodge* at 178 Ajmer Rd, with small rooms with attached bath for Rs 60/80.

Midway between Sadar and Taj Ganj is the *Hotel Akbar Inn* (☎ 36-3212). The small rooms in the separate wing are cheap at Rs 30/45, while those in the main building are

very good value at Rs 80/100 with attached bath.

On Field Marshal Cariappa Rd, in a spacious residential area closer to the Taj and just a few minutes walk from the fort, there are a couple of good places. The friendly *Agra Hotel* (☎ 36-3331) is a large crumbling old place that people either love or hate. There's a good range of rooms from Rs 110/150, all with attached baths. There are views of the Taj from the garden. Right next door is the *Hotel Akbar* (☎ 36-3312), which is a little cheaper and also has a pleasant garden.

Major Bakshi's Tourist Home (☎ 36-3829) has been popular for many years – even Julie Christie has stayed here. The rooms are comfortable and well furnished, and are quite good at Rs 150/250 with attached bath and hot water.

Places to Stay – middle
The *New Bakshi House* (☎ 36-8159) is a very pleasant upmarket guest house at 5 Laxman Nagar, between the railway station and the airport. Comfortable singles/doubles range from Rs 400/500 to Rs 650. The food is excellent and they can also arrange to pick you up from the station or airport.

One of the nicest places in this range is the elderly *Lauries Hotel* (☎ 36-4536) in the Sadar area. The rooms are a tad shabby but the ones at the back are OK. They cost Rs 325/450.

The *Mayur Tourist Complex* (☎ 36-0302) has very pleasant cottages arranged around a lawn and swimming pool, with prices from Rs 400/550.

The *Hotel Amar* (☎ 36-0695) has a popular swimming pool, spa and sauna. Room rates are Rs 700/900 with air-con. At the top of this price range is the *Hotel Mumtaz* (☎ 36-1771) under renovation in an attempt to raise itself from three to five star status. Standard rooms are Rs 1100/1500.

Places to Stay – top end
Agra's five star hotels are generally in the open area south of the Taj. The *Clarks Shiraz Hotel* (☎ 36-1421; fax 36-1620) is fully air-

conditioned, has a swimming pool and singles/doubles cost Rs 1195/2380.

The *Agra Ashok Hotel* (☎ 36-1223; fax 36-1428) is a well managed and pleasant place to stay, or to visit en route to Bharatpur in Rajasthan. Room rates are Rs 1195/2000 for singles/doubles. The *Novotel Agra* (☎ 36-8282), Fatehbad Rd, is a low-rise Mughal-style hotel built around a lawn and swimming pool. Rooms are US$38/75.

The five star hotel with Taj views from most of its rooms is the *Taj View Hotel* (☎ 36-1171; fax 36-1179). It charges US$135/145 for a room where you can admire the Taj from the comfort of your bed. Standard rooms (no view) are US$110/125.

Agra's top hotel is the *Mughal Sheraton* (☎ 36-1701; fax 36-1730) on Fatehbad Rd. The rooms, which cost from US$165/180, are all very well appointed but only the more expensive ones give you a Taj view.

Places to Eat

Taj Ganj Area The tiny *Joney's Place* is one of the area's longest running places. The *Shankari Vegis Restaurant* is a bit better and equally popular.

On the same square as Joney's, the small *Gulshan Lodge Restaurant* is good for a snack. Next door is *Saeed Place* which includes a range of Israeli food. Further west along this street is the *Lucky Restaurant* which claims that its food is so good you'll get your money back if you don't agree.

Honey's Restaurant, near Shanti Lodge, is a small place that's good value – a set breakfast with tomato, eggs, porridge and coffee costs Rs 20.

The *Nice Point Restaurant* near the western gate has good travellers' food. At the eastern gate the *Relax Restaurant* does excellent real coffee and desserts; and there's a pleasant rooftop sitting area.

South of Taj Ganj The *Only Restaurant* is an outdoor place by the roundabout on Taj Rd which has Indian, Chinese and Continental cuisine. Nearby is the equally good *Sonar Restaurant* with excellent Mughlai food.

The *Tourist Rest House* in the Sadar area is a pleasant place to eat. The tables are outside and at night the candles are a nice touch. The *Priya Restaurant*, nearby, advertises 'Delicious Meals & Joy Forever'!

There's a bunch of mid-range restaurants at the western end of Taj Rd, including the *Kwality Restaurant*, the more expensive *Hot Bite*, the open-air *Park Restaurant* and the vegetarian *Lakshmi Vilas Restaurant*.

Zorba the Buddha is an interesting Osho-run vegetarian restaurant. Muesli with fruit, nuts and curd is Rs 20, a lassi is Rs 14. In the same block of shops is the *Savitri Restaurant*, which specialises in barbecue kebabs and chicken tikka; and on the opposite side of the road is the *Chung Wah* Chinese restaurant – it's good value.

The deluxe hotels have excellent food – for a major splurge *Clarks Shiraz* is worth considering. Main dishes here are around Rs 150 and it's Rs 125 for a beer; their lunchtime buffet (Rs 300) is very good.

Agra has a local speciality, the ultra-sweet candied melon called *peitha*.

Things to Buy

Agra is well known for leather goods, jewellery and marble inlay items in the pietra dura style. The Sadar and Taj Ganj areas are the main tourist shopping centres, although the prices here are likely to be more expensive. Around Pratapur, in the old part of Agra, there are many jewellery shops, but precious stones are cheaper in Jaipur.

About one km along the road running from the eastern gate of the Taj is Shilpgram, a crafts village and open-air emporium. At festival times there are live performances by dancers and musicians; the rest of the time there are displays of crafts from all over the country. Prices are certainly on the high side, but the quality is good and the range hard to beat.

Getting There & Away

Air The Indian Airlines office (☎ 36-0948) is at the Clarks Shiraz Hotel. It is open daily from 10 am to 1 pm and from 2 to 5 pm.

AGRA

Indian Airlines flies daily between Agra and Delhi (US$31).

Bus Most buses leave from the Idgah bus terminal. Buses between Delhi and Agra operate about every hour and cost Rs 49; deluxe buses cost Rs 56, and super-deluxe are Rs 60; the trip takes about five hours. From Delhi buses leave from Sarai Kale Khan, the new bus terminal in the south of the city by Nizamuddin railway station.

There are deluxe buses between Agra and Jaipur every 30 minutes for Rs 76; there are also air-con buses for Rs 106. They leave from a small booth right outside the Hotel Sheetal on Ajmer Rd, very close to the Idgah bus terminal.

Train The fastest train between Delhi and Agra is the daily air-con *Shatabdi Express*, which does the trip in a shade under two hours. It leaves Delhi at 6.15 am, returning from Agra at 8.15 pm. The fare is Rs 250 in air-con chair car, and Rs 480 1st class, and this includes meals.

Take great care at New Delhi railway station; pickpockets, muggers and others are very aware that this is a popular tourist route and they work overtime at parting unwary visitors from their valuables.

To Mumbai (Bombay) the journey takes 29 hours at a cost of Rs 198/776 in 2nd/1st class.

The 2308 *Howrah-Jodhpur Express* departs Agra at 8.10 pm, arriving at Jaipur at 4 am, with a connection through to Jodhpur. The fare is Rs 124/460 in 2nd class/air-con sleeper.

Getting Around
The Airport Agra's airport is seven km from the centre of town. Taxis charge around Rs 90 and auto-rickshaws Rs 50.

Taxi & Auto-Rickshaw There are set fares from the Agra Cantonment railway station. Auto-rickshaws charge Rs 15 to any hotel, Rs 45 to the fort and back with a couple of hours at the fort, and Rs 250 for a full day's sightseeing. A taxi to any hotel is Rs 60.

Cycle-Rickshaw & Bicycle You can eas negotiate a full-day rate for a cycle-ricksh (Rs 60 to Rs 100), for which your ricksha wallah will not only take you everywhe but will wait outside while you sightsee even have a meal. How much you p depends on your bargaining ability but ne get in a rickshaw here without first establi ing a price. Being told you can pay 'as y like' does not mean that. For the Taj, a cyc rickshaw is the most environmenta friendly form of transport.

Around Rs 10 should take you from pre well anywhere in Agra to anywhere else, the rickshaw drivers will try for much mo There are plenty of bicycle-rental pla around. The cost is typically Rs 3 per h and Rs 15 per day.

Around Agra

Fatehpur Sikri
Population: 27,500
Telephone Area Code: 05619
Between 1570 and 1585, during the reign Emperor Akbar, the capital of the Mug Empire was situated here, 40 km west Agra. Then, as suddenly and dramatically this new city had been built, it was aba doned, mainly due, it is thought, to dif culties with the water supply. Today it' perfectly preserved example of a Mug city at the height of the empire's splendo

Legend says that Akbar was without male heir and made a pilgrimage to this sp to see the saint Shaikh Salim Chishti. T saint foretold the birth of Akbar's son, future emperor, Jehangir, and in gratitu Akbar named his son Salim. Furthermo Akbar transferred his capital to Sikri a built a new and splendid city.

Most people visit Fatehpur Sikri as a d trip from Agra, but it can be a pleasant pla to stay. Spending the night here would all you to watch the impressive sunset over ruins. The best place is from the top of city walls, a two km walk to the south.

AGRA

Orientation & Information The deserted city lies along the top of a ridge while the modern village, with its bus stand and railway station, is down the ridge's southern side.

Fatehpur Sikri is open from sunrise to sunset and entry is Rs 0.50; free on Friday. There's no charge for a camera unless it's a video (Rs 25). Note that the Jama Masjid and the tomb of Shaikh Salim Chishti are outside the city enclosure; there's no entry fee to visit them.

As Fatehpur Sikri is one of the most perfectly preserved 'ghost towns' imaginable, you may well decide it is worthwhile hiring a guide. Around the ticket office, licensed guides are available; the official charge is set at Rs 48 but if business is slack they ask only about half that. At the Buland Darwaza, the gateway to the mosque and shrine, unlicensed guides will try to lure you into hiring them for around Rs 10 to Rs 20.

Day-trippers in search of toilets or a place to leave their luggage should head for the Maurya Rest House, south of the Jama Masjid. They charge Rs 2 for left luggage.

Getting There & Away The tour buses only stop for an hour or so at Fatehpur Sikri. If you want to spend longer (which is recommended) it is worth taking a bus from Agra's Idgah bus terminal (Rs 10, one hour). You can spend a day in Fatehpur Sikri and continue on to Bharatpur (Rs 7, 45 minutes) in the evening. The train service used to be slow and infrequent but should have improved with the line's conversion to broad gauge.

Glossary

adgaliya – verandah of village hut.

Agnikula – 'Fire Born', name of the mythological race of four Rajput clans who believe that they were manifested from a sacred fire on Mt Abu; one of the three principal races from which Rajputs claim descent.

ahimsa – non-violence and reverence for all life.

andhi – local name for a dust storm in the Thar Desert.

apsara – celestial maiden.

Aryan – Sanskrit word for 'noble'; refers to those who migrated from Persia and settled in northern India.

auto-rickshaw – a noisy three wheel device powered by a two stroke motorcycle engine with a driver up front and seats for two (or sometimes more) passengers behind.

bagh – garden.

baithak – salon in an *haveli* where merchants met their clients.

bandhani – popular form of tie and dye.

banyan – Indian fig tree.

baori – well, particularly a stepwell with landings and galleries, found in Rajasthan and Gujarat.

baraat – marriage party.

bazaar – market area. A market town is called a bazaar.

bhojanalya – basic restaurant or snack bar in Rajasthan; known elsewhere in India as a *dhaba*.

Bhopa – Bhil priest; also traditional storytellers of Rajasthan.

bhuut – ghost.

bichiya – toe ring worn by Rajasthani women.

bo tree – *Ficus religiosa*, the tree under which the Buddha attained enlightenment.

bohara – village moneylender.

bor – forehead ornament worn by Rajasthani women; also known as a *tikka* or *rakhadi*.

Brahma – source of all existence and worshipped as the Creator in the Hindu triad. Brahma is depicted as having four heads (a fifth was burnt by Shiva's 'central eye' when Brahma spoke disrespectfully). His vehicle is a swan or goose.

Brahmin – member of the priest caste, the highest Hindu caste.

Buddha – Awakened One; originator of Buddhism who lived in the 5th century BC regarded by Hindus as the ninth reincarnation of Vishnu.

bund – embankment or dyke.

bunti – wooden block used in block-printing fabric.

caste – a Hindu's hereditary station in life.

chai – tea; the ubiquitous beverage of India

chajeras – the masons employed by wealthy Marwari businessmen of Shekhawati to build their *havelis*.

chakki – handmill used to grind grain.

champleve – method of *meenakari* enamelling.

chapati – unleavened Indian bread.

charpoy – Indian rope bed.

chaupar – town square formed by the inter section of major roads.

chhan – see under *dogla*.

chhapa – wooden block, also known as *bunti*, used to block-print fabric.

chhatri – a cenotaph (literally 'umbrella').

chiteras – painters who painted the walls of the *havelis* in Shekhawati.

choli – blouse worn by Indian women.

chowk – a town square, intersection or marketplace.

chowkidar – caretaker.

chudas – bangles worn by Rajasthani women Worn in great number, the bangles cover the entire arm and increase in diameter along the length of the arm.

chureil – evil spirit. Also known as a *dakin*

cycle-rickshaw – effectively a three wheel bicycle with a seat for two passengers behind the rider.

dacoit – bandit

dakin – evil spirit. See under *chureil*.

dalwar – sword.

330

dargah – shrine or place of burial of a Muslim saint.

darwaza – gateway or door.

dhaba – hole-in-the-wall restaurant or snack bar. Boxed lunches delivered to office workers.

dhobi ghat – the place where clothes are washed.

dhobi-wallah – person who washes clothes.

dhoti – length of fabric worn by men which is drawn up between the legs.

Digambara – sky-clad; a Jain sect whose followers demonstrate their disdain for worldly goods by going naked.

diwan-i-am – public audience hall in a palace.

diwan-i-khas – private audience hall in a palace.

dogla – village building adjacent to a domestic dwelling in which livestock and grain are kept. Also known as a *chhan*.

dosa – paper-thin pancakes made from lentil flour (curried vegetables wrapped inside a dosa make it a *masala dosa*).

durbar – royal court, or maharajas meeting hall; also used to describe a government.

Durga – the Inaccessible; a form of Shiva's wife, Parvati, a beautiful but fierce woman riding a tiger; major goddess of the Shakti cult. (Shakti is the creative/reproductive energy of the gods which often manifests in their spouses.)

durrie – cotton rug.

gaddi – maharaja's throne.

Ganesh – god of wisdom and prosperity. Elephant-headed son of Shiva and Parvati and probably the most popular god in the Hindu pantheon. Also known as Ganapati, his vehicle is a rat. He is depicted as four handed: in one hand he holds a water lily, in another a club, in a third a shell and the fourth a discus.

garh – fort.

Garuda – man-bird vehicle of Vishnu.

ghaghara – very full skirt worn by Rajasthani women. Also known as a *lehanga*.

ghat – steps or landing on a river, range of hills, or road up hills.

ghee – clarified butter.

ghoomer – dance performed by women during festivals and weddings.

Gogaji – 11th century folk hero, believed to have the ability to cure snakebite, who has been deified.

gram panchayat – government at the village level.

Gujjars – people traditionally engaged in animal husbandry.

hathphool – ornament worn on the back of the hand by Rajasthani women.

haveli – traditional mansions with interior courtyards.

Induvansa – Race of the Moon (Lunar Race); one of the three principal races from which Rajputs claim descent.

jagirdari – feudal system of serfdom imposed on the peasants of Rajasthan.

Jagirdars – feudal lords of Rajasthan.

jajman – patron of folk entertainers.

jali – stone or wood tracery used in windows.

Jats – traditionally, people engaged in agriculture. In contemporary Rajasthan, Jats play a strong role in administration and politics.

jauhar – ritual mass suicide by immolation, traditionally performed by Rajput women at times of military defeat to avoid dishonour.

jhonpa – village hut with mud walls and thatched roof.

jogi – priest.

jootis – traditional leather shoes of Rajasthan; men's jootis have curled up toes. Also known as *mojdis*.

Julaha – weaver caste.

kabas – the holy rats which are believed to be the incarnations of storytellers at Karni Mata Temple, Deshnok, near Bikaner.

kalbelia – snake charmer.

kaarkhana – embroidery workshop. A number were established during the Mughal era to train artisans.

Karni Mata – incarnation of Devi worshipped in her temple at Deshnok, near Bikaner.

kashida – embroidery on *jootis* (traditional leather shoes).

kathputli – puppeteer; also known as a *putli-wallah*.

kheis – shawl. Also known as a *pattu*.

kopi – camel-hide water bottle.

kotwali – police station.

Krishna – Vishnu's eighth incarnation, often coloured blue; a popular Hindu deity, he revealed the *Bhagavad Gita* to Arjuna.

Kshatriya – the caste of soldiers and governors, and second in the caste hierarchy. Rajputs claim lineage to the Kshatriyas.

kuldevi – clan goddess. Every family pays homage to a clan goddess.

kund – lake or tank.

kundan – type of jewellery featuring enamelwork *(meenakari)* on one side and precious stones on the other.

kurta – long cotton shirt with either short collar or no collar, worn by men.

lassi – refreshing yoghurt and iced-water drink.

lehanga – see under *ghaghara*.

loharia – form of *bandhani* tie and dye which achieves a ripple effect.

madrassa – Islamic college.

Mahabharata – Great *Vedic* epic of the Bharata dynasty; an epic poem, containing about 10,000 verses, describing the battle between the Pandavas and the Kauravas.

mahal – house or palace.

maharaj kumar – son of a maharaja; prince.

maharaja, maharana, maharao – king.

maharani – wife of a princely ruler or a ruler in her own right.

Mahavir – the 24th and last *tirthankar* (Jain teacher, or prophet).

mandana – folk paintings in red chalk on village dwellings.

mandapa – chamber before the inner sanctum of a temple.

mandir – temple.

Maratha – warlike central Indian people who controlled much of India at various times and who fought against the Mughals and the Rajputs.

marg – major road.

Marwar – kingdom of the Rathore dynasty, which ruled from Mandore, and later Jodhpur.

masuria – finely woven cloth of silk and cotton produced in Kaithoon village in Kota district.

mataji – female priest. Also a respectful form of addressing a mother or older woman.

meenakari – type of enamelwork used on ornaments and jewellery. Jaipur is renowned for its meenakari.

mehfilkhana – Islamic building in which religious songs are sung.

mehndi – intricate henna designs applied by women to their hands and feet for celebrations such as marriages and festivals.

mela – a fair.

Mewar – kingdom of the Sisodia dynasty, which ruled over Udaipur and Chittorgarh.

Moghul – alternative spelling for Mughal.

mojdis – see under *jootis*.

moksha – release from cycle of birth and death.

moosal – pestle.

mosar – death feast.

Mughal – Muslim dynasty of Indian emperors from Babur to Aurangzeb.

Nandi – bull, vehicle of Shiva. Nandi's images are usually found at Shiva temples.

nathdi – nose ornament. Also known as a *laongh* and a *bhanvatiya*.

niwas – house, building.

odhni – headscarf worn by Rajasthani women.

okhli – mortar; bowl for grinding grain with a pestle *(moosal)*.

paag – turban. Also called a *pagri* and a *safa*.

Pabuji – deified folk hero of Rajasthan; particularly revered by the nomadic Bhopas.

pagri – see under *paag*.

pahar – hill.

panchayat sammiti – local government representing several villages.

panghat poojan – ceremony performed at village well following the birth of a child.

pattu – shawl. Also known as a *kheis*.

payal – anklet worn by Rajasthani women.

phad – painted scroll used by Bhopas in

performance to illustrate legends concerned with the life of Pabuji.

pichwai – religious paintings on home-spun cloth, generally illustrating events from the life of Krishna, which are hung behind the image of Sri Nathji at Nathdwara.

pida – low folding chair featuring decorative woodcarving, traditionally made in Shekhawati and Bikaner.

pitar – soul of a dead man.

pitari – soul of a woman who has died before her husband.

pol – gate.

prasaad – sacred food given in offerings to the gods.

puja – literally 'respect'; offering or prayer.

purdah – seclusion; traditionally wives of Rajputs were kept in purdah and seen by no man other than their husband.

putli-wallah – puppeteer; also known as a kathputli.

raj – rule or sovereignty.

raja – king.

Rajput – 'Sons of Princes'; Hindu warrior caste, royal rulers of western India.

Rama – seventh incarnation of Vishnu. His life story is the central theme of the *Ramayana*.

Ramdev – deified folk hero, who, along with his horse, is worshipped in a temple at Ramdevra, near Pokaran.

rani – wife of a king.

reet – bride price; opposite of dowry.

sadar – main.

sadhu – ascetic, holy person, one who is trying to achieve enlightenment; usually addressed as *'swamiji'* or *'babaji'*.

safa – see under *paag*.

sagar – lake, reservoir.

sal – gallery in a palace.

Sanganeri print – famous block-printed fabric of Sanganer village, near Jaipur.

sarangi – stringed folk instrument of Rajasthan.

sati – to become an 'honourable woman' by immolation. Although banned more than a

century ago, the act of sati is occasionally performed.

Scheduled Tribes – government classification for tribal groups of Rajasthan. The tribes are grouped with the lowest casteless class, the Dalits.

shikhar – hunting expedition.

shikhara – temple spire.

Shiva (Siva) – the Destroyer; also the Creator, in which form he is worshipped as a *lingam* (a phallic symbol).

singh – literally 'lion', a surname adopted by Rajputs and Sikhs.

Sufi – ascetic Muslim mystic.

Surya – the sun; a major deity in the *Vedas*.

Suryavansa – Race of the Sun (Solar Race); one of the three principal races from which Rajputs claim descent.

Tejaji – defied folk hero believed to cure snakebite.

tempo – noisy three wheeler public transport vehicle; bigger than an auto-rickshaw.

thakur – nobleman.

thali – traditional South Indian and Gujarati 'all-you-can-eat' vegetarian meal. Thali is actually the name of the plate on which the meal is served. It is also possible to get a non-veg thali.

tirthankars – the 24 great Jain teachers.

tokna – large vessel in which the maharajas' treasurers collected taxes from the peasants.

tonga – two wheeled passenger vehicle drawn by horse or pony.

toran – shield-shaped device above lintels which a bridegroom traditionally pierces with his sword before claiming his bride.

torana – elaborately sculpted gateway before temples.

tripolia – triple gateway.

Vaisya – the caste of tradespeople and farmers; the third caste in the hierarchy.

Varuna – supreme Vedic god; Aryan god of water.

Vishnu – the third in the Hindu trinity of gods along with Brahma and Shiva. The Preserver and Restorer, who so far has nine *avataars* (incarnations): the fish Matsya; the tortoise Kurma; the wild boar Naraha; the man-lion Narasimha; the dwarf Vamana; the Brahmin Parashu-Rama; Rama (of *Ramayana* fame); Krishna; the Buddha.

wallah – literally 'man'. Can be added on to almost anything, thus dhobi-wallah (clothes washer), taxi-wallah, Delhi-wallah.

yagna – self-mortification; holy sacrifice.

zenana – women's quarters in a home or palace.

zila parishad – government at district level.

Index

Text

Boxed Stories